RETHINKING THE COLOR LINE

RETHINKING THE COLOR LINE
Readings in Race and Ethnicity

Charles A. Gallagher
Georgia State University

Mayfield Publishing Company
Mountain View, California
London • Toronto

Copyright © 1999 by Mayfield Publishing Company

Library of Congress Cataloging-in-Publication Data

Rethinking the color line : readings in race and ethnicity / [edited
   by] Charles A. Gallagher.
      p. cm.
   ISBN 0-7674-0268-5
   1. United States—Race relations.   2. United States—Ethnic
relations.   3. Minorities—Civil rights—United States.
I. Gallagher, Charles A. (Charles Andrew)
E184.A1R4485   1999
305.8'00973—dc21   98-44278
                                                            CIP

Manufactured in the United States of America

10 9 8 7 6 5 4 3 2 1

Mayfield Publishing Company
1280 Villa Street
Mountain View, California 94041

Sponsoring editor, Serina Beauparlant; production editor, Lynn Rabin Bauer; manuscript editor, Thomas L. Briggs; design manager and art editor, Susan Breitbard; text and cover designer, Linda Robertson; cover art: *Untitled Jazz Series,* 1987 by Beatrice Mandelman; manufacturing manager, Randy Hurst. The text was set in 10/12 Book Antiqua by Shepherd, Inc., and printed on 45# Highland Plus by Malloy Lithographing.

 This book is printed on recycled paper.

Contents

Constructing a Nonracist World: Obstacles and Opportunities   509

Preface

It is difficult to think about life in America without directly confronting issues of race and ethnicity. Reflect for a moment on how recent events and trends both dominate and alter American social and cultural life: a black Texan is tied to the back of a pick-up truck and dragged to his death by racist whites; the rejection of affirmative action measures in California creates a national dialogue on the extent to which the racial "playing field" is level; tougher immigration laws are called for by politicians, while U.S. farmers and agrabusinesspeople discuss institution of a new *bracero* farm labor program; the media lumps young Asians—a very small part of the U.S. population—into the hip category "Gener-Asian X"; a rash of African American church burnings shocks the nation, although Colin Powell, Denzel Washington, Michael Jordan, and Tiger Woods are consistently voted among America's most celebrated and respected people; and white suburban teenagers continue to be the largest consumers of rap music, yet racially motivated hate crimes have increased on campuses throughout the country. The readings in *Rethinking the Color Line* will allow you to examine the contradictions of race and ethnicity and prepare students to live in an increasingly racially and ethnically diverse society.

Although the media has seized on a U.S. Census Bureau figure that predicts that by the year 2060 whites will be outnumbered by Asians, blacks, Hispanics, and American Indians, this rather simplistic demographic forecast misses the conflicts, contradictions, and cultural convergences that currently define race and ethnic relations in the United States. *Rethinking the Color Line* is designed to help make sense of how race and ethnicity influence aspects of social life in ways that are often made invisible by culture, politics, and economics. This theoretically informed, empirically grounded reader uses a social constructionist perspective to frame and define the concept of race and ethnicity in the United States. The selections should stimulate conversation in the classroom and allow students to think through solutions to what often seem to be intractable problems. As a pedagogical strategy, this text raises a number of questions in the part introductions that guide students through the readings by providing an overview of how each reading is conceptually linked to the others. Each part introduction ends with "Questions to Frame Your Readings," which ask students to compare and contrast each author's position.

It was important to me that my students be exposed to the classic paradigms in the study of race and ethnic relations in the United States. However, just as important was my desire that students be exposed to and explore new theories and paradigms that were challenging, supplanting, and redefining the classic race and ethnicity "canon," which itself changes over time. The biologically based, pseudo-scientific assumptions that defined and guided race and ethnicity scholarship for much of this century have been debunked, discredited, and discarded. What has emerged in the last 30 years are competing narratives of what race and ethnic identity mean and the social pressures that shape those meanings. Post-colonial, post-modern, post-ethnic, class-based, or primordialist perspectives each claim to elucidate how race and ethnicity shape identity construction, gender, political economy, and geo-politics. The modern idea of race and ethnicity has been, and continues to be, thoroughly rethought.

The readings in the first part of this text provide students with the theoretical framework and analytical tools they will use throughout the book. Students come to understand what is meant by race and ethnicity as a social construction. The news, situation comedies, MTV, the racial topography of neighborhoods—each become subjects for sociological scrutiny. *Rethinking the Color Line* allows students to learn how race and ethnicity influence life in ways that many students routinely take for granted. It has been my experience that a majority of students who read these articles internalize a version of the "sociological imagination" that forever changes how they understand race and ethnic relations. Raising consciousness about how each of us influence and in turn are influenced by race and ethnic relations is an explicit goal of this book.

Over the last decade I have had the luxury of testing a large and varied number of readings on hundreds of students in dozens of race and ethnic relations classes at large public universities as well as small, elite liberal arts colleges. The readings in this book represent the final outcome of classroom "hits and misses." I have used classroom experiences, the results of examinations, and how easily students were able to integrate the readings into research papers to gauge (1) the extent to which the reading contributed to students' understanding of a particular theory or concept, (2) if the reading was intellectually engaging, and (3) if it lent itself to active learning in the classroom. If a reading could pass these hurdles in at least three of my classes, then it made it into this book. Teaching at both public universities and private colleges also provided me with the opportunity to observe how students from different regions, class backgrounds, and racial and ethnic identities reacted to the assigned readings. The articles speak to,

challenge, and find common ground among students from racially, ethnically, culturally, and economically diverse backgrounds. *Rethinking the Color Line* is a response to my students' calls for a book that was user-friendly but did not sacrifice intellectual or theoretical rigor.

This book has been designed to be relevant for students on an individual level while also helping them understand that race and ethnic relations are embedded in the institutions that structure their lives. The readings require students to constantly negotiate the tensions between individual agency and the often determining constraints of social structure. The common thread that links these readings is the ongoing debate about the relationship between agency and structure. It is this conceptual framework that will allow students to think about race and ethnicity in fluid rather than static terms.

Acknowledgments

This reader would not have been possible without the input of those who have engaged me in long discussions about race and ethnic relations over the last ten years. I am indebted to: Richard Alba, Amy Ansell, Sam and Linda Chororos, Kevin Delaney, Richard Delgado, James Dievler, Woody Doane, George Dolph, Tom and Maria Gallagher, Henry Giroux, Noel Ignatiev, Charlie Jaret, Magali Larson, George Lipsitz, Jeff Livesay, Joane Nagel, Jennie Randall, David Roediger, Carmen Saia, Stephen Steinberg, France Winddance Twine, Mary Washington, Howie Winant, and Bill Yancey. Thank you all for showing me the way. Thanks also go to Serina Beauparlant, my talented and patient editor at Mayfield.

Alexia Chororos, my partner, is always two steps ahead of me figuring out how the idea of race and ethnicity is constantly being reshaped, refashioned, and rearticulated by politics and popular culture. Thank you for sharing.

This book is dedicated to our newborn, Sophia Mary Gallagher. May the need for you to be part of the struggle for racial and class equality not be as urgent.

My thanks go to the following reviewers who provided suggestions about the form and content of this reader: Richard Alba, State University of New York at Albany; Marcia L. Bellas, University of Cincinnati; Eduardo Bonilla-Silva, University of Michigan; Ashley Doane, University of Hartford; Jennifer L. Eichstedt, Humboldt State University; Emily Noelle Ignacio, Loyola University of Chicago; Marcia Marx, California State University at San Bernardino; Samuel M. Richards, Pennsylvania State University; Garry L. Rolison, California State University at San Marcos; Deidre

A. Royster, University of Massachusetts at Amherst; Gary Sandefur, University of Wisconsin at Madison; Anna M. Santiago, Wayne State University; and Scott Sernau, Indiana University at South Bend.

I welcome any comments, suggestions, or criticism concerning this reader. Please feel free to contact me about which readings work, which do not, or readings I might include in future editions. Please send any comments directly to me. I look forward to your feedback.

Charles A. Gallagher
Department of Sociology
Georgia State University
University Plaza
Atlanta, GA 30303-3083
E-mail: cgallagher@gsu.edu

About the Contributors

Teresa Amott (Reading 20) is associate professor of economics at Bucknell University. She is committed to sharing economic analysis with unions, welfare rights and women's organizations, and other progressive groups. Amott is the co-author of *Race, Gender, and Work: A Multicultural Economic History of Women in the United States* (with Julie Matthaei) and is the author of *Caught in the Crisis: Women in U.S. Economic History,* as well as numerous articles. She is also an editorial associate with *Dollars and Sense* magazine.

Daniel R. Amundson (Reading 31) is research director of the Center for Media and Public Affairs. He is co-author (with S. Robert Lichter) of *Solid Waste Management: Comparing Expert Opinion, Media Coverage, and Public Opinion* (1992).

Elijah Anderson (Reading 27) is the Charles and William L. Day Professor of the Social Sciences, professor of sociology, and director of the Philadelphia Ethnography Project at the University of Pennsylvania. An expert on the sociology of black America, he is the author of *A Place on the Corner: A Study of Black Streetcorner Men* (1978), numerous articles on the black experience, and the forthcoming *The Code of the Streets.* For his ethnographic study *Streetwise: Race, Class, and Change in an Urban Community* (1990), he was honored with the Robert E. Park Award of the American Sociological Association. Anderson is also associate editor of *Qualitative Sociology* and a member of the board of directors of the American Academy of Political and Social Science.

Elliot Aronson (Reading 12) teaches in the Department of Psychology at the University of California, Santa Cruz. His research interests include energy conservation behavior, and he is the author of *The Social Animal* (1992) and *Social Psychology* (1996).

Herbert Blumer (Reading 10) spent most of his professional career at the University of Chicago and the University of California, Berkeley. Blumer established symbolic interactionism as a major sociological perspective in American sociology.

Lawrence Bobo (Reading 9) is a professor of sociology and Afro-American studies and director of graduate studies at Harvard University. His research interests include social psychology, race and ethnic relations, and public opinion. He is the author of *Racial Attitudes in America: Trends and Interpretations, Revised Edition.* Bobo is currently "conducting research in three areas: studies of prejudice and intergroup conflict with an emphasis on black–white relations, American Indian–white relations, and a general mapping of stereotyping and social distance feelings of whites towards African-Americans and Hispanic-Americans."

Edna Bonacich (Reading 19) is a professor of sociology and ethnic studies at the University of California, Riverside. Her research interests include race and ethnic relations, labor, Marxism, social class and inequality, immigration, and social change. She is currently conducting research on issues related to race, class, and gender oppression in the Los Angeles garment industry. She is working with the ILFWU in hopes that the research may benefit the workers. She is the co-editor of *Global Production: The Apparel Industry in the Pacific Rim* (1994) and *The New*

Asian Immigration in Los Angeles and Global Restructuring (1994), and the co-author of *Immigrant Entrepreneurs: The Koreans in Los Angeles, 1965–1982* (1991).

Robert D. Bullard (Reading 18) is a Ware Professor of Sociology and director of the Environmental Justice Resource Center at Clark Atlanta University. He is the author of *Dumping in Dixie: Race, Color, and Environmental Quality* (1990), *Confronting Environmental Racism: Voices from the Grassroots* (1993), *Unequal Protection: Environmental Justice and Communities of Color* (1994), and *Residential Apartheid: The American Legacy* (1994).

Hector Cordero-Guzman (Reading 6) is an urban poverty fellow in the department of Sociology at the University of Chicago and a researcher at the Center for Puerto Rican Studies.

Gregory DeFreitas (Reading 21) is in the department of economics at Hofstra University and is a researcher at the Russell Sage Foundation. He is an expert on Latino employment patterns and immigration.

Benjamin Demott (Reading 28) is emeritus professor at Amherst College. His new books are *The Trouble with Friendship: Why Americans Can't Think Straight About Race* and *Created Equal: Reading and Writing About Class in America.*

Nancy A. Denton (Reading 25) is an associate professor of sociology at the State University of New York, Albany. Her book *American Apartheid* (co-authored with Douglas Massey) won the 1995 Distinguished Scholarly Publication Award from the American Sociological Association.

Judith N. DeSena (Reading 26) teaches at St. John's University and is the author of

Protecting One's Turf: Social Strategies for Maintaining Urban Neighborhoods (1990).

Michael Eric Dyson (Reading 38) teaches media and cultural studies in the communication studies department at the University of North Carolina, Chapel Hill. Dr. Dyson is an ordained Baptist minister, music writer, political activist, and cultural and social critic. In addition to his scholarly writing, including *Reflecting Black: African-American Cultural Criticism,* Dr. Dyson has written for publications such as *The New York Times, Vibe Magazine,* and *Rolling Stone.*

Robert M. Entman (Reading 30) is an associate professor of communication studies at Northwestern University and was a visiting professor at North Carolina State University in 1994–95. He gratefully acknowledges the support of the Chicago Community Trust Human Relations Foundation and the assistance of James B. White in preparing this article.

Yen Le Espiritu (Reading 7) teaches race and ethnic relations and Asian American studies in the ethnic studies department at the University of California, San Diego. She is the author of *Asian American Women and Men: Labor, Laws, and Love* (1997), *Filipino American Lives* (1995), and *Asian American Panethnicity: Bridging Institutions and Identities* (1992). She is also review editor of the *Journal of Asian-American Studies.*

Clairece Booher Feagin (Reading 3) is the author of *What Will School Be Like?* (1991) and co-author of *Stories for Parents* (1990) and *Discrimination American Style: Institutional Racism and Sexism* (1978).

Joe R. Feagin (Reading 3) is a professor of sociology at the University of Florida. He does research mainly on gender and racial discrimination. He has completed a major research project on the discrimination faced by successful black Americans, a major portion of which was published in 1994 as *Living with Racism: The Black Middle Class Experience*. He has also published a book, *White Racism: The Basics* (1995), with coauthor Professor Hernan Vera and has served as scholar-in-residence at the U.S. Commission on Civil Rights. Feagin was nominated for a Pulitzer Prize for *Ghetto Revolts* (1973).

Charles A. Gallagher (Reading 41) is assistant professor of sociology at Georgia State University in Atlanta. He earned his Ph.D. at Temple University in Philadelphia. He is author of numerous articles on the political and cultural meaning whites attach to their race. His book, *Beyond Invisibility: The Meaning of Whiteness in Multiracial America* (New York University Press) will be published in 2000. Gallagher has been twice honored with awards in teaching excellence.

Herbert J. Gans (Reading 16) is the Robert S. Lynd Professor of Sociology at Columbia University. His books include *The Urban Villagers* and *People, Plans and Policies: Essays on Poverty, Racism and Other National Urban Problems*. He is a former president of the American Sociological Association and has received an award for "lifetime contributions to research" from the American Sociological Association's urban section.

Marvin Harris (Reading 1) spent a portion of his life teaching in the anthropology department at Columbia University, where he served as department chair. In 1981, he accepted the position of graduate research professor of anthropology at the University of Florida. Harris is currently chair of the General Anthropology Division of the American Anthropological Association. He is a generalist with an interest in the global processes that account for human origin and the evolution of human cultures. He has

published sixteen books, including *Cannibals and Kings; Culture, People, and Nature;* and *Our Kind.*

Jennifer L. Hochschild (Reading 45) is a professor of politics and public affairs at Princeton University. She is the author of *Facing Up to the American Dream: Race, Class, and the Soul of the Nation* (1995) and the co-editor of *Social Policies for Children* (1996).

bell hooks (Reading 29) is a writer and lecturer who speaks on issues of race, class, and gender. She teaches at the City University of New York Graduate Center. Her books include *Ain't I a Woman, Feminist Theory,* and *Talking Back*. Her column, "Sisters of the Yam," appears monthly in *Z* magazine.

Randall Kennedy (Reading 42) is a native of Washington, DC, who attended St. Albans School, Princeton University, Balliol College of Oxford University (where he was a Rhodes Scholar), and Yale Law School. As a young lawyer, Kennedy clerked for Supreme Court Justice Thurgood Marshall. A trustee of Princeton, he is also a member of the editorial boards of *Dissent, The Nation,* and *The American Prospect*. Kennedy, the author of many articles in legal journals and general interest magazines, has just published his first book, *Race, Crime, and the Law*. He currently lives near Boston with his wife, Yvedt Matory, a cancer surgeon at the Brigham and Women's Hospital, and his son, Henry William Kennedy.

Joleen Kirschenman (Reading 22) is an affiliate of the Center for the Study of Urban Equality at the University of Chicago.

Jonathan Kozol (Reading 15) taught in public schools for several years and is the award-winning author of many books, including *Death at an Early Age, Illiterate America, Free Schools,* and *Rachel and Her Children*.

Maria Krysan (Reading 9) is an assistant professor of sociology at Pennsylvania State University and a research affiliate in its Population Research Institute. She is the co-author of *Racial Attitudes in America: Trends and Interpretations, Revised Edition.*

Richard E. Lapchick (Reading 32) is the director of Northeastern University's Center for the Study of Sport.

Nicholas Lemann (Reading 35) was born and raised in New Orleans. He attended Harvard, graduating in 1976 with a degree in American history and literature. Before joining the staff of *The Atlantic Monthly,* he worked at *The Washington Monthly, Texas Monthly,* and *The Washington Post.* He is the author of the best-selling book *The Promised Land* (1991).

S. Robert Lichter (Reading 31) is the founder of the Center for Media and Public Affairs, a nonpartisan, nonprofit research and educational organization that conducts scientific studies of news and entertainment media. He is the co-author (with Daniel Amundson) of *Solid Waste Management: Comparing Expert Opinion, Media Coverage, and Public Opinion* (1992).

Elizabeth Martínez (Reading 13) is the author of *500 Years of Chicano History,* a regular columnist for *Z* magazine, and an editor of *Crossroads* magazine. She is a lifelong activist in the civil rights and Chicano movements.

Douglas S. Massey (Reading 25) is chair and professor of sociology at the University of Pennsylvania. His book *American Apartheid* (co-authored with Nancy A. Denton) won the 1995 Distinguished Scholarly Publication Award from the American Sociological Association.

Julie Matthaei (Reading 20) is an associate professor of economics at Wellesley College and the author of *An Economic History of Women in America: Women's Work, the Sexual Division of Labor, and the Development of Capitalism.* She is a long-term feminist and has written widely on the political economy of gender and race.

Robert K. Merton (Reading 11) is an adjunct professor at Rockefeller University, a resident scholar at the Russell Sage Foundation, and a professor emeritus at Columbia University. He is an eminent sociological theorist and a well-known defender of sociology as a genuine science. His publications include *On the Shoulders of Giants: A Shandean Postscript* (1965) and *The Sociology of Science: Theoretical and Empirical Investigations* (1973).

Pyong Gap Min (Reading 36) is a professor of sociology at Queens College and the graduate school of the City University of New York. His research interests include Korean small-business and ethnic solidarity, immigrant families, and ethnic attachment among Korean and other Asian American groups. He is the author of *Ethnic Enterprise: Korean Small Business in Atlanta* (1988) and *Middlemen in Contemporary America: Koreans in New York and Los Angeles, 1970–1994.* He edited *Asian Americans: Contemporary Trends and Issues* (1995), to which he contributed several chapters. He received a bachelor's degree from Seoul National University (in Korea) and a master's degree from Georgia State University, both in history, and two Ph.D. degrees from Georgia State University, one in educational philosophy and the other in sociology.

Joane Nagel (Reading 8) is a professor of sociology at the University of Kansas. Her research focuses on the politics of ethnicity. She is the author of "Constructing Ethnicity: Creating and Re-creating Ethnic Identity and Culture" (*Social Problems,* 1994, pp. 152–76) and *American Indian Ethnic Renewal: Red Power and the Resurgence of Identity and*

Culture (Oxford University Press). She is currently working on a book entitled *Masculinity and Nationalism: The Global Politics of Gender and Ethnicity.*

Kathryn M. Neckerman (Reading 22) is an assistant professor of sociology at Columbia University. She writes: "My research interests include education and race and ethnic relations and I am writing a book about minority education in Chicago, 1900–1960." For her latest project, she "interviewed African-American, Latino, and West Indian students who were enrolled in business college to prepare them for white-collar jobs, to see how these students reconciled identity with pressure to 'talk white.'"

Melvin L. Oliver (Reading 44) is on leave from his position as professor of sociology and policy studies at the University of California, Los Angeles. Currently, he is vice president of the Ford Foundation's program Asset Building and Community Development. He was named the 1994 California Professor of the Year by the Carnegie Foundation. Oliver and Thomas M. Shapiro have been awarded the C. Wright Mills Award and the American Sociological Association's Distinguished Scholarly Publication Award for *Black Wealth/White Wealth.*

Michael Omi (Reading 2) is a professor in the Department of Ethnic Studies at the University of California, Berkeley, and the co-author of *Racial Formation in the United States from the 1960s to the 1980s* (1986). He has also written about racial theory and politics, right-wing political movements, Asian Americans and race relations, and race and popular culture. In 1990, he was the recipient of Berkeley's Distinguished Teaching Award.

Howard Pinderhughes (Reading 17) is an assistant professor in the Department of Social and Behavioral Sciences at the University of California, San Francisco, and the author of *Race in the Hood: Conflict and Violence Among Urban Youth.*

Clara E. Rodriguez (Reading 6) is a professor in the Division of Social Sciences at Fordham University. Her major areas of research and interest include race and ethnicity, Latino studies, media, labor markets, and migration.

Lillian B. Rubin (Reading 37) is a practicing psychotherapist and a senior research fellow at the Institute for the Study of Social Change at the University of California, Berkeley. She is an internationally recognized author and social scientist, and has authored numerous books, including *Worlds of Pain: Life in the Working Class* (1976), *Intimate Strangers: Men and Women Together* (1983), *Families on the Fault Line: America's Working Class Speaks About the Family, the Economy, Race, and Ethnicity,* and *Fall Down Seven Times, Get Up Eight* (1966), which presents case histories of people who have transcended very difficult circumstances.

Howard Schuman (Reading 9) is a research scientist at the Institute for Social Research and a professor of sociology, both at the University of Michigan. Together with Charlotte Steeh and others, he is completing a revision of his book *Racial Attitudes in America: Trends and Interpretations,* first published in 1985 (Harvard University Press). He recently wrote a chapter on "Attitudes, Beliefs, and Behavior" for the edited volume *Sociological Perspectives on Social Psychology,* and he continues to write in two other areas: "generations and collective memory" and the "question–answer process in surveys."

Thomas M. Shapiro (Reading 44) is a professor of sociology and anthropology at Northeastern University. Shapiro and Melvin L. Oliver have been awarded the C. Wright Mills Award and the American Sociological

Association's Distinguished Scholarly Publication Award for *Black Wealth/White Wealth*. Shapiro's books include *Population Control Politics: Women, Sterilization, and Reproductive Choice* and *Great Divides: Readings in Social Inequality in the United States*.

Robert Staples (Reading 39) is a professor of sociology at the University of California, San Francisco. He has been the recipient of distinguished achievement awards from Howard University and the National Council on Family Relations. Professor Staples has been published in popular and scholarly periodicals in the United States and around the world. Among his books are *Black Masculinity, The Urban Plantation,* and *Families at the Crossroads*.

Charlotte Steeh (Reading 9) is an associate professor of public administration and urban studies at Georgia State University. She is co-author of *Racial Attitudes in America: Trends and Interpretations*.

Stephen Steinberg (Reading 33) teaches in the Department of Urban Studies at Queens College and the Ph.D. Program in Sociology at the CUNY Graduate Center. His recent book *Turning Back: The Retreat from Racial Justice in American Thought and Policy* received the Oliver Cromwell Cox Award for Distinguished Anti-Racist Scholarship. Other books include *The Ethnic Myth, The Academic Melting Pot,* and *The Tenacity of Prejudice*. In addition to his scholarly publications, he has published articles in *The Nation, New Politics, Reconstruction,* and *The UNESCO Courier*.

Roger Waldinger (Reading 23) is a professor of race/ethnic/minority relations, urban sociology, and migration and immigration at the University of California, Los Angeles. He is the author of *Still the Promised City? New Immigrants and African-Americans in Post-Industrial New York* (1996) and *Ethnic Los Angeles,* co-edited with Medhi Bozorgmehr (1996).

Mary C. Waters (Readings 34 and 40) is a professor of sociology at Harvard University. She is the author of *Ethnic Options: Choosing Identities in America* and the co-author of *From Many Strands: Ethnic and Racial Groups in Contemporary America*. She has consulted with the Census Bureau on issues of measurement of race and ethnicity, and was a member of the National Academy of Science's Study Panel on the Demographic and Economic Consequences of Immigration to the United States. She has been a Guggenheim Fellow and a visiting scholar at the Russell Sage Foundation, and is a member of the International Committee of the Social Science Research Council.

Cornel West (Reading 43) is a professor of Afro-American studies and the philosophy of religion at Harvard University. He is the author of many books and essays, including *Restoring Hope: Conversations on the Future of Black America* (with Shawn Sealey) and *Race Matters*.

William Julius Wilson (Reading 24) is the Malcolm Wiener Professor of Social Policy and the director of the Joblessness and Urban Poverty Research Program at the John F. Kennedy School of Government, Harvard University. He is a MacArthur Prize fellow and the author of *The Declining Significance of Race* and *The Truly Disadvantaged,* among many other books and articles. Wilson's teaching interests include urban poverty, urban race and class relations, and social inequalities and cross-cultural perspective. His current projects include studies of race and the social organization of neighborhoods, the effects of high-risk neighborhoods on adolescent social outcomes, and the new social inequality and race-based social policy.

Howard Winant (Reading 2) is a professor of sociology at Temple University. He is the author of numerous books and articles, including *Racial Formation in the United States from the 1960s to the 1990s* (1994) (with Michael Omi), *Racial Conditions: Politics, Theory, Comparisons* (1994), and *Stalemate: Political Economic Origins of Supply-Side Policy* (1988). Winant states: "My abiding interests are in the sociology of race, particularly in the dynamics of racial politics and the theoretical logic of race. I have conducted research and taught in Brazil and Mexico. My current research focuses on the global dynamics of race at the end of the twentieth century."

Lawrence Wright (Reading 5) is a writer for *The New Yorker.*

Howard Zinn (Reading 4), professor, activist, and author, has dedicated his life to the notion that the knowledge of history is important to people's everyday lives and can be a powerful force for social change. Zinn is a champion of the idea that historical change occurs more through mass movements of ordinary people than through the wisdom and insight of so-called Great Men. His best-known book, *A People's History of the United States,* was one of the first major looks at American history from such a perspective.

RETHINKING THE COLOR LINE

INTRODUCTION
Rethinking the Color Line:
Understanding How Boundaries Shift

The sociological promise implicit in the title, *Rethinking the Color Line,* is that we will explore the contemporary meanings of race and ethnicity and examine how specifically those meanings are shaped by social, political, economic, and cultural forces. This may seem like a straightforward task. It is not. Race and ethnicity are slippery concepts because they are always in a state of flux. Imagine for a moment the shape of the United States as analogous to a definition of race or ethnicity. It may appear that an outline or sketch of the U.S. border, like a definition of race or ethnicity, can be neatly described or mapped out. That is, just as we can imagine the borders of the United States, we can, with reasonable certainty, identify someone as black, white, Asian, or American Indian.

We place people in these racial categories because we have been trained to focus on a combination of traits like skin color, hair texture, and eye shape. After we have placed individuals in racial categories, we typically use cultural markers, such as their ethnic background or ancestry, to further sort them. For instance, if a white person walks into a room, we *see* that individual's race. What happens when he or she starts talking and we pick up on an Irish brogue or a New York City accent or a southern dialect? What happens when the brown woman in front of us in the supermarket talks to the cashier and we recognize her accent as Jamaican or English? We tend to sort first by color and then by cultural background.

Since the founding of the United States more than two hundred years ago, the lines that have defined the nation's borders have been redrawn dozens of times. Just as there was no United States of America prior to 1776, the idea of race as it is currently understood did not exist until the Americas, Africa, and parts of Asia were colonized by the Europeans. The mental map we conjure up of the United States today is only about forty years old. The map was last redrawn in 1959 when Hawaii was admitted into the Union as the fiftieth state. Previously, the map had been redrawn after the Louisiana Purchase of 1803 and again after the Missouri Compromise of 1820, as well as after the admittance of every new state to the Union. And we will have to redraw our mental map yet again if the Commonwealth of Puerto Rico votes to enter the Union as the fifty-first state.

The problem with definitions of race and ethnicity, as with the shape of the United States, is that the borders or contours that give form and meaning to these concepts change over time. A person defined as white in the year 2000 might have been defined as black or Irish or Italian at various times in American history. For example, around the turn of the century, Irish and Italian immigrants were *not* viewed as white when they first arrived in the United States. At that time, members of those groups did not easily fit into the existing racial hierarchy; they were in a racial limbo—not white, not black, not Asian. Their ethnic background—that is, the language, culture, and religious beliefs that distinguished these Irish and Italian immigrants from the dominant group—was used in various ways to define them as a racial group. Within a generation or two, these so-called Irish and Italian racial groups assimilated and were absorbed into the category we now know as white. The journey from being considered not white or racially ambiguous to white was rather swift. It may seem odd, and may even shock our racial sensibilities, to think of Supreme Court Justice Antonin Scalia's or Senator Ted Kennedy's parents or grandparents as possibly being defined as nonwhite Italians or nonwhite Irish at different times in American history. But is a nonwhite Italian or nonwhite Irish any less curious an idea than a black-Irish American or an Asian-Italian American? If one's ethnic identity is subsumed or taken over by a racial identity, the question we need to ask as sociologists is, why?

Just as the shape of the United States has changed over time, so have the definitions of race and ethnicity. Do you think your view of race and ethnicity is different from that of your parents or grandparents? How you understand race and ethnicity reflects a definition specific to this moment in time, one that, in all likelihood, will look quite different in three or four decades. *Rethinking the Color Line* will provide you with a theoretical framework for understanding how and why definitions of race and ethnicity change over time, what sociological forces bring about these changes, and what these categories might look like in the next century.

What these examples suggest, and what many of the readings in *Rethinking the Color Line* consciously explore, is how race and ethnicity are socially constructed. When we say that something is socially constructed, we mean that the characteristics deemed relevant to that definition are based on societal and cultural values. Race and ethnicity are social constructions because their meanings are derived by focusing on arbitrary characteristics that a given society deems socially important. Race and ethnicity are social

products based on cultural values; they are not scientific facts.

Think for a moment about gravity. If you push this book off your desk, do you expect it to fall to the ground? Obviously, you do. If you lived in Brazil or South Africa or Puerto Rico, would you expect the same thing to happen to your book? Of course you would because you know that gravity is a universal constant. However, someone defined as black in the United States could be defined as white in Brazil, Trigueno (intermediate) in Puerto Rico, and "coloured" in South Africa. Gravity is the same everywhere, but racial classifications vary across place and time because definitions of race and ethnicity are based on the physical traits a society chooses to value or devalue. Because each society's values are based on a different set of historical experiences, cultural circumstances, and political definitions, ideas about race and ethnicity can vary quite a bit, not only between countries but within them as well. For example, historically, it was not uncommon for someone to have been socially and legally defined as black in the southern part of the United States but to "pass" for white after migrating north. The beliefs and definitions that undergird the idea of race are very unstable and, as we will see in the readings, quite susceptible to political manipulation.

Racial and ethnic identity is culturally meaningful only because we define and understand it in that way. In other words, race exists because we say race exists. And because the characteristics that make up the idea of race and ethnicity reflect a social process, it is possible to imagine these concepts in a different way. Instead of looking at skin color, facial features, or hair texture as a way to sort individuals, we could create a racial category based on the size of peoples' feet. People with shoe sizes between 4 and 7 would be labeled the Petite Race, those with sizes 8–11 would be designated the Bigger Race, and the 12–15 crowd would be categorized as the Monster Race. Those with feet smaller or larger than the existing categories would be the "Other" Race. Likewise, we could use eye color, height, glove size, or nose length to create racial categories. Because the physical markers we use to define race are arbitrary and have no basis in genetics, biology, anthropology, or sociology, using shoe size as the criterion to fashion a new definition of race would be just as valid as the system currently in place. Similarly, we could redefine ethnicity by changing the focus from language, culture, religion, or nationality as a method of sorting people and instead create categories of people based on the amount of meat they eat or the way they style their hair.

What complicates our ability to accurately and easily map these definitions of race and ethnicity is that the definitions are constantly changing. Are the 30 million Latinos in the United States an ethnic group because they are defined by the U.S. Census Bureau as such, or are Latinos a racial group? If the current census categories of white, black, Asian, and American Indian do not adequately reflect what Latinos experience or how Latinos are viewed by non-Latinos, should a "brown" category be added to the census? Would a newly created "brown" category link Puerto Ricans in New York City with Cuban Americans in Miami and Mexican Americans in San Diego? Why or why not? How should we define the race of a child whose father was Mexican-African

American and whose mother was Japanese-Irish American? What is this child's ethnicity? For that matter, how and in what ways are race and ethnicity related?

In 1903, sociologist W. E. B. Du Bois wrote that "the problem of the twentieth century is the problem of the color-line." It appears that a key problem of the twenty-first century, while different in degree and context from the one Du Bois chronicled, will still be the color line. A topic or issue may not initially seem to be linked to race or ethnicity, but on closer sociological scrutiny, patterns often emerge that make it clear that race and ethnicity matter quite a bit. How do you see race and ethnicity being connected to who gets a good education or adequate health care, who is likely to be poor, where toxic waste sites are built, who gets hired or promoted, or which racial or ethnic groups are more likely to have members sentenced to death and executed? Race and ethnicity are intertwined in every aspect of our lives.

Rethinking the Color Line will provide you with the tools necessary to navigate the complicated and often contradictory meaning of race and ethnicity in the United States. The readings will take you on a sociological journey and explore how you, your classmates, your family, and your friends fit into the racial and ethnic mosaic of the United States. If you focus carefully on the readings and discussion questions, your perspective on race and ethnic relations in the United States will be changed forever.

PART I
Sorting by Color:
Why We Attach Meaning to Race

How would you answer these questions?

Who taught you how to "be" black or American Indian or white or Asian? Did you learn to "do" your race by watching sitcoms on television or by watching your peers in the schoolyard? Was it your parents or an older sibling or cousin who taught you how to act both your age and your race? In what social situations do you think about your racial identity? Is it only when you interact with an individual from a different racial background? Do media events like football games or MTV or the nightly news force you to think about your race, about other racial groups, or about race relations? Do you think about your race while you are in your neighborhood or only when you drive through an area with a different racial population? Were you ever in a social setting in which you were the only person of your color? How did that make you feel?

How did you learn to "be" Korean or Jamaican or German? In what situations do you think about your ancestry? Is it during the holidays or when you spend time with your family? Or has your family been in the United States for so many generations that the family tree linking you to the homeland is unimportant, nonexistent, or untraceable? Does that mean you have a racial identity but not an ethnic identity? Or does "American" best mirror your social identity?

The readings in Part I answer these questions by exposing you to the social theories used to define and understand the dynamics of race and ethnicity. The first three readings examine how the natural variation in human skin color has been used as a way to sort people into groups, create a racial hierarchy, and justify exploitation based on skin color. Marvin Harris explains why white and black and the gradations of color in between are "beautiful" responses to the environment. Michael Omi and Howard Winant explain the emergence of racial categories as a "sociohistoric" process; that is, the way we define ourselves racially reflects a process that was hundreds of years in the making. Joe Feagin and Clairece Booher Feagin provide an overview of the theories central to ethnic and racial studies, theories that will reemerge throughout the book. As you will see, many of the articles in this reader draw on one or more of these theories to explain a particular aspect of race and ethnic relations.

The next five readings draw on the theories outlined in the first section but emphasize the extent to which racial and ethnic identity construction are shaped by politics and culture. Howard Zinn charts the evolution of the idea of race in early U.S. history. Lawrence Wright links the past and present by illustrating how these past definitions of race and ethnicity have been codified by the government but are now being challenged by groups who do not feel their mixed-race backgrounds fit into the government's narrow racial and ethnic categories. As these readings demonstrate, the creation of these categories is as much a historical process as it is a political one. Clara Rodriguez and Hector Cordero-Guzman explain how the social and political organization of slavery in Puerto Rico differed from that in the United States, resulting in an understanding and definition of race that may seem peculiar to those of us accustomed to the white-versus-black view of race relations so dominant in the United States. Finally, although the specific historical circumstances of Asians and American Indians vary, Yen Le Espiritu and Joane Nagel demonstrate how, why, and in what situations racial and ethnic identities are used to organize politically.

QUESTIONS TO FRAME YOUR READINGS

The questions at the end of each part introduction are designed to help you focus on key ideas or themes in the readings.

- If race is not "real" in a scientific sense, why can I look around the classroom or campus and *see* that someone is black or Asian or white? What is the difference between something being "real" and something being a "social construction"?

- How and in what specific ways have definitions of race and ethnicity changed?

- Why was the United States one of the few countries that embraced the "one-drop rule"?

- Why do people often confuse race and ethnicity? Are they ever the same thing? Can you have one and not the other?

- How is it possible to be defined as belonging to one race in one country and to a different race in another country?

- If there is a "social context" to race, as Rodriguez and Cordero-Guzman suggest, what are the sociological factors that make that "context" vary from country to country?

Race and Ethnicity as Sociohistorical Constructions

1

HOW OUR SKINS GOT THEIR COLOR

Marvin Harris

Most human beings are neither very fair nor very dark, but brown. The extremely fair skin of northern Europeans and their descendants, and the very black skins of central Africans and their descendants, are probably special adaptations. Brown-skinned ancestors may have been shared by modern-day blacks and whites as recently as 10,000 years ago.

Human skin owes its color to the presence of particles known as melanin. The primary function of melanin is to protect the upper levels of the skin from being damaged by the sun's ultraviolet rays. This radiation poses a critical problem for our kind because we lack the dense coat of hair that acts as a sunscreen for most mammals. . . . Hairlessness exposes us to two kinds of radiation hazards: ordinary sunburn, with its blisters, rashes, and risk of infection; and skin cancers, including malignant melanoma, one of the deadliest diseases known. Melanin is the body's first line of defense against these afflictions. The more melanin particles, the darker the skin, and the lower the risk of sunburn and all forms of skin

cancer. This explains why the highest rates for skin cancer are found in sun-drenched lands such as Australia, where light-skinned people of European descent spend a good part of their lives outdoors wearing scanty attire. Very dark-skinned people such as heavily pigmented Africans of Zaire seldom get skin cancer, but when they do, they get it on depigmented parts of their bodies—palms and lips.

If exposure to solar radiation had nothing but harmful effects, natural selection would have favored inky black as the color for all human populations. But the sun's rays do not present an unmitigated threat. As it falls on the skin, sunshine converts a fatty substance in the epidermis into vitamin D. The blood carries vitamin D from the skin to the intestines (technically making it a hormone rather than a vitamin), where it plays a vital role in the absorption of calcium. In turn, calcium is vital for strong bones. Without it, people fall victim to the crippling diseases rickets and osteomalacia. In women, calcium deficiencies can result in a deformed birth canal, which makes childbirth lethal for both mother and fetus.

Vitamin D can be obtained from a few foods, primarily the oils and livers of marine fish. But inland populations must rely on the sun's rays and their own skins for the supply of this crucial substance. The particular color of a human population's skin, therefore, represents in large degree a trade-off between the hazards of too much versus too little solar radiation: acute sunburn and skin cancer on the one hand, and rickets and osteomalacia on the other. It is this trade-off that largely accounts for the preponderance of brown people in the world and for the general tendency for skin color to be darkest among equatorial populations and lightest among populations dwelling at higher latitudes.

At middle latitudes, the skin follows a strategy of changing colors with the seasons. Around the Mediterranean basin, for example, exposure to the summer sun brings high risk of cancer but low risk for rickets; the body produces more melanin and people grow darker (i.e., they get suntans). Winter reduces the risk of sunburn and cancer; the body produces less melanin, and the tan wears off.

The correlation between skin color and latitude is not perfect because other factors—such as the availability of foods containing vitamin D and calcium, regional cloud cover during the winter, amount of clothing worn, and cultural preferences—may work for or against the predicted relationship. Arctic-dwelling Eskimo, for example, are not as light-skinned as expected, but their habitat and economy afford them a diet that is exceptionally rich in both vitamin D and calcium.

Northern Europeans, obliged to wear heavy garments for protection against the long, cold, cloudy winters, were always at risk for rickets and osteomalacia from too little vitamin D and calcium. This risk increased sometime after 6000 B.C., when pioneer cattle herders who did not exploit marine resources began to appear in northern Europe. The risk would have been especially great for the brown-skinned Mediterranean peoples who migrated northward along with the crops and farm animals.

Samples of Caucasian skin (infant penile foreskin obtained at the time of circumcision) exposed to sunlight on cloudless days in Boston (42°N) from November through February produced no vitamin D. In Edmonton (52°N) this period extended from October to March. But further south (34°N) sunlight was effective in producing vitamin D in the middle of the winter. Almost all of Europe lies north of 42°N. Fair-skinned, nontanning individuals who could utilize the weakest and briefest doses of sunlight to synthesize vitamin D were strongly favored by natural selection. During the frigid winters, only a small circle of a child's face could be left to peek out at the sun through the heavy clothing, thereby favoring the survival of individuals with translucent patches of pink on their cheeks characteristic of many northern Europeans. (People who could get calcium by drinking cow's milk would also be favored by natural selection.)

If light-skinned individuals on the average had only 2 percent more children survive per generation, the changeover in their skin color could have begun 5,000 years ago and reached present levels well before the beginning of the Christian era. But natural selection need not have acted alone. Cultural selection may also have played a role. It seems likely that whenever people consciously or unconsciously had to decide which infants to nourish and which to neglect, the advantage would go to those with lighter skin, experience having shown that such individuals tended to grow up to be taller, stronger, and healthier than their darker siblings. White was beautiful because white was healthy.

To account for the evolution of black skin in equatorial latitudes, one has merely to reverse the combined effects of natural and cultural selection. With the sun directly overhead most of the year, and clothing a hindrance to work and survival, vitamin D was never in short supply (and calcium was easily obtained from vegetables). Rickets and osteomalacia were rare. Skin cancer was the main problem, and what nature started, culture amplified. Darker infants were favored by parents because experience showed that they grew up to be freer of disfiguring and lethal malignancies. Black was beautiful because black was healthy.

2

RACIAL FORMATIONS

Michael Omi • Howard Winant

In 1982–83, Susie Guillory Phipps unsuccessfully sued the Louisiana Bureau of Vital Records to change her racial classification from black to white. The descendant of an eighteenth-century white planter and a black slave, Phipps was designated "black" in her birth certificate in accordance with a 1970 state law which declared anyone with at least one-thirty-second "Negro blood" to be black. The legal battle raised intriguing questions about the concept of race, its meaning in contemporary society, and its use (and abuse) in public policy. Assistant Attorney General Ron Davis defended the law by pointing out that some type of racial classification was necessary to comply with federal record-keeping requirements and to facilitate programs for the prevention of genetic diseases. Phipps's attorney, Brian Begue, argued that the assignment of racial categories on birth certificates was unconstitutional and that the one-thirty-second designation was inaccurate. He called on a retired Tulane University professor who cited research indicating that most whites have one-twentieth "Negro" ancestry. In the end, Phipps lost. The court upheld a state law which quantified racial identity, and in so doing affirmed the legality of assigning individuals to specific racial groupings.[1]

The Phipps case illustrates the continuing dilemma of defining race and establishing its meaning in institutional life. Today, to assert that variations in human physiognomy are racially based is to enter a constant and intense debate. *Scientific* interpretations of race have not been alone in sparking heated controversy; *religious* perspectives have done so as well.[2] Most centrally, of course, race has been a matter of *political* contention. This has been particularly true in the United States, where the concept of race has varied enormously over time without ever leaving the center stage of US history.

What Is Race?

Race consciousness, and its articulation in theories of race, is largely a modern phenomenon. When European explorers in the

New World "discovered" people who looked different than themselves, these "natives" challenged then existing conceptions of the origins of the human species, and raised disturbing questions as to whether *all* could be considered in the same "family of man."[3] Religious debates flared over the attempt to reconcile the Bible with the existence of "racially distinct" people. Arguments took place over creation itself, as theories of polygenesis questioned whether God had made only one species of humanity ("monogenesis"). Europeans wondered if the natives of the New World were indeed human beings with redeemable souls. At stake were not only the prospects for conversion, but the types of treatment to be accorded them. The expropriation of property, the denial of political rights, the introduction of slavery and other forms of coercive labor, as well as outright extermination, all presupposed a worldview which distinguished Europeans—children of God, human beings, etc.—from "others." Such a worldview was needed to explain why some should be "free" and others enslaved, why some had rights to land and property while others did not. Race, and the interpretation of racial differences, was a central factor in that worldview.

In the colonial epoch science was no less a field of controversy than religion in attempts to comprehend the concept of race and its meaning. Spurred on by the classificatory scheme of living organisms devised by Linnaeus in *Systema Naturae,* many scholars in the eighteenth and nineteenth centuries dedicated themselves to the identification and ranking of variations in humankind. Race was thought of as a *biological* concept, yet its precise definition was the subject of debates which, as we have noted, continue to rage today. Despite efforts ranging from Dr. Samuel Morton's studies of cranial capacity[4] to contemporary attempts to base racial classification on shared gene pools,[5] the concept of race has defied biological definition. . . .

Attempts to discern the *scientific meaning* of race continue to the present day. Although most physical anthropologists and biologists have abandoned the quest for a scientific basis to determine racial categories, controversies have recently flared in the area of genetics and educational psychology. For instance, an essay by Arthur Jensen argued that hereditary factors shape intelligence not only revived the "nature or nurture" controversy, but raised highly volatile questions about racial equality itself.[6] Clearly the attempt to establish a *biological* basis of race has not been swept into the dustbin of history, but is being resurrected in various scientific arenas. All such attempts seek to remove the concept of race from fundamental social, political, or economic determination. They suggest instead that the truth of race lies in the terrain of innate characteristics, of which skin color and other physical attributes provide only the most obvious, and in some respects most superficial, indicators.

Race as a Social Concept

The social sciences have come to reject biologistic notions of race in favor of an approach which regards race as a *social* concept. Beginning in the eighteenth century, this trend has been slow and uneven, but its direction clear. In the nineteenth century Max Weber discounted biological explanations for racial conflict and instead highlighted the social and political factors which engendered such conflict.[7] The work of pioneering cultural anthropologist Franz Boas was crucial in refuting the scientific racism of the early twentieth century by rejecting the connection between race and culture, and the assumption of a continuum of "higher" and "lower" cultural groups. Within the contemporary social science literature, race is assumed to be a variable which is shaped by broader societal forces.

Race is indeed a pre-eminently *socio-historical* concept. Racial categories and the meaning of race are given concrete expression by the specific social relations and historical context in which they are embedded. Racial meanings have varied tremendously over time and between different societies.

In the United States, the black/white color line has historically been rigidly defined and enforced. White is seen as a "pure" category. Any racial intermixture makes one "nonwhite." In the movie *Raintree County,* Elizabeth Taylor describes the worst of fates to befall whites as "havin' a little Negra blood in ya'—just one little teeny drop and a person's all Negra."[8] This thinking flows from what Marvin Harris has characterized as the principle of *hypo-descent:*

> By what ingenious computation is the genetic tracery of a million years of evolution unraveled and each man [sic] assigned his proper social box? In the United States, the mechanism employed is the rule of hypo-descent. This descent rule requires Americans to believe that anyone who is known to have had a Negro ancestor is a Negro. We admit nothing in between. . . . "Hypo-descent" means affiliation with the subordinate rather than the superordinate group in order to avoid the ambiguity of intermediate identity. . . . The rule of hypo-descent is, therefore, an invention, which we in the United States have made in order to keep biological facts from intruding into our collective racist fantasies.[9]

The Susie Guillory Phipps case merely represents the contemporary expression of this racial logic.

By contrast, a striking feature of race relations in the lowland areas of Latin America since the abolition of slavery has been the relative absence of sharply defined racial groupings. No such rigid descent rule characterizes racial identity in many Latin American societies. Brazil, for example, has historically had less rigid conceptions of race, and thus a variety of "intermediate" racial categories exist. Indeed, as Harris notes, "One of the most striking consequences of the Brazilian system of racial identification is that parents and children and even brothers and sisters are frequently accepted as representatives of quite opposite racial types."[10] Such a possibility is incomprehensible within the logic of racial categories in the US.

To suggest another example: the notion of "passing" takes on new meaning if we compare various American cultures' means of assigning racial identity. In the United States, individuals who are actually "black" by the logic of hypo-descent have attempted to skirt the discriminatory barriers imposed by law and custom by attempting to "pass" for white.[11] Ironically, these same individuals would not be able to pass for "black" in many Latin American societies.

Consideration of the term "black" illustrates the diversity of racial meanings which can be found among different societies and historically within a given society. In contemporary British politics the term "black" is used to refer to all nonwhites. Interestingly this designation has not arisen through the racist discourse of groups such as the National Front. Rather, in political and cultural movements, Asian as well as Afro-Caribbean youth are adopting the term as an expression of self-identity.[12] The wide-ranging meanings of "black" illustrate the manner in which racial categories are shaped politically.[13]

The meaning of race is defined and contested throughout society, in both collective action and personal practice. In the process, racial categories themselves are formed, transformed, destroyed and reformed. We use the term *racial formation* to refer to the process by which social, economic and political forces determine the content and importance of racial categories, and by which they are in turn shaped by racial meanings. Crucial to this formulation is the treatment of race as a *central axis* of social relations which cannot be subsumed under or reduced to some broader category or conception.

Racial Ideology and Racial Identity

The seemingly obvious, "natural" and "common sense" qualities which the existing racial order exhibits themselves testify to the effectiveness of the racial formation process in constructing racial meanings and racial identities.

One of the first things we notice about people when we meet them (along with their sex) is their race. We utilize race to provide clues abut *who* a person is. This fact is made painfully obvious when we encounter someone whom we cannot conveniently racially categorize—someone who is, for example, racially "mixed" or of an ethnic/racial group with which we are not familiar. Such an encounter becomes a source of discomfort and momentarily a crisis of racial meaning. Without a racial identity, one is in danger of having no identity.

Our compass for navigating race relations depends on preconceived notions of what each specific racial group looks like. Comments such as, "Funny, you don't look black," betray an underlying image of what black should be. We also become disoriented when people do not act "black," "Latino," or indeed "white." The content of such stereotypes reveals a series of unsubstantiated beliefs about who these groups are and what "they" are like.[14]

In US society, then, a kind of "racial etiquette" exists, a set of interpretative codes and racial meanings which operate in the interactions of daily life. Rules shaped by our perception of race in a comprehensively racial society determine the "presentation of self,"[15] distinctions of status, and appropriate modes of conduct. "Etiquette" is not mere universal adherence to the dominant group's rules, but a more dynamic combination of these rules with the values and beliefs of subordinated groupings. This racial "subjection" is quintessentially ideological. Everybody learns some combination, some version, of the rules of racial classification, and of their own racial identity, often without obvious teaching or conscious inculcation. Race becomes "common sense"—a way of comprehending, explaining and acting in the world.

Racial beliefs operate as an "amateur biology," a way of explaining the variations in "human nature."[16] Differences in skin color and other obvious physical characteristics supposedly provide visible clues to differences lurking underneath. Temperament, sexuality, intelligence, athletic ability, aesthetic preferences and so on are presumed to be fixed and discernible from the palpable mark of race. Such diverse questions as our confidence and trust in others (for example, clerks or salespeople, media figures, neighbors), our sexual preferences and romantic images, our tastes in music, films, dance, or sports, and our very ways of talking, walking, eating and dreaming are ineluctably shaped by notions of race. Skin color "differences" are thought to explain perceived differences in intellectual, physical and artistic temperaments, and to justify distinct treatment of racially identified individuals and groups.

The continuing persistence of racial ideology suggests that these racial myths and stereotypes cannot be exposed as such in the popular imagination. They are, we think, too essential, too integral, to the maintenance of the US social order. Of course, particular meanings, stereotypes and myths can change, but the presence of a *system* of racial meanings and stereotypes, of racial ideology, seems to be a permanent feature of US culture.

Film and television, for example, have been notorious in disseminating images of racial minorities which establish for audiences what people from these groups look like, how they behave, and "who they are."[17] The power of the media lies not only in their ability to reflect the dominant racial ideology, but in their capacity to shape that ideology in the first place. D. W. Griffith's epic *Birth of a Nation,* a sympathetic treatment of the rise of the Ku Klux Klan during Reconstruction, helped to generate, consolidate and "nationalize" images of blacks which had been more disparate (more regionally specific, for example) prior to the film's appearance.[18] In US television, the necessity to define characters in the briefest and most condensed manner has led to the perpetuation of racial caricatures, as racial stereotypes serve as shorthand for scriptwriters, directors and actors, in commercials, etc. Television's tendency to address the "lowest common denominator" in order to render programs "familiar" to an enormous and diverse audience leads it regularly to assign and reassign racial characteristics to particular groups, both minority and majority.

These and innumerable other examples show that we tend to view race as something fixed and immutable—something rooted in "nature." Thus we mask the historical construction of racial categories, the shifting meaning of race, and the crucial role of politics and ideology in shaping race relations. Races do not emerge full-blown. They are the results of diverse historical practices and are continually subject to challenge over their definition and meaning.

Racialization: The Historical Development of Race

In the United States, the racial category of "black" evolved with the consolidation of racial slavery. By the end of the seventeenth century, Africans whose specific identity was Ibo, Yoruba, Fulani, etc., were rendered "black" by an ideology of exploitation based on racial logic—the establishment and maintenance of a "color line." This of course did not occur overnight. A period of indentured servitude which was not rooted in racial logic preceded the consolidation of racial slavery. With slavery, however, a racially based understanding of society was set in motion which resulted in the shaping of a specific *racial* identity not only for the slaves but for the European settlers as well. Winthrop Jordan has observed: "From the initially common term *Christian,* at mid-century there was a marked shift toward the terms *English* and *free.* After about 1680, taking the colonies as a whole, a new term of self-identification appeared—*white.*"[19]

We employ the term *racialization* to signify the extension of racial meaning to a previously racially unclassified relationship, social practice or group. Racialization is an ideological process, an historically specific one. Racial ideology is constructed from pre-existing conceptual (or, if one prefers, "discursive") elements and emerges from the struggles of competing political projects and ideas seeking to articulate similar elements differently. An account of racialization processes that avoids the pitfalls of US ethnic history[20] remains to be written.

Particularly during the nineteenth century, the category of "white" was subject to challenges brought about by the influx of diverse groups who were not of the same Anglo-Saxon stock as the founding immigrants. In the nineteenth century, political and ideological struggles emerged over the classification of Southern Europeans, the Irish and Jews, among other "nonwhite" categories.[21] Nativism was only effectively curbed by the institutionalization of a racial order that drew the color line *around*, rather than *within*, Europe.

By stopping short of racializing immigrants from Europe after the Civil War, and by subsequently allowing their assimilation, the American racial order was reconsolidated in the wake of the tremendous challenge placed before it by the abolition of racial slavery.[22] With the end of Reconstruction in 1877, an effective program for limiting the emergent class struggles of the later nineteenth century was forged: the definition of the working class *in racial terms*—as "white." This was not accomplished by any legislative decree or capitalist maneuvering to divide the working class, but rather by white workers themselves. Many of them were recent immigrants, who organized on racial lines as much as on traditionally defined class lines.[23] The Irish on the West Coast, for example, engaged in vicious anti-Chinese race-baiting and committed many pogrom-type assaults on Chinese in the course of consolidating the trade union movement in California.

Thus the very political organization of the working class was in important ways a racial project. The legacy of racial conflicts and arrangements shaped the definition of interests and in turn led to the consolidation of institutional patterns (e.g., segregated unions, dual labor markets, exclusionary legislation) which perpetuated the color line *within* the working class. Selig Perlman, whose study of the development of the labor movement is fairly sympathetic to this process, notes that:

> The political issue after 1877 was racial, not financial, and the weapon was not merely the ballot, but also "direct action"—violence. The anti-

Chinese agitation in California, culminating as it did in the Exclusion Law passed by Congress in 1882, was doubtless the most important single factor in the history of American labor, for without it the entire country might have been overrun by Mongolian [sic] labor and *the labor movement might have become a conflict of races instead of one of classes*.[24]

More recent economic transformations in the US have also altered interpretations of racial identities and meanings. The automation of southern agriculture and the augmented labor demand of the postwar boom transformed blacks from a largely rural, impoverished labor force to a largely urban, working-class group by 1970.[25] When boom became bust and liberal welfare statism moved rightwards, the majority of blacks came to be seen, increasingly, as part of the "underclass," as state "dependents." Thus the particularly deleterious effects on blacks of global and national economic shifts (generally rising unemployment rates, changes in the employment structure away from reliance on labor intensive work, etc.) were explained once again in the late 1970s and 1980s (as they had been in the 1940s and mid-1960s) as the result of defective black cultural norms, of familial disorganization, etc.[26] In this way new racial attributions, new racial myths, are affixed to "blacks."[27] Similar changes in racial identity are presently affecting Asians and Latinos, as such economic forces as increasing Third World impoverishment and indebtedness fuel immigration and high interest rates, Japanese competition spurs resentments, and US jobs seem to fly away to Korea and Singapore.[28] . . .

Once we understand that race overflows the boundaries of skin color, superexploitation, social stratification, discrimination and prejudice, cultural domination and cultural resistance, state policy (or of any other particular social relationship we list), once we recognize the racial dimension present to some degree in *every* identity, institution and social practice in the United States—once we have done this, it becomes possible to speak of *racial formation*. This recognition is hard-won; there is a continuous temptation to think of race as an *essence*, as something fixed, concrete and objective, as (for example) one of the categories just enumerated. And there is also an opposite temptation: to see it as a mere illusion, which an ideal social order would eliminate.

In our view it is crucial to break with these habits of thought. The effort must be made to understand race as *an unstable and "decentered" complex of social meanings constantly being transformed by political struggle.*

NOTES

1. *San Francisco Chronicle*, 14 September 1982, 19 May 1983. Ironically, the 1970 Louisiana law was enacted to supersede an old Jim Crow statute which relied on the idea of "common report" in determining an infant's race. Following Phipps's unsuccessful attempt to change her classification and have the law declared unconstitutional, a legislative effort arose which culminated in the repeal of the law. See *San Francisco Chronicle*, 23 June 1983.
2. The Mormon church, for example, has been heavily criticized for its doctrine of black inferiority.
3. Thomas F. Gossett notes:
    Race theory . . . had up until fairly modern times no firm hold on European thought. On the other hand, race theory and race prejudice were by no means unknown at the time when the English colonists came to North America. Undoubtedly, the age of exploration led many to speculate on race differences at a period when neither Europeans nor Englishmen were prepared to make allowances for vast cultural diversities. Even though race theories had not then

secured wide acceptance or even sophisticated formulation, the first contacts of the Spanish with the Indians in the Americas can now be recognized as the beginning of a struggle between conceptions of the nature of primitive peoples which has not yet been wholly settled. (Thomas F. Gossett, *Race: The History of an Idea in America* (New York: Schocken Books, 1965), p. 16.)

Winthrop Jordan provides a detailed account of early European colonialists' attitudes about color and race in *White over Black: American Attitudes Toward the Negro, 1550–1812* (New York: Norton, 1977 [1968]), pp. 3–43.
4. Pro-slavery physician Samuel George Morton (1799–1851) compiled a collection of 800 crania from all parts of the world which formed the sample for his studies of race. Assuming that the larger the size of the cranium translated into greater intelligence, Morton established a relationship between race and skull capacity. Gossett reports that:
    In 1849, one of his studies included the following results: The English skulls in his collection proved to be the largest, with an average cranial capacity of 96 cubic inches. The Americans and Germans were rather poor seconds, both with cranial capacities of 90 cubic inches. At the bottom of the list were the Negroes with 83 cubic inches, the Chinese with 82, and the Indians with 79. (Ibid., p. 74.)

On Morton's methods, see Stephen J. Gould, "The Finagle Factor," *Human Nature* (July 1978).
5. Definitions of race founded upon a common pool of genes have not held up when confronted by scientific research which suggests that the differences *within* a given human population are greater than those between populations. See L. L. Cavalli-Sforza, "The Genetics of Human Populations," *Scientific American*, September 1974, pp. 81–89.
6. Arthur Jensen, "How Much Can We Boost IQ and Scholastic Achievement?", *Harvard Educational Review* 39 (1969):1–123.
7. Ernst Moritz Manasse, "Max Weber on Race," *Social Research* 14 (1947):191–221.
8. Quoted in Edward D. C. Campbell, Jr., *The Celluloid South: Hollywood and the Southern Myth* (Knoxville: University of Tennessee Press, 1981), pp. 168–70.

9. Marvin Harris, *Patterns of Race in the Americas* (New York: Norton, 1964), p. 56.
10. Ibid., p. 57.
11. After James Meredith had been admitted as the first black student at the University of Mississippi, Harry S. Murphy announced that he, and not Meredith, was the first black student to attend "Ole Miss." Murphy described himself as black but was able to pass for white and spent nine months at the institution without attracting any notice (ibid., p. 56).
12. A. Sivanandan, "From Resistance to Rebellion: Asian and Afro-Caribbean Struggles in Britain," *Race and Class* 23(2–3) (Autumn–Winter 1981).
13. Consider the contradictions in racial status which abound in the country with the most rigidly defined racial categories—South Africa. There a race classification agency is employed to adjudicate claims for upgrading of official racial identity. This is particularly necessary for the "coloured" category. The apartheid system considers Chinese as "Asians" while the Japanese are accorded the status of "honorary whites." This logic nearly detaches race from any grounding in skin color and other physical attributes and nakedly exposes race as a juridical category subject to economic, social and political influences. (We are indebted to Steve Talbot for clarification of some of these points.)
14. Gordon W. Allport, *The Nature of Prejudice* (Garden City, NY: Doubleday, 1958), pp. 184–200.
15. We wish to use this phrase loosely, without committing ourselves to a particular position on such social psychological approaches as symbolic interactionism, which are outside the scope of this study. An interesting study on this subject is S. M. Lyman and W. A. Douglass, "Ethnicity: Strategies of Individual and Collective Impression Management," *Social Research* 40(2) (1973).
16. Michael Billig, "Patterns of Racism: Interviews with National Front Members," *Race and Class* 20(2) (Autumn 1978):161–79.
17. "Miss San Antonio USA Lisa Fernandez and other Hispanics auditioning for a role in a television soap-opera did not fit the Hollywood image of real Mexicans and had to darken their faces before filming." Model Aurora Garza said that their faces were bronzed with powder because they looked too white. " 'I'm a real Mexican [Garza said] and very dark anyway. I'm even darker right now because I have a tan. But they kept wanting me to make my face darker and darker' " (*San Francisco Chronicle,* 21 September 1984). A similar dilemma faces Asian American actors who feel that Asian character lead roles inevitably go to white actors who make themselves up to be Asian. Scores of Charlie Chan films, for example, have been made with white leads (the last one was the 1981 *Charlie Chan and the Curse of the Dragon Queen*). Roland Winters, who played in six Chan features, was asked by playwright Frank Chin to explain the logic of casting a white man in the role of Charlie Chan: " 'The only thing I can think of is, if you want to cast a homosexual in a show, and get a homosexual, it'll be awful. It won't be funny . . . and maybe there's something there . . .' " (Frank Chin, "Confessions of the Chinatown Cowboy," *Bulletin of Concerned Asian Scholars* 4(3) (Fall 1972)).
18. Melanie Martindale-Sikes, "Nationalizing 'Nigger' Imagery Through 'Birth of a Nation'," paper prepared for the 73rd Annual Meeting of the American Sociological Association, 4–8 September 1978, San Francisco.
19. Jordan, *White over Black,* p. 95; emphasis added.
20. Historical focus has been placed either on particular racially defined groups or on immigration and the "incorporation" of ethnic groups. In the former case the characteristic ethnicity theory pitfalls and apologetics such as functionalism and cultural pluralism may be avoided, but only by sacrificing much of the focus on race. In the latter case, race is considered a manifestation of ethnicity.
21. The degree of antipathy for these groups should not be minimized. A northern commentator observed in the 1850s: "An Irish Catholic seldom attempts to rise to a higher condition than that in which he is placed, while the Negro often makes the attempt with success." Quoted in Gossett, op. cit., p. 288.
22. This analysis, as will perhaps be obvious, is essentially DuBoisian. Its main source will be found in the monumental (and still largely unappreciated) *Black Reconstruction in the United States, 1860–1880* (New York: Atheneum, 1977 [1935]).
23. Alexander Saxton argues that:
    North Americans of European background have experienced three great racial confrontations: with the Indian, with the African, and with the Oriental. Central to each transaction has been a totally one-sided preponderance of

power, exerted for the exploitation of nonwhites by the dominant white society. In each case (but especially in the two that began with systems of enforced labor), white workingmen have played a crucial, yet ambivalent, role. They have been both exploited and exploiters. On the one hand, thrown into competition with nonwhites as enslaved or "cheap" labor they suffered economically; on the other hand, being white, they benefited by that very exploitation which was compelling the nonwhites to work for low wages or for nothing. Ideologically they were drawn in opposite directions. *Racial identification cut at right angles to class consciousness.* (Alexander Saxton, *The Indispensable Enemy: Labor and the Anti-Chinese Movement in California* (Berkeley and Los Angeles: University of California Press, 1971), p. 1; emphasis added.)

24. Selig Perlman, *The History of Trade Unionism in the United States* (New York: Augustus Kelley, 1950), p. 52; emphasis added.

25. Whether southern blacks were "peasants" or rural workers is unimportant in this context. Some time during the 1960s blacks attained a higher degree of urbanization than whites. Before World War II most blacks had been rural dwellers and nearly 80 percent lived in the South.

26. See George Gilder, *Wealth and Poverty* (New York: Basic Books, 1981); Charles Murray, *Losing Ground* (New York: Basic Books, 1984).

27. A brilliant study of the racialization process in Britain, focused on the rise of "mugging" as a popular fear in the 1970s, is Stuart Hall et al., *Policing the Crisis* (London: Macmillan, 1978).

28. The case of Vincent Chin, a Chinese American man beaten to death in 1982 by a laid-off Detroit auto worker and his stepson who mistook him for Japanese and blamed him for the loss of their jobs, has been widely publicized in Asian American communities. On immigration conflicts and pressures, see Michael Omi, "New Wave Dread: Immigration and Intra-Third World Conflict," *Socialist Review* 60 (November–December 1981).

3

THEORETICAL PERSPECTIVES IN RACE AND ETHNIC RELATIONS

Joe R. Feagin • Clairece Booher Feagin

Assimilation and Other Order Perspectives

In the United States much social theorizing has emphasized assimilation, the more or less orderly adaptation of a migrating group to the ways and institutions of an established group. Hirschman has noted that "the assimilation perspective, broadly defined, continues to be the primary theoretical

Joe R. Feagin and Clairece Booher Feagin, *Racial and Ethnic Relations*, 5th edition, pp. 30–56. Copyright © 1996 Prentice-Hall, Inc. Reprinted by permission of Prentice-Hall, Inc., Upper Saddle River, NJ.

framework for sociological research on racial and ethnic inequality." The reason for this dominance, he suggests, is the "lack of convincing alternatives."[1] The English word *assimilate* comes from the Latin *assimulare*, "to make similar."

Robert E. Park

Robert E. Park, a major sociological theorist, argued that European out-migration was a major catalyst for societal reorganization around the globe. In his view intergroup contacts regularly go through stages of a *race relations cycle*. Fundamental social forces such as out-migration lead to recurring cycles in intergroup history: "The race relations cycle which takes the form, to state it abstractly, of *contacts, competition, accommodation* and eventual *assimilation,* is apparently progressive and irreversible."[2] In the contact stage migration and exploration bring people together, which in turn leads to economic competition and thus to new social organization. Competition and conflict flow from the contacts between host peoples and the migrating groups. Accommodation, an unstable condition in the race relations cycle, often takes place rapidly. It involves a forced adjustment by a migrating group to a new social situation. . . . Nonetheless, Park and most scholars working in this tradition have argued that there is a long-term trend toward assimilation of racial and ethnic minorities in modern societies. "Assimilation is a process of interpenetration and fusion in which persons and groups acquire the memories, sentiments, and attitudes of other persons or groups, and, by sharing their experience and history, are incorporated with them in a common cultural life."[3] Even racially subordinate groups are expected to assimilate.[4]

Stages of Assimilation: Milton Gordon

Since Park's pioneering analysis in the 1920s, many U.S. theorists of racial and ethnic relations and numerous textbook writers have adopted an assimilationist perspective, although most have departed from Park's framework in a number of important ways. Milton Gordon, author of the influential *Assimilation in American Life,* distinguishes a variety of initial encounters between race and ethnic groups and an array of possible assimilation outcomes. While Gordon presents three competing images of assimilation—the melting pot, cultural pluralism, and Anglo-conformity—he focuses on Anglo-conformity as the descriptive re-

ality. That is, immigrant groups in the United States, in Gordon's view, have typically tended to give up much of their heritage for the dominant, preexisting Anglo-Saxon core culture and society. The touchstone of adjustment is viewed thus: "If there is anything in American life which can be described as an overall American culture which serves as a reference point for immigrants and their children, it can best be described, it seems to us, as the middle-class cultural patterns of, largely, white Protestant, Anglo-Saxon origins, leaving aside for the moment the question of minor reciprocal influences on this culture exercised by the cultures of later entry into the United States."[5]

Gordon notes that Anglo-conformity has been substantially achieved for most immigrant groups in the United States, especially in regard to cultural assimilation. Most groups following the English have adapted to the Anglo core culture. Gordon distinguishes seven dimensions of adaptation:

1. *cultural assimilation:* change of cultural patterns to those of the core society;
2. *structural assimilation:* penetration of cliques and associations of the core society at the primary-group level;
3. *marital assimilation:* significant intermarriage;
4. *identification assimilation:* development of a sense of identity linked to the core society;
5. *attitude-receptional assimilation:* absence of prejudice and stereotyping;
6. *behavior-receptional assimilation:* absence of intentional discrimination;
7. *civic assimilation:* absence of value and power conflict.[6]

Whereas Park believed structural assimilation, including primary-group ties such as intergroup friendships, flowed from cultural assimilation, Gordon stresses that these are separate stages of assimilation and may take place at different rates.

Gordon conceptualizes structural assimilation as relating to primary-group cliques and relations. Significantly, he does not highlight as a separate type of structural assimilation the movement of a new immigrant group into the *secondary groups* of the host society—that is, into the employing organizations, such as corporations or public bureaucracies, and the critical educational and political institutions. The omission of secondary-structural assimilation is a major flaw in Gordon's theory. Looking at U.S. history, one would conclude that assimilating into the core society's secondary groups does *not necessarily* mean entering the dominant group's friendship cliques. In addition, the dimension Gordon calls *civic assimilation* is confusing since he includes in it "values," which are really part of cultural assimilation, and "power," which is a central aspect of structural assimilation at the secondary-group level.

Gordon's assimilation theory has influenced a generation of researchers. . . . In a recent examination of Gordon's seven dimensions of assimilation, J. Allen Williams and Suzanne Ortega drew on interviews with a midwestern sample to substantiate that cultural assimilation was not necessarily the first type of assimilation to occur. For example, the Mexican Americans in the sample were found to be less culturally assimilated than African Americans, yet were more assimilated structurally. Those of Swiss and Swedish backgrounds ranked about the same on the study's measure of cultural assimilation, but the Swedish Americans were less assimilated structurally. Williams and Ortega conclude that assimilation varies considerably from one group to another and that Gordon's seven types can be grouped into three more general categories of structural, cultural, and receptional assimilation.[7]

In a later book, *Human Nature, Class, and Ethnicity* (1978), Gordon has recognized that his assimilation theory neglects power issues and proposed bringing these into his model, but so far he has provided only a brief and inadequate analysis. Gordon mentions in passing the different resources available to competing racial groups and refers briefly to black-white conflict, but gives little attention to the impact of economic power, inequalities in material resources, or capitalistic economic history on U.S. racial and ethnic relations.[8]

Focused on the millions of white European immigrants and their adjustments, Gordon's model emphasizes *generational* changes within immigrant groups over time. Substantial acculturation to the Anglo-Protestant core culture has often been completed by the second or third generation for many European immigrant groups. The partially acculturated first generation formed protective communities and associations, but the children of those immigrants were considerably more exposed to Anglo-conformity pressures in the mass media and in schools.[9] Gordon also suggests that substantial assimilation along certain other dimensions, such as the civic, behavior-receptional, and attitude-receptional ones, has occurred for numerous European groups. Most white groups have also made considerable progress toward equality at the secondary-structural levels of employment and politics, although the dimensions of this assimilation are neither named nor discussed in any detail by Gordon.

For many white groups, particularly non-Protestant ones, structural assimilation at the primary-group level is underway, yet far from complete. Gordon suggests that substantially complete cultural assimilation (for example, adoption of the English language) along with structural (primary-group) pluralism form a characteristic pattern of adaptation for many white ethnic groups. Even these relatively acculturated groups tend to limit their informal friendships and marriage ties either to their immediate ethnic groups or to *similar* groups that are part of their general religious community. Following Will Herberg, who argued that there are three great community "melting pots" in the United States—Jews, Protestants, and Catholics—Gordon suggests that primary-group ties beyond one's own group are often developed with one's broad socioreligious community, whether that be Protestant, Catholic, or Jewish.[10]

In his influential books and articles Gordon recognizes that structural assimilation has been retarded by racial prejudice and discrimination, but he seems to suggest that non-European Americans, including African Americans, will eventually be absorbed into the core culture and society. He gives the most attention to the gradual assimilation of middle-class non-Europeans. In regard to blacks he argues, optimistically, that the United States has "moved decisively down the road toward implementing the implications of the American credo of [equality and justice] for race relations"—as in employment and housing. This perceived tremendous progress for black Americans has created a policy dilemma for the government: should it adopt a traditional political liberalism that ignores race, or a "corporate liberalism" that recognizes group rights along racial lines? Gordon includes under corporate liberalism government programs of affirmative action, which he rejects.[11] . . .

Some assimilation-oriented analysts such as Gordon and Alba have argued that the once prominent ethnic identities, especially of European American groups, are fading over time. Alba suggests that there is still an ethnic identity of consequence for non-Latino whites, but declares that "a new ethnic group is forming—one based on a vague *ancestry* from anywhere on the European continent."[12] In other words, such distinct ethnic identities as English American and Irish American are gradually becoming only a vague identification as "European American," although Alba emphasizes this as a trend, not a fact. Interestingly, research on intermarriages between members of different white ethnic groups has revealed that large proportions of the children of such marriages see themselves as having multiple ethnic identities, while others choose one of their heritages, or simply "American," as their ethnic identity.[13]

Ethnogenesis and Ethnic Pluralism

Some theorists working in the assimilation tradition reject the argument that most European American groups have become substantially assimilated to a generic Anglo-Protestant or Euro-American identity and way of life. A few have explored models of adjustment that depart from Anglo-conformity in the direction of ethnic or cultural pluralism. Most analysts of pluralism accept some Anglo-conformity as inevitable, if not desirable. In *Beyond the Melting Pot,* Glazer and Moynihan agree that the original customs and home-country ways of European immigrants were mostly lost by the third generation. But this did not mean the decline of ethnicity. The European immigrant groups usually remained distinct in terms of name, identity, and, for the most part, primary-group ties.[14]

Andrew Greeley has developed the interesting concept of *ethnogenesis* and applied it to white immigrant groups, those set off by nationality and religion. Greeley is critical of the traditional assimilation perspective because it assumes "that the strain toward homogenization in a modern industrial society is so great as to be virtually irresistible."[15] Traditionally, the direction of this assimilation in the United States is assumed to be toward the Anglo-Protestant core culture. But from the ethnogenesis perspective, adaptation has meant more than this one-way conformity. The traditional assimilation model does not explain the persistence of ethnicity in the United States—the emphasis among immigrants on ethnicity as a way of becoming American and, in recent decades, the self-conscious attempts to create ethnic identity and manipulate ethnic symbols.[16]

. . . Greeley suggests that in many cases host and immigrant groups had a somewhat similar *cultural* inheritance. For example, some later European immigrant groups had a cultural background initially similar to that of earlier English settlers. As a result of interaction in schools and the influence of the media over several generations the number of cultural traits common to the host and immigrant groups often grew. Yet late in the adaptive process certain aspects of the heritage of the home country remained very important to the character of the immigrant-ethnic group. From this perspective, ethnic groups share traits with the host group *and* retain major nationality characteristics as well. A modern ethnic group is one part home-country heritage and one part common culture, mixed together in a distinctive way because of a unique history of development within the North American crucible.[17]

A number of research studies have documented the persistence of distinctive white ethnic groups such as Italian Americans and Jewish Americans in U.S. cities, not just in New York and Chicago but in San Francisco, New Orleans, and Tucson as well. Yancey and his associates have suggested that ethnicity is an "emergent phenomenon"—that its importance varies in cities and that its character and strength depend on the specific historical conditions in which it emerges and grows.[18]

Some Problems with Assimilation Theories

Most assimilation theorists take as their examples of ethnic adaptation white European groups migrating more or less voluntarily to the United States. But what of the adaptation and assimilation of non-European groups beyond the stage of initial contact? Some analysts of assimilation include non-white groups in their theories, despite the problems that arise from such an inclusion. Some analysts have argued that assimilation, cultural and structural, is the necessary, if long-term, answer to the racial problem in the United States. . . .

More optimistic analysts have emphasized progressive inclusion, which will eventually provide black Americans and other minority groups with full citizenship, in fact as well as principle. For that reason, they expect ethnic and racial conflict to disappear as various groups become fully assimilated into the core culture and society. Nathan Glazer, Milton Gordon, and Talcott Parsons have stressed the egalitarianism of U.S. institutions and what they view as the progressive emancipation of non-European groups. Gordon and others have underscored the gradual assimilation of middle-class black Americans over the last several decades. Full membership for black Americans seems inevitable, notes Parsons, for "the only tolerable solution to the enormous [racial] tensions lies in constituting a single societal community with full membership for all."[19] The importance of racial, as well as ethnic, stratification is expected to decline as powerful, universalistic societal forces wipe out the vestiges of earlier ethnocentric value systems. White immigrants have desired substantial assimilation, and most have been absorbed. The same is expected to happen eventually for non-European groups.

Assimilation theories have been criticized as having an "establishment" bias, as not distinguishing carefully enough between what *has* happened to a given group and what the establishment at some point felt *should have* happened. For example, a number of Asian American scholars and leaders have reacted vigorously to the application of the concept of assimilation to Asian Americans, arguing that the very concept originated in a period (1870–1925) of intense attacks by white Americans on Asian Americans. The term was thus tainted from the beginning by its association with the dominant European American group's ideology that the only "good groups" were those that assimilated (or could assimilate) in Anglo-conformity fashion.

Unlike Park, who paid substantial attention to the historical and world-economy context of migration, many of today's assimilation theorists do not analyze sufficiently the historical background and development of a particular racial or ethnic group within a national or world context. In addition, assimilation analysts such as Gordon tend to neglect the power imbalance and inequality in racial and ethnic relations, which are seen most clearly in the cases of non-European Americans. As Geschwender has noted, "they seem to have forgotten that exploitation is the driving force that gives meaning to the study of racial and ethnic relations."[20]

Biosocial Perspectives

Some U.S. theorists, including assimilationists, now accent a biosocial perspective on racial and ethnic relations. The idea of race and ethnicity being deeply rooted in the biological makeup of human beings is an old European and American notion that has received renewed attention from a few social scientists and biologists in the United States since the 1970s. In *Human Nature, Class, and Ethnicity*, for example, Gordon suggests that ethnic ties are rooted in the "biological organism of man." Ethnicity is a fundamental part of the physiological as well as the psychological self. Ethnicity "cannot be shed by social mobility, as for instance social class background can, since society insists on its inalienable ascription from cradle to grave." What Gordon seems to have in mind is not the old racist notion of the unchanging biological character and separateness of racial groups, but rather the rootedness of intergroup relation, including racial and ethnic relations, in the everyday realities of kinship and other socially constructed group boundaries. Gordon goes further, however, emphasizing that human beings tend to be "selfish, narcissistic and perpetually poised on the edge of aggression." And it is these selfish tendencies that lie behind racial and ethnic tensions.[21] Gordon is here adopting a Hobbesian (dog-eat-dog) view of human nature. . . .

Although decidedly different from the earlier biological theories, the modern biosocial analysis remains problematical. The exact linkages between the deep genetic underpinnings of human nature and concrete racial or ethnic behavior are not spelled out beyond some vague analysis of kin selection and selfish behavior. . . .

Another difficulty with the biosocial approach is that in the everyday world, racial and ethnic relations are *immediately social* rather than biological. As Edna Bonacich has pointed out, many racial and ethnic groups have mixed biological ancestry. Jewish Americans, for example, have a very mixed ancestry: as a group, they share no distinct biological characteristics. Biologically diverse Italian immigrants from different regions of Italy gained a sense of being Italian American (even Italian) in the United States. The bonds holding Jewish Americans together and Italian Americans together were not genetically based or biologically primordial, but rather the result of real *historical* experiences as these groups settled into the United States. Moreover, if ethnicity is primordial in a biological sense, it should always be a prominent force in human affairs. Sometimes ethnicity leads to recurring conflict, as in the case of Jews and Gentiles in the United States; in other cases, as with Scottish and English Americans, it quietly disappears in the assimilation process. Sentiments based on common ancestry are important, but they are activated primarily in the concrete experiences and histories of specific migrating and host groups.[22]

Emphasizing Migration: Competition Theory

. . . The *human ecology* tradition in sociological thought draws on the ideas of Park and other ecologists and emphasizes the "struggle of human groups for survival" within their physical environments. This tradition, which highlights demographic trends such as the migration of groups and population concentration in cities, has been adopted by competition analysts researching racial and ethnic groups.[23]

Competition theorists such as Susan Olzak and Joane Nagel view ethnicity as a social phenomenon distinguished by boundaries of language, skin color, and culture. They consider the tradition of human ecology valuable because it emphasizes the stability of ethnic population boundaries over time, as well as the impact of shifts in these boundaries resulting from migration; ethnic group membership often coincides with the creation of a distinctive group niche in the labor force. Competition occurs when two or more ethnic groups attempt to secure the same resources, such as jobs or housing. Competition theorists have accented the ways in which ethnic group competition and the accompanying ethnic solidarity lead to collective action, mobilization, and protest.[24]

According to competition theorists, collective action is fostered by immigration across borders and by the expansion of once-segregated minorities into the same labor and housing markets to which other ethnic groups have access. A central argument of these theorists is that collective attacks on a subordinate ethnic group—immigrant and black workers, for instance—increase at the local city level when the group moves up and out of segregated jobs and challenges other groups and not, as one might expect, in cities where ethnic groups are locked into residential segregation and poverty. . . .

Competition theorists explicitly contrast their analyses with the power-conflict views we will discuss in the next section, perspectives that emphasize the role of capitalism, economic subordination, and institutionalized discrimination. Competition theorists write about urban ethnic worlds as though institutionalized racism and capitalism-generated exploitation of workers are not major forces in recurring ethnic and racial competition in cities. As we have seen, they emphasize migration and population concentration, as well as other demographic factors. . . .

Power-Conflict Theories

The last few decades have witnessed the development of power-conflict frameworks explaining U.S. racial and ethnic relations, perspectives that place much greater emphasis on economic stratification and power issues than one finds in assimilation and competition theories. Within this broad category of power-conflict theories are a number of subcategories, including the internal colonialism viewpoint, and a variety of class-based and neo-Marxist theories. . . .

Internal Colonialism

Analysts of internal colonialism prefer to see the racial stratification and the class stratification of U.S. capitalism as *separate but related* systems of oppression. Neither should be reduced in social science theories to the other. An emphasis on power and resource inequalities, particularly white-minority inequalities, is at the heart of the internal colonialism model.

The framework of internal colonialism is built in part upon the work of analysts of *external colonialism*—the worldwide imperialism of certain capitalist nations, including the United States and European nations.[25] For example, Balandier has noted that capitalist expansion has affected non-European peoples since the fifteenth century: "Until very recently the greater part of the world population, not belonging to the white race (if we exclude China and Japan), knew only a status of dependency on one or another of the European colonial powers."[26] External colonialism involves the running of a country's economy and politics by an outside colonial power. Many colonies eventually became independent of their colonizers, such as Britain or France, but continued to have their economies directed by the capitalists and corporations of the colonial powers. This system of continuing dependency has been called *neocolonialism.* Neocolonialism is common today where there are few white settlers in the colonized country. Colonies experiencing a large in-migration of white settlers often show a different pattern. In such cases external colonialism becomes *internal colonialism* when the control and exploitation of non-European groups in the colonized country passes from whites in the home country to white immigrant groups within the newly independent country.[27]

Non-European groups entering later, such as African slaves and Mexican farm workers in the United States, can also be viewed in terms of internal colonialism. Internal colonialism here emerged out of classical European colonialism and imperialism and took on a life of its own. The origin and initial stabilization of internal colonialism in North America predate the Revolutionary War. The systematic subordination of non-Europeans began with "genocidal attempts by colonizing settlers to uproot native populations and force them into other regions."[28] Native Americans were killed or driven off desirable lands. Slaves from Africa were a cheap source of labor for capital accumulation before and after the Revolution. Later, Asians and Pacific peoples were imported as contract workers or annexed in an expansionist period of U.S. development. Robert Blauner, a colonialism theorist, notes that agriculture in the South depended on black labor; in the Southwest, Mexican agricultural development was forcibly taken over by European settlers, and later agricultural development was based substantially on cheap Mexican labor coming into what was once northern Mexico.[29]

In exploiting the labor of non-European peoples, who were made slaves or were paid low wages, white agricultural and industrial capitalists reaped enormous profits. From the internal colonialism perspective, contemporary racial and ethnic inequality is grounded in the economic *interests* of whites in low-wage labor—the underpinning of capitalistic economic exploitation. Non-European groups were subordinated to European American desires for *labor* and *land.* Internal colonialism theorists have recognized the central role of *government* support of the exploitation of minorities. The colonial and U.S. governments played an important role in legitimating slavery in the sixteenth through the nineteenth centuries and in providing the government soldiers who subordinated Native Americans across the nation and Mexicans in the Southwest.

Most internal colonialism theorists are not concerned primarily with white immigrant groups, many of which entered the United States after non-European groups were subordinated. Instead, they wish to analyze the establishment of racial stratification and the control processes that maintain persisting white dominance and ideological racism. Stokely Carmichael and Charles Hamilton, who in their writings in the 1960s were among the first to use the term *internal colonialism,* accented institutional racism—discrimination by the white community against blacks as a group.[30] From this perspective African Americans are still a "colony" in the United States in regard to education, economics, and politics. . . .

A Neo-Marxist Emphasis on Class

Analysts of racial and ethnic relations have combined an internal colonialism perspective with an emphasis on class stratification that draws on the Marxist research pioneered by [black sociologists W. E. B.] Du Bois and [Oliver] Cox. Mario Barrera, for example, has suggested that the heart of current internal colonialism is an interactive structure of class *and* race stratification that divides our society. Class, in the economic-exploitation sense of that term, needs to be central to a colonialism perspective. Basic to the U.S. system of internal colonialism are four classes that have developed in U.S. capitalism:

1. *capitalists:* that small group of people who control capital investments and the means of production and who buy the labor of many others;
2. *managers:* that modest-sized group of people who work as administrators for the capitalists and have been granted control over the work of others;
3. *petit bourgeoisie:* that small group of merchants who control their own businesses and do most of their work themselves, buying little labor power from others;
4. *working class:* that huge group of blue-collar and white-collar workers who sell their labor to employers in return for wages and salaries.

The dominant class in the U.S. political-economic system is the capitalist class, which in the workplace subordinates working people, both nonwhite and white, to its profit and investment needs. And it is the capitalists who decide whether and where to create jobs. They are responsible for the flight of capital and jobs from many central cities to the suburbs and overseas.

Barrera argues that each of these classes contains important segments that are set off in terms of race and ethnicity. Figure 1 suggests how this works. Each of the major classes is crosscut by a line of racial segmentation that separates those suffering institutionalized discrimination, such as black Americans and Mexican Americans, from those who do not. Take the example of the working class. Although black, Latino, and other minority workers share a similar *class* position with white workers, in that they are struggling against capitalist employers for better wages and working conditions, they are *also* in a subordinate position because of structural discrimination along racial lines within that working class. Barrera notes that the dimensions of this discrimination often include lower wages for many minority workers, as well as their concentration in lower-status occupations. Many Americans suffer from both class exploitation (as wage workers) and racial exploitation (as workers of color).

Ideology and Oppositional Culture

Internal colonialism theorists have studied the role of cultural stereotyping and ideology in limiting the opportunities of subordinate groups of color. A racist ideology

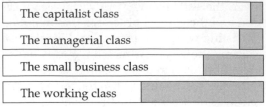

FIGURE 1   The Class and Race Structure of Internal Colonialism. *Note:* Shaded area represents nonwhite segment.

dominates an internal colonialist society, intellectually dehumanizing the colonized. Stereotyping and prejudice, seen in many traditional assimilation theories as more or less temporary problems, are viewed by colonialism analysts as a way of rationalizing exploitation over a very long period, if not permanently. Discrimination is a question not of individual bigots but rather of a system of racial exploitation rationalized by prejudice.[31]

In his book on the English colonization of Ireland, Michael Hechter has developed a theory of internal colonialism that emphasizes how the subordinate group utilizes its own culture to *resist* subordination. Hechter argues that in a system of internal colonialism, cultural as well as racial markers are used to set off subordinate groups such as African Americans in the United States and the Irish in the United Kingdom. Resistance to the dominant group by the subordinate group often takes the form of cultural solidarity in opposition to the dominant culture. This solidarity can become the basis for protest movements by the subordinated group.[32]

Beginning in the 1960s, a number of power-conflict scholars and activists have further developed this idea of *oppositional culture* as a basis for understanding the resistance of non-European groups to the Euro-American core culture. Bonnie Mitchell and Joe Feagin have built on the idea of oppositional culture suggested in the work of Hechter and Blauner.[33] They note that in the centuries of contact before the creation of

the United States, Mexico, and Canada, North America was populated by a diverse mixture of European, African, and Native American cultures. The U.S. nation created in the late 1700s encompassed African enslavement and the genocide of Native Americans. Faced with oppression, these and other victims of internal colonialism have long drawn on their own cultural resources, as well as their distinctive knowledge of Euro-American culture and society, to resist oppression in every way possible.

The cultures of those oppressed by European Americans have not only provided a source of individual, family, and community resistance to racial oppression and colonialism but have also infused, albeit often in unheralded ways, some significant elements into the evolving cultural mix that constitutes the core culture of the United States. The oppositional cultures of colonized groups such as African Americans, Latino Americans, and Native Americans have helped preserve several key elements of U.S. society, including its tradition of civil rights and social justice. Another key element, ironically enough given the usual white image of minority families, is the value of extended kinship relations. The tendency toward extended kin networks is both culturally encouraged and economically beneficial for oppressed minority groups. For example, research on black and Latino communities has found extensive kinship networks to be the basis of social and economic support in difficult times. Native American groups have also been known for their communalism and extended family networks.[34]

. . . This reality contrasts with the exaggerated stereotypes of endemic family pathology in these groups. Internal colonialism theories accent both the oppression of minority Americans and the oppositional cultures that enable minority groups not only to survive but also to resist oppression, passively and actively.

Criticism of Internal Colonialism Theories

. . . Joan Moore has criticized the term *neocolonialism*. As we have noted, a neocolonial situation is one in which a Third World country (for example, an African country) has separated itself politically from a European colonial power but continues to be dependent on that country. The former colony needs "foreign experts." It has a class of indigenous leaders who help the former colonial power exploit the local population. It has a distinct territorial boundary. Moore suggests that this neocolonialism model does not apply very well to subordinate nonwhite groups in the United States, in that these groups are not generally confined to a specific bounded territory, nor do they contain the exploitative intermediary elite of Third World neocolonialism. This space-centered critique has been repeated by Omi and Winant, who argue that the social and spatial intermixing of white and nonwhite groups in the United States casts serious doubt on the internal colonialism argument about territorially bounded colonization.[35]

However, most internal colonialism researchers have recognized the differences between internal colonial and neocolonial oppression. These theorists note that the situations of minority groups in the United States are different from those of, for instance, Africans in a newly independent nation still dependent on a European country. In response to Moore's critique, internal colonialism analysts might argue that there are many aspects of colonialism evident in U.S. racial and ethnic relations; they might emphasize that non-European groups in the United States (1) are usually residentially segregated, (2) are typically "super-exploited" in employment and deficient in other material conditions when compared with white immigrants, (3) are culturally stigmatized, and (4) have had some of their leaders co-opted by whites. While these conditions in the United States are not defined as precisely as they are in the case of Third World neocolonialism, they are similar enough to allow the use of the idea of colonialism to assess racial and ethnic relations in the United States.

The Split Labor Market View: Another Class-Based Theory

Colonialism analysts such as Blauner are sometimes unclear about whether all classes of whites benefit from the colonization of nonwhites, or just the dominant class of capitalist employers. A power-conflict perspective that helps in assessing this question is the *split labor market* view, which treats class in the sense of position in the "means of production." This viewpoint has been defended by Edna Bonacich. She argues that in U.S. society the majority-group (white) workers do not share the interests of the dominant political and economic class, the capitalists. Yet both the dominant employer class and the white part of the working class discriminate against the nonwhite part of the working class.[36]

. . . Bonacich emphasizes that discrimination against minority workers by ordinary white workers seeking to protect their own privileges, however limited these may be, is important. Capitalists bring in nonwhite laborers to decrease labor costs, but white workers resist because they fear job displacement or lower wages. For example, over the last century white workers' unions have restricted the access of black workers to many job ladders, thus splitting the labor market and reducing black incomes. . . . White workers gain and lose from this structural racism. They gain in the short run, because there is less competition for privileged job categories from the nonwhites they have excluded. But they lose in the long run because employers can use this cordoned-off sector of nonwhites to undercut them.[37]

"Middleman" Minorities and Ethnic Enclaves

Drawing on insights of earlier scholars, Bonacich has explored the in-between position, in terms of power and resources, that certain racial and ethnic groups have occupied in stratified societies. These groups find their economic niche serving elites and workers as small-business people positioned between producers and consumers. Some ethnic and racial groups become small-scale traders and merchants doing jobs that dominant groups are not eager to do. For example, many first-generation Jewish and Japanese Americans, excluded from mainstream employment by white Protestants, became small-scale merchants, tailors, restaurant operators, or gardeners. These groups have held "a distinctive class position that is of special use to the ruling class." They "act as a go-between to this society's more subordinate groups."[38]

Bonacich and Modell have found that Japanese Americans fit the middleman minority model. Before World War II Japanese Americans resided in highly organized communities. Their local economies were based on self-employment, including gardening and truck farming, and on other nonindus-trial family businesses. The group solidarity of the first generation of Japanese Americans helped them establish successful small businesses. However, they faced hostility from the surrounding society, and in fact were driven into the businesses they developed because they were denied other employment opportunities. By the second generation there was some breakdown in the middleman position of Japanese Americans, for many of that generation moved into professional occupations outside the niche economy.[39]

Some middleman minorities, such as Jewish and Korean American merchants in central cities, have become targets of hostility from less well off groups, such as poor African Americans. In addition, strong ethnic bonds can make the middleman group an effective competitor, and even Anglo-Protestant capitalists may become hostile toward an immigrant middleman minority that competes too effectively. Thus Jewish Americans have been viewed negatively by better-off Anglo-Protestant merchants, who have the power to discriminate against them, as well as by poor black renters and customers with whom Jews deal as middleman landlords and merchants. . . .

A somewhat similar perspective, *enclave theory*, examines secondary-structural incorporation into the economy, especially the ways in which certain non-European immigrant groups have created social and economic enclaves in cities. Both the middleman and the enclave perspectives give more emphasis to economic inequality and discrimination than assimilation perspectives, and they stress the incorporation of certain groups, such as Asians and Cubans, into the United States through the means of small businesses and specialized ethnic economies. The major differences between the two viewpoints seem to stem from the examples emphasized. Groups accented by enclave theorists, such as Cuban Americans, have created ethnic enclaves that are more than merchant or trading economies—they often include manufacturing enterprises, for example. In addition, ethnic enclaves usually compete with established Anglo-Protestant business elites. In contrast, the middleman minorities and those described as enclave minorities develop trading economies and are likely to fill an economic niche that *complements* that of established white elites. However, the aforementioned research of Bonacich on Jewish Americans suggests that there is little difference between the real-world experiences of those described as middleman minorities. . . .

Women and Gendered Racism: New Perspectives

Most theories of racial and ethnic relations have neglected gender stratification, the hierarchy in which men as a group dominate women as a group in terms of power and resources. In recent years a number of scholars have researched the situations of women within racial and ethnic groups in the United States. Their analyses assess the ways in which male supremacy, or a patriarchal system, interacts with and operates within a system of racial and ethnic stratification. Discussing racial and ethnic cultures around the globe, Adrienne Rich has defined a *patriarchal system* as "a familial-social, ideological, political system in which men—by force, direct pressure, or through ritual, tradition, law and language, customs, etiquette, education, and the division of labor—determine what part women shall or shall not play, and in which the female is everywhere subsumed under the male."[40]

Asking whether racism or patriarchy has been the primary source of oppression, social psychologist Philomena Essed exam-ined black women in the United States and the Netherlands.[41] She found racism and sexism interacting regularly. The oppression of black women can be seen as *gendered racism.* For example, under slavery African American women were exploited not only for labor but also as sex objects for white men. And after slavery they were excluded from most job categories available to white men and white women; major employment changes came only with the civil rights movement of the 1960s. Today racism has many gendered forms. In the U.S. mass media the white female is the standard for female beauty. Minority women are often stereotyped as matriarchs in female-headed families and are found disproportionately in lower-status "female jobs," such as typists. Some women of color are closely bound in their social relations with those who oppress them in such areas as domestic employment ("maids") and other low-paid service work.[42]

In her book *Black Feminist Thought* Patricia Hill Collins argues that a black feminist theoretical framework can help highlight and analyze the negative stereotypes of black women in white society—the stereotypes of the docile mammy, the domineering matriarch, the promiscuous whore, and the irresponsible welfare mother. These severely negative images persist among many whites because they undergird white discrimination against black women in the United States.[43]

Scholars assessing the situations of other women of color, including Native American, Asian, and Latino women, have similarly emphasized the cumulative and interactive character of racial and gender oppression and the necessity of liberating these women from white stereotypes and discrimination. For example, Denise Segura has examined labor-force data on Mexican American women and developed the concept of "triple oppression," the mutually reinforcing and interactive set of race, class, and gender forces whose cumulative effects "place women of color in a subordinate social and economic position relative to men of color and the majority white population."[44]

Class, the State, and Racial Formation

Looking at the important role of governments in creating racial and ethnic designations and institutionalizing discrimination, Michael Omi and Howard Winant have developed a theory of *racial formation.* Racial tensions and oppression, in their view, cannot be explained solely in terms of class or nationalism. Racial and ethnic relations are substantially defined by the actions of governments, ranging from the passing of legislation, such as restrictive immigration laws, to the imprisonment of groups defined as a threat (for example, Japanese Americans in World War II). Although the internal colonialism viewpoint gives some emphasis to the state's role in the exploitation of nonwhite minorities, it has not developed this argument sufficiently.

Omi and Winant note that the U.S. government has shaped the politics of race: the U.S. Constitution and a lengthy series of laws openly defined racial groups and interracial relationships (for example, slavery) in racist terms. The U.S. Constitution counted each African American slave as three-fifths of a person, and the Naturalization Law of 1790 explicitly declared that only *white* immigrants could qualify for naturalization. Many non-Europeans, including Africans and Asians, were prevented from becoming citizens. Japanese and other Asian immigrants, for example, were until the 1950s banned by law from becoming citizens. In 1854 the California Supreme Court ruled that Chinese immigrants should be classified as "Indi-

ans"(!), therefore denying them the political rights available to white Americans.[45]

For centuries, the U.S. government officially favored northern European immigrant groups over non-European and southern European groups such as Italians. For example, the Immigration Act of 1924 was used to exclude Asian immigrants and most immigrants from southern and eastern Europe, whom political leaders in Congress saw as racially inferior and as a threat to their control of the society. North European Americans working through the government thereby shaped the subsequent racial and ethnic mix that is the United States.

Another idea accented by Omi and Winant is that of *social rearticulation,* the recurring historical process of rupturing and reconstructing the understandings of race in this country. The social protest movements of various racial and ethnic groups periodically challenge the governments' definition of racial realities, as well as individual definitions of those realities. The 1960s civil rights movement, for instance, rearticulated traditional cultural and political ideas about race in the United States, and in the process changed the U.S. government and broadened the involvement of minority Americans in the politics of that government. New social movements regularly emerge, sometimes bringing new identities and political norms.[46]

Resistance to the Dominant Group

Recent research has highlighted the many ways in which powerless groups fight back against the powerful. One power-conflict theorist who has made an important contribution to our understanding of how the oppressed react to oppression is James Scott. Influenced by the work of scholars such as John Gaventa on the many "faces of power" Scott has shown that at the heart of much interaction between the powerless and the powerful is intentional deception.[47] For example, the African American slaves were not free to speak their minds to their white masters, but they did create a crucial discourse among themselves that was critical of their white oppressors. Scott cites a proverb of African slaves on the Caribbean island of Jamaica: "Play fool, to catch wise." Looking closely at the lives of slaves and the poor everywhere, Scott has developed the idea of a backstage discourse by the oppressed that includes views that cannot be discussed in public for fear of retaliation. In addition to secret ideological resistance on the part of slaves and other poor people, a variety of other resistance tactics are used, including foot-dragging, pilfering, dissimulation, and flight. Scott cites Afro-Christianity as an example of how African American slaves resisted the "ideological hegemony" (attempts to brainwash) of white slavemasters. In public religious services African American slaves controlled their gestures and facial expressions and pretended to accept Christian preaching about meekness and obedience. Backstage, where no whites were present, Afro-Christianity emphasized "themes of deliverance and redemption, Moses and the Promised Land, the Egyptian captivity, and emancipation."[48] For slaves the Promised Land meant the North and freedom, and the afterlife was often viewed as a place where the slaves' enemies would be severely punished.

Historian Sterling Stuckey has noted that slave spirituals, although obviously affected by Christianity, "take on an altogether new coloration when one looks at slave religion on the plantations where most slaves were found and where African religion, contrary to the accepted scholarly wisdom, was practiced." The religion of African Americans mixed African and European elements from the beginning. Yet at its core

the expressive, often protest-inclined African values prevailed over the European values.[49] Stuckey has shown that African culture and religion were major sources of the slaves' inclination to rebellion. The work of Scott and Stuckey can be linked to the analyses of Hechter and Mitchell and Feagin that we cited previously, for they too have accented the role of an oppositional culture in providing the foundation of resistance to racial oppression.

We can conclude this discussion of the most important critical power-conflict theories by underscoring certain recurring themes:

1. a central concern for racial and ethnic inequalities in economic position, power, and resources;

2. an emphasis on the links of racial inequalities to the economic institutions of capitalism and to the subordination of women under patriarchal systems;

3. an emphasis on the role of the government in legalizing exploitation and segregation and in defining racial and ethnic relations;

4. an emphasis on resistance to domination and oppression by those oppressed.

NOTES

1. Charles Hirschman, "America's Melting Pot Reconsidered," *Annual Review of Sociology* 9 (1983): 397–423.
2. Robert E. Park, *Race and Culture* (Glencoe, IL: Free Press, 1950), p. 150 (italics added).
3. Robert E. Park and Ernest W. Burgess, *Introduction to the Science of Society* (Chicago: University of Chicago Press, 1924), p. 735.
4. Janice R. Hullum, "Robert E. Park's Theory of Race Relations" (M.A. thesis, University of Texas, 1973), pp. 81–88; Park and Burgess, *Introduction to the Science of Society,* p. 760.
5. Milton M. Gordon, *Assimilation in American Life* (New York: Oxford University Press, 1964), pp. 72–73.

6. Ibid., p. 71.

7. Silvia Pedraza, *Political and Economic Migrants in America: Cubans and Mexicans* (Austin: University of Texas Press, 1985), pp. 5–7; Richard Alba, *Ethnic Identity: The Transformation of White America* (New Haven, CT: Yale University Press, 1990), p. 311; J. Allen Williams and Suzanne T. Ortega, "Dimensions of Assimilation," *Social Science Quarterly* 71 (1990):697–709.

8. Milton M. Gordon, *Human Nature, Class, and Ethnicity* (New York: Oxford University Press, 1978), pp. 67–89.

9. Gordon, *Assimilation in American Life,* pp. 78–108.

10. See Will Herberg, *Protestant—Catholic—Jew,* rev. ed. (Garden City, NY: Doubleday, Anchor Books, 1960).

11. Milton M. Gordon, "Models of Pluralism: The New American Dilemma," *Annals of the American Academy of Political and Social Science* 454 (1981):178–88.

12. Alba, *Ethnic Identity,* p. 3.

13. Stanley Lieberson and Mary Waters, "Ethnic Mixtures in the United States," *Sociology and Social Research* 70 (1985):43–53: Cookie White Stephan and Walter Stephan, "After Intermarriage," *Journal of Marriage and the Family* 51 (May 1989):507–519.

14. Nathan Glazer and Daniel P. Moynihan, *Beyond the Melting Pot* (Cambridge, MA: M.I.T. Press and Harvard University Press, 1963).

15. Andrew M. Greeley, *Ethnicity in the United States* (New York: Wiley, 1974), p. 293.

16. Ibid., pp. 295–301.

17. Ibid., p. 309.

18. William L. Yancey, D. P. Ericksen, and R. N. Juliani, "Emergent Ethnicity: A Review and Reformulation," *American Sociological Review* 41 (June 1976):391–93. See also Greeley, *Ethnicity in the United States,* pp. 290–317.

19. Talcott Parsons, "Full Citizenship for the Negro American? A Sociological Problem," in *The Negro American,* edited by Talcott Parsons and Kenneth B. Clark (Boston: Houghton Mifflin, 1965–66), p. 740.

20. James Geschwender, *Racial Stratification in America* (Dubuque, IA: Brown, 1978), p. 58.

21. Gordon, *Human Nature, Class, and Ethnicity,* pp. 73–78. See also Clifford Geertz, "The Integrative Revolution," in *Old Societies and New States,* edited by Clifford Geertz (New York: Free Press, 1963), p. 109.

22. Edna Bonacich, "Class Approaches to Ethnicity and Race," *Insurgent Sociologist* 10 (Fall 1980):11.

23. Frederik Barth, "Introduction," in *Ethnic Groups and Boundaries: The Social Organization of Culture Difference* (Oslo: Universitets Forlaget, 1969), pp. 10–17.

24. Susan Olzak, "A Competition Model of Collective Action in American Cities," in *Competitive Ethnic Relations,* edited by Susan Olzak and Joane Nagel (Orlando, FL: Academic Press, 1986), pp. 17–46.

25. Ronald Bailey and Guillermo Flores, "Internal Colonialism and Racial Minorities in the U.S.: An Overview," in *Structures of Dependency,* edited by Frank Bonilla and Robert Girling (Stanford, CA: privately published by a Stanford faculty–student seminar, 1973), pp. 151–53.

26. G. Balandier, "The Colonial Situation: A Theoretical Approach," in *Social Change,* ed. Immanuel Wallerstein (New York: Wiley, 1966), p. 35.

27. Pablo Gonzalez-Cassanova, "Internal Colonialism and National Development," in *Latin American Radicalism,* edited by Irving L. Horowitz et al. (New York: Random House, 1969), p. 130; Bailey and Flores, "Internal Colonialism," p. 156.

28. Bailey and Flores, "Internal Colonialism," p. 156.

29. Blauner, *Racial Oppression in America,* p. 55. Our analysis of internal colonialism draws throughout on Blauner's provocative discussion.

30. Stokely Carmichael and Charles Hamilton, *Black Power* (New York: Random House, Vintage Books, 1967), pp. 2–7.

31. Guillermo B. Flores, "Race and Culture in the Internal Colony: Keeping the Chicano in His Place," in *Structures of Dependency,* edited by Bonilla and Girling, p. 192.

32. Michael Hechter, *Internal Colonialism* (Berkeley: University of California Press, 1975), pp. 9–12; Michael Hechter, "Group Formation and the Cultural Division of Labor," *American Journal of Sociology* 84 (1978): 293–318; Michael Hechter, Debra Friedman, and Malka Applebaum, "A Theory of Ethnic Collective Action," *International Migration Review* 16 (1982):412–34. See also Geschwender, *Racial Stratification in America,* p. 87.

33. Joe Feagin and Bonnie Mitchell, "America's Non-European Cultures: The Myth of the Melting Pot," in *The Inclusive University: Multicultural Perspectives in Higher Education,* edited by Benjamin Bowser, Gale Auletta, and Terry Jones (forthcoming).

34. Carol B. Stack, "Sex Roles and Survival Strategies in an Urban Black Community," in *Women, Culture and Society,* edited by Michelle Zimbalist Rosaldo and Louise Lamphere (Stanford, CA: Stanford University Press, 1974), p. 128; Ronald Angel and Marta Tienda, "Determinants of Extended Household Structure: Cultural Pattern or Economic Need?" *American Journal of Sociology* 87 (1981–82):1360–83.

35. Joan W. Moore, "American Minorities and 'New Nation' Perspectives," *Pacific Sociological Review* 19 (October 1976):448–55; Michael Omi and Howard Winant, *Racial Formation in the United States* (New York: Routledge & Kegan Paul, 1986), pp. 47–49.

36. Bonacich, "Class Approaches to Ethnicity and Race," p. 14.

37. Barrera, *Race and Class in the Southwest,* pp. 201–203; Bonacich, "Class Approaches to Ethnicity and Race," p. 14.

38. Bonacich, "Class Approaches to Ethnicity and Race," pp. 14–15.

39. Edna Bonacich and John Modell, *The Economic Basis of Ethnic Solidarity* (Berkeley: University of California Press, 1980), pp. 1–37. For a critique, see Eugene Wong, "Asian American Middleman Minority Theory: The Framework of an American Myth," *Journal of Ethnic Studies* 13 (Spring 1985):51–87.

40. Quoted in Michael Albert et al., *Liberating Theory* (Boston: South End Press, 1986), p. 35.

41. Philomena Essed, *Understanding Everyday Racism* (Newbury Park, CA: Sage, 1991), pp. 30–32.

42. Ibid., p. 32.

43. Patricia Hill Collins, *Black Feminist Thought: Knowledge, Consciousness, and the Politics of Empowerment* (Boston: Unwin Hyman, 1990), pp. 40–48.

44. Denise A. Segura, "Chicanas and Triple Oppression in the Labor Force," in *Chicana Voices: Intersections of Class, Race and Gender,* edited by Teresa Cordova et al. (Austin, TX: Center for Mexican American Studies, 1986), p. 48.

45. Omi and Winant, *Racial Formation in the United States,* pp. 75–76.

46. Howard Winant, "Racial Formation Theory and Contemporary U.S. Politics," in *Exploitation and Exclusion,* edited by Abebe Zegeye, Leonard Harris, and Julia Maxted (London: Hans Zell, 1991), pp. 130–40.

47. James C. Scott, *Domination and the Arts of Resistance* (New Haven, CT: Yale University Press, 1990); John Gaventa, *Power and Powerlessness* (Urbana: University of Illinois Press, 1980).

48. Scott, *Domination and the Arts of Resistance,* p. 116.

49. Sterling Stuckey, *Slave Culture* (New York: Oxford University Press, 1987), pp. 27, 42–46.

Race as Chameleon: How the Idea
of Race Changes over Time and Place

4

DRAWING THE COLOR LINE

Howard Zinn

A black American writer, J. Saunders Redding, describes the arrival of a ship in North America in the year 1619:

Sails furled, flag drooping at her rounded stern, she rode the tide in from the sea. She was a strange ship, indeed, by all accounts, a frightening ship, a ship of mystery. Whether she was trader, privateer, or man-of-war no one knows. Through her bulwarks black-mouthed cannon yawned. The flag she flew was Dutch; her crew a motley. Her port of call, an English settlement, Jamestown, in the colony of Virginia. She came, she traded, and shortly afterwards was gone. Probably no ship in modern history has carried a more portentous freight. Her cargo? Twenty slaves.

There is not a country in world history in which racism has been more important, for so long a time, as the United States. And the problem of "the color line," as W. E. B. Du Bois put it, is still with us. So it is more than a purely historical question to ask: How does it start?—and an even more urgent question: How might it end? Or, to put it differently: Is it possible for whites and blacks to live together without hatred?

If history can help answer these questions, then the beginnings of slavery in North America—a continent where we can trace the coming of the first whites and the first blacks—might supply at least a few clues.

Some historians think those first blacks in Virginia were considered as servants, like the white indentured servants brought from Europe. But the strong probability is that, even if they were listed as "servants" (a more familiar category to the English), they were viewed as being different from white servants, were treated differently, and in fact were slaves. In any case, slavery developed quickly into a regular institution, into the normal labor relation of blacks to whites in the New World. With it developed that special racial feeling—whether hatred, or contempt, or pity, or patronization—that accompanied the inferior position of blacks in America for the next 350 years—that combination of inferior status and derogatory thought we call racism.

Everything in the experience of the first white settlers acted as a pressure for the enslavement of blacks.

The Virginians of 1619 were desperate for labor, to grow enough food to stay alive. Among them were survivors from the winter of 1609–1610, the "starving time," when, crazed for want of food, they roamed the woods for nuts and berries, dug up graves to eat the corpses, and died in batches until five hundred colonists were reduced to sixty.

In the *Journals* of the House of Burgesses of Virginia is a document of 1619 which tells of the first twelve years of the Jamestown colony. The first settlement had a hundred persons, who had one small ladle of barley per meal. When more people arrived, there was even less food. Many of the people lived in cavelike holes dug into the ground, and in the winter of 1609–1610, they were

> . . . driven thru insufferable hunger to eat those things which nature most abhorred, the flesh and excrements of man as well of our own nation as of an Indian, digged by some out of his grave after he had lain buried three days and wholly devoured him; others, envying the better state of body of any whom hunger has not yet so much wasted as their own, lay wait and threatened to kill and eat them; one among them slew his wife as she slept in his bosom, cut her in pieces, salted her and fed upon her till he had clean devoured all parts saving her head. . . .

A petition by thirty colonists to the House of Burgesses, complaining against the twelve-year governorship of Sir Thomas Smith, said:

> In those 12 years of Sir Thomas Smith, his government, we aver that the colony for the most part remained in great want and misery under most severe and cruel laws. . . . The allowance in those times for a man was only eight ounces of meale and half a pint of peas for a day . . . mouldy, rotten, full of cobwebs and maggots, loathsome to man and not fit for beasts, which forced many to flee for relief to the savage enemy, who being taken again were put to sundry deaths as by hanging, shooting and breaking upon the wheel . . . of whom one for stealing two or three pints of oatmeal had a bodkin thrust through his tongue and was tied with a chain to a tree until he starved. . . .

The Virginians needed labor, to grow corn for subsistence, to grow tobacco for export. They had just figured out how to grow tobacco, and in 1617 they sent off the first cargo to England. Finding that, like all pleasurable drugs tainted with moral disapproval, it brought a high price, the planters, despite their high religious talk, were not going to ask questions about something so profitable.

They couldn't force Indians to work for them, as Columbus had done. They were outnumbered, and while, with superior firearms, they could massacre Indians, they would face massacre in return. They could not capture them and keep them enslaved; the Indians were tough, resourceful, defiant, and at home in these woods, as the transplanted Englishmen were not.

White servants had not yet been brought over in sufficient quantity. Besides, they did not come out of slavery, and did not have to do more than contract their labor for a few years to get their passage and a start in the New World. As for the free white settlers, many of them were skilled craftsmen, or even men of leisure back in England, who were so little inclined to work the land that John Smith, in those early years, had to declare a kind of martial law, organize them into work gangs, and force them into the fields for survival.

There may have been a kind of frustrated rage at their own ineptitude, at the Indian superiority at taking care of themselves, that made the Virginians especially ready to become the masters of slaves. Edmund Morgan imagines their mood as he writes in his book *American Slavery, American Freedom:*

> If you were a colonist, you knew that your technology was superior to the Indians'. You knew that you were civilized, and they were savages. . . . But your superior technology had proved insufficient to extract anything. The Indians, keeping to themselves, laughed at your superior methods and lived from the land more abundantly and with less labor than you did. . . . And when your own people started deserting in order to live with them, it was too much. . . . So you killed the Indians, tortured them, burned their villages, burned their cornfields. It proved your superiority, in spite of your failures. And you gave similar treatment to any of your own people who succumbed to their savage ways of life. But you still did not grow much corn. . . .

Black slaves were the answer. And it was natural to consider imported blacks as slaves, even if the institution of slavery would not be regularized and legalized for several decades. Because, by 1619, a million blacks had already been brought from Africa to South America and the Caribbean, to the Portuguese and Spanish colonies, to work as slaves. Fifty years before Columbus, the Portuguese took ten African blacks to Lisbon—this was the start of a regular trade in slaves. African blacks had been stamped as slave labor for a hundred years. So it would have been strange if those twenty blacks, forcibly transported to Jamestown, and sold as objects to settlers anxious for a steadfast source of labor, were considered as anything but slaves.

Their helplessness made enslavement easier. The Indians were on their own land.

The whites were in their own European culture. The blacks had been torn from their land and culture, forced into a situation where the heritage of language, dress, custom, family relations, was bit by bit obliterated except for the remnants that blacks could hold on to by sheer, extraordinary persistence.

Was their culture inferior—and so subject to easy destruction? Inferior in military capability, yes—vulnerable to whites with guns and ships. But in no other way—except that cultures that are different are often taken as inferior, especially when such a judgment is practical and profitable. Even militarily, while the Westerners could secure forts on the African coast, they were unable to subdue the interior and had to come to terms with its chiefs.

The African civilization was as advanced in its own way as that of Europe. In certain ways, it was more admirable; but it also included cruelties, hierarchical privilege, and the readiness to sacrifice human lives for religion or profit. It was a civilization of 100 million people, using iron implements and skilled in farming. It had large urban centers and remarkable achievements in weaving, ceramics, sculpture.

European travelers in the sixteenth century were impressed with the African kingdoms of Timbuktu and Mali, already stable and organized at a time when European states were just beginning to develop into the modern nation. In 1563, Ramusio, secretary to the rulers in Venice, wrote to the Italian merchants: "Let them go and do business with the King of Timbuktu and Mali and there is no doubt that they will be well-received there with their ships and their goods and treated well, and granted the favours that they ask. . . ."

A Dutch report, around 1602, on the West African kingdom of Benin, said: "The Towne seemeth to be very great, when you enter it. You go into a great broad street, not paved, which seemeth to be seven or eight times broader than the Warmoes Street in Amsterdam. . . . The Houses in this Towne stand in good order, one close and even with the other, as the Houses in Holland stand."

The inhabitants of the Guinea Coast were described by one traveler around 1680 as "very civil and good-natured people, easy to be dealt with, condescending to what Europeans require of them in a civil way, and very ready to return double the presents we make them."

Africa had a kind of feudalism, like Europe based on agriculture, and with hierarchies of lords and vassals. But African feudalism did not come, as did Europe's, out of the slave societies of Greece and Rome, which had destroyed ancient tribal life. In Africa, tribal life was still powerful, and some of its better features—a communal spirit, more kindness in law and punishment—still existed. And because the lords did not have the weapons that European lords had, they could not command obedience as easily.

In his book *The African Slave Trade,* Basil Davidson contrasts law in the Congo in the early sixteenth century with law in Portugal and England. In those European countries, where the idea of private property was becoming powerful, theft was punished brutally. In England, even as late as 1740, a child could be hanged for stealing a rag of cotton. But in the Congo, communal life persisted, the idea of private property was a strange one, and thefts were punished with fines or various degrees of servitude. A Congolese leader, told of the Portuguese legal codes, asked a Portuguese once, teasingly: "What is the penalty in Portugal for anyone who puts his feet on the ground?"

Slavery existed in the African states, and it was sometimes used by Europeans to justify their own slave trade. But, as Davidson points out, the "slaves" of Africa were more like the serfs of Europe—in other words,

like most of the population of Europe. It was a harsh servitude, but they had rights which slaves brought to America did not have, and they were "altogether different from the human cattle of the slave ships and the American plantations." In the Ashanti Kingdom of West Africa, one observer noted that "a slave might marry; own property; himself own a slave; swear an oath; be a competent witness and ultimately become heir to his master. . . . An Ashanti slave, nine cases out of ten, possibly became an adopted member of the family, and in time his descendants so merged and intermarried with the owner's kinsmen that only a few would know their origin."

One slave trader, John Newton (who later became an antislavery leader), wrote about the people of what is now Sierra Leone:

> The state of slavery, among these wild barbarous people, as we esteem them, is much milder than in our colonies. For as, on the one hand, they have no land in high cultivation, like our West India plantations, and therefore no call for that excessive, unintermitted labour, which exhausts our slaves: so, on the other hand, no man is permitted to draw blood even from a slave.

African slavery is hardly to be praised. But it was far different from plantation or mining slavery in the Americas, which was lifelong, morally crippling, destructive of family ties, without hope of any future. African slavery lacked two elements that made American slavery the most cruel form of slavery in history: the frenzy for limitless profit that comes from capitalistic agriculture; the reduction of the slave to less than human status by the use of racial hatred, with that relentless clarity based on color, where white was master, black was slave.

In fact, it was because they came from a settled culture, of tribal customs and family ties, of communal life and traditional ritual, that African blacks found themselves especially helpless when removed from this. They were captured in the interior (frequently by blacks caught up in the slave trade themselves), sold on the coast, then shoved into pens with blacks of other tribes, often speaking different languages.

The conditions of capture and sale were crushing affirmations to the black African of his helplessness in the face of superior force. The marches to the coast, sometimes for 1,000 miles, with people shackled around the neck, under whip and gun, were death marches, in which two of every five blacks died. On the coast, they were kept in cages until they were picked and sold. One John Barbot, at the end of the seventeenth century, described these cages on the Gold Coast:

> As the slaves come down to Fida from the inland country, they are put into a booth or prison . . . near the beach, and when the Europeans are to receive them, they are brought out onto a large plain, where the ship's surgeons examine every part of everyone of them, to the smallest member, men and women being stark naked. . . . Such as are allowed good and sound are set on one side . . . marked on the breast with a red-hot iron, imprinting the mark of the French, English, or Dutch companies. . . . The branded slaves after this are returned to their former booths where they await shipment, sometimes 10–15 days. . . .

Then they were packed aboard the slave ships, in spaces not much bigger than coffins, chained together in the dark, wet slime of the ship's bottom, choking in the stench of their own excrement. Documents of the time describe the conditions:

> The height, sometimes, between decks, was only eighteen inches; so that the unfortunate human beings could not turn around, or even on their sides, the elevation being less than the breadth of their shoulders; and here they are usually chained to the decks by the neck and legs. In such a place the sense of misery and suffocation is so great, that the Negroes . . . are driven to frenzy.

On one occasion, hearing a great noise from belowdecks where the blacks were chained together, the sailors opened the hatches and found the slaves in different stages of suffocation, many dead, some having killed others in desperate attempts to breathe. Slaves often jumped overboard to drown rather than continue their suffering. To one observer a slave-deck was "so covered with blood and mucus that it resembled a slaughter house."

Under these conditions, perhaps one of every three blacks transported overseas died, but the huge profits (often double the investment on one trip) made it worthwhile for the slave trader, and so the blacks were packed into the holds like fish.

First the Dutch, then the English, dominated the slave trade. (By 1795 Liverpool had more than a hundred ships carrying slaves and accounted for half of all the European slave trade.) Some Americans in New England entered the business, and in 1637 the first American slave ship, the *Desire,* sailed from Marblehead. Its holds were partitioned into racks, 2 feet by 6 feet, with leg irons and bars.

By 1800, 10 to 15 million blacks had been transported as slaves to the Americas, representing perhaps one-third of those originally seized in Africa. It is roughly estimated that Africa lost 50 million human beings to death and slavery in those centuries we call the beginnings of modern Western civilization, at the hands of slave traders and plantation owners in Western Europe and America, the countries deemed the most advanced in the world.

In the year 1610, a Catholic priest in the Americas named Father Sandoval wrote back to a church functionary in Europe to ask if the capture, transport, and enslavement of African blacks was legal by church doctrine. A letter dated March 12, 1610, from Brother Luis Brandaon to Father Sandoval gives the answer:

> Your Reverence writes me that you would like to know whether the Negroes who are sent to your parts have been legally captured. To this I reply that I think your Reverence should have no scruples on this point, because this is a matter which has been questioned by the Board of Conscience in Lisbon, and all its members are learned and conscientious men. Nor did the bishops who were in Sao Thome, Cape Verde, and here in Loando—all learned and virtuous men—find fault with it. We have been here ourselves for forty years and there have been among us very learned Fathers . . . never did they consider the trade as illicit. Therefore we and the Fathers of Brazil buy these slaves for our service without any scruple. . . .

With all of this—the desperation of the Jamestown settlers for labor, the impossibility of using Indians and the difficulty of using whites, the availability of blacks offered in greater and greater numbers by profit-seeking dealers in human flesh, and with such blacks possible to control because they had just gone through an ordeal which if it did not kill them must have left them in a state of psychic and physical helplessness—is it any wonder that such blacks were ripe for enslavement?

And under these conditions, even if some blacks might have been considered servants, would blacks be treated the same as white servants?

The evidence, from the court records of colonial Virginia, shows that in 1630 a white man named Hugh Davis was ordered "to be soundly whipt . . . for abusing himself . . . by defiling his body in lying with a Negro." Ten years later, six servants and "a negro of Mr. Reynolds" started to run away. While the whites received lighter sentences, "Emanuel the Negro to receive thirty stripes and to be burnt in the cheek with the letter R, and to work in shackle one year or more as his master shall see cause."

Although slavery was not yet regularized or legalized in those first years, the lists of servants show blacks listed separately. A law passed in 1639 decreed that "all persons except Negroes" were to get arms and ammunition—probably to fight off Indians. When in 1640 three servants tried to run away, the two whites were punished with a lengthening of their service. But, as the court put it, "the third being a negro named John Punch shall serve his master or his assigns for the time of his natural life." Also in 1640, we have the case of a Negro woman servant who begot a child by Robert Sweat, a white man. The court ruled "that the said negro woman shall be whipt at the whipping post and the said Sweat shall tomorrow in the forenoon do public penance for his offense at James citychurch. . . ."

This unequal treatment, this developing combination of contempt and oppression, feeling and action, which we call "racism"—was this the result of a "natural" antipathy of white against black? The question is important, not just as a matter of historical accuracy, but because any emphasis on "natural" racism lightens the responsibility of the social system. If racism can't be shown to be natural, then it is the result of certain conditions, and we are impelled to eliminate those conditions.

We have no way of testing the behavior of whites and blacks toward one another under favorable conditions—with no history of subordination, no money incentive for exploitation and enslavement, no desperation for survival requiring forced labor. All the conditions for black and white in seventeenth-century America were the opposite of that, all powerfully directed toward antagonism and mistreatment. Under such conditions even the slightest display of humanity between the races might be considered evidence of a basic human drive toward community.

Sometimes it is noted that, even before 1600, when the slave trade had just begun, before Africans were stamped by it—literally and symbolically—the color black was distasteful. In England, before 1600, it meant, according to the Oxford English Dictionary: "Deeply stained with dirt; soiled, dirty, foul. Having dark or deadly purposes, malignant; pertaining to or involving death, deadly; baneful, disastrous, sinister. Foul, iniquitous, atrocious, horribly wicked. Indicating disgrace, censure, liability to punishment, etc." And Elizabethan poetry often used the color white in connection with beauty.

It may be that, in the absence of any other overriding factor, darkness and blackness, associated with night and unknown, would take on those meanings. But the presence of another human being is a powerful fact, and the conditions of that presence are crucial in determining whether an initial prejudice, against a mere color, divorced from humankind, is turned into brutality and hatred.

In spite of such preconceptions about blackness, in spite of special subordination of blacks in the Americas in the seventeenth century, there is evidence that where whites and blacks found themselves with common problems, common work, common enemy in their master, they behaved toward one another as equals. As one scholar of slavery, Kenneth Stampp, has put it, Negro and

white servants of the seventeenth century were "remarkably unconcerned about the visible physical differences."

Black and white worked together, fraternized together. The very fact that laws had to be passed after a while to forbid such relations indicates the strength of that tendency. In 1661 a law was passed in Virginia that "in case any English servant shall run away in company of any Negroes" he would have to give special service for extra years to the master of the runaway Negro. In 1691, Virginia provided for the banishment of any "white man or woman being free who shall intermarry with a negro, mulatoo, or Indian man or woman bond or free."

There is an enormous difference between a feeling of racial strangeness, perhaps fear, and the mass enslavement of millions of black people that took place in the Americas. The transition from one to the other cannot be explained easily by "natural" tendencies. It is not hard to understand as the outcome of historical conditions.

Slavery grew as the plantation system grew. The reason is easily traceable to something other than natural racial repugnance: the number of arriving whites, whether free or indentured servants (under four to seven years contract), was not enough to meet the need of the plantations. By 1700, in Virginia, there were 6,000 slaves, one-twelfth of the population. By 1763, there were 170,000 slaves, about half the population.

Blacks were easier to enslave than whites or Indians. But they were still not easy to enslave. From the beginning, the imported black men and women resisted their enslavement. Ultimately their resistance was controlled, and slavery was established for 3 million blacks in the South. Still, under the most difficult conditions, under pain of mutilation and death, throughout their two hundred years of enslavement in North America, these Afro-Americans continued to rebel. Only occasionally was there an organized insurrection. More often they showed their refusal to submit by running away. Even more often, they engaged in sabotage, slowdowns, and subtle forms of resistance which asserted, if only to themselves and their brothers and sisters, their dignity as human beings.

The refusal began in Africa. One slave trader reported that Negroes were "so wilful and loth to leave their own country, that they have often leap'd out of the canoes, boat and ship into the sea, and kept under water till they were drowned."

When the very first black slaves were brought into Hispaniola in 1503, the Spanish governor of Hispaniola complained to the Spanish court that fugitive Negro slaves were teaching disobedience to the Indians. In the 1520s and 1530s, there were slave revolts in Hispaniola, Puerto Rico, Santa Marta, and what is now Panama. Shortly after those rebellions, the Spanish established a special police for chasing fugitive slaves.

A Virginia statute of 1669 referred to "the obstinacy of many of them," and in 1680 the Assembly took note of slave meetings "under the pretense of feasts and brawls" which they considered of "dangerous consequence." In 1687, in the colony's Northern Neck, a plot was discovered in which slaves planned to kill all the whites in the area and escape during a mass funeral.

Gerald Mullin, who studied slave resistance in eighteenth-century Virginia in his work *Flight and Rebellion,* reports:

> The available sources on slavery in 18th-century Virginia—plantation and county records, the newspaper advertisements for runaways—describe rebellious slaves and few others. The slaves described were lazy and thieving; they feigned illnesses, destroyed crops, stores, tools, and sometimes attacked or killed overseers. They operated blackmarkets in stolen goods.

> Runaways were defined as various types, they were truants (who usually returned voluntarily), "outlaws" . . . and slaves who were actually fugitives: men who visited relatives, went to town to pass as free, or tried to escape slavery completely, either by boarding ships and leaving the colony, or banding together in cooperative efforts to establish villages or hide-outs in the frontier. The commitment of another type of rebellious slave was total; these men became killers, arsonists, and insurrectionists.

Slaves recently from Africa, still holding on to the heritage of their communal society, would run away in groups and try to establish villages of runaways out in the wilderness, on the frontier. Slaves born in America, on the other hand, were more likely to run off alone, and, with the skills they had learned on the plantation, try to pass as free men.

In the colonial papers of England, a 1729 report from the lieutenant governor of Virginia to the British Board of Trade tells how "a number of Negroes, about fifteen . . . formed a design to withdraw from their Master and to fix themselves in the fastnesses of the neighboring Mountains. They had found means to get into their possession some Arms and Ammunition, and they took along with them some Provisions, their Cloths, bedding and working Tools. . . . Tho' this attempt has happily been defeated, it ought nevertheless to awaken us into some effectual measures. . . ."

Slavery was immensely profitable to some masters. James Madison told a British visitor shortly after the American Revolution that he could make $257 on every Negro in a year, and spend only $12 or $13 on his keep. Another viewpoint was of slaveowner Landon Carter, writing about fifty years earlier, complaining that his slaves so neglected their work and were so uncooperative ("either cannot or will not work") that he began to wonder if keeping them was worthwhile.

Some historians have painted a picture—based on the infrequency of organized rebellions and the ability of the South to maintain slavery for two hundred years—of a slave population made submissive by their condition; with their African heritage destroyed, they were, as Stanley Elkins said, made into "Sambos," "a society of helpless dependents." Or as another historian, Ulrich Phillips, said, "by racial quality submissive." But looking at the totality of slave behavior, at the resistance of everyday life, from quiet noncooperation in work to running away, the picture becomes different.

In 1710, warning the Virginia Assembly, Governor Alexander Spotswood said:

> . . . freedom wears a cap which can without a tongue, call together all those who long to shake off the fetters of slavery and as such an Insurrection would surely be attended with most dreadful consequences so I think we cannot be too early in providing against it, both by putting our selves in a better posture of defence and by making a law to prevent the consultations of those Negroes.

Indeed, considering the harshness of punishment for running away, that so many blacks did run away must be a sign of a powerful rebelliousness. All through the 1700s, the Virginia slave code read:

> Whereas many times slaves run away and lie hid and lurking in swamps, woods, and other obscure places, killing hogs, and commiting other injuries to the inhabitants . . . if the slave does not immediately return, anyone whatsoever may kill or destroy such slaves by such ways and means as he . . . shall think fit. . . . If the slave is apprehended . . . it shall . . . be

lawful for the county court, to order such punishment for the said slave, either by dismembering, or in any other way . . . as they in their discretion shall think fit, for the reclaiming any such incorrigible slave, and terrifying others from the like practices. . . .

Mullin found newspaper advertisements between 1736 and 1801 for 1,138 men runaways, and 141 women. One consistent reason for running away was to find members of one's family—showing that despite the attempts of the slave system to destroy family ties by not allowing marriages and by separating families, slaves would face death and mutilation to get together.

In Maryland, where slaves were about one-third of the population in 1750, slavery had been written into law since the 1660s, and statutes for controlling rebellious slaves were passed. There were cases where slave women killed their masters, sometimes by poisoning them, sometimes by burning tobacco houses and homes. Punishments ranged from whipping and branding to execution, but the trouble continued. In 1742, seven slaves were put to death for murdering their master.

Fear of slave revolt seems to have been a permanent fact of plantation life. William Byrd, a wealthy Virginia slaveowner, wrote in 1736:

> We have already at least 10,000 men of these descendants of Ham, fit to bear arms, and these numbers increase every day, as well by birth as by importation. And in case there should arise a man of desperate fortune, he might with more advantage than Cataline kindle a servile war . . . and tinge our rivers wide as they are with blood.

It was an intricate and powerful system of control that the slaveowners developed to maintain their labor supply and their way of life, a system both subtle and crude, involving every device that social orders employ for keeping power and wealth where it is. As Kenneth Stampp puts it:

> A wise master did not take seriously the belief that Negroes were natural-born slaves. He knew better. He knew that Negroes freshly imported from Africa had to be broken into bondage; that each succeeding generation had to be carefully trained. This was no easy task, for the bondsman rarely submitted willingly. Moreover, he rarely submitted completely. In most cases there was no end to the need for control—at least not until old age reduced the slave to a condition of helplessness.

The system was psychological and physical at the same time. The slaves were taught discipline, were impressed again and again with the idea of their own inferiority to "know their place," to see blackness as a sign of subordination, to be awed by the power of the master, to merge their interest with the master's, destroying their own individual needs. To accomplish this there was the discipline of hard labor, the breakup of the slave family, the lulling effects of religion (which sometimes led to "great mischief," as one slaveholder reported), the creation of disunity among slaves by separating them into field slaves and more privileged house slaves, and finally the power of law and the immediate power of the overseer to invoke whipping, burning, mutilation, and death. Dismemberment was provided for in the Virginia Code of 1705. Maryland passed a law in 1723 providing for cutting off the ears of blacks who struck whites, and that for certain serious crimes, slaves should be hanged and the body quartered and exposed.

Still, rebellions took place—not many, but enough to create constant fear among white planters. The first large-scale revolt in the North American colonies took place in New York in 1712. In New York, slaves were 10 percent of the population, the highest proportion in the northern states, where economic conditions usually did not require large numbers of field slaves. About twenty-five blacks and two Indians set fire to a building, then killed nine whites who came on the scene. They were captured by soldiers, put on trial, and twenty-one were executed. The governor's report to England said: "Some were burnt, others were hanged, one broke on the wheel, and one hung alive in chains in the town. . . ." One had been burned over a slow fire for eight to ten hours—all this to serve notice to other slaves.

A letter to London from South Carolina in 1720 reports:

> I am now to acquaint you that very lately we have had a very wicked and barbarous plot of the designe of the negroes rising with a designe to destroy all the white people in the country and then to take Charles Town in full body but it pleased God it was discovered and many of them taken prisoners and some burnt and some hang'd and some banish'd.

Around this time there were a number of fires in Boston and New Haven, suspected to be the work of Negro slaves. As a result, one Negro was executed in Boston, and the Boston Council ruled that any slaves who on their own gathered in groups of two or more were to be punished by whipping.

At Stono, South Carolina, in 1739, about twenty slaves rebelled, killed two warehouse guards, stole guns and gunpowder, and headed south, killing people in their way, and burning buildings. They were joined by others, until there were perhaps eighty slaves in all and, according to one account of the time, "they called out Liberty, marched on with Colours displayed, and two Drums beating." The militia found and attacked them. In the ensuing battle perhaps fifty slaves and twenty-five whites were killed before the uprising was crushed.

Herbert Aptheker, who did detailed research on slave resistance in North America for his book *American Negro Slave Revolts,* found about 250 instances where a minimum of ten slaves joined in a revolt or conspiracy.

From time to time, whites were involved in the slave resistance. As early as 1663, indentured white servants and black slaves in Gloucester County, Virginia, formed a conspiracy to rebel and gain their freedom. The plot was betrayed, and ended with executions. Mullin reports that the newspaper notices of runaways in Virginia often warned "ill-disposed" whites about harboring fugitives. Sometimes slaves and free men ran off together, or cooperated in crimes together. Sometimes, black male slaves ran off and joined white women. From time to time, white ship captains and watermen dealt with runaways, perhaps making the slave a part of the crew.

In New York in 1741, there were ten thousand whites in the city and two thousand black slaves. It had been a hard winter and the poor—slave and free—had suffered greatly. When mysterious fires broke out, blacks and whites were accused of conspiring together. Mass hysteria developed against the accused. After a trial full of lurid accusations by informers, and forced confessions, two white men and two white women were executed, eighteen slaves were hanged, and thirteen slaves were burned alive.

Only one fear was greater than the fear of black rebellion in the new American colonies. That was the fear that discontented whites would join black slaves to overthrow the existing order. In the early years of slavery, especially, before racism as a way of thinking was firmly ingrained, while white indentured servants were often treated as badly as black slaves, there was a possibil-ity of cooperation. As Edmund Morgan sees it:

> There are hints that the two despised groups initially saw each other as sharing the same predicament. It was common, for example, for servants and slaves to run away together, steal hogs together, get drunk together. It was not uncommon for them to make love together. In Bacon's Rebellion, one of the last groups to surrender was a mixed band of eighty negroes and twenty English servants.

As Morgan says, masters, "initially at least, perceived slaves in much the same way they had always perceived servants . . . shiftless, irresponsible, unfaithful, ungrateful, dishonest. . . ." And "if freemen with disappointed hopes should make common cause with slaves of desperate hope, the results might be worse than anything Bacon had done."

And so, measures were taken. About the same time that slave codes, involving discipline and punishment, were passed by the Virginia Assembly,

> Virginia's ruling class, having proclaimed that all white men were superior to black, went on to offer their social (but white) inferiors a number of benefits previously denied them. In 1705 a law was passed requiring masters to provide white servants whose indenture time was up with ten bushels of corn, thirty shillings, and a gun, while women servants were to get 15 bushels of corn and forty shillings. Also, the newly freed servants were to get 50 acres of land.

Morgan concludes: "Once the small planter felt less exploited by taxation and began to prosper a little, he became less turbulent, less dangerous, more respectable. He could begin to see his big neighbor not as an extortionist but as a powerful protector of their common interests."

We see now a complex web of historical threads to ensnare blacks for slavery in America: the desperation of starving settlers, the special helplessness of the displaced African, the powerful incentive of profit for slave trader and planter, the temptation of superior status for poor whites, the elaborate controls against escape and rebellion, the legal and social punishment of black and white collaboration.

The point is that the elements of this web are historical, not "natural." This does not mean that they are easily disentangled, dismantled. It means only that there is a possibility for something else, under historical conditions not yet realized. And one of these conditions would be the elimination of that class exploitation which has made poor whites desperate for small gifts of status, and has prevented that unity of black and white necessary for joint rebellion and reconstruction.

Around 1700, the Virginia House of Burgesses declared:

> The Christian Servants in this country for the most part consists of the Worser Sort of the people of Europe. And since . . . such numbers of Irish and other Nations have been brought in of which a great many have been soldiers in the late warrs that according to our present Circumstances we can hardly governe them and if they were fitted with Armes and had the Opertunity of meeting together by Musters we have just reason to fears they may rise upon us.

It was a kind of class consciousness, a class fear. There were things happening in early Virginia, and in the other colonies, to warrant it.

REFERENCES

APTHEKER, HERBERT, ed. 1974. *A Documentary History of the Negro People in the United States.* Secaucus, NJ: Citadel.

BOSKIN, JOSEPH. 1966. *Into Slavery: Radical Decisions in the Virginia Colony.* Philadelphia: Lippincott.

CATTERALL, HELEN. 1937. *Judicial Cases Concerning American Slavery and the Negro.* 5 vols. Washington, DC: Negro University Press.

DAVIDSON, BASIL. 1961. *The African Slave Trade.* Boston: Little, Brown.

DONNAN, ELIZABETH, ed. 1965. *Documents Illustrative of the History of the Slave Trade to America.* 4 vols. New York: Octagon.

ELKINS, STANLEY. 1976. *Slavery: A Problem in American Institutional and Intellectual Life.* Chicago: University of Chicago Press.

FEDERAL WRITERS PROJECT. 1969. *The Negro in Virginia.* New York: Arno.

FRANKLIN, JOHN HOPE. 1974. *From Slavery to Freedom: A History of American Negroes.* New York: Knopf.

JORDAN, WINTHROP. 1968. *White over Black: American Attitudes Toward the Negro, 1550–1812.* Chapel Hill: University of North Carolina Press.

MORGAN, EDMUND S. 1975. *American Slavery, American Freedom: The Ordeal of Colonial Virginia.* New York: Norton.

MULLIN, GERALD. 1974. *Flight and Rebellion: Slave Resistance in Eighteenth-Century Virginia.* New York: Oxford University Press.

MULLIN, MICHAEL, ed. 1975. *American Negro Slavery: A Documentary History.* New York: Harper & Row.

PHILLIPS, ULRICH B. 1966. *American Negro Slavery: A Survey of the Supply, Employment and Control of Negro Labor as Determined by the Plantation Regime.* Baton Rouge: Louisiana State University Press.

REDDING, J. SAUNDERS. 1973. *They Came in Chains.* Philadelphia: Lippincott.

STAMPP, KENNETH M. 1956. *The Peculiar Institution.* New York: Knopf.

TANNENBAUM, FRANK. 1963. *Slave and Citizen: The Negro in the Americas.* New York: Random House.

5

ONE DROP OF BLOOD

Lawrence Wright

Washington in the millennial years is a city of warring racial and ethnic groups fighting for recognition, protection, and entitlements. This war has been fought throughout the second half of the twentieth century largely by black Americans. How much this contest has widened, how bitter it has turned, how complex and baffling it is, and how far-reaching its consequences are became evident in a series of congressional hearings that began last year in the obscure House Subcommittee on Census, Statistics, and Postal Personnel, which is chaired by Representative Thomas C. Sawyer, Democrat of Ohio, and concluded in November, 1993.

Although the Sawyer hearings were scarcely reported in the news and were sparsely attended even by other members of the subcommittee, with the exception of Representative Thomas E. Petri, Republican of Wisconsin, they opened what may become the most searching examination of racial questions in this country since the sixties. Related federal agency hearings, and meetings that will be held in Washington and other cities around the country to prepare for the 2000 census, are considering not only modifications of existing racial categories but also the larger question of whether it is proper for the government to classify people according to arbitrary distinctions of skin color and ancestry. This discussion arises at a time when profound debates are occurring in minority communities about the rightfulness of group entitlements, some government officials are questioning the usefulness of race data, and scientists are debating whether race exists at all.

Tom Sawyer, forty-eight, a former English teacher and a former mayor of Akron, is now in his fourth term representing the Fourteenth District of Ohio. It would be fair to say that neither the House Committee on Post Office and Civil Service nor the subcommittee that Sawyer chairs is the kind of assignment that members of Congress would willingly shed blood for. Indeed, the attitude of most elected officials in Washington toward the census is polite loathing, because it is the census, as much as any other force in the country, that determines their political futures. Congressional districts rise and fall with the shifting demography of the country, yet census matters rarely seize the front pages of home-town newspapers, except briefly, once every ten years. Much of the subcommittee's business has to do with addressing the safety concerns of postal workers and overseeing federal statistical measurements. The subcommittee has an additional responsibility: it reviews the executive branch's policy about which racial and ethnic groups should be officially recognized by the United States government.

"We are unique in this country in the way we describe and define race and ascribe to it characteristics that other cultures view very differently," Sawyer, who is a friendly man with an open, boyish face and graying black hair, says. He points out that the country is in the midst of its most profound demographic shift since the eighteen-nineties—a time that opened "a period of the greatest immigration we have ever seen, whose numbers have not been matched until right now." A deluge of new Americans from every part of the world is overwhelming our traditional racial distinctions, Sawyer believes. "The categories themselves inevitably reflect the temporal bias of every age," he says. "That becomes a problem when the nation itself is undergoing deep and historic diversification."

Looming over the shoulder of Sawyer's subcommittee is the Office of Management and Budget, the federal agency that happens to be responsible for determining standard classifications of racial and ethnic data. Since 1977, those categories have been set by O.M.B. Statistical Directive 15, which controls the racial and ethnic standards on all federal forms and statistics. Directive 15 acknowledges four general racial groups in the United States: American Indian or Alaskan Native; Asian or Pacific Islander; Black; and White. Directive 15 also breaks down ethnicity into Hispanic Origin and Not of Hispanic Origin. These categories, or versions of them, are present on enrollment forms for schoolchildren; on application forms for jobs, scholarships, loans, and mortgages; and, of course, on United States census forms. The categories ask that every American fit himself or herself into one racial and one ethnic box. From this comes the information that is used to monitor and enforce civil-rights legislation, most notably the Voting Rights Act of 1965, but also a smorgasbord of set-asides and entitlements and affirmative-action programs. "The numbers drive the dollars," Sawyer observes, repeating a well-worn Washington adage.

The truth of that statement was abundantly evident in the hearings, in which a variety of racial and ethnic groups were bidding to increase their portions of the federal pot. The National Coalition for an Accurate Count of Asian Pacific Americans lobbied to add Cambodians and Lao to the nine different nationalities already listed on the census forms under the heading of Asian or Pacific Islander. The National Council of La Raza proposed that Hispanics be considered a race, not just an ethnic group. The Arab American Institute asked that persons from the Middle East, now counted as white, be given a separate, protected category of their own. Senator Daniel K. Akaka, a Native Hawaiian, urged that his people be moved from the Asian or Pacific Islander box to the American Indian or Alaskan Native box. "There is the misperception that Native Hawaiians, who number well over two hundred thousand, somehow 'immigrated' to the United States like other Asian or Pacific Island groups," the Senator testified. "This leads to the erroneous impression that Native Hawaiians, the original inhabitants of the Hawaiian Islands, no longer exist." In the Senator's opinion, being placed in the same category as other Native Americans would help rectify that situation. (He did not mention that certain American Indian tribes enjoy privileges concerning gambling concessions that Native Hawaiians currently don't enjoy.) The National Congress of American Indians would like the Hawaiians to stay where they are. In every case, issues of money, but also of identity, are at stake.

In this battle over racial turf, a disturbing new contender has appeared. "When I received my 1990 census form, I realized that there was no race category for my children," Susan Graham, who is a white woman married to a black man in Roswell, Georgia, testified. "I called the Census Bureau. After checking with supervisors, the bureau finally gave me their answer: the children should take the race of their mother. When I objected and asked why my children should be classified as their mother's race only, the Census Bureau representative said to me, in a very hushed voice, 'Because, in cases like these, we always know who the mother is and not always the father.' "

Graham went on to say, "I could not make a race choice from the basic categories when I enrolled my son in kindergarten in Georgia. The only choice I had, like most other parents of multiracial children, was to leave race blank. I later found that my child's teacher was instructed to choose for him based on her knowledge and observation of my child. Ironically, my child has been white on the United States census, black at school, and multiracial at home—all at the same time."

Graham and others were asking that a "Multiracial" box be added to the racial categories specified by Directive 15—a proposal that alarmed representatives of the other racial groups for a number of reasons, not the least of which was that multiracialism threatened to undermine the concept of racial classification altogether.

According to various estimates, at least seventy-five to more than ninety per cent of the people who now check the Black box could check Multiracial, because of their mixed genetic heritage. If a certain proportion of those people—say, ten per cent—should elect to identify themselves as Multiracial, legislative districts in many parts of the country might need to be redrawn. The entire civil-rights regulatory program concerning housing, employment, and education would have to be reassessed. School-desegregation plans would be thrown into the air. Of course, it is possible that only a small number of Americans will elect to choose the Multiracial option, if it is offered, with little social effect. Merely placing such an option on the census invites people to consider choosing it, however. When the census listed "Cajun" as one of several examples under the ancestry question, the number of Cajuns jumped nearly

two thousand percent. To remind people of the possibility is to encourage enormous change.

Those who are charged with enforcing civil rights laws see the Multiracial box as a wrecking ball aimed at affirmative action, and they hold those in the mixed-race movement responsible. "There's no concern on any of these people's part about the effect on policy—it's just a subjective feeling that their identity needs to be stroked," one government analyst said. "What they don't understand is that it's going to cost their own groups"—by losing the advantages that accrue to minorities by way of affirmative-action programs, for instance. Graham contends that the object of her movement is not to create another protected category. In any case, she said, multiracial people know "to check the right box to get the goodies."

Of course, races have been mixing in America since Columbus arrived. Visitors to Colonial America found plantation slaves who were as light-skinned as their masters. Patrick Henry actually proposed, in 1784, that the State of Virginia encourage intermarriage between whites and Indians, through the use of tax incentives and cash stipends. The legacy of this intermingling is that Americans who are descendants of early settlers, of slaves, or of Indians often have ancestors of different races in their family tree.

Thomas Jefferson supervised the original census, in 1790. The population then was broken down into free white males, free white females, other persons (these included free blacks and "taxable Indians," which meant those living in or around white settlements), and slaves. How unsettled this country has always been about its racial categories is evident in the fact that nearly every census since has measured race differently. For most of the nineteenth century, the census reflected an American obsession with miscegenation. The color of slaves was to be specified as "B," for black, and "M," for mulatto. In the 1890 census, gradations of mulattoes were further broken down into quadroons and octoroons. After 1920, however, the Census Bureau gave up on such distinctions, estimating that three-quarters of all blacks in the United States were racially mixed already, and that pure blacks would soon disappear. Henceforth anyone with any black ancestry at all would be counted simply as black.

Actual interracial marriages, however, were historically rare. Multiracial children were often marginalized as illegitimate half-breeds who didn't fit comfortably into any racial community. This was particularly true of the offspring of black-white unions. "In my family, like many families with African-American ancestry, there is a history of multiracial offspring associated with rape and concubinage," G. Reginald Daniel, who teaches a course in multiracial identity at the University of California at Los Angeles, says. "I was reared in the segregationist South. Both sides of my family have been mixed for at least three generations. I struggled as a child over the question of why I had to exclude my East Indian and Irish and Native American and French ancestry, and could include only African."

Until recently, people like Daniel were identified simply as black because of a peculiarly American institution known informally as "the one-drop rule," which defines as black a person with as little as a single drop of "black blood." This notion derives from a long-discredited belief that each race had its own blood type, which was correlated with physical appearance and social behavior. The antebellum South promoted the rule as a way of enlarging the slave population with the children of slaveholders. By the nineteen-twenties, in Jim Crow America the one-drop rule was well established as the law of the land. It still is, according to a United States Supreme Court decision as late as 1986, which refused to review a lower court's ruling that a Louisiana woman

whose great-great-great-great-grandmother had been the mistress of a French planter was black—even though that proportion of her ancestry amounted to no more than three thirty-seconds of her genetic heritage. "We are the only country in the world that applies the one-drop rule, and the only group that the one-drop rule applies to is people of African descent," Daniel observes.

People of mixed black-and-white ancestry were rejected by whites and found acceptance by blacks. Many of the most notable "black" leaders over the last century and a half were "white" to some extent, from Booker T. Washington and Frederick Douglass (both of whom had white fathers) to W. E. B. Du Bois, Malcolm X, and Martin Luther King, Jr. (who had an Irish grandmother and some American Indian ancestry as well). The fact that Lani Guinier, Louis Farrakhan, and Virginia's former governor Douglas Wilder are defined as black, and define themselves that way, though they have light skin or "European" features, demonstrates how enduring the one-drop rule has proved to be in America, not only among whites but among blacks as well. Daniel sees this as "a double-edged sword." While the one-drop rule encouraged racism, it also galvanized the black community.

"But the one-drop rule is racist," Daniel says. "There's no way you can get away from the fact that it was historically implemented to create as many slaves as possible. No one leaped over to the white community—that was simply the mentality of the nation, and people of African descent internalized it. What this current discourse is about is lifting the lid of racial oppression in our institutions and letting people identify with the totality of their heritage. We have created a nightmare for human dignity. Multiracialism has the potential for undermining the very basis of racism, which is its categories."

But multiracialism introduces nightmares of its own. If people are to be counted as something other than completely black, for instance, how will affirmative-action programs be implemented? Suppose a court orders a city to hire additional black police officers to make up for past discrimination. Will mixed-race officers count? Will they count wholly or partly? Far from solving the problem of fragmented identities, multiracialism could open the door to fractional races, such as we already have in the case of the American Indians. In order to be eligible for certain federal benefits, such as housing-improvement programs, a person must prove that he or she either is a member of a federally recognized Indian tribe or has fifty per cent "Indian blood." One can envision a situation in which nonwhiteness itself becomes the only valued quality, to be compensated in various ways depending on a person's pedigree.

Kwame Anthony Appiah, of Harvard's Philosophy and Afro-American Studies Departments, says, "What the Multiracial category aims for is not people of mixed ancestry, because a majority of Americans are actually products of mixed ancestry. This category goes after people who have parents who are socially recognized as belonging to different races. That's O.K.— that's an interesting social category. But then you have to ask what happens to their children. Do we want to have more boxes, depending upon whether they marry back into one group or the other? What are the children of these people supposed to say? I think about these things because—look, my mother is English; my father is Ghanaian. My sisters are married to a Nigerian and a Norwegian. I have nephews who range from blond-haired kids to very black kids. They are all first cousins. Now, according to the American scheme of things, they're all black—even the guy with blond hair who skis in Oslo. That's what the one-drop rule says. The Multiracial scheme, which is meant to solve anomalies, simply creates more anomalies of its own, and that's because the fundamental concept—that you should be able to assign every American to one of three or four races reliably—is crazy."

These are sentiments that Representative Sawyer agrees with profoundly. He says of the one-drop rule, "It is so embedded in our perception and policy, but it doesn't allow for the blurring that is the reality of our population. Just look at—What are the numbers?" he said in his congressional office as he leafed through a briefing book. "Thirty-eight per cent of American Japanese females and eighteen per cent of American Japanese males marry outside their traditional ethnic and nationality group. Seventy per cent of American Indians marry outside. I grant you that the enormous growth potential of multiracial marriages starts from a relatively small base, but the truth is it starts from a fiction to begin with; that is, what we think of as black-and-white marriages are not marriages between people who come from anything like a clearly defined ethnic, racial, or genetic base."

The United States Supreme Court struck down the last vestige of antimiscegenation laws in 1967, in Loving v. Virginia. At that time, interracial marriages were rare; only sixty-five thousand marriages between blacks and whites were recorded in the 1970 census. Marriages between Asians and non-Asian Americans tended to be between soldiers and war brides. Since then, mixed marriages occurring between many racial and ethnic groups have risen to the point where they have eroded the distinctions between such peoples. Among American Indians, people are more likely to marry outside their group than within it, as Representative Sawyer noted. The number of children living in families where one parent is white and the other is black, Asian, or American Indian, to use one measure, has tripled—from fewer than four hundred thousand in

1970 to one and a half million in 1990—and this doesn't count the children of single parents or children whose parents are divorced.

Blacks are conspicuously less likely to marry outside their group, and yet marriages between blacks and whites have tripled in the last thirty years. Matthijs Kalmijn, a Dutch sociologist, analyzed marriage certificates filed in this country's non-Southern states since the Loving decision and found that in the nineteen-eighties the rate at which black men were marrying white women had reached approximately ten per cent. (The rate for black women marrying white men is about half that figure.) In the 1990 census, six per cent of black householders nationwide had nonblack spouses—still a small percentage, but a significant one.

Multiracial people, because they are now both unable and unwilling to be ignored, and because many of them refuse to be confined to traditional racial categories, inevitably undermine the entire concept of race as an irreducible difference between peoples. The continual modulation of racial differences in America is increasing the jumble created by centuries of ethnic intermarriage. The resulting dilemma is a profound one. If we choose to measure the mixing by counting people as Multiracial, we pull the teeth of the civil-rights laws. Are we ready for that? Is it even possible to make changes in the way we count Americans, given the legislative mandates already built into law? "I don't know," Sawyer concedes. "At this point, my purpose is not so much to alter the laws that underlie these kinds of questions as to raise the question of whether or not the way in which we currently define who we are reflects the reality of the nation we are and who we are becoming. If it does not, then the policies underlying the terms of measurement are doomed to be flawed. What you measure is what you get."

Science has put forward many different racial models, the most enduring being the division of humanity into three broad groupings: the Mongoloid, the Negroid, and the Caucasoid. An influential paper by Masatoshi Nei and Arun K. Roychoudhury, entitled "Gene Differences between Caucasian, Negro, and Japanese Populations," which appeared in *Science,* in 1972, found that the genetic variation among individuals from these racial groups was only slightly greater than the variation within the groups.

In 1965, the anthropologist Stanley Garn proposed hundreds, even thousands, of racial groups, which he saw as gene clusters separated by geography or culture, some with only minor variations between them. The paleontologist Stephen Jay Gould, for one, has proposed doing away with all racial classifications and identifying people by clines—regional divisions that are used to account for the diversity of snails and of songbirds, among many other species. In this Gould follows the anthropologist Ashley Montagu, who waged a lifelong campaign to rid science of the term "race" altogether and never used it except in quotation marks. Montagu would have substituted the term "ethnic group," which he believed carried less odious baggage.

Race, in the common understanding, draws upon differences not only of skin color and physical attributes but also of language, nationality, and religion. At times, we have counted as "races" different national groups, such as Mexicans and Filipinos. Some Asian Indians were counted as members of a "Hindu" race in the censuses from 1920 to 1940; then they became white for three decades. Racial categories are often used as ethnic intensifiers, with the aim of justifying the exploitation of one group by another. One can trace the ominous example of Jews in prewar Germany, who were counted as "Israelites," a religious group, until the Nazis came to power and turned them into a race. Mixtures of first- and second-degree Jewishness were distinguished, much as quadroons and octoroons had been in the United States. In fact, the Nazi experience ultimately caused a widespread reëxamination of the idea of race. Canada dropped the race question from its census in 1951 and has so far resisted all attempts to reinstitute it. People who were working in the United States Bureau of the Census in the fifties and early sixties remember that there was speculation that the race question would soon be phased out in America as well. The American Civil Liberties Union tried to get the race question dropped from the census in 1960, and the State of New Jersey stopped entering race information on birth and death certificates in 1962 and 1963. In 1964, however, the architecture of civil-rights laws began to be erected, and many of the new laws—particularly the Voting Rights Act of 1965—required highly detailed information about minority participation which could be gathered only by the decennial census, the nation's supreme instrument for gathering demographic statistics. The expectation that the race question would wither away surrendered to the realization that race data were fundamental to monitoring and enforcing desegregation. The census soon acquired a political importance that it had never had in the past.

Unfortunately, the sloppiness and multiplicity of certain racial and ethnic categories rendered them practically meaningless for statistical purposes. In 1973, Caspar Weinberger, who was then Secretary of Health, Education and Welfare, asked the Federal Interagency Committee on Education (FICE) to develop some standards for classifying race and ethnicity. An ad-hoc committee sprang into being and proposed to create an intellectual grid that would sort all Americans into five racial and ethnic categories. The first category was American In-

dian or Alaskan Native. Some members of the committee wanted the category to be called Original Peoples of the Western Hemisphere, in order to include Indians of South American origin, but the distinction that this category was seeking was so-called "Federal Indians," who were eligible for government benefits; to include Indians of any other origin, even though they might be genetically quite similar, would confuse the collecting of data. To accommodate the various, highly diverse peoples who originated in the Far East, Southeast Asia, and the Pacific Islands, the committee proposed a category called Asian or Pacific Islander, thus sweeping into one massive basket Chinese, Samoans, Cambodians, Filipinos, and others—peoples who had little or nothing in common, and many of whom were, indeed, traditional enemies. The fact that American Indians and Alaskan Natives originated from the same Mongoloid stock as many of these peoples did not stop the committee from putting them in a separate racial category. Black was defined as "a person having origins in any of the black racial groups of Africa," and White, initially, as "a person having origins in any of the original peoples of Europe, North Africa, the Middle East, or the Indian subcontinent"—everybody else, in other words. Because the Black category contained anyone with any African heritage at all, the range of actual skin colors covered the entire spectrum, as did the White category, which included Arabs and Asian Indians and various other darker-skinned peoples.

The final classification, Hispanic, was the most problematic of all. In the 1960 census, people whose ancestry was Latin-American were counted as white. Then people of Spanish origin became a protected group, requiring the census to gather data in order to monitor their civil rights. But how to define them? People who spoke Spanish? Defining the population that way would have included millions of Americans who spoke the language but had no actual roots in Hispanic culture, and it excluded Brazilians and children of immigrants who were not taught Spanish in their homes. One approach was to count persons with Spanish surnames, but that created a number of difficulties: marriage made some non-Hispanic women into instant minorities, while stripping other women of their Hispanic status. The 1970 census inquired about people from "Central or South America," and more than a million people checked the box who were not Hispanic; they were from Kansas, Alabama, Mississippi—the central and southern United States, in other words.

The greatest dilemma was that there was no conceivable justification for calling Hispanics a race. There were black Hispanics from the Dominican Republic, Argentines who were almost entirely European whites, Mexicans who would have been counted as American Indians if they had been born north of the Rio Grande. The great preponderance of Hispanics are mestizos—a continuum of many different genetic backgrounds. Moreover, the fluid Latin-American concept of race differs from the rigid United States idea of biologically determined and highly distinct human divisions. In most Latin cultures, skin color is an individual variable—not a group marker—so that within the same family one sibling might be considered white and another black. By 1960, the United States census, which counts the population of Puerto Rico, gave up asking the race question on the island, because race did not carry the same distinction there that it did on the mainland. The ad-hoc committee decided to dodge riddles like these by calling Hispanics an ethnic group, not a race.

In 1977, O.M.B. Statistical Directive 15 adopted the FICE suggestions practically verbatim, with one principal exception: Asian Indians were moved to the Asian or Pacific Islander category. Thus, with little political discussion, the identities of Americans were fixed in five broad groupings. Those racial and ethnic categories that were dreamed up almost twenty years ago were not neutral in their effect. By attempting to provide a way for Americans to describe themselves, the categories actually began to shape those identities. The categories became political entities, with their own constituencies, lobbies, and vested interests. What was even more significant, they caused people to think of themselves in new ways—as members of "races" that were little more than statistical devices. In 1974, the year the ad-hoc committee set to work, few people referred to themselves as Hispanic; rather, people who fell into that grouping tended to identify themselves by nationality—Mexican or Dominican, for instance. Such small categories, however, are inconvenient for statistics and politics, and the creation of the meta-concept "Hispanic" has resulted in the formation of a peculiarly American group. "It is a mixture of ethnicity, culture, history, birth, and a presumption of language," Sawyer contends. Largely because of immigration, the Asian or Pacific Islander group is considered the fastest-growing racial group in the United States, but it is a "racial" category that in all likelihood exists nowhere else in the world. The third-fastest-growing category is Other—made up of the nearly ten million people, most of them Hispanics, who refused to check any of the prescribed racial boxes. American Indian groups are also growing at a rate that far exceeds the growth of the population as a whole: from about half a million people in 1960 to nearly two million in 1990—a two-hundred-and-fifty-nine-percent increase, which was demographically impossible. It seemed to be accounted for by improvements in the census-taking procedure and also by the fact that Native Americans had become fashionable, and people now wished to identify with them. To make matters even more confounding, only seventy-four per cent of those who identified themselves as American Indian by race reported having Indian ancestry.

Whatever the word "race" may mean elsewhere in the world, or to the world of science, it is clear that in America the categories are arbitrary, confused, and hopelessly intermingled. In many cases, Americans don't know who they are, racially speaking. A National Center for Health Statistics study found that 5.8 per cent of the people who called themselves Black were seen as White by a census interviewer. Nearly a third of the people identifying themselves as Asian were classified as White or Black by independent observers. That was also true of seventy per cent of people who identified themselves as American Indians. Robert A. Hahn, an epidemiologist at the Centers for Disease Control and Prevention, analyzed deaths of infants born from 1983 through 1985. In an astounding number of cases, the infant had a different race on its death certificate from the one on its birth certificate, and this finding led to staggering increases in the infant-mortality rate for minority populations—46.9 per cent greater for American Indians, 48.8 per cent greater for Japanese-Americans, 78.7 per cent greater for Filipinos—over what had been previously recorded. Such disparities cast doubt on the dependability of race as a criterion for any statistical survey. "It seems to me that we have to go back and reëvaluate the whole system," Hahn says. "We have to ask, 'What do these categories mean?' We are not talking about race in the way that geneticists might use the term, because we're not making any kind of biological assessment. It's closer to self-perceived membership in a population—which is essentially what ethnicity is." There are genetic variations in disease patterns, Hahn points out, and he goes on to say, "But these variations don't always correspond to so-called races.

What's really important is, essentially, two things. One, people from different ancestral backgrounds have different behaviors—diets, ideas about what to do when you're sick—that lead them to different health statuses. Two, people are discriminated against because of other people's perception of who they are and how they should be treated. There's still a lot of discrimination in the health-care system."

Racial statistics do serve an important purpose in the monitoring and enforcement of civil-rights laws; indeed, that has become the main justification for such data. A routine example is the Home Mortgage Disclosure Act. Because of race questions on loan applications, the federal government has been able to document the continued practice of redlining by financial institutions. The Federal Reserve found that, for conventional mortgages, in 1992 the denial rate for blacks and Hispanics was roughly double the rate for whites. Hiring practices, jury selection, discriminatory housing patterns, apportionment of political power—in all these areas, and more, the government patrols society, armed with little more than statistical information to insure equal and fair treatment. "We need these categories essentially to get rid of them," Hahn says.

The unwanted corollary of slotting people by race is that such officially sanctioned classifications may actually worsen racial strife. By creating social-welfare programs based on race rather than on need, the government sets citizens against one another precisely because of perceived racial differences. "It is not 'race' but a *practice* of racial classification that bedevils the society," writes Yehudi Webster, a sociologist at California State University, Los Angeles, and the author of "The Racialization of America." The use of racial statistics, he and others have argued, creates a reality of racial divisions, which then require solutions, such as busing, affirmative action, and multicultural education, all of which are bound to fail, because they heighten the racial awareness that leads to contention. Webster believes that adding a Multiracial box would be "another leap into absurdity," because it reinforces the concept of race in the first place. "In a way, it's a continuation of the one-drop principle. Anybody can say, 'I've got one drop of *something*—I must be multiracial.' It may be a good thing. It may finally convince Americans of the absurdity of racial classification."

In 1990, Itabari Njeri, who writes about interethnic relations for the Los Angeles *Times,* organized a symposium for the National Association of Black Journalists. She recounts a presentation given by Charles Stewart, a Democratic Party activist: "If you consider yourself black for political reasons, raise your hand." The vast majority raised their hands. When Stewart then asked how many people present believed they were of pure African descent, without any mixture, no one raised his hand. Stewart commented later, "If you advocate a category that includes people who are multiracial to the detriment of their black identification, you will replicate what you saw—an empty room. We cannot afford to have an empty room."

Njeri maintains that the social and economic gap between light-skinned blacks and dark-skinned blacks is as great as the gap between all blacks and all whites in America. If people of more obviously mixed backgrounds were to migrate to a Multiracial box, she says, they would be politically abandoning their former allies and the people who needed their help the most. Instead of draining the established categories of their influence, Njeri and others believe, it would be better to eliminate racial categories altogether.

That possibility is actually being discussed in the corridors of government. "It's quite strange—the original idea of O.M.B. Directive 15 has nothing to do with current efforts to 'define' race," says Sally Katzen, the director of the Office of Information and Regulatory Affairs at O.M.B., who has the onerous responsibility of making the final recommendation on revising the racial categories. "When O.M.B. got into the business of establishing categories, it was purely statistical, not programmatic—purely for the purpose of data gathering, not for defining or protecting different categories. It was certainly never meant to *define* a race." And yet for more than twenty years Directive 15 did exactly that, with relatively little outcry. "Recently, a question has been raised about the increasing number of multiracial children. I personally have received pictures of beautiful children who are part Asian and part black, or part American Indian and part Asian, with these letters saying, 'I don't want to check just one box. I don't want to deny part of my heritage.' It's very compelling."

This year, Katzen convened a new interagency committee to consider how races should be categorized, and even whether racial information should be sought at all. "To me it's *offensive*—because I think of the Holocaust—for someone to say what a Jew is," says Katzen. "I don't think a government agency should be defining racial and ethnic categories—that certainly was not what was ever intended by these standards."

Is it any accident that racial and ethnic categories should come under attack now, when being a member of a minority group brings certain advantages? The white colonizers of North America conquered the indigenous people, imported African slaves, brought in Asians as laborers and then excluded them with prejudicial immigration laws, and appropriated Mexican land and the people who were living on it. In short, the nonwhite population of America has historically been subjugated and treated as second-class citizens by the white majority. It is to redress the social and economic inequalities of our history that we have civil-rights laws and affirmative-action plans in the first place. Advocates of various racial and ethnic groups point out that many of the people now calling for a race-blind society are political conservatives, who may have an interest in undermining the advancement of nonwhites in our society. Suddenly, the conservatives have adopted the language of integration, it seems, and the left-leaning racial-identity advocates have adopted the language of separatism. It amounts to a polar reversal of political rhetoric.

Jon Michael Spencer, a professor in the African and Afro-American Studies Curriculum at the University of North Carolina at Chapel Hill, recently wrote an article in *The Black Scholar* lamenting what he calls "the postmodern conspiracy to explode racial identity." The article ignited a passionate debate in the magazine over the nature and the future of race. Spencer believes that race is a useful metaphor for cultural and historic difference, because it permits a level of social cohesion among oppressed classes. "To relinquish the notion of race— even though it's a cruel hoax—at this particular time is to relinquish our fortress against the powers and principalities that still try to undermine us," he says. He sees the Multiracial box as politically damaging to "those who need to galvanize peoples around the racial idea of black."

There are some black cultural nationalists who might welcome the Multiracial category. "In terms of the African-American population, it could be very, very useful, because there is a need to clarify who is in and who is not," Molefi Kete Asante, who is the chairperson of the Department of African-American Studies at Temple University, says. "In fact, I would think they should go further than that—identify those people who are in interracial marriages."

Spencer, however, thinks that it might be better to eliminate racial categories altogether than to create an additional category that empties the others of meaning. "If you had who knows how many thousands or tens of thousands or millions of people claiming to be multiracial, you would lessen the number who are black," Spencer says. "There's no end in sight. There's no limit to which one can go in claiming to be multiracial. For instance, I happen to be very brown in complexion, but when I go to the continent of Africa, blacks and whites there claim that I would be 'colored' rather than black, which means that somewhere in my distant past—probably during the era of slavery—I could have one or more white ancestors. So does that mean that I, too, could check Multiracial? Certainly light-skinned black people might perhaps see this as a way out of being included among a despised racial group. The result could be the creation of another class of people, who are betwixt and between black and white."

Whatever comes out of this discussion, the nation is likely to engage in the most profound debate of racial questions in decades. "We recognize the importance of racial categories in correcting clear injustices under the law," Representative Sawyer says. "The dilemma we face is trying to assure the fundamental guarantees of equality of opportunity while at the same time recognizing that the populations themselves are changing as we seek to categorize them. It reaches the point where it becomes an absurd counting game. Part of the difficulty is that we are dealing with the illusion of precision. We wind up with precise counts of everybody in the country, and they are precisely wrong. They don't reflect who we are as a people. To be effective, the concepts of individual and group identity need to reflect not only who we have been but who we are becoming. The more these categories distort our perception of reality, the less useful they are. We act as if we knew what we're talking about when we talk about race, and we don't."

6

PLACING RACE IN CONTEXT

Clara E. Rodriguez • Hector Cordero-Guzman

Introduction

By the 1960s a consensus had been reached that race as a biological concept was useless (Alland 1971; Harris 1968; Mead et al. 1968; Montagu 1964). There was only one human race and it had infinite variation and some population clusters. Yet, race, as people experience it, is a cultural construct (Sanjek 1990). Thus, how "races" or racial paradigms are determined also varies from culture to culture, as does the meaning of the term "race."

For example, in the United States of America race is conceived as being biologically or genetically based. The White race was defined by the absence of any non-White blood, and, the Black race was defined by the presence of any Black blood. This cultural conception of race differed from that which evolved in Latin America. In Latin America, race may have had blood lines as a referent, but there were also other dimensions brought into "racial classification": for example, class, physical type, and ethnic background. Thus, in the US and in Latin America, two different cultural definitions of "race" arose, each of which took different referents. Each system of racial classification was seen, by those who utilized it, to be the only correct way of viewing individuals.

The fact that popular definitions of "race" vary from culture to culture suggests the importance of historical events, developments or context in determining "race." That there are different systems of racial classification in different countries (and sometimes within countries) is quite counter to the usual perception that most White Americans hold of race in the United States. This is because of the particular way in which race is popularly viewed in the US where race is seen to be genetically based and therefore unchanging. In the words of American sociologists, it is an ascribed characteristic.

An example of how race changes from context to context is the description of the man who, in travelling from Puerto Rico to Mexico to the United States, changes his race from "White to Mulatto to Black" (Mintz 1971). Then there is the case of the Japanese who were accorded the status of honorary Whites in South Africa because of the changing business context. Again, there is the example of the Jews in Europe, who were classified by the Germans as a race apart from other Europeans, despite the fact that they were a group with highly varied phenotypes and quite diverse genetic strains. In nineteenth-century US and in the early twentieth-century immigration laws, race was used to describe not only Blacks and Whites, but also Slavs, Italians, Anglo-Saxons, etc. A basic white-non-white dichotomous categorization was present, but many European groups were also viewed as sub-races, different from Anglo-Saxon stock.

Clara E. Rodriguez and Hector Cordero-Guzman, "Placing Race in Context" from *Ethnic and Racial Studies*, 15, 4, October, 1992, pp. 523–529, 539–541. Copyright © 1992 Routledge. Reprinted by permission.

Given the significance of context in determining popular conceptions of race, it is also important to understand what happens to the conceptions of race and racial self-identity of individuals when they move from a country with one racial paradigm to a country with another. Are dual racial paradigms maintained? Do individuals adhere to their own perceptions of race? What determines whether they adopt or maintain their own perceptions of race? Are responses to questions of racial identity altered depending on how respondents interpret the question and its context?

These issues are brought into sharp relief when studying Puerto Ricans, a group with a history of contact with the US but with a different racial paradigm. In this article we study the way in which Puerto Ricans, who have been exposed to both cultures, identify themselves racially, how they are identified by interviewers and how they think that they would be viewed by North Americans. This research sheds light on these two racial paradigms—that of the US and Puerto Rico—and what happens when they come into contact with each other.

Race in Historical Perspective

Although both the United States and Latin America relied on the importation of African slaves to meet labour needs, the conception and incorporation of peoples of African-descent as a "race" took different directions in the two areas (Denton and Massey 1989; Pitt-Rivers 1975; Wagley 1965). Of special interest is the case of the Spanish Caribbean and, in particular, Puerto Rico. In Puerto Rico race came to be seen as a continuum of categories, with different gradations and shades of colour as the norm. In the US race was conceived as a dichotomous concept in which individuals were envisaged, and legally defined, as being either White or Black. Although both areas had instituted slavery and both had clear demarcations between free whites and slaves, the category "White" included more people in Puerto Rico than it would have done in the United States. In addition, there was a variety of race categories in Puerto Rico and many were fluid.[1]

The population of Puerto Rico is mostly descended from the original Taino Indian settlers, white Spanish colonizers, black slaves brought from Africa, and countless other immigrants. The variety of phenotypes in Puerto Rico, then, is mostly the result of a relatively unexamined history of racial mixing and diverse migratory flows. A number of works have touched on the issue of racial mixing in the island, but there is no real consensus on its extent. Puerto Rican and American researchers at different times have discussed or found Puerto Rico to be everything from a mulatto country to a predominantly white country with small subgroups of blacks and mulattos. Compare, for example, the accounts of Seda Bonilla (1961) with those of Gordon (1949), Mills, Senior and Goldsen (1950), and Senior (1965).

The historical formation of race relations in Puerto Rico was accompanied by the development of a distinct nomenclature to describe the different groups. This nomenclature and the racial discourse in Puerto Rico reflected the fact that race was seen to be multidimensional. This was quite distinct from the conception of race that developed in the United States, where new "racial" categories and terms were not developed. On some occasions the US census did separately count mulattos and other mixtures of European and African peoples, but this practice fluctuated and by 1930 the census used only the "Negro" category to describe those with any trait of African descent (Martin 1990). Thus, the offspring of Native American Indians, Asians or Europeans who intermarried with Blacks would simply be counted as Negro.

The 1896 decision of the US Supreme Court in the *Plessy v Ferguson* case legitimated the more dichotomous black/white view of "race." In this case, the petitioner averred that since he was ". . . seven eighths Caucasian and one eighth African blood; and that the mixture of colored blood was not discernible in him . . . ," he was entitled to the rights and privileges of citizens of the white race. The Supreme Court, however, decided against the plaintiff, thus further legitimating the genetic or blood quantum definition of race and sanctioning Jim Crow legislation (Blaustein and Zangrando 1968). The "separate but equal" doctrine elaborated in *Plessy v Ferguson* regulated the level of contact between White and Black Americans and went so far as to define as "Black" any individual who had even a small fraction of "Black" ancestry (Chang 1985, p. 52).

In Puerto Rico and in other parts of Latin America, race was based more on phenotypic and socio-economic definitions of the person rather than on genotypic definitions. Thus, in the US race is generally seen as a fact of biology, while in many parts of Latin America—particularly in the Spanish Caribbean—a more socio-economic conception of race has been the norm. This more socio-economic conception of race has emphasized dimensions that are freely varying, such as physical appearance (as opposed to genetic make-up), social class, and cultural modes of behaviour. For example, Sanjek (1971, p. 1128) notes that in Brazil classification is affected by contextual variables, that is, by situational and sociological variables that would include

> economic class, the dress, personality, education, and relation of the referent to the speaker; the presence of other actors and their relations to the speaker

and referent; and contexts of speech, such as gossip, insult, joking, showing affection, maintenance of equality or of differential social status, or pointing out the referent in a group.

This perspective of race is opposed to the US conception, which relies mainly on genetic inheritance. In the United States race is an ascribed characteristic that does not change after birth, or from country to country. It is more dependent on a person's supposed genetic make-up and physical appearance than on socio-economic characteristics. The US conception of race with its emphasis on genetic or biological inheritance privileges a static conception of race. One is and always will be the race into which one was born, one is one's blood. This conception also disallows or ignores more contextual definitions.

In many Latin American countries, race is not a meta-concept based on biological categories, but rather a classification dependent on time and context. According to this more fluid view of race, the determination and relative salience of race categories depend not on their "inherent" nature as physical characteristics but on the historical development of the contexts in which these categories are valued. Within this framework, the points of social reference in which a given individual operates are important determinants of racial identity.

A number of arguments seek to account for the different racial conceptions that evolved in the United States and in Puerto Rico. For example, Denton and Massey (1989) cite three elements of the Spanish colonial system that contributed to a greater blending of the peoples in the Spanish Caribbean. First, they argue that the Spanish history of contact with northern African populations made them more tolerant of different colour groups than were northeastern Europeans. Hence, groups of Mediterranean origin, in contrast to northeastern Europeans, tend to see darker people as white. Second, they maintain that the Spanish conceived of slaves and Indians as being subjects or vassals of the crown and as having certain rights. This differed from the North American conception of slaves as being property. (That is not to say, however, that the Spanish treatment of slaves was necessarily more benevolent, merely that it was sanctioned and conceived of differently.) The third factor that Denton and Massey (1989) discuss is the Spanish Catholic Church. They argue that the Church had a central role in the conquest and promoted the conversion, baptism, and attendance of slaves at integrated religious services. Thus, the role of the Church was analogous to that of the Spanish legal code. It promoted ". . . a positive cultural attitude towards persons of color in theory" but failed "to implement the idea in practice."

The history of a country's economic development has also been seen as an important determinant of race relations and racial conceptions. Duany (1985), for example, has argued that Puerto Rico's economy was less dependent on slaves than was that of other countries in the Caribbean. Thus, there was less commitment to slavery as an institution and there were fewer slaves in Puerto Rico, both absolutely and proportionately. This, together with substantial immigration into the island of Europeans and former slaves in the nineteenth century, made for a conception of race that was rather fluid as opposed to strictly dichotomous. Lastly, the greater migration of European women and families to North America as compared with Latin America—where men predominated and European women were scarce—may also have influenced the relations between races and the consequent conceptions of race that evolved.

The differences between these two conceptions of race have been accentuated and made more apparent with the increasing

number of Latinos in the United States. In this article, we explore responses by Puerto Ricans to questions about racial identity. We contend that these responses reflect a conception of race that is different from that generally found in the classical social science literature and from that conventionally held in the US. We also argue that racial identity is contextually influenced, determined and defined.

Race and the United States Census

In the 1980 decennial census results the Puerto Rican conception of race appears to have been manifested. In response to the race item, which asked respondents to identify themselves as White, Black, or Other, 48 per cent of Puerto Ricans living in New York City replied that they were "Other" and wrote in a Spanish descriptor. Another 4 per cent replied that they were "Other" but did not write in any additional comment, 44 per cent said they were "White," and 3.9 per cent said they were "Black." This unique distribution of responses to the race item ran parallel with the national level where a full 40 per cent of all Hispanics (or 7.5 million) replied that they were "Other."

On the national level, where over 60 per cent of the nation's Hispanics are of Mexican origin and Puerto Ricans constitute about 12 per cent, there were similar results. The distribution of Latinos on the race item is particularly surprising in the light of the fact that in no state, including Hawaii, did more than 2 per cent of the general population indicate that they were of "other race" (Rodriguez 1991). See also Denton and Massey (1989) for a detailed discussion of racial identity among Mexican-Americans and Telles and Murguia (1990) for an interesting discussion of the effects of phenotype on the incomes of Mexicans in the United States.

It has been well documented (Denton and Massey 1989; Martin et al. 1988; Tienda and Ortiz 1986) that the Hispanic responses to the race item differed considerably from those of the general population. It is less clear why this is so. One interpretation stresses that the format of the race question may have led to misinterpretation. The question did not include the word race, but rather asked, "Is this person . . . ?" and provided tick-off categories. Included as possible answers were various Asian groups. This may have induced some Latino respondents to respond culturally, namely, to say that they were "Other" and write in "Mexican," "Dominican," etc. (Tienda and Ortiz 1986). In addition, the fact that the race question preceded the Hispanic identifier may have caused a cultural response to the race item. However, Martin et al. (1988) altered the sequence of the race and Hispanic identifier items and found that this affected the responses only of those Hispanics born in the US; it did not affect the tendency of foreign-born Hispanics to report that they were "Other."

Other research also suggests that there are contextual factors that affect the way in which Latinos respond to questions about race. A Content Reinterview Study by census personnel found that of those who reported that they were "Other" in the census, only 10 per cent were similarly classified in the reinterviewing (McKenney, Fernandez and Masamura 1985). Martin et al. (1988, p. 8) conclude: "[I]t appears that many Hispanic people will report themselves as 'Other race' on a self-administered questionnaire, but will be classified as 'White' by enumerators." Chevan (1990) reports on a Current Population Survey in March 1980 in which Hispanics identified themselves overwhelmingly as "White." Thus, in the presence of an interviewer who presented them with four non-Hispanic choices, 97 per cent of Hispanics identified themselves as "White," while "one month later in filling out the Census

form in the privacy of their home, almost 40 per cent of Hispanics chose 'Other' and were prompted to write in the meaning of 'Other' on the form." Of those who specified a meaning 90 per cent wrote in a Hispanic identifier (Chevan 1990, p. 8). . . .

Our results also provide insight into the racial responses by Hispanics reported in the 1980 Census. The findings indicate that, regardless of how the "race" question was asked, many Puerto Ricans chose *not* to use the conventional racial categories of White and Black. The "Other" response did not represent a misunderstanding. Nor did it represent self-classification as a racially intermediate person in all cases. These results suggest a more complex reality than that which assumes that this "Other" response simply represented a misunderstanding of the question, or that it represented a homogeneous middle category of mestizos or mulattos.

The findings indicate that we cannot automatically assume that because Puerto Ricans choose to identify as "Other" they are placing themselves in a racially intermediate situation. For some Puerto Ricans a cultural response also carries a racial implication, that is, they see race and culture as being fused. They emphasize the greater validity of ethnic or cultural identity. Culture is race, regardless of the physical types within the culture.

Others see their culture as representing a "mixed" people. Still others view these concepts as independent, and a cultural response does not imply a racial designation for them. In this latter case, a respondent may identify as "Other-Puerto Rican" because he or she is not culturally or politically like White Americans or Black Americans, regardless of his or her particular race. In essence, the United States of America may choose to divide its culture into White and Black races, but a Puerto Rican will not (Rodriguez et al. 1991).

The findings suggest that race can be viewed in more than one way. For many of our respondents, race was something more than phenotype and genotype and was influenced by contextual factors such as class, education, language, and birthplace. These findings challenge the hegemonic and more static biological view of race prevalent in the US and its data-collection agencies. They challenge the arrogance behind the biological view of race implying, as it does, that there is no other view of race. These findings also raise questions about the extent to which culture, class and race are inextricably tied together even within a classification system that purports to be "biologically" anchored. Thus, "race" in the US may also, in practice, be more of a social construction than is generally admitted.

Acknowledgements

Dr. Clara Rodriguez would like to acknowledge the financial assistance of the Rockefeller Foundation and the Inter-University Program for Latino Research/Social Science Research Council.

Both authors would like to thank the anonymous Referees for the helpful comments made on this article.

NOTES

1. Clearly, the fact that there are different conceptions of race in Puerto Rico and in the US is not meant to imply that there is no racism in Puerto Rico.

REFERENCES

ALLAND, ALEXANDER. 1971. *Human Diversity.* New York: Columbia University Press.

BLAUSTEIN, ALBERT P., and ROBERT L. ZANGRANDO. 1968. *Civil Rights and the American Negro: A Documentary History.* New York: Washington Square Press.

CHANG, HARRY. 1985. "Toward a Marxist Theory of Racism: Two Essays by Harry Chang." *Review of Radical Political Economics,"* 17(3):34–45.

CHEVAN, ALBERT. 1990. "Hispanic Racial Identity: Beyond Social Class." Paper presented at the American Sociological Association meetings, Washington, DC, 14 August 1990.

DENTON, NANCY, and DOUGLAS S. MASSEY. 1989. "Racial Identity Among Caribbean Hispanics: The Effect of Double Minority Status on Residential Segregation." *American Sociological Review* 54:790–808.

DUANY, JORGE. 1985. "Ethnicity in the Spanish Caribbean: Notes on the Consolidation of Creole Identity in Cuba and Puerto Rico, 1762–1868." *Ethnic Groups* 6:99–123.

GORDON, MAXINE W. 1949. "Race Patterns and Prejudice in Puerto Rico," *American Sociological Review* 14:294–301.

HARRIS, MARVIN. 1968. *Patterns of Race in the Americas.* New York: Walker.

MARTIN, ELIZABETH, THERESA J. DeMAIO, and PAMELA C. CAMPANELLI. 1990. "Context Effects for Census Measures of Race and Hispanic Origin." *Public Opinion Quarterly* 54(4):551–66.

McKENNEY, NAMPEO R., EDWARD W. FERNANDEZ, and WILFRED T. MASAMURA. 1985. "The Quality of the Race and Hispanic Origin Information Reported in the 1980 Census," Proceedings of the Survey Research Methods Section (American Statistical Association), pp. 46–50.

MEAD, MARGARET, THEODOSIUS DOBZHANSKY, ETHEL TOBACH, and ROBERT LIGHT, eds. 1968. *Science and the Concept of Race.* New York: Columbia University Press.

MILLS, C. WRIGHT, CLARENCE SENIOR, and ROSE GOLDSEN. 1950. *The Puerto Rican Journey: New York's Newest Migrants.* New York: Harper & Row.

MINTZ, SIDNEY W. 1971. "Groups, Group Boundaries and the Perception of Race." *Comparative Studies in Society and History* 13(4):437–50.

MONTAGU, ASHLEY, ed. 1964. *The Concept of Race.* New York: Free Press.

PITT-RIVERS, JULIAN. 1975. "Race, Color and Class in Central America and the Andes." In *Majority and Minority,* edited by Norman Yetman and C. Hoy Steele. Boston: Allyn & Bacon.

RODRIGUEZ, CLARA E. 1974. "Puerto Ricans: Between Black and White." *New York Affairs* I(4):92–101.

———. 1991. *Puerto Ricans: Born in the USA.* Boulder, CO: Westview Press.

RODRIGUEZ, CLARA E., AIDA CASTRO, OSCAR GARCIA, and ANALISA TORRES. 1991. "Latino Racial Identity: In the Eye of the Beholder?" *Latino Studies Journal* 2(3):33–48.

SANJEK, ROGER. 1971. "Brazilian Racial Terms: Some Aspects of Meaning and Learning." *American Anthropology* 73(5):1126–43.

———. 1990. "Conceptualizing Caribbean Asians: Race, Acculturation, Creolization." Asian/American Center Working Papers, Queens College/City University of New York.

SEDA BONILLA, E. 1961. "Social Structure and Race Relation." *Social Forces* 40:141–48.

SENIOR, CLARENCE. 1965. *Strangers, Then Neighbors: From Pilgrims to Puerto Ricans.* Chicago: Quadrangle.

TELLES, EDWARD, and EDWARD MURGUIA. 1990. "Phenotypic Discrimination and Income Differences Among Mexican Americans." *Social Science Quarterly* 71(4):682–96.

TIENDA, MARTA, and VILMA ORTIZ. 1986. " 'Hispanicity' and the 1980 Census." *Social Science Quarterly* 67:3–20.

WAGLEY, CHARLES. 1965. "On the Concept of Social Race in the Americas." In *Contemporary Cultures and Societies of Latin America: A Reader in the Social Anthropology of Middle and South America and the Caribbean,* edited by Dwight B. Heath and Richard N. Adams. New York: Random House.

7

ASIAN AMERICAN PANETHNICITY
Bridging Institutions and Identities

Yen Le Espiritu

Goals, Definitions, and Scope

Pan-Asian American ethnicity is the development of bridging organizations and solidarities among several ethnic and immigrant groups of Asian ancestry. Although subject to the same general prejudice and similar discriminatory laws, Asians in the United States have rarely conceived of themselves as a single people and many still do not. "Asiatic," "Oriental," and "Mongolian" were merely convenient labels used by outsiders to refer to all Asians. The development of panethnicity among Asian Americans has a short his-

Yen Le Espiritu, *Asian American Panethnicity,* Temple University Press, 1992, pp. 14–52. Copyright © 1992 by Temple University. Reprinted by permission of Temple University Press.

tory. While examples of white oppression of Asian Americans stretch back over a century, a meaningful pan-Asian movement was not constructed until the late 1960s (Daniels 1988, p. 113). This [reading] tells the story of this construction—of the resultant unity and division, and corresponding benefits and costs. The emphasis here is on the *political* nature of panethnicity, that is, on the distribution and exercise of, and the struggle for, power and resources inside and outside the community. Panethnicity is political not only because it serves as a basis for interest group mobilization but also because it is linked with the expansion of the role of the polity (Enloe 1980, p. 5).

Panethnicity has not been well studied. Moreover, the few existing works on panethnicity have dealt primarily with Native

American and Latino American panethnicities (Cornell 1988; Nagel 1982; Padilla 1985). Except for several essays from the proponents of the 1960s Asian American movement (Uyematsu 1971; P. Wong 1972), the process of pan-Asianization has not been well documented. While social scientists have devoted substantial attention to individual Asian groups (Bonacich and Modell 1980; Kim 1981; Montero 1979), few have focused on Asian Americans as a collectivity. Yet a host of pan-Asian organizations testify to the salience of pan-Asian consciousness, as do the numerous cooperative efforts by Asian American groups and organizations on behalf of both subgroup and pan-Asian interests.

There are two dimensions of groupness: the conceptual and the organizational. The conceptual refers to individual behavior and attitude—the ways group members view themselves; the organizational refers to political structures—the ways groups are organized as collective actors. The boundaries of these two dimensions usually but do not necessarily coincide (Cornell 1988, p. 72). Some key indicators of pan-Asian consciousness include self-identification, pan-Asian residential, friendship, and marriage patterns, and membership in pan-Asian organizations. Given the multiple levels of Asian American ethnicity, a study of individual ethnicity can also document "ethnic switching"—the relabeling of individuals' ethnic affiliation to meet situational needs. That is, a person is a Japanese American or an Asian American depending on the ethnic identities available to him or her in a particular situation. Sometimes the individual has a choice, and sometimes not (see Nagel 1986, pp. 95–96). While recognizing the importance of the conceptual dimension of panethnicity, this work is primarily a study of the organizational dimension: the institutionalization of Asian American consciousness, and not the state of panethnic consciousness itself. Thus, most of the evidence is drawn from the level of formal organizations. The research methods are basically those of the historically grounded community study, combining organization archives, public records, interviews with the leaders of organizations, participant observation, and library research.

Naturally, the rank and file's level of Asian American consciousness influences its institutionalization. On the other hand, grass-roots consciousness does not necessarily precede the process of organizational consolidation. As this study documents, panethnic organizations need not merely reflect existing panethnic consciousness but can also generate and augment it. In building themselves, pan-Asian organizations also build pan-Asian consciousness. Thus, the organizational level is intrinsically worthy of examination because it tells us about the directions of the populations supposedly represented.

Moreover, pan-Asian institutions cannot survive without support; their very existence presupposes some amount of consensus. One research strategy would be to quantify this consensus. Another would be to identify the individuals who may have vested interests in promoting pan-Asian ethnicity, and in so doing name the dominant groups and sectors in the pan-Asian coalitions. The research question then becomes not who identifies with pan-Asian ethnicity, but who benefits the most from it—and at whose expense? Such an approach allows us to look beyond numbers to the power struggles and the resultant intergroup conflicts and competition.

The influx of the post-1965 Asian immigrants and refugees—who are distinct in ethnic and class composition from the more "established" Asian Americans—has exacerbated intergroup conflicts. The determination of what and whose interests will be defended often factionalizes the pan-Asian collectivity, as newcomers and old-timers pursue their separate goals (Lopez and Espiritu 1990, p. 206). On the other hand, the pan-Asian concept is now so well institutionalized that new Asian immigrants and refugees often encounter extensive pressure to consider themselves Asian Americans, regardless of whether or not they see themselves in such terms. For example, Southeast Asian refugees have had to adopt the Asian American designation because this category resonates in the larger society (Hein 1989; Skinner and Hendricks 1979). Accordingly, this study examines the benefits as well as the limitations of pan-Asian coalitions.

Scholars and laypersons alike have argued that Asian Americans are not a panethnic group because they do not share a common culture (Ignacio 1976; Trottier 1981). While Native Americans can trace their common descent to their unique relationship to the land, and Latino Americans to their common language, Asian Americans have no readily identifiable symbols of ethnicity. This view involves the implicit assumption that ethnic boundaries are unproblematic. However, as Frederick Barth (1969) suggested, when ethnic boundaries are strong and persistent, cultural solidarity will result. But ethnic groups that are merging need not exhibit such solidarity. Discussing the ongoing efforts to build an Asian American culture, John Liu (1988 pp. 123–24) stated, "The admonition that we can no longer assume that Asian Americans share a common identity and culture is not a setback in our efforts, but rather a reminder that the goals we set for ourselves need to be constantly struggled for."

The construction of pan-Asian ethnicity involves the creation of a common Asian American heritage out of diverse histories. Part of the heritage being created hinges on what Asian Americans share: a history of exploitation, oppression, and discrimination. However, individuals' being treated alike does not automatically produce new groups. "Only when people become aware of being treated alike on the basis of some arbitrary criterion do they begin to establish identity on that basis" (Shibutani and Kwan 1965, p. 210). For Asian Americans, this "arbitrary criterion" is their socially defined racial distinctiveness, or their imposed identity as "Asians." As such, an important task for pan-Asian leaders is to define racist activities against one Asian American subgroup as hostilities against all Asian Americans. In her call for pan-Asian organization, Amy Uyematsu (1971, pp. 10–11) referred to the internment of Japanese Americans as a "racist treatment of *'yellows,'* " and the mistreatment of Chinese immigrants in 1885 as mistreatment of *Asians* in America (emphasis mine). More recently, Asian American leaders characterized the 1982 fatal beating of Chinese American Vincent Chin as a racial attack against all Asian Americans (Zia 1984). Thus, following Barth (1969), the task at hand is to document the process of culture building and its function in the construction and maintenance of panethnic boundaries—not to define and inventory cultural symbols. . . .

Social and Demographic Changes: Setting the Context

Although Asians in the United States have long been engaged in political action, their efforts never drew public attention until the 1960s (Chan 1991, p. 171). Prompted by broader political struggles and internal demographic changes, college students of Asian ancestry spearheaded the Asian American movement. Critical to its development was the mobilization of American blacks. Besides offering tactical lessons, the civil rights and the Black Power movements had a profound impact on the consciousness of Asian Americans, sensitizing them to racial issues (Uyematsu 1971). The anticolonial nationalist movements in Asia also stirred racial and cultural pride and provided a context for the emergence of the Yellow Power movement (P. Wong 1972). Influenced by these broader political struggles, Americans of Asian ancestry united to denounce racist institutional structures, demand new or unattended rights, and assert their cultural and racial distinctiveness. Normal urban issues such as housing, education, and social welfare began to take on ethnic coloration.

While important, these broader societal developments alone do not explain why the Asian American movement became panethnic. To understand this development, we first need to understand the underlying social and demographic factors that allowed pan-Asianism to take root in the 1960s but not earlier. Before World War II, pan-Asian unity was not feasible because the predominantly foreign-born Asian population did not share a common language. During the postwar years, increasing intergroup communication and contact facilitated the emergence of a pan-Asian consciousness. The breakdown of economic and residential barriers during the postwar period provided the first opportunity for an unprecedented number of Asian Americans to come into intimate, sustained contact with the larger society—and with one another.

From an Immigrant to a Native Population

Before 1940, the Asian population in the United States was primarily an immigrant population. Immigrant Asians faced practical barriers to pan-Asian unity. Foremost was their lack of a common language. Old national rivalries were another obstacle, as many early Asian immigrants carried the political memories and outlook of their homelands. For example, Japan's occupation of Korea resulted in pervasive anti-Japanese sentiments among Koreans in the United States. According to Brett Melendy

(1977, p. 155), "Fear and hatred of the Japanese appeared to be the only unifying force among the various Korean groups through the years." Moreover, these historical enmities and linguistic and cultural differences reinforced one another as divisive agents.

During the postwar period, due to immigration restrictions and the growing dominance of the second and third generations, American-born Asians outnumbered immigrants. The demographic changes of the 1940s were pronounced. During this decade, nearly twenty thousand Chinese American babies were born. For the first time, the largest five-year cohort of Chinese Americans was under five years of age (Kitano and Daniels 1988, p. 37). By 1960, approximately two-thirds of the Asian population in California had been born in the United States (Ong 1989, pp. 5–8). As the Asian population became a native-born community, linguistic and cultural differences began to blur. Although they had attended Asian-language schools, most American-born Asians possessed only a limited knowledge of their ethnic language (Chan 1991, p. 115). By 1960, with English as the common language, persons from different Asian backgrounds were able to communicate with one another (Ling 1984, p. 73), and in so doing create a common identity associated with the United States.

Moreover, unlike their immigrant parents, native-born and American-educated Asians could muster only scant loyalties to old world ties. Historical antagonisms between their mother countries thus receded in importance (P. Wong 1972, p. 34). For example, growing up in America, second-generation Koreans "had difficulty feeling the painful loss of the homeland and understanding the indignity of Japanese domination" (Takaki 1989, p. 292). Thus, while the older generation of Koreans hated all Japanese, "their children were much less hostile or had no concern at all" (Melendy 1977,

p. 156). As a native-born Japanese American community advocate explained, "By 1968, we had a second generation. We could speak English; so there was no language problem. And we had little feelings of historical animosity" (Kokubun interview).

As national differences receded in subjective importance, generational differences widened. For the most part, American-born Asians considered themselves to have more in common with other American-born Asians than they did with foreign-born compatriots. According to a third-generation Japanese American who is married to a Chinese American, "As far as our experiences in America, I have more things in common than differences with a Chinese American. Being born and raised here gives us something in common. We have more in common with each other than with a Japanese from Japan, or a Chinese from China" (Ichioka interview). Much to their parents' dismay, young Asian Americans began to choose their friends and spouses from other Asian groups. Eui-Young Yu (1983, p. 47) related that second- and third-generation Koreans "identify and intermingle as much with other Asian minorities as with fellow Koreans, especially with the Japanese and Chinese." Similarly, Stephen Fugita and David O'Brien (1991, p. 146) reported that the Sansei (third-generation) were much more likely than the Nisei (second-generation) to see themselves as Asian Americans. This muting of cultural and historical divisions distressed their parents, who, more often than not, had supported these divisions for most of their lives. As a young Chinese American asserted:

> My parents mean well and I try to respect them, but they do not understand what it's all about. We have buried the old hatreds between Chinese and Japanese, and my friends and I must go beyond our parents' "hang-ups." My

mother is upset because I'm engaged to a Japanese girl but she knows she can do nothing about it. (Cited in Weiss 1974, p. 235)

The Watershed of World War II

Before World War II, Asian immigrant communities were quite distinct entities, isolated from one another and from the larger society. Because of language difficulties, prejudice, and lack of business opportunities elsewhere, there was little chance for Asians in the United States to live outside their ethnic enclaves (Yuan 1966, p. 331). Shut out of the mainstream of American society, the various immigrant groups struggled separately in their respective Chinatowns, Little Tokyos, or Manilatowns. Stanford Lyman (1970, pp. 57–63) reported that the early Chinese and Japanese communities in the western states had little to do with one another—either socially or politically. Although statistical data do not exist, ethnographic accounts confirm the ethnic homogeneity of each early Asian immigrant community. For example, according to a study of New York's Chinatown in the 1890s, "The entire triangular space bounded by Mott, Pell, and Doyers Streets and Chatham Square is given to the exclusive occupancy of these Orientals" (cited in Yuan 1966, p. 323). Within these enclaves, diversity among Asian nationalities was more salient than commonality.

Economic and residential barriers began to crumble after World War II. The war against Nazism called attention to racism at home and discredited the notions of white superiority. The fifteen years after the war was a period of largely positive change as civil rights statutes outlawed racial discrimination in employment as well as housing (Daniels 1988, ch. 7). Popular attitudes were also changing. Polls taken during World War II showed a distinct hostility toward

Japan: 74 percent of the respondents favored either killing off all Japanese, destroying Japan as a political entity, or supervising it. On the West Coast, 97 percent of the people polled approved of the relocation of Japanese Americans. In contrast, by 1949, 64 percent of those polled were either friendly or neutral toward Japan (Feraru 1950).

During the postwar years, Asian American residential patterns changed significantly. Because of the lack of statistical data, a longitudinal study of the changing residential patterns of Asian Americans cannot be made. However, descriptive accounts of Asian American communities indicate that these enclaves declined in the postwar years. Edwin Hoyt (1974, p. 94) reported that in the 1940s, second-generation Chinese Americans moved out of the Chinatowns. Although they still came back to shop or to see friends, they lived elsewhere. In 1940, Rose Hum Lee found twenty-eight cities with an area called Chinatown in the United States. By 1955, Peter Sih found only sixteen (Sung 1967, pp. 143–44). New York's Chinatown exemplifies the declining significance of Asian ethnic enclaves. In 1940, 50 percent of the Chinese in New York City lived in its Chinatown; by 1960, less than one-third lived there (Yuan 1966, p. 331). Similarly, many returning Japanese Americans abandoned their prewar settlement in old central cities and joined the migration to suburbia (Daniels 1988, p. 294). In the early 1970s, Little Tokyo in Los Angeles remained a bustling Japanese American center, "but at night the shop owners [went] home to the houses in the suburbs" (Hoyt 1974, p. 84).

Although single-ethnic communities were still the norm, residential segregation between Asian nationalities declined in the postwar years. Formerly homogeneous, the ethnic enclaves started to house other Asian groups—as well as non-Asian groups. In 1957, driving past 7th and H streets in Washington, D.C., Betty Lee Sung (1967, pp. 142–43) reported, "I passed the length of Chinatown before I suddenly realized that the place was almost deserted. The faces that I did see on the street were not Chinese but Filipinos." In 1970, due to the influx of Japanese and Filipinos, there was a proposal to rename Oakland Chinatown "Asian-town" (Sano 1970). Multigroup urban centers also emerged. Paul Wong (1972, p. 34) reported that since the early 1960s, Asian Americans of diverse national origins have moved into the suburbs outside the major Asian communities such as Berkeley or San Mateo, California. Although a small proportion of the local population, these Asian Americans tended to congregate in pockets; consequently, in some residential blocks a majority of the residents were Asian Americans.

Moreover, recent research on suburban segregation indicates that the level of segregation between certain Asian American groups is often less than that between them and non-Asians. Using Standard Metropolitan Statistical Area (SMSA) data for 1960, 1970, and 1980, Frankie Lam (1986) computed indices of dissimilarity (ID) among Chinese, Japanese, black, and white Americans in 822 suburbs. As indicated in Table 1, from 1960 to 1980 the level of segregation between Chinese and Japanese Americans was much less than that between these two groups and blacks and, in one case, less than that between these groups and whites. But the actual level of segregation is only one issue. The decline of segregation over time is another. From 1960 to 1980, Chinese segregation from the Japanese shows a more pronounced decline (−14.14) than that of Chinese or Japanese from whites (−10.61 and −7.23 respectively) and from blacks (−4.59 and −2.65 respectively). Though not comprehensive, these studies together suggest that Asian residential segregation declined in the postwar years.

As various Asian groups in the United States interacted, they became aware of common problems and goals that tran-

TABLE 1 Mean Segregation Indices for Chinese and Japanese Americans in 822 U.S. Suburbs, 1960, 1970, and 1980

Ethnic Groups	1960	1970	1980	Change, 1960–80
Chinese–White	38.83	31.45	28.22	−10.61
Chinese–Black	54.02	50.42	49.43	−4.59
Japanese–White	34.00	22.16	26.77	−7.23
Japanese–Black	48.62	48.46	45.97	−2.65
Chinese–Japanese	39.11	27.70	24.97	−14.14

Source: Lam (1986: tables 1, 2, and 3).

scended parochial interests and historical antagonisms. One recurrent problem was employment discrimination. According to a 1965 report published by the California Fair Employment Practices Commission, for every $51 earned by a white male Californian, Japanese males earned $43 and Chinese males $38—even though Chinese and Japanese American men had become slightly better educated than the white majority (Daniels 1988, p. 315). Moreover, although the postwar period marked the first time that well-trained Chinese and Japanese Americans could find suitable employment with relative ease, they continued to be passed over for promotion to administrative and supervisory positions (Kitano and Daniels 1988, p. 47). Asians in the United States began to see themselves as a group that shared important common experiences: exploitation, oppression, and discrimination (Uyematsu 1971).

Because inter-Asian contact and communication were greatest on college campuses, pan-Asianism was strongest there (P. Wong 1972, pp. 33–34). Exposure to one another and to the mainstream society led some young Asian Americans to feel that they were fundamentally different from whites. Disillusioned with the white society and alienated from their traditional communities, many Asian American student activists turned to the alternative strategy of pan-Asian unification (Weiss 1974, pp. 69–70).

The Construction of Pan-Asian Ethnicity

Although broader social struggles and internal demographic changes provided the impetus for the Asian American movement, it was the group's politics—confrontational and explicitly pan-Asian—that shaped the movement's content. Influenced by the internal colonial model, which stresses the commonalities among "colonized groups," college students of Asian ancestry declared solidarity with fellow Asian Americans— and with other Third World minorities (Blauner 1972, ch. 2). Rejecting the label "Oriental," they proclaimed themselves "Asian American." Through pan-Asian organizations, publications, and Asian American studies programs, Asian American activists built pan-Asian solidarity by pointing out their common fate in American society. The pan-Asian concept enabled diverse Asian American groups to understand their "unequal circumstances and histories as being related" (Lowe 1991, p. 30).

From "Yellow" to "Asian American"

Following the example of the Black Power movement, Asian American activists spearheaded their own Yellow Power movement to seek "freedom from racial oppression through the power of a consolidated yellow people" (Uyematsu 1971, p. 12). In the summer of 1968, more than one hundred students of diverse Asian backgrounds attended an "Are You Yellow?" conference at UCLA to discuss issues of Yellow Power, identity, and the war in Vietnam (Ling 1989, p. 53). In 1970, a new pan-Asian organization in northern California called itself the "Yellow Seed" because "Yellow [is] the common bond between Asian-Americans and Seed symboliz[es] growth as an individual and as an alliance" (Masada 1970). This "yellow" reference was dropped when Filipino Americans rejected the term, claiming that they were brown, not yellow (Ignacio 1976, p. 84; Rabaya 1971, p. 110). At the first Asian American national conference in 1972, Filipino Americans "made it clear to the conferees that we were 'Brown Asians' " by forming a Brown Asian Caucus (Ignacio 1976, pp. 139–41). It is important to note, however, that Filipino American activists did not reject the term "yellow" because they objected to the pan-Asian framework. Quite the contrary, they rejected it because it allegedly excluded them from that grouping (Rabaya 1971, p. 110).

Other community organizers used the term "Oriental" to define their organizations and service centers. In Southern California, the Council of Oriental Organizations (COO) became the political base for the diverse Asian American communities. In 1968, COO lobbied for federal funding to establish the Oriental Service Center in Los Angeles County, serving Chinese, Japanese, Filipinos, and Koreans. But Asian American activists also rejected *Oriental* because the term conjures up images of "the sexy Susie Wong, the wily Charlie Chan, and the evil Fu Manchu" (Weiss 1974, p. 234). It is also a term that smacks of European colonialism and imperialism: *Oriental* means "East"; Asia is "east" only in relationship to Europe, which was taken as the point of reference

(Browne 1985). To define their own image and to claim an *American* identity, college students of Asian ancestry coined the term *Asian American* to "stand for all of us Americans of Asian descent" (Ichioka interview). While *Oriental* suggests passivity and acquiescence, *Asian Americans* connotes political activism because an Asian American "gives a damn about his life, his work, his beliefs, and is willing to do almost anything to help Orientals become Asian Americans" (cited in Weiss 1974, p. 234).

The account above suggests that the creation of a new name is a significant symbolic move in constructing an ethnic identity. In their attempt to forge a pan-Asian identity, Asian American activists first had to coin a composite term that would unify and encompass the constituent groups. Filipino Americans' rejection of the term "yellow" and the activists' objection to the cliché-ridden *Oriental* forced the group to change its name to Asian American. . . . It is noteworthy that while *Yellow, Oriental,* and *Asian American* connote different ideologies, all three terms signify panethnicity. . . .

Conclusion

The development of a pan-Asian consciousness and constituency reflected broader societal developments and demographic changes, as well as the group's political agenda. By the late 1960s, pan-Asianism was possible because of the more amicable relationships among the Asian countries, the declining residential segregation among diverse Asian groups in America, and the large number of native-born, American-educated political actors. Disillusioned with the larger society and estranged from their traditional communities, third- and fourth-generation Asian Americans turned to the alternative strategy of pan-Asian unification. Through pan-Asian organizations, media, and Asian American Studies programs, these political activists assumed the role of "cultural entrepreneurs" consciously creating a community of culture out of diverse Asian peoples. This process of pan-Asian consolidation did not proceed smoothly nor did it encompass all Asian Americans. Ethnic chauvinism, competition for scarce resources, and class cleavages continued to divide the subgroups. However, once established, the pan-Asian structure not only reinforced the cohesiveness of already existing networks but also expanded these networks. Although first conceived by young Asian American activists, the pan-Asian concept was subsequently institutionalized by professionals and community groups, as well as government agencies. The confrontational politics of the activists eventually gave way to the conventional and electoral politics of the politicians, lobbyists, and professionals, as Asian Americans continued to rely on the pan-Asian framework to enlarge their political capacities.

REFERENCES

BARTH, FREDERICK. 1969. *Ethnic Groups and Boundaries.* Boston: Little, Brown.

BLAUNER, ROBERT. 1972. *Racial Oppression in America.* New York: Harper & Row.

BONACICH, EDNA, and JOHN MODELL. 1980. *The Economic Basis of Ethnic Solidarity: A Study of Japanese Americans.* Berkeley: University of California Press.

BROWNE, BLAIN T. 1985. "A Common Thread: American Images of the Chinese and Japanese, 1930–1960." Ph.D. dissertation, University of Oklahoma.

CHAN, SUCHENG. 1991. *Asian Americans: An Interpretive History.* Boston: Twayne.

CORNELL, STEPHEN. 1988. *The Return of the Native: Native American Political Resurgence.* New York: Oxford University Press.

DANIELS, ROGER. 1988. *Asian America: Chinese and Japanese in the United States Since 1850.* Seattle: University of Washington Press.

ENLOE, CYNTHIA H. 1980. *Police, Military, and Ethnicity: Foundations of State Power.* New Brunswick, NJ: Transaction Books.

FERARU, ARTHUR N. 1950. "Public Opinion Polls on Japan." *Far Eastern Survey* 19(10):101–103.

FUGITA, STEPHEN S., and DAVID J. O'BRIEN. 1991. *Japanese American Ethnicity: The Persistence of Community.* Seattle: University of Washington Press.

HEIN, JEREMY. 1989. "States and Political Migrants: The Incorporation of Indochinese Refugees in France and the United States." Ph.D. dissertation, Northwestern University.

HOYT, EDWIN P. 1974. *Asians in the West.* New York: Thomas Nelson.

IGNACIO, LEMUEL F. 1976. *Asian Americans and Pacific Islanders (Is There Such an Ethnic Group?)* San Jose, CA: Pilipino Development Associates.

KIM, ILLSOO. 1981. *New Urban Immigrants: The Korean Community in New York.* Princeton, NJ: Princeton University Press.

KITANO, HARRY H. L., and ROGER DANIELS. 1988. *Asian Americans: Emerging Minorities.* Englewood Cliffs, NJ: Prentice-Hall.

LAM, FRANKIE. 1986. "Suburban Residential Segregation of Chinese and Japanese Americans, 1960, 1970, and 1980." *Sociology and Social Research* 70(4):263–65.

LING, SUSIE HSIUHAN. 1984. "The Mountain Movers: Asian American Women's Movement in Los Angeles." *Amerasia Journal* 15(1):51–67.

LIU, JOHN. 1988. "The Relationship of Migration Research to Asian American Studies: Unity and Diversity Within the Curriculum." Pp. 117–25 in *Reflections on Shattered Windows,* edited by Gary Okihiro, Shirley Hune, Arthur Hansen, and John Liu. Pullman: Washington State University Press.

LOPEZ, DAVID, and YEN ESPIRITU. 1990. "Panethnicity in the United States: A Theoretical Framework." *Ethnic and Racial Studies* 13(2):198–224.

LOWE, LISA. 1991. "Heterogeneity, Hybridity, Multiplicity: Marking Asian American Differences." *Diaspora* 1:24–44.

LYMAN, STANFORD M. 1970. *The Asian in the West.* Reno and Las Vegas: Desert Research Institute, University of Nevada.

MASADA, SABURO. 1970. "Stockton's Yellow Seed." *Pacific Citizen,* 9 October.

MELENDY, H. BRETT. 1977. *Asians in America: Filipinos, Koreans, and East Indians.* Boston: Twayne.

MONTERO, DARRELL. 1979. *Vietnamese Americans: Patterns of Resettlement and Socioeconomic Adaptations in the United States.* Boulder, CO: Westview Press.

NAGEL, JOANE. 1982. "The Political Mobilization of Native Americans." *Social Science Journal* 19:37–45.

———. 1986. "The Political Construction of Ethnicity." Pp. 93–112 in *Competitive Ethnic Relations,* edited by Susan Olzal and Joane Nagel. San Diego: Academic Press.

ONG, PAUL. 1989. "California's Asian Population: Past Trends and Projections for the Year 2000." Los Angeles: Graduate School of Architecture and Urban Planning.

PADILLA, FELIX M. 1985. *Latino Ethnic Consciousness: The Case of Mexican Americans and Puerto Ricans in Chicago.* Notre Dame, IN: Notre Dame University Press.

RABAYA, VIOLET. 1971. "I Am Curious (Yellow?)." Pp. 110–11 in *Roots: An Asian American Reader,* edited by Amy Tachiki, Eddie Wong, and Franklin Odo. Los Angeles: UCLA Asian American Studies Center.

SANO, ROY. 1970. "Asiantown in Oakland." *Pacific Citizen,* 4 August.

SHIBUTANI, TAMOTSU, and KIAN M. KWAN. 1965. *Ethnic Stratification.* New York: Macmillan.

SKINNER, KENNETH, and GLEN HENDRICKS. 1979. "The Shaping of Self-Identity Among Indochinese Refugees." *Journal of Ethnic Studies* 7:25–41.

SUNG, BETTY LEE. 1967. *Mountain of Gold: The Story of the Chinese in America.* New York: Macmillan.

TAKAKI, RONALD. 1989. *Strangers from a Different Shore: A History of Asian Americans.* Boston: Little, Brown.

TROTTIER, RICHARD. 1981. "Charters of Panethnic Identity: Indigenous American Indians and Immigrant Asian Americans." Pp. 271–305 in *Ethnic Change,* edited by Charles F. Keyes. Seattle: University of Washington Press.

UYEMATSU, AMY. 1971. "The Emergence of Yellow Power in America." Pp. 9–13 in *Roots: An Asian American Reader,* edited by Amy Tachiki, Eddie Wong, and Franklin Odo. Los Angeles: UCLA Asian American Studies Center.

WEISS, MELFORD S. 1974. *Valley City: A Chinese Community in America.* Cambridge, MA: Schenkman.

WONG, PAUL. 1972. "The Emergence of the Asian American Movement." *Bridge* 2(1):33–39.

YU, EUI-YOUNG. 1983. "Korean Communities in America: Past, Present, and Future." *Amerasia Journal* 10(2):23–51.

YUAN, D. Y. 1966. "Chinatown and Beyond: The Chinese Population in Metropolitan New York." *Phylon* 23(4):321–32.

ZIA, HELEN. 1984. "The Real Violence." *Bridge* 9(2):18–23.

8

AMERICAN INDIAN ETHNIC RENEWAL
Politics and the Resurgence of Identity

Joane Nagel

This paper examines the phenomenon of ethnic identity change and the role of politics in prompting the reconstruction of individual ethnicity. Specifically, I examine recent demographic trends in the American Indian population to understand the conditions and factors that lead individuals to change their racial identity.[1] Between 1960 and 1990, the number of Americans reporting American Indian as their race in the U.S. Census more than tripled, growing from 523,591 to 1,878,285. This increase cannot be accounted for by the usual explanations of population growth (e.g., increased births, decreased deaths). Researchers have concluded that much of this population growth must have resulted from "ethnic switching," where individuals who identified their race as non-Indian (e.g., White) in an earlier census, switched to "Indian" race in a later census. Why are more and more Americans reporting their race as American Indian?

My research draws on historical analyses and interview data, and combines a social constructionist model of ethnic identity with a social structural approach to ethnic change. I argue that the increase in American Indian ethnic identification reflected in the U.S. Census is an instance of "ethnic renewal." Ethnic renewal refers to both individual and collective processes. *Individual ethnic renewal* occurs when an individual acquires or asserts a new ethnic identity by reclaiming a discarded identity, replacing or amending an identity in an existing ethnic repertoire, or filling a personal ethnic void. Reclaiming a discarded identity might entail resuming religious observances or "retraditionalization" (e.g., the return to orthodoxy by American Jews). Replacing an identity in an existing ethnic repertoire might involve religious conversion (e.g., the conversion to Islam by Christian African Americans); amending an existing ethnic repertoire might involve exploring a new side of one's family tree and including that nationality or ethnicity among one's working ethnic identities (e.g., the taking on of Armenian ethnicity by an Irish Armenian American already involved in Irish American ethnic life). Filling a personal ethnic void might entail adopting a new ethnic identity for the first time (e.g., Americans reconnecting with their ethnic "roots" and joining ethnic social, political, or religious organizations). *Collective ethnic renewal* involves the reconstruction

Joane Nagel, "American Indian Ethnic Renewal: Politics and the Resurgence of Identity," *American Sociological Review*, 1995. Vol. 60, December, pp. 947–965. Copyright © 1995 by American Sociological Review. Reprinted with permission.

[1]Consistent with the usage of native and non-native scholars, I use the terms "American Indian," "Indian," "Native American" and "native" interchangeably to refer to the descendants of the aboriginal inhabitants of North America. I also use the terms "race" and "ethnicity" somewhat interchangeably, although I view ethnicity as the broader concept subsuming race, which generally refers to visible (often skin color) distinctions among populations. Ethnicity can refer not only to somatic or physical differences, but also to differences in language, religion, or culture. I acknowledge the importance, some would say preeminence, of race in historical and contemporary American ethnic relations.

of an ethnic community by current or new community members who build or rebuild institutions, culture, history, and traditions (Nagel 1994, forthcoming).

My thesis is that ethnic renewal among the American Indian population has been brought about by three political forces: (1) federal Indian policy, (2) American ethnic politics, and (3) American Indian political activism. Federal Indian policies have contributed to the creation of an urban, intermarried, bicultural American Indian population that lives outside traditional American Indian geographic and cultural regions. For these individuals, American Indian ethnicity has been more optional than for those living on reservations. Changes in American political culture brought about by the ethnic politics of the civil rights movement created an atmosphere that increased ethnic consciousness, ethnic pride, and ethnic mobilization among all ethnic groups, including American Indians. The resulting "Red Power" Indian political activist movement of the 1960s and 1970s started a tidal wave of ethnic renewal that surged across reservation and urban Indian communities, instilling ethnic pride and encouraging individuals to claim and assert their "Indianness." . . .

Background

Negotiating and Changing Individual and Collective Identities

In the past 30 years, our understanding of ethnicity has increasingly stressed the socially constructed character of ethnicity. The pioneering work of Fredrik Barth (1969) shows ethnicity to be situational and variable. Many studies have followed that have found ethnicity to be more emergent than primordial, ethnic group boundaries to be more fluid than fixed, ethnic conflicts to

arise more from clashes of contemporary interests than from ancient animosities, ethnic history and culture to be routinely revised and even invented, and the central essence of ethnicity—ethnic identity—to be multifaceted, negotiable, and changeable (see Conzen et al. 1992; Sollors 1989).

It is this last assertion—that one ethnic identity can be exchanged for another—that runs most against the grain of common wisdom. Sociologists have long identified forms of ethnic change associated with intergroup contact, such as assimilation, accommodation, and acculturation (Glazer and Moynihan 1963; Gordon 1961; Park 1928). These processes have been seen as long-term, often intergenerational, frequently involving the dissolution or blending of immigrant or minority ethnicities into a larger dominant ethnicity or nationality (e.g., from "Indian" to "White" or from "Irish" to "American"). In the case of ethnic renewal, however, individuals adopt a *nondominant* ethnic identity, and thus move from membership in a dominant group to become part of a minority or subnational group (e.g., from "White" to "Indian" or from "American" to "Irish American" or "Jewish American"). This resurgence of nondominant ethnic identity does not fit clearly into traditional models of ethnic change which carry a heavy presumption that ethnic change invariably moves in the direction of assimilation (i.e., from minority to majority).

Opportunities for individual ethnic change vary. Certainly some people, for instance, American Whites, have a wide menu of "ethnic options" from which they are free to choose (Waters 1990). It is more difficult for members of other racial or ethnic groups to change their ethnicity, particularly communities of color. This is because in the United States such groups confront a world of "hypodescent," where one drop of particular blood (African, Asian) dictates a specific ethnic group membership, leaving limited options for individual members (see Davis 1991; Harris 1964). European Americans and African Americans represent two ends of an ethnic ascription continuum, in which Whites are always free to remember their ancestry and Blacks are never free to forget theirs. These ethnic boundaries are maintained and policed by both Blacks and Whites, although their content and location can change over time (see Collas 1994 for a discussion of "transgressing racial boundaries"). . . .

American Indian Ethnicity: Opting for an Indian Identity

American Indians reside at the intersection of two racial regimes: hypodescent and self-identification. In some portions of the United States Indianness is strongly socially ascribed and often mandatory (e.g., in the Southwest or the Northern Plains). In these settings Indian ethnicity is regulated in two ways. The first is informal and external to Indian communities, and involves ascription mainly, though not exclusively, by non-Indians. In this instance of classic hypodescent, any visible "Indianness" labels an individual as "Indian." The second, more formal way American Indian ethnicity is regulated can be both internal and external to native communities, and involves official membership in Indian tribes. In this case, tribal, state, and/or federal governments recognize an individual as an "enrolled" member or not.

In much of the United States, however, American Indian ethnicity is largely a matter of individual choice; "Indian" ethnicity is an ethnic option that an individual can choose or not. This is *not* to say that *anyone* can choose to be an Indian or that all observers will unanimously confirm the validity of that choice. Indeed, there is enormous controversy among native people about

who should be considered an Indian for purposes of receiving tribal services, federal benefits, affirmative action consideration, or rights to participate in tribal governments (Larimore and Waters 1993; Reynolds 1993; Snipp 1993).

An important point to make here about supratribal "American Indian" ethnicity is that it is purely a social construction. That is, the Native American population is comprised of many linguistic, cultural, and religious groups, more than 300 of which are separately recognized by federal or state governments in the lower 48 states (with many more in Alaska and Hawaii); each group has its own political, legal, and police system, economy, land base, and sovereign authority. Around two-thirds of American Indians identified in the U.S. Censuses are official members of these recognized communities (Snipp 1989). Thus, when we speak of an "American Indian" race or ethnicity, we are of necessity referring to a group of individuals from various tribal backgrounds, some of whom speak native languages, most of whom converse in English, some of whom live on or regularly visit reservation "homelands," most of whom live off-reservation, some of whom participate in tribal community life, most of whom live in urban areas.

Despite this diversity, researchers assert that, indeed, there are "Indians," and this all-encompassing category can be seen as an "ethnic group."[2] For instance, Deloria (1992) argues that as American Indians became increasingly involved in off-reservation political and economic life after World War II, they came to see themselves as minority group members and as part of the larger American ethnic mosaic. In fact, many Native Americans carry within their portfolio of

---

[2]Some native scholars and commentators have taken offense at the notion that Indians are a "mere" ethnic group, arguing that they are instead, sovereign nations (Deloria and Lytle 1984; Morris 1989; Stiffarm and Lane 1992; Trask 1990, 1991).

ethnic identities (which may include identities based on kin or clan lineage, tribe, reservation, language, and religion) a supratribal or pan-Indian "Indian" identity, which is often reserved for use when interacting with non-Indians. Finally, as further evidence of the existence of an "American Indian" ethnic group, in recent decades increasing percentages of Americans who identify their race as "Indian" fail to specify a tribal affiliation, suggesting that their primary ethnic identity is supratribal or "Indian" (Masumura and Berman 1987).[3]

Patterns of American Indian Identification, 1960–1990

The U.S. Census provides data for examining both ethnic choice and ethnic ascription in American society. Beginning in 1960, the Census Bureau moved from a system where enumerators assigned each person a race to a system that permitted individual racial self-identification. This move from ascription to racial choice opened the door to individual racial "switching," especially for those ethnic categories not strongly governed by social conventions of hypodescent. Table 1 shows the growth in the American Indian Census population from 1900 to 1990.

Between 1970 and 1980, the American Indian population increased the most: The population grew from 792,730 in 1970 to 1,364,033 in 1980, an increase of 72 percent. Researchers wondered what accounted for this growth. They searched for the usual explanations: increased birthrates, decreased death rates, immigration, changes in census coding procedures.[4] As these explanations were examined one by one and each failed to

TABLE 1   American Indian Population, 1900–1990

Census Year	Population Size	Percent Change from Previous Year
1900	237,196	—
1910	276,927	17
1920	244,437	–13
1930	343,352	40
1940	345,252	1
1950	357,499	4
1960	523,591	46
1970	792,730	51
1980	1,364,033	72
1990	1,878,285	38

Sources: For 1900–1970, Thornton (1987, p. 160); for 1980 and 1990, U.S. Bureau of the Census (1991, table 1).

account for Indian population growth, researchers looked to alternative, more sociological explanations. For instance, Passel and Berman (1986) and Deloria (1986) argue that the unexplained percentage of Indian population growth is the result of " 'recruitment,' i.e., changes in self-definition" by individuals from non-Indian in one census to Indian in the next (Passel and Berman 1986, p. 164). Thornton (1987) suggests that such increases are the result of " 'biological migration': the migration of non-Indian genes into the American Indian population" (p. 174), the offspring of whom identify themselves as Indian. Steiner (1967) characterizes individuals likely to be included in the ranks of the unaccounted for Indian population as "new Indians"—urban, educated, and multicultural—people whom Snipp (1989) describes as "individuals who in an earlier era of American history would have 'passed' unrecognized into white society" (p. 57). Eschbach (1992) depicts the In-

---

[3]In 1980, about one-fifth of U.S. Census respondents who identified their race as "American Indian" did not report a tribe (U.S. Bureau of the Census 1981).
[4]Researchers believe that the racial self-reporting introduced by the U.S. Census in 1960 contributed to the 46 percent increase from 1950 to 1960. After 1960, how-

---

ever, census coding procedures were no longer a major explanation for American Indian population growth (see Eschbach 1992; Passel and Berman 1986; Snipp 1989; Stiffarm and Lane 1992; Thornton 1987, 1990; U.S. Bureau of the Census 1988).

dian population explosion as the result of "new identification" by Americans of varying degrees of Indian ancestry who formerly reported a non-Indian race, but who changed their race to "Indian" in a later census. And, finally, there is the somewhat unkind, informal description of newly identified census Indians as "wannabes," non-Indian individuals who want to be American Indian and thus identify themselves as such (Deloria 1981, p. 140; Giago 1991; Taliman 1993, p. 10).

Describing the "New" Indian Population

Although researchers seem to agree that individual ethnic change is an important factor in the recent growth of the American Indian population, the reasons remain unclear. Phrased as research questions, we might ask: Who are these "new" Indians? And, what motivates them to change their ethnicity? . . .

. . . During the 1960–1990 period, the urban Indian population increased 720 percent compared to a 218 percent increase in rural areas (Sorkin 1978, p. 10; U.S. Bureau of the Census 1989, p. 150; 1992). Thus, *the "new" Indians are much more likely to live in urban areas than rural areas.*

There are also regional differences in Indian population growth. Passel and Berman (1986) compared 1970–1980 population growth rates in "Indian states" with those in "non-Indian states,"[5] and found that the In-

dian population was growing twice as fast in non-Indian states: A 114 percent increase occurred in non-Indian states compared to only a 56 percent increase in Indian states. Eschbach (1995, p. 103) examined population growth rates in regions of the country with states containing historically small Indian populations similar to Passel and Berman's "non-Indian states."[6] He found that population growth in these regions during the period from 1960 to 1990 was six times greater than in the regions containing states with historical Indian populations. These two studies strongly suggest that *the "new" Indians are much more likely to be from states with historically small Indian populations.*

Researchers have also found that Indian population growth is associated with racial intermarriage. American Indians have very high intermarriage rates compared to other racial groups. For instance, Snipp (1989, p. 157) compared rates of intermarriage of Blacks, Whites, and Indians in the 1980 Census and found that nearly half of Indians were intermarried (48 percent) compared to only 2 percent of Blacks and 1 percent of Whites. . . . The implication of this research on Indian intermarriage is that *the "new" Indians in the 1970, 1980, and 1990 Censuses are more likely to be intermarried.*

The race assigned to children in mixed marriages provides another important piece of information about the characteristics of the fastest growing segment of the American Indian population. Where hypodescent does not dictate the race of mixed race children, parents may choose their child's race. In 1980 and 1990, mixed Indian–non-Indian

[5]Indian states are those states with a native population of 3000 or more in 1950: Alaska, Arizona, Idaho, Michigan, Minnesota, Montana, Nebraska, Nevada, New Mexico, New York, North Carolina, North Dakota, Oklahoma, Oregon, South Dakota, Utah, Washington, Wisconsin, and Wyoming; California was excluded because it "behaved demographically over the last three decades much like a typical 'non-Indian' state" (Passel and Berman 1986, p. 171).

[6]The correspondence between Passel and Berman (1986) and Eschbach (1995) is close, but not perfect. For instance, Passel and Berman's "Indian" states of Michigan, Nebraska, and New York are contained in Eschbach's six non-Indian regions, and unlike Passel and Berman, Eschbach includes California as an Indian region. I follow Passel and Berman in excluding California from Indian regions.

couples assigned the race of the Indian parent to only about half of their offspring. . . . Further, those regions with the greatest Indian population growth were areas where children of mixed marriages were *less likely* to be classified by their parents as Indians. These findings suggest that *the "new" Indians are more likely to assign a non-Indian race to their mixed offspring*.

Finally, we come to that major indicator of assimilation—native language loss. Indian language usage has declined dramatically in the past century . . . 74 percent of American Indians spoke only English in their homes (U.S. Bureau of the Census 1989, p. 203); by 1990, the percentage had risen to 77 percent (U.S. Bureau of the Census 1992, p. 66). Snipp (1989) found, not surprisingly, that native language usage varies by region, with Native Americans from regions with historically large Indian populations much more likely to speak an Indian language than are those from historically non-Indian regions.[7] As Indian population growth is highest in these non-Indian regions, we can conclude that *the "new" Indians are quite likely to speak only English*.

Adding the above data together, a picture emerges of the fastest growing segment of the Native American population: Compared to the total American Indian population, these Indians are more urban, more concentrated in non-Indian states without reservation communities, more often intermarried, less likely to assign their mixed offspring an Indian race, and more likely to speak only English. These characteristics are all descriptive of a population more "blended" into the American demographic and cultural mainstream than their reservation co-ethnics, more likely to have more flexible conceptions of self, residing in parts of the country that permit a wide range of ethnic options. In other words, under the proper conditions, the fastest growing portions of the American Indian population are available for ethnic renewal.

Accounting for American Indian Ethnic Renewal

What *are* the conditions that promote American Indian ethnic renewal? Restated, what has motivated these new Indians to change their ethnicity? The answers to this question can be found in policy and politics: federal Indian policy, American ethnic politics, and Native American political activism.

Federal Indian Policy

Beginning in the nineteenth century, federal Indian policy was designed to assimilate American Indians into the Euro-American cultural mainstream (e.g., through forced English language acquisition, Anglo-centric education in Indian boarding and day schools, and reservation land reduction programs). Despite a brief pause in federal assimilation programs during the "New Deal" era,[8] the net result of decades of federal Indian policy was the creation of an English-speaking, bicultural, multi-tribal American Indian population living in U.S. cities. World War II also spurred the urbanization and acculturation of the Native American population, as Indians volunteered and were drafted into the military and non-enlisted native workers left reservations for wartime industrial jobs in urban areas.

---

[7]For instance, Snipp (1989, pp. 175–76) reports that in the Mountain states 62.0 percent of Indians report speaking a native language at home, compared to only 3.6 percent in the South Atlantic states.

[8]For instance, the Indian Reorganization Act of 1934 (IRA) reaffirmed tribal rights. Many critics maintain that the IRA was also an acculturation program of sorts, because it created tribal "councils" with "chairmen" linked to the Bureau of Indian Affairs (Champagne 1986; Deloria and Lytle 1984).

Many of these Indian veterans and workers never returned to the reservation (Bernstein 1986; Nash 1985). Post–World War II programs for job training and urban relocation were specifically designed to reduce reservation populations during the "termination" era of federal Indian policy, and provided a further push in the reservation-urban Indian population stream.[9] For instance, Sorkin (1978) estimates that from 1952 to 1972, federal programs relocated more than 100,000 American Indians to a number of targeted cities, including Chicago, Cleveland, Dallas, Denver, Los Angeles, Oakland, Oklahoma City, Phoenix, Salt Lake City, San Francisco, San Jose, Seattle, and Tulsa (Sorkin 1978, chap. 3). By 1970, nearly half of American Indians lived in cities as a result of relocation programs and other general urbanization processes. The combined result of decades of these federal Indian policies was the creation of an urbane, educated, English-speaking Indian constituency that was available for mobilization when the civil rights era arrived in the 1960s.

Not only did federal Indian policy help urbanize the Indian population, many programs had a major impact on the organizational fabric of urban Indian life. For instance, relocation programs directly funded the creation and operation of a number of Indian centers in both relocation target cities and cities near large reservation populations (Ablon 1965). These centers were established to provide services and meeting places for burgeoning urban Indian populations. Further, as an indirect consequence of relocation efforts, other urban Indian organizations blossomed: intertribal clubs, bars, athletic leagues, beauty contests, powwows, and dance groups, as well as Indian newspapers and newsletters, social service agencies, political organizations, and Christian churches (Guillemin 1975; Hertzberg 1971; Mucha 1983; Steele 1975; Weibel-Orlando 1991).

In a few urban areas, some of these organizations had a specific tribal character and were frequented only by members of a particular tribe (Hodge 1971). However, the vast majority of urban Indian organizations were intertribal and had names reflecting their inclusionary character: the Cleveland American Indian Center, the *Inter-Tribal Tribune* (newsletter of the Heart of American Indian Center, Kansas City), the Los Angeles American Indian Bowling League, the Many Trails Indian Club, the First Southern Baptist Indian Church (Weibel-Orlando 1991). In such intertribal organizations, many urban Indians "sought refuge from the terrible loss of identity that marked modern urban existence" (Clark 1988, p. 289). The diverse organizations that populated the urban Indian organizational landscape formed the core of an intertribal network and informal communication system in urban Indian communities. They were important building blocks in the development of a supratribal level of Indian identity and the emergence of a pan-Indian culture, both of which were essential ingredients in the Red Power political mobilization of the 1960s.

American Ethnic Politics

Two forces converged in the 1960s to end the assimilationist thrust of federal Indian policy and to set in motion the contemporary period of American Indian ethnic renewal.

---

[9]The "termination" era in federal Indian policy began in 1946 with the creation of the Indian Claims Commission, which was designed to settle all Indian land claims, and so to begin a process of ending (terminating) the federal-Indian trust relationship. Termination policies were unofficially suspended when the Kennedy administration took office in 1961, although a number of tribes were terminated after that date. A 1970 statement by President Richard M. Nixon that embraced Indian "self-determination" marked the official turning point in federal Indian policy, shifting it from "termination" to "self-determination" (see Cohen [1982] for a summary of federal Indian policy).

One was the civil rights movement and the shifts in American social and political culture that followed in its wake. The other was President Lyndon Johnson's solution to the problem of race in America—the Great Society, the War on Poverty, and the civil rights legislation of the 1960s. The fluctuating currents of cultural change and reform politics that marked the 1960s were responded to by increasingly cosmopolitan and sophisticated American Indians who lobbied successfully to send federal War on Poverty and community development resources into impoverished urban and reservation communities (Deloria 1978, p. 88; Witt 1968, p. 68).

This mix of volatile ethnic politics and an explosion of federal resources, many earmarked for minority programs, combined with earlier federal Indian policies, which had concentrated large numbers of tribally diverse, educated, acculturated, and organizationally connected Indians in American cities. The result: a large-scale mobilization of urban Indians marked by a rapid growth of political organizations, newspapers, and community programs. To grasp fully these dynamic changes in many American communities, Indian and non-Indian, it is important to recall the atmosphere of the 1960s. As Hugh Davis Graham (1990) writes in the Introduction to *The Civil Rights Era:*

> This is a story about a rare event in America: a radical shift in national social policy. Its precondition was a broader social revolution, the black civil rights movement that surged up from the South, followed by the nationwide rebirth of the feminist movement. (p. 3)

The demographic changes that underlay the rise of Black militancy in American cities, namely, the "great Black migration" from the rural south to the urban north (Cloward and Piven 1975; Edsall and Edsall 1991;

Lemann 1991), were paralleled by the movement of American Indians off the reservations. The federal response to Black protest—civil rights legislation and the War on Poverty—spilled over into other minority communities, including American Indian communities, which were quickly mobilizing in the wake of Black insurgency. The ethnic militancy of the 1960s redefined mainstream America as "White" and exposed and challenged its racial hegemony. For America's ethnic minorities it was a time to cast off negative stereotypes, to reinvent ethnic and racial social meanings and self-definitions, and to embrace ethnic pride. For American Indians it marked the emergence of supratribal identification, the rise of Indian activism, and a period of increased Indian ethnic pride. Despite their often brutal treatment by United States' authorities and citizens throughout American history, American Indians have ironically, but consistently occupied a romanticized niche in the American popular media and imagination (Berkhofer 1978). The durable symbolic value of the American Indian as a cultural icon was further enhanced by the increased ethnic pride characterizing the civil rights era. The result increased the appeal of Indian ethnicity for many individuals, and no doubt contributed to the resurgence of Indian self-identification.

In addition to the symbolic allure of Indian ethnicity, there were also material incentives. Castile (1992) notes the connection between these ideational and material realms, commenting that American Indians were able "to manipulate their symbolic position [in American history and society] in ways that grant[ed] them a political leverage far greater than their numbers justif[ied]. By keeping a sharp eye on the political waves of ethnicity, which they [could] not raise themselves, shrewd timing . . . allow[ed] them to ride those waves and maximize their impact in positive ways" (p. 183). American Indians indeed were able to navigate the changing currents of American ethnic politics, and their successes resulted in increased federal spending on Indian affairs, making American Indian identification a more attractive ethnic option for many Americans of Indian descent. The settlement of land claims by the Indian Claims Commission and the U.S. federal court system during the 1970s and 1980s was another important source of funds for Indian communities. Churchill (1992) reports that more than $128 million in Indian land claims awards were disbursed between 1946 and 1970, and by 1978 the total amount of claims awards exceeded $657 million (also see Lurie 1978, p. 101). In addition, a number of major land claims were settled during the early 1980s, some of which involved large controversial settlements. Most notable are the claims of Maine's Passamaquoddy and Penobscot tribes, who in 1980 recovered 300,000 acres of land and received a payment of $27 million (see Jaimes 1992).

Increased federal spending in general and land claim awards in particular, along with the inclusion of Indians in many affirmative action and minority set-aside programs, contributed to the American Indian ethnic resurgence in part because they increased both the symbolic and the potential material value of Indian ethnicity. Individuals of Indian ancestry became more willing to identify themselves as Indians, whether or not such identification was a strategy to acquire a share of real or putative land claims awards or other possible ethnically-allocated rewards (such as scholarships, mineral royalties, employment preference). It was in this atmosphere of increased resources, ethnic grievances, ethnic pride, and civil rights activism that Red Power burst on the scene in the late 1960s and galvanized a generation of Native Americans. The rest of the country watched as the media covered such events as the occupation of Alcatraz Island, the takeover of the Bureau of Indian Affairs headquarters in Washington, D.C., and the siege at Wounded Knee.

American Indian Activism: Red Power

The shifting political culture and protest climate of the 1960s and 1970s spawned many Indian activist organizations, such as the American Indian Movement (AIM) and the National Indian Youth Council, and produced a number of Indian protest actions: the 19-month occupation of Alcatraz Island which began in 1969; the 1972 Trail of Broken Treaties which culminated in a week-long occupation of the Bureau of Indian Affairs in Washington, D.C.; the 71-day siege at Wounded Knee, South Dakota in 1973; the 1975 shoot-out on the Pine Ridge Reservation in South Dakota which resulted in the imprisonment of Leonard Peltier; and numerous protest events in cities and on reservations around the United States, concluding with the 1978 Longest Walk to Washington, D.C. These events and this era stand out boldly in the publications and accounts of Native Americans living at that time, particularly native youth (see Crow Dog and Erdoes 1990; Fortunate Eagle 1992). Red Power played an important symbolic role in motivating individual ethnic renewal on the part of Indian participants and observers; this ethnic renewal took two forms, and both forms are relevant to the argument I present here.

The first type of individual ethnic renewal involves individuals who most likely would have identified themselves as Indians in earlier censuses, and thus is best summarized as a resurgence in ethnic pride which did not involve taking on a new ethnic identity (e.g., does not involve racial switching). Instead, this type of individual ethnic renewal involved a reaffirmation, reconstruction, or redefinition of an individual's ethnicity. For example, the slogan, "I'm Black and I'm proud" reflected such a redefinition of "Negro" in the U.S. in the 1960s. These individuals did not change their race, rather they changed the *meaning* of their race. This parallels the resurgence of Native American ethnic pride among individuals who already identified themselves as "Indian."

The second type of individual ethnic renewal involves individuals who would *not* have identified themselves as Indian in earlier censuses, but rather would have "passed" into the non-Indian race categories. For these individuals, a resurgence of ethnic pride meant not only redefining the worth and meaning of their ancestry, but also involved laying a new claim to that ancestry by switching their race on the census form from non-Indian to Indian. This type of individual ethnic renewal is, I believe, reflected in census data; but currently the data do not exist for evaluating directly the influences of federal Indian policy, the ethnic politics of the civil rights era, or the rise of Indian activism on this kind of ethnic renewal. Such an evaluation would require examining the backgrounds and beliefs of those individuals who changed their race from non-Indian to Indian in the 1970, 1980, and 1990 Censuses. As Sandefur and McKinnell (1986) state, "it is not possible to know from census data who has changed his or her racial identification since a previous census" (p. 348). Indeed, researchers are awaiting such a definitive study. Snipp (1993) notes, while it is plausible that census increases reflect the fact that "more mixed ancestry persons are identifying themselves as American Indians than in the past, . . . [it] is virtually impossible to prove" (p. 16; also see Harris 1994, p. 592; Thornton, Sandefur and Snipp 1991, p. 365). . . .

Conclusion

The rise in American Indian ethnic identification during the last three decades has resulted from a combination of factors in American politics. Assimilationist federal Indian policies helped to create a bicultural, intermarried, mixed race, urban Indian population living in regions of the country where ethnic options were most numerous; this was a group "poised" for individual ethnic renewal. The ethnic politics of the civil rights era encouraged ethnic identification, the return to ethnic roots, ethnic activism, and provided resources for mobilizing ethnic communities; thus, the climate and policies of civil rights provided individuals of native ancestry (and others as well) symbolic and material incentives to claim or reclaim Indian ethnicity. Red Power activism during the 1960s and 1970s further raised Indian ethnic consciousness by dramatizing long held grievances, communicating an empowered and empowering image of Indianness, and providing Native Americans, particularly native youth, opportunities for action and participation in the larger Indian cause. Together then, federal Indian policies, ethnic politics, and American Indian activism provided the rationale and motivation for individual ethnic renewal.

The overall explanation of the resurgence of American Indian ethnicity I offer here can be seen as part of a general model of ethnic renewal. The impact of federal Indian policies on American Indian ethnic renewal represents an instance of the political construction of ethnicity (i.e., the ways in which political policy, the structure of political opportunity, and patterns of political culture shape ethnic boundaries in society). The impact of events in this larger political arena on Indian ethnic activism and identity illustrates the role of politics and political culture in ethnic mobilization (i.e., the power of political *zeitgeist* and shifting political definitions to open windows of opportunity for ethnic activists and to affirm and render meaningful their grievances and claims). The impact of Red Power on American Indian ethnic consciousness reveals the role of human agency in individual and collective redefinition and empowerment (i.e., the power of activism to challenge prevailing policies, to encourage ethnic awareness, and to foster ethnic community-building). This model of ethnic renewal suggests that, given the capacity of individuals to reinvent themselves and their communities, ethnicity occupies an enduring place in modern societies.

REFERENCES

ABLON, JOAN. 1965. "American Indian Relocation: Problems of Dependency and Management in the City." *Phylon* 66:362–71.

BARTH, FREDRIK. 1969. *Ethnic Groups and Boundaries.* Boston, MA: Little, Brown.

BERKHOFER, ROBERT F. 1978. *The White Man's Indian: Images of the American Indian from Columbus to the Present.* New York: Knopf.

BERNSTEIN, ALISON RICKY. 1986. "Walking in Two Worlds: American Indians and World War Two." Ph.D. dissertation, Department of History, Columbia University, New York.

CASTILE, GEORGE P. 1992. "Indian Sign: Hegemony and Symbolism in Federal Indian Policy." Pp. 163–86 in *State and Reservation: New Perspectives on Federal Indian Policy,* edited by G. P. Castile and R. L. Bee. Tucson: University of Arizona Press.

CHAMPAGNE, DUANE. 1986. "American Indian Values and the Institutionalization of IRA Governments." Pp. 25–34 in *American Indian Policy and Cultural Values: Conflict and Accommodation* (Contemporary American Indian Issues Series No. 6), edited by J. R. Joe. Los Angeles: American Indian Studies Center, UCLA Publications Services Department.

CHURCHILL, WARD. 1992. "The Earth Is Our Mother: Struggles for American Indian Land and Liberation in the Contemporary United States." Pp. 139–88 in *The State of Native America: Genocide, Colonization, and Resistance,* edited by M. A. Jaimes. Boston: South End Press.

CLARK, BLUE. 1988. "Bury My Heart in Smog: Urban Indians." Pp. 278–91 in *The American Indian Experience. A Profile: 1524 to the Present,* edited by P. Weeks. Arlington Heights, IL: Forum Press.

CLOWARD, RICHARD A., and FRANCES FOX PIVEN. 1975. *The Politics of Turmoil: Poverty, Race, and the Urban Crisis.* New York: Vintage Books.

COHEN, FELIX S. 1982. *Felix S. Cohen's Handbook of Federal Indian Law.* Charlottesville, VA: Michie Bobbs-Merrill.

COLLAS, SARA. 1994. "Transgressing Racial Boundaries: The Maintenance of the Racial Order." Paper presented at the annual meeting of the American Sociological Association, August 8, Los Angeles.

CONZEN, KATHLEEN N., DAVID A. GERBER, EWA MORAWSKA, GEORGE E. POZZETTA, and RUDOLPH J. VECOLI. 1992. "The Invention of Ethnicity: A Perspective from the U.S.A." *Journal of American Ethnic History* 12:3–41.

CROW DOG, MARY, and RICHARD ERDOES. 1990. *Lakota Woman.* New York: Grove Weidenfeld.

DAVIS, JAMES F. 1991. *Who Is Black? One Nation's Definition.* University Park: Pennsylvania State University.

DELORIA, VINE, JR. 1978. "Legislation and Litigation Concerning American Indians." *The Annals of the American Academy of Political and Social Science* 436:88–96.

———. 1981. "Native Americans: The American Indian Today." *The Annals of the American Academy of Political and Social Sciences* 454:139–49.

———. 1986. "The New Indian Recruits: The Popularity of Being Indian." *Americans Before Columbus* 14:3, 6–8.

———. 1992. "American Indians." Pp. 31–52 in *Multiculturalism in the United States: A Comparative Guide to Acculturation and Ethnicity,* edited by J. D. Buenker and L. A. Ratner. Westport, CT: Greenwood Press.

DELORIA, VINE, JR., and CLIFFORD LYTLE. 1984. *The Nations Within: The Past and Future of American Indian Sovereignty.* New York: Pantheon Books.

EDSALL, THOMAS B., and MARY D. EDSALL. 1991. *Chain Reaction: The Impact of Race, Rights, and Taxes on American Politics.* New York: Norton.

ESCHBACH, KARL. 1992. "Shifting Boundaries: Regional Variation in Patterns of Identification as American Indians." Ph.D. dissertation, Department of Sociology, Harvard University, Cambridge, MA.

———. 1995. "The Enduring and Vanishing American Indian: American Indian Population Growth and Intermarriage in 1990." *Ethnic and Racial Studies* 18:89–108.

FORTUNATE EAGLE, ADAM. 1992. *Alcatraz! Alcatraz! The Indian Occupation of 1969–71.* San Francisco: Heyday Books.

GIAGO, TIM. 1991. "Big Increases in 1990 Census Not Necessarily Good for Tribes." *Lakota Times,* March 12, p. 3.

GLAZER, NATHAN, and DANIEL P. MOYNIHAN. 1963. *Beyond the Melting Pot.* Cambridge, MA: Harvard University Press.

GORDON, MILTON. 1961. "Assimilation in America: Theory and Reality." *Daedalus* 90:263–85.

GRAHAM, HUGH DAVIS. 1990. *The Civil Rights Era: Origins and Development of National Policy, 1960–1972.* New York: Oxford University Press.

GUILLEMIN, JEANNE. 1975. *Urban Renegades: The Cultural Strategy of American Indians.* New York: Columbia University Press.

HARRIS, DAVID. 1994. "The 1990 Census Count of American Indians: What Do the Numbers Really Mean?" *Social Science Quarterly* 75: 580–93.

HARRIS, MARVIN. 1964. *Patterns of Race in the Americas.* New York: Norton.

HERTZBERG, HAZEL. 1971. *The Search for an American Indian Identity: Modern Pan-Indian Movements.* Syracuse, NY: Syracuse University Press.

HODGE, WILLIAM H. 1971. "Navajo Urban Migration: An Analysis from the Perspective of the Family." Pp. 346–92 in *The American Indian in Urban Society,* edited by J. O. Waddell and O. M. Watson. Boston: Little, Brown.

JAIMES, M. ANNETTE. 1992. "Federal Indian Identification Policy: A Usurpation of Indigenous Sovereignty in North America." Pp. 123–28 in *The State of Native America: Genocide, Colonization, and Resistance,* edited by M. A. Jaimes. Boston: South End Press.

LARIMORE, JIM, and RICK WATERS. 1993. "American Indians Speak Out Against Ethnic Fraud in College Admissions." Paper presented at a conference sponsored by the American Council on Education: "Educating One-Third of a Nation IV: Making Our Reality Match Our Rhetoric," October 22, Houston.

LEMANN, NICHOLAS. 1991. *The Promised Land: The Great Black Migration and How It Changed America.* New York: Knopf.

LURIE, NANCY O. 1978. "The Indian Claims Commission." *The Annals of the American Academy of Political and Social Science* 436:97–110.

MASUMURA, WILLIAM, and PATRICIA BERMAN. 1987. "American Indians and the Census." Unpublished manuscript.

MORRIS, GLENN T. 1989. "The International Status of Indigenous Nations within the United States." Pp. 1–14 in *Critical Issues in Native North America* (Document No. 62), edited by W. Churchill. Copenhagen, Denmark: International Work Group for Indigenous Affairs.

MUCHA, JANOSZ. 1983. "From Prairie to the City: Transformation of Chicago's American Indian Community." *Urban Anthropology* 12:337–71.

NAGEL, JOANE. 1994. "Constructing Ethnicity: Creating and Recreating Ethnic Identity and Culture." *Social Problems* 41:1001–26.

———. Forthcoming. *American Indian Ethnic Renewal: Red Power and the Resurgence of Identity and Culture.* New York: Oxford University Press.

NASH, GERALD D. 1985. *The American West Transformed: The Impact of the Second World War.* Bloomington: Indiana University Press.

PARK, ROBERT E. 1928. *Race and Culture.* Glencoe, IL: Free Press, 1950.

PASSEL, JEFFREY S., and PATRICIA A. BERMAN. 1986. "Quality of 1980 Census Data for American Indians." *Social Biology* 33:163–82.

REYNOLDS, JERRY. 1993. "Indian Writers: Real or Imagined." *Indian Country Today,* September 8, pp. A1, A3.

SANDEFUR, GARY D., and TRUDY McKINNELL. 1986. "American Indian Intermarriage." *Social Science Research* 15:347–71.

SNIPP, C. MATTHEW. 1989. *American Indians: The First of This Land.* New York: Russell Sage Foundation.

———. 1993. "Some Observations about the Racial Boundaries and the Experiences of American Indians." Paper presented at the University of Washington, April 22, Seattle.

SOLLORS, WERNER, ed. 1989. *The Invention of Ethnicity.* New York: Oxford University Press, 1989.

SORKIN, ALAN L. 1978. *The Urban American Indian.* Lexington, MA: Lexington Books.

STEELE, C. HOY. 1975. "Urban Indian Identity in Kansas: Some Implications for Research." Pp. 167–78 in *The New Ethnicity: Perspectives from Ethnology,* edited by J. W. Bennett. St. Paul, MN: West.

STEINER, STANLEY. 1967. *The New Indians.* New York: Harper & Row.

STIFFARM, LENORE A., and PHIL LANE, JR. 1992. "The Demography of Native North America: A Question of American Indian Survival." Pp. 23–53 in *The State of Native America: Genocide, Colonization, and Resistance,* edited by M. A. Jaimes. Boston: South End Press.

TALIMAN, VALORIE. 1993. "Lakota Declaration of War." *News from Indian Country* 7:10.

THORNTON, RUSSELL. 1987. *American Indian Holocaust and Survival.* Norman: University of Oklahoma Press.

———. 1990. *The Cherokees: A Population History.* Lincoln: University of Nebraska Press.

THORNTON, RUSSELL, GARY D. SANDEFUR, and C. MATTHEW SNIPP. 1991. "American Indian Fertility Patterns: 1910 and 1940–1980." *American Indian Quarterly* 15:359–67.

THORNTON, RUSSELL, C. MATTHEW SNIPP, and NANCY BREEN. 1990. "Appendix: Cherokees in the 1980 Census." Pp. 178–203 in *The Cherokees: A Population History,* edited by R. Thornton. Lincoln: University of Nebraska Press.

TRASK, HAUNANI-KAY. 1990. "Politics in the Pacific Islands: Imperialism and Native Self-Determination." *Amerasia* 16:1–19.

———. 1991. "Natives and Anthropologists: The Colonial Struggle." *The Contemporary Pacific* 3:159–67.

U.S. BUREAU OF THE CENSUS. 1981. *American Indian Population Estimates by Tribe.* U.S. Bureau of the Census, Washington, DC. Unpublished tables.

———. 1988. *We, the First Americans.* Washington, DC: Government Printing Office.

———. 1989. *Census of Population, Subject Reports, Characteristics of American Indians by Tribes and Selected Areas, 1980.* Washington, DC: Government Printing Office.

———. 1991. "Census Bureau Releases 1990 Census Counts on Specific Racial Groups" (Census Bureau Press Release CB91–215, Wednesday, June 12). U.S. Bureau of the Census, Washington, DC.

———. 1992. *Census of the Population, General Population Characteristics, American Indian and Alaskan Native Areas, 1990.* Washington, DC: Government Printing Office.

WATERS, MARY C. 1990. *Ethnic Options: Choosing Identities in America.* Berkeley: University of California Press.

WEIBEL-ORLANDO, JOAN. 1991. *Indian Country, L.A.: Maintaining Ethnic Community in Complex Society.* Champaign: University of Illinois Press.

WITT, SHIRLEY HILL. 1968. "Nationalistic Trends among American Indians." Pp. 53–75 in *The American Indian Today,* edited by S. Levine and N. O. Lurie. Deland, FL: Everett/Edwards.

PART II
Prejudice and Discrimination

Imagine you are a 57-year-old white vice president with Friendly Bank. You earn a considerable amount of money, have large mortgage and car payments, and support four kids, two of whom are in college. You are the primary breadwinner in your family. At lunch, your boss asks you about the new manager you will be hiring. He hints to you in a subtle way, a way you could never prove in court, that he has had bad experiences working with Asian Americans and would be extremely upset if one was hired. You are not racist toward Asians. You do, however, need this job, your family needs to eat, two of your children are in college, and you are at an age at which moving from one job to another would be both difficult and costly. Of the three hundred or so people who apply for this position, several Asian American candidates appear to be highly qualified, and one unquestionably would make an excellent bank manager. Would you turn a blind eye to the resumes of the Asian Americans or would you hire the most qualified person, even if that meant hiring an Asian American and being marginalized or conveniently downsized by your boss?

How do feelings of antipathy toward or dislike of a group of people because of their skin color, ethnicity, or religion culminate in actions against members of that group? As the preceding example indicates, individuals may act in discriminatory ways and not be prejudiced or racist. Conversely, someone may be prejudiced and racist toward a group and not discriminate. The black shoe salesperson who does not like whites may still sell a white customer a pair of shoes in order to earn a commission.

Prejudice and discrimination are linked in complicated ways. In Reading 9, "The Complexity of Race Relations," Howard Schuman and associates use longitudinal, or decade-by-decade, survey data to chart how the racial attitudes of whites toward blacks and Asians have improved in the United States. Their findings are quite impressive. Since World War II, whites' views on integration, interracial marriage, voting for nonwhite politicians, and sharing social space with blacks and Asians suggest that whites are gradually embracing the idea of a color-blind society.

However, things, particularly attitudes, are not always as they seem. Such findings are encouraging only if you believe that respondents' answers are an accurate reflection of what they really think or feel. Perhaps these trends reflect pressure to conform to what respondents believe is a socially desirable attitude. Typically, individuals want to present themselves to others in a positive way. This pressure to conform may lead respondents to conveniently forget or tightly monitor racist or prejudiced beliefs. Are answers to questions about racial attitudes merely a reflection of what takes place in the abstract, unnatural interview setting, or are these responses a valid and reliable window into Americans' racial attitudes? Frankly, social scientists are not always sure. To further complicate matters, it's not clear what connection, if any, exists between attitudes and action or between prejudice and discrimination.

Demonstrating a strong, consistent causal link between attitudes and actions has proved elusive in the social sciences. The proposition that actions flow from attitudes may seem straightforward, but as we will see in the readings, it is not. It seems logical that individuals would behave in a manner consistent with their attitudes, opinions, or beliefs about a particular topic. If, for example, you define yourself as not being racist, you would not engage in racial discrimination. But as the example about the vice president of Friendly Bank suggests, various social and economic pressures mediate what we would like to do, what we should do, and what we actually do.

Prejudice and discrimination takes many forms. The first five readings in Part II examine those forms and the way certain social and structural conditions can create an environment in which prejudice and discrimination are likely to emerge. As mentioned previously, Howard Schuman and colleagues use survey research findings to trace shifts in the racial attitudes of whites. In an insightful and classic piece of sociology, Herbert Blumer explains race prejudice (racism) as a reflection of how individuals place themselves in a racial hierarchy relative to other racial groups they encounter. That is, individuals attempt to maintain privilege and status by reserving the "prerogatives" of their racial group, even if they are not consciously aware of it. Robert Merton provides examples of the social context in which a nonprejudiced individual like our vice president at Friendly Bank might act in a discriminatory fashion. Like Merton, Elliot Aronson outlines how prejudice and discrimination are often rooted in efforts to maintain privileges or advantages that accrue to individuals because of their skin color. Finally, Elizabeth Martínez reminds us that racism, prejudice, and discrimination are not solely black–white issues, although one might draw that conclusion based on how race and ethnicity are covered in the media.

The next five articles in Part II focus on how a particular social environment shapes both our own behavior and attitudes and the way others see us. Joe Feagin explores how racism directed at middle- and upper-middle-class blacks plays out in ways that whites do not, cannot, or will not see. Jonathan Kozol and Herbert Gans each examine how structural inequality disproportionately affects racial minorities in the United States. Not only does institutional racism result in a two-tiered educational system, but poverty provides various social "functions" to the nonpoor—not the least of which is a sense of superiority. In a timely and insightful article, Howard Pinderhughes describes how acting in a racist fashion provides status for the poor white youths. Finally, Robert Bullard details how poor and nonwhite neighborhoods are disproportionately exposed to toxic waste— perhaps the most obvious way in which social space gets colored.

QUESTIONS TO FRAME YOUR READINGS

- How is it possible for you to think about your race or ethnic identity in individual terms but to see others as part of a racial group?

- What racialized situations have you been in where social, economic, or peer pressure forced you to do something you did not want to do?

- Have you ever defined your racial or ethnic group membership in such a way as to heighten your group's status at the expense of another?

- In a number of these readings, some people seem to benefit from engaging in racist behavior. What structural changes could you suggest that would shift their energies from something negative to something positive?

"Some of My Best Friends Are . . .": Linking Group Position to Attitudes and Action

9

THE COMPLEXITY OF RACE RELATIONS

Howard Schuman • Charlotte Steeh • Lawrence Bobo • Maria Krysan

Seek simplicity and distrust it.
— A. N. WHITEHEAD

Color and other racial identifications are such powerful ascriptive markers that nobody can fully escape them, regardless of their pursuits or achievements in life. The late Secretary of Commerce Ronald Brown kept in his desk a news photograph from a Midwestern paper that had been sent to him by Colin Powell. The picture was of Mr. Brown, but the caption identified him as General Powell. Attached to the clipping was a handwritten note from Powell: "Ron, they *still* can't tell us apart" (*New York Times*, April 4, 1996, p. A10). Such perceived similarities in appearance, and the complementary distinction between whites and blacks, are fundamental in the United States, as they are to varying degrees in other parts of the world.[1]

There is no evidence that this virtually absolute differentiation of the American population has been reduced by the changes of the last half century, though it has no doubt been further complicated by the increase in several Asian, Hispanic, and other minorities. Indeed, the black-white division may even have deepened in some respects as a result of the growth of black consciousness and the use of racial enumeration as a way of monitoring progress in civil rights. Americans are not much more color-blind today than they ever were, and despite some growth in the rate of racial intermarriage (Harrison and Bennett 1995), a melting-pot solution to racial differences in the United States is not likely to occur in the foreseeable future.

What *has* changed over the past half century is the normative definition of appropriate relations between blacks and whites. Whereas discrimination against, and enforced segregation of, black Americans were taken for granted by most white Americans as recently as the World War II years, today the norm holds that black Americans deserve the same treatment and respect as whites, and in addition that racial integration in all public spheres of life is a desirable goal. . . . How far back in time the development of the new norm goes, and what led to both the initial and the continuing movement of whites toward acceptance of the principle of equal treatment are interesting questions, but available survey data do not allow us to answer them very well.[2] In any case, the more pressing problem here is the meaning for the present of this great normative shift and its implications for the future.

Do the changes in individual attitudes that flow from the larger normative shift mean anything outside the survey interview? It is difficult to believe that they do not, for the evidence is all around us of important and pervasive changes in the relations between blacks and whites in the United States. Beyond the total elimination of a vast structure of legal segregation throughout the South and Southwest and within the U.S. armed forces, there is an abundance of *non*survey evidence of genuine change in white actions toward blacks. Black Americans today hold a wide range of high elected and appointed political positions, and not by any means only in areas with black majorities. African Americans are also prominent in television and film, in major universities and colleges, and to a greater or lesser degree in many other public spheres of life.[3] In most of these spheres they are still greatly underrepresented in proportion to their numbers in the total population, and the large black lower class is almost totally excluded from participation in this change. But these crucial qualifications do not alter the fact that actual change in public life over the past half century has been very substantial. Only because so much of the population of the United States—both black and white—is now too young to have any memory of race relations circa 1940 or even 1960 can there be any doubt about the magnitude of the change.

The tendency to look for exact consistency between attitudes and behavior also misses a useful distinction that can be made between literal consistency and correlational consistency (Schuman and Johnson 1976). The former asks whether people do what they say they will do; the latter asks

whether people are ordered or ranked in the same way along both attitude and behavioral dimensions. . . .

In other words, attitude measures can be seen as tapping broad currents of social change, though of course imperfectly, and if they show correlational consistency we should be able at the same time to see similar trends in directly relevant behaviors. . . .

Yet even where behavior is consistent correlationally with attitudes, one can still ask whether changes in either survey responses *or* public behavior represent a true inner transformation by white Americans. Or are the changes a kind of veneer that conceals continued profound racism on the part of most or all white Americans? This is a complex question: in the language of social science, it asks whether the new norm has been internalized. One legitimate response is to insist that the change in public norms is important in itself, especially as it is reflected in white actions. If a white president appoints a black general to the position of chief of staff of the armed forces, or if a substantial part of a white electorate votes for a black gubernatorial or congressional candidate, we may never know whether they do so because in their hearts they are genuinely nondiscriminatory, or because they have temporarily put aside their deep racism to make that particular decision. But all of us conform to norms that we may or may not have internalized deeply, yet that guide our actions in ways that are of considerable consequence for our relations with others. Myrdal spoke of the American Dilemma as being "in the heart of the American," but what he surely meant was that it was located in the values and norms of our society, and that most Americans are capable of feeling pressure from these values and norms—if not out of personal guilt, then from social shaming when they are blatantly violated. We should not overpsychologize the problem of comformity to social norms, as though each of us has either internalized a norm completely or chosen to ignore it completely.

Another approach to the same issue is to acknowledge that white persons who respond to a survey question on the principle of school integration by saying "blacks and whites should go to the same schools" doubtless run the full gamut from those deeply committed to that idea to those who feel quite otherwise but are embarrassed to admit it to an interviewer. However, most Americans, black as well as white, probably fall somewhere in the middle: they feel some genuine belief in the norm but also have other beliefs and preferences that put them in conflict on the issue. It is clear from the combination of questions we have examined that many white respondents do feel conflict about school integration and similar issues, and that their responses in support of integration in principle are unlikely to be translated directly and completely into action. It is therefore important to try to understand—and to measure—the sources of these conflicts.

One such source is the fact that questions like the one about blacks and whites going to the same schools are too simple, asking in dichotomous form about "segregation" versus "integration," without defining these abstractions or allowing consideration of either the amount or the form of integration. The questions we reviewed on white willingness to be personally involved in integration, as well as other survey data (Farley et al. 1994; Levine 1971; Rothbart 1976; Smith 1981), make it quite clear that whites are much more positive toward a situation with a white majority and a black minority than toward one defined as fifty-fifty or certainly one with a black majority. Given the history of white dominance in this country and the persistence of color as a significant dividing line, this is not a surprising finding; nor is it out of keeping with the way majority ethnic groups behave in other countries, including black African countries. These propensities are at least as much a matter of power and control and of fear of being controlled by others as they are of "prejudice" as a separate and self-contained psychological state.

One sign of this fact of political life about intergroup relations in America is the ability of a black candidate frequently to obtain more white votes when blacks are clearly in the minority than when blacks approach a majority (Hacker 1995). White voting in the latter instances tends to be determined not so much by attitudes toward the race of the candidate as by the perceived balance of power between blacks and whites as groups. For a similar reason, Colin Powell has appeared attractive as a presidential candidate to many white Americans in part because he did not ever suggest that he represented or would represent blacks as a collective political force.

Resistance to government intervention in support of black employment, school integration, or open housing is probably at least partly due to the same perceived conflict between blacks and whites as competing groups, which in turn is based on the way in which physical appearance shapes personal identification of individuals with one group or the other and its political positions. The identification can range from a relatively innocuous form, much like boosting one's hometown sports team, all the way to the most extreme forms of ethnocentrism. Thus many questions about government intervention can be understood as implying large-scale group change, and they suggest a degree of integration that many whites are reluctant to accept, at least at this point in time.

Norms, Preferences, and Personal Conflicts

As we consider the implications of attitudes based on norms, it is useful to get some sense of their generality and of the distinction that many people make between larger societal norms and those attitudes that reflect personal preferences or more local norms. As Myrdal (1944) clearly recognized, a great deal of social behavior is a compromise between the two. We summarize below a series of experimental investigations that show both the power and limitations of norms of equal treatment and the importance of distinguishing them from personal preferences. The experiments focused on issues of residential discrimination, but would apply in other spheres as well.[4]

Individual vs. Group Rights

The first experiment was developed to test the intuitively attractive notion that there would be more support for the right of a single black family to move into an all-white neighborhood than there is for a broad open housing law, which at that point in time (1986) showed an approximately 50-50 division of opinion by whites. First, the focus on a single black family points up forcefully the implications of the norm of equal treatment for real individuals. Second, by keeping the focus on a single family, there should be somewhat less concern about rapid transformation of a neighborhood from entirely or largely white to majority black, as might be implied by an open housing law. However, the initial results of the experiment were unexpected and led to surprising directions.

Half of a national telephone sample was randomly assigned to answer the Open Housing question, and half was assigned to answer a specially written question about a single black family. Moreover, unlike the typical survey interview, we explicitly instructed interviewers to allow and immediately record any volunteered answer that did not fit the alternatives offered to respondents. This change in procedure proved instructive.

There is, as predicted, a great deal more support for government enforcement of the rights of a single black family than for a general open housing law. Of those making a clear choice, 80 percent express support for government enforcement of the rights of a single black family, as against only 61 percent who support a general open housing law, a difference that is highly significant statistically. Taken by itself, this finding indicates that when the focus is on an individual or an individual family, the norm of equal treatment has greater efficacy than when a more general racial transformation is proposed.

A large proportion of respondents (35 percent) who were asked the question about the single black family avoided choosing either of the alternatives offered, whereas only a tiny fraction (7 percent) failed to give a direct answer to the question about open housing laws. Most of those who volunteered their own response to the single family question claimed to favor the right of a black family to live wherever it wished *but* also opposed any use of government power to enforce that right. Such answers, quite overt rather than concealed, show respondents who are trying to conform to the norm of equal treatment yet avoid committing themselves to government enforcement of that norm. The responses emphasize the conflict in the minds of about a quarter of the white population between support of a principle and support of its implementation through government action. . . .

Our results thus far indicate that when blacks are involved, a substantial portion of the white population either opposes residential integration or tries to have it both ways by supporting the goal but not the means to equal treatment. Is this a sign of the special barriers erected against African Americans? A series of further experiments indicates that the implications are different than they initially appeared. We first considered the possibility that white American "racism" applies to *all* nonwhite groups. We repeated the previous experiment with a new variation: half of a national sample was asked the question about a single black family; the other half was asked the same question about another nonwhite group, a single Japanese-American family, on the assumption that white resistance would be somewhat less in this case. To our surprise, there was no difference approaching statistical significance between the two distributions (enforcement vs. all nonenforcement responses combined), and the trend is in the direction of greater support for enforcement in the case of the black family.

Next, in order to allow for the possibility that white opposition to enforcement of equal rights may have roots in a still broader ethnocentrism (Adorno et al. 1950), a further experiment was carried out. A "Jewish family" was substituted for a "Japanese-American family" and a "Christian neighborhood" was substituted for a "white neighborhood." The comparison was again with the parallel question about a single black family and a white neighborhood.[5] And again we discovered that there was no significant difference between the two questions: no greater willingness to enforce equal treatment for the Jewish family than for the black family.

Finally, we carried out a still more extreme experiment that reversed the issue posed between Jews and non-Jews. This time the question about the single black family was compared with a parallel question about enforcing the right of a single Christian family to move into a previously all-Jewish neighborhood. The basic finding remained the same: the distribution of answers to the two questions does not differ significantly, and in fact the trend is toward more support for the black family than for the presumably white, Christian family.

In sum, there is little evidence from this series of experiments that opposition to enforcement of a single black family's right to move into a white neighborhood represents simply a form of antiblack sentiment. On the contrary, there is evidence that it reflects a more general resistance to government enforcement of equal treatment in residential integration, though not necessarily rejection of the desirability of equal treatment. This conclusion fits our impressions based on occasional monitoring of the actual interviews and also the impressions of the interviewers themselves. Opposition to government enforcement in this area of life takes on the force of a principle for many respondents, regardless of the group involved and regardless of what may seem a contradiction inherent in statements by many of these same people that all individuals should be allowed to live where they wish.[6]

Norms vs. Preferences

Given the patterns of actual segregation in the United States, it is difficult to believe that there is the same resistance on the part of whites to Japanese-American or Jewish families moving into a previously white, non-Jewish neighborhood as there is to blacks (Farley and Frey 1994; see also Thomas Wilson 1996). How can we explain that fact if the same degree of adherence to the norm of equal treatment is found regardless of the ethnic group involved? A further experiment casts some light on this question.

The new experiment shifted attention from "rights" to "preferences." This time half the respondents were asked if they would "mind a lot, a little, or not at all" if a black family moved next door, and the other half was asked a parallel question about a Japanese-American family's moving next door. (The word "mind" was intended to emphasize personal preference rather than a general norm.) Moreover, the experiment was carried out twice, once with the addition of a phrase stating that the family moving next door would have "the same income and education" as the respondent, and a second time without that phrase.

There is noticeably (and significantly) less personal objection to a Japanese-American family's moving next door than to a black family's, and this is true regardless of whether or not the income and education of the new neighbors are equated to the respondent's income and education. Thus our earlier finding that acceptance of equal treatment and support for government enforcement do not vary by racial or ethnic group is indeed restricted to these normative issues, since personal preferences *do* vary by the race of the group mentioned. The distinction here is reminiscent of one made [previously] between attitudes based on norms and attitudes based on personal preferences, though that is not meant to be an absolute distinction: insofar as attitudes based on norms are deeply internalized, they become personal, while at the same time even the most personal attitudes are almost always shaped by the larger culture (that is, by norms). . . .

This series of experiments indicates something of the complexity of the forces that are likely to operate in real situations when neighborhood integration becomes a concrete issue. The norm of equal treatment is one such force and we believe that it has some efficacy, but obviously it is not the only factor influencing the outcome. Perceptions of social class differences clearly play a role, so that the potential similarity of a new black (or Japanese American or any other) neighbor in these terms is likely to influence concrete behavior on the part of those already making up the neighborhood. Still an additional element derives from the level of personal preference, and it is important to recognize that some whites who do not seem to distinguish among different groups when considering government enforcement of the norm of equal treatment do make such distinctions when answering in terms

of their own preferences.[7] Thus it is not, or not only, a matter of respondents' concealing preferences, but of their overtly making a distinction between their preferences and what they think they ought to do in a situation. Finally, we should add a further important complication that we deliberately eliminated in these experiments: the proportion of blacks likely to move into a previously white neighborhood makes a considerable difference to white respondents (Farley et al. 1978; Farley et al. 1994).

In real life, all the above elements come into play. Moreover, the balance among them is likely to be greatly affected by the positions taken by community leaders, as well as by external laws and government actions, whether wanted or not. Our survey data can help identify the elements that enter the picture, as they have done in these experiments, but they cannot lead to simple predictions about outcomes. If the experiments are repeated over time, however, it should be possible to measure changes in the balance of the forces.

Of course, neighborhood integration, or indeed an even broader perspective on racial integration, omits other major issues of race in America. Not even mentioned in the evidence just reviewed are the social and economic obstacles faced by a substantial proportion of the black population, obstacles that may have little to do directly with issues of integration. Most relevant here from our earlier chapters and from writings by other social scientists are findings about white explanations for black disadvantage (see Kluegel and Smith 1986). It is particularly important to recall that racial discrimination is not seen by whites as the major factor in racial inequalities, despite the evidence of continuing discrimination. Furthermore, there are signs that whites increasingly believe that discrimination has virtually disappeared in the United States, or has now been reversed and favors African Americans. This leads to even more emphasis on the attribution of all problems to failures of black motivation and effort. Only with regard to making greater investment in education does there seem to be much white support for further intervention to improve the standard of living and opportunities for blacks at the bottom of the socioeconomic ladder. Since the majority of blacks do believe that discrimination is still a major factor in American racial relations, both the causes and the solutions for racial problems in the United States are perceived from quite different perspectives by most members of the two racial groups.

Epilogue: History and Social Psychology

. . . The data and interpretations we have discussed are efforts to view from one vantage point the complex and changing meaning of race in America.

When President Truman's Committee on Civil Rights reported in 1947, Jim Crow laws were still alive and constituted in many places an unchallenged set of social rules. Black Americans were second-class citizens, mostly impoverished, poorly educated, and widely disdained by the white majority. The prosperity and social dislocation brought about by World War II, the importance of the black labor force to the war effort, the growing influence of black urban voters within the Democratic coalition, the heightened impatience of black leaders (driven in part by their increasingly urban, educated, and politicized constituencies), and the need of the United States as the self-proclaimed leader of the Free World to rid itself of racial bigotry, were some of the factors that placed a challenge to Jim Crow high on the national

agenda. Other evidence suggests that this was also part of a larger ideological transformation that affected attitudes toward other minorities as well (for example, toward Jews, and eventually toward women and other disadvantaged groups).

Many of those who tried to understand America's glaring racial discrimination in the postwar era emphasized prejudice as the core of the problem. Prejudice, in turn, was regarded primarily as the product of ignorance. From this standpoint, prejudice could be attacked by teaching tolerance and by facilitating contact between blacks and whites in ways not structured by Jim Crow. The emotional roots of white contempt for blacks depended upon the regular symbolic humbling of blacks through petty exclusions, separate and starkly unequal facilities, a demand for traditional deference, and even lynchings in parts of the country. If the government could intervene in these practices, both the symbolic and the concrete social relations required by Jim Crow would be weakened. Contact on new terms would gradually reduce the level of prejudice and set us on the path toward becoming a color-blind society.

In many ways, this analysis of the American racial dilemma bore fruit in the 1940s, 1950s, and early 1960s. The slow, steady decline of norms supporting prejudice is consistent with, for example, the strong educational differentials in response to racial principle items, the liberalizing impact of the cohort-replacement process, the positive changes in the attitudes of individuals, the nearly complete rejection of biological arguments for white racial superiority, and an increasing recognition of the importance of black-white relations to U.S. world leadership. It is understandable that one of the most forceful governmental statements opposing segregation came from nine white male Supreme Court justices in 1954—individuals likely to be sensitive to changes in both social norms and national needs insofar as they can be construed as relevant to law.

These shifts in public opinion seemed to support Myrdal's view that, at core, Americans maintained a value for equality (surely equality before the law). This value would break through more plainly as soon as the intellectual and emotional underpinnings of prejudice began to dissipate. Government played its role through court decisions (like the *Brown* ruling) and executive actions (like Truman's order to desegregate the armed forces). Prejudice seemed an enemy that could be overcome. Categorical inequalities overtly premised upon notions of innate inferiority fell as the government intervened, backed by public attitudes that not only increasingly rejected such views but were moving toward full endorsement of the principle of racial equality. This process was fueled by insistent and often integrated civil rights demonstrations, which not only focused national attention upon black grievances but served an educational purpose and pressed the government to act more urgently in racial matters.

There was a growing consensus to all of this, and in the late 1960s the government began to move beyond the paradigm of reducing prejudice through ending discrimination—though this goal had by no means been achieved—to the often implicit paradigm of increasing the economic and political standing of blacks; that is, to treating the race problem as a matter of social inequality as well as of prejudice. But during these same years, the civil rights movement was becoming not only more visible but also more variegated. In many of its important branches, it was no longer itself integrated. The thrust of the demand for change was decreasingly toward integration and increasingly toward redistribution. The sudden outburst and then decline of the riots and the Black Power Movement; the assassination of Martin Luther King, which si-

lenced the most widely listened to voice for nonviolent racial change; and Richard Nixon's victory over Hubert Humphrey, the national white political figure most closely associated with civil rights legislation, were both symbols and partial causes of a halt, or at least a pause, in government action in favor of racial equality. The later election of more conservative presidents and legislatures placed further brakes on change.

Moreover, the issues shifted from removing an absolute color bar to eliminating the pervasive inequalities that the bar had furthered. There were no longer struggles over allowing *one* or *two* black students to enroll at a public university; instead, there were struggles over city-wide desegregation plans. Our data indicate that survey researchers were attentive, though not always quickly so, to these changing issues and social contexts. Questions on the implementation of racial principles were asked beginning around 1964. The results showed that enthusiasm for large-scale policy change was less strong than the support of broad principles of equal treatment. Still later, questions concerning the causes of black disadvantage and questions about strong forms of affirmative action issues were added, in both cases producing evidence that a large part of the white population was reluctant to go beyond supporting more general principles of equal treatment, and indeed was coming to think that those principles were already in effect throughout much of the society.

The changes of the past half century are seldom of transparent meaning for students of racial attitudes. Nonetheless, our examination of the attitudinal record—this venture in historical social psychology—points to some important considerations for those grappling with racial inequality today. To the extent that public attitudes are important, it is possible to bring societal pressure, indeed public shame, on any white American who clearly discriminates against blacks, provided that the discrimination can be brought to light, as in videotapes of police beatings, audiotapes of corporate obstruction of equal opportunity laws, or public remarks that impugn African Americans. The application of the term "racist" to a person or an organization is itself a severe sanction in most parts of the country. Such pressures will not always be successful, but they often are and they are not a trivial force. Moreover, there is willingness to go further and to elect black leaders, provided they offer assurance that their concern clearly includes whites equally with blacks.[8]

But beyond the enforcement of norms of equal treatment, there seems to be little public support for any but remedial forms of special training to help disadvantaged African Americans, or perhaps for broader programs that can be described in ways that do not emphasize race. It is not likely that affirmative action plans that call for clear forms of preferential treatment of blacks will survive for long outside a few insulated places (for example, academic departments in liberal universities), except where clear and recent discrimination has been documented. Exactly how the black underclass can escape from its present cycle of poverty, crime, and hopelessness is unclear, and this in turn adds to the alienation of the black middle class from white society.[9] There is no real sign that the larger white public is prepared to see norms of equal treatment reconceptualized to support substantial steps toward drastically reducing economic and social inequality in this country. It would be worth trying to present questions to the white population that succinctly point to the basic problem of disappearing employment opportunities for lower-class blacks in central cities: perhaps then there would be greater support for government efforts to create substitute training and jobs.

A final word about our own research. In terms of the data on which this book is based, we must recognize that not only do our attitude questions measure changes over time, but the changes themselves affect our surveys. We pointed out earlier that a question first asked in 1964 about federal intervention in the area of employment may have shifted somewhat in meaning over the years. It asked: "Should the government in Washington see to it that black people get fair treatment in jobs, or is this not the federal government's business?" When the question was first posed in the mid-1960s, "fair treatment" could be assumed to refer to "equal treatment," but by the 1990s "fair treatment" could be taken by some proportion of the population—both black and white—to mean affirmative action in the sense of compensatory preferential treatment. In this case, and in some others as well, surveys reflect change not only in terms of the movement of percentages across tables and graphs, but by the new meanings that questions take on for those who are asked to answer them.[10]

NOTES

1. Rigid categorization can be enforced even where the physical signs of race lead in an opposite direction, as in the occasional case of someone who seems white in appearance but either elects or is forced to be viewed as black. One striking account can be found in an autobiography by Williams (1995) with the subtitle *The True Story of a White Boy Who Discovered He Was Black.* The clear contrast of racial identity with the "symbolic ethnicity" of many white Americans is discussed by Waters (1990).
2. The normative change was clearly a broad one that extended to other minorities besides blacks (see, for example, Stember et al. 1966).
3. Ironically, one recent commentator considers the success of some blacks and the portrayal of friendly black-white relations in the media to be dangerous, since they allow the white population to ignore the tremendous

obstacles faced by the larger black lower class (DeMott 1995).

4. The experiments were first reported in Schuman and Bobo (1988), which includes some additional analysis.

5. All Jewish respondents were omitted from this comparison and from the one described below.

6. Despite these results, which are important in themselves, we suspect that our hypothesis about the difference between application of the norm of equal treatment to a single person and application to a large group is likely to prove correct, and that our original way of operationalizing that distinction was not adequate, perhaps because the Open Housing question itself is already written with something of a focus on individuals.

7. We do not actually ask the same white individuals both types of questions, but since the two samples were drawn to represent the same population of individuals, one can reasonably draw this inference.

8. Of course, there are individuals and groups, mostly well outside the American mainstream, that continue to be openly racist in words and actions. But despite the individual tragedies that such virulent racism can produce—as in the random assassination of a black couple in 1995 by two army paratroopers—one should not give extreme deviance a larger social significance than it deserves. One can see this even more clearly in the case of another group: Jews represent a minority that has been highly successful and highly assimilated in almost all respects, yet one that is still the target of hostility and occasional violence from scattered extremist groups. Sometimes such hostility occurs because of progress toward incorporating a racial or ethnic minority into the larger society, which becomes a threat to those who feel themselves estranged from what they see the society becoming (Green et al. 1996).

9. A short but sensitive description of this complex of problems is found in Anderson's (1990) ethnographic account of one such area in Philadelphia, and of course there are other large-scale research efforts such as Thomas Wilson (1996).

10. We also increasingly feel that questions asked on racial issues have lacked useful variation in format. More scales like that for the NORC Residential Choice question would be of value, and more attention should be paid experimentally to what happens when middle alternative and no opinion options are offered. Scattered throughout this book are hints that a good deal can be learned about the *strength* of racial attitudes by such variations, as distinct from simple dichotomous questions and also from the multi-item indexes sometimes made up of such questions.

REFERENCES

ADORNO, T. W., E. FRENKEL-BRUNSWIK, D. J. LEVINSON, and R. N. SANFORD. 1950. *The Authoritarian Personality.* New York: Harper.

ANDERSON, ELIJAH. 1990. *Streetwise: Race, Class, and Change in an Urban Community.* Chicago: University of Chicago Press.

DEMOTT, BENJAMIN. 1995. *The Trouble with Friendship: Why Americans Can't Think Straight About Race.* New York: Atlantic Monthly Press.

FARLEY, REYNOLDS, HOWARD SCHUMAN, SUZANNE BIANCHI, DIANE COLASANTO, and SHIRLEY HATCHETT. 1978. "Chocolate City, Vanilla Suburbs: Will the Trend Toward Racially Separate Communities Continue?" *Social Science Research* 7:319–44.

FARLEY, REYNOLDS, CHARLOTTE STEEH, MARIA KRYSAN, TARA JACKSON, and KEITH REEVES. 1994. "Stereotypes and Segregation: Neighborhoods in the Detroit Area." *American Journal of Sociology* 100:750–80.

GREEN, DONALD P., ROBERT P. ABELSON, MARGARET GARNER, JOHN GLASER, ANDREW RICH, and AMY RICHMOND. 1996. "Cultural Encroachment and Hate Crime: An Ecological Analysis of Crossburnings in North Carolina." Paper presented at the Annual Meeting of the American Criminal Justice Society, Boston.

HACKER, ANDREW. 1995. *Two Nations: Black and White, Separate, Hostile, Unequal.* New York: Ballantine Books.

HARRISON, RODERICK J., and CLAUDETTE E. BENNETT. 1995. "Racial and Ethnic Diversity." In *State of the Union: America in the 1990s,* Vol. 2: *Social Trends,* edited by Reynolds Farley. New York: Russell Sage Foundation.

LEVINE, ROBERT E. 1971. "The Silent Majority: Neither Simple nor Simple Minded." *Public Opinion Quarterly* 33:571–77.

MYRDAL, GUNNAR. 1994. *An American Dilemma: The Negro Problem and Modern Democracy.* 2 vols. New York: Harper & Brothers.

ROTHBART, MYRON. 1976. "Achieving Racial Equality: An Analysis of Resistance to Social Reform." In *Towards the Elimination of Racism.* New York: Pergamon Press.

SCHUMAN, HOWARD, and LAWRENCE BOBO. 1988. "Survey-Based Experiments on White Racial Attitudes Toward Residential Integration." *American Journal of Sociology* 94:273–99.

SCHUMAN, HOWARD, and MICHAEL P. JOHNSON. 1976. "Attitudes and Behavior." *Annual Review of Sociology* 6:161–207.

SMITH, A. WADE. 1981. "Racial Tolerance as a Function of Group Position." *American Sociological Review* 46:558–73.

STEMBER, CHARLES HERBERT, et al. 1996. *Jews in the Mind of America.* Boston: Beacon Press.

WATERS, MARY C. 1990. *Ethnic Options: Choosing Identities in America.* Berkeley: University of California Press.

WILLIAMS, GREGORY HOWARD. 1995. *Life in the Color Line: The True Story of a Boy Who Discovered That He Was Black.* New York: Dutton.

WILSON, THOMAS. 1996. "Cohort and Prejudice: Whites' Attitudes Toward Blacks, Hispanics, Jews, and Asians." *Public Opinion Quarterly* 60:253–74.

10

RACE PREJUDICE AS A SENSE OF GROUP POSITION

Herbert Blumer

In this paper I am proposing an approach to the study of race prejudice different from that which dominates contemporary scholarly thought on this topic. My thesis is that race prejudice exists basically in a sense of group position rather than in a set of feelings which members of one racial group have toward the members of another racial group. This different way of viewing race prejudice shifts study and analysis from a preoccupation with feelings as lodged in individuals to a concern with the relationship of racial groups. It also shifts scholarly treatment away from individual lines of experience and focuses interest on the collective process by which a racial group comes to define and redefine another racial group. Such shifts, I believe, will yield a more realistic and penetrating understanding of race prejudice.

There can be little question that the rather vast literature on race prejudice is dominated by the idea that such prejudice exists fundamentally as a feeling or set of feelings lodged in the individual. It is usually depicted as consisting of feelings such as antipathy, hostility, hatred, intolerance, and aggressiveness. Accordingly, the task of scientific inquiry becomes two-fold. On one hand, there is a need to identify the feelings which make up race prejudice—to see how they fit together and how they are supported by other psychological elements, such as mythical beliefs. On the other hand, there is need of showing how the feeling complex has come into being. Thus, some scholars trace the complex feelings back chiefly to innate dispositions; some trace it to personality composition, such as authoritarian personality; and others regard the feelings of prejudice as being formed

Herbert Blumer "Race Prejudice as a Sense of Group Position" from *The Pacific Sociological Review,* Vol. 1, No. 1, Spring 1958, pp. 3–7. Reprinted by permission of the Pacific Sociological Association.

through social experience. However different may be the contentions regarding the make-up of racial prejudice and the way in which it may come into existence, these contentions are alike in locating prejudice in the realm of individual feeling. This is clearly true of the work of psychologists, psychiatrists, and social psychologists, and tends to be predominantly the case in the work of sociologists.

Unfortunately, this customary way of viewing race prejudice overlooks and obscures the fact that race prejudice is fundamentally a matter of relationship between racial groups. A little reflective thought should make this very clear. Race prejudice presupposes, necessarily, that racially prejudiced individuals think of themselves as belonging to a given racial group. It means, also, that they assign to other racial groups those against whom they are prejudiced. Thus, logically and actually, a scheme of racial identification is necessary as a framework for racial prejudice. Moreover, such identification involves the formation of an image or a conception of one's own racial group and of another racial group, inevitably in terms of the relationship of such groups. To fail to see that racial prejudice is a matter (a) of the racial identification made of oneself and of others, and (b) of the way in which the identified groups are conceived in relation to each other, is to miss what is logically and actually basic. One should keep clearly in mind that people necessarily come to identify themselves as belonging to a racial group; such identification is not spontaneous or inevitable but a result of experience. Further, one must realize that the kind of picture which a racial group forms of itself and the kind of picture which it may form of others are similarly products of experience. Hence, such pictures are variable, just as the lines of experience which produce them are variable.

The body of feelings which scholars, today, are so inclined to regard as constituting the substance of race prejudice is actually a resultant of the way in which given racial groups conceive of themselves and of others. A basic understanding of race prejudice must be sought in the process by which racial groups form images of themselves and of others. This process, as I hope to show, is fundamentally *a collective process*. It operates chiefly through the public media in which individuals who are accepted as the spokesmen of a racial group characterize publicly another racial group. To characterize another racial group is, by opposition, to define one's own group. This is equivalent to placing the two groups in relation to each other, or defining their positions *vis-à-vis* each other. It is the *sense of social position* emerging from this collective process of characterization which provides the basis of race prejudice. The following discussion will consider important facets of this matter.

I would like to begin by discussing several of the important feelings that enter into race prejudice. This discussion will reveal how fundamentally racial feelings point to and depend on a positional arrangement of the racial groups. In this discussion I will confine myself to such feelings in the case of a dominant racial group.

There are four basic types of feeling that seem to be always present in race prejudice in the dominant group. They are (1) a feeling of superiority, (2) a feeling that the subordinate race is intrinsically different and alien, (3) a feeling of proprietary claim to certain areas of privilege and advantage, and (4) a fear and suspicion that the subordinate race harbors designs on the prerogatives of the dominant race. A few words about each of these four feelings will suffice.

In race prejudice there is a self-assured feeling on the part of the dominant racial group of being naturally superior or better. This is commonly shown in a disparagement of the qualities of the subordinate racial group. Condemnatory or debasing traits, such as laziness, dishonesty, greediness, unreliability, stupidity, deceit and immorality, are usually imputed to it. The second feeling, that the subordinate race is an alien and fundamentally different stock, is likewise always present. "They are not of our kind" is a common way in which this is likely to be expressed. It is this feeling that reflects, justifies, and promotes the social exclusion of the subordinate racial group. The combination of these two feelings of superiority and of distinctiveness can easily give rise to feelings of aversion and even antipathy. But in themselves they do not form prejudice. We have to introduce the third and fourth types of feeling.

The third feeling, the sense of proprietary claim, is of crucial importance. It is the feeling on the part of the dominant group of being entitled to either exclusive or prior rights in many important areas of life. The range of such exclusive or prior claims may be wide, covering the ownership of property such as choice lands and sites; the right to certain jobs, occupations or professions; the claim to certain kinds of industry or lines of business; the claim to certain positions of control and decision-making as in government and law; the right to exclusive membership in given institutions such as schools, churches and recreational institutions; the claim to certain positions of social prestige and to the display of the symbols and accoutrements of these positions; and the claim to certain areas of intimacy and privacy. The feeling of such proprietary claims is exceedingly strong in race prejudice. Again, however, this feeling even in combination with the feeling of superiority and the feeling of distinctiveness does not explain race prejudice. These three feelings are present frequently in societies showing no prejudice, as in certain forms of feudalism, in caste relations, in societies of chiefs and commoners, and under many settled relations of conquerors and conquered. Where claims are solidified into a structure which

is accepted or respected by all, there seems to be no group prejudice.

The remaining feeling essential to race prejudice is a fear or apprehension that the subordinate racial group is threatening, or will threaten, the position of the dominant group. Thus, acts or suspected acts that are interpreted as an attack on the natural superiority of the dominant group, or an intrusion into their sphere of group exclusiveness, or an encroachment on their area of proprietary claim are crucial in arousing and fashioning race prejudice. These acts mean "getting out of place."

It should be clear that these four basic feelings of race prejudice definitely refer to a positional arrangement of the racial groups. The feeling of superiority places the subordinate people *below;* the feeling of alienation places them *beyond;* the feeling of proprietary claim excludes them from the prerogatives of position; and the fear of encroachment is an emotional recoil from the endangering of group position. As these features suggest, the positional relation of the two racial groups is crucial in race prejudice. The dominant group is not concerned with the subordinate group as such but it is deeply concerned with its position *vis-à-vis* the subordinate group. This is epitomized in the key and universal expression that a given race is all right in "its place." The sense of group position is the very heart of the relation of the dominant to the subordinate group. It supplies the dominant group with its framework of perception, its standard of judgment, its patterns of sensitivity, and its emotional proclivities.

It is important to recognize that this sense of group position transcends the feelings of the individual members of the dominant group, giving such members a common orientation that is not otherwise to be found in separate feelings and views. There is likely to be considerable difference between the ways in which the individual members of the dominant group think and feel about the subordinate group. Some may feel bitter and hostile, with strong antipathies, with an exalted sense of superiority and with a lot of spite; others may have charitable and protective feelings, marked by a sense of piety and tinctured by benevolence; others may be condescending and reflect mild contempt; and others may be disposed to politeness and considerateness with no feelings of truculence. These are only a few of many different patterns of feeling to be found among members of the dominant racial group. What gives a common dimension to them is a sense of the social position of their group. Whether the members be humane, or callous, cultured or unlettered, liberal or reactionary, powerful or impotent, arrogant or humble, rich or poor, honorable or dishonorable—all are led, by virtue of sharing the sense of group position, to similar individual positions.

The sense of group position is a general kind of orientation. It is a general feeling without being reducible to specific feelings like hatred, hostility or antipathy. It is also a general understanding without being composed of any set of specific beliefs. On the social psychological side it cannot be equated to a sense of social status as ordinarily conceived, for it refers not merely to vertical positioning but to many other lines of position independent of the vertical dimension. Sociologically it is not a mere reflection of the objective relations between racial groups. Rather, it stands for "what ought to be" rather than for "what is." It is a sense of where the two racial groups *belong*.

In its own way, the sense of group position is a norm and imperative—indeed a very powerful one. It guides, incites, cows, and coerces. It should be borne in mind that this sense of group position stands for and involves a fundamental kind of group affiliation for the members of the dominant racial group. To the extent they recognize or feel themselves as belonging to that group they will automatically come under the influence of the sense of position held by that group. Thus, even though given individual members may have personal views and feelings different from the sense of group position, they will have to conjure with the sense of group position held by their racial group. If the sense of position is strong, to act contrary to it is to risk a feeling of self-alienation and to face the possibility of ostracism. I am trying to suggest, accordingly, that the locus of race prejudice is not in the area of individual feeling but in the definition of the respective positions of the racial groups.

The source of race prejudice lies in a felt challenge to this sense of group position. The challenge, one must recognize, may come in many different ways. It may be in the form of an affront to feelings of group superiority; it may be in the form of attempts at familiarity or transgressing the boundary line of group exclusiveness; it may be in the form of encroachment at countless points of proprietary claim; it may be a challenge to power and privilege; it may take the form of economic competition. Race prejudice is a defensive reaction to such challenging of the sense of group position. It consists of the disturbed feelings, usually of marked hostility, that are thereby aroused. As such, race prejudice is a protective device. It functions, however shortsightedly, to preserve the integrity and the position of the dominant group.

It is crucially important to recognize that the sense of group position is not a mere summation of the feelings of position such as might be developed independently by separate individuals as they come to compare themselves with given individuals of the subordinate race. The sense of group position refers to the position of group to group, not to that of individual to individual. Thus, *vis-à-vis* the subordinate racial group the unlettered individual with low status in the dominant racial group has a sense of group position common to that of the elite of his group. By virtue of sharing this sense of position such an individual, despite his low status, feels that members of the subordinate group, however distinguished and accomplished, are somehow inferior, alien, and properly restricted in the area of claims. He forms his conception as a representative of the dominant group; he treats individual members of the subordinate group as representative of that group.

An analysis of how the sense of group position is formed should start with a clear recognition that it is an historical product. It is set originally by conditions of initial contact. Prestige, power, possession of skill, numbers, original self-conceptions, aims, designs and opportunities are a few of the factors that may fashion the original sense of group position. Subsequent experience in the relation of the two racial groups, especially in the area of claims, opportunities and advantages, may mould the sense of group position in many diverse ways. Further, the sense of group position may be intensified or weakened, brought to sharp focus or dulled. It may be deeply entrenched and tenaciously resist change for long periods of time. Or it may never take root. It may undergo quick growth and vigorous expansion, or it may dwindle away through slow-moving erosion. It may be firm or soft, acute or dull, continuous or intermittent. In short, viewed comparatively, the sense of group position is very variable.

However variable its particular career, the sense of group position is clearly formed by a running process in which the dominant racial group is led to define and redefine the subordinate racial group and the relations between them. There are two important aspects of this process of definition that I wish to single out for consideration.

First, the process of definition occurs obviously through complex interaction and communication between the members of the dominant group. Leaders, prestige bearers, officials, group agents, dominant individuals and ordinary laymen present to one another characterizations of the subordinate group and express their feelings and ideas on the relations. Through talk, tales, stories, gossip, anecdotes, messages, pronouncements, news accounts, orations, sermons, preachments and the like definitions are presented and feelings are expressed. In this usually vast and complex interaction separate views run against one another, influence one another, modify each other, incite one another and fuse together in new forms. Correspondingly, feelings which are expressed meet, stimulate each other, feed on each other, intensify each other and emerge in new patterns. Currents of view and currents of feeling come into being; sweeping along to positions of dominance and serving as polar points for the organization of thought and sentiment. If the interaction becomes increasingly circular and reinforcing, devoid of serious inner opposition, such currents grow, fuse and become strengthened. It is through such a process that a collective image of the subordinate group is formed and a sense of group position is set. The evidence of such a process is glaring when one reviews the history of any racial arrangement marked by prejudice.

Such a complex process of mutual interaction with its different lines and degrees of formation gives the lie to the many schemes which would lodge the cause of race prejudice in the make-up of the individual— whether in the form of innate disposition, constitutional make-up, personality structure, or direct personal experience with members of the other race. The collective image and feelings in race prejudice are forged out of a complicated social process in which the individual is himself shaped and organized. The scheme, so popular today, which would trace race prejudice to a so-called authoritarian personality shows a grievous misunderstanding of the simple essentials of the collective process that leads to a sense of group position.

The second important aspect of the process of group definition is that it is necessarily concerned with *an abstract image* of the subordinate racial group. The subordinate racial group is defined as if it were an entity or whole. This entity or whole—like the Negro race, or the Japanese, or the Jews—is necessarily an abstraction, never coming within the perception of any of the senses. While actual encounters are with individuals, the picture formed of the racial group is necessarily of a vast entity which spreads out far beyond such individuals and transcends experience with such individuals. The implications of the fact that the collective image is of an abstract group are of crucial significance. I would like to note four of these implications.

First, the building of the image of the abstract group takes place in the area of the remote and not of the near. It is not the experience with concrete individuals in daily association that gives rise to the definitions of the extended, abstract group. Such immediate experience is usually regulated and orderly. Even where such immediate experience is disrupted the new definitions which are formed are limited to the individuals involved. The collective image of the abstract group grows up not by generalizing from experiences gained in close, first-hand contacts but through the transcending characterizations that are made of the group as an entity. Thus, one must seek the central stream of definition in those areas where the dominant group as such is characterizing the subordinate group as such. This occurs in the "public arena" wherein the spokesmen appear as representatives and agents of the dominant group. The extended public arena is constituted by such things as legislative assemblies, public meetings, conventions, the press, and the printed word. What goes on in this public arena attracts the attention of large numbers of the dominant group and is felt as the voice and action of the group as such.

Second, the definitions that are forged in the public arena center, obviously, about matters that are felt to be of major importance. Thus, we are led to recognize the crucial role of the "big event" in developing a conception of the subordinate racial group. The happening that seems momentous, that touches deep sentiments, that seems to raise fundamental questions about relations, and that awakens strong feelings of identification with one's racial group is the kind of event that is central in the formation of the racial image. Here, again, we note the relative unimportance of the huge bulk of experiences coming from daily contact with individuals of the subordinate group. It is the events seemingly loaded with great collective significance that are the focal points of the public discussion. The definition of these events is chiefly responsible for the development of a racial image and of the sense of group position. When this public discussion takes the form of a denunciation of the subordinate racial group, signifying that it is unfit and a threat, the discussion becomes particularly potent in shaping the sense of social position.

Third, the major influence in public discussion is exercised by individuals and groups who have the public ear and who are felt to have standing, prestige, authority and power. Intellectual and social elites, public figures of prominence, and leaders of powerful organizations are likely to be the key figures in the formation of the sense of group position and in the characterization of the subordinate group. It is well to note this in view of the not infrequent tendency of students to regard race prejudice as growing out of the multiplicity of experiences and attitudes of the bulk of the people.

Fourth, we also need to perceive the appreciable opportunity that is given to strong interest groups in directing the lines of discussion and setting the interpretations that arise in such discussion. Their self-interests may dictate the kind of position they wish the dominant racial group to enjoy. It may be a position which enables them to retain certain advantages, or even more to gain still greater advantages. Hence, they may be vigorous in seeking to manufacture events to attract public attention and to set lines of issue in such a way as to predetermine interpretations favorable to their interests. The role of strongly organized groups seeking to further special interest is usually central in the formation of collective images of abstract groups. Historical records of major instances of race relations, as in our South, or in South Africa, or in Europe in the case of the Jew, or on the West Coast in the case of the Japanese, show the formidable part played by interest groups in defining the subordinate racial group.

I conclude this highly condensed paper with two further observations that may throw additional light on the relation of the sense of group position to race prejudice. Race prejudice becomes entrenched and tenacious to the extent the prevailing social order is rooted in the sense of social position. This has been true of the historic South in our country. In such a social order race prejudice tends to become chronic and impermeable to change. In other places the social order may be affected only to a limited extent by the sense of group position held by the dominant racial group. This I think has been true usually in the case of anti-Semitism in Europe and this country. Under these conditions the sense of group position tends to be weaker and more vulnerable. In turn, race prejudice has a much more variable and intermittent career, usually becoming pronounced only as a consequence of grave disorganizing events that allow for the formation of a scapegoat.

This leads me to my final observation which in a measure is an indirect summary. The sense of group position dissolves and race prejudice declines when the process of running definition does not keep abreast of major shifts in the social order. When events touching on relations are not treated as "big events" and hence do not set crucial issues in the arena of public discussion; or when the elite leaders or spokesmen do not define such big events vehemently or adversely; or where they define them in the direction of racial harmony; or when there is a paucity of strong interest groups seeking to build up a strong adverse image for special advantage—under such conditions the sense of group position recedes and race prejudice declines.

The clear implication of my discussion is that the proper and fruitful area in which race prejudice should be studied is the collective process through which a sense of group position is formed. To seek, instead, to understand it or to handle it in the arena of individual feeling and of individual experience seems to me to be clearly misdirected.

11

DISCRIMINATION AND THE AMERICAN CREED

Robert K. Merton

The primary function of the sociologist is to search out the determinants and consequences of diverse forms of social behavior. To the extent that he succeeds in fulfilling this role, he clarifies the alternatives of organized social action in a given situation and of the probable outcome of each. To this extent, there is no sharp distinction between pure research and applied research. Rather, the difference is one between research with direct implications for particular problems of social action and research which is remote from these problems. Not infrequently, basic research which has succeeded only in clearing up previously confused concepts may have an immediate bearing upon the problems of men in society to a degree not approximated by applied research oriented exclusively to these problems. At least, this is the assumption underlying the present paper: clarification of apparently unclear and confused concepts in the sphere of race and ethnic relations is a step necessarily prior to the devising of effective programs for reducing intergroup conflict and for promoting equitable access to economic and social opportunities. . . .

The American Creed: As Cultural Ideal, Personal Belief and Practice

The American creed as set forth in the Declaration of Independence, the preamble of the Constitution and the Bill of Rights has often been misstated. This part of the cultural heritage does *not* include the patently false assertion that all men are created equal in capacity or endowment. It does *not* imply that an Einstein and a moron are equal in intellectual capacity or that Joe Louis and a small, frail Columbia professor (or a Mississippian Congressman) are equally endowed with brawny arms harboring muscles as strong as iron bands. It does *not* proclaim universal equality of innate intellectual or physical endowment.

Instead, the creed asserts the indefeasible principle of the human right to full equity—the right of equitable access to justice, freedom and opportunity, irrespective of race or religion or ethnic origin. It proclaims further the universalist doctrine of the dignity of the individual, irrespective of the groups of which he is a part. It is a creed announcing full moral equities for all, not an absurd myth affirming the equality of intellectual and physical capacity of all men everywhere. And it goes on to say that though men differ in innate endowment, they do so as individuals, not by virtue of their group memberships.

Viewed sociologically, the creed is a set of values and precepts embedded in American culture, to which Americans are expected to conform. It is a complex of affirmations, rooted in the historical past and ceremonially celebrated in the present, partly enacted in the laws of the land and partly not. Like all creeds, it is a profession of faith, a part of cultural tradition sanctified by the larger traditions of which it is a part.

It would be a mistaken sociological assertion, however, to suggest that the creed is a fixed and static cultural constant, unmodified in the course of time, just as it would be an error to imply that as an integral part of culture, it evenly blankets all subcultures of the national society. It is indeed dynamic, subject to change and in turn promoting change in other spheres of culture and society. It is, moreover, unevenly distributed throughout the society, being institutionalized as an integral part of local culture in some regions of the society and rejected in others.

. . . Learned men and men in high public positions have repeatedly observed and deplored the disparity between ethos and behavior in the sphere of race and ethnic relations. In his magisterial volumes on the American Negro, for example, Gunnar Myrdal called this gulf between creed and conduct "an American dilemma," and centered his attention on the prospect of narrowing or closing the gap. The President's Committee on Civil Rights, in their report to the nation, and . . . President [Truman] himself, in a message to Congress, have called public attention to this "serious gap between our ideals and some of our practices."

But as valid as these observations may be, they tend so to simplify the relations between creed and conduct as to be seriously misleading both for social policy and for social science. All these high authorities notwithstanding, the problems of racial and ethnic inequities are not expressible as a discrepancy between high cultural principles and low social conduct. It is a relation not between two variables, official creed and private practice, but between three: first, the cultural creed honored in cultural tradition and partly enacted into law; second, the beliefs and attitudes of individuals regarding the principles of the creed; and third, the actual practices of individuals with reference to it.

Once we substitute these three variables of cultural ideal, belief and actual practice for the customary distinction between the two variables of cultural ideals and actual practices, the entire formulation of the problem becomes changed. We escape from the virtuous but ineffectual impasse of deploring the alleged hypocrisy of many Americans into the more difficult but potentially effectual realm of analyzing the problem in hand.

To describe the problem and to proceed to its analysis, it is necessary to consider the official creed, individuals' beliefs and attitudes concerning the creed, and their actual behavior. Once stated, the distinctions are readily applicable. Individuals may *recognize* the creed as part of a cultural tradition, *without having any private conviction of its moral validity or its binding quality.* Thus, so far as the beliefs of individuals are concerned, we can identify two types: those who genuinely believe in the creed and those who do not (although some of these may, on public or ceremonial occasions, profess adherence to its principles). Similarly, with respect to actual practices: conduct may or may not conform to the creed. But, and this is the salient consideration: *conduct may or may not conform with individuals' own beliefs concerning the moral claims of all men to equal opportunity.*

Stated in formal sociological terms, this asserts that attitudes and overt behavior vary independently. *Prejudicial attitudes need not coincide with discriminatory behavior.* The implications of this statement can be drawn out in terms of a logical syntax whereby the variables are diversely combined, as can be seen in the following typology.

By exploring the interrelations between prejudice and discrimination, we can identify four major types in terms of their attitudes toward the creed and their behavior with respect to it. Each type is found in every region and social class, though in varying numbers. By examining each type, we shall be better prepared to understand their interdependence and the appropriate types of action for curbing ethnic discrimination. The folklabels for each type are intended to aid in their prompt recognition.

Type I: The Unprejudiced Non-Discriminator or All-Weather Liberal

These are the racial and ethnic liberals who adhere to the creed in both belief and practice. They are neither prejudiced nor given to discrimination. Their orientation toward the creed is fixed and stable. Whatever the environing situation, they are likely to abide by their beliefs: hence, the *all-weather* liberal.

This is, of course, the strategic group which *can* act as the spearhead for the progressive extension of the creed into effective practice. They represent the solid foundation both for the measure of ethnic equities which now exist and for the future enlargement of these equities. Integrated with the creed in both belief and practice, they would seem most motivated to influence others toward the same democratic outlook. They represent a reservoir of culturally legitimatized goodwill which can be channeled into an active program for extending belief in the creed and conformity with it in practice.

Most important, as we shall see presently, the all-weather liberals comprise the group which can so reward others for conforming with the creed, as to transform deviants into conformists. They alone can provide the positive social environment for the other types who will no longer find it ex-

pedient or rewarding to retain their prejudices or discriminatory practices.

But though the ethnic liberal is a *potential* force for the successive extension of the American creed, he does not fully realize this potentiality in actual fact, for a variety of reasons. Among the limitations on effective action are several fallacies to which the ethnic liberal seems peculiarly subject. First among these is the *fallacy of group soliloquies.* Ethnic liberals are busily engaged in talking to themselves. Repeatedly, the same groups of like-minded liberals seek each other out, hold periodic meetings in which they engage in mutual exhortation and thus lend social and psychological support to one another. But however much these unwittingly self-selected audiences may reinforce the creed among themselves, they do not thus appreciably diffuse the creed in belief or practice to groups which depart from it in one respect or the other.

More, these group soliloquies in which there is typically wholehearted agreement among fellow-liberals tend to promote another fallacy limiting effective action. This is the *fallacy of unanimity.* Continued association with like-minded individuals tends to produce the illusion that a large measure of consensus has been achieved in the community at large. The unanimity regarding essential cultural axioms which obtains in these small groups provokes an overestimation of the strength of the movement and of its effective inroads upon the larger population which does not necessarily share these creedal axioms. Many also mistake participation in the groups of like-minded individuals for effective action. Discussion accordingly takes the place of action. The reinforcement of the creed for oneself is mistaken for the extension of the creed among those outside the limited circle of ethnic liberals.

Arising from adherence to the creed is a third limitation upon effective action, the *fallacy of privatized solutions* to the problem. The ethnic liberal, precisely because he is at one with the American creed, may rest content with his own individual behavior and thus see no need to do anything about the problem at large. Since his own spiritual house is in order, he is not motivated by guilt or shame to work on a collective problem. The very freedom of the liberal from guilt thus prompts him to secede from any *collective* effort to set the national house in order. He essays a *private* solution to a *social* problem. He assumes that numerous individual adjustments will serve in place of a collective adjustment. His outlook, compounded of good moral philosophy but poor sociology, holds that each individual must put his own house in order and fails to recognize that privatized solutions cannot be effected for problems which are essentially social in nature. For clearly, if each person *were* motivated to abide by the American creed, the problem would not be likely to exist in the first place. It is only when a social environment is established by conformists to the creed that deviants can in due course be brought to modify their behavior in the direction of conformity. But this "environment" can be constituted only through collective effort and not through private adherence to a public creed. Thus we have the paradox that the clear conscience of many ethnic liberals may promote the very social situation which permits deviations from the creed to continue unchecked. Privatized liberalism invites social inaction. Accordingly, there appears the phenomenon of the inactive or passive liberal, himself at spiritual ease, neither prejudiced nor discriminatory, but in a measure tending to contribute to the persistence of prejudice and discrimination through his very inaction.

The fallacies of group soliloquy, unanimity and privatized solutions thus operate to make the potential strength of the ethnic liberals unrealized in practice.

It is only by first recognizing these limitations that the liberal can hope to overcome them. With some hesitancy, one may suggest initial policies for curbing the scope of the three fallacies. The fallacy of group soliloquies can be removed only by having ethnic liberals enter into organized groups not comprised merely by fellow-liberals. This exacts a heavy price on the liberal. It means that he faces initial opposition and resistance rather than prompt consensus. It entails giving up the gratifications of consistent group support.

The fallacy of unanimity can in turn be reduced by coming to see that American society often provides large rewards for those who express their ethnic prejudice in discrimination. Only if the balance of rewards, material and psychological, is modified will behavior be modified. Sheer exhortation and propaganda are not enough. Exhortation verges on a belief in magic if it is not supported by appropriate changes in the social environment to make conformity with the exhortation rewarding.

Finally, the fallacy of privatized solutions requires the militant liberal to motivate the passive liberal to collective effort, possibly by inducing in him a sense of guilt for his unwitting contribution to the problems of ethnic inequities through his own systematic inaction.

One may suggest a unifying theme for the ethnic liberal: goodwill is not enough to modify social reality. It is only when this goodwill is harnessed to social-psychological realism that it can be used to reach cultural objectives.

Type II: The Unprejudiced Discriminator or Fair-Weather Liberal

The fair-weather liberal is the man of expediency who, despite his own freedom from prejudice, supports discriminatory practices when it is the easier or more profitable course. His expediency may take the form of holding his silence and thus implicitly acquiescing in expressions of ethnic prejudice by others or in the practice of discrimination by others. This is the expediency of the timid: the liberal who hesitates to speak up against discrimination for fear he might lose status or be otherwise penalized by his prejudiced associates. Or his expediency may take the form of grasping at advantages in social and economic competition deriving solely from the ethnic status of competitors. This is the expediency of the self-assertive: the employer, himself not an anti-Semite or Negrophobe, who refuses to hire Jewish or Negro workers because "it might hurt business"; the trade union leader who expediently advocates racial discrimination in order not to lose the support of powerful Negrophobes in his union.

In varying degrees, the fair-weather liberal suffers from guilt and shame for departing from his own effective beliefs in the American creed. Each deviation through which he derives a limited reward from passively acquiescing in or actively supporting discrimination contributes cumulatively to this fund of guilt. He is, therefore, peculiarly vulnerable to the efforts of the all-weather liberal who would help him bring his conduct into accord with his beliefs, thus removing this source of guilt. He is the most amenable to cure, because basically he wants to be cured. His is a split conscience which motivates him to cooperate actively with those who will help remove the source of internal conflict. He thus represents the strategic group promising the largest returns for the least effort. Persistent re-affirmation of the creed will only intensify his conflict; but a long regimen in a favorable social climate can be expected to transform the fair-weather liberal into an all-weather liberal.

Type III: The Prejudiced Non-Discriminator or Fair-Weather Illiberal

The fair-weather illiberal is the reluctant conformist to the creed, the man of prejudice who does not believe in the creed but conforms to it in practice through fear of sanctions which might otherwise be visited upon him. You know him well: the prejudiced employer who discriminates against racial or ethnic groups until a Fair Employment Practice Commission, able and willing to enforce the law, puts the fear of punishment into him; the trade union leader, himself deeply prejudiced, who does away with Jim Crow in his union because the rank-and-file demands that it be done away with; the businessman who foregoes his own prejudices when he finds a profitable market among the very people he hates, fears or despises; the timid bigot who will not express his prejudices when he is in the presence of powerful men who vigorously and effectively affirm their belief in the American creed.

It should be clear that the fair-weather illiberal is the precise counterpart of the fair-weather liberal. Both are men of expediency, to be sure, but expediency dictates different courses of behavior in the two cases. The timid bigot conforms to the creed only when there is danger or loss in deviations, just as the timid liberal deviates from the creed when there is danger or loss in conforming. *Superficial similarity in behavior of the two in the same situation should not be permitted to cloak a basic difference in the meaning of this outwardly similar behavior,* a difference which is as important for social policy as it is for social science. Whereas the timid bigot is under strain when he conforms to the creed, the timid liberal is under strain when he deviates. For ethnic prejudice has deep roots in the character structure of the fair-weather bigot, and this will find overt expression unless there are powerful countervailing forces, institutional, legal and interpersonal. He does not accept the moral legitimacy of the creed; he conforms because he must, and will cease to conform when the pressure is removed. The fair-weather liberal, on the other hand, is effectively committed to the creed and does not require strong institutional pressure to conform; continuing interpersonal relations with all-weather liberals may be sufficient.

This is the one critical point at which the traditional formulation of the problem of ethnic discrimination as a departure from the creed can lead to serious errors of theory and practice. Overt behavioral deviation (or conformity) may signify importantly different situations, depending upon the underlying motivations. Knowing simply that ethnic discrimination is rife in a community does not, therefore, point to appropriate lines of social policy. It is necessary to know also the distribution of ethnic prejudices and basic motivations for these prejudices as well. Communities with the same amount of overt discrimination may represent vastly different types of problems, dependent on whether the population is comprised by a large nucleus of fair-weather liberals ready to abandon their discriminatory practices under slight interpersonal pressure or a large nucleus of fair-weather illiberals who will abandon discrimination only if major changes in the local institutional setting can be effected. Any statement of the problem as a gulf between creedal ideals and prevailing practice is thus seen to be overly-simplified in the precise sense of masking this decisive difference between the type of discrimination exhibited by the fair-weather liberal and by the fair-weather illiberal. That the gulf-between-ideal-and-practice does not adequately describe the nature of the ethnic problem will become more apparent as we turn to the fourth type in our inventory of prejudice and discrimination.

Type IV: The Prejudiced Discriminator or the All-Weather Illiberal

This type, too, is not unknown to you. He is the confirmed illiberal, the bigot pure and unashamed, the man of prejudice consistent in his departure from the American creed. In some measure, he is found everywhere in the land, though in varying numbers. He derives large social and psychological gains from his conviction that "any white man (including the village idiot) is 'better' than any nigger (including George Washington Carver)." He considers differential treatment of Negro and white not as "discrimination," in the sense of unfair treatment, but as "discriminating," in the sense of showing acute discernment. For him, it is as clear that one "ought" to accord a Negro and a white different treatment in a wide diversity of situations, as it is clear to the population at large that one "ought" to accord a child and an adult different treatment in many situations.

This illustrates anew my reason for questioning the applicability of the unusual formula of the American dilemma as a gap between lofty creed and low conduct. For the confirmed illiberal, ethnic discrimination does *not* represent a discrepancy between *his* ideals and *his* behavior. His ideals proclaim the right, even the duty, of discrimination. Accordingly, his behavior does not entail a sense of social deviation, with the resultant strains which this would involve. The ethnic illiberal is as much a conformist as the ethnic liberal. He is merely conforming to a different cultural and institutional pattern which is centered, not about the creed, but about a doctrine of essential inequality of status ascribed to those of diverse ethnic and racial origins. To overlook this is to overlook the well-known *fact* that our national culture is divided into a number of local subcultures which are not consistent among themselves in all respects. And again, to fail to take this fact of different subcultures into account is to open the door for all manner of errors of social policy in attempting to control the problems of racial and ethnic discrimination.

This view of the all-weather illiberal has one immediate implication with wide bearing upon social policies and sociological theory oriented toward the problem of discrimination. The extreme importance of the social surroundings of the confirmed illiberal at once becomes apparent. For as these surroundings vary, so, in some measure, does the problem of the consistent illiberal. The illiberal, living in those cultural regions where the American creed is widely repudiated and is no effective part of the subculture, has his private ethnic attitudes and practices supported by the local mores, the local institutions and the local power-structure. The illiberal in cultural areas dominated by a large measure of adherence to the American creed is in a social environment where he is isolated and receives small social support for his beliefs and practices. In both instances, the *individual* is an illiberal, to be sure, but he represents two significantly different *sociological types*. In the first instance, he is a *social conformist,* with strong moral and institutional reinforcement, whereas in the second, he is a *social deviant,* lacking strong social corroboration. In the one case, his discrimination involves him in further integration with his network of social relations; in the other, it threatens to cut him off from sustaining interpersonal ties. In the first cultural context, personal change in his ethnic behavior involves alienating himself from people significant to him; in the second context, this change of personal outlook may mean fuller incorporation in groups meaningful to him. In the first situation, modification of his ethnic views requires him to take the path of greatest resistance whereas in the second, it may mean the path of least resistance. From all this, we may surmise that any social policy aimed at changing the behavior and perhaps the attitudes of the all-weather illiberal will have to take into account the cultural and social structure of the area in which he lives. . . .

Implications of the Typology for Social Policy

. . . In approaching problems of policy, two things are plain. First, these should be considered from the standpoint of the militant ethnic liberal, for he alone is sufficiently motivated to engage in positive action for the reduction of ethnic discrimination. And second, the fair-weather liberal, the fair-weather illiberal and the all-weather illiberal represent types differing sufficiently to require diverse kinds of treatment.

Treatment of the Fair-Weather Liberal

The fair-weather liberal, it will be remembered, discriminates only when it appears expedient to do so, and experiences some measure of guilt for deviating from his own belief in the American creed. He suffers from this conflict between conscience and conduct. Accordingly, he is a relatively easy target for the all-weather liberal. He represents the strategic group promising the largest immediate returns for the least effort. Recognition of this type defines the first task for the militant liberal who would enter into a collective effort to make the creed a viable and effective set of social norms rather than a ceremonial myth. . . .

Since the fair-weather liberal discriminates only when it seems rewarding to do so, the crucial need is so to change social situations that there are few occasions in which discrimination proves rewarding and many in which it does not. This would suggest that ethnic liberals self-consciously and deliberately seek to draw into the social groups where they constitute a comfortable majority a number of the "expedient discriminators." This would serve to counteract the dangers of self-selection through which liberals come to associate primarily with like-minded individuals. It would, further, provide an interpersonal and social environment for the fair-weather liberal in which he would find substantial social and psychological gains from abiding by his own beliefs, gains which would more than offset the rewards attendant upon occasional discrimination. It appears that men do not long persist in behavior which lacks social corroboration.

We have much to learn about the role of numbers and proportions in determining the behavior of members of a group. But it seems that individuals generally act differently when they are numbered among a minority rather than the majority. This is not to say that minorities abdicate their practices in the face of a contrary-acting majority, but only that the same people are subjected to different strains and pressures according to whether they are included in the majority or the minority. And the fair-weather liberal who finds himself associated with militant ethnic liberals may be expected to forego his occasional deviations into discrimination; he may move from category II into category I. . . .

Treatment of the Fair-Weather Illiberal

Because his *beliefs* correspond to those of the full-fledged liberal, the fair-weather liberal can rather readily be drawn into an interpersonal environment constituted by those of a comparable turn of mind. This would be more difficult for the fair-weather illiberal, whose beliefs are so fully at odds with those of ethnic liberals that he may, at first, only be alienated by association with them. If the initial tactic for the fair-weather liberal, therefore, is a change in interpersonal environment, the seemingly most appropriate tactic for the fair-weather illiberal is a change in the institutional and legal environment. It is, indeed, probably this type which liberals implicitly have in mind when they expect significant changes in behavior to result from the introduction of controls on ethnic discrimination into the legal machinery of our society.

For this type—and it is a major limitation for planning policies of control that we do not know his numbers or his distribution in the country—it would seem that the most effective tactic is the institution of legal controls administered with strict efficiency. This would presumably reduce the amount of *discrimination* practiced by the fair-weather illiberal, though it might *initially* enhance rather than reduce his *prejudices*. . . .

A second prevalent tactic for modifying the prejudice of the fair-weather illiberal is that of seeking to draw him into interethnic groups explicitly formed for the promotion of tolerance. This, too, seems largely ineffectual, since the deeply prejudiced individual will not enter into such groups of his own volition. As a consequence of this process of self-selection, these tolerance groups soon come to be comprised by the very ethnic liberals who initiated the enterprise.

This barrier of self-selection can be partially hurdled only if the ethnic illiberals are brought into continued association with militant liberals in groups devoted to significant common values, quite remote from objectives of ethnic equity as such. Thus, as our Columbia-Lavanburg researches have found, many fair-weather illiberals *will* live in interracial housing projects in order to enjoy the rewards of superior housing at a given rental. And some of the illiberals thus brought into personal contact with various ethnic groups under the auspices of prestigeful militant liberals come to modify their prejudices. It is, apparently, only through interethnic collaboration, initially enforced by pressures of the situation, for immediate and significant objectives (other than tolerance) that the self-insulation of the fair-weather illiberal from rewarding interethnic contacts can be removed.

But however difficult it may presently be to affect the *prejudicial sentiments* of the fair-weather illiberal, his *discriminatory practices* can be lessened by the uniform, prompt and prestigeful use of legal and institutional sanctions. The critical problem is to ascertain the proportions of fair-weather and all-weather illiberals in a given local population in order to have some clue to the probable effectiveness or ineffectiveness of anti-discrimination legislation.

Treatment of the All-Weather Illiberal

It is, of course, the hitherto confirmed illiberal, persistently translating his prejudices into active discrimination, who represents the most difficult problem. But though he requires longer and more careful treatment, it is possible that he is not beyond change. In every instance, his social surroundings must be assiduously taken into account. It makes a peculiarly large difference whether he is in a cultural region of bigotry or in a predominantly "liberal" area, given over to verbal adherence to the American creed, at the very least. As this cultural climate varies, so must the prescription for his cure and the prognosis for a relatively quick or long delayed recovery.

In an unfavorable cultural climate—and this does not necessarily exclude the benign regions of the Far South—the immediate resort will probably have to be that of working through legal and administrative federal controls over extreme discrimination, with full recognition that, in all probability, these regulations will be systematically evaded for some time to come. In such cultural regions, we may expect nullification of the law as the common practice, perhaps as common as was the case in the nation at large

with respect to the Eighteenth Amendment, often with the connivance of local officers of the law. The large gap between the new law and local mores will not *at once* produce significant change of prevailing practices; token punishments of violations will probably be more common than effective control. At best, one may assume that significant change will be fitful, and excruciatingly slow. But secular changes in the economy may in due course lend support to the new legal framework of control over discrimination. As the economic shoe pinches because the illiberals do not fully mobilize the resources of industrial manpower nor extend their local markets through equitable wage-payments, they may slowly abandon some discriminatory practices as they come to find that these do not always pay—even the discriminator. So far as discrimination is concerned, organized counteraction is possible and some small results may be expected. But it would seem that wishes father thoughts, when one expects basic changes in the immediate future in these regions of institutionalized discrimination.

The situation is somewhat different with regard to the scattered, rather than aggregated, ethnic illiberals found here and there throughout the country. Here the mores and a social organization oriented toward the American creed still have some measure of prestige and the resources of a majority of liberals can be mobilized to isolate the illiberal. In these surroundings, it is possible to move the all-weather illiberal toward Type III—he can be brought to conform with institutional regulations, even though he does not surrender his prejudices. And once he has entered upon this role of the dissident but conforming individual, the remedial program designed for the fair-weather illiberal would be in order.

12

CAUSES OF PREJUDICE

Elliot Aronson

As we have seen, one determinant of prejudice in a person is a need for self-justification. . . . we have seen that, if we have done something cruel to a person or a group of people, we derogate that person or group in order to justify our cruelty. If we can convince ourselves that a group is unworthy, subhuman, stupid, or immoral, it helps *us* to keep from feeling immoral if we enslave members of that group, deprive them of a decent education, or murder them. We can then continue to go to church and to feel like good Christians, because it isn't a fellow human we've hurt. Indeed, if we're skillful enough, we can even convince ourselves that the barbaric slaying of old men, women, and children is a Christian virtue—as the crusaders did when, on the way to the holy land, they butchered European Jews in the name of the Prince of Peace. Again, as we have seen, this form of self-justification serves to intensify subsequent brutality.

Of course, there are other human needs in addition to self-justification. For example, there are status and power needs. Thus, an individual who is low on the socioeconomic hierarchy may need the presence of a downtrodden minority group in order to be able to feel superior to somebody. Several studies have shown that a good predictor of prejudice is whether or not a person's social status is low or declining. Regardless of whether it is prejudiced against blacks[1] or

against Jews,[2] if a person's social status is low or declining, that individual is apt to be more prejudiced than someone whose social status is high or rising. It has been found that people who are at or near the bottom in terms of education, income, and occupation not only are the highest in their dislike of blacks but also are the ones most likely to resort to violence in order to prevent the desegregation of schools.[3]

These findings raise some interesting questions. Are people of low socioeconomic and educational status more prejudiced because (1) they need someone to feel superior to, (2) they most keenly feel competition for jobs from minority-group members, (3) they are more frustrated than most people and therefore more aggressive, or (4) their lack of education increases the probability of their taking a simplistic stereotypical view of the world? It is difficult to disentangle these variables, but it appears that each of these phenomena contributes to prejudice. Indeed, there is no single cause of prejudice. Prejudice is determined by a great many factors. Let's look at some of these major determinants.

. . . We will look at four basic causes of prejudice: (1) economic and political competition or conflict, (2) displaced aggression, (3) personality needs, and (4) conformity to existing social norms. These four causes are not mutually exclusive—indeed, they may all operate at once—but it would be helpful to determine how important each cause is, because any action we are apt to recommend in an attempt to reduce prejudice will depend on what we believe to be the major cause of prejudice. Thus, for example, if I believe bigotry is deeply ingrained in the human personality, I might throw my hands up in despair and conclude that, in the absence of deep psychotherapy, the majority of prejudiced people will always be prejudiced. This would lead me to scoff at attempts to reduce prejudice by reducing competitiveness or by attempting to counteract the pressures of conformity.

Economic and Political Competition

Prejudice can be considered to be the result of economic and political forces. According to this view, given that resources are limited, the dominant group might attempt to exploit or derogate a minority group in order to gain some material advantage. Prejudiced attitudes tend to increase when times are tense and there is conflict over mutually exclusive goals. This is true whether the goals are economic, political, or ideological. Thus, prejudice has existed between Anglo and Mexican-American migrant workers as a function of a limited number of jobs, between Arabs and Israelis over disputed territory, and between Northerners and Southerners over the abolition of slavery. The economic advantages of discrimination are all too clear when one looks at the success certain craft unions have had, over the years, in denying membership to women and members of ethnic minorities, thus keeping them out of the relatively high-paying occupations the unions control. For example, the decade between the mid-1950s and the mid-1960s was one of great political and legal advancement for the civil rights movement. Yet in 1966 only 2.7 percent of union-controlled apprenticeships were filled with black workers—an increase of only 1 percent over the preceding ten years. Moreover, in the mid-1960s, the U.S. Department of Labor surveyed four major cities in search of minority-group members serving as apprentices among union plumbers, steamfitters, sheetmetal workers, stone masons, lathers, painters, glaziers, and operating engineers. In the four cities, they failed to find a single black person thus employed. Clearly, prejudice pays off for some people.[4] While the 1970s and 1980s have produced significant changes in many of these statistics, they also show that the situation remains far from equitable for minority groups.

Discrimination, prejudice, and negative stereotyping increase sharply as competition for scarce jobs increases. In one of his classic early studies of prejudice in a small industrial town, John Dollard documented the fact that, although there was initially no discernible prejudice against Germans in the town, it came about as jobs became scarce:

> Local whites largely drawn from the surrounding farms manifested considerable direct aggression toward the newcomers. Scornful and derogatory opinions were expressed about these Germans, and the native whites had a satisfying sense of superiority toward them. . . . The chief element in the permission to be aggressive against the Germans was rivalry for jobs and status in the local woodenware plants. The native whites felt definitely crowded for their jobs by the entering German groups and in case of bad times had a chance to blame the Germans who by their presence provided more competitors for the scarcer jobs. There seemed to be no traditional pattern of prejudice against Germans unless the skeletal suspicion against all outgroupers (always present) can be invoked in its place.[5]

Similarly, the prejudice, violence, and negative stereotyping directed against Chinese immigrants in the United States fluctuated wildly throughout the nineteenth century—spurred largely by changes in economic competition. For example, when the Chinese were attempting to mine gold in California, they were described as "depraved and vicious . . . gross gluttons . . . bloodthirsty and inhuman."[6] However, just a decade later, when they were willing to accept dangerous and arduous work building the transcontinental railroad—work that Caucasian Americans were unwilling to undertake—they were generally regarded as sober, industrious, and law-abiding. Indeed, Charles Crocker, one of the western railroad tycoons, wrote: "They are equal to the best white men. . . . They are very trusty, very intelligent and they live up to their contracts."[7] After the completion of the railroad, however, jobs became more scarce; moreover, when the Civil War ended, there was an influx of former soldiers into an already tight job market. This was immediately followed by a dramatic increase in negative attitudes toward the Chinese: The stereotype changed to "criminal," "conniving," "crafty," and "stupid."

These data suggest that competition and conflict breed prejudice. Moreover, this phenomenon transcends mere historical significance—it seems to have enduring psychological effects as well. In a survey conducted in the 1970s, most anti-black prejudice was found in groups that were just one rung above the blacks socioeconomically. And, as we might expect, this tendency was most pronounced in situations in which whites and blacks were in close competition for jobs.[8] At the same time, there is some ambiguity in interpreting the data, because in some instances the variables of competition are intertwined with such variables as educational level and family background.

In order to determine whether competition causes prejudice in and of itself, an experiment is needed. But how can we proceed? Well, if conflict and competition lead to prejudice, it should be possible to produce prejudice in the laboratory. This can be done by the simple device of (1) randomly assigning people of differing backgrounds to one of two groups, (2) making those two groups distinguishable in some arbitrary way, (3) putting those groups into a situation in which they are in competition with each other, and (4) looking for evidence of prejudice. Such an experiment was conducted by Muzafer Sherif and his colleagues[9] in the natural environment of a Boy Scout camp. The subjects were normal, well-adjusted, twelve-year-old boys who were randomly assigned to one of two groups, the *Eagles* and the *Rattlers*. Within each group, the youngsters were taught to cooperate. This was largely done through arranging activities that made each group highly interdependent. For example, within each group, individuals cooperated in building a diving board for the swimming facility, preparing group meals, building a rope bridge, and so on.

After a strong feeling of cohesiveness developed within each group, the stage was set for conflict. The researchers arranged this by setting up a series of competitive activities in which the two groups were pitted against each other in such games as football, baseball, and tug-of-war. In order to increase the tension, prizes were awarded to the winning team. This resulted in some hostility and ill will during the games. In addition, the investigators devised rather diabolical devices for putting the groups into situations specifically designed to promote conflict. In one such situation, a camp party was arranged. The investigators set it up so that the *Eagles* were allowed to arrive a good deal earlier than the *Rattlers*. In addition, the refreshments consisted of two vastly different kinds of food: About half the food was fresh, appealing, and appetizing; the other half was squashed, ugly, and unappetizing. Perhaps because of the general competitiveness that already existed, the early arrivers confiscated most of the appealing refreshments, leaving only the less interesting, less appetizing, squashed, and damaged food for their adversaries. When the *Rattlers* finally arrived and saw how they had been taken advantage of, they were understandably annoyed—so annoyed they began to call the exploitive group rather uncomplimentary names. Because the *Eagles* believed they deserved what they got (first come, first served), they resented this treatment and responded in kind. Name calling escalated into food throwing, and within a very short time a full-scale riot was in progress.

Following this incident, competitive games were eliminated and a great deal of social contact was initiated. Once hostility had been aroused, however, simply eliminating the competition did not eliminate the hostility. Indeed, hostility continued to escalate, even when the two groups were engaged in such benign activities as sitting around watching movies. Eventually, the investigators succeeded in reducing the hostility. Exactly how this was accomplished will be discussed later. . . .

The "Scapegoat" Theory of Prejudice

In [an earlier discussion] . . . I made the point that aggression is caused, in part, by frustration and such other unpleasant or aversive situations as pain or boredom. . . . We saw [that] there is a strong tendency for a frustrated individual to lash out at the cause of his or her frustration. Frequently, however, the cause of a person's frustration is either too big or too vague for direct retaliation. For example, if a six-year-old boy is humiliated by his teacher, how can he fight back? The teacher has too much power. But this frustration may increase the probability of his aggressing against a less powerful bystander—even if the bystander has noth-

ing to do with his pain. By the same token, if there is mass unemployment, who is the frustrated, unemployed worker going to strike out against—the economic system? The system is much too big and much too vague. It would be more convenient if the unemployed worker could find something or someone less vague and more concrete to blame. The president? He's concrete, all right, but also much too powerful to strike at with impunity.

The ancient Hebrews had a custom that is noteworthy in this context. During the days of atonement, a priest placed his hands on the head of a goat while reciting the sins of the people. This symbolically transferred the sin and evil from the people to the goat. The goat was then allowed to escape into the wilderness, thus cleansing the community of sin. The animal was called a scapegoat. In modern times the term *scapegoat* has been used to describe a relatively powerless innocent who is made to take the blame for something that is not his or her fault. Unfortunately, the individual is not allowed to escape into the wilderness but is usually subjected to cruelty or even death. Thus, if people are unemployed, or if inflation has depleted their savings, they can't very easily beat up on the economic system—but they can find a scapegoat. In Nazi Germany, it was the Jews; in nineteenth-century California, it was Chinese immigrants; in the rural South, it was black people. Some years ago, Carl Hovland and Robert Sears[10] found that, in the period between 1882 and 1930, they could predict the number of lynchings in the South in a given year from a knowledge of the price of cotton during that year. As the price of cotton dropped, the number of lynchings increased. In short, as people experienced an economic depression, they probably experienced a great many frustrations. The frustrations apparently resulted in an increase in lynchings and other crimes of violence.

Otto Klineberg,[11] a social psychologist with a special interest in the cross-cultural aspects of prejudice, describes a unique scapegoating situation in Japan. The Eta or Burakumin are a group of two million outcasts, scattered throughout Japan. They are considered unclean and fit only for certain undesirable occupations. As you might imagine, the Eta usually live in poor, slum areas. Their IQ scores are, on average, sixteen points lower than that of other Japanese. Eta children are absent from school more often and their delinquency rate is three times higher than other Japanese children. For a non-Eta to marry an Eta is taboo, although there is some "passing." For an Eta to "pass" is relatively easy because there are *no inherited racial or physical differences* between the Eta and other Japanese. The Eta are an invisible race—an outgroup defined more by social class than physical characteristics. They can only be identified because of their distinctive speech pattern (which has developed from years of nonassociation with other Japanese) and their identity papers. Although the historical origins of the Eta are unclear, they probably occupied the lower rungs of the socioeconomic ladder until an economic depression led to their complete expulsion from Japanese society. Now the Japanese consider the Eta to be "innately inferior," thus justifying further scapegoating and discrimination.

It is difficult to understand how the lynching of blacks or the mistreatment of the Eta could be due only to economic competition. There is a great deal of emotion in these actions that suggests the presence of deeper psychological factors in addition to economics. Similarly, the zeal with which Nazis carried out their attempt to erase all members of the Jewish ethnic group (regardless of economic status) strongly suggests that the phenomenon was not exclusively economic or political, but was (at least in part) psychological.[12] Firmer evidence for the existence of psychological processes comes from a well-controlled experiment by Neal Miller and Richard Bugelski.[13] Individuals were asked to state their feelings about various minority groups. Some of the subjects were then frustrated by being deprived of an opportunity to attend a film and were given an arduous and difficult series of tests instead. They were then asked to restate their feelings about the minority groups. These subjects showed some evidence of increased prejudicial responses following the frustrating experience. A control group that did not go through the frustrating experience did not undergo any change in prejudice.

Additional research has helped to pin down the phenomenon even more precisely. In one experiment,[14] white students were instructed to administer a series of electric shocks to another student as part of a learning experiment. The subjects had the prerogative to adjust the intensity of the shocks. In actuality, the learner was an accomplice of the experimenter who (of course) was not really connected to the apparatus. There were four conditions: The accomplice was either black or white; he was trained to be either friendly or insulting to the subject. When he was friendly, the subjects administered slightly *less* intense shocks to the black student; when he insulted them, they administered far more intense shocks to the black student than to the white student. In another experiment,[15] college students were subjected to a great deal of frustration. Some of these students were highly anti-Semitic; others were not. The subjects were then asked to write stories based on pictures they were shown. For some subjects, the characters in these pictures were assigned Jewish names; for others, they were not. There were two major findings: (1) After being frustrated, anti-Semitic subjects wrote stories that directed more aggression toward the Jewish characters than did people who were not anti-Semitic; and (2) there was no difference between the anti-Semitic students and the others when the characters they were writing about were not identified as Jewish. In short, frustration or anger leads to a specific aggression—aggression against an outgroup member.

The laboratory experiments help to clarify factors that seem to exist in the real world. The general picture of scapegoating that emerges is that individuals tend to displace aggression onto groups that are disliked, that are visible, and that are relatively powerless. Moreover, the form the aggression takes depends on what is allowed or approved by the ingroup in question: In society, lynchings of blacks and pogroms against Jews are not frequent occurrences, unless they are deemed appropriate by the dominant culture or subculture.

The Prejudiced Personality

As we have seen, the displacement of aggression onto scapegoats may be a human tendency, but not all people do it to a like degree. We have already identified socioeconomic status as a cause of prejudice. Also, we have seen that people who dislike members of a particular outgroup are more apt to displace aggression onto them than are people who do not dislike members of that outgroup. We can now carry this one step further. There is some evidence to support the notion of individual differences in a general tendency to hate. In other words, there are people who are predisposed toward being prejudiced, not solely because of immediate external influences, but because of the kind of people they are. Theodor Adorno and his associates[16] refer to these individuals as "authoritarian personalities." Basically, authoritarian personalities have the following characteristics. They tend to be rigid in their beliefs; they tend to possess "conventional" values; they are intolerant of weak-

ness (in themselves as well as in others); they tend to be highly punitive; they are suspicious; and they are respectful of authority to an unusual degree. The instrument developed to determine authoritarianism (called the *F* scale) measures the extent to which each person agrees or disagrees with such items as these:

1. Sex crimes such as rape and attacks on children deserve more than mere imprisonment; such criminals ought to be publicly whipped, or worse.

2. Most people don't realize how much our lives are controlled by plots hatched in secret places.

3. Obedience and respect for authority are the most important virtues children should learn.

A high degree of agreement with such items indicates authoritarianism. The major finding is that people who are high on authoritarianism do not simply dislike Jews or dislike blacks, but, rather, they show a consistently high degree of prejudice against *all* minority groups.

Through an intense clinical interview of people high and low on the *F* scale, Adorno and his colleagues have traced the development of this cluster of attitudes and values to early childhood experiences in families characterized by harsh and threatening parental discipline. Moreover, people high on the *F* scale tend to have parents who use love and its withdrawal as their major way of producing obedience. In general, authoritarian personalities, as children, tend to be very insecure and highly dependent on their parents; they fear their parents and feel unconscious hostility against them. This combination sets the stage for the emergence of an adult with a high degree of anger, which, because of fear and insecurity, takes the form of displaced aggression against powerless groups, while the individual maintains an outward respect for authority.

Although research on the authoritarian personality has added to our understanding of the possible dynamics of prejudice, it should be noted that the bulk of the data are correlational. That is, we know only that two variables are related—we cannot be certain what causes what. Consider, for example, the correlation between a person's score on the *F* scale and the specific socialization practices he or she was subjected to as a child. Although it is true that adults who are authoritarian and highly prejudiced had parents who tended to be harsh and to use "conditional love" as a socialization technique, it is not necessarily true that this is what *caused* them to develop into prejudiced people. It turns out that the parents of these people tend, themselves, to be highly prejudiced against minority groups. Accordingly, it may be that the development of prejudice in some people is due to conformity through the process of *identification*. . . . That is, a child might consciously pick up beliefs about minorities from his or her parents because the child identifies with them. This is quite different from, and much simpler than, the explanation offered by Adorno and his colleagues, which is based on the child's unconscious hostility and repressed fear of his or her parents.

This is not to imply that, for some people, prejudice is not rooted in unconscious childhood conflicts. Rather, it is to suggest that many people may have learned a wide array of prejudices on Mommy's or Daddy's knee. Moreover, some people may conform to prejudices that are limited and highly specific, depending upon the norms of their subculture. Let's take a closer look at the phenomenon of prejudice as an act of conformity.

Prejudice Through Conformity

It is frequently observed that there is more prejudice against blacks in the South than in the North. This often manifests itself in stronger attitudes against racial integration. For example, in 1942, only 4 percent of all southerners were in favor of the desegregation of transportation facilities, while 56 percent of all northerners were in favor of it.[17] Why? Was it because of economic competition? Probably not; there is more prejudice against blacks in those southern communities in which economic competition is low than in those northern communities in which economic competition is great. Are there relatively more authoritarian personalities in the South than in the North? No. Thomas Pettigrew[18] administered the *F* scale widely in the North and in the South and found the scores about equal for northerners and southerners. In addition, although there is more prejudice against blacks in the South, there is *less* prejudice against Jews in the South than there is in the nation as a whole; the prejudiced personality should be prejudiced against everybody—the southerner isn't.

How then do we account for the animosity toward blacks that exists in the South? It could be due to historical causes: the blacks were slaves, the Civil War was fought over the issue of slavery, and so on. This could have created the climate for greater prejudice. But what sustains this climate? One possible clue comes from the observation of some rather strange patterns of racial segregation in the South. One example, a group of coal miners in a small mining town in West Virginia, should suffice. The black miners and the white miners developed a pattern of living that consisted of total and complete integration while they were under the ground, and total and complete segregation while they were above the ground. How can we account for this inconsistency? If you truly hate someone, you want to keep away from him—why associate with him below the ground and not above the ground?

Pettigrew has suggested that the explanation for these phenomena is *conformity*. In this case, people are simply conforming to the norms that exist in their society (above the ground!). The historical events of the South set the stage for greater prejudice against blacks, but it is conformity that keeps it going. Indeed, Pettigrew believes that, although economic competition, frustration, and personality needs account for some prejudice, the greatest proportion of prejudiced behavior is a function of slavish conformity to social norms.

How can we be certain conformity is responsible? One way is to determine the relation between a person's prejudice and that person's general pattern of conformity. For example, a study of interracial tension in South Africa[19] showed that those individuals who were most likely to conform to a great variety of social norms also showed a higher degree of prejudice against blacks. In other words, if conformists are more prejudiced, the suggestion is that prejudice may be just another thing to conform to. Another way to determine the role of conformity is to see what happens to people's prejudice when they move to a different area of the country. If conformity is a factor in prejudice, we would expect individuals to show dramatic increases in their prejudice when they move into areas in which the norm is more prejudicial, and to show dramatic decreases when they are affected by a less prejudicial norm. And that is what happens. In one study, Jeanne Watson[20] found that people who had recently moved to New York City and had come into direct contact with anti-Semitic people became more anti-Semitic themselves. In another study, Pettigrew found that, as southerners entered the army and came into contact with a less discriminatory set of social norms, they became less prejudiced against blacks.

The pressure to conform can be relatively overt, as in the Asch experiment. On the other hand, conformity to a prejudicial norm might simply be due to the unavailability of accurate evidence and a prepon-

derance of misleading information. This can lead people to adopt negative attitudes on the basis of hearsay. Examples of this kind of stereotyping behavior abound in the literature. For example, consider Christopher Marlowe's *The Jew of Malta* or William Shakespeare's *The Merchant of Venice.* Both of these works depict the Jew as a conniving, money-hungry, cringing coward. We might be tempted to conclude that Marlowe and Shakespeare had had some unfortunate experiences with unsavory Jews, which resulted in these bitter and unflattering portraits—except for one thing: The Jews had been expelled from England some three hundred years before these works were written. Thus, it would seem that the only thing with which Marlowe and Shakespeare came into contact was a lingering stereotype. Tragically, their works not only reflected the stereotype but undoubtedly contributed to it as well.

Even casual exposure to bigotry can affect our attitudes and behavior toward a group that is the victim of prejudice. For example, research has demonstrated that merely overhearing someone use a derogatory label—such as a racial or ethnic epithet—toward a given group can increase our likelihood of viewing someone from that group—or someone merely *associated* with that group—in a negative light. In one experiment,[21] Shari Kirkland and her co-researchers asked subjects to read a transcript of a criminal trial in which a white defendant was represented by a black attorney, whose picture was attached to the trial transcript. While reading the transcript, the subject "overhears" a brief exchange between two experimental confederates, who are posing as subjects. Some subjects hear the first confederate call the black lawyer a "nigger," while other subjects hear the confederate call him a "shyster." In both conditions, the second confederate expresses agreement with the first confederate's derogatory opinion of the black lawyer. With this conformity dynamic in place, the experimenters then asked the subject to evaluate the attorney and the defendant. An analysis of these ratings revealed that subjects who overheard the racial slur rated the black lawyer more negatively than those who overheard a derisive comment that was not related to the lawyer's race. Moreover, the white defendant received particularly harsh verdicts and highly negative evaluations from subjects who heard the racial slur against the black attorney. This latter finding indicates that conformity to the prejudiced norms can have damaging effects that extend beyond the initial target of racism.

Bigoted attitudes can also be fostered intentionally by a bigoted society that institutionally supports these attitudes. For example, a society that supports the notion of segregation through law and custom is supporting the notion that one group is inferior to another. A more direct example: One investigator[22] interviewed white South Africans in an attempt to find reasons for their negative attitudes toward blacks. He found that the typical white South African was convinced that the great majority of crimes were committed by blacks. This was erroneous. How did such a misconception develop? The individuals reported they saw a great many black convicts working in public places—they never saw any white convicts. Doesn't this prove blacks are convicted of more crimes than whites? No. In fact, the rules forbade white convicts from working in public places! In short, a society can *create* prejudiced beliefs by its very institutions. In our own society, forcing blacks to ride in the back of the bus, keeping women out of certain clubs, preventing Jews from staying at exclusive hotels are all part of our recent history—and create the illusion of inferiority or unacceptability.

NOTES

1. J. Dollard, *Class and Caste in a Southern Town* (New Haven, CT: Yale University Press, 1987).

2. B. Bettelheim and M. Janowitz, *Social Change and Prejudice, Including Dynamics of Prejudice* (New York: Free Press, 1964).

3. M. Tumin, P. Barton, and B. Burrus, "Education, Prejudice, and Discrimination: A Study in Readiness for Desegregation," *American Sociological Review* 23 (1958):41–49.

4. M. Levitas, *America in Crisis* (New York: Holt, Rinehart & Winston, 1969).

5. J. Dollard, "Hostility and Fear in Social Life," *Social Forces* 17 (1938):15–26.

6. E. Roberts, quoted by P. Jacobs and S. Landau, *To Serve the Devil*, Vol. 2 (New York: Vintage Books, 1971), p. 71.

7. C. Crocker, quoted by Jacobs and Landau, *To Serve the Devil*, Vol. 2, p. 81.

8. A. Greeley and P. Sheatsley, "The Acceptance of Desegregation Continues to Advance," *Scientific America* 225(6) (1971):13–19; see also R. D. Vanneman and T. F. Pettigrew, "Race and Relative Deprivation in the Urban United States," *Race* 13 (1972):461–86.

9. M. Sherif, O. J. Harvey, B. J. White, W. Hood, and C. Sherif, *Intergroup Conflict and Cooperation: The Robbers Cave Experiment* (Norman: University of Oklahoma Institute of Intergroup Relations, 1961).

10. C. Hovland and R. Sears, "Minor Studies of Aggression: Correlation of Lynchings with Economic Indices," *Journal of Psychology* (1940):301–10.

11. O. Klineberg, "Black and White in International Perspective," *American Psychologist* 26 (1971):119–28.

12. A. Speer, *Inside the Third Reich: Memoirs,* trans. R. Winston and C. Winston (New York: Macmillan, 1970).

13. N. Miller and R. Bugelski, "Minor Studies in Aggression: The Influence of Frustrations Imposed by the In-group on Attitudes Expressed by the Out-group," *Journal of Psychology* 25 (1948):437–42.

14. R. Rogers and S. Prentice-Dunn, "Deindividuation and Anger-Mediated Interracial Aggression: Unmasking Regressive Racism," *Journal of Personality and Social Psychology* 41 (1981):63–73.

15. D. Weatherly, "Anti-Semitism and the Expression of Fantasy Aggression," *Journal of Abnormal and Social Psychology* 62 (1961): 454–57.

16. T. Adorno, E. Frenkel-Brunswick, D. Levinson, and R. N. Sanford, *The Authoritarian Personality* (New York: Harper, 1950).

17. Greeley and Sheatsley, "Acceptance of Desegregation."

18. T. F. Pettigrew, "Regional Differences in Anti-Negro Prejudice," *Journal of Abnormal and Social Psychology* 59 (1959):28–36.

19. T. F. Pettigrew, "Personality and Sociocultural Factors and Intergroup Attitudes: A Cross-National Comparison," *Journal of Conflict Resolution* 2 (1958):29–42.

20. J. Watson, "Some Social and Psychological Situations Related to Change in Attitude," *Human Relations* 3 (1950):15–56.

21. S. L. Kirkland, J. Greenberg, and T. Pyszczynski, "Further Evidence of the Deleterious Effects of Overheard Derogatory Ethnic Labels: Derogation Beyond the Target," *Personality and Social Psychology Bulletin* 13 (1987): 216–27.

22. I. MacCrone, *Race Attitudes in South Africa* (London: Oxford University Press, 1937).

13

BEYOND BLACK/WHITE
The Racisms of Our Time

Elizabeth Martínez

By Way of Introduction

Let me begin by admitting that I have an axe to grind. A bell to toll, a *grito* to shout, a banner to wave. The banner was fashioned during 10 years in the Black civil rights–human rights movement followed by 10 years in the Chicano *movimiento*. Those years taught that liberation has similar meanings in both histories: an end to racist oppression, the birth of collective self-respect, and a dream of social justice. Those years taught that alliances among progressive people of color can and must help realize the dream.

Such alliances require a knowledge and wisdom that we have yet to attain. For the present, it remains painful to see how divide-and-conquer strategies succeed among our peoples. It is painful to see how prejudice, resentment, petty competitiveness, and sheer ignorance fester. It is positively pitiful to see how often we echo Anglo stereotypes about one another.

All this suggests that we urgently need some fresh and fearless thinking about racism at this moment in history. Fresh thinking might begin with analyzing the strong tendency among Americans to frame racial issues in strictly Black-white terms. Do such terms make sense when changing demographics point to a U.S. population that will be 32% Latino, Asian/Pacific American, and Native American—that is, neither Black nor white—by the year 2050? Not to mention the increasing numbers of mixed people who incorporate two, three, or more "races" or nationalities? Don't we need to imagine multiple forms of racism rather than a single, Black-white model?

Practical questions related to the fight against racism also arise. Doesn't the exclusively Black-white framework discourage

Elizabeth Martínez, "Beyond Black/White: The Racisms of Our Time" from *Social Justice*, Vol. 20, Nos. 1–2, 1993. Reprinted by permission of Social Justice, Box 40601, San Francisco, CA 94140.

perception of common interests among people of color—primarily in the working class—and thus sustain White Supremacy? Doesn't the view of institutionalized racism as a problem experienced only by Black people isolate them from potential allies? Doesn't the Black-white definition encourage a tendency often found among people of color to spend too much energy understanding our lives in relation to Whiteness, obsessing about what the White will think? That tendency is inevitable in some ways: the locus of power over our lives has long been white (although big shifts have recently taken place in the color of capital) and the oppressed have always survived by becoming experts on the oppressor's ways. But that can become a prison of sorts, a trap of compulsive vigilance. Let us liberate ourselves, then, from the tunnel vision of Whiteness and behold the colors around us!

To criticize the Black-white framework is not simply a resentful demand from other people of color for equal sympathy, equal funding, equal clout, equal patronage. It is not simply us-too resentment at being ignored or minimized. It is not just another round of mindless competition in the victimhood tournament. Too often we make the categories of race, class, gender, sexuality, age, physical condition, etc., contend for the title of "most oppressed." Within "race," various population groups then compete for that top spot. Instead, we need to understand that various forms and histories of oppression exist. We need to recognize that they include differences in extent and intensity. Yet pursuing some hierarchy of competing oppressions leads us down dead-end streets where we will never find the linkage between oppressions or how to overcome them.

The goal in reexamining the Black-white definition is to find an effective strategy for vanquishing an evil that has expanded rather than diminished in recent years.

Three recent developments come to mind. First is the worldwide economic recession in which the increasingly grim struggle for sheer survival encourages the scapegoating of working-class people—especially immigrants, especially those of color—by other working-class people. This has become so widespread in the West that a Klan cross-burning in London's Trafalgar Square or on Paris' Champs Élysée doesn't seem hard to imagine. The globalization of racism is mounting rapidly.

Second, and relatedly, the reorganization of the international division of labor continues, with changing demands for workers that are affecting demographics everywhere. History tells us of the close relationship between capital's need for labor and racism. If that relationship changes, so may the nature of racism.

Finally, in the U.S., we have passed through a dozen years of powerful reaction against the civil-rights agenda set in the 1960s. This has combined with the recession's effects and other socioeconomic developments to make people go into a defensive, hunkering-down mode, each community on its own, at a time when we need more rather than less solidarity. Acts of racist violence now occur in communities that never saw them before (although they always could have happened). An intensification of racism is upon us.

We see it in the anti-immigrant emotions being whipped up and new divisions based on racism and nativism. We see escalating white fears of becoming the minority population, the minority power, after centuries of domination. As U.S. demographics change rapidly, as the "Latinization" of major regions and cities escalates, a cross fire of fears begins to crackle. In that climate the mass media breed both cynical hopelessness and fear. Look only at the October 1992 *Atlantic* magazine cover proclaiming "BLACKS

VS. BROWNS: Immigration and the New American Dilemma" for one chilling symptom of an assumed, inevitable hostility.

Today the task of building solidarity among people of color promises to be more necessary and difficult than ever. An exclusively Black-white definition of racism makes our task all the harder. That's the banner that will be raised here: an urgent need for 21st-century thinking, which can move us beyond the Black-white framework without negating its central, historical role in the construction of U.S. racism. We do need much more understanding of how racism and its effects developed, not only similarly, but also differently for different peoples according to whether they were victimized by genocide, enslavement, or colonization in various forms.

Greater solidarity among peoples of color must be hammered out, painstakingly. With solidarity a prize could be won even bigger than demolishing racism. The prize could be a U.S. society whose national identity not only ceases to be white, but also advances beyond "equality"—beyond a multiculturalism that gives people of color a respect equal to whites. Toni Morrison has written eloquently in *Playing in the Dark* of this goal from an Africanist perspective: "American means white, and Africanist people struggle to make the term applicable to themselves with ethnicity and hyphen after hyphen after hyphen. . . . In the scholarship on the formation of an American character [a] . . . major item to be added to the list must be an Africanist presence—decidedly not American, decidedly other" (Morrison 1992, p. 47).

We need to dream of replacing the white national identity with an identity grounded in cultures oriented to respect for all forms of life and balance rather than domination as their guiding star. Such cultures, whose roots rest in indigenous, precolonial societies of the Americas and Africa, can help define a new U.S. identity unshackled from the capitalist worldview. Still alive today, they color my banner bright.

Let us begin that dialogue about the exclusively Black-white model of racism and its effects with the question: does that definition prevail and, if so, why?

Alas, it does prevail. Major studies of "minorities" up to 1970 rarely contain more than a paragraph on our second largest "minority," Mexican-Americans (Blauner 1972, p. 165). In two dozen books of 1960s movement history, I found inadequate treatment of the Black Civil Rights Movement, but almost total silence about the Chicano, Native American, and Asian American movements of those years (Martínez 1989). Today, not a week goes by without a major media discussion of race and race relations that totally ignores the presence in U.S. society of Native Americans, Latinos, Asian/Pacific Americans, and Arab-Americans.

East Coast–based media and publishers are the worst offenders. Even a progressive magazine like *The Nation* can somehow publish a special issue entitled "The Assault on Equality: Race, Rights, and the New Orthodoxy" (December 9, 1991) containing only two brief phrases relating to people of color other than African-Americans in 27 pages. Outbreaks of Latino unrest or social uprising, such as we saw in the Mt. Pleasant section of Washington, D.C., make little if any dent. New York, that center of ideological influence, somehow remains indifferent to the fact that in 1991, Latinos totaled 24.4% of its population while Asians formed 6.9%.

Even in California, this most multinational of the states, where Latinos have always been the most numerous population of color, it is not rare for major reports on contemporary racial issues to stay strictly inside the Black-white framework. Journalists in San Francisco, a city almost half Latino or Asian/Pacific-American, can see no need to acknowledge "This article will be about African-Americans, only"—which would be quite acceptable—in articles on racial issues. At best we may hear that after-thought construction, "Blacks and other minorities."

Again, momentous events that speak to Latino experience of racist oppression fail to shake the prevailing view. Millions of Americans saw massive Latino participation in the April 1992 Los Angeles uprising on their TV screens. Studies show that, taken as a whole, the most heavily damaged areas of L.A. were 49% Latino, and the majority of people arrested were Latino (Pastor 1993). Yet the mass media and most people have continued to view that event as "a Black riot."

Predominantly Anglo left forces have not been much better than the mainstream and liberals. The most consistently myopic view could be heard from the Communist Party U.S.A., which has seen the African-American experience as the only model of racism. Left groups that adopted the Black Nation thesis rarely analyzed the validity of Chicano nationalism in the Southwest, or advocated giving lands back to the Native Americans, or questioned the "model minority" myth about Asian/Pacific Americans.

A semi-contemptuous indifference toward Latinos—to focus on this one group—has emanated from institutions in the dominant society for decades. Echoing this attitude are many individual Anglos. To cite a handful of personal experiences: Anglos will admit to having made a racist remark or gesture toward an African-American much more quickly than toward a Latino. Or if you bring up some Anglo's racist action toward a Latino, they will change the subject almost instantly to racism toward a Black person. Or they may respond to an account of police brutality toward Latinos with some remark of elusive relevance about Spanish crimes against indigenous people in the Americas.

A stunning ignorance also prevails. Race-relations scholar Robert (Bob) Blauner has rightly noted that:

> Even informed Anglos know almost nothing about La Raza, its historical experience, its present situation. . . . And the average citizen doesn't have the foggiest notion that Chicanos have been lynched in the Southwest and continue to be abused by the police, that an entire population has been exploited economically, dominated politically, and raped culturally. (Blauner 1972, p. 166)

Above all, there seems to be little comprehension of what it means to suffer total disenfranchisement in the most literal sense. Millions of Latinos, like many Asian/Pacific Americans, lack basic political rights. They are often extremely vulnerable to oppression and the most intense oppression occurs when people have problems of legal status. This means the borderlands, where vulnerability rests on having formal admission documents or not. Aside from South Africa's pass system, it is hard to imagine any mechanism in modern times so well designed to control, humiliate, and disempower vast numbers of workers than the border and its requirements.

Why the Black-White Framework?

Three of the reasons for the Black-white framework of racial issues seem obvious: numbers, geography, and history. African-Americans have long been the largest population of color in the U.S.; only recently has this begun to change. Also, African-Americans have long been found in sizable numbers in most of the United States, including major cities. On the other hand, Latinos—to focus on this group—are found primarily in the Southwest plus parts of the

Northwest and Midwest and they have been (wrongly) perceived as a primarily rural people—therefore of less note.

Historically, it has been only 150 years since the U.S. seized half of Mexico and incorporated those lands and their peoples into this nation. The Black/white relationship, on the other hand, has long been entrenched in the nation's collective memory. White enslavement of Black people together with white genocide against Native Americans provided the original models for racism as it developed here. Slavery and the struggle against it form a central theme in this country's only civil war—a prolonged, momentous conflict—and continuing Black rebellion. Enslaved Africans in the U.S. and African-Americans have created an unmatched history of massive, persistent, dramatic, and infinitely courageous resistance, with individual leaders of worldwide note. They cracked the structure of racism in this country during the first Reconstruction and again during the second, the 1960s Civil Rights Movement, as no other people of color have done.

Interwoven with these historical factors are possible psychological explanations of the Black-white definition. In the eyes of Jefferson and other leaders, Native Americans did not arouse white sexual anxieties or seem a threat to racial purity, as did Blacks. In any case, White Supremacy's fear of Indian resistance had greatly diminished by the late 1800s as a result of relentless genocide accompanied by colonization. Black rebelliousness, on the other hand, remains an inescapable nightmare to the dominant white society. There is also the fact that contemporary Black rebellion has been urban: right in the Man's face, scary.

A relative indifference toward Mexican people developed in Occupied America in the late 1800s. Like the massacre of Indians and enslavement of Africans, the successful colonization of Mexicans in what became the Southwest was key to U.S. economic growth. One would expect to see racist institutions and ideology emerge, and so they did in certain areas. Yet even in places like the Texas borderlands, where whites have historically reviled and abused Latinos, the Mexican presence didn't arouse a high level of white sexual anxiety and other irrational fears. Today Latinos often say Anglo attitudes make them feel they are less hated than dismissed as inconsequential. "There's no Mau-Mau factor," observed a Black friend half-humorously about Latino invisibility.

Of course there may be an emergent Mau-Mau factor, called demographics. Anglo indifference to Latinos may be yielding to a new fear. The white response to anticipation of becoming a minority during one's own lifetime is often panic as well as hatred and those "hordes" at the gate are of colors other than Black. But the new frenzy has yet to show the same fear-stricken face toward Latinos—or Asian/Pacific Americans—as toward African-Americans.

Robert Blauner, an Anglo and one of the few authors on racism to have examined the Black-white framework, looks at these psychological factors as revealed in literature:

> . . . We buy black writers, not only because they can write and have something to say, but because the white racial mind is obsessed with blackness. . . . Mexican-Americans, on the other hand, have been unseen as individuals and as a group. . . . James Baldwin has pointed to the deep mutual involvement of black and white in America. The profound ambivalence, the love-hate relationship, which Baldwin's own work expresses and dissects, does not exist in the racism that comes down on La Raza. . . . Even the racial stereotypes that plague Mexican-Americans tend to lack those positive attributes that mark antiblack

fantasies—supersexuality, inborn athletic and musical power, natural rhythm. Mexicans are dirty, lazy, treacherous, thieving bandits—and revolutionaries. (Blauner 1972, pp. 163–64)

(Not that I would want to choose between having Rhythm or Roaches.)

A final reason for the Black-white framework may be found in the general U.S. political culture, which is not only white-dominated, but also embraces an extremely stubborn form of national self-centeredness. This U.S.-centrism has meant that the political culture lacks any global vision other than relations of domination. In particular, the U.S. has consistently demonstrated contempt for Latin America, its people, their languages, and their issues. The U.S. refuses to see itself as one nation sitting on a continent with 20 others whose dominant languages are Spanish and Portuguese. That myopia has surely nurtured the Black-white framework for racism.

The Culture of Color

Color is crucial to understanding the Black-white framework of racial issues. Early in this nation's history, Benjamin Franklin perceived a tri-racial society based on skin color—"the lovely white," black, and "tawny," as Ron Takaki tells us in *Iron Cages.* Echoing this triad, we still have the saying "If you're white, you're all right; if you're Black, get back; if you're brown, stick around." As that old saying indicates, racism is experienced differently by Native Americans, African-Americans, Latinos, and Asian/Pacific Americans. In the case of Latinos, we find them somewhat more likely to be invisibilized—rendered "unseen"— than problemized (with thanks to writer/ activist Linda Burnham for that concept). Color explains much of this.

The relatively light skin and "Caucasian" features of many Latinos mean they are less threatening in the eyes of white racism and can even "pass"—unnoticed, invisible—much more often than African-Americans. Obviously this carries certain advantages in a racist society. Many Latinos would like to pass, work hard to assimilate, and succeed.

Until 1990 the U.S. Census categorized Latinos as "White," and even in that year it generated mass confusion on this issue: today the common term "Non-Hispanic Whites" certainly suggests a view of Latinos as white. At the same time, a 1992 poll of Latinos has shown an unexpectedly strong lack of self-identification as such. More than 90%, for example, said they did not belong to any ethnic organizations and less than 13% participated in any political activities organized around their national groups.

The term Hispanic (Her Panic, His Panic), whose emergence accompanied the rise of a Latino middle-class in the late 1970s to 1980s, encourages the wannabe whites/don't wannabe Indians. Always the unspoken goal has been to sidestep racist treatment, and who can be criticized for that? But we must also recognize the difference between those whom racism's obsession with color allows to try, and those with no such choice. "Passing" is an option for very few African-Americans. If it is possible for some Latinos to assimilate, one cannot say that of most African-Americans; they can only accommodate.

Latinos themselves buy into the hierarchy of color. Too often we fail to recognize the way in which we sustain racism ideologically. We do it when we express prejudice against those among us who look *indio,* mulatto, or just Black. We do it when we favor being lighter. Such prejudice dehumanizes fellow human beings, it divides our forces in the struggle for justice, and must be confronted. . . .

The Color of Culture

If there is a culture of color in these racist United States, is it possible we also have a color of culture?

In trying to understand the Black/white construct, one might distinguish between racial oppression (derived from physical appearance, especially skin color), and national minority oppression (derived from cultural differences or nationality). According to these criteria Latinos—like Asian/Pacific Americans—would be victims of national minority rather than racial oppression. Racism itself, then, would indeed be strictly white on Black.

Does the distinction hold? Do Latinos suffer for reasons of culture and nationality, but not for their "race"?

On one hand, cultural difference (especially language) and nationality are indeed used in oppressing a colonized people like Mexicans or those of Mexican descent in the U.S. The right to speak Spanish on the job or in a school playground has been historically denied. A Spanish accent (though not a British or French accent) is a liability in many professional situations. Children are ridiculed at school for bringing Mexican lunches, their names are Anglicized by white teachers, humiliation is daily fare. Later in life, they will be treated as foreigners; citizens will be denied citizen rights and noncitizens will be denied human rights.

Culturally, Latinos are seen as exotica, outside the mainstream, alien. They speak a funny language, some say (the most beautiful in the world, others say), and nobody outside the barrio can understand their best jokes, their beloved play-on-words, or self-mocking style. This isolation largely results from tactics of self-defense: culture has provided a long-standing survival mechanism for many people of Latino origin in a hostile world. It is a mechanism whose strength has continued to flow, given the proximity of Mexico, Central America, and the Caribbean to the United States. Latino efforts to move from outside to inside have intensified in the last 25 years and will continue, but the sense of inhabiting a culturally distinct world remains, especially in newer generations.

Latinos are acknowledged—if at all—in a ghettoized cultural framework: as actors, filmmakers, musicians, and other kinds of artists; as a growing market with great promise if one caters to its cultural characteristics; perhaps as an "ethnic" electoral force—or, on the negative side, as immigrants who speak a "foreign" language and "swarm" across the border; as urban gang-bangers with a culture of their own, *órale* Eddie Olmos! Even when these attitudes are not actively hostile, they are dehumanizing.

Does all this mean Latinos suffer for their culture and nationality, but not for their "race"? If we look at social conditions, at the actual experience of Latinos in the U.S., it makes more sense to conclude that the presence of national minority oppression doesn't signify the absence of racial oppression. It makes more sense to understand "racial" in terms of peoplehood and not only a supposed biology.

Social conditions affirm that combination of national, cultural, and racial oppression. The statistics for Latinos are grim: their national poverty rate (27%), high school drop-out rate (36%), and child poverty rate (42%) are even higher than for African-Americans, according to news reports on the 1990 Census. They are now reported to experience the most discrimination in housing markets of any U.S. population group (Lueck 1991).

Life-endangering racism is not rare for Latinos in the Southwest, especially near the border, and especially for those who are poor and working class. For decades, Anglos in Texas, Arizona, and California have enslaved, tortured, and murdered Latinos because their victims were nonwhite "foreigners." Hundreds of Mexicans were lynched between 1847 and 1935, if not later.

On a recent visit, San Diego County in California felt to me for Mexicans and Central Americans like Mississippi felt for Blacks in the 1960s. Five years ago, in that county a pair of middle-class white youths spied two young, documented Latinos standing by the roadside; one shot them dead and later explained to the judge that he did it because he "didn't like Mexicans." Such attitudes are even more common in that county today. In urban areas Latinos number high among the victims of Los Angeles Police Department and Sheriff's Department brutality. It's far from chic to be a spic, as poet Gerardo Navarro rhymed it sardonically.

The borderlands remain the locus of the most intense oppression, for that is where Latinos are most vulnerable by virtue of nationality—with or without documents. Agents of the Border Patrol, the largest police force in the U.S., murder Latinos with impunity. Killing Latinos as they try to run back to Mexico, running them down with official vehicles, forcing them into the river to drown—all these seem to be favorite Border Patrol pastimes.

Women are among those most brutally abused at the border; their victimization has only recently attracted public attention. Officials rape and then sometimes murder Latinas trying to cross the border, at will. Latina women contracted in their home countries as housekeepers have been raped on the day of arrival here at a new job; worked 14 to 16 hours a day, seven days a week; never paid promised wages; and kept isolated from possible sources of assistance. What happens to young, "illegal" children has included separation from parents and being jailed.

Latino men, women, and children are victimized on the basis of nationality and culture, rendered vulnerable by their lack of documents and scant knowledge of English or of local institutions. More often than not, they are rendered additionally vulnerable by their skin color and other physical features. Nationality then combines with a nonwhite (though not Black) physical appearance to subject them to an oppression that is a form of racism. Even if a nonwhite appearance is lacking, however, nationality and culture create a separate peoplehood as the basis for oppression.

In a land where the national identity is white, nationality and race become interchangeable. We live today with a white definition of citizenship, which generates a racist dynamic. Think about our words, our codes, in the media and conversation. "Immigrants" today means only two things: Mexicans and Central Americans, or Asians. It doesn't mean French or Irish or Serbian people who have come to relocate (a nicer word than "immigrate").

A rigid line cannot be drawn between racial and national oppression when all victims are people of color. Both are racism, and in combination they generate new varieties of racism. All this suggests why we need to understand more than the Black-white model today.

Racism Evolves

Racism evolves; as editor David Goldberg points out in his book *Anatomy of Racism*, it has no single, permanently fixed set of characteristics. New forms are being born today out of global events, in particular from the new international division of labor. He writes:

> . . . all forms of racism may be linked in terms of their exclusionary or inclusionary undertakings. A major historical shift has been from past racist forms defining and fueling expansionist colonial aims

and pursuits to contemporary expressions in nationalist terms. Insistence on racial inferiority in the past fed colonial appetites and imperialist self-definition. Racism is taken now to be expressed increasingly in terms of isolationist nationalist self-image, of cultural differentiation tied to custom, tradition, and heritage, and of exclusionary immigration policies, anti-immigrant practices and criminality. (Goldberg 1990, p. xiv)

The increasing equation of racism with nationalism is spotlighted by the title of Paul Gilroy's provocative book, *There Ain't No Black in the Union Jack.* We need to look at that equation more closely here in the U.S. The challenge is to understand such new developments and to draw strength from our understanding. The challenge is to abandon a dead-end dualism that comprises two White Supremacist inventions: Blackness and Whiteness. The challenge is to extend a dialectical reach.

Black/white are real poles—but not the only poles. To organize against racism, as people in SNCC (the Student Nonviolent Coordinating Committee) used to say, Blackness is necessary but not sufficient. They were thinking of class, as I remember; today we can also think of other colors, other racisms. In doing so, we have to proceed with both boldness and infinite care. Talking race in these United States is an intellectual minefield; for every social observation, one can find three contradictions and four necessary qualifications. Crawling through the complexity, it helps to think: keep your eye on the prize, which is uniting against the monster.

REFERENCES

BLAUNER, ROBERT. 1972. P. 165 in *Racial Oppression in America.* New York: Harper & Row.

GOLDBERG, DAVID THEO, ed. 1990. *Anatomy of Racism.* Minneapolis: University of Minnesota Press.

HAYES-BAUTISTA, DAVID, and GREGORY RODRIGUEZ. 1993. "Latinos Are Redefining Notions of Racial Identity." *Los Angeles Times,* 15 January.

LUECK, T. J. 1991. "U.S. Study Finds Hispanic Minority Most Often Subject to Victimization." *New York Times,* 3 November.

MARTÍNEZ, ELIZABETH. 1989. "A Certain Absence of Color." *Social Justice* 16:4.

MORRISON, TONI. 1992. *Playing in the Dark: Whiteness and the Literary Imagination.* Cambridge, MA: Harvard University Press.

PASTOR, MANUEL, JR. 1993. *Latinos and the L.A. Uprising.* Los Angeles: Tomas Rivera Center (TRC) Study, Occidental College.

The Color of Space

14

THE CONTINUING SIGNIFICANCE OF RACE
Antiblack Discrimination in Public Places

Joe R. Feagin

Title II of the 1964 Civil Rights Act stipulates that "all persons shall be entitled to the full and equal enjoyment of the goods, services, facilities, privileges, advantages, and accommodations of any place of public accommodation . . . without discrimination or segregation on the ground of race, color, religion, or national origin." The public places emphasized in the act are restaurants, hotels, and motels, although racial discrimination occurs in many other public places. Those black Americans who would make the greatest use of these public accommodations and certain other public places would be middle-class, i.e., those with the requisite resources. . . .

Discrimination can be defined in social-contextual terms as "actions or practices carried out by members of dominant racial or ethnic groups that have a differential and negative impact on members of subordinate racial and ethnic groups" (Feagin and Eckberg 1980, pp. 1–2). This differential treatment ranges from the blatant to the subtle

(Feagin and Feagin 1986). Here I focus primarily on blatant discrimination by white Americans targeting middle-class blacks. Historically, discrimination against blacks has been one of the most serious forms of racial/ethnic discrimination in the United States and one of the most difficult to overcome, in part because of the institutionalized character of color coding. I focus on three important aspects of discrimination: (1) the variation in sites of discrimination; (2) the range of discriminatory actions; and (3) the range of responses by blacks to discrimination.

Sites of Discrimination

There is a spatial dimension to discrimination. The probability of experiencing racial hostility varies from the most private to the most public sites. If a black person is in a relatively protected site, such as with friends at home, the probability of experiencing hostility and discrimination is low. The probability increases as one moves from friendship settings to such outside sites as the workplace, where a black person typically has contacts with both acquaintances and strangers, providing an interactive context with greater potential for discrimination.

In most workplaces, middle-class status and its organizational resources provide some protection against certain categories of discrimination. This protection probably weakens as a black person moves from those work and school settings where he or she is well-known into public accommodations such as large stores and city restaurants where contacts are mainly with white strangers. On public streets blacks have the greatest public exposure to strangers and the least protection against overt discriminatory behavior, including violence. A key feature of these more public settings is that they often involve contacts with white strangers who react primarily on the basis of one ascribed characteristic. The study of the micro-life of interaction between strangers in public was pioneered by Goffman (1963, 1971) and his students, but few of their analyses have treated hostile discriminatory interaction in public places. A rare exception is the research by Gardner (1980; see also Gardner 1988), who documented the character and danger of passing remarks by men directed against women in unprotected public places. Gardner writes of women (and blacks) as "open persons," i.e. particularly vulnerable targets for harassment that violates the rules of public courtesy.

The Range of Discriminatory Actions

In his classic study, *The Nature of Prejudice,* Allport (1958, pp. 14–5) noted that prejudice can be expressed in a series of progressively more serious actions, ranging from antilocution to avoidance, exclusion, physical attack, and extermination. Allport's work suggests a continuum of actions from avoidance, to exclusion or rejection, to attack. In his travels in the South in the 1950s a white journalist who changed his skin color to black encountered discrimination in each of these

categories (Griffin 1961). In my data, discrimination against middle-class blacks still ranges across this continuum: (1) avoidance actions, such as a white couple crossing the street when a black male approaches; (2) rejection actions, such as poor service in public accommodations; (3) verbal attacks, such as shouting racial epithets in the street; (4) physical threats and harassment by white police officers; and (5) physical threats and attacks by other whites, such as attacks by white supremacists in the street. Changing relations between blacks and whites in recent decades have expanded the repertoire of discrimination to include more subtle forms and to encompass discrimination in arenas from which blacks were formerly excluded such as formerly all-white public accommodations.

Black Responses to Discrimination

Prior to societal desegregation in the 1960s much traditional discrimination, especially in the South, took the form of an asymmetrical "deference ritual" in which blacks were typically expected to respond to discriminating whites with great deference. . . . Such rituals can be seen in the obsequious words and gestures—the etiquette of race relations—that many blacks, including middle-class blacks, were forced to utilize to survive the rigors of segregation (Doyle 1937). However, not all responses in this period were deferential. From the late 1800s to the 1950s, numerous lynchings and other violence targeted blacks whose behavior was defined as too aggressive (Raper 1933). Blauner's (1989) respondents reported acquaintances reacting aggressively to discrimination prior to the 1960s.

Deference rituals can still be found today between some lower-income blacks and their white employers. In her northeastern study Rollins (1985, p. 157) found black maids regularly deferring to white employers. Today, most discriminatory interaction no longer involves much asymmetrical deference, at least for middle-class blacks. Even where whites expect substantial deference, most middle-class blacks do not oblige. For middle-class blacks contemporary discrimination has evolved beyond the asymmetrical deference rituals and "No Negroes served" type of exclusion to patterns of black-contested discrimination. . . .

Some white observers have suggested that many middle-class blacks are paranoid about white discrimination and rush too quickly to charges of racism (Wieseltier 1989, June 5; for male views of female "paranoia" see Gardner 1988). But the daily reality may be just the opposite, as middle-class black Americans often evaluate a situation carefully before judging it discriminatory and taking additional action. This careful evaluation, based on past experiences (real or vicarious), not only prevents jumping to conclusions, but also reflects the hope that white behavior is not based on race, because an act not based on race is easier to endure. After evaluation one strategy is to leave the site of discrimination rather than to create a disturbance. Another is to ignore the discrimination and continue with the interaction, a "blocking" strategy similar to that Gardner (1980, p. 345) reported for women dealing with street remarks. In many situations resigned acceptance is the only realistic response. More confrontational responses to white actions include verbal reprimands and sarcasm, physical counterattacks, and filing lawsuits. Several strategies may be tried in any given discriminatory situation. In crafting these strategies middle-class blacks, in comparison with less privileged blacks, may draw on middle-class resources to fight discrimination.

The Research Study

To examine discrimination, I draw primarily on 37 in-depth interviews from a larger study of 135 middle-class black Americans in Boston, Buffalo, Baltimore, Washington, D.C., Detroit, Houston, Dallas, Austin, San Antonio, Marshall, Las Vegas, and Los Angeles. . . .

Although all types of mistreatment are reported, there is a strong relationship between type of discrimination and site, with rejection/poor-service discrimination being most common in public accommodations and verbal or physical threat discrimination by white citizens or police officers most likely in the street. [Table 1, p. 136.] . . .

The most common black responses to racial hostility in the street are withdrawal or a verbal reply [Table 2, p. 136]. In many avoidance situations (e.g., a white couple crossing a street to avoid walking past a black college student) or attack situations (e.g., whites throwing beer cans from a passing car), a verbal response is difficult because of the danger or the fleeting character of the hostility. A black victim often withdraws, endures this treatment with resigned acceptance, or replies with a quick verbal retort. In the case of police harassment, the response is limited by the danger, and resigned acceptance or mild verbal protests are likely responses. Rejection (poor service) in public accommodations provides an opportunity to fight back verbally—the most common responses to public accommodations discrimination are verbal counterattacks or resigned acceptance. Some black victims correct whites quietly, while others respond aggressively and lecture the assailant about the discrimination or threaten court action. A few retaliate physically. Examining materials in these 37 interviews . . . we will see that the depth and complexity of contemporary black middle-class responses to white

TABLE 1 Percentage Distribution of Discriminatory Actions by Type and Site: Middle-Class Blacks in Selected Cities, 1988–1990

	Site of Discriminatory Action	
Type of Discriminatory Action	*Public Accommodations*	*Street*
Avoidance	3	7
Rejection/poor service	79	4
Verbal epithets	12	25
Police threats/harassment	3	46
Other threats/harassment	3	18
Total	100	100
Number of actions	34	28

TABLE 2 Percentage Distribution of Primary Responses to Discriminatory Incidents by Type and Site: Middle-Class Blacks in Selected Cities, 1988–1990

Response to Discriminatory	Site of Discriminatory Incident	
Incident	*Public Accommodations*	*Street*
Withdrawal/exit	4	22
Resigned acceptance	23	7
Verbal response	69	59
Physical counterattack	4	7
Response unclear	—	4
Total	100	99
Number of responses	26	27

discrimination accents the changing character of white-black interaction and the necessity of continual negotiation of the terms of that interaction.

Responses to Discrimination: Public Accommodations

Two Fundamental Strategies: Verbal Confrontation and Withdrawal

In the following account, a black news director at a major television station shows the interwoven character of discriminatory action and black response. The discrimination took the form of poor restaurant service, and the responses included both suggested withdrawal and verbal counterattack.

He [her boyfriend] was waiting to be seated. . . . He said, "You go to the bathroom and I'll get the table. . . ." He was standing there when I came back; he continued to stand there. The restaurant was almost empty. There were waiters, waitresses, and no one seated. And when I got back to him, he was ready to leave, and said, "Let's go." I said, "What happened to our table?" He wasn't seated. So I said, "No, we're not leaving, please." And he said, "No, I'm leaving." So we went outside and we talked about it. And what I said to him was, you have to be aware of the possibilities that this is not the first time that this has happened at this restaurant or at other restaurants, but this is the first time it has happened to a black news director here or someone who could make an issue of it, or someone who is prepared to make an issue of it.

So we went back inside after I talked him into it and, to make a long story short, I had the manager come. I made most of the people who were there (while conducting myself professionally the whole time) aware that I was incensed at being treated this way. . . . I said, "Why do you think we weren't seated?" And the manager said, "Well, I don't really know." And I said, "Guess." He said, "Well I don't know, because you're black?" I said, "Bingo. Now isn't it funny that you didn't guess that I didn't have any money" (and I opened up my purse) and I said, "because I certainly have money. And isn't it odd that you didn't guess that it's because I couldn't pay for it because I've got two American Express cards and a Master Card right here. I think it's just funny that you would have assumed that it's because I'm black." . . . And then I took out my card and gave it to him and said, "If this happens again, or if I hear of this happening again, I will bring the full wrath of an entire news department down on this restaurant." And he just kind of looked at me. "Not [just] because I am personally offended. I am. But because you have no right to do what you did, and as a people we have lived a long time with having our rights abridged. . . ." There were probably three or four sets of diners in the restaurant and maybe five waiters/

waitresses. They watched him standing there waiting to be seated. His reaction to it was that he wanted to leave. I understood why he would have reacted that way, because he felt that he was in no condition to be civil. He was ready to take the place apart and . . . sometimes it's appropriate to behave that way. We hadn't gone the first step before going on to the next step. He didn't feel that he could comfortably and calmly take the first step, and I did. So I just asked him to please get back in the restaurant with me, and then you don't have to say a word, and let me handle it from there. It took some convincing, but I had to appeal to his sense of, this is not just you, this is not just for you. We are finally in a position as black people where there are some of us who can genuinely get their attention. And if they don't want to do this because it's right for them to do it, then they'd better do it because they're afraid to do otherwise. If it's fear, then fine, instill the fear.

This example provides insight into the character of modern discrimination. The discrimination was not the "No Negroes" exclusion of the recent past, but rejection in the form of poor service by restaurant personnel. The black response indicates the change in black-white interaction since the 1950s and 1960s, for discrimination is handled with vigorous confrontation rather than deference. The aggressive black response and the white backtracking underscore Brittan and Maynard's (1984, p. 7) point that black-white interaction today is being renegotiated. It is possible that the white personnel defined the couple as "poor blacks" because of their jeans, although the jeans were fashionable and white patrons wear jeans. In comments not quoted here the news director rejects such an explanation. She forcefully articulates a theory of rights—a response that signals the critical impact of civil rights laws on the thinking of middle-class blacks. The news director articulates the American dream: she has worked hard, earned the money and credit cards, developed the appropriate middle-class behavior, and thus has under the law a *right* to be served. There is defensiveness in her actions too, for she feels a need to legitimate her status by showing her purse and credit cards. One important factor that enabled her to take such assertive action was her power to bring a TV news team to the restaurant. This power marks a change from a few decades ago when very few black Americans had the social or economic resources to fight back successfully. . . .

The confrontation response is generally so costly in terms of time and energy that acquiescence or withdrawal are common options. An example of the exit response was provided by a utility company executive in an east coast city:

> I can remember one time my husband had picked up our son . . . from camp; and he'd stopped at a little store in the neighborhood near the camp. It was hot, and he was going to buy him a snowball. And the proprietor of the store—this was a very old, white neighborhood, and it was just a little sundry store. But the proprietor said he had the little window where people could come up and order things. Well, my husband and son had gone into the store. And he told them, "Well, I can't give it to you here, but if you go outside to the window, I'll give it to you." And there were other [white] people in the store who'd been served [inside]. So, they just left and didn't buy anything.

. . . This site differed from the previous example in that the service was probably not of long-term importance to the black family passing through the area. In the previous site the possibility of returning to the restaurant for business or pleasure, may have contributed to the choice of a confrontational response. The importance of the service is a likely variable affecting black responses to discrimination in public accommodations. . . .

The complex process of evaluation and response is described by a college dean, who commented generally on hotel and restaurant discrimination encountered as he travels across the United States:

> When you're in a restaurant and . . . you notice that blacks get seated near the kitchen. You notice that if it's a hotel, your room is near the elevator, or your room is always way down in a corner somewhere. You find that you are getting the undesirable rooms. And you come there early in the day and you don't see very many cars on the lot and they'll tell you that this is all we've got. Or you get the room that's got a bad television set. You know that you're being discriminated against. And of course you have to act accordingly. You have to tell them, "Okay, the room is fine, [but] this television set has got to go. Bring me another television set." So in my personal experience, I simply cannot sit and let them get away with it [discrimination] and not let them know that I know that that's what they are doing. . . .
>
> When I face discrimination, first I take a long look at myself and try to determine whether or not I am seeing what I think I'm seeing in 1989, and if it's something that I have an option [about]. In other words, if I'm at a store making a purchase, I'll simply walk away from it. If it's at a restaurant where I'm not getting good ser-

vice, I first of all let the people know that I'm not getting good service, then I [may] walk away from it. But the thing that I have to do is to let people know that I know that I'm being singled out for a separate treatment. And then I might react in any number of ways—depending on where I am and how badly I want whatever it is that I'm there for.

This commentary adds another dimension to our understanding of public discrimination, its cumulative aspect. Blacks confront not just isolated incidents—such as a bad room in a luxury hotel once every few years—but a lifelong series of such incidents. Here again the omnipresence of careful assessments is underscored. The dean's interview highlights a major difficulty in being black—one must be constantly prepared to assess accurately and then decide on the appropriate response. This long-look approach may indicate that some middle-class blacks are so sensitive to white charges of hypersensitivity and paranoia that they err in the opposite direction and fail to see discrimination when it occurs. In addition, as one black graduate student at a leading white university in the Southeast put it: "I think that sometimes timely and appropriate responses to racially motivated acts and comments are lost due to the processing of the input." The "long look" can result in missed opportunities to respond to discrimination.

Using Middle-Class Resources for Protection

One advantage that middle-class blacks have over poorer blacks is the use of the resources of middle-class occupations. A professor at a major white university commented on the varying protection her middle-class status gives her at certain sites:

If I'm in those areas that are fairly protected, within gatherings of my own group, other African Americans, or if I'm in the university where my status as a professor mediates against the way I might be perceived, mediates against the hostile perception, then it's fairly comfortable. . . . When I divide my life into encounters with the outside world, and of course that's ninety percent of my life, it's fairly consistently unpleasant at those sites where there's nothing that mediates between my race and what I have to do. For example, if I'm in a grocery store, if I'm in my car, which is a 1970 Chevrolet, a real old ugly car, all those things—being in a grocery store in casual clothes, or being in the car—sort of advertises something that doesn't have anything to do with my status as far as people I run into are concerned.

Because I'm a large black woman, and I don't wear whatever class status I have, or whatever professional status [I have] in my appearance when I'm in the grocery store, I'm part of the mass of large black women shopping. For most whites, and even for some blacks, that translates into negative status. That means that they are free to treat me the way they treat most poor black people, because they can't tell by looking at me that I differ from that.

This professor notes the variation in discrimination in the sites through which she travels, from the most private to the most public. At home with friends she faces no problems, and at the university her professional status gives her some protection from discrimination. The increase in unpleasant encounters as she moves into public accommodations sites such as grocery stores is attributed to the absence of mediating factors such as clear symbols of middle-class status—displaying the middle-class symbols may provide some protection against discrimination in public places. . . .

Responses to Discrimination: The Street

Reacting to White Strangers

As we move away from public accommodations settings to the usually less protected street sites, racial hostility can become more fleeting and severer, and thus black responses are often restricted. The most serious form of street discrimination is violence. Often the reasonable black response to street discrimination is withdrawal, resigned acceptance, or a quick verbal retort. The difficulty of responding to violence is seen in this report by a man working for a media surveying firm in a southern industrial city:

> I was parked in front of this guy's house. . . . This guy puts his hands on the window and says, "Get out of the car, nigger." . . . So, I got out, and I thought, "Oh, this is what's going to happen here." And I'm talking fast. And they're, "What are you doing here?" And I'm, "This is who I am. I work with these people. This is the man we want to put in the survey." And I pointed to the house. And the guy said, "Well you have an out-of-state license tag, right?" "Yea." And he said, "If something happened to you, your people at home wouldn't know for a long time, would they?" . . . I said, "Look, I deal with a company that deals with television. [If] something happens to me, it's going to be a national thing." . . . So, they grab me by the lapel of my coat, and put me in front of my car. They put the blade on my zipper. And now I'm thinking

about this guy that's in the truck [behind me], because now I'm thinking that I'm going to have to run somewhere. Where am I going to run? Go to the police? [laughs] So, after a while they bash up my headlight. And I drove [away].

Stigmatized and physically attacked solely because of his color, this man faced verbal hostility and threats of death with courage. Cautiously drawing on his middle-class resources, he told the attackers his death would bring television crews to the town. This resource utilization is similar to that of the news director in the restaurant incident. Beyond this verbal threat his response had to be one of caution. For most whites threatened on the street, the police are a sought-after source of protection; this is often not the case. . . .

Responses to Discrimination by White Police Officers

Most middle-class blacks do not have such governmental authority as their personal protection. In fact, white police officers are a major problem. Encounters with the police can be life-threatening and thus limit the range of responses. A television commentator recounted two cases of police harassment when he was working for a survey firm in the mid-1980s. In one of the incidents, which took place in a southern metropolis, he was stopped by several white officers:

> "What are you doing here?" I tell them what I'm doing here. . . . And so me spread on top of my car. [What had you done?] Because I was in the neighborhood, I left this note on these peoples' house: "Here's who I am. You weren't here, and I will come back in thirty minutes." [Why were they searching you?] They don't know. To

me, they're searching, I remember at that particular moment when this all was going down, there was a lot of reports about police crime on civilians. . . . It took four cops to shake me down, two police cars, so they had me up there spread out. I had a friend of mine with me who was making the call with me, because we were going to have dinner together, and he was black, and they had me up, and they had him outside. . . . They said, "Well, let's check you out." . . . And I'm talking to myself, and I'm not thinking about being at attention, with my arms spread on my Ford [a company car], and I'm sitting there talking to myself, "Man, this is crazy, this is crazy."

[How are you feeling inside?] Scared. I mean real scared. [What did you think was going to happen to you?] I was going to go to jail. . . . Just because they picked me. Why would they stop me? It's like, if they can stop me, why wouldn't I go to jail, and I could sit there for ten days before the judge sees me. I'm thinking all this crazy stuff. . . . Again, I'm talking to myself. And the guy takes his stick. And he doesn't whack me hard, but he does it with enough authority to let me know they mean business. "I told you stand still; now put your arms back out." And I've got this suit on, and the car's wet. And my friend's hysterical. He's outside the car. And they're checking him out. And he's like, "Man, just be cool, man." And he had tears in his eyes. And I'm like, oh, man, this is a nightmare. This is not supposed to happen to me. This is not my style! And so finally, this other cop comes up and says, "What have we got here Charlie?" "Oh, we've got a guy here. He's running through the neighbor-

hood, and he doesn't want to do what we tell him. We might have to run him in." [You're "running through" the neighborhood?] Yeah, exactly, in a suit in the rain?! After they got through doing their thing and harassing me, I just said, "Man, this has been a hell of a week."

And I had tears in my eyes, but it wasn't tears of upset. It was tears of anger; it was tears of wanting to lash back. . . . What I thought to myself was, man, blacks have it real hard down here. I don't care if they're a broadcaster; I don't care if they're a businessman or a banker. . . . They don't have it any easier than the persons on skid row who get harassed by the police on a Friday or Saturday night.

It seems likely that most black men—including middle-class black men—see white police officers as a major source of danger and death. (See "Mood of Ghetto America" 1980, June 2, pp. 32–34; Louis Harris and Associates 1989; Roddy 1990, August 26.) Scattered evidence suggests that by the time they are in their twenties, most black males, regardless of socioeconomic status, have been stopped by the police because "blackness" is considered a sign of possible criminality by police officers (Moss 1990; Roddy 1990, August 26). This treatment probably marks a dramatic contrast with the experiences of young white middle-class males. In the incident above the respondent and a friend experienced severe police maltreatment—detention for a lengthy period, threat of arrest, and the reality of physical violence. The coping response of the respondent was resigned acceptance somewhat similar to the deference rituals highlighted by Goffman. The middle-class suits and obvious corporate credentials (for example, survey questionnaires and company car) did not protect the two black men. The final comment suggests a disappointment that middle-class status brought no reprieve from police stigmatization and harassment. . . .

Conclusion

I have examined the sites of discrimination, the types of discriminatory acts, and the responses of the victims and have found the color stigma still to be very important in the public lives of affluent black Americans. The sites of racial discrimination range from relatively protected home sites, to less protected workplace and educational sites, to the even less protected public places. The 1964 Civil Rights Act guarantees that black Americans are "entitled to the full and equal enjoyment of the goods, services, facilities, privileges, advantages, and accommodations" in public accommodations. Yet the interviews indicate that deprivation of full enjoyment of public facilities is not a relic of the past: deprivation and discrimination in public accommodations persist. Middle-class black Americans remain vulnerable targets in public places. Prejudice-generated aggression in public places is, of course, not limited to black men and women—gay men and white women are also targets of street harassment (Benokraitis and Feagin 1986). Nonetheless, black women and men face an unusually broad range of discrimination on the street and in public accommodations.

The interviews highlight two significant aspects of the additive discrimination faced by black Americans in public places and elsewhere: (1) the cumulative character of an *individual's* experiences with discrimination; and (2) the *group's* accumulated historical experiences as perceived by the individual. A retired psychology professor who has worked in the Midwest and Southwest commented on the pyramiding of incidents:

I don't think white people, generally, understand the full meaning of racist discriminatory behaviors directed toward Americans of African descent. They seem to see each act of discrimination or any act of violence as an "isolated" event. As a result, most white Americans cannot understand the strong reaction manifested by blacks when such events occur. They feel that blacks tend to "over-react." They forget that in most cases, we live lives of quiet desperation generated by a litany of *daily* large and small events that whether or not by design, remind us of our "place" in American society.

Particular instances of discrimination may seem minor to outside white observers when considered in isolation. But when blatant acts of avoidance, verbal harassment, and physical attack combine with subtle and covert slights, and these accumulate over months, years, and lifetimes, the impact on a black person is far more than the sum of the individual instances.

The historical context of contemporary discrimination was described by the retired psychologist, who argued that average white Americans

. . . ignore the personal context of stimulus. That is, they deny the historical impact that a negative act may have on an individual. "Nigger" to a white may simply be an epithet that should be ignored. To most blacks, the term brings into sharp and current focus all kinds of acts of racism—murder, rape, torture, denial of constitutional rights, insults, limited opportunity structure, economic problems, unequal justice under the law and a myriad of . . . other racist and discriminatory acts that occur daily in the lives of *most* Americans of African descent— including professional blacks.

Particular acts, even antilocution that might seem minor to white observers, are freighted not only with one's past experience of discrimination but also with centuries of racial discrimination directed at the entire group, vicarious oppression that still includes racially translated violence and denial of access to the American dream. Anti-black discrimination is a matter of racial-power inequality institutionalized in a variety of economic and social institutions over a long period of time. The microlevel events of public accommodations and public streets are not just rare and isolated encounters by individuals; they are recurring events reflecting an invasion of the microworld by the macroworld of historical racial subordination.

REFERENCES

ALLPORT, GORDON. 1958. *The Nature of Prejudice.* Abridged. New York: Doubleday Anchor Books.

BENOKRAITIS, NIJOLE, and JOE R. FEAGIN. 1986. *Modern Sexism: Blatant, Subtle and Covert Discrimination.* Englewood Cliffs, NJ: Prentice-Hall.

BLAUNER, BOB. 1989. *Black Lives, White Lives.* Berkeley: University of California Press.

BRITTAN, ARTHUR, and MARY MAYNARD. 1984. *Sexism, Racism and Oppression.* Oxford: Basil Blackwell.

DOYLE, BERTRAM W. 1937. *The Etiquette of Race Relations in the South.* Port Washington, NY: Kennikat Press.

FEAGIN, JOE R., and DOUGLAS ECKBERG. 1980. "Prejudice and Discrimination." *Annual Review of Sociology* 6:1–20.

FEAGIN, JOE R., and CLAIRECE BOOHER FEAGIN. 1986. *Discrimination American Style,* rev. ed. Melbourne, FL: Krieger.

GARDNER, CAROL BROOKS. 1980. "Passing By: Street Remarks, Address Rights, and the Urban Female." *Sociological Inquiry* 50:328–56.

———. 1988. "Access Information: Public Lies and Private Peril." *Social Problems* 35:384–97.

GOFFMAN, ERVING. 1956. "The Nature of Deference and Demeanor." *American Anthropologist* 58:473–502.

GRIFFIN, JOHN HOWARD. 1961. *Black Like Me.* Boston: Houghton Mifflin.

"The Mood of Ghetto America." 1980. *Newsweek,* 2 June, pp. 32–4.

MOSS, E. YVONNE. 1990. "African Americans and the Administration of Justice." Pp. 79–86 in *Assessment of the Status of African-Americans,* edited by Wornie L. Reed. Boston: University of Massachusetts, William Monroe Trotter Institute.

RAPER, ARTHUR F. 1933. *The Tragedy of Lynching.* Chapel Hill: University of North Carolina Press.

RODDY, DENNIS B. 1990. "Perceptions Still Segregate Police, Black Community." *The Pittsburgh Press,* 26 August, p. B1.

ROLLINS, JUDITH. 1985. *Between Women.* Philadelphia: Temple University Press.

WIESELTIER, LEON. 1989. "Scar Tissue." *New Republic,* 5 June, pp. 19–20.

15

SAVAGE INEQUALITIES

Jonathan Kozol

In a country where there is no distinction of class," Lord Acton wrote of the United States 130 years ago, "a child is not born to the station of its parents, but with an indefinite claim to all the prizes that can be won by thought and labor. It is in conformity with the theory of equality . . . to give as near as possible to every youth an equal stake in life."[1] Americans, he said, "are unwilling that any should be deprived in childhood of the means of competition."

It is hard to read these words today without a sense of irony and sadness. Denial of "the means of competition" is perhaps the single most consistent outcome of the education offered to poor children in the schools of our large cities; and nowhere is this pattern of denial more explicit or more absolute than in the public schools of New York City.

Average expenditures per pupil in the city of New York in 1987 were some $5,500. In the highest spending suburbs of New York (Great Neck or Manhasset, for example, on Long Island) funding levels rose above $11,000, with the highest districts in the state at $15,000.[2] "Why . . .", asks the city's Board of Education, "should our students receive less" than do "similar students" who live elsewhere? "The inequity is clear."[3]

But the inequality to which these words refer goes even further than the school board may be eager to reveal. "It is perhaps the supreme irony," says the nonprofit Community Service Society of New York, that "the same Board of Education which perceives so clearly the inequities" of funding between separate towns and cities "is perpetuating similar inequities" right in New York. And, in comment on the Board of Education's final statement—"the inequity is clear"—the CSS observes, "New York City's poorest . . . districts could adopt that eloquent statement with few changes."

New York City's public schools are subdivided into 32 school districts. District 10 encompasses a large part of the Bronx but is, effectively, two separate districts. One of these districts, Riverdale, is in the northwest section of the Bronx. Home to many of the city's most sophisticated and well-educated families, its elementary schools have relatively few low-income students. The other section, to the south and east, is poor and heavily nonwhite.

The contrast between public schools in each of these two neighborhoods is obvious to any visitor. At Public School 24 in Riverdale, the principal speaks enthusiastically of his teaching staff. At Public School 79, serving poorer children to the south, the principal says that he is forced to take the "tenth-best" teachers. "I thank God they're still breathing," he remarks of those from whom he must select his teachers.

Some years ago, District 10 received an allocation for computers. The local board decided to give each elementary school an equal number of computers, even though the schools in Riverdale had smaller classes and far fewer students. When it was pointed out that schools in Riverdale, as a result, had twice the number of computers in proportion to their student populations as the schools in the poor neighborhoods, the chairman of the local board replied, "What is fair is what is determined . . . to be fair."

The superintendent of District 10, Fred Goldberg, tells *The New York Times* that "every effort" is made "to distribute resources equitably." He speculates that some gap might exist because some of the poorer schools need to use funds earmarked for computers to buy basic supplies like pens and paper. Asked about the differences in teachers noted by the principals, he says there are no differences, then adds that next year he'll begin a program to improve the quality of teachers in the poorer schools. Questioned about differences in physical appearances between the richer and the poorer schools, he says, "I think it's demographics."[4]

Sometimes a school principal, whatever his background or his politics, looks into the faces of the children in his school and offers a disarming statement that cuts through official ambiguity. "These are the kids most in need," says Edward Flanery, the principal of one of the low-income schools, "and they get the worst teachers." For children of diverse needs in his overcrowded rooms, he says, "you need an outstanding teacher. And what do you get? You get the worst."

In order to find Public School 261 in District 10, a visitor is told to look for a mortician's office. The funeral home, which faces Jerome Avenue in the North Bronx, is easy to identify by its green awning. The school is next door, in a former roller-skating rink. No sign identifies the building as a school. A metal awning frame without an awning supports a flagpole, but there is no flag.

In the street in front of the school there is an elevated public transit line. Heavy traffic fills the street. The existence of the school is virtually concealed within this crowded city block.

In a vestibule between the outer and inner glass doors of the school there is a sign with these words: "All children are capable of learning."

Beyond the inner doors a guard is seated. The lobby is long and narrow. The ceiling is low. There are no windows. All the teachers that I see at first are middle-aged white women. The principal, who is also a white woman, tells me that the school's "capacity" is 900 but that there are 1,300 children here. The size of classes for fifth and sixth grade children in New York, she says, is "capped" at 32, but she says that class size in the school goes "up to 34." (I later see classes, however, as large as 37.) Classes for younger children, she goes on, are "capped at 25," but a school can go above this limit if it puts an extra adult in the room. Lack of space, she says, prevents the school from operating a pre-kindergarten program.

I ask the principal where her children go to school. They are enrolled in private school, she says.

"Lunchtime is a challenge for us," she explains. "Limited space obliges us to do it in three shifts, 450 children at a time."

Textbooks are scarce and children have to share their social studies books. The principal says there is one full-time pupil counselor and another who is here two days a week: a ratio of 930 children to one counselor. The carpets are patched and sometimes taped together to conceal an open space. "I could use some new rugs," she observes.

To make up for the building's lack of windows and the crowded feeling that results, the staff puts plants and fish tanks in the corridors. Some of the plants are flourishing. Two boys, released from class, are in a corridor beside a tank, their noses pressed against the glass. A school of pinkish fish inside the tank are darting back and forth. Farther down the corridor a small Hispanic girl is watering the plants.

Two first grade classes share a single room without a window, divided only by a blackboard. Four kindergartens and a sixth grade class of Spanish-speaking children have been packed into a single room in which, again, there is no window. A second grade bilingual class of 37 children has its own room but again there is no window.

By eleven o'clock, the lunchroom is already packed with appetite and life. The kids line up to get their meals, then eat them in ten minutes. After that, with no place they can go to play, they sit and wait until it's time to line up and go back to class.

On the second floor I visit four classes taking place within another undivided space. The room has a low ceiling. File cabinets and movable blackboards give a small degree of isolation to each class. Again, there are no windows.

The library is a tiny, windowless and claustrophobic room. I count approximately 700 books. Seeing no reference books, I ask a teacher if encyclopedias and other reference books are kept in classrooms.

"We don't have encyclopedias in classrooms," she replies. "That is for the suburbs."

The school, I am told, has 26 computers for its 1,300 children. There is one small gym and children get one period, and sometimes two, each week. Recess, however, is not possible because there is no playground. "Head Start," the principal says, "scarcely exists in District 10. We have no space."

The school, I am told, is 90 percent black and Hispanic; the other 10 percent are Asian, white or Middle Eastern.

In a sixth grade social studies class the walls are bare of words or decorations. There seems to be no ventilation system, or, if one exists, it isn't working.

The class discusses the Nile River and the Fertile Crescent.

The teacher, in a droning voice: "How is it useful that these civilizations developed close to rivers?"

A child, in a good loud voice: "What kind of question is that?"

In my notes I find these words: "An uncomfortable feeling—being in a building with no windows. There are metal ducts across the room. Do they give air? I feel asphyxiated. . . ."

On the top floor of the school, a sixth grade of 30 children shares a room with 29 bilingual second graders. Because of the high class size there is an assistant with each teacher. This means that 59 children and four grown-ups—63 in all—must share a room that, in a suburban school, would hold no more than 20 children and one teacher. There are, at least, some outside windows in this room—it is the only room with windows in the school—and the room has a high ceiling. It is a relief to see some daylight.

I return to see the kindergarten classes on the ground floor and feel stifled once again by lack of air and the low ceiling. Nearly 120 children and adults are doing what they can to make the best of things: 80 children in four kindergarten classes, 30 children in the sixth grade class, and about eight grown-ups who are aides and teachers. The kindergarten children sitting on the worn rug, which is patched with tape, look up at me and turn their heads to follow me as I walk past them.

As I leave the school, a sixth grade teacher stops to talk. I ask her, "Is there air conditioning in warmer weather?"

Teachers, while inside the building, are reluctant to give answers to this kind of question. Outside, on the sidewalk, she is less constrained: "I had an awful room last year. In the winter it was 56 degrees. In the summer it was up to 90. It was sweltering."

I ask her, "Do the children ever comment on the building?"

"They don't say," she answers, "but they know."

I ask her if they see it as a racial message.

"All these children see TV," she says. "They know what suburban schools are like. Then they look around them at their school. This was a roller-rink, you know. . . . They don't comment on it but you see it in their eyes. They understand."

On the following morning I visit P.S. 79, another elementary school in the same district. "We work under difficult circumstances," says the principal, James Carter, who is black. "The school was built to hold one thousand students. We have 1,550. We are badly overcrowded. We need smaller classes but, to do this, we would need more space. I can't add five teachers. I would have no place to put them."

Some experts, I observe, believe that class size isn't a real issue. He dismisses this abruptly. "It doesn't take a genius to discover that you learn more in a smaller class. I have to bus some 60 kindergarten children elsewhere, since I have no space for them. When they return next year, where do I put them?

"I can't set up a computer lab. I have no room. I had to put a class into the library. I have no librarian. There are two gymnasiums upstairs but they cannot be used for sports. We hold more classes there. It's unfair to measure us against the suburbs. They have 17 to 20 children in a class. Average class size in this school is 30.

"The school is 29 percent black, 70 percent Hispanic. Few of these kids get Head Start. There is no space in the district. Of 200 kindergarten children, 50 maybe get some kind of preschool."

I ask him how much difference preschool makes.

"Those who get it do appreciably better. I can't overestimate its impact but, as I have said, we have no space."

The school tracks children by ability, he says. "There are five to seven levels in each grade. The highest level is equivalent to 'gifted' but it's not a full-scale gifted program. We don't have the funds. We have no science room. The science teachers carry their equipment with them."

We sit and talk within the nurse's room. The window is broken. There are two holes in the ceiling. About a quarter of the ceiling has been patched and covered with a plastic garbage bag.

"Ideal class size for these kids would be 15 to 20. Will these children ever get what white kids in the suburbs take for granted? I don't think so. If you ask me why, I'd have to speak of race and social class. I don't think the powers that be in New York City understand, or want to understand, that if they do not give these children a sufficient education to lead healthy and productive lives, we will be their victims later on. We'll pay the price someday—in violence, in economic costs. I despair of making this appeal in any terms but these. You cannot issue an appeal to conscience in New York today. The fair-play argument won't be accepted. So you speak of violence and hope that it will scare the city into action."

While we talk, three children who look six or seven years old come to the door and ask to see the nurse, who isn't in the school today. One of the children, a Puerto Rican girl, looks haggard. "I have a pain in my tooth," she says. The principal says, "The nurse is out. Why don't you call your mother?" The child says, "My mother doesn't have a phone." The principal sighs. "Then go back to your class." When she leaves, the principal is angry. "It's amazing to me that these children ever make it with the obstacles they face. Many *do* care and they *do* try, but there's a feeling of despair. The parents of these children want the same things for their children that the parents in the suburbs want. Drugs are not the cause of this. They are the symptom. Nonetheless, they're used by people in the suburbs and rich people in Manhattan as another reason to keep children of poor people at a distance."

I ask him, "Will white children and black children ever go to school together in New York?"

"I don't see it," he replies. "I just don't think it's going to happen. It's a dream. I simply do not see white folks in Riverdale agreeing to cross-bus with kids like these. A few, maybe. Very few. I don't think I'll live to see it happen."

I ask him whether race is the decisive factor. Many experts, I observe, believe that wealth is more important in determining these inequalities.

"This," he says—and sweeps his hand around him at the room, the garbage bag, the ceiling—"would not happen to white children."

In a kindergarten class the children sit cross-legged on a carpet in a space between two walls of books. Their 26 faces are turned up to watch their teacher, an elderly black woman. A little boy who sits beside me is involved in trying to tie bows in his shoelaces. The children sing a song: "Lift Every Voice." On the wall are these handwritten words: "Beautiful, also, are the souls of my people."

In a very small room on the fourth floor, 52 people in two classes do their best to teach and learn. Both are first grade classes. One, I am informed, is "low ability." The other is bilingual.

"The room is barely large enough for one class," says the principal.

The room is 25 by 50 feet. There are 26 first graders and two adults on the left, 22 others and two adults on the right. On the wall there is the picture of a small white child, circled by a Valentine, and a Gainsborough painting of a child in a formal dress.

"We are handicapped by scarcity," one of the teachers says. "One fifth of these children may be at grade level by the year's end."

A boy who may be seven years old climbs on my lap without an invitation and removes my glasses. He studies my face and runs his fingers through my hair. "You have nice hair," he says. I ask him where he lives and he replies, "Times Square Hotel," which is a homeless shelter in Manhattan.

I ask him how he gets here.

"With my father. On the train," he says.

"How long does it take?"

"It takes an hour and a half."

I ask him when he leaves his home.

"My mother wakes me up at five o'clock."

"When do you leave?"

"Six-thirty."

I ask him how he gets back to Times Square.

"My father comes to get me after school."

From my notes: "He rides the train three hours every day in order to attend this segregated school. It would be a shorter ride to Riverdale. There are rapid shuttle-vans that make that trip in only 20 minutes. Why not let him go to school right in Manhattan, for that matter?"

At three o'clock the nurse arrives to do her recordkeeping. She tells me she is here three days a week. "The public hospital we use for an emergency is called North Central. It's not a hospital that I will use if I am given any choice. Clinics in the private hospitals are far more likely to be staffed by an experienced physician."

She hesitates a bit as I take out my pen, but then goes on: "I'll give you an example. A little girl I saw last week in school was trembling and shaking and could not control the motions of her arms. I was concerned and called her home. Her mother came right up to school and took her to North Central. The intern concluded that the child was upset by 'family matters'— nothing more—that there was nothing wrong with her. The mother was offended by the diagnosis. She did not appreciate his words or his assumptions. The truth is, there was nothing wrong at home. She brought the child back to school. I thought that she was ill. I told her mother, 'Go to Montefiore.' It's a private hospital, and well respected. She took my advice, thank God. It turned out that the child had a neurological disorder. She is now in treatment.

"This is the kind of thing our children face. Am I saying that the city underserves this population? You can draw your own conclusions."

Out on the street, it takes a full half hour to flag down a cab. Taxi drivers in New York are sometimes disconcertingly direct in what they say. When they are contemptuous of poor black people, their contempt is unadorned. When they're sympathetic and compassionate, their observations often go right to the heart of things. "Oh . . . they neglect these children," says the driver. "They leave them in the streets and slums to live and die." We stop at a light. Outside the window of the taxi, aimless men are standing in a semicircle while another man is working on his car. Old four-story buildings with their windows boarded, cracked or missing are on every side.

I ask the driver where he's from. He says Afghanistan. Turning in his seat, he gestures at the street and shrugs. "If you don't, as an American, begin to give these kids the kind of education that you give the kids of Donald Trump, you're asking for disaster."

Two months later, on a day in May, I visit an elementary school in Riverdale. The dogwoods and magnolias on the lawn in front of P.S. 24 are in full blossom on the day I visit. There is a well-tended park across the street, another larger park three blocks away. To the left of the school is a playground for small children, with an innovative jungle gym, a slide and several climbing toys. Behind the school there are two playing fields for older kids. The grass around the school is neatly trimmed.

The neighborhood around the school, by no means the richest part of Riverdale, is nonetheless expensive and quite beautiful. Residences in the area—some of which are large, free-standing houses, others condominiums in solid red-brick buildings—sell for prices in the region of $400,000; but some of the larger Tudor houses on the winding and tree-shaded streets close to the school can cost up to $1 million. The excellence of P.S. 24, according to the principal, adds to the value of these homes. Advertisements in *The New York Times* will frequently inform prospective buyers that a house is "in the neighborhood of P.S. 24."

The school serves 825 children in the kindergarten through sixth grade. This is approximately half the student population crowded into P.S. 79, where 1,550 children fill a space intended for 1,000, and a great deal smaller than the 1,300 children packed into the former skating rink; but the principal of P.S. 24, a capable and energetic man named David Rothstein, still regards it as excessive for an elementary school.

The school is integrated in the strict sense that the middle- and upper-middle-class white children here do occupy a building that contains some Asian and Hispanic and black children; but there is little integration in the classrooms since the vast majority of the Hispanic and black children are assigned to "special" classes on the basis of evaluations that have classified them "EMR"—"educable mentally retarded"—or else, in the worst of cases, "TMR"—"trainable mentally retarded."

I ask the principal if any of his students qualify for free-lunch programs. "About 130 do," he says. "Perhaps another 35 receive their lunches at reduced price. Most of these kids are in the special classes. They do not come from this neighborhood."

The very few nonwhite children that one sees in mainstream classes tend to be Japanese or else of other Asian origins.

Riverdale, I learn, has been the residence of choice for many years to members of the diplomatic corps.

The school therefore contains effectively two separate schools: one of about 130 children, most of whom are poor, Hispanic, black, assigned to one of the 12 special classes; the other of some 700 mainstream students, almost all of whom are white or Asian.

There is a third track also—this one for the students who are labeled "talented" or "gifted." This is termed a "pull-out" program since the children who are so identified remain in mainstream classrooms but are taken out for certain periods each week to be provided with intensive and, in my opinion, excellent instruction in some areas of reasoning and logic often known as "higher-order skills" in the contemporary jargon of the public schools. Children identified as "gifted" are admitted to this program in first grade and, in most cases, will remain there for six years. Even here, however, there are two tracks of the gifted. The regular gifted classes are provided with only one semester of this specialized instruction yearly. Those very few children, on the other hand, who are identified as showing the most promise are assigned, beginning in the third grade, to a program that receives a full-year regimen.

In one such class, containing ten intensely verbal and impressive fourth grade children, nine are white and one is Asian. The "special" class I enter first, by way of contrast, has twelve children of whom only one is white and none is Asian. These racial breakdowns prove to be predictive of the schoolwide pattern.

In a classroom for the gifted on the first floor of the school, I ask a child what the class is doing. "Logic and syllogisms," she replies. The room is fitted with a planetarium. The principal says that all the elementary schools in District 10 were given the same planetarium ten years ago but that certain schools, because of overcrowding, have been forced to give them up. At P.S. 261, according to my notes, there was a domelike space that had been built to hold a planetarium, but the planetarium had been removed to free up space for the small library collection. P.S. 24, in contrast, has a spacious library that holds almost 8,000 books. The windows are decorated with attractive, brightly colored curtains and look out on flowering trees. The principal says that it's inadequate, but it appears spectacular to me after the cubicle that holds a meager 700 books within the former skating rink.

The district can't afford librarians, the principal says, but P.S. 24, unlike the poorer schools of District 10, can draw on educated parent volunteers who staff the room in shifts three days a week. A parent organization also raises independent funds to buy materials, including books, and will soon be running a fund-raiser to enhance the library's collection.

In a large and sunny first grade classroom that I enter next, I see 23 children, all of whom are white or Asian. In another first grade, there are 22 white children and two others who are Japanese. There is a computer in each class. Every classroom also has a modern fitted sink.

In a second grade class of 22 children, there are two black children and three Asian children. Again, there is a sink and a computer. A sixth grade social studies class has only one black child. The children have an in-class research area that holds some up-to-date resources. A set of encyclopedias (World Book, 1985) is in a rack beside a window. The children are doing a Spanish language lesson when I enter. Foreign languages begin in sixth grade at the school, but Spanish is offered also to the kindergarten children. As in every room at P.S. 24, the window shades are clean and new, the floor is neatly tiled in gray and green, and there is not a single light bulb missing.

Walking next into a special class, I see twelve children. One is white. Eleven are black. There are no Asian children. The room is half the size of mainstream classrooms. "Because of overcrowding," says the principal, "we have had to split these rooms in half." There is no computer and no sink.

I enter another special class. Of seven children, five are black, one is Hispanic, one is white. A little black boy with a large head sits in the far corner and is gazing at the ceiling.

"Placement of these kids," the principal explains, "can usually be traced to neurological damage."

In my notes: "How could so many of these children be brain-damaged?"

Next door to the special class is a woodworking shop. "This shop is only for the special classes," says the principal. The children learn to punch in time cards at the door, he says, in order to prepare them for employment.

The fourth grade gifted class, in which I spend the last part of the day, is humming with excitement. "I start with these children in the first grade," says the teacher. "We pull them out of mainstream classes on the basis of their test results and other factors such as the opinion of their teachers. Out of this group, beginning in third grade, I pull out the ones who show the most potential and they enter classes such as this one."

The curriculum they follow, she explains, "emphasizes critical thinking, reasoning and logic." The planetarium, for instance, is employed not simply for the study of the universe as it exists. "Children also are designing their own galaxies," the teacher says.

A little girl sitting around a table with her classmates speaks with perfect poise: "My name is Susan. We are in the fourth grade gifted program."

I ask them what they're doing and a child says, "My name is Laurie and we're doing problem-solving."

A rather tall, good-natured boy who is half-standing at the table tells me that his name is David. "One thing that we do," he says, "is logical thinking. Some problems, we find, have more than one good answer. We need to learn not simply to be logical in our own thinking but to show respect for someone else's logic even when an answer may be technically incorrect."

When I ask him to explain this, he goes on, "A person who gives an answer that is not 'correct' may nonetheless have done some interesting thinking that we should examine. 'Wrong' answers may be more useful to examine than correct ones."

I ask the children if reasoning and logic are innate or if they're things that you can learn.

"You know some things to start with when you enter school," Susan says. "But we also learn some things that other children don't."

I ask her to explain this.

"We know certain things that other kids don't know because we're *taught* them."

She has braces on her teeth. Her long brown hair falls almost to her waist. Her loose white T-shirt has the word TRI-LOGIC on the front. She tells me that Tri-Logic is her father's firm.

Laurie elaborates on the same point: "Some things you know. Some kinds of logic are inside of you to start with. There are other things that someone needs to teach you."

David expands on what the other two have said: "Everyone can think and speak in logical ways unless they have a mental problem. What this program does is bring us to a higher form of logic."

The class is writing a new "Bill of Rights." The children already know the U.S. Bill of Rights and they explain its first four items to me with precision. What they are examining today, they tell me, is the very *concept* of a "right." Then they will create their own compendium of rights according to their own analysis and definition. Along one wall of the classroom, opposite the planetarium, are seven Apple II computers on which children have developed rather subtle color animations that express the themes—of greed and domination, for example—that they also have described in writing.

"This is an upwardly mobile group," the teacher later says. "They have exposure to whatever New York City has available. Their parents may take them to the theater, to museums. . . ."

In my notes: "Six girls, four boys. Nine white, one Chinese. I am glad they have this class. But what about the others? Aren't there ten black children in the school who could enjoy this also?"

The teacher gives me a newspaper written, edited and computer-printed by her sixth grade gifted class. The children, she tells me, are provided with a link to kids in Europe for transmission of news stories.

A science story by one student asks if scientists have ever falsified their research. "Gregor Mendel," the sixth grader writes, "the Austrian monk who founded the science of genetics, published papers on his work with peas that some experts say were statistically too good to be true. Isaac Newton, who formulated the law of gravitation, relied on unseemly mathematical sleight of hand in his calculations. . . . Galileo Galilei, founder of modern scientific method, wrote about experiments that were so difficult to duplicate that colleagues doubted he had done them."

Another item in the paper, also by a sixth grade student, is less esoteric: "The Don Cossacks dance company, from Russia, is visiting the United States. The last time it toured America was 1976. . . . The Don Cossacks will be in New York City for two weeks at the Neil Simon Theater. Don't miss it!"

The tone is breezy—and so confident! That phrase—"Don't miss it!"—speaks a volume about life in Riverdale.

"What makes a good school?" asks the principal when we are talking later on. "The building and teachers are part of it, of course. But it isn't just the building and the teachers. Our kids come from good families and the neighborhood is good. In a three-block area we have a public library, a park, a junior high. . . . Our typical sixth grader reads at eighth grade level." In a quieter voice he says, "I see how hard my colleagues work in schools like P.S. 79. You have children in those neighborhoods who live in virtual hell. They enter school five years behind. What do they get?" Then, as he spreads his hands out on his desk, he says: "I have to ask myself why there should be an elementary school in District 10 with fifteen hundred children. Why should there be an elementary school within a skating rink? Why should the Board of Ed allow this? This is not the way that things should be."

Stark as the inequities in District 10 appear, educators say that they are "mild" in comparison to other situations in the city. Some of the most stunning inequality, according to a report by the Community Service Society, derives from allocations granted by state legislators to school districts where they have political allies. The poorest districts in the city get approximately 90 cents per pupil from these legislative grants, while the richest districts have been given $14 for each pupil.

Newspapers in New York City have reported other instances of the misallocation of resources. "The Board of Education," wrote the *New York Post* during July of 1987, "was hit with bombshell charges yesterday that money earmarked for fighting drug abuse and illiteracy in ghetto schools was funneled instead to schools in wealthy areas."

In receipt of extra legislative funds, according to the *Post,* affluent districts were funded "at a rate 14 times greater than low-income districts." The paper said the city's poorest areas were underfunded "with stunning consistency."

The report by the Community Service Society cites an official of the New York City Board of Education who remarks that there is "no point" in putting further money "into some poor districts" because, in his belief, "new teachers would not stay there." But the report observes that, in an instance where beginning teacher salaries were raised by nearly half, "that problem largely disappeared"—another interesting reminder of the difference money makes when we are willing to invest it. Nonetheless, says the report, "the perception that the poorest districts are beyond help still remains. . . ." Perhaps the worst result of such beliefs, says the report, is the message that resources would be "wasted on poor children." This message "trickles down to districts, schools, and classrooms." Children hear and understand this theme—they are poor investments—and behave accordingly. If society's resources would be wasted on their destinies, perhaps their own determination would be wasted too. "Expectations are a powerful force . . . ," the CSS observes.

Despite the evidence, the CSS report leans over backwards not to fuel the flames of racial indignation. "In the present climate," the report says, "suggestions of racism must be made with caution. However, it is inescapable that these inequities are being perpetrated on [school] districts which are virtually all black and Hispanic. . . ." While the report says, very carefully, that there is no "evidence" of "deliberate in-dividual discrimination," it nonetheless concludes that "those who allocate resources make decisions over and over again which penalize the poorest districts." Analysis of city policy, the study says, "speaks to systemic bias which constitutes a conspiracy of effect. . . . Whether consciously or not, the system writes off its poorest students."[5]

NOTES

1. Lord Acton cited: George Alan Hickrod, "Reply to the 'Forbes' Article," *Journal of School Finance* 12 (1987).
2. Per-pupil spending, New York City and suburbs: Office for Policy Analysis and Program Accountability, New York State Board of Education, "Statistical Profiles of School Districts" (Albany: 1 January 1989). Numbers cited are for 1986–1987 school year.
3. Question asked by New York City Board of Education and response of Community Service Society: Community Service Society of New York, "Promoting Poverty: The Shift of Resources Away from Low-Income New York City School Districts" (New York: 1987).
4. Contrasts between Schools in District 10, statements of principals and superintendent: *The New York Times,* January 2, 1987. District 10 Superintendent Fred Goldberg resigned under pressure in 1991. A highly respected veteran of the New York City public schools, he struck me, in the course of an April 1990 interview, as an enlightened educator caught up in a compromising situation that was not of his own making. Educators in New York believe that he was made to pay an unfair price for the profound racism rooted in the city's public schools.
5. Inequities in New York City Schools: *The New York Times,* 2 July 1987; *New York Post,* 2 July 1987; *The* (New York) *City Sun,* 15–21 July 1987; "Promoting Poverty" (Community Service Society of New York), cited above.

16

POSITIVE FUNCTIONS OF THE UNDESERVING POOR
Uses of the Underclass in America

Herbert J. Gans

I. Introduction

Poverty, like any other social phenomenon, can be analyzed in terms of the *causes* which initiate and perpetuate it, but once it exists, it can also be studied in terms of the consequences or *functions* which follow. These functions can be both *positive* and *negative*, adaptive and destructive, depending on their nature and the people and interests affected.

Poverty has many negative functions (or dysfunctions), most for the poor themselves, but also for the nonpoor. Among those of most concern to both populations, perhaps the major one is that a small but visible proportion of poor people is involved in activities which threaten their physical safety, for example street crime, or which deviate from important norms claimed to be "mainstream," such as failing to work, bearing children in adolescence and out of wedlock, and being "dependent" on welfare. In times of high unemployment, illegal and even legal immigrants are added to this list for endangering the job opportunities of native-born Americans.

Furthermore, many better-off Americans believe that the number of poor people who behave in these ways is far larger than it actually is. More important, many think that poor people act as they do because of

moral shortcomings that express themselves in lawlessness or in the rejection of mainstream norms. Like many other sociologists, however, I argue that the behavior patterns which concern the more fortunate classes are *poverty-related*, because they are, and have historically been, associated with poverty. After all, mugging is only practiced by the poor. They are in fact caused by poverty, although a variety of other causes must also be at work since most poor people are not involved in any of these activities, including mugging.

Because their criminal or disapproved behavior is ascribed to moral shortcomings, the poor people who resort to it are often classified as unworthy or *undeserving*. For example, even though the failure of poor young men (or women) to work may be the effect of a lack of jobs, they are frequently accused of laziness, and then judged undeserving. Likewise, even though poor young mothers may decide not to marry the fathers of their children, because they, being jobless, cannot support them, the women are still accused of violating conventional familial norms, and also judged undeserving. Moreover, once judged to be undeserving, poor people are then no longer thought to be deserving of public aid that is financially sufficient and secure enough to help them escape poverty.

Judgments of the poor as undeserving are not based on evidence, but derive from a stereotype, even if, like most others, it is a stereotype with a "kernel of truth" (e.g., the monopolization of street crime by the poor). Furthermore, it is a very old stereotype;

Herbert J. Gans, "Positive Functions of the Undeserving Poor" from *Politics and Society*, Vol. 22, No. 3, September 1994, pp. 269–283. Copyright © 1994 by Sage Publications. Reprinted by permission of Sage Publications, Inc.

Cicero already described the needy of Rome as criminals.[1] By the middle of the sixteenth century, complicated laws to distinguish between the deserving and undeserving were in existence.[2] However, the term undeserving poor was first used regularly in England in the 1830s, at the time of the institution of the Poor Law.[3]

In America, a series of other, more specific, terms were borrowed or invented, with new ones replacing old ones as conditions and fashions changed.[4] Such terms have included *beggar, pauper,* the *dangerous class, rabble, vagabond* and *vagrant,* and so on, which the United States borrowed from Europe. America also invented its own terms, including *shiftless, tramp,* and *feeble-minded,* and in the late twentieth century, terms like *hard-core, drifter, culturally deprived*—and most recently, *underclass.*[5] Nonetheless, in terms of its popular uses and the people to whom it is applied, the term underclass differs little from its predecessors.[6]

It is not difficult to understand why people, poor and more fortunate, are fearful of street crime committed by poor people, and even why the jobless poor and welfare recipients, like paupers before them, may be perceived as economic threats for not working and drawing on public funds, at least in bad economic times. Also, one can understand why other forms of poverty-related behavior, such as the early sexual activity of poor youngsters and the dramatic number of poor single-parent families, are viewed as moral threats, since they violate norms thought to uphold the two-parent nuclear family and related normative bases of the social order. However, there would seem to be no inherent reason for exaggerating these threats, for example, in the case of welfare recipients who obtain only a tiny proportion of governmental expenditures, or more generally, by stereotyping poor people as undeserving without evidence of what they have and have not done, and why.

One reason, if not the only one, for the exaggeration and the stereotyping, and for the continued attractiveness of the concept of the undeserving poor itself, is that undeservingness has a number of *positive* functions for the better-off population. Some of these functions, or uses, are positive for everyone who is not poor, but most are positive only for some people, interest groups, and institutions, ranging from moderate income to wealthy ones. Needless to say, that undeservingness has uses for some people does not justify it; the existence of functions just helps to explain why it persists.

My notion of function, or empirically observable adaptive consequence, is adapted from the classic conceptual scheme of Robert K. Merton.[7] My analysis will concentrate on those positive functions which Merton conceptualized as *latent,* which are unrecognized and/or unintended, but with the proviso that the functions which are identified as latent would probably not be abolished once they were widely recognized. Positive functions are, after all, also benefits, and people are not necessarily ready to give up benefits, including unintended ones, even if they become aware of them.[8]

The rest of this article deals only with the functions of the poor labeled undeserving. It can also be read as a sequel to an earlier article, in which I analyzed the positive functions of poverty without distinguishing between the deserving and undeserving poor.[9]

II. Functions of the Undeserving Poor[10]

I will discuss five sets of positive functions: microsocial, economic, normative-cultural, political, and macrosocial, which I divide into 13 specific functions, although the sets are arbitrarily chosen and interrelated, and I could add many more functions. The functions are not listed in order of importance, for such a listing is not possible without empirical research on the various beneficiaries of undeservingness.

Two Microsocial Functions

1. *Risk reduction.* Perhaps the primary use of the idea of the undeserving poor, primary because it takes place at the microsocial scale of everyday life, is that it distances the labeled from those who label them. By stigmatizing people as undeserving, labelers protect themselves from the responsibility of having to associate with them, or even to treat them like moral equals, which reduces the risk of being hurt or angered by them. Risk reduction is a way of dealing with actual or imagined threats to physical safety, for example from people who might be muggers, or cultural threats attributed to poor youngsters or normative ones imagined to come from welfare recipients. All pejorative labels and stereotypes serve this function, which may help to explain why there are so many such labels.

2. *Scapegoating and displacement.* By being thought undeserving, the stigmatized poor can be blamed for virtually any shortcoming of everyday life which can be credibly ascribed to them—violations of the laws of logic or social causation notwithstanding. Faulting the undeserving poor can also support the desire for revenge and punishment. In a society in which punishment is reserved for legislative, judicial, and penal institutions, *feelings* of revenge and punitiveness toward the undeserving poor supply at least some emotional satisfaction.

Since labeling poor people undeserving opens the door for nearly unlimited scapegoating, the labeled are also available to serve what I call the displacement function. Being too weak to object, the stigmatized poor can be accused of having caused social problems which they did not actually cause

and can serve as cathartic objects on which better-off people can unload their own problems, as well as those of the economy, the polity, or of any other institution, for the shortcomings of which the poor can be blamed.

Whether societywide changes in the work ethic are displaced on to "shiftlessness," or economic stagnation on to "welfare dependency," the poor can be declared undeserving for what ails the more affluent. This may also help to explain why the national concern with poor Black unmarried mothers, although usually ascribed to the data presented in the 1965 Moynihan Report, did not gather steam until the beginning of the decline of the economy in the mid-1970s. Similarly, the furor about poor "babies having babies" waited for the awareness of rising adolescent sexual activity among the better-off classes in the 1980s—at which point rates of adolescent pregnancy among the poor had already declined. But when the country became ambivalent about the desirability of abortions, the issue was displaced on the poor by making it almost impossible for them to obtain abortions.

Many years ago, James Baldwin, writing in *The Fire Next Time,* illustrated the displacement function in racial terms, arguing that, as Andrew Hacker put it, Whites "need the 'nigger' because it is the 'nigger' within themselves that they cannot tolerate. Whatever it is that Whites feel 'nigger' signifies about Blacks—lust and laziness, stupidity or squalor—in fact exists within themselves. . . . By creating such a creature, Whites are able to say that because only members of the Black race can carry that taint, it follows that none of its attributes will be found in White people."[11]

Three Economic Functions

3. *Economic banishment and the reserve army of labor.* People who have successfully

been labeled as undeserving can be banished from the formal labor market. If young people are designated "school dropouts," for example, they can also be thought to lack the needed work habits, such as proper adherence to the work ethic, and may not be offered jobs to begin with. Often, they are effectively banished from the labor market before entering it because employers imagine them to be poor workers simply because they are young, male, and Black.[12] Many ex-convicts are declared unemployable in similar fashion, and some become recidivists because they have no other choice but to go back to their criminal occupations.

Banishing the undeserving also makes room for immigrant workers, who may work for lower wages, are more deferential, and are more easily exploitable by being threatened with deportation. In addition, banishment helps to reduce the official jobless rate, a sometimes useful political function, especially if the banished drop so completely out of the labor force that they are not even available to be counted as "discouraged workers."

The economic banishment function is in many ways a replacement for the old reserve army of labor function, which played itself out when the undeserving poor could be hired as strikebreakers, as defense workers in the case of sudden wartime economic mobilization, as "hypothetical workers," who by their very presence could be used to depress the wages of other workers, or to put pressure on the unions not to make wage and other demands. Today, however, with a plentiful supply of immigrants, as well as of a constantly growing number of banished workers who are becoming surplus labor, a reserve army is less rarely needed—and when needed, can be recruited from sources other than the undeserving poor.[13]

Welfare recipients may, however, turn out to continue to be a part of the reserve army. Currently, they are encouraged to stay out of the labor market by remaining eligible for the Medicaid benefits they need for their children only if they remain on welfare.[14] Should the Clinton administration welfare reform program become reality, however, welfare recipients, who will be required to work for the minimum wage or less, could exert pressure on the wages of the employed, thus bringing them right back into the reserve army.

4. *Supplying illegal goods.* The undeserving poor who are banished from other jobs remain eligible for work in the manufacture and sale of illegal goods, including drugs. Although it is estimated that 80 percent of all illegal drugs are sold to Whites who are not poor, the sellers are often people banished from the formal labor market.[15] Other suppliers of illegal goods include the illegal immigrants, considered undeserving in many American communities, who work for garment industry sweatshops manufacturing clothing under illegal conditions.

5. *Job creation.* Perhaps the most important economic function of the undeserving poor today is that their mere presence creates jobs for the better-off population, including professional ones. Since the undeserving poor are thought to be dangerous or improperly socialized, their behavior either has to be modified so that they act in socially approved ways, or they have to be isolated from the deserving sectors of society. The larger the number of people who are declared undeserving, the larger also the number of people needed to modify and isolate as well as control, guard, and care for them. Among these are the social workers, teachers, trainers, mentors, psychiatrists, doctors and their support staffs in juvenile training centers, "special" schools, drug treatment centers, and penal behavior modification institutions, as well as the police, prosecutors, defense attorneys, judges, court officers, probation personnel and others who constitute

the criminal courts, and the guards and others who run the prisons.

Jobs created by the presence of undeserving poor also include the massive bureaucracy of professionals, investigators, and clerks who administer welfare. Other jobs go to the officials who seek out poor fathers for child support monies they may or may not have, as well as the welfare office personnel needed to take recipients in violation of welfare rules off the rolls, and those needed to put them back on the rolls when they reapply. In fact, one can argue that some of the rules for supervising, controlling, and punishing the undeserving poor are more effective at performing the latent function of creating clerical and professional jobs for the better-off population than the manifest function of achieving their official goals.

More jobs are created in the social sciences and in journalism for conducting research about the undeserving poor and producing popular books, articles, and TV documentaries for the more fortunate who want to learn about them. The "job chain" should also be extended to the teachers and others who train those who serve, control, and study the undeserving poor.

In addition, the undeserving poor make jobs for what I call the salvation industries, religious, civil, or medical, which also try to modify the behavior of those stigmatized as undeserving. Not all such jobs are paid, for the undeserving poor also provide occasional targets for charity and thus offer volunteer jobs for those providing it—and paid jobs for the professional fundraisers who obtain most of the charitable funds these days. Among the most visible volunteers are the members of "cafe" and "high" society who organize and contribute to these benefits.[16]

Three Normative Functions

6. *Moral legitimation.* Undeservingness justifies the category of deservingness and

thus supplies moral and political legitimacy, almost by definition, to the institutions and social structures that include the deserving and exclude the undeserving.[17] Of these structures, the most important is undoubtedly the class hierarchy, for the existence of an undeserving class or stratum legitimates the deserving classes, if not necessarily all of their class-related behavior.[18] The alleged immorality of the undeserving also gives a moral flavor to, and justification for, the class hierarchy, which may help to explain why upward mobility itself is so praiseworthy.[19]

7. *Norm reinforcement.* By violating, or being imagined as violating, a number of mainstream behavioral patterns and values, the undeserving poor help to reaffirm and reinforce the virtues of these patterns—and to do so visibly, since the violations by the undeserving are highly publicized. As Emile Durkheim pointed out nearly a century ago, norm violations and their punishments also provide an opportunity for preserving and reaffirming the norms. This is not insignificant, for norms sometimes disparaged as "motherhood" values gain new moral power when they are violated, and their violators are stigmatized.

If the undeserving poor can be imagined to be lazy, they help to reaffirm the Protestant work ethic; if poor single-parent families are publicly condemned, the two-parent family is once more legitimated as ideal. In the 1960s, middle-class morality was sometimes criticized as culturally parochial and therefore inappropriate for the poor, but since the 1980s, mainstream values have once more been regarded as vital sources of behavioral guidance for them.[20]

Enforcing the norms also contributes further to preserving them in another way, for one of the standard punishments of the undeserving poor for misbehaving—as well as a standard obligation in exchange for help—is practicing the mainstream norms, including those that the members of the mainstream may only be preaching, and that might die out if the poor were not required to incorporate them in their behavior. Old work rules that can no longer be enforced in the rest of the economy can be maintained in the regulations for workfare; old-fashioned austerity and thrift are built into the consumption patterns expected of welfare recipients. Economists like to argue that if the poor want to be deserving, they should take any kind of job, regardless of its low pay or demeaning character, reflecting the work ethic which economists themselves have never practiced.

Similarly, welfare recipients may be removed from the rolls if they are found to be living with a man—but the social worker who removes them has every right to cohabit and not lose his or her job. In most states, welfare recipients must observe rules of housecleaning and child care that middle-class people are free to ignore without being punished. While there are many norms and laws governing child care, only the poor are monitored to see if they obey these. Should they use more physical punishment on their children than social workers consider desirable, they can be charged with child neglect or abuse and can lose their children to foster care.[21]

The fact is that the defenders of such widely preached norms as hard work, thrift, monogamy, and moderation need people who can be accused, accurately or not, of being lazy, spendthrift, promiscuous, and immoderate. One reason that welfare recipients are a ready target for punitive legislation is that politicians, and most likely some of their constituents, imagine them to be enjoying leisure and an active sex life at public expense. Whether or not very many poor people actually behave in the ways that are judged undeserving is irrelevant if they can be imagined as doing so. Once imagining and stereotyping are allowed to take over, then judgments of undeservingness can be

made without much concern for empirical accuracy. For example, in the 1990s, the idea that young men from poor single-parent families were highly likely to commit street crimes became so universal that the news media no longer needed to quote experts to affirm the accuracy of the charge.

Actually, most of the time most of the poor are as law abiding and observant of mainstream norms as are other Americans. Sometimes they are even more observant; thus the proportion of welfare recipients who cheat is always far below the percentage of taxpayers who do so.[22] Moreover, survey after survey has shown that the poor, including many street criminals and drug sellers, want to hold respectable jobs like everyone else, hope someday to live in the suburbs, and generally aspire to the same American dream as most moderate and middle-income Americans.[23]

8. *Supplying popular culture villains.* The undeserving poor have played a long-term role in supplying American popular culture with villains, allowing the producers of the culture both to reinforce further mainstream norms and to satisfy audience demands for revenge, notably by showing that crime and other norm violations do not pay. Street criminals are shown dead or alive in the hands of the police on local television news virtually every day, and more dramatically so in the crime and action movies and television series.

For many years before and after World War II, the criminal characters in Hollywood movies were often poor immigrants, frequently of Sicilian origin. Then they were complemented for some decades by communist spies and other Cold War enemies who were not poor, but even before the end of the Cold War, they were being replaced by Black and Hispanic drug dealers and gang leaders.

At the same time, however, the popular culture industry has also supplied music and other materials offering marketable cultural and political protest which does not reinforce mainstream norms, or at least not directly. Some of the creators and performers come from poor neighborhoods, however, and it may be that some rap music becomes commercially successful by displacing on ghetto musicians the cultural and political protest of record buyers from more affluent classes.[24]

Three Political Functions

9. *Institutional scapegoating.* The scapegoating of the undeserving poor mentioned in Function 2 above also extends to institutions which mistreat them. As a result, some of the responsibility for the existence of poverty, slums, unemployment, poor schools, and the like is taken off the shoulders of elected and appointed officials who are supposed to deal with these problems. For example, to the extent that educational experts decide that the children of the poor are learning disabled or that they are culturally or genetically inferior in intelligence, attempts to improve the schools can be put off or watered down.

To put it another way, the availability of institutional scapegoats both personalizes and exonerates social systems. The alleged laziness of the jobless and the anger aimed at beggars take the heat off the failure of the economy, and the imagined derelictions of slum dwellers and the homeless, off the housing industry. In effect, the undeserving poor are blamed both for their poverty and also for the absence of "political will" among the citizenry to do anything about it.

10. *Conservative power shifting.* Once poor people are declared undeserving, they also lose their political legitimacy and whatever little political influence they had before they were stigmatized. Some cannot vote, and many do not choose to vote or mobilize because they know politicians do not listen to their demands. Elected officials might ignore them even if they voted or mobilized, because these officials and the larger polity cannot easily satisfy their demands for economic and other kinds of justice.[25] As a result, the political system is able to pay additional attention to the demands of more affluent constituents. It can therefore shift to the "right."

The same shift to the right also takes place ideologically. Although injustices of poverty help justify the existence of liberals and the more radical left, the undeserving poor themselves provide justification and opportunities for conservatives to attack their ideological enemies on their left. When liberals can be accused of favoring criminals over victims, their accusers can launch and legitimate incursions on the civil liberties and rights of the undeserving poor, and concurrently on the liberties and rights of defenders of the poor. Moreover, the undeservingness of the poor can be used to justify attacks on the welfare state. Charles Murray understood the essence of this ideological function when he argued that welfare and other welfare state legislation for the poor only increased the number of poor people.[26]

11. *Spatial purification.* Stigmatized populations are often used, deliberately or not, to stigmatize the areas in which they live, making such areas eligible for various kinds of purification. As a result, "underclass areas" can be torn down and their inhabitants moved to make room for more affluent residents or higher taxpayers.

However, such areas can also be used to isolate stigmatized poor people and facilities by selecting them as locations for homeless shelters, halfway houses for the mentally ill or for ex-convicts, drug treatment facilities, and even garbage dumps, which have been forced out of middle- and working-class areas following NIMBY (not in my backyard) protests. Drug dealers and other sellers of illegal goods also find a haven in areas stigmatized as underclass areas, partly because these supply some customers, but also because police protection in such areas is usually minimal enough to allow illegal activities without significant interference from the law.[27] In fact, municipalities would face major economic and political obstacles to their operations without stigmatized areas in which stigmatized people and activities can be located.

Two Macrosocial Functions

12. *Reproduction of stigma and the stigmatized.* For centuries now, undeservingness has given rise to policies and agencies which are manifestly set up to help the poor economically and otherwise to become deserving, but which actually prevent the undeserving poor from being freed of their stigma, and which also manage, unwittingly, to see to it that their children face the same obstacles.[28] In some instances, this process works so speedily that the children of the stigmatized face "anticipatory stigmatization," among them the children of welfare recipients who are frequently predicted to be unable to learn, to work, and to remain on the right side of the law even before they have been weaned.

If this outcome were planned deliberately, one could argue that politically and culturally dominant groups are reluctant to give up an easily accessible and always available scapegoat. In actuality, however, the reproduction function results unwittingly from other intended and seemingly popular practices. For example, the so-called War on Drugs, which has unsuccessfully sought to keep hard drugs out of the United States, but has meanwhile done little to provide drug treatment to addicts who want it, thereby aids the continuation of addiction, street crime, and a guaranteed prison population, not to mention the vari-

ous disasters that visit the families of addicts and help to keep them poor.

The other major source of reproducing stigma and the stigmatized is the routine activities of the organizations which service welfare recipients, the homeless, and other stigmatized poor, and end up mistreating them.[29] For one thing, such agencies, whether they exist to supply employment to the poor or to help the homeless, are almost certain to be underfunded because of the powerlessness of their clientele. No organization has ever had the funds or power to buy, build, or rehabilitate housing for the homeless in sufficient number. Typically, they have been able to fund or carry out small demonstration projects.

In addition, organizations which serve stigmatized people often attract less well-trained and qualified staff than those with high-status clients, and if the clients are deemed undeserving, competence may become even less important in choosing staff.[30] Then too, helping organizations generally reflect the societal stratification hierarchy, which means that organizations with poor, low-status clients frequently treat them as undeserving. If they also fear some of their clients, they may not only withhold help, but attack the clients on a preemptive strike basis. Last but not least, the agencies that serve the undeserving poor are bureaucracies which operate by rules and regulations that routinize the work, encourage the stability and growth of the organizations, and serve the needs of their staffs before those of their clients.

When these factors are combined, as they often are, and become cumulative, as they often do, it should not be surprising that the organizations cut off escape routes from poverty not only for the clients, but in doing so, also make sure that some of their children remain poor as well.

13. *Extermination of the surplus.* In earlier times, when the living standards of all

poor people were at or below subsistence, many died at an earlier age than the better off, thus performing the set of functions for the latter forever associated with Thomas Malthus. Standards of living, even for the very poor, have risen considerably in the last century, but even today, morbidity and mortality rates remain much higher among the poor than among moderate-income people. To put it another way, various social forces combine to do away with some of the people who have become surplus labor and are no longer needed by the economy.

Several of the killing illnesses and pathologies of the poor change over time; currently, they include AIDS, tuberculosis, hypertension, heart attacks, and cancer, as well as psychosis, substance abuse, street crime, injury and death during participation in the drug trade and other underworld activities, and intraclass homicide resulting from neighborhood conflicts over turf and "respect." Whether the poor people whose only problem is being unfairly stereotyped and stigmatized as undeserving die earlier than other poor people is not known.[31]

Moreover, these rates can be expected to remain high or even to rise as rates of unemployment—and of banishment from the labor force—rise, especially for the least skilled. Even the better-off jobless created by the downsizing of the 1990s blame themselves for their unemployment if they cannot eventually find new jobs, become depressed, and in some instances begin the same process of being extruded permanently from the labor market experienced by the least skilled of the jobless.

In effect, contemporary advanced capitalism may well have created the conditions for a new Malthusian hypothesis. In any case, the early departure of poor people from an economy and society which do not need them is useful for those who remain. Since the more fortunate classes have already developed a purposive blindness to the structural causes of unemployment and to the poverty-related causes of pathology and crime that follow, those who benefit from the current job erosion and the possible extermination of the surplus labor may not admit it consciously either. Nonetheless, those left over to compete for scarce jobs and other resources will have a somewhat easier time in the competition, thus assigning undeservingness a final positive function for the more fortunate members of society.[32]

III. Conclusion

I have described thirteen of the more important functions of the undeserving poor, enough to support my argument that both the idea of the undeserving poor and the stigmas with which some poor people are thus labeled may persist in part because they are useful in a variety of ways to the people who are not poor.

This analysis does not imply that undeservingness will or should persist. Whether it *will* persist is going to be determined by what happens to poverty in America. If it declines, poverty-related crime should also decline, and then fewer poor people will probably be described as undeserving. If poverty worsens, so will poverty-related crime, as well as the stereotyping and stigmatization of the poor, and any worsening of the country's economy is likely to add to the kinds and numbers of undeserving poor, if only because they make convenient and powerless scapegoats.

The functions that the undeserving poor play cannot, by themselves, perpetuate either poverty or undeservingness, for as I noted earlier, functions are not causes. For example, if huge numbers of additional unskilled workers should be needed, as they were for the World War II war effort, the undeserving poor will be welcomed back into the labor force, at least temporarily. Of course, institutions often try to survive once they have lost both their reasons for existence and their functions. Since the end of the Cold War, parts of the military-industrial establishment both in the United States and Russia have been campaigning for the maintenance of some Cold War forces and weapons to guarantee their own futures, but these establishments also supply jobs to their national economies, and in the United States, for the constituents of elected officials. Likewise, some of the institutions and interest groups that benefit from the existence of undeservingness, or from controlling the undeserving poor, may try to maintain undeservingness and its stigma. They may not even need to, for if Emile Durkheim was right, the decline of undeservingness would lead to the criminalization, or at least stigmatization, of new behavior patterns.

Whether applying the label of undeservingness to the poor *should* persist is a normative question which ought to be answered in the negative. Although people have a right to judge each other, that right does not extend to judging large numbers of people as a single group, with one common moral fault, or to stereotyping them without evidence either about their behavior or their values. Even if a case could be made for judging large cohorts of people as undeserving, these judgments should be distributed up and down the socioeconomic hierarchy, requiring Americans also to consider whether and how people in the working, middle, and upper classes are undeserving.

The same equality should extend to the punishment of crimes. Today, many Americans and courts still treat white-collar and upper-class criminals more leniently than poor ones. The public excuse given is that the street crime of the undeserving poor involves violence and thus injury or death, but as many students of white-collar and corporate crime have pointed out, these also hurt

and kill people, and often in large numbers, even if they do so less directly and perhaps less violently.

Changes also need to be made in the American conception of deviance, which like that of other countries, conflates people whose behavior is *different* with those whose behavior is socially *harmful*. Bearing children without marriage is a long-standing tradition among the poor. Born of necessity rather than preference, it is a poverty-related practice, but it is not, by itself, harmful, or at least not until it can be shown that either the children—or the moral sensibilities of the people who oppose illegitimacy—are significantly hurt. Poor single-parent families are hardly desirable, but as the lack of condemnation of more affluent single-parent families should suggest, the major problem of such families is not the number of parents, actual or surrogate, in the family, but its poverty.

Finally, because many of the poor are stereotyped unjustly as undeserving, scholars, writers, journalists, and others should launch a systematic and public effort to deconstruct and delegitimate the notion of the undeserving poor. This effort, which is necessary to help make effective antipoverty programs politically acceptable again, should place the following five ideas on the public agenda and encourage discussion as well as dissemination of available research.

The five ideas, all discussed earlier in this article, are that (1) the criminal and deviant behavior among the poor is largely poverty related rather than the product of free choice based on distinctive values; (2) the undeservingness of the poor is an ancient stereotype, and like all stereotypes, it vastly exaggerates the actual dangers that stem from the poor; (3) poverty-related deviance is not necessarily harmful just because it does not accord with mainstream norms; (4) the notion of undeservingness survives in part because of the positive functions it has for the better-off population; and (5) the only certain way to eliminate both this notion and the functions is to eliminate poverty.[33]

NOTES

1. However, Cicero had a distinctive perspective; in today's terminology, he was a slumlord. See R. A. Brunt, *Social Conflicts in the Roman Republic* (New York: Norton), pp. 128–29.

2. Sidney Webb and Beatrice Webb, *English Poor Law History, Part I: The Old Poor Law* (Hamden, CT: Shoestring Press, 1963 [1927]), pp. 20–50.

3. However, the *Oxford English Dictionary,* compiled by J. A. Simpson and E. S. Weiner (New York: Oxford University Press, 1989), 19:996, already has a 1647 reference to beggars as undeserving, and the adjective itself was earlier used to refer to nonpoor people, for example, by Shakespeare.

4. David Matza, "Poverty and Disrepute," in *Contemporary Social Problems,* 2nd ed., edited by Robert K. Merton and Robert A. Nisbet (New York: Harcourt Brace & World, 1966), pp. 619–66.

5. These terms were often, but not exclusively, applied to the poor "races" who arrived in the nineteenth and early twentieth century from Ireland, Germany and later, Eastern and Southern Europe. They have also been applied, during and after slavery, to Blacks. Nonetheless, the functions to be discussed in this article are consequences of poverty, not of race, even though a disproportionate rate of those "selected" to be poor have always been darker-skinned than the more fortunate classes.

6. See Michael B. Katz, *The Undeserving Poor: From the War on Poverty to the War on Welfare* (New York: Pantheon Books, 1989), chap. 5; Herbert J. Gans, "The Dangers of the Underclass," in my *People, Plans and Policies* (New York: Columbia University Press and Russell Sage Foundation), chap. 21. The popular definition of underclass must be distinguished from Gunnar Myrdal's initial, scholarly one, which viewed the underclass as a stratum driven to the margins or out of the labor force by what are today called the postindustrial and global economies. Gunnar Myrdal, *Challenge to Affluence* (New York: Pantheon Books, 1963), p. 10 and passim.

Myrdal's definition viewed the underclass as victims of economic change, and said nothing about its moral state.

7. Robert K. Merton, "Manifest and Latent Functions," in his *Social Theory and Social Structure: Toward the Codification of Social Research* (Glencoe, IL, 1949), chap. 1.

8. Actually, some of the functions that follow may in fact have been intended by some interest groups in society, but neither intended nor recognized by others, adding an interesting conceptual variation—and empirical question—to Merton's dichotomy.

9. Herbert J. Gans, "The Positive Functions of Poverty," *American Journal of Sociology* 78(2) (1972):275–89. That article also had another purpose, to show that functional analysis could come to liberal or radical conclusions, to counter the charge commonly launched against functional analysis that it is inherently conservative or supportive of the status quo. That article, like its present complement, was a straightforward analysis, written sans irony, even though the analysis of latent functions often becomes a debunking exercise that can take on an unintentionally ironic tone.

10. For brevity's sake, I will hereafter refer to the undeserving poor instead of the poor labeled undeserving, but I always mean the latter.

11. Hacker is paraphrasing Baldwin. Andrew Hacker, *Two Nations: Black and White, Separate, Hostile, Unequal* (New York: Scribner, 1992), p. 61. Mark Stern applies the displacement function to the economy of the 1990s, writing that "if economic dislocation . . . and urban restructuring were taking their toll on all of us, perhaps it was reassuring to imagine that there was a class at the bottom . . . whose vices made us look virtuous." Mark Stern, "Poverty and Family Composition Since 1940," in *The 'Underclass' Debate: Views from History,* edited by Michael B. Katz (Princeton, NJ: Princeton University Press, 1993), p. 253.

12. Kathryn M. Neckerman and Joleen Kirschenman, "Hiring Strategies, Racial Bias and Inner-City Workers," *Social Problems* 38(4) (1991):433–47.

13. Dahrendorf has suggested, surely with Marx's *Lumpenproletariat* in mind, that when the very poor are excluded from full citizenship, they can become "a reserve army for demonstrations . . . including soccer violence, race riots, and running battles with the police." Ralf Dahrendorf, *Law and Order*

(London: Stevens, 1985), p. 107. He is writing with Europe in mind, however.

14. Consequently, they are part of the reserve army only if and when they also work off-the-books in the informal economy. For the argument that recipients are permanently part of the reserve army, see Frances F. Piven and Richard A. Cloward, *Regulating the Poor: The Functions of Public Welfare*, 2nd ed. (New York: Pantheon Books, 1993).

15. Ron Harris, "Blacks Feel Brunt of Drug War," *Los Angeles Times*, 22 April 1990, p. 1.

16. While most charity benefits target the deserving poor, they are also held for poor AIDS victims and the homeless, who are considered undeserving, at least by some members of the better-off classes. The undeserving poor who are served by these charities thus help to justify the continued existence of these upper-class "societies."

17. Since political legitimacy is involved here, these functions could also be listed among the political ones below.

18. That many of the undeserving poor, and literally those of the underclass, are also thought to be *declasse*, adds to the moral and political legitimacy of the rest of the class system.

19. Although Marxists might have been expected to complain that the notion of the undeserving poor enables the higher classes to create a split in the lower ones, instead Marxist theory creates a mirror image of the capitalist pattern. In declaring undeserving the owners of the means of production, and sometimes the entire bourgeoisie, the theorists ennobled the working class and the poor together with it. Nonetheless, Marx found it necessary to make room for the *Lumpenproletariat*, although for him if not all of his successors, its moral failures were largely determined by the needs of Marxist ideology, just as those of the undeserving poor were shaped by capitalist ideology.

20. See Isabel Sawhill, "The Underclass: An Overview," *The Public Interest* 96 (1989): 3–15. For a contrary analysis, which finds and criticizes the acceptance of poverty-related deviance as normal, see Daniel P. Moynihan, "Defining Deviancy Down," *American Scholar* 62(1) (1993):17–30.

21. Poor immigrants who still practice old-country discipline norms are particularly vulnerable to being accused of child abuse.

22. Teresa Funiciello, *Tyranny of Kindness: Dismantling the Welfare System to End Poverty in America* (New York: Atlantic Monthly Press, 1993), p. 60.

23. See Mark R. Rank, *Living on the Edge: The Realities of Welfare in America* (New York: Columbia University Press, 1994), p. 93.

24. A sizable proportion of the blues, country music, cowboy songs, and jazz of earlier eras was originally composed and played in prisons, brothels, and slum area taverns. It is probably not coincidental that as far back as the eighteenth century, at least, English "actors, fencers, jugglers, minstrels, and in fact all purveyors of amusements to common folk," were thought undeserving by the higher classes. Webb and Webb, *English Poor Law History*, p. 354.

25. In addition, the undeserving poor make a dangerous constituency. Politicians who say kind words about them or who act to represent their interests are likely to be attacked for their words and actions. Jesse Jackson was hardly the first national politician to be criticized for being too favorable to the poor.

26. Charles Murray, *Losing Ground: American Social Policy, 1950–1980* (New York: Basic Books, 1984). Myron Magnet went him one step better, blaming the increase in undeservingness also on various unnamed radicals associated with the conservative image of the 1960s. Myron Magnet, *The Dream and the Nightmare: The Sixties' Legacy to the Underclass* (New York: Morrow, 1993).

27. Since even middle-class drug buyers are willing to travel to underclass areas for drugs, neighborhoods convenient to expressways and bridges that serve the suburbs often become major shopping centers for hard drugs.

28. It is well known that many policies and agencies reproduce the positions and statuses of the people they are asked to raise, notably the public schools.

29. For some examples of the literature on client mistreatment, see Michael B. Katz, *In the Shadow of the Poor House: A Social History of Welfare in America* (New York: Basic Books, 1986); Michael Lipsky, *Street Level Bureaucracy: Dilemmas of the Individual in Public Services* (New York: Russell Sage Foundation, 1980); Piven and Cloward, *Regulating the Poor*, chaps. 4 and 5; and for mistreatment of the homeless, Elliot Liebow, *Tell Them Who I Am: The Lives of Homeless Women* (New York: Free Press, 1993), chap. 4.

30. They may also attract young professionals with reforming or missionary impulses, but many of them either burn out or leave for financial reasons when they begin to raise families.
31. Poor Blacks and members of some other racial minorities pay additional "health penalties" for being non-White.
32. Killing off the undeserving poor may conflict with the prior function (see Function 12) of reproducing them, but functional analysis describes consequences which do not have to be logically consistent. Moreover, since turning poor people into undeserving ones can be a first step toward eliminating them, Functions 12 and 13 may even be logically consistent.
33. A fuller discussion of policy proposals will appear in my forthcoming book, *Ending the War against the Poor.*

17

THE ANATOMY OF RACIALLY MOTIVATED VIOLENCE IN NEW YORK CITY
A Case Study of Youth in Southern Brooklyn

Howard Pinderhughes

Ethnic diversity in New York City has been described in many ways, from a "melting pot" to a "gorgeous mosaic." But in the spring of 1990, the melting pot seemed on the verge of boiling over; the mosaic ripped apart by racial tension. Three news stories filled the pages of the city's major newspapers: the Bensonhurst murder trial, the rape case of the Central Park jogger, and the boycott of two Korean grocery stores in Flatbush. Each of these events symbolized a growing problem in New York City and the nation as a whole—racial tension, conflict, and confrontation had increased and hate violence was on the rise.

Howard Pinderhughes, "The Anatomy of Racially Motivated Violence in New York City" from *Social Problems*, Vol. 40, No. 4, November 1993, pp. 478–492. Copyright © 1993 by The Society for the Study of Social Problems. Reprinted by permission of the University of California Press Journals.

As a result of the public perception that the racial situation in the city was spiralling out of control, David Dinkins, the first African-American mayor in the city's history, made a public plea for ethnic and racial harmony. In his speech, the mayor called for calm and cooperation. His appeal assumed that the rise in racial conflict resulted from prejudice—which could be resolved if people would simply try to get along and be more tolerant of other groups.

The mayor's speech, and reports which followed analyzing the city's racial climate, made no attempt to explain the causes of deteriorating race relations in the city. There was no analysis of the complex network of interrelated factors which combined to produce an alarming increase in bias related violence. The fact that young people perpetrate the majority of racially motivated attacks was not discussed. Nor were the content and substance of racial attitudes among youth in the city examined. There was no discussion of the structural factors which created fertile soil for racial animosity—a prominent concern more than three years earlier when, on 20 December 1986, a group of over twenty white youths attacked three black men in the Howard Beach section of New York City.

In the wake of the death of one of the Howard Beach victims, Michael Griffith, the eyes of the entire nation focused on race relations in New York. The incident shocked the city and the rest of the country. Racial murders were supposed to be a thing of the past—part of the dark days of segregation in the South, perpetrated by small town whites in anonymous sheets. Yet, this was the North, the nation's largest city, the lap of liberalism.

In hindsight, the Howard Beach incident should have been a warning signal. Howard Beach was the first high profile incident in an alarming increase in bias related crimes in New York and throughout the country. It was one of 235 racially motivated crimes investigated by the New York City Human Rights Commission in 1986.

This study uses statistics collected by the New York City Police Department Bias Unit and the Human Rights Commission which establish a dramatic increase in the number of verified bias incidents. It is virtually impossible to determine unconditionally that this increase in verified cases is the result of an actual increase in the number of bias crimes perpetrated. The increase in verified incidents could be the result of increased reporting. However, the evidence strongly suggests a rise in racially motivated violence. Interviews with representatives of the New York City Police Department, the Human Rights Commission, youth program coordinators, school teachers, administrators, and officials yielded different interpretations of the meaning of the increase. Human Rights Commission officials argue that there was an increase. Further, most of the individuals interviewed for the present study who worked with youth agreed that there had been an increase in racial tension, conflict, and violence; New York City youths confirmed this conclusion. In 1987, the number of racially motivated crimes shot up to 463, and reached 550 in 1988.

Two differences in the character of bias motivated crimes of the last five years, as compared to the three previous years, are the racial and ethnic backgrounds of the victims and the types of attacks. In 1982, 50 percent of the confirmed bias motivated crimes were characterized as anti-Semitic and the vast majority were directed against property. This trend continued through 1985; after that point, blacks became the number one target of bias related crimes and the percentage of physical assaults increased significantly. Of the 500 reported ethnically or racially motivated attacks in 1987, 118 victims were white, 220 were black, 82 were Jewish, and 33 were Latino.

The present pattern reveals a rise in physical bias related attacks, with people of color and gays and lesbians as the primary targets. Attacks occurred in many different neighborhoods and in all five boroughs of the city. Victims and assailants came from many different backgrounds. The one common feature of the assailants was their age. Over 70 percent of those arrested for perpetrating bias crimes in 1987 and 1988 were under the age of 20.

One of the most infamous bias incidents was the racial murder of Yusuf Hawkins which took place in Bensonhurst, Brooklyn. On 23 August 1989, Yusuf Hawkins and two companions were in Bensonhurst looking for a used car when they were attacked by a mob of over 20 white youths. In the trial which followed, the incident was presented in the courtroom and media as a tragic one-night occurrence which happened almost accidentally. The incident was presented as the result of a confluence of factors which included Hawkins and his companions being "in the wrong place at the wrong time"—walking down a street in Bensonhurst where the mob of young whites mistook them for another group of blacks they believed were coming into the neighborhood to cause trouble.

In this article, I argue that such racial violence in New York City is the result of a combination of factors shaping the behavior of youth in the city. These factors include (1) structural conditions, (2) ethnic and racial attitudes, and (3) peer group participation and community sentiment. I argue that bleak structural economic conditions have laid the foundation for racial conflict by leaving some young people with extremely uncertain futures. The anxieties and fears of these youth about their futures are directed at other racial groups they view as threats. Peer groups reinforce negative attitudes towards other ethnic and racial groups and facilitate violence. White youths who live in close-knit ethnic communities which fear blacks and other minorities are supported in keeping unwanted minorities out of their neighborhoods. The article challenges the popular view of the Bensonhurst incident as an aberration. Data from interviews with white youth from southern Brooklyn reveal a consistent pattern of racially motivated violence linked to specific factors.

Scholars have reported a strong and steady change in the attitudes of U.S. whites towards the principle of racial equality in the last thirty years (Kinder and Sears 1981; Schuman, Steeh, and Bobo 1985; Sheatsley 1966; Taylor, Sheatsley, and Greeley 1978). Schuman, Steeh, and Bobo (1985) point to an important finding in their study of racial attitudes in the United States: positive trends in attitudes of whites towards blacks have largely been the result of cohort replacement rather than individual attitude change. They predict that this trend will not continue, which is consistent with the pattern of in-creased racial conflict among youth in New York City.

Traditionally, social scientific examinations of race relations and racial attitudes have focused either on adults or young children. Little has been written about adolescence, although this is obviously a crucial period for identity development and attitude formation. In contrast, this study focuses directly on adolescents. It combines elements of Blumer's (1985) theory of racism as a sense of group position, Omi and Winant's (1986) theory of ideology's role in producing racial meanings, and competition theory which analyzes racial violence as the result of ethnic competition activated by the rising supply of low wage labor due to immigration and the migration of blacks into tight labor markets. I argue that racial conflict and violence result from a combination of structural conditions of intense competition, racialized ideologies, and racial and ethnic identities which incorporate negative attitudes towards other groups.

Methodology

The data analyzed in this article were drawn from a larger study conducted in 1990 of ethnic and racial attitudes among youth and the rise in racial conflict in New York City. That study examined the attitudes of 270 youths between the ages of 14 and 21, from 37 different neighborhoods in New York City, in a purposive sample. The sample came from a wide range of ethnic and racial backgrounds, including significant numbers of Italians, African Americans, Puerto Ricans, Jews, Albanians, and Irish.

This article focuses on a subsample of 88 participants in a youth program in southern Brooklyn. The program works primarily with white delinquents in an educational setting, offering an alternative high school program for at-risk youth and a GED program.

Participants generally resided in the surrounding communities of Gravesend, Bensonhurst, Sheepshead Bay, and Canarsie. The sample limitations make it difficult to generalize beyond the groups represented and impossible to generalize about all youth in the city of New York. The sample *is*, however, representative of a small universe of neighborhood youth who have had trouble in school, have dropped out, and/or who spend significant time "hanging out" on the streets.

Two methods were used to collect data on ethnic and racial attitudes. First, a survey questionnaire to gather general demographic data (socioeconomic background, ethnic and racial identity, age) and a short survey of attitudes towards other groups were developed. The survey instrument used a combination of questions from "The Study of High School Students and Educational Staff on Prejudice and Race Relations" (Martin Luther King, Jr. Institute for Nonviolence 1990), and questions developed specifically for this study. The questionnaire was field tested and revised accordingly.

Second, focus group interviews were conducted, using open-ended questions designed to elicit information about the youths' views of race relations. Interviews were structured and data were analyzed in accordance with established methodological guidelines for focus groups (Krueger 1988; Morgan 1988). Eleven focus groups were conducted, ranging in size from five to seventeen participants.[1] The interviews were conducted immediately after the administration of the survey, lasted between 45 and 90 minutes, and were tape-recorded. Tapes of the interviews were transcribed and analyzed systematically for patterns and trends of responses. The patterns were established

through a content analysis of the data which entailed systematic coding.

The interviews followed a set guideline of open-ended questions structured around four themes: (1) the state of race relations in New York City; (2) relations among youths of different ethnic and racial backgrounds; (3) relations among different ethnic and racial groups in respondents' neighborhoods; and (4) the future of race relations in the city. Data from the focus group interviews provided detailed information about the substance and content of ethnic and racial attitudes among youth in New York City. Finally, data from the focus group interviews were compared to survey data to confirm patterns of attitudes about race and ethnicity.

A Brief History of Structural Conditions in New York City

In the past 20 years, significant demographic changes have taken place in the composition of New York City's population. As a result of the massive outmigration of New Yorkers to the suburbs and other parts of the state and nation, between 1970 and 1980 the population per square mile declined between 5 and 20 percent in four of the five boroughs, with an overall reduction of 800,000, or 10.4 percent. Much of this decline was the result of "white flight," the movement from the city of middle- and upper-income families to escape the rapidly increasing numbers of African Americans and Latinos and the social problems whites associated with this demographic change. During that same period, the population of people of color grew by one million. From 1965 to 1980, the foreign-born population increased by almost one million. Most of these immigrants arrived from Third World nations; of the 772,040 immigrants who are classified by

---

[1] Twenty-three focus groups were conducted in the larger study.

their country of origin, close to 80 percent (598,500) were from Third World countries (New York City Department of Planning 1985).[2] Meanwhile, working- and lower-class families in New York City found it increasingly difficult to locate or maintain affordable housing. Beginning in the 1980s, neighborhoods in all five boroughs were gradually, but steadily converted from lower- and working-class tracts to middle- and upper-income tracts. Wealthier people, whose resources allowed them to move out of the city when threatened with the encroachment of "undesirable" groups, returned to the urban areas from which they fled in the 1950s and 1960s as these areas became "gentrified." As a result of the conversion of existing rental units to co-ops and condominiums, the proportion of households that owned their homes increased by 2.5 percent from 1981 to 1987 (Harris 1991). By 1987, vacancy rates for inexpensive apartments throughout the city were low: less than 1 percent for apartments asking below $300; below 2.5 percent for those asking between $300 and $500; and 4.28 percent for apartments asking more than $500 (Stegman 1988). The result was an intensification of the housing shortage for lower- and working-class people and a dramatic increase in the number of homeless people. By the end of the 1980s, the stage had been set for intensified competition for housing and employment among New York City's diverse working- and lower-class communities.

Beginning in the late 1960s, the city's economy underwent a profound restructuring, which has been analyzed as a simulta-neous process of decay and growth (Drennan 1991). Although the manufacturing sector was in serious decline during the last two decades, during the same period, the finance and service industries experienced rapid expansion. Between 1969 and 1977, New York City lost over 600,000 jobs, primarily in the manufacturing sector (Drennan 1991); the largest decline was in manufacturing jobs in Brooklyn and the Bronx (Harris 1991). As a result, after a decade of expansion in the 1960s, employment decreased steadily from 1969 to 1977. Although the number of workers increased from 1978 to 1984, this increase was almost exclusively in the service sector. The highest percentage of these jobs was in business and related professional services. Jobs in business, professional, social and religious services, education, media, and health care accounted for 76 percent of the increase. Even though some of these were clerical, janitorial, and support jobs, the prospects for working-class youth remained severely restricted. Although some sectors of New York's population benefited from this decade of economic expansion, poverty increased from 15 percent in 1975, about 20 percent over the national average, to 23 percent in 1987, almost twice the national average (Mollenkopf and Castells 1991). Unemployment rates have been consistently higher in New York City than the rest of the state and the nation. While the city's unemployment rate dropped from 11.2 percent in 1976 to 8.9 percent in 1984, New York City has remained among the top ten cities in the United States in unemployment. Among youth under 20, unemployment rates are as high as 22.2 percent for whites and 47.5 percent for blacks. The employment to population ratio, a more reliable indicator of actual employment, decreased steadily from 1967 to 1984. In 1984, the ratio in New York City was below the U.S. average in all categories. Thus, only 49.1 percent of whites, 47 percent

---

[2]The U.S. Bureau of the Census estimated a slight increase in the city's overall population between 1980 and 1990. This recent increase is attributed to a reversal of the trend of urban flight by the white middle class, combined with a continued influx of new immigrants to the city. Nevertheless, the demographic changes in the last 30 years have made non-Hispanic whites a minority of the city's population (Mollenkopf and Castells 1991).

of blacks, and 42 percent of Latinos were working. Among those below the age of 20, less than 20 percent were working, compared to the national average of almost 44 percent (U.S. Department of Labor 1986).

At the time when competition for employment intensified, the dropout rate among the city's youth increased from 13.5 percent in 1983 to 25 percent in 1987. The situation was worst for black and Puerto Rican youth, with official dropout rates of 24.3 and 31.3 percent respectively (New York Times 21 June 1988). Italian Americans are now the third most likely group to drop out of high school. The percentage of white students in the New York City public schools decreased steadily, from 62.7 percent in 1960 to 23.7 percent in 1980. In addition, the percentage of white students in the New York City public schools steadily decreased from 63 percent in 1960 to 23 percent in 1980 (New York City Board of Education 1984). Whereas whites were the majority in 1960, and remained the single largest group in 1970, by 1980 they were a distinct minority in the city's public schools. By the late 1980s, though the racial composition differed from school to school, schools in Brooklyn were 25 percent white (Sullivan 1989).

For youth living in southern Brooklyn's white working-class neighborhoods, these structural changes were ominous developments which reinforced fears, already widespread in their communities, of other racial groups.

Community Sentiment in Southern Brooklyn

Bensonhurst, Sheepshead Bay, Gravesend, and Canarsie are adjacent communities; they are part of a strip of white ethnic, primarily working-class, predominantly Italian-American and Jewish neighborhoods stretching across the southern section of Brooklyn. Bensonhurst is 89.2 percent white, second only to neighboring Bay Ridge among the 18 community board districts in Brooklyn in its percentage of whites. The Sheepshead Bay and Gravesend areas are 86.1 percent white and Canarsie is 76.8 percent white (Stegman 1988). Bensonhurst is one of only three areas in the entire city with no appreciable black population; Sheepshead Bay and Gravesend are 3.0 percent black and Canarsie is 14.3 percent black.

For the most part, these four neighborhoods are stable working-class communities, which have some of the lowest in-migration (influx of new residents) rates of any of the predominantly white communities in New York City (Stegman 1988). Yet, in 1986, the median household income in Bensonhurst was $16,000, as contrasted with the citywide median of $20,000, well below the median household income of $25,000 for whites in New York City. The median household income in Sheepshead Bay and Gravesend was $20,000, and in Canarsie it was $24,000.

Many of the residents in these four neighborhoods used to live in other parts of New York City, especially central Brooklyn and Queens. In a classic case of neighborhood racial succession, many of these families moved out of their previous neighborhoods 30 to 40 years ago when African Americans, Puerto Ricans, and West Indians began to move in. This historical experience profoundly affected the attitudes and sentiments of these whites towards other groups. All minority groups, but particularly African Americans, were perceived as a direct threat to the quality of neighborhood life, as intruders who had the potential to ruin the stable, safe, close-knit ethnic niche the white community had taken years to establish.

These attitudes and sentiments have been well documented by Rieder (1985) in *Canarsie: The Jews and Italians of Brooklyn*

Against Liberalism, which focuses on the Canarsie community which has a similar history and demographic composition to Gravesend, Sheepshead Bay, and Bensonhurst. Rieder found that Italian and Jewish residents in Canarsie viewed maintaining the ethnic and racial composition of their neighborhood as the most important factor for community harmony. Canarsie residents viewed African Americans and Puerto Ricans with mistrust, fear, and loathing as the harbingers of neighborhood deterioration, crime, decay and chaos. A July 1988 article in the *Wall Street Journal* painted a similar portrait of Bensonhurst.

Both Bensonhurst and Canarsie include housing projects, whose residents are primarily African American, located on the northeast fringes of the neighborhoods. In both communities these housing projects have become the focal points of racial animosity and conflict. White residents view the projects as the first foothold gained by poor African Americans encroaching on their communities. For their part, African-American residents in the projects describe their situation as reminiscent of the European Jewish ghettos where residents could not venture outside after dark for fear of being attacked. The Marlboro housing project, located on the border between Gravesend and Bensonhurst, has been at the center of much of the racial conflict in these two predominantly white communities. White youths interviewed in this study revealed a deep distrust and antagonism toward racial minorities in their community generally, and in these projects specifically.

The Attitudes of Community Youth

Analysis of the data revealed that the attitudes of the white youths in Bensonhurst and Gravesend were influenced by their neighborhoods' histories of racial tension

and neighborhood defense. They had grown up in close-knit, exclusively white communities which distrusted strangers and feared blacks. Consequently, these youths displayed a distrust of all outsiders, and of blacks particularly.

The youths interviewed in the study were surprisingly open in discussing and describing their feelings about racial tension in New York City. All of the young people had strong opinions about race relations and believed that they had worsened in the past decade and that racial tensions in the city were high.

The youths listed five factors which they perceived were the cause of heightened racial tensions in New York City: (1) the deteriorating economic situation, (2) blacks starting trouble, (3) a media which favors blacks, (4) racial prejudice, and (5) black political and economic power in the city.

One important finding of the study is that these young people felt they were the victims of favoritism towards blacks, reverse discrimination, double standards, and increasing black power in the city.

> Everybody is leaning over backwards to give the blacks everything. They get all the jobs. They get all the attention from the mayor. These days white people don't have a chance. Because blacks are controlling the city. You got your black mayor. The main police chief is black. They never do nothin' for us.

> You know I been lookin' for work for awhile, but I can't get a job 'cause they're givin' them all to the black people.

The sense of victimization was heightened by the youths' fear that blacks were "taking over the city."

> You know, Italians used to run this city. We didn't have any problems 'cause we had political juice [power]. Now the

blacks have taken over and we don't get nothin' from the politicians.

The election of a black mayor, David Dinkins, was viewed as strengthening the political and economic power of blacks in New York City. The youths believed the mayor was working only to help black people and that the city government was being run by black people, for black people. The mayor's victory fueled preexisting prejudices and fears among whites that blacks were gaining control of New York City, which would make it more difficult for working-class whites like them to maintain the ethnic composition of their neighborhoods, and as importantly to achieve economic and job security.

> My father told me that [as a result of the new black mayor] they are going to fire all the white construction workers in the city and hire all black guys.

> Dinkins, he's all for the blacks, 100 percent. Not like Ed Koch who used to care about people in white neighborhoods.

> Youth 1: Koch, he was for everybody. He went out into the neighborhoods and talked to people one on one.

> Youth 2: When Dinkins was elected I wanted to move out of the city.

> Youth 3: The black people will get more attention than they already receive— they get power.

> Youth 2: That's right, the black people really think they got it now.

The youths consistently described economic constraints and problems as the primary reasons for racial problems in the city.

> The situation is more racial because the economy has changed. Some people are out of work and they want to have some fun.

> People in my neighborhood don't like how things are going. There aren't enough jobs. You got all these homeless people. When things get bad, it gets tense. Especially when the blacks get all of the attention. Except when some black guy gets beat up or somethin'. Then everybody's lookin' at us and callin' us racist.

Although they lacked a developed analysis or ideology, these teens felt they were in unfair competition with other groups, particularly blacks, whom they saw as benefiting from "special" treatment.

The attitudes of the youth towards blacks were clearly linked to their sense of the position of whites vis-a-vis blacks in the city. Blumer states that "it is the sense of social position emerging from this collective process of characterization which provides the basis of racial prejudice" (Blumer 1958:4). This held true for these white youths; their attitudes towards blacks were significantly influenced by their perception that blacks were achieving success at the expense of whites. The following quotes from several interviews illustrate this perception.

> The situation is much worse for white people than it used to be. There is more competition. They are going to give blacks more jobs because people will be afraid of calling it racial.

> Companies have to give certain jobs to blacks even though they don't qualify as much as the whites, and I don't think that's fair.

> If there is a white and a black going after the same job, and they don't hire the black, the black might make something out of it. The white person might let it pass.

> Why is it that black people think we owe them something?

Youth 1: How come when somebody white gets shot, we don't make a big deal about it?

Youth 2: We don't do nothing, we all sit on our asses.

Youth 3: We should be fighting for our rights.

Youth 4: That's right, fight back.

Youth 3: Instead of fighting among ourselves, we need to get together and fight back.

The interviews also revealed that the youths perceived blacks as benefiting from preferential treatment in the media. They consistently described the media as distorting the image of white youth and white communities, unfairly portraying young whites, and misrepresenting young black males. They had a strong perception that the media only showed the bad things that happened in their neighborhoods and reported events as racially motivated which they felt were not. They strongly believed there should be "more equal and fair media coverage."

The media is more worried about what white people are doing to blacks than what black people are doing to whites.

If a white person attacks a black person, they throw the book at him. Meanwhile black kids are getting away with murder and nobody says anything about it, not the media, not the police, nobody.

There's a double standard in the media. If a black kid gets jumped by a bunch of white kids, they say it's racial. Friends of mine get jumped by black kids all the time and no one describes it as racial.

The media is pushing the black people's case and it's pissing off white people.

The media makes a little issue into a big racial shit.

Many of the young people described crimes committed by blacks as the main reason for racial tension in the city. There was a widespread feeling that blacks were violent troublemakers who were especially dangerous and bold in large groups. Many told stories and anecdotes about blacks committing crimes which went unpunished by the police or school administrators. The youths uniformly described blacks who ventured into their neighborhoods as "looking for trouble." According to them, *everybody* in their community believed that the only reason for blacks to come into their neighborhoods was to commit crimes. Consequently, they felt they had the right and obligation to defend their territory against blacks; that it was up to them to "stop the blacks"; that if they attacked these outsiders, they would send a message to all blacks from outside the neighborhood to stay out of their communities.

A group of black kids come into your neighborhood—they are looking for trouble. Why else are they there?

The police know the blacks don't belong in our neighborhoods—everybody knows if they are here they must be looking for trouble. It's up to us to make sure they stay out of our neighborhood.

What is a 16 year old kid [Yusuf Hawkins] without a driver's license doing walking into an all white neighborhood at 9:30 at night looking for a used car? He was out looking for trouble and he found it. Those guys did what they had to do.

If they are stupid enough to walk, one person, at night—they're not looking for a fight but they are stupid and crazy. They should know that they don't belong there.

If a white guy walks on my block, nobody will say anything to him. But if a black guy walks on my block everybody puts their heads out the window to make sure he leaves the block.

Yeah, if a black guy comes around, they are usually trying to rob or beat up on people. They would call the cops on a black guy if they see him. The black guy is probably better off if the cops show up than if the Avenue X boys find him first.

Blacks just keep stealing everybody's sneakers. They will kill you for your sneakers. They start a lot of trouble. If they want trouble, they're going to get trouble.

These statements illustrate the youths' desire to maintain their neighborhoods' ethnic and racial composition. Their statements were consistent with the survey data. While the overwhelming majority (80 percent) agreed that people have the right to live wherever they choose, 51 percent agreed that it is better to have people of the same race living in the same neighborhoods and disagreed that it is better to have mixed neighborhoods with people of different racial and ethnic backgrounds. Thirty-eight percent of the youths agreed that whites, blacks, Asians, and Hispanics should stay in their own neighborhoods. Fifteen percent agreed that people have a right to physically prevent people who are different from them from coming into their neighborhoods.

The Importance of Peer Groups

Like young people everywhere, the youths from these neighborhoods hung out together. Analysis of the interviews reveals that negative attitudes towards blacks served a social cohesion function within peer groups. The youths explained that the expression of negative attitudes towards blacks and other people of color provided status and respect and "proof positive that they are down with the program."

The link between these attitudes and the individual and group identities of the white youths is very strong. Many of the youths interviewed had dropped out of high school and many had behavioral problems in school and on the streets. Consequently, they often were viewed by adult members of their community as "hoodlums" or "outcasts"; many were also alienated from their families. These young white men repeatedly stated that other community residents held such opinions of them.

With my friends I get respect. I can't talk to my mother, that's why I moved out when I was fifteen. The rest of the people in my neighborhood think I'm crazy. They think we are bums who hang out on the street and cause trouble. In some ways they're right.

In this context, their primary positive reinforcement was on the street, hanging out with other neighborhood teens. As a result, they were constantly trying to prove themselves worthy to their peers. In the context of the street, that proof lay in their ability to express the peer group's collective ideology and a willingness to back up those ideas with brute force ranging from harassment to mayhem, and sometimes even murder.

In the focus group interviews, several youths revealed that they were "going on missions." When asked to explain what "missions" were, one young Bensonhurst man described how informal groups of neighborhood teens would get together at night to hang out. After several hours of drinking or taking drugs, the group would look for people to harass and beat up.

> We'll just be hanging out, partying. And somebody will say "hey, let's go on a mission." That's when you go look for people who don't belong in the neighborhood and you beat 'em up. Sometimes, they go out lookin' for blacks to jump. Sometimes they look for anybody who ain't supposed to be there.

The rest of the group responded with noticeable enthusiasm to discussing missions. They seemed excited by descriptions of late night searches for individuals who "did not belong in the neighborhood." They talked openly and excitedly about going on missions, and the entire ambience of the interview changed as they began to describe them in detail.

At first, the youths steadfastly proclaimed that there was nothing "racial" about the missions. They argued the media was responsible for making things "look racial"; they were simply "defending their neighborhood" and would attack whites as well as blacks since their main objective was to "take care of outsiders." However, analysis of the interview data revealed that the perception that missions were not racially motivated was contradicted by the youths' descriptions of nightly group activities, which included regular searches for people of color, particularly blacks.

> If we fight against Bay Parkway, that's because we don't like each other. When we fight the blacks, it's because we don't like their color. All of Bensonhurst unites against them.
>
> Youth 1: Every weekend, me and him and a group of others would go out and get racial with—against Mexicans.
>
> Youth 2: It wasn't really racial . . .

> Youth 1: Oh, yeah, we were racial. Alright, would you call this racial? Every Mexican we see, no matter what they were doing, if they weren't doing nothing, we'd still beat 'em up.
>
> You go out and you're lookin for people. The best is if you catch a couple of black guys. Or if you can't find no blacks, maybe you find an Indian or an Arab or a Dominican.

The youth described a hierarchy of desirable targets for assault. Blacks were their primary targets. If they could not find a black person, then a Dominican, a Pakistani, or an Indian would do. The list varied in its order of preference, with the exception that blacks were always at the top of the list. The youth said they would attack other whites as well, but only if they were from a rival neighborhood that had started trouble in their neighborhood.

> Blacks, Pakistanis, everybody gets a little bit, racial slurs—like that. And if you're really hyped, you fuck them up good. Especially Dominicans.
>
> We go after a lot of people. But, it's the blacks, mostly, who you want to take care of.
>
> Youth 1: The problem is mostly with blacks. There is not as much problem between whites and Asians or whites and Hispanics.
>
> Youth 2: We don't have no problem with Asians.

Their language reflected how central race was to their outlook towards other groups. It provides an illustration of what Omi and Winant call "racialization," defined as "the extension of racial meaning to a previously unclassified relationship, social practice or group" (1986:64). These youths described their actions towards other groups as "getting racial"—an indication of missions' racially motivated character and of the perceived meaning of racial differences with the people of color they attacked. Racial differences were the critical motivating factor. Italian, Jewish, and a few light-skinned Puerto Rican youths all engaged in these activities, some in mixed ethnic groups.

The youths seemed to get a sense of self-worth and individual power from going on missions which was lacking in their lives. A sense of group cohesion and solidarity was heightened if the victim was from a racial or ethnic group high on the list of desirable targets. Recall that these young people consistently expressed feelings of economic and political powerlessness and frustration. Feelings of powerlessness, stemming from their economic positions and prospects and from their social positions within their own communities, appear to contribute to the visceral nature of their racial attitudes.

Analysis of the interviews shows that the missions gave these teens a sense of power. They seemed to describe themselves as itching to feel the elation of the power, control, and status which would result from administering a beating to a neighborhood intruder, usually while primed with alcohol and/or drugs.

What emerges from an analysis of white youths in South Brooklyn, is a picture of the relationship between their (1) negative attitudes and actions towards other groups, (2) individual identities, (3) developing ethnic identities, and (4) perceptions of themselves in their communities and in society more generally. Racism and racial violence are essentially group activities rarely perpetrated by a single individual. For these young people, establishing a strong, cohesive individual and group identity required showing the rest of the group that they were "down with the program." In this case, the program includes concrete proof of being tough, hating the appropriate enemies, and a readiness to take those enemies on to defend principles and turf.

> You go on missions to impress your friends. You get a name as a tough guy who is down with the neighborhood and down with his people.
>
> You prove you're a real Bensonhurst Italian who don't take no shit, who don't let the wrong kind of people into the neighborhood.
>
> You do it to feel powerful, to feel like you're somebody. So people will respect you.
>
> Youth 1: You do it cause you want to be cool.
>
> Youth 2: To get out their frustrations.
>
> Youth 3: Because there is nothing else to do.

The Importance of Community Support

The study subjects claimed they fought to "protect the neighborhood" and for "unity in their community." Delinquent behavior had been translated into acts of neighborhood defense. The language the youths used reflected a feeling of responsibility for protecting their community, defending their turf, and keeping undesirable outsiders (i.e., people of color) out of their neighborhood. Numerous statements about how they "did what they had to do," reveal this rationalization.

> I did what I had to do. I have a reputation as a tough guy who defends the neighborhood and I want to keep it. People know when you've taken care of people who don't belong in the neighborhood. You get respect. Especially if it is some of the blacks from Marlboro projects.

When you're hanging out with your partners and you see somebody who don't belong on your block, like a black guy or a Dominican, and you do him [beat him up], you feel real together. Everybody's together doing what we have to do.

Everybody in the neighborhood knows what the deal is. The police don't care about it unless somebody gets killed. Everybody else figures we're just doing them a favor. As long as we don't bother neighborhood folks, it's no problem.

The youths clearly see themselves as defending the community from individuals and groups they believe do not belong in their neighborhoods. Consequently, they can explain and justify their actions as "helpful" to the community and in sync with its sentiments and values.

Like many teens, these youths engage in behaviors which are aimed at proving themselves worthy to their peers. In this context, they demonstrate their toughness and hatred of certain groups by beating them up.

By interpreting racially motivated behavior as beneficial to the community, the youths gain a sense of self-worth. This is reinforced by positive feedback from their peers and from some members of the community. I encountered evidence of support in discussions with various community residents. These discussions included one shopowner who was disgusted with the activities of the youths and complained that the problem was neighborhoodwide.

The problem is that some of the people around here like what they are doing. People don't want blacks around here and these kids keep them out. These kids even get rewards from some of the shopowners for taking care of blacks who look suspicious. A fellah up the street gives away free pizza, if you can believe it.

Conclusion

The white youths from southern Brooklyn interviewed for this study provide important insights into racially motivated attacks and partly explain the increase in bias related violence in New York City. The analysis reveals four major factors contributing to involvement in racially motivated attacks: (1) structural economic conditions; (2) the societal racial climate and ideology; (3) the history of neighborhood race relations and the community's racial ideology; (4) participation in neighborhood-based peer groups.

Economic conditions are an important factor. These young people face extremely uncertain futures. In the last 15 to 20 years, industrial jobs have disappeared from the city's economy at an alarming rate and the employment prospects for working-class youth, particularly males, are constricted. Competition for employment in New York City was accompanied by an increase in the dropout rate from 13 percent in 1983 to 25 percent in 1987. These conditions laid the foundation for rising ethnic and racial violence by increasing anxiety and competition between groups. Most of the youths in this study had done poorly in school or had dropped out completely, placing them in a precarious position in a labor market which places a high value on education. As a result of changes in the labor market, jobs like those of their parents and older brothers or sisters are no longer available. These young people believe jobs are scarce for whites because of special treatment towards blacks. In their view, affirmative action functions as reverse discrimination against whites, and Third World immigrants take away additional jobs and invade their neighborhoods. They perceive *themselves* as disadvantaged, while people of color gain political and economic power by getting special treatment.

In addition, the attitudes of these white youths reflect the neoconservative ideas and principles which have achieved prominence on a national level in debates over civil rights, affirmative action, and racial inequality. In the last ten years, neoconservative ideology has emerged as a strong current in public policy, academia, and politics (Omi and Winant 1986). The public positions taken by the Reagan and Bush administrations on these issues; the emerging theories of neoconservative scholars such as Sowell (1990), Murray (1984), and Glazer (1975); and the imagery and language of the 1988 Bush campaign and of politicians such as Jesse Helms and David Duke all lend credence to a sense of victimization and provide a target for anger, frustration, and economic anxiety. While these teens were not well informed about the specifics of neoconservative analysis, they related to its images and symbols; for example, a black person getting a job that a white person was more qualified for; blacks getting preferential treatment; young black males as criminals; black and Puerto Rican families as welfare dependent, single-parent households with a violent culture and unclean habits. Several young whites referred to Professor Michael Levin in discussing the violent, criminal danger blacks posed to their neighborhood.[3] These ideologies fuel the perception that African Americans have power. In this context, the youths view their violent actions as "fighting back," though

the tragic reality is that African Americans and other people of color lack the power to deter racially motivated attacks and therefore are vulnerable targets.

Another contributing factor is the close-knit ethnic communities with histories of "flight" from neighborhoods where African Americans and other minorities have moved in. Though community members frown on delinquent activities, there is evidence of tacit support for the role these young people play in keeping unwanted minorities out of their neighborhoods. There is no doubt that the youths believe neighborhood residents either look the other way or directly support their attacks on "unwanted" nonwhite outsiders.

For example, much of the Bensonhurst community rallied to the defense of the white youths involved in the attack on Yusuf Hawkins, staunchly proclaiming that the incident was not racially motivated. A cloak of silence was placed over the events of 23 August 1989, based on an implicit understanding that the participants were not to be criticized openly. In one focus group interview, a young woman inadvertently broke this code of silence and was immediately rebuked with angry stares and verbal reminders of the code.

Other evidence of tacit community support for the youths' activities can be drawn from an analysis of previous incidents. All four communities have a history of racial tensions marked in the 1970s and 1980s by frequent racial violence at their high schools (Wall Street Journal 1988). In 1982, an African-American transit worker was attacked and killed by a mob of whites. In 1988, on three separate occasions, flyers asserting that "Orientals" were trying to take over the neighborhood and encouraging residents to boycott Asian businesses and to refuse to sell their homes to Asians were distributed throughout the neighborhood (Mayor's Advisory Council on Community

---

[3]Michael Levin is a professor of philosophy at the City University of New York. In the spring of 1990, he became the center of controversy when he gave several lectures and interviews in which he stated that whites have justifiable fear of young black males because they have a higher propensity to be violent. Among other measures, Levin advocated specific subway cars for young black males—a position which resonated deeply with the youths involved in this study.

Relations 1989). There was little coordinated neighborhood response to these incidents. In the absence of community control over racial violence, the youth of Bensonhurst and Gravesend felt encouraged and supported in their racially motivated actions.

Since the murder of Yusuf Hawkins in August 1989, Bensonhurst has been the focus of nationwide attention. As a result, the people of Bensonhurst, as well as the surrounding white working-class communities, are extremely sensitive to the issue of race. Many residents complain that their neighborhood has been unfairly labeled as a "racist community." One of the difficulties in discussing community collusion is that it treats the neighborhood as an exception; it appears more racist than other neighborhoods in South Brooklyn or in other parts of New York City.

In fact, labeling Bensonhurst as a "racist community" shifts the analysis from wider conditions and factors to an analysis of the people of Bensonhurst—from a systematic and generalizable examination of the problem to a more microscopic, individual analysis. What sets Bensonhurst apart is simply that Yusuf Hawkins died there. The statements of youths elsewhere in southern Brooklyn reveal that racially motivated attacks occur regularly in other white ethnic communities.

As in all communities, the number of youths involved in violent activity is small. However, in white ethnic communities in South Brooklyn, they serve a function; in the case of Bensonhurst and Howard Beach they have a profound effect on how the communities are viewed by outsiders. The actions of the youths are well known in other parts of the city. As a result, these communities have a reputation throughout New York City for being inhospitable to African Americans. This reputation helps to deter African Americans and other minorities from settling in or even visiting these communities.

Finally, the peer groups of these white youths reinforce negative attitudes and thereby facilitate violence against other ethnic and racial groups. The youths gain a positive sense of themselves, a more cohesive group solidarity, and a heightened sense of identity from participating in group attacks against people or groups from different ethnic and racial backgrounds. Through peer group membership and activity these youths develop a racialized perspective concretized through group action.

The most powerful motivations for white youths to participate in acts of racial violence were turf defense, personal power, self-worth, and the need to belong to a group. Ethnic and racial attitudes were directly linked to these issues and were imparted by family, friends, the community, and the wider society; attitudes were internalized through participation in peer groups. Maintenance of these attitudes was clearly linked to developing a racialized self-identity and ethnic identity; internalizing and exhibiting the image of a tough, important, powerful member of the neighborhood who defended the community and received its tacit support was part of the identification process.

Processes of affiliation are often linked to processes of differentiation (Pinderhughes 1982). In this case, the process of differentiation from African Americans and other groups by white youths is linked to the process of affiliation with the neighborhood and ethnic group. Thus, these Italian and Jewish working-class youths from Gravesend and Bensonhurst believe that disliking blacks is part of what it means to be a "good" Italian or Jew within the context of their community place and role. For many, the street has replaced the home and the school as the context in which identity is developed; neighborhood peers supply values and models.

However, the behavior of these young people is an extension of neighborhood and societal attitudes and ideologies which have been translated to the street. Messages from parents, community residents, and political representatives at many different levels have been incorporated into a street ideology which provides justifications for racial violence.

The research findings support the hypothesis that a combination of structural factors, neighborhood influences, and peer group dynamics produce ethnic and racial conflict among youth. Deteriorating economic prospects for teens have raised anxieties and fears and have fueled competition with other youth. Community sentiments and peer group participation direct these anxieties and fears against other ethnic and racial groups by encouraging an oppositional sense of group position and linking group membership to particular racial attitudes. The peer group provides a mechanism for expressing negative attitudes towards other groups in the form of ethnic and racial violence, which is seen by the youth as a defense of turf and neighborhood.

In conclusion, the process of racial conflict can only be understood by examining how a number of factors *combine* to produce ethnic and racial conflict. None of the factors alone can plausibly explain the presence or absence of conflict. For example, not all Italian or Jewish youth have negative attitudes towards blacks. Only when ethnicity is combined with neighborhood support and participation in peer groups which encourage and facilitate these attitudes is there the potential for ethnic and racial violence. All working-class white youths from Bensonhurst do not have negative attitudes towards blacks. Nor do all white youths who do poorly in school or who drop out have negative attitudes towards blacks. However, an Italian or Jewish youth who is from a neighborhood with a history of conflict with blacks, does poorly in school or has dropped out, spends time on the street with a neighborhood-based peer group with an established oppositional sense of ethnic group position and that sees itself as threatened by members of another group is more likely to have negative attitudes towards blacks and to engage in acts of racial violence.

Finally, the problem of racially motivated violence is not isolated to the white communities of southern Brooklyn. The same factors which result in racial conflict and violence in southern Brooklyn are present or developing in many communities with different ethnic and racial compositions. Until the factors discussed in this paper are addressed comprehensively, they will continue to provide the foundation for persistent racial violence in communities across the country.

REFERENCES

BLUMER, HERBERT. 1958. "Race Prejudice as a Sense of Group Position." *Pacific Sociological Review* 1:3–7.

DRENNAN, MATTHEW. 1991. "The Decline and Rise of the New York Economy." Pp. 25–42 in *Dual City: Restructuring New York,* edited by John Mollenkopf and Manuel Castells. New York: Russell Sage Foundation.

GLAZER, NATHAN. 1975. *Affirmative Discrimination.* New York: Basic Books.

HARRIS, RICHARD. 1991. "The Geography of Employment and Residence in New York Since 1950." Pp. 129–52 in *Dual City,* edited by Mollenkopf and Castells.

KINDER, D., and D. SEARS. 1981. "Prejudice and Politics: Symbolic Racism Versus Racial Threats to the Good Life." *Journal of Personality and Social Psychology* 40:414–31.

KRUEGER, RICHARD. 1988. *Focus Groups: A Practical Guide for Applied Research.* Newbury Park, CA: Sage.

Martin Luther King, Jr., Institute for Nonviolence. 1990. "A Study of New York City High School Students and Educational Staff on Prejudice and Race Relations." Unpublished document.

The Mayor's Advisory Council on Community Relations. 1989. *Final Report.* New York: Office of the Mayor of the City of New York.

MOLLENKOPF, JOHN, and MANUEL CASTELLS, eds. 1991. Introduction to *Dual City: Restructuring New York.* New York: Russell Sage Foundation.

MORGAN, DAVID. 1988. *Focus Groups as Qualitative Research.* Newbury Park, CA: Sage.

MURRAY, CHARLES. 1984. *Losing Ground: American Social Policy 1950–1980.* New York: Basic Books.

New York City Board of Education, Office of Student Information Services. 1984. *Annual Pupil Ethnic Census, 1960–1983.* New York: New York City Board of Education.

New York City Department of Planning, Population Division and Office of Immigrant Affairs. 1985. Unpublished Report.

New York Times. 1988. "Dropout Rate for Hispanic Teenagers Is Highest in New York." 21 June.

OMI, M., and H. WINANT. 1986. *Racial Formation in the United States: From the 1960s to the 1980s.* New York: Routledge & Kegan Paul.

PINDERHUGHES, CHARLES. 1982. "Paired Differential Bonding in Biological, Psychological, and Social Systems." *The American Journal of Social Psychiatry* 2:5–14.

RIEDER, JONATHAN. 1985. *Canarsie: The Jews and Italians of Brooklyn Against Liberalism.* Cambridge, MA: Harvard University Press.

SCHUMAN, HOWARD, CHARLOTTE STEEH, and LAWRENCE BOBO. 1985. *Racial Attitudes in America.* Cambridge, MA: Harvard University Press.

SHEATSLEY, PAUL. 1966. "White Attitudes Toward the Negro. *Daedalus* 95:217–38.

SOWELL, THOMAS. 1990. *Preferential Policies.* New York: Morrow.

STEGMAN, MICHAEL. 1988. *Housing and Vacancy Report: New York City, 1987.* New York: City of New York Department of Housing Preservation and Development.

STEINBERG, STEPHEN. 1981. *The Ethnic Myth.* New York: Atheneum.

SULLIVAN, MERCER. 1989. *Getting Paid: Youth Crime and Work in the Inner City.* Ithaca, NY: Cornell University Press.

TAYLOR, D., P. SHEATSLEY, and A. GREELEY. 1978. "Attitudes Toward Racial Integration." *Scientific American* 238:42–49.

U.S. Department of Labor, Bureau of Labor Statistics. 1986. *Current Population Survey.* Washington, DC: U.S. Government Printing Office.

Wall Street Journal. 1988. "Turf Defenders: The Mood Gets Nasty in City Neighborhoods as Racial Tension Rises—Working-Class Bensonhurst, Next to New York Ghetto, Fears Drugs and Crime." 25 July.

18

ANATOMY OF ENVIRONMENTAL RACISM AND THE ENVIRONMENTAL JUSTICE MOVEMENT

Robert D. Bullard

Communities are not all created equal. In the United States, for example, some communities are routinely poisoned while the government looks the other way. Environmental regulations have not

Robert Bullard, ed., *Confronting Environmental Racism: Voices from the Grassroots*, 1993, pp. 15–39. Reprinted by permission from the publisher, South End Press, 116 Saint Botolph Street, Boston, MA 02115.

uniformly benefited all segments of society. People of color (African Americans, Latinos, Asians, Pacific Islanders, and Native Americans) are disproportionately harmed by industrial toxins on their jobs and in their neighborhoods. These groups must contend with dirty air and drinking water—the byproducts of municipal landfills, incinerators, polluting industries, and hazardous waste treatment, storage and disposal facilities.

Why do some communities get "dumped on" while others escape? Why are environmental regulations vigorously enforced in some communities and not in others? Why are some workers protected from environmental threats to their health while others (such as migrant farmworkers) are still being poisoned? How can environmental justice be incorporated into the campaign for environmental protection? What institutional changes would enable the United States to become a just and sustainable society? What community organizing strategies are effective against environmental racism? These are some of the many questions addressed in this [reading].

This [reading] sketches out the basic environmental problems communities of color face, discusses how the mainstream environmental movement does not provide an adequate organizational base, analysis, vision, or strategy to address these problems, and, finally, provides a glimpse of several representative struggles within the grassroots environmental justice movement. For these purposes, the pervasive reality of racism is placed at the very center of the analysis.

Internal Colonialism and White Racism

The history of the United States has long been grounded in white racism. The nation was founded on the principles of "free land" (stolen from Native Americans and Mexicans), "free labor" (cruelly extracted from African slaves), and "free men" (white men with property). From the outset, institutional racism shaped the economic, political, and ecological landscape, and buttressed the exploitation of both land and people. Indeed, it has allowed communities of color to exist as internal colonies characterized by dependent (and unequal) relationships with the domi-

nant white society or "Mother Country." In their 1967 book, *Black Power*, Carmichael and Hamilton were among the first to explore the "internal" colonial model as a way to explain the racial inequality, political exploitation, and social isolation of African Americans. As Carmichael and Hamilton write:

> The economic relationship of America's black communities [to white society] . . . reflects their colonial status. The political power exercised over those communities goes hand in glove with the economic deprivation experienced by the black citizens.
>
> Historically, colonies have existed for the sole purpose of enriching, in one form or another, the "colonizer"; the consequence is to maintain the economic dependency of the "colonized." (pp. 16–17)

Generally, people of color in the United States—like their counterparts in formerly colonized lands of Africa, Asia, and Latin America—have not had the same opportunities as whites. The social forces that have organized oppressed colonies internationally still operate in the "heart of the colonizer's mother country" (Blauner 1972, p. 26). For Blauner, people of color are subjected to five principal colonizing processes: they enter the "host" society and economy involuntarily; their native culture is destroyed; white-dominated bureaucracies impose restrictions from which whites are exempt; the dominant group uses institutionalized racism to justify its actions; and a dual or "split labor market" emerges based on ethnicity and race. Such domination is also buttressed by state institutions. Social scientists Omi and Winant (1986, pp. 76–78) go so far as to insist that "every state institution is a racial institution." Clearly, whites receive benefits from racism, while people of color bear most of the cost.

Environmental Racism

Racism plays a key factor in environmental planning and decisionmaking. Indeed, environmental racism is reinforced by government, legal, economic, political, and military institutions. It is a fact of life in the United States that the mainstream environmental movement is only beginning to wake up to. Yet, without a doubt racism influences the likelihood of exposure to environmental and health risks and the accessibility to health care. Racism provides whites of all class levels with an "edge" in gaining access to a healthy physical environment. This has been documented again and again.

Whether by conscious design or institutional neglect, communities of color in urban ghettos, in rural "poverty pockets," or on economically impoverished Native-American reservations face some of the worst environmental devastation in the nation. Clearly, racial discrimination was not legislated out of existence in the 1960s. While some significant progress was made during this decade, people of color continue to struggle for equal treatment in many areas, including environmental justice. Agencies at all levels of government, including the federal EPA, have done a poor job protecting people of color from the ravages of pollution and industrial encroachment. It has thus been an up-hill battle convincing white judges, juries, government officials, and policymakers that racism exists in environmental protection, enforcement, and policy formulation.

The most polluted urban communities are those with crumbling infrastructure, ongoing economic disinvestment, deteriorating housing, inadequate schools, chronic unemployment, a high poverty rate, and an overloaded health-care system. Riot-torn South Central Los Angeles typifies this urban neglect. It is not surprising that the "dirtiest" zip code in California belongs to the mostly African-American and Latino neighborhood in that part of the city (Kay 1991a). In the Los Angeles basin, over 71 percent of the African Americans and 50 percent of the Latinos live in areas with the most polluted air, while only 34 percent of the white population does (Mann 1991; Ong and Blumenberg 1990). This pattern exists nationally as well. As researchers Wernette and Nieves note:

> In 1990, 437 of the 3,109 counties and independent cities failed to meet at least one of the EPA ambient air quality standards . . . 57 percent of whites, 65 percent of African Americans, and 80 percent of Hispanics live in 437 counties with substandard air quality. Out of the whole population, a total of 33 percent of whites, 50 percent of African Americans, and 60 percent of Hispanics live in the 136 counties in which two or more air pollutants exceed standards. The percentage living in the 29 counties designated as nonattainment areas for three or more pollutants are 12 percent of whites, 20 percent of African Americans, and 31 percent of Hispanics. (pp. 16–17)

Income alone does not account for these above-average percentages. Housing segregation and development patterns play a key role in determining where people live. Moreover, urban development and the "spatial configuration" of communities flow from the forces and relationships of industrial production which, in turn, are influenced and subsidized by government policy (Feagin 1988; Gottdiener 1988). There is widespread agreement that vestiges of race-based decisionmaking still influence housing, education, employment, and criminal justice. The same is true for municipal services such as garbage pickup and disposal, neighborhood sanitation, fire and police protection, and library services. Institutional racism influences decisions on local land use, enforcement of environmental regulations, industrial facility siting, management of economic vulnerability, and the paths of freeways and highways.

People skeptical of the assertion that poor people and people of color are targeted for waste-disposal sites should consider the report the Cerrell Associates provided the California Waste Management Board. In their 1984 report, *Political Difficulties Facing Waste-to-Energy Conversion Plant Siting,* they offered a detailed profile of those neighborhoods most likely to organize effective resistance against incinerators. The policy conclusion based on this analysis is clear. As the report states:

> All socioeconomic groupings tend to resent the nearby siting of major facilities, but middle and upper socioeconomic strata possess better resources to effectuate their opposition. Middle and higher socioeconomic strata neighborhoods should not fall within the one-mile and five-mile radius of the proposed site. (p. 43)

Where then will incinerators or other polluting facilities be sited? For Cerrell Associates, the answer is low-income, disempowered neighborhoods with a high concentration of nonvoters. The ideal site, according to their report, has nothing to do with environmental soundness but everything to do with lack of social power. Communities of color in California are far more likely to fit this profile than are their white counterparts.

Those still skeptical of the existence of environmental racism should also consider the fact that zoning boards and planning commissions are typically stacked with white developers. Generally, the decisions of these bodies reflect the special interests of the individuals who sit on these boards. People of color have been systematically excluded from these decisionmaking boards, commissions, and governmental agencies (or allowed only token representation). Grassroots leaders are now demanding a shared role in all the decisions that shape their communities. They are challenging the intended or unintended racist assumptions underlying environmental and industrial policies.

Toxic Colonialism Abroad

To understand the global ecological crisis, it is important to understand that the poisoning of African Americans in South Central Los Angeles and of Mexicans in border *maquiladoras* have their roots in the same system of economic exploitation, racial oppression, and devaluation of human life. The quest for solutions to environmental problems and for ways to achieve sustainable development in the United States has considerable implications for the global environmental movement.

Today, more than 1,900 *maquiladoras,* assembly plants operated by American, Japanese, and other foreign countries, are located along the 2,000-mile U.S.-Mexico border (Center for Investigative Reporting 1990; Sanchez 1990; Zuniga 1992, p. 22A). These plants use cheap Mexican labor to assemble products from imported components and raw materials, and then ship them back to the United States (Witt 1991). Nearly half a million Mexicans work in the *maquiladoras.* They earn an average of $3.75 a day. While these plants bring jobs, albeit low-paying ones, they exacerbate local pollution by overcrowding the border towns, straining sewage and water systems, and reducing air quality. All this compromises the health of workers and nearby community residents. The Mexican environmental regulatory agency is understaffed and ill-equipped to adequately enforce the country's laws (Working Group on Canada–Mexico Free Trade 1991).

The practice of targeting poor communities of color in the Third World for waste disposal and the introduction of risky technologies from industrialized countries are forms of "toxic colonialism," what some activists have dubbed the "subjugation of people to an ecologically-destructive economic order by entities over which the people have no control" (Greenpeace 1992, p. 3). The industrialized world's controversial Third World dumping policy was made public by the release of an internal, December 12, 1991, memorandum authored by Lawrence Summers, chief economist of the World Bank. It shocked the world and touched off a global scandal. Here are the highlights:

> "Dirty" Industries: Just between you and me, shouldn't the World Bank be encouraging MORE migration of the dirty industries to the LDCs [Less Developed Countries]? I can think of three reasons:
>
> 1. The measurement of the costs of health impairing pollution depends on the foregone earnings from increased morbidity and mortality. From this point of view a given amount of health impairing pollution should be done in the country with the lowest cost, which will be the country with the lowest wages. I think the economic logic behind dumping a load of toxic waste in the lowest wage country is impeccable and we should face up to that.
>
> 2. The costs of pollution are likely to be non-linear as the initial increments of pollution probably have very low cost. I've always thought that under-polluted areas in Africa are vastly UNDER-polluted; their air quality is probably vastly inefficiently low compared to Los Angeles or Mexico City. Only the lamentable facts that so much pollution is generated by non-tradable industries (transport, electrical

> generation) and that the unit transport costs of solid waste are so high prevent world welfare-enhancing trade in air pollution and waste.
>
> 3. The demand for a clean environment for aesthetic and health reasons is likely to have very high income elasticity. The concern over an agent that causes a one in a million change in the odds of prostate cancer is obviously going to be much higher in a country where people survive to get prostate cancer than in a country where under 5 [year-old] mortality is 200 per thousand. Also, much of the concern over industrial atmosphere discharge is about visibility impairing particulates. These discharges may have very little direct health impact. Clearly trade in goods that embody aesthetic pollution concerns would be welfare enhancing. While production is mobile the consumption of pretty air is a non-tradable.
>
> The problem with the arguments against all of these proposals for more pollution in LDCs (intrinsic rights to certain goods, moral reasons, social concerns, lack of adequate markets, etc.) could be turned around and used more or less effectively against every Bank proposal . . .

Beyond the Race vs. Class Trap

Whether at home or abroad, the question of who *pays* and who *benefits* from current industrial and development policies is central to any analysis of environmental racism. In the United States, race interacts with class to create special environmental and health vulnerabilities. People of color, however, face elevated toxic exposure levels even when social class variables (income, education, and occupational status) are held constant (Bryant and Mohai 1992). Race has been found to be an independent factor, not reducible to class, in predicting the distribution of 1) air pollution in our society (Freeman 1972; Gelobter 1988; Gianessi, Peskin, and Wolff 1979; Wernette and Nieves 1992); 2) contaminated fish consumption (West, Fly, and Marans 1990); 3) the location of municipal landfills and incinerators (Bullard 1983, 1987, 1990, 1991); 4) the location of abandoned toxic waste dumps (United Church of Christ Commission for Racial Justice 1987); and 5) lead poisoning in children (Agency for Toxic Substances and Disease Registry 1988).

Lead poisoning is a classic case in which race, not just class, determines exposure. It affects between three and four million children in the United States—most of whom are African Americans and Latinos living in urban areas. Among children five years old and younger, the percentage of African Americans who have excessive levels of lead in their blood far exceeds the percentage of whites at all income levels (Agency for Toxic Substances and Disease Registry 1988, p. I12).

The federal Agency for Toxic Substances and Disease Registry found that for families earning less than $6,000 annually an estimated 68 percent of African-American children had lead poisoning, compared with 36 percent for white children. For families with incomes exceeding $15,000, more than 38 percent of African-American children have been poisoned, compared with 12 percent of white children. African-American children are two to three times more likely than their white counterparts to suffer from lead poisoning independent of class factors.

One reason for this is that African Americans and whites do not have the same opportunities to "vote with their feet" by leaving unhealthy physical environments. The ability of an individual to escape a health-threatening environment is usually correlated with income. However, racial barriers make it even harder for millions of African Americans, Latinos, Asians, Pacific Islanders, and Native Americans to relocate. Housing discrimination, redlining, and other market forces make it difficult for millions of households to buy their way out of polluted environments. For example, an affluent African-American family (with an income of $50,000 or more) is as segregated as an African-American family with an annual income of $5,000 (Denton and Massey 1988; Jaynes and Williams 1989). Thus, lead poisoning of African-American children is not just a "poverty thing."

White racism helped create our current separate and unequal communities. It defines the boundaries of the urban ghetto, *barrio*, and reservation, and influences the provision of environmental protection and other public services. Apartheid-type housing and development policies reduce neighborhood options, limit mobility, diminish job opportunities, and decrease environmental choices for millions of Americans. It is unlikely that this nation will ever achieve lasting solutions to its environmental problems unless it also addresses the system of racial injustice that helps sustain the existence of powerless communities forced to bear disproportionate environmental costs.

The Limits of Mainstream Environmentalism

Historically, the mainstream environmental movement in the United States has developed agendas that focus on such goals as wilderness and wildlife preservation, wise resource management, pollution abatement, and population control. It has been primarily supported by middle- and upper-middle-class whites. Although concern for the environment cuts across class and racial lines, ecology activists have traditionally been individuals with above-average education, greater access to economic resources, and a greater sense of personal power (Bachrach and Zautra 1985; Bullard 1990; Bullard and Wright 1987; Buttel and Flinn 1978; Dunlap 1987; Mohai 1985, 1990; Morrison 1980, 1986).

Not surprisingly, mainstream groups were slow in broadening their base to include poor and working-class whites, let alone African Americans and other people of color. Moreover, they were ill-equipped to deal with the environmental, economic, and social concerns of these communities. During the 1960s and 1970s, while the "Big Ten" environmental groups focused on wilderness preservation and conservation through litigation, political lobbying, and technical evaluation, activists of color were engaged in mass direct action mobilizations for basic civil rights in the area of employment, housing, education, and health care. Thus, two parallel and sometimes conflicting movements emerged, and it has taken nearly two decades for any significant convergence to occur between these two efforts. In fact, conflicts still remain over how the two groups should balance economic development, social justice, and environmental protection.

In their desperate attempt to improve the economic conditions of their constituents, many African-American civil rights and political leaders have directed their energies toward bringing jobs to their communities. In many instances, this has been achieved at great risk to the health of workers and the surrounding communities. The promise of jobs (even low-paying and hazardous ones) and of a broadened tax base has enticed several economically impoverished, politically powerless communities of color both in the United States and around the world (Bryant and Mohai 1992; Bullard 1990; Center for Investigative Reporting and Bill Moyers 1990). Environmental job blackmail is a fact of life. You can get a job, but only if you are willing to do work that will harm you, your families, and your neighbors.

Workers of color are especially vulnerable to job blackmail because of the greater threat of unemployment they face compared to whites and because of their concentration in low-paying, unskilled, nonunionized occupations. For example, they make up a large share of the nonunion contract workers in the oil, chemical, and nuclear industries. Similarly, over 95 percent of migrant farmworkers in the United States are Latino, African-American, Afro-Caribbean, or Asian, and African Americans are overrepresented in high-risk, blue-collar, and service occupations for which a large pool of replacement labor exists. Thus, they are twice as likely to be unemployed as their white counterparts. Fear of unemployment acts as a potent incentive for many African-American workers to accept and keep jobs they know are health threatening. Workers will tell you that "unemployment and poverty are also hazardous to one's health." An inherent conflict exists between the interests of capital and that of labor. Employers have the power to move jobs (and industrial hazards) from the Northeast and Midwest to the South and Sunbelt, or they may move the jobs offshore to Third World countries where labor is even cheaper and where there are even fewer health and safety regulations. Yet, unless an environmental movement emerges that is capable of addressing these economic concerns, people of color and poor white workers are likely to end up siding with corporate managers in key conflicts concerning the environment.

Indeed, many labor unions already moderate their demands for improved work-safety and pollution control whenever the economy is depressed. They are afraid of layoffs, plant closings, and the relocation of industries. These fears and anxieties of labor are usually built on the false but understandable assumption that environmental regulations inevitably lead to job loss (Brown 1980, 1987).

The crux of the problem is that the mainstream environmental movement has not sufficiently addressed the fact that social

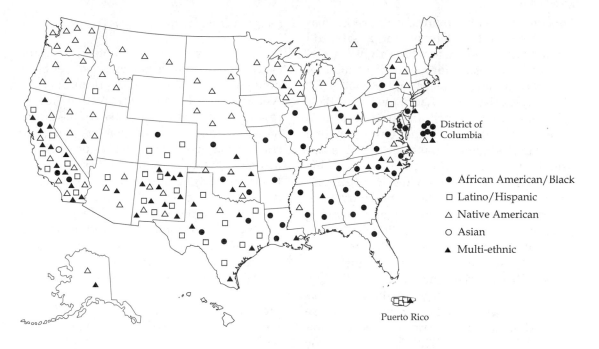

District of Columbia

● African American/Black
□ Latino/Hispanic
△ Native American
○ Asian
▲ Multi-ethnic

Puerto Rico

inequality and imbalances of social power are at the heart of environmental degradation, resource depletion, pollution, and even overpopulation. The environmental crisis can simply not be solved effectively without social justice. As one academic human ecologist notes, "Whenever [an] in-group directly and exclusively benefits from its own overuse of a shared resource but the costs of that overuse are 'shared' by out-groups, then in-group motivation toward a policy of resource conservation (or sustained yields of harvesting) is undermined" (Catton 1982).

The Movement for Environmental Justice

As this [reading] testifies, activists of color have begun to challenge both the industrial polluters and the often indifferent mainstream environmental movement by actively fighting environmental threats in their communities and raising the call for environmental justice. This groundswell of environmental activism in African-American, Latino, Asian, Pacific Islander, and Native-American communities is emerging all across the country. While rarely listed in the standard environmental and conservation directories, grassroots environmental justice groups have sprung up from Maine to Louisiana and Alaska (see map).

These grassroots groups have organized themselves around waste-facility siting, lead contamination, pesticides, water and air pollution, Native self-government, nuclear testing, and workplace safety (Alston 1990; Bryant and Mohai 1992; Bullard 1990, 1992). People of color have invented and, in other cases, adapted existing organizations to meet the disproportionate environmental challenges they face. A growing number of grassroots groups and their leaders have adopted confrontational direct action strategies similar to those used in earlier civil rights conflicts. Moreover, the increasing documentation of environmental racism has strengthened the demand for a safe and healthy environment as a basic right of all individuals and communities (Bryant and Mohai forthcoming; Bullard and Wright 1987, 1990; Commission for Racial Justice 1991).

Drawing together the insights of *both* the civil rights and the environmental movements, these grassroots groups are fighting hard to improve the quality of life for their residents. As a result of their efforts, the environmental justice movement is increasingly influencing and winning support from more conventional environmental and civil rights organizations. For example, the National Urban League's *1992 State of Black America* included—for the first time in the seventeen years the report has been published—a chapter on the environmental threats to the African-American community (Bullard 1992b). In addition, the NAACP, ACLU, and NRDC led the fight to have poor children tested for lead poisoning under Medicaid provisions in California. The class-action lawsuit *Matthews v. Coye*, settled in 1991, called for the state of California to screen an estimated 500,000 poor children for lead poisoning at a cost of $15 to $20 million (Lee 1992). The screening represents a big step forward in efforts to identify children suffering from what federal authorities admit is the number one environmental health problem of children in the United States. For their part, mainstream environmental organizations are also beginning to understand the need for environmental justice and are increasingly supporting grassroots groups in the form of technical advice, expert testimony, direct financial assistance, fundraising, research, and legal assistance. Even the Los Angeles chapter of the wilderness-focused Earth First! movement worked with community groups to help block the incinerator project in South Central Los Angeles.

Case Studies from the Grassroots

For all of their current and potential significance, however, little research has yet been done on these African-American, Latino, Asian, Pacific Islander, and Native American organizations which make up the grassroots environmental justice movement. The research discussed here focuses on environmentally threatened communities of color in Houston (TX), Dallas (TX), Los Angeles (CA), Richmond (CA), Kettleman City (CA), Alsen (LA), and Rosebud (SD). Each of these communities is embroiled in a wide range of environmental disputes against both government and private industry.

We had three major objectives in looking at these nine communities: 1) to examine the organizations and the dispute mechanisms people of color use in resolving environmental conflicts, 2) to explore the conditions and circumstances under which communities of color mobilize against an environmental threat, and 3) to assess the level of external support that grassroots groups of color receive from environmental, social justice, and other groups. To gather this information, in-depth interviews were conducted with opinion leaders, who were identified through a "reputational" approach. We started out with a small number of local informants. The informants were asked to "identify the *most* influential person or persons who had played a role in resolving the local dispute." These influential leaders were later asked the same question, and this second group of leaders was also interviewed.

The interviews focused on a number of key issue areas, including the nature of the dispute, leadership and external support, opposition tactics, and dispute outcomes. The questions included: Were the environmental problems caused by the government and/or corporations? Did the dispute in-

TABLE 1   Summary of Community Disputes

Group (Year Founded), Location	Type of Dispute	Facility
Northeast Community Action Group (1979), Houston, TX	Solid waste landfill	Existing
Neighborhood Committee on Lead Pollution (1981), Dallas, TX	Lead smelter	Existing
West Dallas Coalition for Environmental and Economic Justice (1989), Dallas, TX	Lead smelter	Existing
Coalition for Community Action (1979), Alsen, LA	Hazardous waste incinerator	Existing
Concerned Citizens of South Central Los Angeles (1985), Los Angeles, CA	Solid waste incinerator	Proposed
Mothers of East Los Angeles (1985), Los Angeles, CA	Hazardous waste incinerator	Proposed
People for Clean Air and Water (1990), Kettleman City, CA	Hazardous waste incinerator	Proposed
West County Toxics Coalition (1989), Richmond, CA	Petrochemical refinery	Existing
Good Road Coalition (1991), Rosebud, SD	Solid waste landfill	Proposed

volve a proposed or existing facility? Was the community group started as an environmental group? Do its leaders and members see themselves as environmentalists? Were equity and social justice concerns dominant organizing themes? Who led the local citizen opposition in the disputes? What kind of support did the local groups receive from environmental and other organizations? What tactics did the groups use? Which were most effective? How was the dispute resolved?

A summary of the various communities, grassroots groups, and types of environmental disputes included in this study are presented in Table 1. Here is a more detailed overview of each community's situation.

Houston: In the 1970s, Houston was dubbed the "golden buckle" of the Sunbelt (Bullard 1987, 1990). In 1982, it became the nation's fourth largest city with 1.7 million inhabitants. Its black community of some 450,000 is the largest in the South. For decades, Houston boasted that it was the only major city without zoning. During the "boom" years of the 1970s, this no-zoning policy contributed to haphazard and irrational land-use planning and infrastructure chaos (Bullard 1983). A mostly African-American suburban neighborhood was selected as the site for a municipal landfill. The Northeast Community Action Group (NECAG) formed to block the construction of the landfill.

Dallas: Dallas is the seventh largest city in the nation with a population of just under one million. The 265,594 African Americans who live in Dallas represent 29.4 percent of the city's population. West Dallas is one of many segregated black enclaves in the city. It has a population of 13,161, of which 85 percent is black. The neighborhood has lived with a polluting lead smelter for five decades (Bullard 1990; Nauss 1983). Early on, West Dallas residents formed the Neighborhood Coalition on Lead Pollution to get the smelter closed and the area cleaned up. Another group, West Dallas Coalition for Environmental Justice, continued the fight after the Neighborhood Coalition for Lead Pollution was disbanded.

Alsen (LA): Alsen is an unincorporated community on the Mississippi River several miles north of Baton Rouge, Louisiana's state capital. It had a population of 1,104 individuals in 1980, of which 98.9 percent were African Americans. Alsen lies at the beginning of "Cancer Alley," the 85-mile stretch of land from Baton Rouge to New Orleans, an area that accounts for one-fourth of the nation's petrochemical production (see Anderson, Dunn, and Alabarado 1985; Bullard 1990; Bullard and Wright 1990; Maraniss and Weisskopf 1987). Much of Louisiana's hazardous waste is disposed of in the Rollins Environmental Services incinerators located near Alsen. The residents formed Coalition for Community Action to challenge the Rollins hazardous waste incinerator operation.

Los Angeles: Los Angeles is the nation's second largest city with a population of 3.5 million. It is one of the nation's most culturally and ethnically diverse big cities. People of color (Latinos, Asians, Pacific Islanders, African Americans, and Native Americans) now constitute 63 percent of the city's population. Residents of South Central Los Angeles, a neighborhood that is over 52 percent African-American and about 44 percent Latino, was slated to host the city's first state-of-the-art municipal solid waste incinerator. Local residents organized Concerned Citizens of South Central Los Angeles to fight the incinerator (Blumberg and Gottlieb 1989; Hamilton 1990; Russell 1989; Sanchez 1988).

Just as Los Angeles's largest African-American community was selected as a site for a city-sponsored municipal incinerator, East Los Angeles, the city's largest Latino community, was chosen as a site for a hazardous waste incinerator (Russell 1989). Officially, the incinerator was planned for Vernon, an industrial suburb that has only 96 people. But several East Los Angeles neighborhoods (made up of mostly Latino residents) are located only a mile away and downwind from the proposed site. The group Mothers of East Los Angeles (MELA) took the lead in fighting the proposed hazardous waste site (Pardo 1991).

Richmond (CA): Richmond has a population of 80,000. Over half are African Americans and about 10 percent are Latinos. Most of the African-American population live next to the city's petrochemical corridor—a cluster of 350 facilities that handle hazardous waste (Citizens for a Better Environment 1989). The five largest industrial polluters in the city are the Chevron oil refinery, Chevron Ortho pesticide plant, Witco Chemical, Airco Industrial Gases, and an ICI pesticide plant (formerly Stauffer Chemical). Chevron Ortho generates over 40 percent of the hazardous waste in Richmond. The bulk of it is incinerated on the plant's grounds. Local citizens founded the West County Toxics Coalition to address the problem of toxic emissions.

Kettleman City (CA): Kettleman City is a small farmworker community of approximately 1,200. Over 95 percent of the residents are Latino. It is home to a hazardous waste landfill operated by the world's largest waste-disposal company, Chemical Waste Management (see Corwin 1991; Siler 1991). The company proposed that a new incinerator be built in Kettleman City. Residents organized an opposition group called El Pueblo para el Aire y Agua Limpio (People for Clean Air and Water).

Rosebud Reservation (SD): As state environmental regulations have become more stringent in recent years, Native-American reservations have become prime targets of waste-disposal firms (Beasley 1990; Kay 1991b; Tomsho 1990). Many waste-disposal companies have attempted to skirt state regulations (which are often tougher than the federal regulations) by targeting Native lands (Angel 1992). Because of their quasi-independent status, Native-American reservations are not covered by state environmental regulations. The threat to Native lands exists for the Mohawk Indians in New York to the Mission Indians (i.e., Campo, La Posta, Los Coyotes, Morongo, Pala, and

Soboda) in southern California to the Gwichin people in Alaska (Kay 1991b). The problem is typified in the case of the Rosebud Reservation in South Dakota. RSW, a Connecticut-based company, proposed in 1991 to build a 6,000-acre municipal landfill on Sioux lands (Daschle 1991). Local residents founded the Good Road Coalition to block the landfill.

What We Learned

Eight of the nine community opposition groups were started as environmental groups. Mothers of East Los Angeles was the only exception. It grew out of a six-year dispute involving a proposed 1,450-bed state prison in East Los Angeles (Pardo 1991). MELA also fought a proposed underground pipeline through their neighborhood. Its fight against the incinerator is an extension of this earlier battle.

All of the groups have multi-issue agendas and incorporate social justice and equity as their major organizing themes. The leaders see their communities as "victims" and are quick to make the connection between other forms of discrimination, the quality of their physical environment, and the current dispute. Some of the leaders have worked in other organizations that fought discrimination in housing, employment, and education.

It is clear that the local grassroots activists in the impacted communities provided the essential leadership in dealing with the disputes. The typical grassroots leader was a woman. For example, women led the fight in seven of the nine cases examined. Only the West Dallas Coalition for Environmental Justice and Richmond's West County Toxics Coalition were headed by men.

Women activists were quick to express their concern about the threat to their family, home, and community. The typical organizer found leadership thrust upon her by immediate circumstances with little warning or prior training for the job. Lack of experience, however, did not prove an insurmountable barrier to successful organizing.

The manner in which the local issue was framed appears to have influenced the type of leadership that emerged. Local activists immediately turned their energies to what they defined as environmental discrimination, for discrimination is a fact of life in all of these communities. Most people of color face it daily.

The quest for environmental justice thus extends the quest for basic civil rights. Actions taken by grassroots activists to reduce environmental inequities are consistent with the struggle to end the other forms of social injustice found throughout our society—in housing, education, employment, health care, criminal justice, and politics.

The mainstream environmental groups do not have a long history of working with African-American, Latino, Asian, Pacific Islander, and Native-American groups. For the most part, they have failed to adequately address environmental problems that disproportionately impact people of color. Despite some exceptions, the national groups have failed to sufficiently make the connection between key environmental and social justice issues.

The experience of the organizations discussed here suggests that the situation is beginning to change for the better. While still too little, the mainstream environmental movement's support of environmental justice struggles has visibly increased between the first Earth Day in 1970 and Earth Day 1990. Certainly, the early environmental struggles by communities of color were less likely than more recent ones to attract significant support from the mainstream groups.

Because of the redefinition of "environmentalism" spurred on by grassroots challenges to the elitism and environmental racism of the mainstream groups, more mainstream groups now acknowledge and try to address the widespread inequities throughout our society. Many of these groups are beginning to understand and embrace the cause of social justice activists mobilizing to protect their neighborhoods from garbage dumps or lead smelters. These first steps have been a long time in coming, however. For many conservationists, the struggle for social justice is still seen as separate from environmental activism. Because of this, environmental activists of color have usually had better luck winning support for their cause by appealing to more justice-oriented groups. For example, Houston's Northeast Community Action Group (NECAG) was able to enlist support from a number of local social justice activists in their dispute with Browning-Ferris Industries. The antidiscrimination theme was a major tool in enlisting the Houston Black United Front (an African-American self-help group), the Harris County Council of Organizations (an African-American voter education and political group), and a Houston chapter of ACORN (Association of Community Organizations for Reform Now).

The situation in Dallas somewhat resembled that found in Houston. Leaders of West Dallas's Neighborhood Committee on Lead Pollution received no assistance from any outside environmental group in resolving their dispute. Instead, they relied exclusively on the grassroots self-help group, the Common Ground Community Economic Development Corporation, to get their grievances publicly aired. Common Ground not surprisingly has a long history of working on equity issues in the city's African-American community.

The Neighborhood Committee on Lead Pollution disbanded after the lead-smelter dispute was resolved. In 1989, the West Dallas Coalition for Environmental Justice, a multiracial group, formed to fill the leadership vacuum. It pressed for cleanup of the RSR site in West Dallas, closure of the Dixie Metals lead smelter in Dallas's East Oak Cliff neighborhood, and pollution prevention measures for the remaining industries in the neighborhood. The multiracial coalition has about 700 members and 20 volunteers. It has worked closely with Common Ground and Texas United, a grassroots environmental group affiliated with the Boston-based National Toxics Campaign. The local Sierra Club also wrote several letters endorsing the actions taken by the West Dallas group to get their neighborhood cleaned up.

Leaders in Alsen, on the other hand, did receive support (although late in their struggle) from several environmental groups. Rollins' proposal to burn PCBs in the Alsen incinerator had gotten the attention of several national environmental groups, including Greenpeace, Citizens' Clearinghouse for Hazardous Waste, and the National Toxics Campaign.

Alsen residents also enlisted the support of the Louisiana Environmental Action Network (a mostly white group) and Gulf Coast Tenants Organization (a mostly African-American group). Gulf Coast has, for example, led Earth Day "toxics marches" from New Orleans to Baton Rouge.

The four California community groups examined in this study all had great success in getting support from and forming alliances with both grassroots and national environmental groups. Again, the level of outside support was greatest for the groups fighting new facilities proposals.

The African-American leaders of Concerned Citizens of South Central Los Angeles found allies and built strong working relationships with a diverse set of international, national, and grassroots environmental groups. Greenpeace was the first national group to join Concerned Citizens in their fight to kill LANCER 1 (Blumberg and Gottlieb 1989; Russell 1989). Others joined later, including Citizens for a Better Environment (CBE), National Health Law Program, and the Center for Law in the Public Interest. Concerned Citizens also forged alliances with two white Westside "slow-growth" groups: Not Yet New York (a coalition of environmental and homeowner groups) and the anti-incineration group California Alliance in Defense of Residential Environments (CADRE).

Mothers of East Los Angeles lined up the support of groups such as Greenpeace, the Natural Resources Defense Council, the Environmental Policy Institute, the Citizens' Clearinghouse on Hazardous Waste, the National Toxics Campaign, and the Western Center on Law and Poverty. These allies provided valuable technical advice, expert testimony, lobbying, research, and legal assistance.

The Kettleman City dispute attracted widespread attention and became a topic on prime-time newscasts. The local group, El Pueblo para el Aire y Agua Limpio (People for Clean Air and Water), got a lot of support from both national and grassroots environmental and social justice groups. The dispute brought together environmental leaders of color from inside and outside California. The decision to site a hazardous waste incinerator in Kettleman City also acted as a rallying point for many environmental justice groups ranging from Greenpeace to the Albuquerque-based Southwest Network for Environmental and Economic Justice (a coalition of environmental activists of color from eight states in the Southwest).

The Richmond-based West County Toxics Coalition was founded with assistance from the National Toxics Campaign. It then got the Sierra Club (headquartered just across the Bay in San Francisco) involved in their struggle. The San Francisco–based Citizens for a Better Environment (CBE) furnished the group with technical assistance and documentation of the local environ-

mental problem (see the 1989 report *Richmond at Risk*). The report offers graphic evidence of the threat posed by polluting industries in the city's African-American and Latino communities.

Disputes involving Native lands present special problems to conventional environmental movements. Given the long history of exploitation and genocide directed at Native Americans by whites, environmental disputes take on larger historical and cultural meanings. However, the Good Road Coalition was able to enlist the support of Greenpeace activists and two Native-American groups (the Indigenous Environmental Network and the Natural Resource Coalition).

Organizing Tactics

The grassroots environmental groups and their allies have used a wide range of tactics to fend off what they see as a threat to family, home, and community. The leaders have borrowed many of their tactics from the earlier civil rights movement. All of the groups have used public protest, demonstrations, petitions, lobbying, reports and fact-finding, and hearings to educate the community and intensify public debate on the dispute. In addition, leaders organized community workshops and neighborhood forums to keep local residents informed on the disputes and new developments.

All of the grassroots groups targeted local, state, and federal governments for their direct or indirect influence in siting and enforcement decisions. For example, the leaders of Houston's Northeast Community Action Group directed their actions toward both the local and state government bodies responsible for permitting the facility.

A number of tangible results emerged from the Houston dispute. First, the Houston City Council, acting under intense political pressure from local residents, passed a resolution in 1980 that prohibited city-owned garbage trucks from dumping at the controversial landfill in the Northwood Manor subdivision. Second, the council also passed an ordinance restricting the construction of solid-waste sites near public facilities such as schools and parks. (This action was nothing less than a form of protective zoning.) And, third, the Texas Department of Health updated its requirements for landfill permit applicants. Applications now must include detailed land-use, economic impact, and sociodemographic data on areas where proposed municipal solid-waste landfills are to be sited.

The Neighborhood Committee on Lead Pollution challenged the Dallas Health Department for its lax enforcement of the city's lead ordinance and the repeated violations by the nearby smelter. Grassroots leaders in West Dallas extended their influence beyond the neighborhood by pressuring the Dallas mayor to appoint a government-sanctioned city-wide task force (the Dallas Alliance Environmental Task Force) to address lead contamination. The impetus for the task force came from the local West Dallas group.

The two Los Angeles neighborhood groups also sought to have the city intervene in their dispute. The LANCER dispute was injected into local city politics and became a contributing factor in both the defeat of the pro-LANCER City Council President Pat Russell and the election of environmental advocate Ruth Galanter. Concerned Citizens of South Central Los Angeles and its allies proved that local citizens can fight city hall and win. Opponents of the city-initiated incinerator project applied pressure on key elected officials, including Mayor Tom Bradley. Bradley reversed his position and asked the city council to kill the project, which had been in the planning stage since 1969 and included a commitment to contribute $12 million (Russell 1989).

Mothers of East Los Angeles, in its struggle, targeted the South Coast Air Quality Management District (AQMD), the California Department of Health Services (DHS), and the U.S. Environmental Protection Agency (EPA)—the agencies responsible for awarding a permit for the Vernon hazardous waste incinerator project. The facility was to be California's first "state-of-the-art" toxic-waste incinerator.

To block the project, Mothers of East Los Angeles and its allies arranged for more than 500 residents to attend a 1987 DHS hearing on it. They pressed their demands in other public forums as well. The alliance questioned DHS's 1988 decision that allowed California Thermal Treatment Services (CTTS) to move the project forward without preparing an environmental impact report (EIR). The City of Los Angeles, MELA, and others joined in a lawsuit to review the decision. The federal EPA, however, approved the permit without an EIR.

This prompted California Assemblywoman Lucille Roybal-Allard to lead a successful fight to change the California law and require EIRs for all toxic waste incinerators. In December 1988, as CTTS was about to start construction, the AQMD decided that the company should do the environmental studies and redesign its original standards to meet the new, more stringent clean air regulations. CTTS legally challenged the AQMD's decision all the way up to the State Supreme Court and lost.

The Coalition for Community Action (Alsen, LA) focused its attack on the Louisiana Department of Environmental Quality and its less-than-enthusiastic enforcement of air quality standards in North Baton Rouge and the African-American communities affected by emissions from the nearby polluting industries. The group also worked on getting the federal EPA more actively involved in pollution prevention efforts in "Cancer Alley."

Richmond's West County Toxics Coalition worked to get both state and federal government agencies involved in reducing emissions from the nearby polluting industries. On the other hand, Kettleman City's People for Clean Air and Water focused its attention on the Kings County Board of Supervisors, the California Department of Health Services, and the federal EPA.

The Native Americans who founded the Good Road Coalition appealed to their Tribal Council (the government of the sovereign Sioux Nation on the Rosebud Reservation) to rescind the contract signed with RSW to build the 6,000-acre landfill on the reservation. Tribal Chairman Ralph Moran had supported the construction. It is interesting that six of the nine grassroots groups used litigation as a tactic. The three groups that did not were the West Dallas Coalition for Environmental Justice (its predecessor had already filed a lawsuit), Richmond's West County Toxics Coalition, and Rosebud's Good Road Coalition. All of the groups that filed lawsuits used their own lawyers. Three of them (Concerned Citizens of South Central Los Angeles, Mothers of East Los Angeles, and People for Clean Air and Water) applied to public interest law centers to file their lawsuits.

The West Dallas and East Los Angeles groups were joined in their lawsuits by the local government: both the city of Dallas and the Texas Attorney General joined the West Dallas plaintiffs, while the city of Los Angeles joined MELA.

Three of the neighborhood groups (the two in West Dallas and the one in Richmond) used negotiations as a dispute resolution tactic. The West Dallas groups were able to negotiate two different cleanup plans—the first in 1984, the second in 1992.

Richmond's West County Toxics Campaign brought in the Reverend Jesse Jackson of the National Rainbow Coalition to negotiate with Chevron, the major polluter in the community. Richmond's Mayor George Livingston helped arrange the May 7, 1990 meeting with Chevron that included representatives from the West County Toxics Coalition, the National Rainbow Coalition, and the Sierra Club. Jackson described the negotiations as a "test case, a test example, both with dangers and possibilities." He and the West County Toxics Coalition presented Chevron with a six-point plan (Reed 1990, p. A1):

- Annually set aside 1 percent of the cost of Chevron's proposed $1 billion modernization for a cleanup fund. The fund should employ Richmond's unemployed to help clean up the environment, and should also be used to finance health care and new pollution-reduction technology;
- Establish a 24-hour, fully funded clinic to provide medical attention to those harmed by the dozens of polluting industries in Richmond;
- Reduce the tons of toxic waste destroyed in Chevron's Ortho Chemical plant incinerator. (Chevron, which currently burns about 75,000 tons annually in the furnace, is seeking state permits to double the incinerator's capacity);
- Bring together representatives of other polluting industries and pressure them to reduce their companies' toxic emissions;
- Divest from South Africa; and
- Negotiate a timetable for accomplishing the above goals.

Nobody knows what these negotiations will yield or how long it will take to get tangible results. Nevertheless, both sides appear willing to talk. Of course, talking about emission reduction is different from actual emission reduction. But the Coalition and its allies did get Chevron to agree not to bring in outside waste to burn at the Richmond site.

The other concrete result of the negotiations was an agreement to meet again to negotiate specifics. Nevertheless, the meeting itself represented a major community victory in that the West County Toxics Coalition finally won the right to bargain with Chevron, something local leaders had unsuccessfully attempted to do since 1987.

Resolutions and Outcomes

These case studies demonstrate that African Americans, Latino Americans, and Native Americans are actively pursuing strategies to improve the overall quality of life in their neighborhoods. The grassroots leaders have not waited for "outsiders" or "elites" to rush to their rescue; they have taken the initiative themselves.

As expected, the groups had more success in blocking proposed facilities than closing those already operating. The West Dallas residents were successful in shutting down the lead smelter and in winning an out-of-court settlement worth over $45 million—one of the largest awards ever in a lead pollution case in the country. It was made on behalf of 370 children—almost all of whom were poor, black residents of the West Dallas public housing project—and 40 property owners.

The lawsuit was finally settled in June 1983 when RSR agreed to a soil cleanup program in West Dallas, a blood-testing program for the children and pregnant women, and the installation of new antipollution equipment. The equipment, however, was never installed. In May 1984 the Dallas Board of Adjustments, a city agency responsible for monitoring land-use violations, requested that the city attorney order the smelter permanently closed for violating the zoning code. It had operated in the neighborhood for some 50 years without the necessary use permits.

The 1984 lead cleanup proved inadequate. A more comprehensive cleanup of West Dallas was begun in December 1991—20 years after the first government study of lead smelters. Some 30,000 to 40,000 cubic yards (roughly 1,800 truckloads) of lead-tainted soil are to be removed from several West Dallas sites, including schoolyards and about 140 private homes (Loftis 1992). The project will cost between $3 and $4 million. The contaminated soil was originally planned to be shipped to a landfill in Monroe, Louisiana—a city that is 60 percent African-American.

The municipal landfill in Houston, the hazardous waste incinerator in Alsen, and the petrochemical plant (and on-site hazardous waste incinerator) in Richmond are still operating. Although the three groups and their allies fell short of completely eliminating the threat by bringing about actual plant closures, they were able to extract concessions from the polluting industries in the form of capacity reduction and emission controls. In Alsen, after more than six years, a 1987 out-of-court settlement was reached between Rollins and the residents. It was reported to be worth an average of $3,000 per resident. The company was also required to reduce emissions from its facilities.

Construction of four proposed facilities was prevented: the two waste facilities in Los Angeles (South Central and East Los Angeles), the one on Rosebud Reservation in South Dakota, and the one in Kettleman City. The two lawsuits filed on behalf of South Central and East Los Angeles residents never reached the trial or settlement stage, for the two construction proposals were withdrawn. The city-sponsored LANCER project was killed by the mayor and city council. In May 1991, CTTS decided to "throw in the towel" because the lawsuits threatened to drive up costs beyond the $4 million the company had already spent on the project (Dolan 1991). The Vernon hazardous waste incinerator became a dead issue.

On the other hand, the Good Road Coalition blocked plans to build the 6,000-acre landfill on the Rosebud Reservation through the electoral process. A majority of the residents voted the proposal down. In 1991, former tribal chairman Ralph Moran, who had favored the landfill proposal, was defeated in the tribal primary election and residents convinced the tribal council to cancel the agreement to build the facility. The proposal was resurrected in 1992 in yet another offer to the tribal council by RSW. Again, the plan was rejected by the council.

Although part of the lawsuit involving the Kettleman City incinerator dispute is still pending, People for Clean Air and Water won a major victory in delaying construction. A superior court judge in January 1992 overturned the Kings County Board of Supervisors' approval of the Kettleman City incinerator, citing its detrimental impact on air quality in the agriculture-rich Central Valley of California.

The judge ruled that Kings County's environmental impact report was inadequate and that county leaders had failed to involve the local residents in the decision by not providing Spanish translations of material about the project. This court ruling represents a victory since the waste-disposal company must now begin the permit process all over again if it is still interested in siting the facility.

Conclusion

The mainstream environmental movement has proven that it can help enhance the quality of life in this country. The national membership organizations that make up the mainstream movement have clearly played an important role in shaping the nation's environmental policy. Yet, few of these groups have actively involved themselves in environmental conflicts involving communities of color. Because of this, it's unlikely that we will see a mass influx of people of color into the national environmental groups any time soon. A continuing growth in their own grassroots organizations is more likely. Indeed, the fastest growing segment of the environmental movement is made up by the grassroots groups in communities of color which are increasingly linking up with one another and with other community-based groups. As long as U.S. society remains divided into separate and unequal communities, such groups will continue to serve a positive function.

It is not surprising that indigenous leaders are organizing the most effective resistance within communities of color. They have the advantage of being close to the population immediately affected by the disputes they are attempting to resolve. They are also completely wedded to social and economic justice agendas and familiar with the tactics of the civil rights movement. This makes effective community organizing possible. People of color have a long track record in challenging government and corporations that discriminate. Groups that emphasize civil rights and social justice can be found in almost every major city in the country.

Cooperation between the two major wings of the environmental movement is both possible and beneficial, however. Many environmental activists of color are now getting support from mainstream organizations in the form of technical advice, expert testimony, direct financial assistance, fundraising, research, and legal assistance. In return, increasing numbers of people of color are assisting mainstream organizations to redefine their limited environmental agendas and expand their outreach by serving on boards, staffs, and advisory councils. Grassroots activists have thus been the most influential activists in placing equity and social justice issues onto the larger environmental agenda and democratizing and diversifying the movement as a whole. Such changes are necessary if the environmental movement is to successfully help spearhead a truly global movement for a just, sustainable, and healthy society and effectively resolve pressing environmental disputes. Environmentalists and civil rights activists of all stripes should welcome the growing movement of African Americans, Latinos, Asians, Pacific Islanders, and Native Americans who are taking up the struggle for environmental justice.

REFERENCES

Agency for Toxic Substances and Disease Registry. 1988. *The Nature and Extent of Lead Poisoning in Children in the United States:* A reprint to Congress. Atlanta: U.S. Department of Health and Human Services.

ALSTON, DANA. 1990. *We Speak for Ourselves: Social Justice, Race, and Environment.* Washington, DC: Panos Institute.

ANDERSON, BOB, MIKE DUNN, and SONNY ALABARADO. 1985. "Prosperity in Paradise: Louisiana's Chemical Legacy." *Morning Advocate,* 25 April.

ANGEL, BRADLEY. 1992. *The Toxic Threat to Indian Lands: A Greenpeace Report.* San Francisco: Greenpeace.

BACHRACH, KENNETH M., and ALEX J. ZAUTRA. 1985. "Coping with Community Stress: The Threat of a Hazardous Waste Landfill." *Journal of Health and Social Behavior* 26 (June):127–41.

BEASLEY, CONGER, JR. 1990. "Of Poverty and Pollution: Deadly Threat on Native Lands." *Buzzworm* 2 (September-October):39–50.

BLAUNER, ROBERT. 1972. *Racial Oppression in America.* New York: Harper & Row.

BLUMBERG, MICHAEL, and ROBERT GOTTLIEB. 1989. *War on Waste: Can America Win Its Battle with Garbage?* Washington, DC: Island Press.

BROWN, MICHAEL H. 1980. *Laying Waste: The Poisoning of America by Toxic Chemicals.* New York: Pantheon Books.

———. 1987. *The Toxic Cloud: The Poisoning of America's Air.* New York: Harper & Row.

BRYANT, BUNYAN, and PAUL MOHAI. 1992. *Race and the Incidence of Environmental Hazards.* Boulder, CO: Westview Press.

BULLARD, ROBERT D. 1983. "Solid Waste Sites and the Black Houston Community." *Sociological Inquiry* 53 (Spring):273–88.

———. 1987. *Invisible Houston: The Black Experience in Boom and Bust.* College Station: Texas A&M University Press.

———. 1990. *Dumping in Dixie: Race, Class, and Environmental Quality.* Boulder, CO: Westview Press.

———. 1991. "Environmental Justice for All." *EnviroAction,* Environmental News Digest for the National Wildlife Federation (November).

BULLARD, ROBERT D., and BEVERLY H. WROGHT. 1987. "Blacks and the Environment." *Humboldt Journal of Social Relations* 14:165–84.

BUTTEL, FREDERICK, and WILLIAM L. FLINN. 1978. "Social Class and Mass Environmental Beliefs: A Reconsideration." *Environment and Behavior* 10 (September):433–50.

CARMICHAEL, S., and C. V. HAMILTON. 1967. *Black Power.* New York: Vintage Books.

CATTON, WILLIAM. 1982. *Overshoot: The Ecological Basis of Revolutionary Change.* Chicago: University of Illinois Press.

Center for Investigative Reporting and Bill Moyers. 1990. *Global Dumping Grounds: The International Trade in Hazardous Waste.* Washington, DC: Seven Locks Press.

DASCHLE, THOMAS. 1991. "Dances with Garbage." *Christian Science Monitor,* 14 February.

DENTON, NANCY A., and DOUGLAS S. MASSEY. 1988. "Residential Segregation of Blacks, Hispanics, and Asians by Socioeconomic Class and Generation." *Social Science Quarterly* 69:797–817.

DOLAN, MAURA. 1991. "Toxic Waste Incinerator Bid Abandoned." *Los Angeles Times,* 24 May.

DUNLAP, RILEY E. 1987. "Public Opinion on the Environment in the Reagan Era: Polls, Pollution, and Politics." *Environment* 29:6–11, 31–37.

FEAGIN, JOE R. 1988. *Free Enterprise City: Houston in Political and Economic Perspective.* Englewood Cliffs, NJ: Prentice-Hall.

FREEMAN, MYRICK A. 1971. "The Distribution of Environmental Quality." In *Environmental Quality Analysis,* edited by Allen V. Kneese and Blair T. Bower. Baltimore: Johns Hopkins University Press for Resources for the Future.

GIANESSI, LEONARD, H. M. PESKIN, and E. WOLFF. 1979. "The Distributional Effects of Uniform Air Pollution Policy in the U.S." *Quarterly Journal of Economics* (May):281–303.

GOTTDIENER, MARK. 1988. *The Social Production of Space.* Austin: University of Texas Press.

GREENPEACE. 1992. "The 'Logic' Behind Hazardous Waste Export." *Greenpeace Waste Trade Update* (First Quarter):1–2.

HAMILTON, CYNTHIA. 1990. "Women, Home, Community." *Race, Poverty, and the Environment Newsletter* 1 (April).

JAYNES, GERALD D., and ROBIN M. WILLIAMS, Jr. 1989. *A Common Destiny: Blacks and American Society.* Washington, DC: National Academy Press.

KAY, JANE. 1991a. "Fighting Toxic Racism: L.A.'s Minority Neighborhood Is the 'Dirtiest' in the State." *San Francisco Examiner,* 7 April.

———. 1991b. "Indian Lands Targeted for Waste Disposal Sites." *San Francisco Examiner,* 10 April.

LEE, BILL LANN. 1992. "Environmental Litigation on Behalf of Poor, Minority Children: *Matthew v. Coye:* A Case Study." Paper presented at the Annual Meeting of the American Association for the Advancement of Science, Chicago, April.

LOFTIS, RANDY LEE. 1992. "Louisiana OKs Dumping of Tainted Soil." *Dallas Morning News,* 12 May, pp. A1, A30.

MARANISS, DAVID, and MICHAEL WEISSKOPF. 1987. "Jobs and Illness in Petrochemical Corridor." *Washington Post,* 22 December.

MOHAI, PAUL. 1985. "Public Concern and Elite Involvement in Environmental Conservation." *Social Science Quarterly* 66 (December):820–38.

———. 1990. "Black Environmentalism." *Social Science Quarterly* 71 (April):744–65.

MORRISON, DENTON E. 1980. "The Soft Cutting Edge of Environmentalism: Why and How the Appropriate Technology Notion Is Changing the Movement." *Natural Resources Journal* 20 (April):275–98.

———. 1986. "How and Why Environmental Consciousness Has Trickled Down." Pp. 187–220 in *Distributional Conflict in Resource Policy,* edited by Allan Schnaiberg, Nicholas Watts, and Klaaus Zimmerman. New York: St. Martin's Press.

NAUSS, D. W. 1983. "The People vs. the Lead Smelter." *Dallas Times Herald,* 17 July.

OMI, MICHAEL, and HOWARD WINANT. 1986. *Racial Formation in the United States: From the 1960s to the 1980s.* Routledge & Kegan Paul.

PARDO, MARY. 1990. "Mexican American Women Grassroots Community Activists: Mothers of East Los Angeles." *Frontiers: A Journal of Women's Studies* 11 (January):1–6.

REED, DAN. 1990. "Jackson to Chevron: Clean Up." *West County Times,* 8 May, p. A1.

RUSSEL, DICK. 1989. "Environmental Racism." *Amicus Journal* 11 (February):22–32.

SANCHEZ, JESUS. 1988. "The Environment: Whose Movement?" *California Tomorrow* 3:10–17.

SANCHEZ, ROBERTO. 1990. "Health and Environmental Risks of the Maquiladora in Mexicali." *Natural Resources Journal* 30 (Winter):163–86.

TOMSHO, ROBERT. 1990. "Dumping Grounds: Indian Tribes Contend with Some of the Worst of America's Pollution." *Wall Street Journal,* 29 November.

WERNETTE, D. R., and L. A. NIEVES. 1992. "Breathing Polluted Air." *EPA Journal* 18 (March–April):16–17.

WEST, PAT C., F. Fly, and R. MARANS. 1989. "Minority Anglers and Toxic Fish Consumption: Evidence from a State-Wide Survey in Michigan." Pp. 108–122 in *The Proceedings of the Michigan Conference on Race and the Incidence of Environmental Hazards,* edited by B. Bryant and P. Mohai. Ann Arbor: University of Michigan School of Natural Resources.

WITT, MATTHEW. 1991. "An Injury to One Is a Gravio a Todo: The Need for a Mexico–U.S. Health and Safety Movement." *New Solutions: A Journal of Environmental and Occupational Health Policy* 1 (March):28–33.

Working Group on Canada–Mexico Free Trade. 1991. "Que Pasa? A Canada–Mexico 'Free' Trade Deal." *New Solutions: A Journal of Environmental and Health Policy* 2 (January):10–25.

ZUNIGA, JO ANN. 1992. "Watchdog Keeps Tabs on Politics of Environment Along Border." *Houston Chronicle,* 24 May, p. A22.

PART III

Race and Ethnicity in Social Institutions

Answer the questions that follow.

1. As of 1999, what percentage of the United States do you think was:
   a. black _____%
   b. white _____%
   c. Asian _____%
   d. American Indian _____%
   e. Latino _____%

2. Who are your three best friends? _____ _____ _____

3. Does the unemployment rate in the United States vary by color or ethnicity? _____

Each of your answers, whether you realize it or not, reflects how you have been shaped by social institutions. Compare your answers on item 1 to the correct percentages as enumerated by the U.S. Bureau of the Census: 12.7 percent black, 82.6 percent white, 3.8 percent Asian/Pacific Islander, 0.9 percent American Indian, and 11 percent Latino. (These numbers add up to more than 100 percent because Latinos can be any race.)

Did your estimates of the size of these groups differ from the actual numbers? If you said that the black population was around 30 percent or that the Asian population was 10 percent, your answer was similar to the average American response. How do you explain the fact that most people in the United States almost triple-count the black and Asian population? From a sociological perspective, what does the overcounting of the nonwhite population mean?

Item 2 asked you to list your three best friends. How many of the people you listed are from a different race? How many are the same sex as you? If you don't have any best friends who are from a racial background different from your own, why not? Do you only have friends of the same sex? Why?

With regard to item 3, the unemployment rate in the United States does vary by color or ethnicity, with blacks and Latinos twice as likely as whites to be unemployed. How is the unemployment rate linked to how close people live to areas of high job growth, and how are both of these factors linked to race and ethnicity?

The answers to these questions reflect the ways in which institutions shape how we view the world. Your beliefs, opinions, and attitudes, and the "commonsense" knowledge that guides your moment-to-moment understanding of the world—all may seem to be highly individualistic. Upon closer sociological inspection, however, we see that it is institutions and other social arrangements that influence, mediate, and structure how we think about and come to understand the world in which we live. Think for a moment about your answers to the preceding questions. People of all colors typically overestimate the nonwhite population and underestimate the white population. Perhaps you overestimated the nonwhite population because you live in an all-black or all-Latino neighborhood. When you look out the window or walk down the street, you see that everyone in your neighborhood is like you. That local information is then used to make a judgment about the rest of the United States.

But what if you are white and you over-estimated the nonwhite population? How do you explain doubling or tripling the black or Asian population? Do you get your information about other racial groups second-hand, from watching television? Might there be a difference between the media's portrayal of race and ethnic relations and what is actually taking place in society?

If you do live in a racially segregated neighborhood, might that explain why your best friends are all the same color as you? Do you think you might have close friends from different racial backgrounds if your high school or neighborhood was racially integrated? Why is it that compared to white areas or the suburbs, jobs are often not as plentiful or as well paying in black or Latino neighborhoods?

In Part III, we focus on how race and ethnic identity intersect with the labor market, where and why individuals live where they do, and how the media shapes our views on race and ethnic relations. The first six readings examine why the economic and occupational outcomes for individuals vary by race and ethnicity. Edna Bonacich draws on the history of how whites and blacks have been pitted against one another in what she calls a "split labor market" to help explain a black rate of unemployment double that of whites. Julie Matthaei and Teresa Amott detail how Asian women were exploited economically, socially, and sexually by all those who could profit from their immigration to the United States. Gregory DeFreitas traces the emergence of the Hispanic American labor force. Joleen Kirschenman and Kathryn Neckerman focus on hiring practices in Chicago to reveal the extent to which employers use stereotypes as a way to exclude blacks, particularly black men. Roger Waldinger and William J. Wilson provide historical and contemporary examples of how employment opportunities have changed over time. Waldinger examines the different occupational niches that ethnic and racial groups occupied in New York City, while Wilson demonstrates that the poorest, most isolated, and disproportionately black parts of the nation's inner cities face a crisis of joblessness.

The next three readings reveal a nation highly segregated by race and ethnicity. Douglas Massey and Nancy Denton argue that residential segregation results in a loss of occupational and educational mobility for racial minorities and cuts off communities from "mainstream" America. Judith DeSena traces the informal mechanisms individuals and organizations use to keep the "wrong" people out of their neighborhoods. Elijah Anderson explains how many poor, young African Americans use fear and intimidation as a way to gain respect among their peers.

The final five readings in Part III explore how our views on race and ethnicity are shaped by the media. Benjamin DeMott suggests that two versions of racial and ethnic relations exist in the United States—the one manufactured by Hollywood and the one that we actually live in. Author bell hooks examines how white entertainers create and maintain this schism by using racially coded symbols in blatant and subtle ways to "spice up" their performances. The readings by Robert Entman and by S. Robert Lichter and Daniel R. Amundson focus on the invidious ways in which blacks in the nightly news and Latinos in television programming are reduced to a series of degrading stereotypes. Each of these readings asks us to consider how representations of race and ethnicity on the nightly news or on situation comedies shapes our worldview. Finally, Richard Lapchick and David Stuckey report on the status of minority groups "behind the scene" in professional sports—specifically, baseball, football, and basketball.

QUESTIONS TO FRAME
YOUR READINGS

- Why is it that even during times of low unemployment, blacks and Latinos are twice as likely to be unemployed as whites?

- Why might women of color be doubly disadvantaged in the labor market in terms of race and gender?

- Do people *choose* to live in racially segregated neighborhoods, or are there other social forces at work? What are they?

- Is the media's representation of racial groups or race relations accurate? Are race relations better or worse than the media would have us believe?

Economy and Work

19

ADVANCED CAPITALISM AND BLACK/WHITE RACE RELATIONS IN THE UNITED STATES
A Split Labor Market Interpretation

Edna Bonacich

Currently one of the most noteworthy features of the position of black people in the United States is a high degree of unemployment running at roughly twice the white rate and aggravated by higher black than white hidden unemployment (Ross 1967). This has not always been the case. According to Killingsworth (1968, p. 2):

> The roughly two-to-one ratio between white and Negro unemployment rates has been widely publicized, and some otherwise well-informed persons have formed the impression that this relationship has "always" existed—at least as far back as the figures go. That is not so. The two-to-one ratio first appeared in 1954, and it has persisted through good years and bad since then. But the ratio was only about 160 in the 1947–49 period; the 1940 Census reported a ratio of 118, and the 1930 Census showed a ratio of 92.

Edna Bonacich, "Advanced Capitalism and Black/White Race Relations in the United States" from *American Sociological Review,* Vol. 41, February 1976, pp. 34–51. Copyright © 1976 by American Sociological Association. Reprinted by permission.

Unemployment statistics as currently defined were not collected prior to 1940; however, earlier censuses computed the proportion of the population which was gainfully employed. The complement of this figure gives us not only the proportion unemployed (defined as persons in the labor force who are out of work) but also those who have not entered the labor force. As a measure of unemployment, it has the advantage of not omitting hidden unemployment, and disadvantage of including those who would genuinely not be part of the labor force (such as students and the independently wealthy). Table 1 presents the census findings on black versus white proportion not gainfully employed for males ten years and older. It is evident that black rates were lower than white and that lower black "unemployment" was not a regionally restricted phenomenon. In a word, there appears to have been a reversal in the relative rate of unemployment for blacks and whites. From 1940, black unemployment exceeds white and climbs rapidly to the current two-to-one ratio. The reversal took place some time during the 1930s.

The rise in relative unemployment among blacks raises a question regarding

TABLE 1　Proportion of Males Ten Years Old or Over Not Gainfully Employed, 1910–1930, by Region

		Black	White*	Black White
1910		12.6	20.6	.61
1920		18.9	22.2	.85
1930		19.8	24.2	.82
1920	North	13.5	21.6	.62
	West	10.5	21.3	.49
	South	20.0	23.7	.84
1930	North	17.5	24.1	.73
	West	18.2	23.4	.78
	South	20.4	24.9	.82

Source: U.S. Department of Commerce, Bureau of Census. *Negroes in the United States, 1920–32.* Washington, DC: 1935, p. 28.

*White rates are based on combining native-born and foreign-born whites.

the role of race in advanced capitalism. While black slavery and share-cropping were of unambiguous benefit to the owners of land and capital, the gains from high unemployment in one segment of the population are less evident. Two approaches to this question can be distinguished in the literature. One sees a continued advantage to the employer in keeping blacks as a marginal workforce, useful for dealing with economic fluctuations and helping to divide and weaken the working class (e.g., Baron 1971, p. 34; Gordon 1972, pp. 53–81; Reich 1972; Tabb 1970, pp. 26–27). The other, exemplified by Willhelm (1971), asserts that the technology of advanced capitalism has lessened the need for unskilled labor, which was the primary role played by blacks in the past. Blacks have become useless to the economy and to the capitalist class and, combining this fact with persistent racism, may even face genocide. . . .

Each of these approaches has problems. It takes some convoluted reasoning to find the interests of the employer served by unemployment, and one could argue with equal cogency that his interests are hurt by reduction in "surplus value" to be expropriated (Harris 1972), by the decline of a market and by the creation of a dangerously dissatisfied element in the population. In addition, it is difficult to see why black unemployment would be more beneficial to the capitalist class now than it was before 1940.

Interpreting black disadvantage as a product of technological advances, rather than a planned strategy of capitalists, makes more sense on the surface; but this approach errs in the opposite direction in treating technology as an impersonal force which imposes itself on society without human choice. Technology should be seen as a resource which parties can use in a variety of ways to further their interests, or which they may choose not to use if their interests are harmed by its introduction. Thus, despite the availability of labor-saving technology, the South African economy tends to be under-mechanized in large measure because African labor is so cheap that mechanization does not pay (van den Berghe 1967, p. 185). In addition, there is no reason to assume that technological advances inevitably displace the unskilled. During the 1920s and 1930s there was considerable technological innovation in certain industries in the United States. For example, the meat-packing industry rationalized its production process through the introduction of some machinery and an assembly line (disassembly in this case). The craft of meat-cutting was divided into fairly simple activities enabling unskilled and semi-skilled labor to be used in place of skilled labor. This mechanization may be seen, in part, as an attack on craft unions and the power they wielded by controlling access to training in complex skills (Tuttle 1970a, pp. 89–90).

In order to understand the shift to high unemployment of blacks in advanced capitalism we need to look behind the process of automation in the post–World War II era.

Who would profit by automation of industries? Why did technological advances during this period hurt unskilled (and disproportionately black) labor? The answers lie in the historical evolution of class conflict in this country. The period between World War I and the New Deal was characterized by a racially split labor market, encouraging the employment of black "cheap labor" but also generating considerable conflict. New Deal labor legislation temporarily helped to resolve the conflicts but created pressure to mechanize unskilled work, as well as other forces, which threw blacks out of work. This paper attempts to trace the dominant forces at work during this evolution.

The Split Labor Market: World War I to the New Deal

A split labor market refers to a difference in the price of labor between two or more groups of workers, holding constant their efficiency and productivity (Bonacich 1972). The price differential includes not only wages but any costs incurred by the employer connected with his labor supply, such as housing, recruitment, training and discipline. A racially (black/white) split labor market began with slavery (Bonacich 1975) and persisted well into the twentieth century in industrial America. During the period under investigation the price difference showed most clearly in wage rates and degree of unionization.

Wages

Northern and southern states differ in the degree to which racial wage differentials were openly drawn but both regions show various more covert means of maintaining a difference. In the South blacks sometimes received lower wages than whites for the same work. Table 2 illustrates this difference

TABLE 2 Average Daily Pay Rate for White and Black Workers in the Building Trades in Virginia, 1927

Occupations	White Rate	Black Rate
Apprentices	$ 3.35	$3.00
Bricklayers	11.00	9.60
Carpenters	6.24	4.22
Cement Workers	6.33	4.42
Helpers	3.37	3.08
Laborers	3.25	3.06
Lathers	6.08	5.40
Painters & Decorators	4.00	5.81
Plasterers	9.26	9.12
Plumbers & Gas Fitters	4.04	4.49
Sheet Metal Workers	4.75	6.16
Miscellaneous	4.29	2.75

Source: Reid (1969, p. 17).

in the Virginia building trades using data (described as "the most complete data on variations between the wages of white and Negro workers") from the reports of the Commissioner of Labor of Virginia (Reid 1969, p. 17). Alternatively, blacks and whites had different job titles and were paid at different wage rates (Table 3), yet it is not clear that the "value" of the work in the production process was any less for black workers than for white workers.

The northern picture is more complicated. Blacks and whites doing the same work in the same plant rarely were paid different wages. But a wage differential appears in two more disguised forms. First, as in the South, one finds racial segregation by job title, with "black" jobs generally paying less. For example, a steel foundry in Chicago employing 135 people in 1927, 35 of whom were black, paid white workers an average of $37 a week and black workers an average of $29 (Spero and Harris 1966, p. 175). . . .

Such discrepancies are typical and generally accounted for by the fact that blacks were concentrated in unskilled and semi-skilled jobs; but job classifications are sometimes arbitrary and a "skill" may require

TABLE 3 Average Daily Pay Rate for White and Black Workers in the Foundry Industry, Birmingham, Alabama, 1926

White		Black	
Craft	*Rate*	*Craft*	*Rate*
Machinists	$6.16	Molder's Helpers	$3.60
Molders	6.32	Clippers	3.60
Pattern Makers	6.48	Crane Operators	5.00
Blacksmiths	6.48	Cupola Tenders	3.85
Electricians	6.32	Rammers	4.00
Carpenters	6.00	Pit Foremen	4.50
Core Makers	6.32	Core Foremen	5.00
Core Foremen	5.75		

Source: Adapted from Spero and Harris (1966, p. 170).

very little training. For example, Bailer (1943, p. 421) points out that before World War II only 10 percent of jobs in the automobile industry required more than one year of training or experience.

The second indirect form of wage differential appears in segregation by firm, i.e., black workers are employed by firms which pay a lower wage rate than firms employing white workers even though they may be engaged in the same work. According to Hill (cited in Reid 1969, p. 16), "working as the only wage earners of a business such as building tradesmen, laundresses, garment workers, the rule is to force upon [black workers] smaller compensation than white would get."

Some may argue that, despite apparent similarities in job title, black workers were less efficient to employ and that wages reflect "productivity." Black and white labor would be equal in price to the employer, the higher wages of whites being balanced by their greater efficiency. By and large the evidence goes against this supposition. For example, the Chicago Commission of Race Relations (1922, pp. 373–78) sent questionnaires to 137 firms and interviewed 93 employers concerning their experiences with black workers. Their conclusion was that

"despite occasional statements that the Negro is slow or shiftless, the volume of evidence before the Commission shows that Negroes are satisfactory employees and compare favorably with other racial groups" (Chicago Commission 1922, p. 378). It seems reasonable to conclude that the causes of the wage differential lie elsewhere.

Unions

More important than wage differences, in the period under investigation, was a difference in labor militance. White workers were more likely than blacks to form unions, to make demands for improved conditions (including wages) and to engage in costly strikes. This militance threatened to raise the price of labor substantially. If black labor was less militant, it would be cheaper to employ.

The picture of black union activity is complicated by the fact that a number of "white" unions openly excluded blacks while many others discriminated more covertly (Wesley 1927, pp. 254–81). It may be that this discrimination entirely accounts for black underrepresentation in the unions. However, each group entered the situation with a different historical experience which, I would argue, shaped their initial orientation towards unions. And as we shall see, union discrimination was partly a product as well as a cause of black anti-unionism.

Greater white worker recognition of class conflict with the capitalist class was partly a product of longer experience in the industrial labor market. When they were raw immigrants, Europeans had also played a "cheap labor" role. But the wartime decline in immigration, coupled with the Immigration Act of 1924, meant that the white work force was becoming increasingly seasoned. Not-so-new immigrants began to join or form labor organizations and make demands for higher wages and improved work conditions. For example, in the organizing campaign of 1918 in the steel industry, white immigrants were the first to respond (Brody 1960, pp. 223–24). In addition, unlike the blacks, some white immigrants came from countries where the concept of a politically active working class was well developed. These elements were feared by capital and denounced as un-American and communist. The exclusion of European immigrants in 1924 was, perhaps, not only a reaction by "native" labor to the threat of undercutting, but also a response by capital to the dangers of a "corrupting" element in the work force.

Some blacks had been members of the industrial proletariat for years and were at least as class conscious as white workers. But with the coming of World War I a large, impoverished peasantry entered both northern and southern industrial labor markets for the first time. This class was vulnerable to exploitation as cheap labor.

At least three factors were at work making blacks more "exploitable." First, they tended to be desperately poor; jobs and wage levels which were distasteful to some seemed attractive to them. . . . Wages for farm labor in the South were around 75 cents a day compared to 40 cents to $1.00 an hour for unskilled labor in Chicago (Spear 1967,

p. 156). What looked undesirable to many white workers looked like a "golden opportunity" to black migrants from the South (Spero and Harris 1966, p. 114). At least at the outset, their discontent would be lower.

A second factor was a tradition of paternalism in the South, begun under slavery but extending well beyond it. Mixed with a hearty dose of intimidation by southern landowners there was, nonetheless, a personal relationship between employer and employee which sometimes bound the worker to his employer. Black workers were not accustomed to intervening organizations, like unions, which expressed an explicitly antagonistic relationship to the employer. They had not had much exposure to the ideals and goals of organized labor. "The attachment which the Negro had been taught to feel for his employer in the South was quickly sensed and exploited by northern industrialists" (Cayton and Mitchell 1970, p. 61).

Third, a long history of discrimination and hostility by white labor led black workers to be chary of joining their organizations. It was in part the product of a split labor market begun under slavery (Bonacich 1975) which led white workers to erect defensive barriers against the threat of being undermined, and this history created considerable black suspicion against the unions.

Precise figures on union membership are difficult to obtain, but scraps of information have come down to us from past studies. . . . In 1930, according to Wolters (1970a, pp. 138–39), the NAACP calculated that a maximum of three percent of the 1,500,000 nonagricultural black workers were in unions and almost half of these were in the Brotherhood of Sleeping Car Porters. The country-wide rate of union membership in non-agricultural work in 1930 was around ten percent.

In New York, a 1919 survey found that less than .003 percent of black women working in 217 industrial establishments were union members. "Even in the shops where the white women were well organized, Negro women working there seldom held union membership" (Franklin 1936, p. 96). A 1928 survey, also conducted in New York and this time not restricted to women, found that 3.8 percent of union members were black while the 1930 census revealed the black proportion of gainful workers in the city was 14.1 percent. "This leaves no doubt that on the whole Negro workers were far less organized than others" (Franklin 1936, p. 114).

There are important exceptions to this picture. Some black workers were active union members and even leaders in the "white" labor movement. Black workers sometimes organized their own unions either under the umbrella of the American Federation of Labor or independently. The former arrangement was not very satisfactory (Spero and Harris 1966, pp. 95–101). Black locals were chartered directly by the AFL, an organization which could not negotiate wage rates itself. They were dependent on agreements arrived at by the white unions and did little to improve black bargaining power. Independent black unionism was not much more successful (Spero and Harris 1966, pp. 116–27). Many of these unions failed after brief histories. The most successful, the Brotherhood of Sleeping Car Porters, was unable to bring off a threatened strike and eventually requested affiliation with the AFL (Marshall 1965, p. 26).

Lack of unionization among blacks affected their bargaining position which in turn affected wage levels. . . . The Shipbuilding Labor Adjustment Board, created during World War I, accepted the southern system of dividing work into black and white, unequally paid, occupations. "Since most Negroes in the industry were unorganized, they had no representation on the Board, and hence no opposition to such plans was voiced" (Rubin 1970, p. 38).

In sum, a lesser degree of involvement in labor unions meant that black workers could be used by employers to cut costs. This was achieved both by avoiding demands for improved wages and work conditions, and by avoiding the costs of labor conflict itself.

Dynamics

Split labor markets develop dynamics which can perpetuate or increase the original price differential. The chief parties to the interaction are capital, higher priced labor and cheap labor. A schematic representation of the interactions for the post–World War I period is presented in Figure 1.

Figure 1 begins with the class conflict between capital and white labor (1). Efforts by white workers to improve their position, especially through militant trade unionism, threatened to drive up the price of labor. Capital, in an effort to keep costs down, sought an alternative labor supply which would be cheaper (2). Blacks were facing economic displacement in the South while European sources were drying up. Besides, for reasons suggested above, blacks seemed an ideal group with whom to fight the aspirations of white labor (3). That they were so used is demonstrated by three types of evidence: the use of black strike-breakers, the displacement of white workers with black and efforts to gain the loyalty of the black community.

Strike-Breaking

The use of blacks as strike-breakers was not uncommon during this period. According to Jacobson (1968, p. 5), "In strikebound plants employers found it easier to recruit strike-breakers among Negroes who never developed a trade union consciousness and could see no reason why they should forsake a

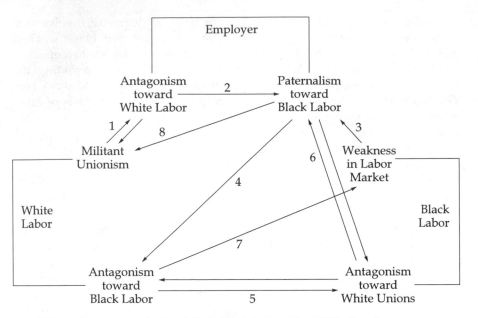

FIGURE 1 Interactions in the Split Labor Market, World War I to the New Deal.

much needed day's pay for a white man's union." . . .

Perhaps the most important use of black strike-breaking occurred in the great steel strike of 1919. Foster (1920, p. 206) reports that blacks already working in the steel mills were less likely to participate in the strike (e.g., in the Homestead Steel Works 1,737 of the 14,687 employees were black but only eight joined the unions and one struck; among white unskilled workers in the same plant at least 75 percent joined the unions and 90 percent struck). In addition, 30,000 to 40,000 blacks were brought into the mills from outside as strike-breakers, some from northern cities, and most from the South. Black strike-breakers "were used in all the large districts and were a big factor in breaking the strike" (Foster 1920, p. 207).

Displacement

Strike-breaking sometimes proves to be a short-term relationship in that strikers may return to their position once the conflict is resolved. A more stable relationship with black labor also emerged in the form of substituting black for white in non-strike situations. . . .

[E]xamples are found in a variety of industries. For instance, in the metal industry during the fall of 1916 the Aluminum Ore Company of East St. Louis "embarked upon a policy of increasing the Negro labor force in order to limit the future demands of white workers" (Rudwick 1964, pp. 16–17). In November 1916 they increased the number of black employees from 10–12 to 280; in December, to 410; in February 1917 to 470. In the bituminous coal industry, there was an increase in the use of black labor, in part because of "the ease with which Negro labor, because of limited industrial opportunity and low economic standards, can be used in labor difficulties" (Spero and Harris 1966, p. 208). . . . In general, "employers came to refer to their Negro help as 'strike insurance'" (Cayton and Mitchell 1970, p. x).

The great migration of blacks northwards during and after World War I must be understood in this context. Not only were economic conditions bad in the rural South, but positive inducements were being offered by industrial employers. Labor recruiters were sent South to encourage migration (Brody 1960, pp. 184–85; Spear 1967, p. 133). While recruitment was partly a product of labor shortage caused by the war and the decline in European immigration, it is also evident that employers saw in this black "industrial reserve" a population which could be used to keep out unions and displace troublesome and increasingly expensive white labor.

Loyalty

Displacement was sometimes accompanied by efforts to gain the loyalty of the black work force, thereby forestalling the development of unions among them and maintaining the "cheap labor" status. . . . On a larger scale, employers would make overtures to black workers and community leaders, giving money and urging workers to come to the employer for aid. Leaders in the black community would, in turn, urge black workers to be a docile and loyal work-force, keeping faith with the employer.

In the Chicago meat-packing industry, for example, packers "made financial efforts to obtain good relationships with institutions in the black community such as the YMCA and the churches" (Fogel 1970, p. 32). Their efforts bore fruit. When faced with a strike in 1921, the packers had black ministers read messages to their congregants urging them not to join the strike. The Urban League supplied the packers with 450 strike-breakers. "The dependence of the League upon wealthy whites for financial support . . . may have influenced its actions" (Fogel 1970, p. 35).

One of the most outstanding cases of paternalism occurred in the automobile industry. The Ford Company, especially at its Rouge plant, "followed a definite policy of employing Negroes in all capacities" (Bailer 1943, p. 422). As a result, "Negroes have traditionally shown greater loyalty to Ford than to any other automobile manufacturer" (Bailer 1944, p. 554), and this loyalty enabled Ford to resist unionization of his plants. . . .

Another facet of paternalism was the development of "industrial representation plans" or company unions. "Migrant Negroes from the South proved peculiarly susceptible to this form of organization" (Cayton and Mitchell 1970, p. 61), and they received support from some black community leadership. . . .

Needless to say, not all black leadership responded to paternalistic overtures by capital, but a significant element did. According to Foster (1920, p. 210), "It is a lamentable fact, well known to all organizers who have worked in industries employing considerable numbers of negroes, that there is a large and influential black leadership, including ministers, politicians, editors, doctors, lawyers, social workers, etc., who as a matter of race tactics are violently opposed to their people going into the trade unions." Even black nationalist Marcus Garvey took an anti-union, pro-employer, stance. He saw the white capitalist as a friend of black workers because of the latter's relative cheapness and advocated a strategy of continued undercutting. "If the Negro takes my advice he will organize by himself and keep his scale of wage a little lower than the whites . . . By doing so he will keep the good will of the white employer" (Spero and Harris 1966, p. 136).

The substitution of black labor for white was, in part, accompanied by the process, described earlier, of division of skills into simpler, assembly line tasks. Black migrants were largely unskilled while the union movement's strength lay in controlling access to training in complex skills. A way of cracking the unions' power was to break down the skills and substitute unskilled labor. Black labor was not the only source of substitution, but it was an important and growing element.

Returning to Figure 1, the efforts to develop the black labor force aroused the ire of white labor (4) which felt a threat to their efforts to improve their lot. The antagonism towards black workers was not simply race prejudice but a fear that blacks, because of their weakness in the labor market, could be used by capital as a tool to weaken or destroy their organizations or take away their jobs. As Spero and Harris (1966, p. 128) state: "The use of Negroes for strike breaking has . . . led the white trade unionist to regard the black workers as an enemy of the labor movement." White workers reacted by trying to exclude black workers or to keep them restricted to certain jobs. (See Bonacich 1972 for a more thorough discussion of the reasoning behind these reactions.)

Black workers came on the industrial scene unfamiliar, for the most part, with the aspirations of organized labor. They were not an easy element to organize to start out with, but whatever potential for organization was present was discouraged by white union antipathy and exclusion (5). Union policies frequently meant that black workers had no alternative but to turn to strikebreaking as the only means of entering white-dominated lines of work. Sometimes even strike-breaking did not secure long-term employment as white workers roared back, anxious to see them dismissed.

Interaction 5 was mutually reinforcing. Blacks distrusted the unions because they discriminated, and the unions discriminated because blacks didn't support them. The circle of antagonism was difficult to break out of. Even if the unions opened their doors, as was not uncommon, black workers were apt to view the action as self-serving, to protect the unions from scabbing by blacks. It would take more than non-discrimination to end the distrust, and many white unionists were not willing even to take the first step of lowering the barriers to membership.

The policies of the employer fed the division between black and white workers (6). Employer paternalism led black workers to feel they had more to gain by allying with capital than with white labor. Besides, behind it lay a veiled threat: blacks would be hired and given preference over white workers so long as they remained out of the unions. . . .

The antagonism of the labor movement to black workers weakened still further the latter's position in the labor market (7). White labor severely restricted the alternatives of black labor by maintaining control over important lines of work. The perpetuation of the black labor force in a weak position kept them as a target group for capital's efforts to undermine the union movement. Finally, to close the "system," the efforts by capital to utilize black labor to their detriment added to the militance of white workers (8). Strikes were sometimes called over this very issue, which could unite white workers in a common grievance (Tuttle 1970a, pp. 107–108).

This interpretation of the division between black and white workers differs from one which sees it as created by the capitalist class to "divide and rule." If employers create a price differential, they must be paying one group of workers more than they have to, which would only be rational if paying more to one group enabled them to pay another substantially less. Capital would have to be "bribing" white labor to help keep black labor cheap. Such a convoluted strategy may indeed be in operation, but a number of facts argue against it. First, as we have seen, workers do not enter the labor market with a clean slate upon which the employer arbitrarily marks his price; there are forces which differentiate the labor force before he touches it. Second, a strategy of bribery is hard to combine with the facts of displacement and strike-breaking. If capital wanted to keep white labor loyal why undermine them? Third, the evidence suggests that bribery and the exacting of loyalty were strategies directed more toward cheap labor than higher priced labor. As a means of maintaining labor costs as low as possible, this makes more sense.

What fits the evidence better is a picture of a capitalist class faced with (rather than creating) a labor market differentiated in terms of bargaining power (or price). Capital turns toward the cheaper labor pool as a more desirable work force, a choice consistent with the simple pursuit of higher profits. Higher priced labor resists being displaced, and the racist structures they erect to protect themselves are antagonistic to the interests of capital.

Effects of the Split Labor Market

The "system" described above had implications for black labor force participation. Blacks were more desirable employees than whites which helps to explain their higher employment rates in 1920 and 1930. However, considerable conflict was generated in the process and some of the nation's worst race riots occurred during this period. East St. Louis erupted in 1917 (Rudwick 1964). Twenty-six riots broke out in 1919 (Lee and Humphrey 1968, p. ix), the most destructive in Chicago (Chicago Commission 1922; Tuttle 1970b). Detroit and Harlem blew up in 1925 and 1935, respectively. The importance of labor conflict in these riots is subject to some dispute. Undoubtedly, they were complex affairs with more than a single cause. However, the East St. Louis riot was directly precipitated by the introduction of blacks to break a strike at the Aluminum Ore Company (Marshall 1965, p. 22), and Tuttle

(1970a; 1970b, pp. 108–56) argues convincingly that the Chicago riot of 1919 was intimately tied to labor conflict, especially in the stockyards.

Another negative effect was the precipitous decline of the trade union movement. Union membership reached a peak of 5,047,800 in 1920. It dropped sharply to 3,622,000 by 1923 and continued falling to 3,442,600 in 1929 and 2,973,000 in 1933 (Bernstein 1950, p. 2; 1960, p. 84). "By 1930 union membership constituted a bare 10.2 percent of the more than 30 million nonagricultural employees counted in the census, a marked drop from 19.4 percent in 1920" (Bernstein 1960, p. 84).

I am not suggesting that the decline was entirely a product of the black/white split labor market. This was an era of virtually unrestrained union-busting and the use by employers of every device imaginable to keep independent labor organizations out of their plants (Bernstein 1950, pp. 7–14). However, the split labor market played a part in the decline.

Industrial unions suffered most. Craft unions which were able to maintain control over access to training, in the building trades, printing trades and railways, held their membership or increased it (Bernstein 1960, p. 86). The unions which survived the open-shop drives of the corporations were those which discriminated most severely against blacks (Jacobson 1968, p. 4; Marshall 1965, pp. 22–23), suggesting that discrimination by the unions was not a totally irrational short-term reaction.

Protection as a Resolution

White labor had dealt with this problem in a variety of ways in the past. Two prominent strategies were exclusion (keeping blacks out of the territory) and caste (dividing "white work" from "black work," so that cheaper blacks were not substitutable). By

the 1930s, the former strategy had failed totally, and a caste arrangement was holding
only in its strongest bastions. These resolutions could too easily be attacked by capital.
A new solution was called for.

The New Deal provided such a solution
in the form of protection by the Federal Government. Section 7a of the National Industrial Recovery Act (1933) reads as follows:

> (1) That employees shall have the right
> to organize and bargain collectively
> through representatives of their own
> choosing, and shall be free from the
> interference, restraint, or coercion of
> employers of labor, or their agents, in
> the designation of such representatives
> or in self-organization or in other con-
> certed activities for the purpose of col-
> lective bargaining or mutual aid or
> protection; (2) that no employee and no
> one seeking employment shall be re-
> quired as a condition of employment to
> join any company union or to refrain
> from joining, organizing, or assisting a
> labor organization of his choosing; and
> (3) that employers shall comply with
> the maximum hours of labor, minimum
> rates of pay, and other conditions of
> employment approved or prescribed
> by the President.

Thus, it protected unions from employer efforts to undermine them, ensured the right
of independent unions to organize and bargain collectively and outlawed sweatshops
and cheap labor. Although the NIRA was
shot down by the Supreme Court in 1935,
these principles were kept alive in other legislation such as the National Labor Relations
(Wagner) Act of 1935 and the Fair Labor
Standards Act of 1938.

The racially split labor market was not
the only precipitant of these laws, but it was
one of their major beneficiaries. In effect,
they legislated it out of existence, making it
illegal for employers to use blacks as strike-

breakers or "strike insurance," denying the
legitimacy of the company union and taking
away the advantage to be had in paying
blacks lower wages for longer hours. Protective legislation ideally made the price of labor equal regardless of race.

This ideal was not totally realized in
practice. The process of establishing protective barriers took time and was never complete. Powerful capitalists were often able to
by-pass the laws or find loopholes in them.
One important standout was Henry Ford,
and a split labor market pattern continued
into the early 1940s in the automobile industry (Bailer 1944). . . . Despite loopholes
and evasions, protection for the unions
gradually came to be enforced in most of the
major industries in the nation.

Short-Term Effects (1935–1945)

In the short run, protective legislation dramatically altered the split labor market.
The New Deal brought black and white labor closer together than ever before, enabling them to form a "radical coalition"
(Bonacich 1975).

The labor movement received a tremendous spurt from protective legislation. The
American Federation of Labor took advantage of the new laws and began organizing
campaigns. During two months in 1933, for
example, they moved from a membership of
2,126,798 to 3,926,796 (Cayton and Mitchell
1970, p. 123), but most of the new vigor was
associated with the emergence of a new organization, the Congress of Industrial Organizations. Denouncing craft unionism and
advocating broad-based industrial unions,
the CIO successfully penetrated the automobile, steel, rubber, electrical goods and meat-
packing industries by 1940. The AFL
responded by moving more toward industrial unionism. Between them total union
membership rose from 2,805,000 in 1933 to

8,410,000 in 1941. The latter figure represents 23 percent of non-agricultural workers (Dubofsky 1970, pp. 12–14).

Black workers were not excluded from this new development. A shift in orientation was evident in both camps. White labor became more active in recruiting black support, and the black community became more supportive of organized labor.

The shift in white labor was especially noticeable in the CIO. This organization adopted many programs to attract blacks including "financial contributions to organizations like the NAACP and Negro churches and newspapers, the adoption of equalitarian racial resolutions, the use of Negroes to organize in Negro communities, the creation of the Committee to Abolish Racial Discrimination, and interlocking officials between unions and such organizations as the NAACP and the National Urban League" (Marshall 1965, pp. 38–39). . . .

At first the black community feared protective legislation, believing it would strengthen the AFL without stopping it from discriminating against blacks. Efforts were made to introduce an amendment to the Wagner Act outlawing racial discrimination, but to no avail (Wolters 1970a). These early suspicions gradually disappeared especially with the emergence of the CIO. . . . While exact figures are not available, one estimate gives black union membership in 1930 as around 56,000. By 1940, it had risen to 600,000 and during World War II reached 1,250,000 (Marshall 1965, p. 49).

The short-term emergence of a radical coalition provides support for our previous analysis. The fact that blacks could be used as cheap labor contributed to white union antagonism towards them. When the cheap labor status was made illegal and "management . . . ended its conspicuous relations with the black community and no longer demanded or commanded loyalty" (Olson 1970, p. 163), unions could accept black workers much more warmly, with ramifications for how black workers responded. In addition, when the option of siding with the employer was removed, black workers had every reason to join forces enthusiastically with organized labor. Franklin's description (1936, p. 266) of the effect of the New Deal and its immediate aftermath in New York applies to the nation as a whole: "The role of the Negro worker as a strike-breaker has about come to an end." In terms of Figure 1, the split labor market interactions had been short-circuited at arrow 2.

Long-Term Effects: Fighting the High Cost of Labor

Protective legislation swung the balance of power in the class struggle between capital and labor towards the labor side, but it could not be expected that the capitalist class would accept such a state of affairs lying down. Protective legislation drove up the price of labor, threatening the very existence of firms throughout the economic spectrum.

Wolters (1970b, p. 119) describes the impact of the New Deal on a small cotton textile mill in Greensboro, Georgia:

> Before the NRA, the daily wage of workers in this mill was about seventy-five cents for a ten-hour day; afterward, wages ranged from $2 to $2.40 for an eight-hour day. The machinery in this mill was obsolete, and the firm had been able to compete with more modernized mills only because labor costs were so low. With the coming of the NRA the mill at Greensboro had three choices: to maintain employment, pay code wages, and operate at a loss; to ignore the NRA stipulation; or to install more productive machinery and pay code wages to fewer workers.

Oppenheimer (1974, p. 11) makes a similar point for the garment industry. Sweatshops in the Northeast, which became organized and had safety features introduced, then faced competition from sweatshops in the Far East. . . .

At least three options were open to the capitalist class. (Of course, not every capitalist had all three alternatives available.) First, they could relocate part of the industrial process overseas to make use of cheaper foreign labor. Second, they could relocate internally to those sectors of the economy where organized labor and/or protection had not yet penetrated. And third, they could mechanize, displacing jobs which had previously been performed by "cheap labor." These processes all had a negative impact on black employment.

Relocation Overseas

Treating the late 1960s, Jaleé (1973, p. 80) points out that roughly 20 percent of American investment in manufacturing industry went abroad. At that time a high proportion went to Europe which "has the use of cheaper labor than in the United States" (Jaleé 1973, p. 82). Today the "runaway shop" is found wherever cheap labor is available. "Smith-Corona makes typewriters in Italy. U.S. Plywood makes veneers in Peru, South Korea, and Nigeria. National Cash Register has plants in Taiwan and Japan. Sears Roebuck manufactures shoes in Spain . . . Heinz makes tomato paste in Portugal and cans pineapple in Mexico" (Zimmerman et al. 1973, p. 6), and so forth.

The runaway shop has hurt black unskilled and semi-skilled labor disproportionately, partly because white labor is more concentrated in the production of goods with high technological content, which are more likely to be produced here. For example, in moving a radio plant to Taiwan at the cost of 7,000 American jobs, Zenith reported that 38 percent of those laid off would be

blacks (Zimmerman et al. 1973, p. 8). Black workers in the United States are in competition with overseas labor at the same level of skill but overseas labor is considerably cheaper to employ.

Internal Relocation

There remains gaps and loopholes in the present protective structure, and capital has moved internally to avail itself of these. An illustration is provided by the meat-packing industry, the major industrial employer of blacks before the New Deal. Since the late 1940s and early 1950s, the big meat-packing cities of Chicago, Kansas City, East St. Louis and Omaha, have lost meat-packing plants—particularly to the South where hourly wages are $1.86 compared to $3.08 in the Midwest. By 1947 the large midwestern packers were all unionized and could not themselves take advantage of cheaper labor elsewhere. But small, low-cost operators could open without unions to serve local and regional markets. Between 1946 and 1965, the four largest packers were forced to close a net 250 plants, and the industry became decentralized. Black workers were adversely affected by this shift. In 1950 the big midwestern cities employed 16,960 blacks in meat-packing. By 1960 the number had declined to 10,350. While black workers did not lose a disproportionate number of jobs, their overrepresentation in the industry meant a greater impact on group unemployment (Fogel 1970, pp. 58–65). In this particular case internal relocation took advantage of another segment of black workers: non-union, southern women (Fogel 1970, pp. 65–66). Other minorities, such as Mexican illegal aliens and poor immigrants from other countries, have played a part in this type of displacement (e.g., Lan 1971 on the use of Chinese "sweatshop" labor in the San Francisco garment industry). Regardless of where new sources of cheap labor came from, the losers have been black industrial workers who had made important gains under the New Deal.

Given that cheap labor jobs are still scattered through the economy, why do the black urban unemployed not flock to them? The answer, I believe, lies in two inter-related factors. First, black industrial workers, unlike new immigrants, had come, during the late 1930s and early 1940s, to develop a working class consciousness. They rejected the sweatshop as had white workers before them. Employers have long justified the use of cheap minority labor on the grounds that "whites will not do the work." The same can be said of blacks today. Both groups are unwilling to work under rough conditions for low wages. If the job were "decent," they would willingly do it. The availability of a "cheap labor" alternative enables the employer to avoid improving the job and raising wages (Abrams and Abrams 1975, pp. 24–26).

The second factor is "welfare." This institution may, in part, be seen as a mechanism which keeps people from having no alternative but the sweatshop. It is part of the apparatus which protects organized labor from being undercut. Protective legislation would be totally ineffective if large segments of the population were close to starvation. Employers would by-pass the laws and the starving people would gladly avail themselves of the jobs, however dreadful and low-paying. Of course, this phenomenon does occur in the United States, e.g., among many Mexican illegal immigrants (Samora 1971). But a significant difference between black and immigrant poor lies in legal status. Blacks are unambiguously eligible for various forms of welfare and unemployment compensation which many new immigrants, particularly illegals, are not. Blacks have an "alternative" to the sweatshop.

Internal relocation helps to perpetuate a "dual labor market," i.e., a division of the economy into central and peripheral industries, the former offering higher wage, union jobs, and the latter relying on cheap,

nonunion labor. If they try to escape the welfare trap, black workers tend to get locked into the peripheral economy with a ceiling on opportunities for advancement. (There is an extensive and growing literature on this topic partially reviewed by Gordon 1972, pp. 43–52).

The persistence of peripheral or marginal firms operating on cheap labor means that a split labor market is not dead in this country. Protective legislation has changed its shape somewhat, increasing the segregation, by industry and plant, of higher priced from cheap labor. And the ethnic composition of cheap labor has shifted away from blacks to some extent (Oppenheimer 1974, p. 16) to other nonwhite immigrants. But the New Deal did not, in the long run, successfully eradicate the problem.

Automation

The move to automate does not arise simply as a response to technological innovation. Rather it is, at least in part, a response to rising labor costs. In the steel industry for instance, rising wages have led to an increase in capital relative to labor. "The United Steelworkers are resigned to continued long-term shrinkage of its core membership in basic steel" (Averitt 1968, p. 147). . . .

A number of authors trace a link between automation and black unemployment (e.g., Ferman et al. 1968, pp. 276–77; Willhelm 1971, pp. 188–224). Northrup (1965, p. 87) sums up the situation well:

> An important factor in the Negro unemployment problem was industry's substitution of machinery for unskilled labor. Ever higher minimum wages, the rapid rise under union pressure of unskilled labor rates, and the competition from West European and Japanese industry (with the much lower labor rates paid in these countries) all spurred this labor-replacement program.

Negroes laid off as a result of these developments and young Negroes who found that industry was no longer hiring the unskilled became significant proportions of the hardcore, long-term unemployed.

To the three processes must be added certain "rigidities" in the system which make blacks suffer disproportionately from displacement. For example, poor ghetto schools make it more difficult for blacks to move out of the unskilled ranks. Union seniority rules, which may be "universalistic" and protect against the employer's natural desire to lay off his oldest, most expensive workers, may in practice have racist consequences because of the trend towards later entrance to industrial work among blacks. Similarly, discrimination in apprenticeship programs hurts black acquisition of skills while unions perceive efforts to change their rules as "union busting" (Strauss and Ingerman 1968). And residential restrictions make it difficult for black workers to follow decentralizing industries as they flee highly taxed central cities.

Conclusion

Let us return to the two approaches to the question of high black unemployment in advanced capitalism presented at the beginning of the paper. The first suggested that significant elements in the white community, especially the corporate capitalist class, benefited from black unemployment. While there may be indirect sources of gain, the conclusion to be drawn from this paper would be that large capitalists are unable to take advantage of ghetto labor and abandon it to marginal enterprises. The second argument, that technological advance has left blacks useless to the economy, gained some support, but I hope to have shown that it was not the product of impersonal economic forces. Rather, it was one effect of a complex history of class struggle.

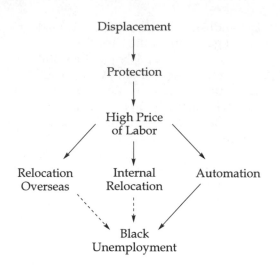

FIGURE 2   The Historical Development of Black Unemployment.

This history is summarized in Figure 2. The "displacement" phase was one in which blacks were desirable employees relative to whites but threatened the gains of the latter. Protective legislation equalized the two groups in terms of labor price but also drove up the price of labor, leading capital to seek cheaper alternatives. As a result, black labor has been by-passed for machines and other cheap labor groups, here and abroad, creating a class of hard-core unemployed in the ghettos. This reality took a while to emerge after the New Deal and only became full-blown in the mid-1950s when black unemployment reached its current two-to-one ratio. The timing helps to explain the rising despair of the 1960s.

Our conclusion is not cause for optimism over solving the problems of split labor markets. Immediately after the New Deal, it appeared they could be eradicated by government intervention, but the passing years have shown this to be a false hope. As long as there is "cheap labor" anywhere in the world, there may not be a solution within capitalism.

REFERENCES

ABRAMS, ELLIOTT, and FRANKLIN S. ABRAMS. 1975. "Immigration Policy—Who Gets In." *Public Interest* 38:3–29.

AVERITT, ROBERT T. 1968. *The Dual Economy: The Dynamics of American Industry Structure*. New York: Norton.

BAILER, LLOYD H. 1943. "The Negro Automobile Worker." *Journal of Political Economy* 51:415–28.

———. 1944. "The Automobile Unions and Negro Labor." *Political Science Quarterly* 59:548–77.

BARON, HAROLD M. 1972. "The Demand for Black Labor: Historical Notes on the Political Economy of Racism." *Radical America* 5:1–46.

BERNSTEIN, IRVING. 1950. *The New Deal Collective Bargaining Policy*. Berkeley: University of California Press.

———. 1960. *The Lean Years: A History of the American Worker 1920–1933*. Cambridge, MA: Riverside Press.

BONACICH, EDNA. 1972. "A Theory of Ethnic Antagonism: The Split Labor Market." *American Sociological Review* 37:547–59.

———. 1976. "Abolition, the Extension of Slavery, and the Position of Free Blacks: A Study of Split Labor Markets in the United States, 1830–1863." *American Journal of Sociology* 81:601–628.

BRODY, DAVID. 1960. *Steelworkers in America: The Nonunion Era*. Cambridge, MA: Harvard University Press.

CAYTON, HORACE R., and GEORGE S. MITCHELL. 1970 [1939]. *Black Workers and the New Unions*. Westport, CT: Negro Universities Press.

CHICAGO COMMISSION OF RACE RELATIONS. 1922. *The Negro in Chicago: A Study of Race Relations and a Race Riot*. Chicago: University of Chicago Press.

DUBOFSKY, MELVYN. 1970. *American Labor Since the New Deal*. Chicago: Quadrangle.

FERMAN, LOUIS A., JOYCE L. KORNBLUH, and J. A. MILLER, eds. 1968. *Negroes and Jobs*. Ann Arbor: University of Michigan Press.

FOGEL, WALTER A. 1970. *The Negro in the Meat Industry*. Philadelphia: University of Pennsylvania Press.

FOSTER, WILLIAM Z. 1920. *The Great Steel Strike and Its Lessons*. New York: Huebsch.

FRANKLIN, CHARLES L. 1936. *The Negro Labor Unionist of New York: Problems and Conditions Among Negroes in the Labor Unions in Manhattan with Special Reference to the N.R.A. and Post-N.R.A. Situations*. New York: Columbia University Press.

GORDON, DAVID M. 1972. *Theories of Poverty and Underemployment*. Lexington, MA: Heath.

HARRIS, DONALD J. 1972. "The Black Ghetto as Colony: A Theoretical Critique and Alternative Formulation." *Review of Black Political Economy* 2:3–33.

JACOBSON, JULIUS, ed. 1968. *The Negro and the American Labor Movement*. Garden City, NY: Doubleday Anchor.

JALEÉ, PIERRE. 1973. *Imperialism in the Seventies*. New York: Third Press.

KILLINGSWORTH, CHARLES C. 1968. *Jobs and Income for Negroes*. Ann Arbor: University of Michigan Press.

LAN, DEAN, 1971. "The Chinatown Sweatshops." *Amerasia Journal* 1:40–57.

LEE, ALFRED McCLUNG, and NORMAN D. HUMPHREY. 1968. *Race Riot (Detroit, 1943)*. New York: Octagon.

MARSHALL, RAY. 1965. *The Negro and Organized Labor*. New York: Wiley.

NORTHRUP, HERBERT R. 1965. "Equal Opportunity and Equal Pay." Pp. 85–107 in *The Negro and Equal Opportunity*, edited by H. R. Northrup and Richard L. Rowan. Ann Arbor, MI: Bureau of Industrial Relations.

OLSON, JAMES S. 1970. "Race, Class, and Progress: Black Leadership and Industrial Unionism, 1936–1945." Pp. 153–64 in *Black Labor in America*, edited by Milton Cantor. Westport, CT: Negro Universities Press.

OPPENHEIMER, MARTIN. 1974. "The Sub-Proletariat: Dark Skins and Dirty Work." *Insurgent Sociologist* 4:7–20.

REICH, MICHAEL. 1972. "Economic Theories of Racism." Pp. 67–79 in *Schooling in a Corporate Society*, edited by Martin Carnoy. New York: McKay.

REID, IRA DE A. 1969 [1930]. *Negro Membership in American Labor Unions*. New York: Negro Universities Press.

ROSS, ARTHUR M. 1967. "The Negro in the American Economy." Pp. 3–48 in *Employment, Race, and Poverty*, edited by Arthur M. Ross and Herbert Hill. New York: Harcourt, Brace & World.

ROWAN, RICHARD L. 1968. *The Negro in the Steel Industry*. Philadelphia: University of Pennsylvania Press.

RUBIN, LESTER. 1970. *The Negro in the Shipbuilding Industry*. Philadelphia: University of Pennsylvania Press.

RUDWICK, ELLIOTT M. 1964. *Race Riot at East St. Louis, July 2, 1917*. Carbondale: Southern Illinois University Press.

SAMORA, JULIAN. 1971. *Los Mojados: The Wetback Story*. Notre Dame, IN: University of Notre Dame Press.

SAXTON, ALEXANDER. 1971. *The Indispensible Enemy: Labor and the Anti-Chinese Movement in California*. Berkeley: University of California Press.

SPEAR, ALLAN H. 1967. *Black Chicago: The Making of a Negro Ghetto, 1890–1920*. Chicago: University of Chicago Press.

SPERO, STERLING D., and ABRAM L. HARRIS. 1966 [1931]. *The Black Worker: The Negro and the Labor Movement*. Port Washington, NY: Kennikat.

STRAUSS, GEORGE, and SIDNEY INGERMAN. 1968. "Public Policy and Discrimination in Apprenticeship." Pp. 198–322 in *Negroes and Jobs*, edited by Louis Ferman, Joyce Kornbluh, and J. A. Miller. Ann Arbor: University of Michigan Press.

TABB, WILLIAM K. 1970. *The Political Economy of the Black Ghetto*. New York: Norton.

TUTTLE, WILLIAM M., JR. 1970a. "Labor Conflict and Racial Violence: The Black Worker in Chicago, 1897–1904." Pp. 53–85 in *Black Labor in America*, edited by Milton Cantor. Westport, CT: Negro Universities Press.

———. 1970b. *Race Riot: Chicago in the Red Summer of 1919*. New York: Atheneum.

U.S. DEPARTMENT OF LABOR. 1974. *Manpower Report of the President*. Washington, DC: U.S. Government Printing Office.

VAN DEN BERGHE, PIERRE L. 1967. *South Africa: A Study in Conflict*. Berkeley: University of California Press.

WESLEY, CHARLES H. 1927. *Negro Labor in the United States, 1850–1925*. New York: Vanguard.

WILLHELM, SIDNEY M. 1971. *Who Needs the Negro?* Garden City, NY: Doubleday Anchor.

WOLTERS, RAYMOND. 1970a. "Closed Shop and White Shop: The Negro Response to Collective Bargaining, 1933–1935." Pp. 137–52 in *Black Labor in America*, edited by Milton Cantor. Westport, CT: Negro Universities Press.

———. 1970b. *Negroes and the Great Depression: The Problem of Economic Recovery*. Westport, CT: Greenwood.

WORTHMAN, PAUL. 1970. "Black Workers and Labor Unions in Birmingham, Alabama, 1897–1904." Pp. 53–85 in *Black Labor in America*, edited by Milton Cantor. Westport, CT: Negro Universities Press.

ZIMMERMAN, MITCH, and the UNITED FRONT PRESS STAFF. 1973. *International Runaway Shop*. San Francisco: United Front Press.

20

RACE, GENDER, WORK
The History of Asian and Asian-American Women

Julie Matthaei • Teresa Amott

From 1840 until the Second World War, Asian immigrants—first Chinese, then Japanese, and finally Filipinos—were recruited into the western United States (US)

Julie Matthaei and Teresa Amott, *Race, Gender, Work*, pp. 61–80. Copyright © 1990 by South End Press. Reprinted by permission from the publisher, South End Press, 116 Saint Botolph Street, Boston, MA 02115.

and Hawaii as a low-wage, second-class labour force. Unlike white immigrants, they were not seen as permanent settlers and laws specially restricted their rights. Only Asian Americans born in the US were accepted as citizens; the immigrants were permanent "aliens," and whites were able to pass numerous laws to discriminate against them (for example, preventing them from purchasing lands) simply by referring to their alien status. They faced vicious discrimination from white workers (who resented their low-wage competition and their use as strike-breakers), from white employers (who found them less attractive as they began to form effective labour organisations) and from self-employed whites (who resented Asian successes in small businesses). From the late nineteenth century until the Depression, there were broad-based white movements to try and restrict Asian immigration and even to send migrants back to Asia. In response to these pressures, between 1850 and 1950, federal and state governments passed about fifty laws aimed at restricting and subordinating Asian immigrants. Anti-Asian sentiment culminated in laws excluding further immigration: Chinese immigration was cut off in 1882 and 1892; Japanese in 1907, 1908 and 1924; Indian in 1917, and Filipino in 1934.

Initially, the numbers of women relative to men were low—one to nineteen among the Chinese in 1860, for example. Employers sought out single male workers, most of whom came as "sojourners," planning to return home after they had made their fortunes. Although laws and experiences with women's immigration varied between the groups, all faced the difficulty of forming families across the ocean—miscegenation laws prevented marriage with white women—especially when further immigration was cut off. For all groups, it took decades before a sizeable second generation of Asians was born.*

Chinese-American Women

In the mid-nineteenth century, the needs of US capitalists for cheap labour coincided with economic crisis and massive dislocation in China, compounded of internal rebellion, loss of peasant lands to large landowners and the Opium wars, in which China was forced to cede territory, including Hong Kong, to the British. To take advantage of the situation, western firms set up a lucrative "coolie" trade (literally "bitter labour"), aided by highly-paid Chinese middlemen who recruited workers and contracted them out. While physical coercion was not unknown, most Chinese men came to the US voluntarily, if forced by desperate economic straits, expecting to strike it rich on "Gold Mountain" (as they called San Francisco) and return.

Chinese workers were especially attractive to US and Hawaiian employers who could contract mainly young, able-bodied men whose children and wives were prevented from joining them. By 1852, 11,787 Cantonese Chinese had come to the United States, only seven of whom were women.[1] Since the costs of producing another generation of workers and caring for the dependants were borne in China, employers could keep wages low, and the men were ideal for migrant farm work, mining and railroad construction, where a mobile work-force was needed. Finally, Chinese men were desirable because of their experience in China, working in "excavation work in hilly terrain" and in sugar cultivation.

Early Chinese Male Employment

Chinese men first came to the US in large numbers in the late 1840s, during the Gold Rush; by 1860, they comprised 10 per cent of California's population and almost 25 per cent of its labour force. In the next twenty years, another 105,000 immigrated. Independent white miners had exhausted most lands, and mining companies used the Chinese as contract labourers to search for the dregs, primarily in California but also in other northwest states. A second wave of Chinese workers came to work on the most

---

*There is some difficulty in characterising Asians in the US as Asians or Asian Americans. Generally, we will describe immigrants as Asians and second generation and on (i.e. those born in the US of Asian parentage) Asian-American.

dangerous segment of the transcontinental railroad, through the Rockies—thousands lost their lives in this work. Chinese men were also employed in San Francisco's woollen mills as a cheap substitute for white workers: "Stop paying American workmen three dollars a day and substitute Chinamen at a dollar and a quarter, and then you will make money," urged businessman Louis McLane.[2] They were also concentrated in citrus- and celery-harvesting, fishery work and cigar-making, and urban Chinese men could be found in the cigar, slipper, sewing and shoe-making industries.

Although most Chinese immigrants worked as low-paid wage workers, some were able to work for themselves. Some miners, especially the early migrants, laboured independently, even if under debt. In response to the shortage of domestic servants, Chinese men set up hundreds of small laundry businesses in San Francisco. Many were successful in truck gardening and large-scale tenant farming, and others accumulated large amounts of land to farm and ranch. Chinese fishermen in southern California villages successfully exported millions of dollars worth of abalone and shrimp annually in the 1870s and 1880s. In urban Chinatowns, too, there were many small Chinese businesses: 1878 San Francisco boasted grocers, restaurants, apothecaries, fancy goods and jewelry stores, for example. Although women were fewer in number, their unpaid labour as wives was crucial for the success of many of these small businesses.

Wealthy Chinese import-export merchants from the scholar-gentry class formed the elite of nineteenth-century communities in the US. Although they differed from the mass of Chinese immigrants in class, culture and language, they dominated the Chinese political organisations, including the patriarchal clan organisations and the secret societies. Some merchants were also capitalist producers, hiring poor Chinese at meagre wages to produce goods such as cigars and garments. Others became rich by contracting out Chinese workers to white capitalists, or by profiting from prostitution. Merchants' wives lived sheltered lives, cared for by servants and filling their time with decorative needlework and socialising with others of their class.

On the plantations of the Hawaiian sugar industry, Chinese, and later Japanese and Filipinos, were used in large numbers. From the 1850s to 1870s, Chinese men (an estimated 93 per cent of immigrants were men)[3] were the largest group of workers. Many married Hawaiian women, but a few immigration companies did encourage men to bring their wives, with an eye both to using female labour in the fields and to encouraging stability among the workers.

The majority of women immigrants in Hawaii were Cantonese, many of whose feet had been bound. "Lily feet," as they were called, were desirable among brides, even though they made walking unassisted very difficult and painful, so women with bound feet performed light work such as cane cutting and stripping. Southern Chinese women, however, did not practise footbinding, and they worked in the fields alongside their husbands.

The Split-Household Family, the Gum-Shan-Poo and Prostitution

In nineteenth century China, marriages were arranged between parents: the couple met on the day of their marriage, and then moved to the husband's town to live with his parents. Village leaders pressured the male emigrant to marry and attempt to conceive a male descendant before he left. The emigrant had to promise to send money for his family and village, and his wife and children remained in his parents' home to guarantee his cooperation with the arrangement.

The migration of Chinese women into the US was kept to a trickle by a combination of factors: the economic motives of family patriarchs in China, the view that it was indecent for a woman to travel abroad, reports of sexual molestation by sailors and anti-Chinese violence in the US, and contractors' and employers' insistence on single men. What Evelyn Nakano Glenn has called a "split-household family system" was created,[4] and some families remained split through many generations. Thousands of Chinese women led the life of a Gum-Shan-Poo, a "Golden Mountain lady," married to a man who lived and worked in the US and who returned seldom, if ever.

Most immigrant men were able to send enough money home to keep their families alive, supplementing whatever a wife and children could provide for themselves through subsistence farming or other means. Emigrants who could afford to returned for visits and to father children—boy children often joined their fathers in the US when of age. However, when the flow of money stopped during times of war or natural disaster, families in China were left in dire straits, and "became refugees or were compelled to sell their belongings, homes, children, or even themselves to stay alive."[5]

Prostitution of Chinese women in the US developed and thrived within this split-family situation, and it was encouraged by white capitalists, who wanted to keep wives and children from immigrating and increasing labour costs, and by racist whites, who wanted to keep the Chinese from reproducing in the US.[6] In the early years, a few Chinese women came to the US of their own accord and worked independently. Ah Toy arrived in San Francisco in 1849 to "better her condition," worked as a prostitute, and then became the madam of a brothel of Chinese women.[7] Soon, however, the Chinese secret societies or tongs took over and organised the lucrative trade—between 1852

and 1873, the Hip Yee Tong imported an estimated 6,000 women (87 per cent of all Chinese women arrivals).[8]

Male Chinese purchasing agents for the tongs went to Canton and Hong Kong to recruit young girls into prostitution. Sometimes the exchange was open: agents bought girls from poor families as outright slaves or under contract for an average of four and a half years. When the contract expired, a prostitute was theoretically free, but other rules, which lengthened the years of contract if she was ill or had a child, made such freedom difficult to achieve. When they arrived in California, the girls were sold to wealthy Chinese as concubines, to higher-class brothels reserved only for Chinese men, or to "inferior dens of prostitution which served a racially mixed clientele."[9] Not only the Hip Yee Tong made money on the trade: white policemen were paid off (at $10 a head), white lawyers and customs officials grew rich as increasingly restrictive immigration codes were passed, and Chinatown landlords (over 90 per cent of land was owned by whites) were able to charge brothel owners exorbitant rents.

Chinese prostitutes worked in conditions far inferior to those of white prostitutes. No wages were paid, although gifts could be kept, and in the daytime they were forced to do sewing work subcontracted out to their employers. Those in low-grade brothels lived locked in tiny rooms, often facing dim alleyways, and some were shipped into mining camps, where their treatment was especially harsh.

While many Chinese prostitutes were never able to free themselves, almost all found ways to keep their daughters out of prostitution. White society, however, saw it as natural for Chinese women—"the Chinese are lustful and sensual in their dispositions; every female is a prostitute of the basest order," said the New York *Tribune* in 1856.[10] Indeed, the immorality of

Chinese prostitution was cited as one of the reasons to stop Chinese immigration in 1882, although white prostitution was equally prevalent.

Organised Chinese prostitution began to decline in the 1870s as whites passed laws against it and then ended Chinese immigration in 1882, and as a result of raids by Chinese missionaries. More and more Chinese women were married and worked as homemakers. In cities, they also worked for pay at home, doing laundry or sewing, rolling cigars, making slippers or taking in boarders; in rural areas, they earned income from gardening, fishing or raising livestock. Chinese women were also servants, cooks and farm labourers, and a few fished, mined, ran lodging houses or worked on the railroads.

The Anti-Chinese Movement

By the 1870s, US whites began a movement against the Chinese. Town after town passed laws which pushed them out of mining. Although the essential motive seems to have been economic self-interest, it was combined with virulent racism. An Arizona editorial called Chinese "filthy," "heathens," "disgusting" and "barbarous"; a Montana journalist wrote: "We don't mind hearing of a Chinaman being killed now and then. . . . Don't kill them unless they deserve it, but when they do—why kill 'em lots."[11] All over the West they were expelled from small towns and rural areas in what the Chinese called "the Great Driving Out."

Sinophobia was also strong among urban whites in California, fuelled by the use of Asian workers as strike-breakers or low-wage competition. The white Workingmen's Party of California led the assault, with "The Chinese Must Go" as its slogan; it called the Chinese "the most debased order of humanity known to the civilised world."[12] Political and labour leaders incited violence—in one of the worst episodes, a white mob attacked the Los

Angeles Chinatown in 1871, lynching nineteen people and stealing $40,000 in cash.[13]

White activism resulted in numerous anti-Chinese laws in states and localities, especially in California. Taking advantage of the alien status of Asians, California state laws levied special taxes on them, preventing them from testifying against whites (by declaring them American Indians) and buying land (from 1913 to the 1950s), and legalised their exclusion from public schools, among other things. And Chinese immigration itself was terminated in 1882 by the Chinese Exclusion Act. As a result of such laws and of anti-Chinese sentiment, the Chinese-American community actually contracted from 124,000 in 1890 to a low of 85,000 in 1920, rising again only very gradually, to 106,000 in 1940.[14] West Coast and Hawaiian employers turned to Japan for their cheap labour.

The 1882 Exclusion Act prevented single Chinese women as well as the wives of US residents (except those of merchants) from immigrating, solidifying the sex imbalance. Those sojourners who now wished to send for their wives could not do so. Further, miscegenation laws (in operation until 1967) prevented Chinese men from marrying white women—only a few married Indian, African-American or Mexican women. Most Chinese men who had migrated to the US single could only start a family by going to China, marrying and returning, leaving their wives and future children there. Thus, the split-household family system continued over generations, well into the twentieth century. In one typical family history, a 21-year-old college student in the 1980s was the first in four generations of split families to be born in the US.

During the "Great Driving Out" of the late nineteenth century, many Chinese lost their land and businesses and moved into the urban ghettos, "Chinatowns." The proportion of Chinese farm labourers fell, as did the number of Chinese wage-workers in urban areas, as white workers prevented white capitalists from hiring them. Chinese capitalists could not offer many jobs because white consumers boycotted Chinese-made products. Many Chinese women, however, continued to work as seamstresses, in canning or as domestics—garment work was especially common, some girls beginning to work as young as 7 years of age. In 1938, in the middle of the Depression, Chinese women garment workers employed by the National Dollar Stores organised their own union chapter, went on strike for thirteen weeks and won a contract and better wages and working conditions.

Many Chinese were able to circumvent the restricted labour market by forming small businesses, despite white hostility—in 1937, in San Antonio, Texas, the Chinese community stopped a drive to push Chinese out of the grocery business. Most Chinese businesses were in Chinatowns, but not all—for instance, some Chinese set up small shops in the South to serve blacks, who were refused by whites.

Once Chinese men registered as merchants, they could send for their wives and children. "Small-producer" families were formed, much like the white family businesses in colonial times. Super-self-exploitation of the whole family was necessary to turn a profit. One Chinese woman from Boston's Chinatown described her family's laundry business in the 1930s and 1940s: it employed all four children and both parents, and the work day was 7 A.M. to midnight, six days a week; the children worked the same hours, except for school and a short nap, and did their homework from midnight to 2 A.M.

The Second World War Watershed and the New Immigrants

The Second World War proved to be a watershed. Since Japan had invaded China in 1931, Chinese Americans, for once, felt a common interest with the US when war was declared on Japan after the bombing of Pearl Harbour in 1941, and both women and men served in the armed forces. The labour shortage created by the war forced the US government to prohibit discrimination against Chinese and Chinese-American workers in defence industries. Chinese-American women workers were finally allowed into office work outside Chinatowns. Jobs in the civil service, professional fields and factories also opened up—and the new stereotype of Chinese-American women as obedient "office wives" was formed.

Political alliance with China and Madame Chiang Kai-shek's visit to the US further eased anti-Chinese-American sentiment. In 1943, the Chinese Exclusion Act was repealed: Chinese were put under the racial quota system for immigration (allowing 105 Chinese immigrants a year) and Chinese immigrants became eligible for citizenship if they could prove they had entered before 1924, or had come in under the new laws as permanent residents. A later amendment to the "War Brides Act" also allowed Chinese servicemen, once they had become citizens, to bring their wives and children to the US. Many rushed to China to marry before the Act expired in 1949.

For five years, almost all the immigrants from China were women and children. Upon arrival, they were interrogated to prove their right to immigrate and some were detained or harassed. In 1948, Leong Bick Ha hanged herself in an immigration detention centre after being held three months there. One hundred Chinese women detainees protested her death with a day-long hunger strike. Finally, in response to adverse publicity and public pressure, the Immigration and Naturalisation Service ended its policy of detaining Chinese immigrants, after over 100 years of the inhuman practice. Subsequent immigration acts—in 1952 and 1965—eased the sex imbalance in the Chinese American community.

The Chinese immigration of the 1940s and 1950s, however, was small compared to that after the 1965 Immigration Act. The Chinese-American population quadrupled between 1960 and 1985, from 236,084 to 1,079,400.[15] But the specific provisions of the laws created two very different communities: the "Uptown" and the "Downtown" Chinese. On the one hand, elite professionals, particularly scientists and engineers, have been actively encouraged by the US government. On the other, a substantial proportion of the immigration quota is allocated to relatives of Chinese already settled in the US—mostly poor, rural Cantonese who had resettled in Hong Kong.

The "Uptown" Chinese, many of them women, come with considerable resources, and their experiences have raised average income statistics for Chinese Americans, giving the false impression of upward mobility in the US. Actually, the "Uptown" Chinese were already educationally and socially elevated in Taiwan and China, and have simply transferred that status. And, indeed, discrimination has ensured the downward mobility even of such model immigrants.

The "Downtown" Chinese, on the other hand, live and work in Chinatowns—where they need not know English—and have revitalised these areas, which had been declining as second-generation Chinese moved out. But garment sweatshops and other Chinatown employment, in restaurants and laundries, are often part of the "underground economy," unprotected by labour laws. While the garment workers have become increasingly militant, Chinese women have taken the lead in struggles over community control and education in Chinatowns across the US. In Los Angeles, in the 1970s, the Chinatown Education Project won improved education for Chinatown children, and in Boston, Chinese women led the fight for local input into "urban renewal" plans that threatened Chinatown. Chinese immigrant women

organised "It's Time," a New York City group serving tenants, mostly from the Chinese community, facing evictions, harassment and deteriorating buildings.

Japanese-American Women

Japanese workers were not sought until Chinese immigration was stopped in 1882. Although similarities existed between Japanese and Chinese immigration—contract work in Hawaii and on the West Coast, limitations on immigration as a result of US racism, initial unbalanced sex ratios—there were also profound differences. Japanese women were key to these differences, since they came in greater numbers than Chinese women and came earlier in the immigration period.

For the Japanese government, which first permitted and later encouraged emigration to the US, it was seen as a solution to the growing problem of landlessness, while the remittances of the emigrants were looked upon as an important source of income to impoverished families.[16] In contrast to Chinese emigrants, most of those who left Japan were literate, including the women—an education was deemed to make them good wives and wise mothers. Such education had much in common with the nineteenth-century cult of domesticity. As among whites, however, not all women were able to live their lives according to such precepts; for the vast majority of peasants and tenant farmers, backbreaking work for economic survival took precedence over notions of womanhood.

By 1910, there were over 72,000 Japanese in the continental US, mostly educated young, single males who worked as unskilled labourers on the railroads and in the mines, as gardeners or laundrymen, as "houseboys" in domestic service or as field hands. Conditions for the field hands were harsh, and many workers died from the heat, beriberi and tuberculosis. According to one account from the 1890s: During those days around Fresno, labourers did not even carry blankets. They slept in the field with what they had on. They drank river water brought in by irrigation ditches. . . . If they ate supper, it consisted of flour dumplings in a soup seasoned with salt."[17] Nearly all these agricultural workers were recruited by Japanese labour contractors who earned high incomes by charging the workers not only a daily commission, withheld from their wages, but also medical fees and service fees for sending money back to families in Japan.

Some "Issei" (first-generation immigrants) were able to set up small businesses, including laundries, hotels and stores, catering primarily for Japanese clients who faced discrimination by white-owned businesses. And by 1900, there was a sizeable number of Japanese sharecroppers and tenant farmers.

Issei Women, Prostitution and "Picture Brides"

During the early years, most Japanese migrants were men—in 1900, there were twenty-five Japanese men for every woman. Most women immigrants came as part of families and worked in agriculture, as domestic servants and alongside their husbands in small family businesses. The most common form of non-agricultural employment for Japanese women was domestic service.

However, as with the Chinese, the unbalanced sex ratio made prostitution a thriving business. The first reports of the presence of Japanese prostitutes date back to the 1880s.[18] Many of the women were abducted or tricked into coming; others were sold into prostitution by their impoverished families. Once they arrived in the US the women were often held in bondage by *amegoro*, pimps who used physical intimidation and lived off their prostitutes' earnings.

Prostitution was fairly strictly segregated by race: *Hakujin-tori* catered to whites, *Shinajin-tori* to Chinese and *Nihonjin-tori* to Japanese.

In the 1890s, San Francisco and Seattle newspapers began to publish a series of sensationalist articles about the presence of Japanese prostitutes. The Japanese government adopted a number of measures to stem their immigration to the US, fearing that exclusionary measures would be imposed on the mass of Japanese immigrants, as they had on the Chinese. Japanese student leaders in San Francisco petitioned the Japanese Foreign Ministry, claiming the women were "a blot on our national image and national morality" and that "if this notorious vice spreads, America will adopt measures against us in the same manner as she did formerly against the Chinese."[19] However, Japanese leaders' attempts to protect their communities by dissociating themselves from Chinese immigrants failed and Japanese workers and farmers became the targets of racist violence and agitation. In 1907, the Japanese government was finally forced by the US to limit the emigration of Japanese men, and entry was closed to the unskilled. But the entry of wives and relatives was still permitted. With the exclusive immigration of Japanese women, the ratio of men to women began to fall, and by 1920, 34 per cent of the Japanese immigrant community was female.[20]

Of the women who entered the US between 1909 and 1920, over half—an estimated 23,000[21]—were "picture brides" who had never seen their husbands. The picture-bride practice was a variation on the traditional Japanese marriage form, in which families selected marriage partners for their children using go-betweens. The picture brides tended to come from the same backgrounds as the men they married, who, typically, were approximately ten years their senior and had lived in the US for a while. The Japanese government regulated the practise of photo marriage in a number of ways: men were required to show evidence of stable employment and have savings of anywhere from $800 to $1,000—labourers were ineligible until 1915. The brides had to pass physical examinations and be no more than thirteen years younger than their husbands.

Women became picture brides for a number of reasons. Most obeyed their parents, since "to refuse would have been an act of filial disobedience, a grave moral offence;"[22] others came to help their families by remitting money back to Japan. One traveller described her thoughts:

> gazing upon the rising majestic Mount Fuji in a cloudless sky aboard the ship, I made a resolve. For a woman who was going to a strange society and relying upon an unknown husband whom she had married through photographs, my heart had to be as beautiful as Mount Fuji. I resolved that the heart of a Japanese woman had to be sublime, like that soaring majestic figure, eternally constant through wind and rain, heat and cold. Thereafter, I never forgot that resolve on the ship, enabling me to overcome sadness and suffering.[23]

When they arrived, picture brides, having been subjected to degrading inspections, saw their husbands for the first time at the station. Until 1917, the US government did not recognise photo marriages as legal, so group marriages were conducted on arrival. Once outfitted in uncomfortable western clothing, picture brides followed their husbands to their new homes. According to Evelyn Nakano Glenn:

> Some went to remote labour camps that were built for railroad workers in the Mountain states, coal miners in Wyoming, sugar beet field hands in

Utah and Idaho, labourers in lumbering camps and sawmills in Washington, and fish cannery workers in Alaska. Others, particularly those who stayed in California, went into the fields where their husbands tilled the soil as tenant farmers. In addition to working alongside their husbands, women in labour camps and farms often drew their own water, gathered wood to cook and heat the house, and fought to keep dirt out of houses that were little more than shacks. . . . Women whose husbands resided in urban areas were more fortunate. They too worked long hours and kept house in crowded quarters, but conditions were less primitive, and the presence of an ethnic community eased their adjustment.[24]

Although most marriages were stable, some women deserted their husbands, often for another man. Accurate figures are impossible to obtain, but such desertion was common enough to feature frequently in the Japanese press. The close network of Japanese associations (local and business associations, language schools, temples, churches) which regulated and controlled community life were often involved in apprehending such couples, eager to uphold the strict moral tone of the community and concerned that such incidents reflected badly on the Japanese in general.

Then, in 1920, the picture-bride practice was ended, in response to a new wave of anti-Japanese sentiment—the brides, it was claimed by one Californian senator, were breeding a new generation of US citizens who would take over agricultural land.[25] The Japanese associations and the Japanese government stopped issuing passports to picture brides—and over 24,000 single male Issei were left stranded in the US without possibility of marriage, since the vast majority of them could not afford to return to Japan to find a wife.[26]

Agriculture and Economic Advance

Women played a key role in shaping the economic status of Japanese America, since their presence made it possible for Japanese Americans to enter agriculture. The unpaid family labour of women and children "allowed Issei truck farmers to compete effectively with white farmers, enabling them to gain a dominant share of the produce market."[27] The Japanese success in agriculture was impressive: from thirty-seven Japanese farms in California in 1900, the number grew to over 1800 by 1910. By 1920, Japanese farms produced one-third of the truck crops in California. This success was the result of a labour-intensive, high-yield style of farming, very different from most of California agriculture, which tended to use more machinery and larger plots of land, and generated low yields.

This success was threatened in 1913 when California and other western states passed a series of laws banning aliens "ineligible for citizenship" from purchasing land or leasing it for more than three years. But Japanese agriculture continued to expand between 1914 and 1920, largely because Japanese bought land in the names of "Nisei" (the second generation, born on US soil and, hence, US citizens) or through land companies set up to circumvent the ban. The passage of yet another law, in 1920, aimed at plugging these loopholes, led Japanese farmers to develop a variety of new strategies to stay in agriculture. Besides forming land companies and issuing stock to Nisei or other US citizens, some Japanese farmers found Nisei middlemen to lease land and then hire them as managers or foremen. Others entered into oral agreements with landowners, who publicly hired the Japanese farmer as an employee, but privately permitted them to sharecrop or tenant farm. Whites entered these arrangements for economic reasons: Japanese farmers were so skilled at intensive cultivation that they were able to pay higher rents and achieve higher yields—in essence, they paid a "racial rent premium."

The Second World War and the Aftermath

Japanese Americans had achieved great economic success by 1940, but bitter times were ahead. The bombing of Pearl Harbour in 1941 set in motion a war not only between Japan and the US but also against Japanese Americans in the US. Immediately, their economic assets were frozen and hundreds of community leaders were rounded up and detained. Then, in February 1942, the "evacuation" of 110,000 Issei and Nisei from the coastal areas of Washington, Oregon and California was authorised on the grounds of potential sabotage and espionage. (During the course of the war, not one such incident was ever reported.) In one week families had to dispose of possessions, close up businesses and report to a temporary assembly centre. Farmers who had invested years of painstaking effort in raising orchards from seedlings had to sell them quickly, at low prices. Once they arrived at the assembly centre, Japanese Americans were tagged like luggage and transported to ten "permanent relocation camps" in Utah, Arizona, Colorado, California, Wyoming, Idaho and Arkansas.

The camps, which held an average of 10,000 people each and were situated in desert or swamp areas where temperatures fluctuated between freezing and boiling, were surrounded by barbed wire and patrolled by armed guards. Camp life was extraordinarily difficult. Families lived in tar-paper barracks divided into rooms housing an average of eight people. Walls did not reach the ceiling, latrines and showers had few or no partitions, and all meals were eaten in large communal mess halls. Adult internees were expected to work, for very low wages, at jobs such as cooking, farming, teaching and providing medical care.

Despite these conditions, Matsumoto suggests that camp life produced some aspects of equality for Issei and Nisei women.[28] And since they were now able to meet young men on their own, Nisei women moved further away from traditional Japanese practices of arranged marriages. Also, the war had generated such a severe labour shortage that the War Relocation Authority, which oversaw the camps, soon began to let internees leave to do domestic, agricultural or factory labour. Issei parents were reluctant to let their daughters go, but their hopes for the future rested on the Nisei generation, and so women were able to leave for schooling and on work releases. Although most work release requests were for domestic servants, Nisei women also found clerical and factory jobs. Some internees left to join the armed forces. Nearly 3,000 Nisei men from the camps joined other Hawaii and US Nisei in the segregated 442nd Combat Team, which became the most highly decorated combat unit of the war,[29] while 100 Nisei women joined the Women's Army Corps.[30] White newspapers refused to print the names of the Nisei war dead.

In 1945, the War Relocation Authority ended the West Coast exclusion and began closing the camps. By then, over a third of adult internees had already left. Japanese Americans returned to a dramatically altered way of life. Much agricultural land had been lost, along with businesses and homes, and whites in many of their former home towns greeted them with signs warning "No Japanese Welcome." Thus, the end of internment also saw the end of the highly segregated Japanese America, concentrated in the Pacific Northwest and in Japanese-owned or -operated businesses. Although many remained on the West Coast, others dispersed across the US: some of those who had been relocated to the Midwest or the East remained there; others found that their small farms had been displaced by competition from huge corporate farms; still others left the Japanese ghetto in cities like San Francisco and Oakland to disperse throughout the city.

The ban on Japanese immigration was lifted in 1952 with the McCarran-Walter Act (the Japanese quota, however, was only 100 persons); this act also struck down racial barriers to naturalisation, making those born in Japan but living in the US finally eligible for US citizenship. The 1965 Immigration Act further opened up immigration to Asians by eliminating the quota system, but, in contrast to the Chinese-American and Filipino-American communities, the Japanese-American community has not experienced a huge second wave of immigration in response to the act.

The Japanese America of the 1970s and 1980s is dramatically different from that of the prewar period. Most Japanese Americans do not live in ethnic ghettos, and although they continue to experience discrimination and racist violence, they rank in the upper middle class economically.

Filipina-American Women

A major cause of Filipino migration to the US prior to the Second World War has been the US colonisation of the Philippines from 1898 onwards, which followed centuries of Spanish colonisation. The US used the islands for agricultural export crops, as Spain had done before, and also as a growing market for US manufactured goods. Already, by the early years of the twentieth century the Filipino economy was in a shambles, following years of fighting and epidemics of cholera. Land ownership became increasingly concentrated and poverty, landlessness and tenancy grew in the rural areas. Along with the English-language public schools set up by the US, the stage was set for the first wave of Filipino migration. But whereas Chinese and Japanese immigrants were "aliens," their colonial status made Filipinos US nationals, with the right to immigrate freely to the US. At the same time, they could be kept at the very bottom of the economic hierarchy because they were not allowed to naturalise unless they had served in the US Navy.

Apart from recruitment to the Hawaiian sugar plantations after first Chinese and then Japanese immigration had been halted, Filipinos sought an education in the US. In the early 1900s, an estimated 14,000 Filipino young men, backed by the immense financial sacrifices of their families, came to study, most working as domestic servants to pay their way. This group of young Filipino men was joined, in the 1920s, by 16,000 from Hawaii and 9,000 from Asia. Of the 24,000 Filipinos who entered California between 1925 and 1929, only 1,300 were women. Most Filipinos found jobs at the bottom of the economic hierarchy: in agriculture, as servants, in hotels or restaurants, or in the Alaskan canneries.

Women, Family and Work

There were very few Filipinas in the US until the Second World War: in 1930, the male/female ratio was 14 to 1.[31] Perhaps the most important reason was that employers preferred single men (although, in response to worker unrest and strikes in 1920 and 1924, planters—supposedly to calm the workers—shipped in about 3,000 Filipinas). Also, Filipinos planned to return home; indeed, many did. Another factor was the different family structure in the Philippines, compared to China and Japan. When a Filipina marries, her ties with her blood family remain equal in importance to those with her husband's families. Hence, Filipinas

may have been unwilling to migrate as part of a nuclear family—many waited for their husbands in the Philippines, similar to the Chinese Gum-Shan-Poo. Most Filipinos and Filipinas were Catholic as a result of Spanish colonisation, and divorce was unacceptable. Men who were successful financially tended to return home to their wives and families or to marry; those who stayed in Hawaii or in the continental US tended to remain single, often forming stable households together and paying prostitutes or "taxi-dance girls" for their company.

White racism against Filipinos was organised by the anti-Asian movement. At a 1930 House Committee on immigration hearing, Fred Hart of Salinas claimed: "The Filipinos are poor labour and a social menace as they will not leave our white girls alone and frequently intermarry."[32] Whites verbally harassed Filipinos on the streets, calling them "go-go" and "monkey," and refused to allow them in their restaurants, barbershops, cinemas, swimming pools and tennis courts.

In the Second World War, young Filipino Americans were drafted and others found work in war-related industry. In Hawaii, planters contracted them out to war industries, but paid them their former wages and pocketed the difference. One tangible result of the war was an act in 1946 which finally allowed Filipinos who had entered the US before 1934 to naturalise, thus giving them the right to vote for the first time and freeing them from the restrictions of the Alien Land Laws.

Some new immigration, especially of women, accompanied these changes. During the war, many men in the Philippines had enlisted in the US navy, even though they were confined to stewards' jobs. Many of these veterans applied for citizenship when a 1942 Act of Congress permitted foreign veterans to naturalise. Then the 1947-amended War Brides Act allowed Filipino-American citizens who had served in the war to bring wives in as citizens. Filipinos, often in their 50s and 60s, returned to the Philippines to find wives.

Many Filipinas were, by this time, eager to come, convinced by colonial ideology that "all Americans were beautiful and rich and that America must be like heaven." Most wives ended up working in agriculture or in canneries with their husbands on the West Coast, as domestic servants in cities, or in family businesses. Large numbers of Filipinas came to the US after the Second World War, some as the wives of white servicemen who were stationed in the Philippines: over 63,000 arrived between 1950 and 1980.[33]

The third wave of Filipinos, following the 1965 Immigration Act with its provisions for Filipino immigration—for family reunification, or for professional workers—has created a bipolar income and job distribution among new immigrants, similar to that experienced by the Chinese. Family reunification provisions have allowed the relatives of present Filipino Americans to join their families. Most of these are poor, although many have basic education in English from their Philippine schools. The other, highly visible group of Filipino immigrants, however, is made up of well-trained scientific professionals for whom demand had grown sharply in the US during the 1960s, particularly medical personnel, many of whom are women. However, severe institutional discrimination ensures that they earn far less than their white counterparts, so that the economic situation of these professional Filipino immigrants is far from rosy.

War Brides and the Sexploitation of Asian Women

Apart from the institutionalised racism and high levels of racist violence meted out to Asian communities generally, Asian-American women have faced a special kind of discrimination. The US involvement in wars in Asia—the Second World War in Japan and the Philippines, the Korean War and the Vietnam War—and US bases in those countries have placed generations of US non-Asian servicemen in contact with Asian women, mostly as prostitutes or teahouse girls. Amerasian children abound in Korea and Vietnam, ostracised by the local communities. Many of the 200,000 Japanese, Korean, Vietnamese, Thai and Filipino women who married white US servicemen and came to live in the US, many on military bases, lead difficult lives, due to language difficulties, lack of familiarity with US ways and psycho-social isolation. Many husbands, far from assisting their wives' efforts to adapt, become abusive or disenchanted; unaware of their legal rights, wives have been divorced without their knowledge, lost financial support and custody of their children and even faced deportation.

Thousands more difficult relationships between new immigrant Asian women and white men have been produced by the recent growth of the mail-order bride industry, which supplies Asian women as wives to non-Asian US and European men. Unlike long-distance arranged marriages or wife-sales of the past, which located wives of the same racial/ethnic background as the men, the mail-order marriage business is centred on the presumed difference of Asian women from US women. One survey of the men involved found that they "see the women's liberation movement as the cause of their problems. They start with certain negative stereotypes of American women as aggressive, selfish, not family oriented. Then they add positive stereotypes of Asian women—family centred, undemanding, untouched by women's liberation."[34]

The women involved, mostly extremely poor Filipinas, respond to advertisements placed by agencies in local newspapers which offer prospective husbands in the US (and in Europe). The agencies compile catalogues with the women's pictures, descriptions and addresses, which they sell to US men for about $150; the men write to the women who interest them, "fall in love by mail," and marry. An estimated 2,000–3,000 US men find wives in this way each year. Many mail-order brides complain of beatings by their husbands, but fear deportation if they ask for help. Siriporn Skrobanek, a founder of the Women's Information Center in Bangkok, Thailand, views these marriages as "another form of economic exploitation of the periphery by the centre, one which is so intensive that women in the peripheral countries have to sell their labour and sexuality to men on a commercial marriage market."

The sexual stereotypes of Asian women affect Asian-American women in the economic and legal arenas. As Germaine Wong points out:

> The men who used Asian-Pacific women as prostitutes very likely feel today, consciously or not, that Asian-Pacific-American women are beneath their dignity; that we do not value ourselves because we are "willing" to sell ourselves so cheaply; that we are only good for meeting their base needs; etc., etc.
>
> The men who saw Asian-Pacific women in places like tea houses may have come to expect us to be good, faithful, uncomplaining, totally compliant, self-effacing, gracious servants who will do anything and everything to please, entertain, and make them feel comfortable and carefree. All of this they had for "free" when buying drinks or a meal; in present-day circumstances they expect this behaviour to come "free" for the salary paid in exchange for work performed. They

expect Asian-Pacific women to be like this "by nature"; it is part of the charm of the Oriental culture.[35]

These stereotypes reinforce Asian women's segregation in office work. Assuming Asian-American women to be particularly pleasing and unaggressive, employers deny them pay rises and claim they lack the leadership qualities needed for executive jobs. These stereotypes have also led to sexual harassment of Asian-American women by police, and women reporting such incidents do not receive justice from the courts because of "the prostitute stereotype."[36]

. . .

Asian patriarchal practices, white society's racism, and the special sexploitation of Asian women have led increasing numbers of Asian-American women to become active in Asian civil rights organising, in Asian women's movements, and in Asian lesbian and gay groups. They face many impediments: hostility from Asian men (who criticise Asian feminists and lesbians for destroying Asian community solidarity), the racism of white women (few of whom have any knowledge of the history or present status of Asian-American women), vast differences among them (from ethnicity and language to class and sexuality), and the needs of many Asian-American women, still, to focus on economic survival. Nevertheless, Asian-American women have started Asian women's studies courses and study groups; writers' groups, such as the Pacific Asian American Women's Writers West; health and mental health projects and advocacy groups, such as the Pacific Asian Shelter for Battered Women in Los Angeles and the Asian Pacific Outreach Center in Long Beach; and regional feminist organisations, such as the National Organisation of Pan Asian Women, the National Network of Asian and Pacific Women, and Asian American Women United. Asian lesbians have formed political networks such as ALOEC (Asian Lesbians of the East Coast), which has created a slide-show of Asian lesbian history in India, China and Japan. Further, Asian feminists have begun to join in coalitions with other feminists of colour, in spite of historical differences and antagonisms.

In her "Letter to Ma," Merle Woo tells her:

> Do you realise, Ma, that I could never have reacted the way I have if you had not provided for me the opportunity to be free of the binds that have held you down . . . ? Because of your life, because of the physical security you have given me . . I saw myself as having worth: now I . . . see our potential, and fight for just that kind of social change that will reaffirm me, my race, my sex, my heritage. And while I affirm myself, Ma, I affirm you.[37]

REFERENCES

For this excerpt most of the references have been eliminated for reasons of space. In addition to the works cited below, see also Jayjia Hsia, *Asian Americans in higher education and at work* (New Jersey, 1988); H. B. Melendy, *Asians in America: Filipinos, Koreans and East Indians* (Boston, 1977); A. T. Moriyama, *Imingaisha: Japanese emigration companies and Hawaii 1894–1908* (Honolulu, 1985); A. J. A. Pido, *The Filipinos in America: macro/micro dimensions of immigration and integration* (New York, 1986); A. Saxton, *The indispensable enemy: labor and the anti-Chinese movement* (Berkeley, 1971); B. L. Sung, *A survey of Chinese-American manpower and employment* (New York, 1977); R. V. Vallangca, *Pinoy: the first wave (1898–1941)* (San Francisco, 1977). For more information, see the complete work.

1. Paul C. P. Siu, *The Chinese Laundryman: A Study of Social Isolation* (New York, 1987), pp. 44–45.
2. Ibid., p. 49.
3. John Liu, "Race, Ethnicity, and the Sugar Plantation System: Asian Labor in Hawaii, 1850–1900," in *Labor Immigration Under Capitalism: Asian Workers in the United States before World War II,* edited by Lucie Cheng and Edna Bonacich (Berkeley, 1984), p. 195.
4. Evelyn Nakano Glenn, "Split Household, Small Producer and Dual Wage Earner: An Analysis of Chinese-American Family Strategies," *Journal of Marriage and the Family* (February 1983).
5. June Mei, "Socioeconomic Origins of Emigration: Guangdong to California, 1850–1882," in *Labor Immigration Under Capitalism,* ed. Cheng and Bonacich, p. 240.
6. Lucie Cheng, "Free, Indentured, Enslaved: Chinese Prostitutes in Nineteenth-Century America," in *Labor Immigration Under Capitalism,* ed. Cheng and Bonacich.
7. Judy Yung, *Chinese Women of America: A Pictorial History* (Seattle, 1986), pp. 14–15.
8. Cheng, "Free, Indentured, Enslaved," in *Labor Immigrants Under Capitalism,* ed. Cheng and Bonacich.
9. Ibid., p. 411.
10. June Mei, "Socioeconomic Developments Among the Chinese in San Francisco, 1848–1906," in *Labor Immigration Under Capitalism,* ed. Cheng and Bonacich. Diane Mei, Lin Mark and Ginger Chih, *A Place Called Chinese America* (Organization of Chinese Americas, 1982), pp. 54–56; Roger Daniels, *The Politics of Prejudice: The Anti-Japanese Movement in California and the Struggle for Japanese Exclusion* (New York, 1969), pp. 81–83.
11. Stanford Lyman, "Strangers in the City: The Chinese in the Urban Frontier," in *Roots: An Asian American Reader,* edited by Amy Tachiki, Eddie Wong and Franklin Odo with Buck Wong (UCLA Asian American Studies Center, 1971), pp. 159–87.
12. Ibid., p. 173.
13. Ibid., p. 174 and Siu, *The Chinese Laundryman,* p. 50.
14. Calculated from tables 2.1 and 2.5 in Bonacich; numbers include Hawaii.
15. Peter Kwong, *The New Chinatown* (New York, 1987), p. 22.
16. Alan Moriyama, "The Causes of Emigration," in *Labor Immigration Under Capitalism,* ed. Cheng and Bonacich.
17. Yuji Ichioka, *The Issei: The World of the First Generation Japanese Immigrants 1885–1924* (New York, 1988), p. 83.
18. The following material on prostitutes comes from Yuji Ichioka, "Ameyuki-san: Japanese Prostitutes in Nineteenth Century America," *Amerasia* 4(1), (1977).
19. Ichioka, *The Issei,* p. 39.

20. Yukiko Hanawa, *The Several Worlds of Issei Women* (dissertation, Dept. of Asian Studies, California State University, 1982), p. 51.

21. Evelyn Nakano Glenn, "The Dialectics of Wage Work: Japanese American Women and Domestic Service, 1905–40," and Alan Moriyama, "The Causes of Emigration: The Background of Japanese Emigration to Hawaii 1885–94," pp. 268–70, both in *Labor Immigration Under Capitalism*, ed. Cheng and Bonacich.

22. Ichioka, *The Issei*, p. 345.

23. Emma Gee, "Issei Women," in *Counterpoint: Perspectives on Asian America*, edited by Emma Gee (Los Angeles, Asian American Studies Center, 1976), p. 11.

24. Evelyn Nakano Glenn, *Issei, Nisei, War Bride: Three Generations of Japanese Women in Domestic Service* (Philadelphia, 1986), pp. 47–48.

25. Ichioka, *The Issei*, p. 173.

26. Ibid., p. 175.

27. Victor Nee, and Herbert Y. Wong, "Asian American Socioeconomic Achievement: The Strength of the Family Bond," *Sociological Perspectives* 28(3), (July 1985), p. 294.

28. Valerie Matsumoto, "Japanese American Women During World War II," *Frontiers* 8(1), (1984).

29. Roger Daniels, *Asian America: Chinese and Japanese in the United States Since 1850* (Seattle, 1988), pp. 252–54.

30. Ibid., p. 285.

31. Violet Rabaya, "Filipino Immigration: The Creation of a New Social Problem," in *Roots*, ed. Tachiki et al., pp. 188–200.

32. Brett Melendy, *Asians in America: Filipinos, Koreans and East Indians* (Boston, 1977), p. 67.

33. Elaine Kim, *With Silk Wings* (San Francisco, 1983), pp. 120–30.

34. Lisa Belkin, "The Mail-Order Marriage Business," *New York Times Magazine*, 11 May 1986, p. 51.

35. Germaine Wong, "Impediments to Asian-Pacific-American Women Organizing," in *Conference on the Educational and Occupational Needs of Asian-Pacific-American Women* (National Institute of Education, October 1980), p. 93.

36. Diane Yen-Mei Wong, "Asian/Pacific American Women: Legal Issues," in U.S. Commission on Civil Rights, *Civil Rights Issues of Asian and Pacific Americans*, pp. 142, 146.

37. Merle Woo, "Letter to Ma," in *This Bridge Called My Back*, edited by Gloria Anzaldua and Cherie Moraga (Watertown, MA, 1981).

21

THE EMERGENCE OF THE HISPANIC AMERICAN LABOR FORCE

Gregory DeFreitas

By almost every measure of socioeconomic well-being, the Spanish-origin population of the United States is today at a considerable disadvantage relative to non-Hispanic whites. The statistical overview in Table 1 shows that in the late 1980s, the average Hispanic family had an income ($20,306) over one-third lower than non-Hispanic whites. One in every four Hispanic families was below the official government poverty line, compared with only 8.2 percent of whites. Despite a nearly identical labor force participation rate, Spanish-origin workers were less than half as likely as non-Hispanic whites to hold managerial

Gregory DeFreitas, *Inequality at Work: Hispanics in the U.S. Labor Force.* Copyright © 1991 by Gregory DeFreitas. Reprinted courtesy of the author.

TABLE 1 Selected Social and Economic Characteristics of Whites, Blacks, and Hispanics,[a] March 1988

	White	Black	All Hispanic	Mexican	Puerto Rican	Cuban	Other Latin American	Other Hispanic
Population (000's)	205,233	29,847	19,431	12,110	2,471	1,035	2,242	1,573
Age								
Median	33.0	27.2	25.5	23.9	24.9	38.7	27.6	29.7
16–24 (%)	13.9	15.6	17.0	17.8	16.7	12.9	18.4	13.4
Years of Schooling Completed[b]								
Median	12.7	12.4	12.0	10.8	12.0	12.4	12.4	12.4
12 or more (%)	78.4	64.6	50.9	44.6	50.7	60.5	63.8	65.2
16 or more (%)	20.5	10.7	10.0	7.1	9.6	17.2	16.5	14.0
Labor Force Status[c]								
In civilian labor force (%)	65.5	62.8	65.5	67.0	53.2	65.3	72.4	62.6
Unemployed (%)	5.0	12.8	8.5	9.8	9.2	3.1	4.8	9.2
Profsnl. or manager (%)	26.6	16.0	14.1	11.2	17.4	25.2	13.0	23.4
Median Earnings[d]								
Males	$21,348	14,344	13,599	11,791	15,672	16,634	13,105	15,574
Females	$11,105	10,984	9,188	7,912	11,327	11,364	8,056	11,239
Family Income[e]								
Median	$32,274	18,098	20,306	19,968	15,185	27,294	22,939	21,196
Below poverty level (%)	8.2	29.9	25.8	25.5	37.9	13.8	18.9	26.1
Family Type								
5 or more persons (%)	12.9	19.6	225.7	31.6	16.4	34.4	25.5	13.7
Female head, no husband present (%)	12.9	42.8	23.4	18.5	44.0	16.1	24.4	26.1

[a]Persons of Spanish origin may be of any race.

[b]Persons 25 years old and over.

[c]Civilian population 16 years old and over. Managerial and professional employees expressed as percentage of employed persons.

[d]Annual wages and salaries of civilian workers 15 and over in 1987.

[e]Income and poverty figures for the calendar year 1987.

Source: U.S. Bureau of the Census (1989a, 1989b).

TABLE 2   Migration and Language Characteristics of Persons by Race and Type of Spanish Origin, 1980

	White	Black	All Hispanic	Mexican	Puerto Rican	Cuban	Other Hispanic
All Persons							
Foreign born (%)[a]	3.8	2.8	28.6	26.0	48.6	77.9	39.4
Living abroad in 1975 (%)	1.0	1.1	8.8	7.4	10.2	5.6	12.5
Persons 16 Years Old and Over							
Fluency in English (%)							
Speak only English	93.1	96.1	19.7	19.5	11.4	7.3	29.3
Speak very well	5.0	2.6	38.0	39.6	41.0	41.4	30.9
Speak well	1.3	0.9	21.1	20.8	27.0	22.7	17.9
Speak poorly or not at all	0.5	0.3	21.2	20.1	20.7	28.6	22.0

[a]*Note:* In the case of Puerto Ricans those born on the island are here listed as "foreign born" (though they are U.S. citizens).

Source: U.S. Bureau of the Census (1984a: U.S. Summary Vol.) and 1980 Public Use Microdata.

or professional jobs and nearly twice as likely to be unemployed.

Among the factors often thought to underlay such disparities are differences in age, schooling, family composition, migration, and language ability. Hispanics, with a median age of 25, are younger than non-Hispanic whites and blacks by an average of eight years and two years, respectively. Among adults ages 25 and older, 77 percent of non-Hispanic whites and 63 percent of blacks have completed high school, but only one-half of Hispanics. The latter are also the least likely to be college graduates. Families headed by a person of Spanish origin are twice as likely as whites to be stretching their incomes over five or more members, and nearly twice as likely to be female-headed. Finally, nearly three-tenths of Hispanics were born outside the continental United States, and 31 percent of these have only been in the country five years or less (Table 2). This is reflected in the fact that, in response to a 1980 census question, only one in five Hispanics said English was their sole language and only three in five were very fluent in English.

Among Hispanics, there are marked differences among the various national-origin groups. Mexicans are by far the most numerous, accounting for 62.6 percent of the total. Puerto Ricans represent another 12.2 percent, followed by Central and South Americans (11.4 percent), the other Hispanic category (8.4 percent), and Cubans (5.4 percent).[1] Despite gradual geographic dispersion over time, Mexicans, Central Americans, and other Hispanics remain largely concentrated in the Southwest, Puerto Ricans and most South Americans in New York and a few other northeastern cities, and Cubans in south Florida.

The two largest groups are also the most disadvantaged: they have lower median incomes and higher unemployment and poverty rates than all others of Spanish origin. At $15,185, Puerto Ricans' median family income is less than half that of non-Hispanic whites and almost $3,000 below the black average. Some 38 percent of Puerto Rican families live under the poverty line, a rate over four and one-half times that of whites and 8 percentage points higher than that of blacks.

At the other extreme, Cubans have an average family income that is one-third above the all-Hispanic median and less than $3,000 short of the non-Hispanic white level. Cuban workers' average earnings are also well above the average, as is the percentage employed in professional or managerial occupations. Their poverty rate is by far the lowest of all Hispanic ethnic groups and the fraction unemployed is almost identical to the non-Hispanic white rate.

This [reading] aims to provide the historical perspective necessary to an understanding of these current patterns. It briefly traces the historical emergence of the principal ethnic subgroups of the Spanish-origin work force. Each section ends with a review of the latest research findings on the economic characteristics of each group's recent immigrants.

Mexican Americans

The origins of the Mexican American population are woven inextricably into the political and economic history of the American Southwest. Until the middle of the nineteenth century, this region was the northern tier of Mexico, a newly independent nation sharing the same continent with the United States but little else. Both began as European colonies, but the early American economy was shaped by England, when it was the most advanced industrial and commercial power of the age, while Spain was still a backward mercantilist colonizer stressing resource and labor exploitation at the expense of local economic development. Mexico was further disadvantaged by the fact that it did not gain independence from Spain until nearly a half century after U.S. independence, and at far greater human cost (500,000 deaths, an estimated one-tenth of its population). In the century following independence, 1821–1920, Mexico was repeatedly the victim of military invasion, at an

average rate of about once every decade. The most costly of these came from the United States. First, a series of armed expeditions, often encouraged by Washington, led to the secession of Texas from Mexico in 1836. Then in 1846, one year after annexing Texas, President James Polk exploited a minor incident as a pretext to start a full-scale war. The Mexican War ended with the Treaty of Guadalupe Hidalgo (known to generations of Mexican historians as "the amputation of 1848"), which stripped the country of nearly one-half of its national territory: the area that would become Arizona, California, New Mexico, and large parts of Colorado, Nevada, and Utah. Although the treaty included guarantees from the victor to protect the civil, cultural, language, and property rights of the 80,000 to 100,000 Mexicans who stayed on in the region, there is ample historical evidence of widespread, often brutal violations of these little-enforced provisions in the years that followed.[2]

If one looked solely at official immigration statistics, it would appear that significant Mexican migration into the Southwest began only in the 1920s. But that simply reflects the fact that port-of-entry stations were not established until 1894 and that the only Mexicans officially counted as "immigrants" before 1908 were the small numbers arriving at U.S. seaports. The actual growth of the region's Mexican-origin population can perhaps be most clearly understood by distinguishing five main phases: the "open door" period (1848–1916); the selective screening period (1917–1929); the "Great Repatriation" (1930–1941); the *bracero* program (1942–1964); and the modern period, years of quotas and economic crisis (1965–1990).

1848–1916

The same year that Mexico lost its northern states also saw the beginning of migration to the United States by Mexican workers. The California Gold Rush of 1848 drew some 20,000 northward in the next two years, most from the silver regions of Sonora and Zacatecas.[3] After 1850, Mexican miners also found work in the mines of Nevada, southern Arizona, and Colorado.

Following the Civil War, a number of developments occurred with fundamental importance for the emergence of mass migration. In Mexico, the land policies of the Porfirio Diaz dictatorship (1876–1911) opened the way for speculators and foreign interests to acquire millions of hectares of farm and pastoral lands, including communal peasant holdings. By the turn of the century, about 90 percent of the land was controlled by only 5 percent of the families, and the large landless population thereby created was forced to find new means of survival.[4]

The size of the population grew at an unprecedented rate in these same years, jumping from 9 million in 1876 to 15 million by 1910. However, it was concentrated far from the northern border; while the population density in 1890 averaged about 90 persons per square mile in the central region, it was below 3 in the big semidesert border state of Sonora.[5] But in the 1880s, American companies began developing mines in Sonora and paid high wages to attract a labor force. Both Mexicans from the interior and Americans from Arizona responded, and a two-way population movement emerged between Arizona towns like Tucson, Tombstone, and Douglas and Sonoran towns and rancherias. This movement was greatly accelerated by completion of the U.S. campaign to forcibly evict the last Native American Indian tribes active in the Southwest and by construction of the first cross-border railroads. In 1884, Mexico City was linked to El Paso, and through that rail hub to Los Angeles and the Midwest. By the end of the decade, American labor agents were active in such recruit-ing centers as El Paso and Laredo organizing migrant work forces needed to pick cotton, clear land for farms and pastures, and build and maintain the new railroads. Seasonal labor was thus already quite common throughout the region when the first systematic study of Mexican migration was made for the U.S. Department of Labor in 1908. As the report observed:

> The Mexicans who cross the border to work are either making their first trip to the United States or are making a second or third seasonal visit from the interior of Mexico or are of that big class of American-Mexican frontier residents who reside intermittently in either country. These last are apt to travel widely or work regularly, except during cotton-picking time in Texas and in Oklahoma; their migratory habits are not of recent origin and they are not vacating old industries in Mexico to enter new occupations in the United States.[6]

The growth of the Mexican migrant population was made possible by the "open door" immigration policy of the federal government throughout the nineteenth century. Aside from the Alien and Sedition Acts of 1798 (repealed in 1800), immigration into the United States was unrestricted for most of the nation's first century.[7] Selective screening began only in 1875 with a statute banning immigration by convicts and prostitutes. In 1882 the first general immigration law was enacted. It imposed a head tax (50 cents) on each immigrant and added to the list of proscribed entrants the insane and others likely to become public charges. In the spring of that year, Congress approved the Chinese Exclusion Acts, culminating years of increasingly violent nativist hostility and discrimination against Chinese immigrants in California. Besides prejudice against their non-European customs and religions, this legislation reflected the fact that, after their early period of employment largely in mining and railroad construction, the Chinese tended to settle in towns and cities where natives came to see them as competitors for jobs. Also, like the later Japanese immigrants (whose entry would be curtailed by a 1907–08 bilateral "gentlemen's agreement"), their efforts to buy property and become self-employed put them in competition with powerful business interests. Although Mexicans were also victimized by discrimination and were resented by some native workers, they remained far more rural, short-term migrants, and demand for them rose as employers in agriculture lost their Asian work forces.

Two legislative changes that had the potential to begin limiting entry from Mexico occurred in 1885 and 1891. The former year saw passage of the Alien Contract Labor Law, banning direct contracting of alien workers by American employers. While congressional advocates claimed it would assuage the rising fears of some indigenous workers that immigrants were taking jobs from them and driving down wage levels, it was enforced with great discretion and with negligible effect on Mexicans. Part of the reason for this was a loophole in the law: a violation was said to occur only when a migrant arrived at the border with a pre-arranged U.S. employment contract. American employers simply instructed their labor agents to wait until migrants had stepped over the border before signing them up for work. Also, until 1891, enforcement of immigration law was left to individual states. That year the federal government assigned this responsibility to a new Bureau of Immigration (initially set up within the Treasury Department). The enabling legislation also provided for regulation of overland immigration from Mexico and Canada. It was not, however, Mexicans that were to be kept out but rather any Chinese or other proscribed groups trying to circumvent the

tighter inspections at seaports. The 1,945-mile border with Mexico remained largely unguarded until 1924, when the small mounted patrol (never more than 75 men) active since 1904 was replaced by a new U.S. Border Patrol (initially 450 men, their numbers doubled by 1930).[8]

1917–1929

At the beginning of this century, the Rio Grande was still an open border for the Mexican workers moving back and forth across it regularly. In 1908, the first year in which border posts were authorized to make full counts of overland migration, 6,067 Mexican immigrants were recorded.[9] But by 1917 three times as many migrants were arriving and the 1920s saw an average of over 72,000 per year. One reason for this growth was no doubt the increased refugee outflows caused by the turmoil of the Mexican Revolution of 1910–1917. But the dominant forces were those on the demand side. This period saw especially rapid economic growth in the Southwest with the completion of huge irrigation systems. The need for large numbers of laborers to work the millions of acres of new farmland was made all the more urgent by the onset of World War I. The United States' entry into the war in 1917 drew millions of rural workers into uniform or into the generally more skilled, higher-paying jobs in defense plants. The resulting labor shortage seemed likely to worsen due to a law passed that same year requiring prospective immigrants to pass a literacy test and pay an eight-dollar entry tax before admission could be granted. However, President Wilson not only had this waived for Mexican immigrants but authorized an "Emergency Labor Program" in which the U.S. Employment Service itself acted as a labor contractor to recruit more such workers.

Mexico was also exempted (along with other Western Hemisphere nations) from the ethnocentric national origins quota system created by the immigration acts of 1921 and 1924. This system, which was to remain in place for the next 40 years, was designed to cut the high volume of Southern and Eastern European entrants. Migration of workers from Mexico was thus able to fill many of the new unskilled jobs in the Southwest generated by the 1920s boom.[10] Mexican migration jumped from just over 91,000 in 1915–1919 to 255,774 in the first half of the twenties, and another 498,945 entrants were recorded between 1925 and 1929.[11]

This period marked the beginning of two trends that were to become increasingly important in later years. First, the wartime labor shortage opened a wider spectrum of jobs for Mexican workers (as for women and blacks). Significant numbers were for the first time in demand by such manufacturing industries as auto, food-processing, iron, and steel. Such jobs both introduced them to new sectors of the American labor market and began to disperse the Mexican population beyond the rural border areas into other states and cities.[12] The higher earnings offered farther inland, especially in industry, were of course a key motivating factor behind this transition. In 1920, real hourly wages (valued in 1967 U.S. dollars) in Mexico averaged only about 20 to 25 cents in agriculture and 50 to 75 cents in industry (factories, mines, railroads), while the average industrial wage in the United States was three to four dollars.[13]

In addition, the distinction between "legal" and "illegal" immigration only began to gain currency at this time. The tightening of immigration restrictions in 1917–1924 made the formerly straightforward act of immigration a cumbersome process demanding birth certificates, evidence of good mental and physical health, proof that one would not become a public charge, visa fees, and entry taxes. For the poor, illiterate peasants long accustomed to free movement into the territories of the Mexican Cession, these new requirements might well have seemed unnecessary administrative interference. Up to this time the border was little more than an imaginary line through a unified Mexican–Anglo economy in which the migrant work force had become incorporated as a vital component. The repeated *ad hoc* exemptions of Mexicans in past immigration policy no doubt stemmed from an awareness of their importance. After its enormous investment, both military and economic (particularly the massive federal land grants to the new railroads), in the region, Washington viewed business access to a low-wage labor reserve as crucial to profitable business expansion in the Southwest.[14] The government was also certainly not unaware of the fact that, in the 1920s, nearly all American foreign investments were in either Mexico, Canada, or Cuba. Good relations were especially important with revolutionary Mexico because it posed the greatest potential danger of nationalization of American-owned oil fields, mines, and ranches.

1929–1941

With the onset of the Great Depression, the border gates swung shut. Rather than seek a legislative quota for Mexican admissions, the State Department simply used its administrative powers to tighten visa standards. In addition, in 1929 the Registry Act was passed, which for the first time made illegal immigration by an individual a misdemeanor, punishable by up to one year in prison and a maximum fine of $1,000.

As the unemployment rate continued surging upward, both federal and local officials sought to slash the number of immigrants still in the United States. What followed was the controversial "Mexican Repatriation" of the early 1930s. This appears to have occurred in two main phases. Late 1929 to mid-1931 was a period of largely voluntary return migration by about 200,000 *repatriados* unable to find work, of whom three-fourths relied entirely on their own resources or those offered by Mexican mutual-aid societies and Mexico's consular force. From the middle of 1931 on, the deepening depression led overburdened states and cities, denied any significant relief aid from the government of President Hoover, to begin offering various subsidies (e.g., small cash grants, rail tickets, food parcels for the journey home) to aliens who would return to Mexico. The federal government's main contribution was to announce a stepped-up deportation drive, which actually deported relatively few but probably frightened many thousands into fleeing on their own. An estimated one-half million returned to Mexico in the years 1929–37, with 138,519 leaving at the peak in 1931.[15]

1942–1964

United States entry into the Second World War at the end of 1941 reversed this process with remarkable speed. Another labor shortage occurred for much the same reasons as in 1917–18, but was intensified by the government's drastic decision to force 100,000 Japanese and Japanese Americans into concentration camps. Under mounting pressure from southwestern business, President Franklin Roosevelt, in August, 1942, signed a bilateral agreement with Mexico for another emergency wartime program of importing labor. This was known as the *bracero* program (from the Spanish for "working hand"). It recruited 52,000 workers in its first year, half for crop harvesting and the rest for railway maintenance. Although the agreement stipulated that those in the program were to be given the same wages and employment protections as Americans in comparable jobs, the Labor Department relied largely on "self-policing"; abuses appear to have been widespread. Nevertheless, and despite mounting opposition by organized labor, the program was renewed after the war. As the economy began its extraordinary postwar expansion, which was to produce a doubling of real GNP between 1946 and 1966, business leaders lobbied hard for a continued supply of low-wage migrant labor. The U.S. labor market tightened after the war (the annual civilian unemployment rate was below 4 percent from 1943 to 1948) and employers sought to prolong the employment of *braceros* as long as possible. One avenue many followed was to request that the Immigration and Naturalization Service adjust their migrant workers' status from temporary *braceros* to permanent resident immigrants. Or course, the more permanent migrants become in a receiving country the more they will seek to have their families join them. In this way the *bracero* program expanded the volume of legal entry from Mexico. It stimulated increased illegal entry as well, since those not granted legal status for themselves or their relatives by the U.S. Immigration and Naturalization Service (INS) were often encouraged by their employers to enter surreptitiously. In addition, since many more job-seekers traveled to the program's recruitment stations (concentrated near the border) than were selected, unsuccessful candidates often joined the illegal influx. Before its demise in late 1964, the *bracero* program was importing over 400,000 per year at its peak in 1956–1959. In many of its 23 years the number of persons apprehended for illegal entry from Mexico exceeded the number of legal *bracero* entrants.[16]

1965–1990

The end of the *bracero* program coincided with the beginning of a new American immigration system. In 1965, Congress, under

TABLE 3   Immigrants Admitted to the U.S., 1961–88, by Region and Country of Origin (in thousands)

Place of Origin	1961–70	1971–80	1981–88
All Countries	3,321.7	4,493.3	4,710.6
Europe	1,238.6	801.3	510.3
Asia	445.3	1,633.8	2,166.7
Central America	97.7	132.4	211.5
El Salvador	15.0	34.4	76.6
Guatemala	15.4	25.6	36.5
Panama	18.4	22.7	22.2
Nicaragua	10.1	13.0	23.7
South America	228.3	284.4	311.3
Colombia	70.3	77.6	85.0
Ecuador	37.0	50.2	36.1
Peru	18.6	29.1	38.5
Argentina	42.1	25.1	16.9
Cuba	256.8	276.8	138.5
Dominican Republic	94.1	148.0	182.8
Mexico	443.3	637.2	569.1

Source: U.S. Immigration and Naturalization Service (1988, 1989a).

pressure from the Civil Rights movement and the booming economy's demand for labor, abolished the racist national-origins quotas in favor of a new set of criteria stressing family reunification. Since the system went fully into effect in 1968, permanent residence status has been granted according to a set of seven preference categories so designed that about 9 out of 10 places have gone to relatives of U.S. residents, the residual divided between refugees and the small number admitted on occupational grounds. Annual limits were established for the Eastern (170,000) and Western (120,000) Hemispheres, as well as annual numeric quotas of 20,000 per country from the Eastern Hemisphere. But the exemption of immediate relatives of U.S. citizens and of many political refugees from these limits has enabled annual inflows to far exceed the nominal 290,000 ceiling. The result has been not only an additional 100,000 or more legal entrants per year but also a dramatic compositional change: as Table 3 shows, the proportion from Europe declined

from 59 percent of those arriving in the 1950s to only 18 percent of entrants in the 1970s, while the Asian share leapt from 6.2 percent to 36 percent and the Latin American percentage from 22 to 40.

Of all the countries in the world, Mexico has consistently sent the largest number of immigrants here since 1965. Over 443,000 were admitted legally in the 1960s, another 637,000 in the 1970s, and more have entered from that one country in the 1980s than from all the European nations combined (Table 3). This was for a time thought to reflect the exemption of Western Hemisphere nations from the 20,000 per-country maximum. But new legislation extended this same quota to the Western Hemisphere in 1977. The immediate result was a drop in the number of legal entrants from Mexico of 24 percent from the year before. Nevertheless, 44,600 Mexican immigrants were admitted in 1977 and the following year over 90,000 immigrated—the highest number of any postwar year. The principal reason for this increase is that, while many workers from Mexico return home after only a few years employment in the United States, enough settled here over the long history of this migration to have created a large resident population by the 1960s. The 1960 census counted 575,902 U.S. residents who were born in Mexico and over twice as many others (1,160,090) with one or both parents born there. Ten years later, these numbers had risen to 759,711 and 1,579,440.[17] The 1965 legal changes thus made possible the entry of large numbers on the nonquota visas set aside for reunification of immediate family members.

Still, the supply of visas fell far short of the demand and thousands continued to enter without legal documents. A large number were former participants in the *bracero* program denied readmission after the program ended. In the course of the program's more than two decades, involving 4.5 million participants, information on job opportunities in the United States and on the easiest methods to enter and find work had been widely disseminated in Mexico, stimulating increased illegal migration. Border apprehensions rose from 55,349 in 1965 to over a million per year in the late 1970s.

But the recent patterns of legal and illegal immigration cannot be explained independently of labor supply conditions in Mexico. Like the United States, Mexico experienced a remarkable period of economic growth between World War II and the mid-sixties. The rate of growth in real Gross Domestic Product (GDP) averaged an impressive 6 percent annually in the 1940s. During the years of "stabilizing development" from 1954 to 1971, average annual real GDP growth was 6 to 8 percent and inflation was held to an average rate below 5 percent. Industrial output jumped fivefold between 1940 and 1965. Significant progress was also recorded in education and health. The percentage of the population (ages six and over) who were illiterate fell from 58.3 percent in 1940 to 28.3 percent in 1970. Average life expectancy at birth rose from only 38.9 years to 60.2 between 1940 and 1970. And the falling mortality rate helped the population more than double in size, from 19.6 million in 1940 to 42 million just a quarter century later.[18]

However, the postwar development strategy also produced severe structural problems and greater income inequality, as was to become painfully evident in the spiraling economic crises of the 1970s and 1980s. Successive governments relied heavily on attracting foreign investment, which nearly doubled in volume (in U.S. dollars) in the course of the 1950s and then nearly tripled in the sixties. Over 70 percent of the investment was from a single country, the United States, and U.S.-based companies had by 1970 acquired control of over 50 percent of such key industries as aluminum, automobiles, computers, electrical machinery, industrial chemicals, mining, and pharmaceuticals.[19] Of the country's biggest 100 industrial firms, 47 were foreign owned. From the revenue earned in their Mexican operations, the outflow of their payments to foreign investors was, on average, three to four times larger than the profits reinvested in Mexico.[20] The strong preference of these firms for importing new capital for their plants accounted for an estimated one-third of the country's widening trade deficit in the 1970s. The concentration of agricultural investments in export-oriented crops at the expense of corn and other mass subsistence crops led to sharply rising agricultural imports, which actually exceeded the value of agricultural exports by the early 1980s.[21] The nation's trade deficit in 1980 was four times its 1970 level and growing.

Since much of the postwar investment boom was directed at capital-intensive rather than labor-intensive industries, employment and wage benefits were relatively slim for the bulk of the population. This was especially dramatic in agriculture, where employment dropped by 900,000 in the 1960s, despite the continuing increase in the rural population. Among those with jobs, the all-industry real wage was cut in half between 1939 and 1946 and rose so slowly thereafter that it did not reach the 1939 level again until 1968. The far more rapid increases in returns to capital had the effect of worsening the already severe inequality of income. In 1950 the richest 10 percent of families received 49 percent of all family income, the poorest 10 percent only 2.7 percent.[22] But by 1969 the top decile had increased its share still more to 51 percent as that of the bottom decile shrank to 2 percent. In fact, the richest 5 percent captured a share (36 percent) of income that year that was more than twice as large as the shares of the bottom 50 percent of families combined. The expanded stock of educational and health care services were also distributed in a sharply skewed manner, both regionally and socioeconomically, greatly favoring urban middle- and upper-class families.[23]

The impetus for emigration provided by these trends was greatly intensified by the U.S. recession of 1973–75. It was to be expected that Mexico, by now tightly integrated with the American economy, would be adversely affected. But this proved to be the beginning of a crisis of startling depth and duration. A massive wage of bankruptcies and capital flight forced the Mexican government to seek foreign financial aid. Under pressure from the International Monetary Fund, it adopted an austerity program and devalued the peso by almost 100 percent late in 1976. This in turn nearly doubled import costs and the real value of the foreign debt, as well as slashing the purchasing power of personal incomes. Salaried workers watched their real earnings plummet 36 percent between 1978 and 1980, and the mass of nonunionized private sector laborers unprotected by wage indexation programs suffered even more.[24] The underemployment rate climbed to an estimated 50.3 percent of the labor force.[25] According to the World Bank measure of poverty-level income, more than one out of every three Mexican families were poor in 1977.

Despite some recovery in GDP growth rates from expanded oil production in the late seventies, the "economic crisis" had, by the early eighties, deteriorated into a "national emergency." The onset of a steep fall in world oil prices, rising interest rates, and a severe American recession in 1982 pushed Mexico into its worst depression since the 1930s. Nearly 1 million lost their jobs and the inflation rate topped 100 percent. When, in August 1982, the Lopez Portillo administration revealed that it was unable to meet payments due on the $66 billion public debt for at least three months, a worldwide financial crisis was threatened. The $10 billion international bailout that followed saved the banking industry but still left the nation deeply in debt, its export earnings mortgaged long into the future. The three peso devaluations that year completed a 10-fold decline in its exchange value with the dollar since 1976. What this meant for workers and the unemployed was that the purchasing power of their peso incomes was dropping at the same time that the relative value of the dollars that could be earned north of the border increased.

In the United States, the public concern about undocumented immigration that had been growing since the mid-seventies was intensified by reports by the U.S. Immigration and Naturalization Service of a surge in illegal entrants from Mexico during the 1982 crisis. With the unemployment rate at a postwar high, the argument (heard in every recession of at least the last century) that new immigrants were depressing natives' wages and job opportunities won new popularity. A lengthy congressional drive (starting in the late 1970s) to punish firms employing undocumented workers culminated in November of 1986 when President Reagan signed the Immigration Reform and Control Act (IRCA).

IRCA's two main components are (1) a requirement that all nonfarm employers hiring new workers (after November 1986) obtain at least two documents from each of them verifying that they are citizens or aliens with legal authorization to work. For each worker, a new form (called I-9) must be signed by the employer verifying that the required documents have been examined. Employers are obligated to keep this form for at least three years and may not dispose of it until one year after the relevant employee has stopped working for the firm. Firms violating the law were made subject to fines of from $250 to $10,000 and those engaging in a "pattern and practice" of violations could be sentenced to up to six months in prison. Aliens found to use false documents to get a job can be fined up to $2,000 and imprisoned for up to two years. (2) A general amnesty program was established for a one-year period during which legal status as a Temporary Resident Alien (TRA) was to be granted those undocumented migrants who provided evidence of continuous residence in the United States since January 1, 1982. After 18 months in TRA status, aliens would then be allowed to apply for permanent residence alien status. Applications for amnesty were only accepted through May 4, 1988 and full enforcement of employer sanctions began the following month.

Of the 1.75 million undocumented TRA applicants who filed by the deadline, about three out of four were from Mexico. Another 1.3 million sought the Special Agricultural Worker (SAW) amnesty before its deadline date of November 30, 1988. The SAW amnesty could be obtained by producing evidence that an alien had worked in perishable agriculture in the United States for at least 90 days in the 12 months ended May 1, 1986.

Although the INS identified nearly 400,000 of these as potentially fraudulent claims, it investigated only a tiny fraction, citing inadequate staff after three years of budget cuts. Nine out of 10 amnesty applications in both programs were approved in 1989.[26]

The Mexican-origin population in the United States had grown to 12.1 million by 1988. Our knowledge of its demographic and socioeconomic characteristics has improved considerably over the past decade, thanks both to expanded government data collection and to a new wave of social science research on immigration and ethnic minorities. The component of this population about which we know the least is, of course, the undocumented. Nevertheless, a body of generally consistent findings has emerged in the literature on their number and their salient features. First, contrary to the high speculative figures cited throughout the public debates of the 1970s and early eighties, Census Bureau demographers estimated that there were probably no more than about 3.5 million undocumented aliens in the United States in 1980, of whom about half came from Mexico.[27] The number of new illegal entrants from Mexico in the early 1980s each year was estimated by Passel and Woodrow (1987) to have averaged about 140,000 per year. In light of the 3 million who actually surfaced to take advantage of the amnesty program in 1987–89, the Census Bureau's figures do not appear to have been nearly as far off the mark as many critics long thought.

Research in the 1930s and 1940s suggested that the majority of the undocumented originated in only four Mexican states—Guanajuato, Jalisco, Michoacan, and Nuevo Leon—only the last of which bordered the United States. Since then there has been increasing evidence of a widening distribution of migrants across the country.

Samora's (1971) study of a sample of 493 Mexicans apprehended for illegal entry in 1969 found that only 30 percent had been born in these four states. The largest number (representing 18.5 percent of the total) were from the northern border state of Chihuahua, and four other border states together accounted for 14.2 percent. Likewise, in a study of 481 undocumented Mexicans apprehended in 1975, North and Houston (1976) found that only one-third were from the four states that had supplied most prewar emigrants.[28] Chihuahua accounted for 11.2 percent of the sample, and four other border states for another 16.4 percent. Unlike the Samora data, North and Houston had information on the state of residence before emigration, not the state of birth. Their findings thus reflect the growing internal movement of the Mexican population toward the northern centers of rapid industrialization and urbanization.

The undocumented population from Mexico has long had a larger fraction with rural backgrounds than any other major sending country. In the North–Houston sample, most hailed from small- or medium-sized towns and nearly half worked in agriculture before emigrating. Two-thirds were from hometowns with populations of 2,500 or more and 9 percent were from cities of over 1 million. In contrast, over half of those interviewed who were from other Western Hemisphere nations (85 percent of whom were from other Spanish-speaking countries) originated in cities of over a million inhabitants.

The Mexican migrants interviewed were also largely young and male. Nearly 47 percent were between 16 and 24 years old. The mean age (27.6) was far below the U.S. average that year (39). The fact that 9 out of 10 were male doubtless reflects the way in which the sample was collected. Only those aliens already on U.S. soil and apprehended by the INS were included. Migrants denied admission at a port of entry are not counted as apprehensions by the INS. Since the INS estimates that a sizable portion of those denied admission are women, reliance on apprehension data entails a sampling bias toward males.

Over 43 percent of the Mexicans interviewed had completed fewer than five years of schooling, and another 42 percent had only between five and eight years. Fewer than 1 percent had received any higher, post-secondary education, compared with over 27 percent of the American labor force in 1973. The mean number of years of educational attainment was 4.9 among the undocumented, 7.5 years lower than the U.S. average. The lower the schooling level, the weaker the knowledge of English. Three out of four said they spoke it "very badly" or "not at all" and another 15.3 percent "not very well." Only 1.5 percent spoke English "very well."

Despite the average undocumented Mexican's relatively young age, limited schooling, and unfamiliarity with English, other characteristics could count in his favor with American employers. First, most are experienced workers, with a mean of nine and one-half years of paid employment behind them in Mexico. Almost 7 percent had white-collar occupations and a substantial number had industrial experience. Nearly 13 percent were formerly machine operatives, another 11.8 percent nonfarm laborers, and 15 percent skilled craftsmen. They also tended to have considerable familiarity with the U.S. labor market and a support network of friends, relatives, and other migrants. Nearly 58 percent said they knew other undocumented migrants in their hometown and 54 percent had lived with other migrants while in the United States. Almost one in every three had relatives living north of the border. Of all migrants of all nationalities interviewed, 45 percent had found their most recent U.S. job through friends or relatives and over half of the respondents had undocumented coworkers. Mexicans were three times more likely than others to work alongside fellow migrants. Finally, most had ample cause to be highly motivated job-seekers and workers. The trek into the United States is risky and costly, usually demanding the investment of much of one's own meager funds together with loans from relatives and others. The debts and other obligations incurred by the typical migrant were such that 9 out of 10 Mexicans reported they sent money home and the average monthly remittance ($169) was over a third of mean monthly earnings. At home were an average of over five dependents per migrant, most relying on these remittances for over half their needs.

In the United States, most of the undocumented succeeded not only in earning far higher wages than were available in Mexico but in working nearly continuously throughout their stay. The average duration of residence before apprehension by the INS of those in the North–Houston study was 2.4 years, of which an estimated 2.1 years were occupied by paid employment. More than one in five had the same job for two years or more. And for most the new jobs represented upward occupational mobility. The proportion doing farm labor (27 percent) was cut to nearly half that in their pre-migration job distribution, an identical fraction found manufacturing jobs, and one-fifth went into construction. They were still eight times more likely than Americans to be farm workers. But the longer an individual's residence in the United States, the less likely he or she was still a farm laborer: of those who stayed two years or more, only 11 percent were still in agriculture, while 39 percent worked in manufacturing.

Still, only 1.2 percent were hired into white-collar jobs, and the mean hourly wage was $2.34, only about half that of the average male production worker in the United States at the time. Nearly one of every four

was paid below the legal minimum wage. The fact that an equal fraction was regularly paid in cash probably reflects the intention of many American employers to avoid leaving any documented proof of exploitative wages. Below-minimum pay was most common in agriculture and in nonunion workplaces. But only 1 in 10 of the undocumented had been represented by an American labor union.

Despite the impression one might get from all the attention given the undocumented, the clear majority of Mexican-born residents of the United States are legal aliens or naturalized citizens. Compared with the undocumented, they are far more likely to come from urban areas of Mexico, have more schooling, and higher average skill levels. This has been confirmed by a unique longitudinal data set that tracks a large sample of individuals admitted to the United States with legal immigrant status between 1973 and 1974. As reported by Portes and Bach (1985), the sample consisted of 822 Mexican immigrants first interviewed in El Paso and Laredo, as well as 590 Cubans interviewed in Miami. Their study sample was restricted to males who were between the ages of 18 and 60 and household heads (i.e., not dependent on others for their livelihood). In addition to the 1973–74 interviews, the same individuals were reinterviewed in 1976 and again in 1979.[29]

Like the undocumented in the North–Houston survey, the legal migrant sample reflected the northward population shift in Mexico. Although three-tenths of their fathers came from the four states that dominated prewar emigration, only 22.3 percent of the sons lived in these states by their sixteenth birthday and only 11.1 percent still lived there just prior to moving to the United States. Almost three out of four were born in one of the northern states. Over 30 percent lived in Chihuahua alone just before emigrating. Nearly 47 percent of the sample were born in a town or city of 10,000 or more inhabitants and 19.2 percent in large cities of 100,000 or more. Rural-urban migration resulted in one-half reporting residence in a large city by the time of emigration.

The educational attainment of these migrants was certainly low by U.S. standards, but it surpassed that of their parents and that of their undocumented countrymen. Only 2.4 percent had no formal education. Nearly two-thirds completed at least primary school, one-fourth completed secondary school, 9 percent finished postsecondary business or vocational training, and 3.6 percent attended a university. Just as their fathers had schooling and occupational levels above average for Mexico at the time, so also did their sons. Only 34.4 percent of the fathers and 11.5 percent of their sons were farm laborers. Almost one in four sons held manufacturing jobs and 46.2 percent were skilled workers, artisans, or semiskilled urban laborers before emigrating.

Seven out of 10 in the sample had lived in the United States before their legal entry as immigrants in 1973–74, the majority for between one and three years. The importance of return migration to the volume of legal immigration increased with the 1965 legal reforms in the American admissions criteria. The long tradition of Mexican migration into the Southwest meant that many south of the border had relatives already in the United States who could aid their entry. Others could take advantage of the relatively porous border to live and work in the country illegally for a time so as to acquire the social and economic contacts needed to gain legal admission later. Information about survival in the American labor market was available from the many former migrants who had returned home. Cornelius (1978) found that half of a sample of Mexican immigrants entering the United States since 1969 had fathers who themselves once

worked here. Portes and Bach made a valuable effort to distinguish the returnees from the 30 percent of their sample who only entered the country for the first time once they could be admitted legally. They found first-time immigrants tended to be younger and slightly better educated than returnees. Their background was more urban and their fathers held more skilled occupations.

Both first-time migrants and returnees were able to rely on cross-border social networks. Only 2 percent of the 1973–74 cohort had no relatives or friends to meet them when they entered the United States. They arrived remarkably well informed about the work they could expect to do. Nearly 8 in 10 knew where their American employer lived. And comparisons of their occupational expectations, as stated in 1973–74, with their actual occupations in 1976 and 1979 showed a close correspondence emerging in most categories the longer their stay. The most unexpected outcome was the 51.5 percent hired into semiskilled urban jobs by 1976. This was twice the proportion in such jobs in Mexico, but as more moved into skilled and service employment, by 1979 the fraction in semiskilled work fell almost to two-fifths.

Ethnic networks extended into most migrants' workplaces. A majority (54 percent) of those interviewed said they worked primarily among Mexican coworkers. These firms were mainly small- to medium-sized, with those whose work forces consisted of 6–20 employees accounting for one-fifth of the Mexican sample and firms with 21–100 employees accounting for another one-fourth of the sample. Only 15.1 percent worked in firms owned by a Mexican national or a Mexican American. Likewise, the respondents reported that in their community they made consumer purchases overwhelmingly in stores owned by non-Mexicans. Even when buying small items, only 27.7 percent bought primarily from Mexican-run stores. This is unsurprising in light of the low rate of self-employment (5.5 percent in 1979) among the migrants.

Finally, despite the generally weak presence of labor unions in the Southwest, over one-fourth of the Mexican workers surveyed were union members. And, when a local union was present at their workplaces, 9 out of 10 migrants joined. In light of the oft-cited difficulties of organizing immigrants, particularly those isolated on farms or in small businesses, this finding may seem quite surprising. In fact, Mexican immigrants have a long history of participation in southwestern union organizing and strikes stretching back to the early years of this century, when Mexican miners were active in the Industrial Workers of the World (IWW). But their role in the union movement only began to attract public attention in the 1960s as a result of the United Farm Workers (UFW) Organizing Committee's grape boycott. Since that time, while the crisis of the national union movement has deepened, Mexican workers have often been at the forefront of organizing activities among low-wage firms in the region. James Cockcroft (1986) has documented their efforts in restaurants, hotels, garment, auto assembly, ship building, and other industries during the 1970s and early 1980s. The evidence of the recent past, coupled with their steadily growing numeric importance in the work force, suggests that Mexican Americans may play a pivotal role in any future reversal of union fortunes.

Puerto Ricans

The Puerto Rican population on the U.S. mainland is only about one-fifth as numerous as Mexican Americans, with marked political, cultural, and economic differences. Nonetheless, both originate from former Spanish colonies that were invaded by the U.S. military and strongly influenced there-

after by American economic development. From Columbus's landing in 1493 until the end of the eighteenth century, Spain's interest in the island was largely confined to its small gold deposits and strategic location on the main sea lane to Europe. After only 30 years of colonization, the native Indian population (an estimated 30,000 Tainos) had been decimated by forced labor and smallpox, the gold mines were exhausted, and the economy was consigned to two centuries of economic stagnation. Despite the use of low-cost Indian and African slave labor to raise cattle and grow sugarcane, the island remained so poor that the costs of the San Juan military garrison and the colonial administration had to be regularly subsidized by the Viceroyship of Mexico.

As the demands on the Spanish treasury mounted late in the eighteenth century, the Crown sought to stimulate greater Puerto Rican self-financing by liberalizing trade relations, allowing European settlers to buy some of the land long monopolized by the state, and offering incentives to new immigration. The result was a larger increase in population growth (in both absolute and percentage terms) in the last 35 years of the century than in all of the previous 250. Colonial restrictions relaxed even more as increasing amounts of Spain's resources were required to fight Napoleon's invasion in 1809 and the Latin American wars of independence that raged until 1824. The economy began to shift from subsistence production to a stronger export orientation, led by expanding sales of sugar (and its rum and molasses by-products) to the United States. Sugar haciendas acquired a growing share of the island's cultivable land, and their increased labor needs (intensified by the decline of the slave trade) were met by the creation of a large, landless wage-labor force. "Antivagrancy" laws (the *libreta* system) were put into effect to coerce the sizable number of squatters and free peasant small-holders to work on the haciendas. But in the 1870s, increased competition from European beet sugar and from low-cost cane producers using new extraction technologies overwhelmed the backward Puerto Rican industry. The investment funds it needed for modernization were unavailable, thanks to Spain's colonial policy of siphoning off any agricultural surplus and suppressing development of indigenous credit institutions.

Coffee displaced sugar as the leading export crop in the last third of the nineteenth century and in so doing moderated the pace of capitalist agricultural development. While still furthering the growth of a wage-labor force, the coffee industry also created parallel opportunities for small-scale subsistence farming. This resulted from the custom of protecting coffee plants by growing them interspersed with other crops, like bananas and plantains. Coupled with the modest capital requirements for preparing coffee for the market, this enabled many independent peasants to produce both a cash crop and the foods needed for their family's subsistence.

By the end of the nineteenth century, the island's embryonic capitalist economy strained against Spain's continuing commercial, credit, and political restrictions. Many of the immigrants who had fueled the country's population and economic growth were refugees from other rebellious colonies, and their conservatism long contained the developing nationalist movement. But as the economic power of the merchants and large landowners increased, so did their demands for greater independence. Fearing the loss of one of its last imperial possessions, Spain agreed in 1897 to a Charter of Autonomy, which provided for popular election of a bicameral legislature with extensive powers over taxation, budgeting, trade, tariffs, and commercial treaties.

On July 28, 1898, just eight days after the first meeting of the elected Puerto Rican legislature, 16,000 American troops invaded Puerto Rico. In one of the last acts of the Spanish-American War, the United States expended only 21 days and four American lives to seize the island. With the construction of the Panama Canal already planned, Puerto Rico held great strategic value in addition to its demonstrated economic potential. The new legislature was closed down and for the next two years the island was under direct U.S. military control. In May 1900, military rule was replaced by civilian rule, but the key civilians were all Americans and presidential appointees. The 1900 Foraker Act delineated the exhaustive U.S. control over the new colony (formally called a "non-incorporated territory"): the dollar was to replace the local peso as the sole monetary unit, all tariff setting and treaty making were put in American hands, all goods traded with the mainland had to be carried on American-owned ships, English was made the official language of instruction (though only a handful of local teachers spoke it), and, in perhaps the most insulting decree of all, the island's name was Americanized to "Porto" Rico—the official spelling until 1932.

Puerto Rican protests that Spanish colonialism had simply been replaced by American colonialism found an increasingly sympathetic audience in Washington once the mobilization for World War I began. The island's work force was seen as a means to cope with worsening U.S. labor shortages, and the island's role as a coaling station for American warships assumed new importance with the sighting of German submarines in the Caribbean. In March 1917, one month before the United States entered the war, the Jones Act became law. This expanded Puerto Rican political rights to the extent that it authorized a new elective, bicameral legislature, gave all males (but not females) ages 21 and over voting rights, and granted U.S. citizenship to all Puerto Ricans from this point onward. But the U.S.. president and Congress retained final veto power over all bills passed by the island legislature, and all the colonial economic controls defined by the Foraker Act were continued. This remained the legal structure for U.S.–Puerto Rican relations from 1917 to 1947.

The American takeover immediately accelerated the transformation of Puerto Rico into an agrarian capitalist economy. The flourishing coffee industry was singled out for contraction in favor of an extraordinary expansion of sugar production. Two of the biggest markets for Puerto Rican coffee were quickly lost when Cuba and Spain, viewing the island as a foreign possession after 1898, substantially raised their tariffs on its coffee. The United States proved to be no help in compensating for these lost sales. Never an important market for the strong Puerto Rican coffee, it imported weaker South American coffees at lower prices. Washington refused to grant special tariff protection to Puerto Rican coffee, leaving it uncompetitive with its rivals. Coffee's share of total island exports collapsed from 60 percent in 1897 to 19.5 percent in 1901, and kept falling to a mere 2.5 percent in 1928.[30]

In sharp contrast, Puerto Rican sugar was granted protection from foreign competitors behind high tariff walls. The reason was not difficult to discern. The American taste for sugar had, by the turn of the century, made it the world's second biggest consumer (per capita), exceeded only by Great Britain. American investors rushed in to buy up the best Puerto Rican land and quickly dominated the industry. Four giant U.S. corporations controlled 24 percent of all cane land by 1930 and produced over half the local ground sugar. Since the majority of sugar exports had long gone to the mainland, the expansion of sugar rapidly increased the economy's dependence on the American market: only one-fifth of the island's trade was with the United States in 1897, but by 1900 that share had leapt to 68 percent. By 1930, the United States accounted for 96 percent of Puerto Rico's exports and 87 percent of its imports.[31]

In addition to sugar, two other industries, tobacco and needlework, attracted U.S. investment capital, which initiated the development of the island's manufacturing sector. Cigar production was transformed from strictly artisan techniques to mechanized factory-based methods dependent only on wage labor. Needlework followed a similar path from a rural cottage industry to large-scale textile production. But the tobacco boom did not survive the 1920s, owing to the steep decline in cigar sales as American consumption and production of cigarettes grew. Textile production began to thrive only in the years after the Great Depression.

The U.S. authorities could claim credit for important advances in schooling, health care, and basic infrastructural investments. After over 400 years of Spanish colonialism, in 1898 the island had an illiteracy rate of 80 percent and smallpox was rampant. Between the U.S. invasion and 1910, the number of public schools had nearly doubled, the illiteracy rate was cut to 66.5 percent, and a smallpox vaccination program succeeded in lowering the mortality rate. Spanish neglect of the transportation infrastructure was reflected in the fact that only 159 miles of railroad (in several different segments) had been built by 1897, on an island of 3,435 square miles. The United States had expanded the total track miles to 923 by 1930.[32]

But the rate of improvement slowed sharply after the first three or four years. By 1920, the illiteracy rate was still 61 percent, in part because only about two-fifths of rural children were enrolled in a school, mainly in half-day programs, and only one in six stayed beyond the third grade. The average mortality rate fell so slowly, that in 1920 it was still twice the U.S. level. And most of the additional railroads built were owned and largely used for freight haulage by the major sugar corporations. Likewise, non–Puerto Rican absentee owners controlled shipping, banking, and public utilities.[33]

This dependent status made it inevitable that the onset of the Great Depression in the United States would quickly inflict severe damage on the island's export-oriented economy. Between 1929 and 1933, Puerto Rico's nominal GNP fell by one-fourth and per capita income tumbled 30 percent. U.S. Secretary of the Interior Harold Ickes, whose office oversaw American policy toward the island, wrote in 1935:

> Puerto Rico . . . has been the victim of the *laissez-faire* economy which has developed the rapid growth of great absentee owned sugar corporations, which have absorbed much land formerly belonging to small independent growers and who in consequence have been reduced to virtual economic serfdom. While the inclusion of Puerto Rico within our tariff walls has been highly beneficial to the stockholders of those corporations, the benefits have not been passed down to the mass of Puerto Ricans. These on the contrary have seen the lands on which they formerly raised subsistence crops, given over to sugar production while they have been gradually driven to import all their food staples, paying for them the high prices brought about by the tariff. There is today more widespread misery and destitution and far more unemployment in Puerto Rico than at any previous time in its history.[34]

With the standard of living reduced to the level prevailing at the turn of the century and foreign economic domination as complete as it had been under Spanish rule, the depression ignited nationalist movements seeking political independence and economic restructuring. Labor organizations won growing support and launched a strike wave against the giant sugar corporations. By the end of the decade, a powerful new labor confederation (the CGT) had been formed, uniting a wide array of trades under the banner of industrial unionism.

The United States' entry into World War II coincided with the start of a sustained period of economic reorganization in Puerto Rico. In 1941, Luis Munoz Marin of the Popular Democratic Party (PPD) began 24 consecutive years as the top elected official and embarked upon an ambitious program of land reform and government-led industrialization. The fact that Washington went along with this policy no doubt stemmed in part from its concern that undermining the reformist PPD would tip the political balance in favor of the more radical parties demanding home rule. The presence of German submarines in the Caribbean early in the war reemphasized the island's strategic value to the United States. At the same time, with most of the government's attention focused on the Pacific and Atlantic theaters, it left Puerto Rico with considerable autonomy throughout the war. Finally, the new American governor appointed in 1941 was Rexford Tugwell, an early New Dealer in the Roosevelt administration who was predisposed to using interventionist government policies to promote economic stability and growth.

The Munoz program proceeded through two overlapping phases. The initial period (1941–47) focused on land reform and government-led development of infrastructure and of state-owned factories. This was replaced by "Operation Bootstrap" (*Operacion Manos a la Obra*), begun in 1947 to attract foreign investment. The land reform program involved government purchases of corporate-owned farms of 500 acres or more.

Some were reorganized as large worker-managed enterprises, while others were distributed in small parcels to entitled landless farm laborers. However, the program was ended after less than six years, with two-thirds of the large farms still in corporate hands. It was a victim of scarce funds and the government's decision to allocate more resources to its industrialization program. The latter was an import-substitution strategy based on new government-financed and government-operated corporations. Though limited to only four areas (clay building materials, glass products, paperboard, and shoes), it faced mounting opposition from mainland corporations throughout the 1940s. They starved the state enterprises of needed inputs and boycotted their output. The government retreated from this approach and, from the mid-forties on, concentrated mainly on infrastructural improvement to attract foreign investments.

In May of 1947, the Puerto Rican legislature passed the Industrial Incentive Act, inaugurating "Operation Bootstrap." Under its provisions, qualified foreign investors were granted tax-exempt status for 10 years, and a partial exemption for another 3. They also received valuable government benefits such as free use of buildings, utilities, work-training programs, and low-interest loans. The program was initially viewed as temporary, with all exemptions to end by the early 1960s. But the threat by many firms to relocate as soon as their exemptions expired led to new legislation in 1954 and 1963 extending and liberalizing the tax holidays. For example, from 1963 on, foreign investment in less-developed areas outside the main cities could be exempted from all taxes for up to 17 years. For U.S. corporations this meant that virtually all their Puerto Rican income was tax-free, since IRS regulations had long exempted income from Puerto Rican subsidiaries from any U.S. federal income tax.

The rapid industrialization that followed inspired talk of a new "capitalist showcase" in the Caribbean. Between 1948 and 1963 GDP more than doubled, gross investment and exports nearly quadrupled, the contribution of industry to GDP jumped 50 percent and the agricultural share fell by the same amount.[35] Two-thirds of the new foreign firms located in the four biggest cities, which quickly became population magnets. The percentage of the population in urban areas rose from 30.3 percent in 1940 to 44.2 percent in 1960, then climbed in the sixties to nearly 60 percent by the decade's end.

This transformation imposed some serious long-term costs. Among the most obvious was the increase in the already enormous external control over the economy. By 1963 non–Puerto Rican firms accounted for about three-fifths of all manufacturing sales, value-added, and employment. Only four years later, their share had risen to about 70 percent.[36] Ironically, the island's control of its economy was declining just as its formal political autonomy was increasing. In August 1947, President Truman signed legislation that, for the first time, allowed Puerto Ricans to popularly elect their governor. Two years later Public Law 600 gave them the right to draft their own constitution. And in July 1952, 54 years after the U.S. invasion, the island's official status was changed from territory to "commonwealth." But de facto control has stayed with the U.S. Congress and the president, who retain veto power over all legislation and over any proposed changes in the constitution (which have always been rejected). Though the old Jones Act of 1917 has formally been replaced by Federal Relations Law, most of its restrictive provisions live on.

One of the costliest failures of Operation Bootstrap was in the area of job creation. The program was based on the conviction that, since agriculture could not absorb all the country's surplus workers, it should be ignored in favor of maximum attention to rapid industrialization. The subsequent neglect helped speed agriculture's decline: its contribution to total GNP dropped from 17.5 percent to 3.6 percent between 1950 and 1980, and its share of all employment shrank from 36 percent to only 5.3 percent.[37] Until the early 1960s, most of the new investment attracted by the government incentives was in labor-intensive industries, particularly textiles and apparel. By the end of the decade, apparel alone accounted for nearly one-fifth of all manufacturing firms and the same fraction of total employment. Though such growth was acclaimed as the result of Operation Bootstrap, Taylor (1957) found that the industry's relatively low wage scale represented a larger subsidy to investors than tax exemptions. It also appears that almost half of the added jobs in tax-exempt firms simply replaced jobs lost in the largely local firms, who were placed at a competitive disadvantage by the lowered tax costs of their rivals. Manufacturing employment in tax-exempt firms increased by 37,300 from 1947 to 1957, but fell 16,000 over the same period in nonexempt firms.[38]

Of the new jobs that were created in the postwar years, a disproportionately large number were given to women. As the government figures in Table 4 show, women have long had lower rates of unemployment than men on the island. Male discouragement over their inferior job prospects may help explain the remarkable decline in the fraction of Puerto Rican men active in the labor force. In 1950, nearly four out of five males living in Puerto Rico were employed or searching for a job, a labor force participation rate less than 7 percentage points below the American average for all males. As is well known, male participation rates in the United States slowly declined in the

postwar period (to 77.4 percent by 1980), largely because of expanded schooling and the Social Security program's work disincentives for the elderly. But the male rate in Puerto Rico fell far more sharply, to only 60.7 percent by 1980. In three decades, the gap between the U.S. and the Puerto Rican rates more than doubled in size. This cannot be blamed on work disincentives tied to federal transfer programs, because most programs, such as food stamps, were extended to the island in only the early 1970s, and all were, of course, also available to men in the United States whose participation rates nevertheless did not fall as rapidly as those of Puerto Ricans. Nor can it be attributed to increased school enrollment, since this expanded far more on the mainland than on the island. In fact, the secular decline in male labor force participation began in Puerto Rico at least as early as 1910. The best available estimates indicate that of males 10 years old and over, an astonishing 94.4 percent were economically active on the island that year.[39] But by 1920, this rate had fallen to 88.3 percent and it kept declining to 82.1 percent 10 years later. By 1940, nearly one in four males (24.2 percent) were no longer active in the labor force. Since the male school enrollment rate rose only from 12.4 percent to 13.5 percent between 1910 and 1940, the most likely source of this trend is instead the structural transformation of the Puerto Rican economy begun by the U.S. takeover, which created far too few new jobs for males to replace those destroyed in agriculture.

The bias toward female employment in new manufacturing jobs has been investigated by Safa (1985) through interviews with a sample of female workers in three plants of an island garment firm in 1980. The oldest plant, in the large western city of Mayaguez, was found to employ mainly older, married, urban women. Production was increasingly being shifted to the other

TABLE 4   Labor Force Status, Income, and Poverty, Mainland U.S. and Puerto Rico, 1950–80

	1950	1960	1970	1980
Labor Force[a]				
Participation Rate (%)				
Males				
US	86.4	83.3	79.7	77.4
Puerto Rico	79.5	72.4	65.6	60.7
Females				
US	33.9	37.7	43.3	51.5
Puerto Rico	27.6	22.5	26.0	27.8
Unemployment Rate (%)				
Males				
US	5.1	5.4	4.4	6.9
Puerto Rico	14.0	13.9	11.0	19.5
Females				
US	5.7	5.9	5.9	7.4
Puerto Rico	9.5	11.2	9.0	12.3
Median Income[b]				
Males				
US	$2434	4103	6444	12192
Puerto Rico	$434	987	2259	4314
Females				
US	$1029	1357	2328	5263
Puerto Rico	$247	471	1321	2775
Families				
US	$3073	5660	9596	20835
Puerto Rico	NA	1268	3063	5923
Families Below Poverty				
Level (%)				
US	NA	NA	11.6	9.6
Puerto Rico	NA	NA	59.6	58.0

[a]Civilian population 14 years old and over, 1950–60; ages 16 and over for 1970–80. Annual average participation and unemployment rates from Current Population Survey. On comparability of U.S. and Puerto Rican data collection, see U.S. Department of Commerce (1979), pp. 590–602.
[b]Income and poverty estimates are for the last calendar year before each census.
Source: U.S. Bureau of the Census (1953, 1964, 1973, 1984a and 1984b) and Puerto Rican Department of Labor and Human Resources, Bureau of Labor Statistics.

two new plants located in the countryside several miles from the city. These plants were far more likely to hire young, single women from nearby rural areas, for two main reasons. First, the younger the employee the lower the firm's costs incurred in contributions to maternity and retirement benefits. Second, interviews with management revealed a perception of such women as more docile than either older women or men. And this appeared to be confirmed by the young women interviewed, who indicated high degrees of job satisfaction, few complaints about management, and a strong work ethic.

How can this be, in an industry that is the lowest paying on the island, paying an average salary of only $4,885 in 1977?[40] Safa attributes the attitudes of these youth to their vital role in supporting typically large rural households. Four of five surveyed lived in households of four or more persons, of which half had seven or more persons. A large fraction of their fathers were displaced agricultural workers now relying on Social Security, food stamps, and their children's earnings. Ninety percent of the young women said it was easier for a woman to find employment than for a man. But, despite the male's declining status as a wage earner, women accepted the traditional patriarchal hierarchy of the peasant family, both before and after marriage (when dominant authority passed from father to husband). Of all the households Safa sampled with working daughters, three-fourths of these women contributed earnings that accounted for 50 percent or more of total household income. They were able to devote their full energy to their jobs because child care and other household responsibilities were largely assumed by unemployed family members, as well as by other relatives in the close-knit kinship networks in which nearly all live in these rural communities.

Besides reliance on the employment of daughters or wives, supplemented by income transfers, the other principal response of men to the island's declining male employment prospects has been emigration. In the Safe study, over three-fifths of the women surveyed had husbands or brothers who had left the island for the United States.[41]

From the early 1960s, Operation Bootstrap shifted its promotional efforts to attracting capital-intensive firms in industries like petrochemicals, electrical machinery, and pharmaceuticals. This was defended as a means to increase the number of skilled, high-wage jobs available and to moderate the economy's cyclical vulnerability. Not surprisingly, the average employment of firms in the program began falling: from 1947 to 1961 they employed an average of 70 workers each, but by the late sixties the average was only 33.3.[42] It had been hoped that capital-intensive firms would create significant indirect spinoff effects on employment. Local "backward-linked" firms would emerge to provide them raw materials and intermediate inputs, and "forward-linked" firms would profit from marketing and distributing their output. But by the 1970s, it was clear that foreign corporations could remain isolated from the rest of the Puerto Rican economy because they already had well-established relations with suppliers and distributors in their home country.

The oil crisis of 1973–74 and the worldwide recession that followed put an abrupt end to the island's high output and investment growth. Real GNP, which had grown at average annual rates of 6.1 percent from 1947 to 1963 and 6.6 percent from 1963 to 1973, slowed to a mere 1 percent growth rate from 1973 to 1977. Real per capita GNP actually fell 2 percent during the mid-seventies.[43] The official unemployment rate jumped to over 16 percent in 1976 and exceeded 23 percent in 1983. Average family income on the island fell from 32 percent of the U.S. income level to 28.4 percent between 1970 and 1980, and the family poverty rate in 1980 (58 percent) was six times the American level (Table 4). With the island's unemployment and poverty reaching levels of the sort not seen in the United States since the Great Depression, Washington resorted to massive issuance of food stamps as its principal relief assistance. The first coupons were introduced on the island in September 1974. In their first full year of distribution, food stamps were issued to more than one-fourth of the population. By

1980, over 58 percent were using the coupons and another 10–20 percent were sufficiently poor to qualify for the program, though they were not then recipients.[44]

The failure of the postwar development strategy to create adequate job growth left many with only one reasonable option besides dependence on government transfers: emigration. Puerto Ricans have been moving to the U.S. mainland since the early nineteenth century, but migration, both within the island and abroad, was greatly accelerated by the American invasion. The vast expansion of coastal sugar production at the expense of the inland coffee industry forced large numbers of rural subsistence and coffee farmers to leave the western and central coffee belt to seek work in the coastal canefields or the tobacco factories of the urban San Juan–Rio Piedras area. As unemployment became a growing problem, many left for jobs on the farms and in the mines of Cuba and Hispaniola. Over 5,000 Puerto Ricans were recruited to work on the sugar plantations of Hawaii in 1900–1901. And these years also saw the first small numbers of craftsmen and tobacco workers migrate to New York City, home of a tiny Puerto Rican community founded by early anticolonial political exiles. But the 1910 census counted only 1,513 Puerto Ricans in the country.

World War I brought some 12,000 to 13,000 to the mainland to help fill wartime labor shortages. Another 18,000 Puerto Ricans were inducted into the U.S. military during the war (though, like blacks, they were forced into segregated units). The 1920 census reported that, of the 11,811 Puerto Ricans in the United States, two-thirds of them were in New York City where they congregated in the Harlem and Brooklyn Navy Yard areas. The granting of U.S. citizenship in 1917 freed Puerto Ricans of the visa and other restrictions hindering other migrants. But they still faced a five-day, 1,600-mile sea voyage to New York, which was beyond the means of many. The Great Depression actually caused net return migration from the mainland in every year from 1931 to 1934. The annual number traveling to the mainland was below 30,000 throughout the 1920s and 1930s and net migration (the difference between departures from the island and arrivals) did not exceed 9,000 per year until 1945.[45]

The Second World War and the postwar economic boom in the United States sparked the first mass migration from the island. Frequent commercial airline flights became available only at that time, making the trip relatively brief and affordable. Even as late as 1970, the one-way fare could be under $50 and a ticket could be had on credit from travel agencies for as little as $5 down payment.[46] The number traveling to the mainland more than doubled between 1945 and 1946 and passed the 100,000 mark for the first time the following year. Net migration, a mere 500 persons in 1941, climbed to 33,086 in 1949. Between 1940 and 1950 the census recorded a fourfold increase in the number of Puerto Rican residents in the United States. But the postwar peak in net migration was not reached until 1953, when 74,603 more arrived on the mainland than departed. For the decade as a whole, net migration totaled 461,000. The outflow from the island slowed to 144,724 in the 1960s, but by the end of the decade the census counted 1,429,369 residents of Puerto Rican origin. During the 1970s, for the first time since the Great Depression, more returned to the island (a net outflow of over 158,000) than stayed. But the 1980s saw a revival of the secular pattern of positive net migration.

As the postwar migration has continued, the island-born component of the Puerto Rican population in the United States has decreased and the geographic dispersion of the population has increased. Three-fourths of Puerto Ricans counted in the 1950 U.S. census were born on the island as were 69.3 percent of the 1960 count. But by 1970 this percentage had fallen to 54.8 percent and it dropped slightly below the 50 percent mark for the first time in 1980. While the arrival point for most migrants still tends to be New York City, Puerto Ricans now live in all of the 50 states. The fraction concentrated in New York State fell from four-fifths of all Puerto Ricans in 1940 and 1950 to 69 percent in 1960. By 1980 about half continued to live in the state, with large contingents in New Jersey, California, Florida, and Illinois.

The sudden influx of large numbers of migrants sparked public controversy about their implications for the New York economy. Some critics claimed they were akin to the "new immigration" of Eastern and Southern Europeans at the turn of the century; like them, it was said, the latest migrants were largely Catholics, from low-skill rural backgrounds, and many were dark skinned. The first major study of the initial postwar influx was organized at Columbia University by C. Wright Mills, Clarence Senior, and Rose Goldsen (1950). Interviews of a large sample of persons living in Spanish Harlem and the Morrisania section of the Bronx in 1947 produced information on about 5,000 Puerto Ricans. Just over one-third of their sample was nonwhite (20 percent blacks and 16 percent "mixed blood"), a slightly higher fraction than on the island. But 91 percent of the total study group had lived in urban areas of the island before migrating, two-thirds in either of the two largest cities, San Juan and Ponce. These were not primarily unstable, transient families: four out of five had lived in the same place in Puerto Rico for at least 10 years prior to emigrating and a higher percentage were married than in the general population. In part this reflects migrants' older average age, 24, four years above the island average.

Mills, Senior, and Goldsen also found evidence that, before emigration, most were better educated and employed in more skilled jobs than the average urban Puerto Rican. The illiteracy rate was 8 percent among migrants, compared with 17 percent in San Juan and 32 percent islandwide in 1940. Only 4 percent had been unemployed just prior to migrating, and nearly three out of four had been employed in an uninterrupted full-year job. About 29 percent of the male migrants and 68 percent of females had worked in manufacturing at home, higher proportions than their nonmigrant countrymen. Most of these were in skilled or semiskilled occupations.

Though these early migrants had superior educational and employment credentials than the average Puerto Rican at the time, many were at a substantial disadvantage in the United States. Their average illiteracy rate was twice that of the overall New York City population. On arrival in New York, the majority experienced downward mobility into semiskilled operative or service occupations.

The Columbia study remains a unique source of information on the earliest years of the postwar migration, though caution must always be exercised when interpreting results from samples, such as this one, derived through the nonrandom "snowball" method (locating additional subjects through relatives and various community networks). However, 1950 census data on the educational attainment of Puerto Ricans on the mainland and on the island seem consistent with the view that the early migrants came from the better-educated strata. The average amount of schooling completed by island-born Puerto Ricans living on the mainland in 1950 was 8.4 years, two years more than the island average.[47]

As with any large-scale migration from a small country, it was to be expected that as it continued there would be regression toward the mean levels of schooling and occupation. Thus, by the late 1950s, there were reports of relatively fewer migrants than before from the largest cities and top skill groups.[48] In the late 1970s, by contrast, it was widely believed on the island that the worsening recession was forcing a "brain drain" of much of the business and academic elite who had resisted emigrating earlier. But research comparing the educational and occupational distributions of migrants with the population of Puerto Rico has found that, after adjusting for age differences, there has been little change in the relative selectivity of migration between the late 1950s and the early eighties.[49]

Cubans

Most of the Cuban population of the United States traces its American roots back less than a generation. On the eve of the 1959 revolution, it numbered little more than 30,000. It had taken over half a century to increase by 19,000 over the 1900 census count (11,081). But from 1959 to 1980 about 1 in every 10 Cubans left the island and the number living in the United States leapt to over 600,000. The migration occurred through a number of distinct periods, each conditioned by the course of the revolution and by the state of U.S.–Cuban relations.

The first phase, from early 1959 to October 1962, was one of rapid socioeconomic transformation in Cuba and of growing American hostility to the Castro government. Throughout 1959 and most of 1960, commercial air travel was readily available and the right to exit was unrestricted. But of the roughly 215,000 who left for the United States from 1959 to 1962, fewer than one-fifth of the departures occurred in the first two years.[50] The pace of emigration began to quicken noticeably in the waning months of 1960 with the announcement of a wide-ranging Urban Reform Law. Emigration took off on a sustained increase in 1961, the

year in which diplomatic relations were broken off between Havana and Washington and the U.S.-backed invasion at the Bay of Pigs was defeated. Exit and financial restrictions were tightened that year, but direct flights to Miami were not suspended until the Cuban Missile Crisis in October of 1962.

From November 1962 through August 1965, immigration to the United States was possible only by the indirect approach of first securing approval for travel to a third country, or by surreptitious means. The outflow during this period was only about 69,000.

Fidel Castro's speech of September 28, 1965, inaugurated a lengthy period of freer exit. From September through November about 5,000 relatives of exiles already in the United States were allowed to leave from the port of Camarioca. Then, in December, a "memorandum of understanding" between the United States and Cuba instituted an airlift between Varadero Beach, Cuba and Miami. With two flights each day until the airlift's termination in April 1973, over 340,000 migrated.

The period from May 1973 to April 1980 saw a reimposition of the 1962–65 ban on direct flights. The Cuban government permitted a number of political prisoners to emigrate in both 1978 and 1979. In addition to clandestine exits and travelers coming via third countries (particularly Spain), this produced a total of only about 34,500 migrants in the course of these eight years.

The largest Cuban emigration in a single year took place between April 21 and September 26, 1980, from the port of Mariel. Sparked by the occupation of the Peruvian embassy in Havana, the government opened the port to unlimited emigration. With a recession underway in the United States, the Carter administration reflected widespread misgivings about any large new influx by declaring a ceiling of 3,500 refugee admissions. But this was soon eliminated and special processing camps were quickly set up.

Although a U.S. naval blockade was begun on May 14 to dissuade others from joining the boatlift, and though Mariel harbor was closed from September 27 on, some 124,769 left for the United States in this period.

Who were the Cuban migrants? Thanks to a number of research studies conducted at different stages of the migration, a great deal is known about their demographic and socioeconomic features. The richest source of information on the earliest exiles is the study by Fagen, Brody, and O'Leary (1968) on Cubans who arrived from 1959 to the end of 1961 and registered at the Cuban Refugee Center (CRC) in Miami. From samples of the subpopulation of 59,682 registrants who were previously employed or employable, they reported that the refugees were far more likely to be relatively well educated urban professionals than was the average island resident.

While their findings show that the farther down the socioeconomic ladder one looked the larger the fraction of people who stayed in Cuba, Fagen, Brody, and O'Leary were impressed by the presence of migrants from many different strata:

Although the refugee community contains the majority of living members of the Batistiano establishment, corrupt politicians, profiteers, landowners, and gangsters, most of the exiles come from the inclusive social sectors that were squeezed, pressured, or deprived by the revolution not because their members wholeheartedly supported the old order, but because they stood in the way of the new. The Castro government became so radical and reorganized society so thoroughly that almost all social sectors from blue-collar workers through professionals experienced the impact of some revolutionary program in a negative way. Of course, not all negative experiences with revolutionary programs resulted in self-imposed exile, both because of the counterbalancing effect of positive experiences and because of the psychological, physical, and political barriers to leaving the island.[51]

In fact, their findings understated the dominance of high-income emigres in this first wave because their data included only those who registered with the CRC. Since the center was expressly devoted to aiding those without substantial assets or immediate job prospects, the 23 percent of all 1958–61 migrants from the island who chose not to register were likely (as the authors themselves recognized) to be the rich and well connected who fled during the early days of the Castro government. Restrictions on taking personal funds and property from the island were not made stringent until mid-1961.

Later cohorts, while still characterized by educational and occupational backgrounds well above the average in Cuba, have tended to come from more heterogeneous urban sectors than did earlier waves. This reflects in part the dramatic economic shifts undertaken in Cuba in the late sixties. Real national income and consumption expanded from 1962 to 1965, then began to fall sharply. The government responded in 1966 by inaugurating a new, more radical strategy to contract the scope of the private sector in order to reallocate more resources to the public sector. Urban trade and services were rapidly transformed and the resultant increase in middle-class emigration is reflected in the Portes–Bach survey of Cubans arriving in the United States in 1973 and 1974. One-fourth of the males interviewed had worked in white-collar or minor professional jobs at home and another one-fifth had held intermediate service jobs. The modal occupation was the crafts group, accounting for one-fourth of the total. The average level of educational attainment was 9 years. Over one-fifth (22 percent) had completed 12 or more years of school, about five times the average in Cuba. But this represented a decline from the early 1960s, when over one-third of migrants from Cuba reported 12 or more years of educational attainment.[52]

Despite negative publicity claiming that the 1980 wave of "Marielitos" was drawn disproportionately from the Cuban underclass, a survey of a sample of 5,700 found that most had very similar characteristics to earlier cohorts.[53] This was especially true of the 62,000 who arrived in the first few weeks of the exodus and were processed and released in Miami. A large fraction were families being reunited with relatives in the United States. Few had been unemployed in Cuba, and their occupational distribution was much like that of those leaving the island in the early seventies. The later arrivals who were processed at military camps in the North had a larger proportion of younger, nonwhite, unattached males and about one in six had a prison record in Cuba. But overall the refugees processed at the camps had largely urban backgrounds of steady employment, mainly in skilled crafts jobs in manufacturing or construction. Over 9 percent were professional, technical, or kindred workers, of whom the most common specific occupations were teachers, nurses, entertainers, and accountants.

Compared with Mexicans immigrating at the same time, the 1973–74 Cuban cohort averaged three more years schooling. Professional and proprietary occupations accounted for 11 percent of Cubans' premigration positions but for only 1 percent in the Mexican sample. A mere 2 percent of the Cubans had been farm workers, compared with 12 percent of the Mexicans. The main occupational similarity between the two nationalities was in the proportions from skilled blue-collar backgrounds.

Although 9 out of 10 Cubans arriving in the early seventies had no previous experi-ence in the United States, only 6 of the original 586 surveyed by Portes and Bach had no friends or relatives waiting for them at destination. One in four had over 20 friends or relatives already in the country.[54] This is comparable to the finding from a 1968 survey of the large Cuban population in West New York, New Jersey. Nearly 93 percent of the migrants interviewed reported that some family members were waiting for them when they arrived. Almost two-thirds had found jobs through the help of relatives.[55]

The first few years in the American labor market involved downward occupational mobility for many Cubans with high-status positions back home. The proportion of the 1973–74 cohort in white-collar jobs fell from 25 percent before migration to about 10 percent in the United States in both 1976 and 1979. Only 4.6 percent were in professional positions in the United States by 1976, compared with 8.5 percent who held such jobs before leaving Cuba. But some recovery (to 6.4 percent) was evident three years later. By far the largest change was the fourfold increase (to 34.5 percent in 1979) in the share of Cubans in semiskilled industrial work. The greatest stability was in craft positions: the 22.8 percent of 1979 jobs in crafts fields was almost identical to the premigration level. Occupational mobility does not appear to have come at the price of frequent unemployment. Three out of four of Cuban men reinterviewed in 1979 said they had not been unemployed a single time during the past six years in the United States and another 15 percent had only one jobless spell.[56]

Like Mexican workers, Cubans work primarily in small- to medium-sized firms staffed by large proportions of other Hispanics. In 1979, 59 percent of the 1973–74 Cuban cohort reported that most of their coworkers were Cuban. But a very important distinction is evident in the ownership of the businesses they work for. Nearly two out of five Cubans worked in a Cuban-owned firm in

1976, and by 1979 this was the case for 49 percent of the Cuban sample.[57] This is consistent with the remarkable increase recorded in the rate of self-employment among Cuban migrants, from 7.6 percent to 21.2 percent between 1976 and 1979.[58] Not only are Cubans more likely to work for their countrymen than are Mexican immigrants, but they are also more likely to patronize Hispanic-owned stores for both small items and consumer durables.

Other Latin Americans

The most rapidly growing component of the Hispanic immigrant population in recent years is the influx from Latin American nations other than Cuba and Mexico. Excluding the latter two, the countries of Central America, South America, and the Spanish-speaking Caribbean were the source of 564,800 legal immigrants in the 1970s and another 705,800 from 1981 through 1988 (Table 3). The average number entering the United States each year from the region jumped 57 percent between the seventies and the eighties, almost five times faster than the Mexican rate of increase. Despite the recency of this migration, by 1988 Central and South Americans numbered some 2.2 million—one in every nine Hispanic Americans.

Dominicans

More Hispanics have immigrated to the United States from the Dominican Republic since 1960 than from any other foreign country except Mexico and Cuba. The 1980 census counted 169,147 Dominican-born residents on the American mainland, of whom over half had arrived during the seventies. Another 183,000 migrated between 1981 and 1988, representing one-fourth of all migration from Latin America (aside from Mexico and Cuba) in this period.

One reason for the unusually large inflows from this small Caribbean island is a close relationship with its immediate neighbor, Puerto Rico. Barely 15 minutes apart by airplane, the two have long been tied by trade and migration. The fact that the Dominican income per capita ($790 in 1985) has averaged only one-third that of Puerto Rico in recent years has drawn many Dominicans to San Juan and other cities in search of work.[59] While the island's limited employment opportunities lead some to return home, others continue on from Puerto Rico to the United States. Since air flights to the mainland from Puerto Rico are considered "U.S. domestic travel" and Puerto Ricans are not required to show passports before boarding, some Dominicans have attempted to enter by illegally misrepresenting their nationality. Recent estimates by Larson and Sullivan (1987) suggest that contrary to widely quoted claims that there are 300,000 or more undocumented Dominicans, the actual number is more likely a quite small part of the overall Dominican influx.[60] Others who intermarry with Puerto Ricans gain preference in obtaining legal entry status.

The increase in political instability from the early 1960s is another oft-cited factor used to explain the upsurge in emigration. The 1961 assassination of the long-reigning dictator Trujillo was followed by five years of political turmoil and economic stagnation. The democratic election of Juan Bosch as the new leader in 1963 was nullified by his overthrow only seven months later by traditional forces opposed to his populist program. In 1965, widespread fears of a military coup sparked the "April Revolution," which, in turn, prompted the United States to launch a counterrevolutionary invasion on behalf of a conservative faction. The late sixties and early seventies witnessed sizable inflows of foreign investment in mining, sugar, communications, tourism, and other industries. But the period was also one of harsh repression in which an estimated 600 to 700 political activists and their relatives "disappeared" or were found murdered. And a sizable share of the returns from economic expansion were widely reported to have been diverted into luxury imports and military corruption.

Those who have left for the United States appear to be drawn disproportionately from the urban, better-educated, white-collar segment of the republic. This emerges clearly from the analysis by Ugalde, Bean, and Cardenas (1979) of a large national survey of 25,000 island households in 1974. The survey, called *Diagnos,* was conducted by the Ministry of Health and included a series of questions about household members who traveled overseas planning to stay there for over a year. Brief tourist and business trips were thereby excluded. If the migrant had not returned by the time of the survey, other household members were asked to provide information on him or her. Of course, the survey had the limitation that it completely missed those cases where the entire household had migrated and was still out of the country in 1974. But it provided a wealth of information on about 125,000 household members.

The survey results show that, of household heads, only 32 percent of nonmigrants were born in a city, compared with 59 percent of migrants. Another 17 percent of migrants, though not city-born, were urban residents in the period before emigrating. The middle and upper social strata account for the bulk of migrants. In a country with a literacy rate of only 61 percent among nonmigrants, 96 percent of migrants were literate and 31 percent had some university training— 10 times the nonmigrant percentage.

When questioned about the main reason for leaving their homeland, most cited economic rather than political reasons. Thirty percent moved because of unemployment and another 30 percent left in search of

higher incomes. The study's authors note that political persecution may be more likely to force the migration of entire households, who would not be included in this survey. And they point out the interrelationship between political conditions and economic prospects. Indeed, since such a large fraction of these urban, well-educated individuals cited unemployment as the cause of their emigration, it is likely that they were victims of a "middle-class bottleneck" in the government's development strategy.[61] Their economic frustrations could well have been fused with political frustrations, given the effort so many invested in the 1963 election of Bosch and in the 1965 nationalist rebellion.

The survey also provided the strongest evidence to date that Dominicans, like Mexicans and Puerto Ricans, average high rates of return migration. About 39 percent of migrants had returned home by the time of the survey. The largest fraction of middle- and upper-class returnees were those who had completed studies in the United States. Lower-class migrants were more likely to be target earners who returned to the island after accumulating sufficient savings.[62]

In the United States, Dominicans are among the most geographically concentrated of all immigrant groups. In 1980, New York State was the home of 86.5 percent of them, with most living in the Washington Heights area of upper Manhattan or in the Corona section of Queens. The employment experiences of both legal and undocumented Dominicans in the city have been investigated by Grasmuck (1984). She supervised a 1981 project in which seven Dominican interviewers questioned a sample of 301 of their countrymen, of whom 57 percent were documented and the remainder undocumented immigrants. The survey was designed to try to oversample the undocumented and was collected through the chain or "snowball" procedure of locating subjects through community institutions and kinship networks. This approach has the advantage of often insuring greater access to individuals underrepresented in government surveys, but the disadvantage of lacking the desirable statistical property of random sampling.

Like the *Diagnos* findings, the New York sample came from urban areas of the republic and had educational and occupational backgrounds well above the island norm. Contrary to stereotypes, the undocumented exceeded legal immigrants in all of these background characteristics. While three-fourths of legal Dominican migrants had urban origins and their average educational attainment was 7.9 years, 86 percent of the undocumented came from a city and they averaged 8.4 years of schooling. The fraction of each group in a professional, technical, or kindred occupation at home was 26 percent of undocumented males and 29.2 percent of undocumented females, compared with only 11.1 percent and 17.9 percent of legal males and females, respectively. But the undocumented were considerably more likely to be unemployed prior to migration.

In New York, legal and illegal entrants become similarly concentrated in low-wage manual manufacturing jobs in firms with largely Hispanic work forces. Nearly half of males and three-fifths of females interviewed were in blue-collar jobs as craftsmen, operatives, or laborers. Professional or technical jobs were found by only 10.5 percent of males and 3 percent of females. The majority of both the documented and the undocumented worked in firms in which over half of their coworkers and their supervisors were Dominicans or other Hispanics. However, clear distinctions by immigration status emerge when one's focus narrows to firm-level conditions. The undocumented were substantially more likely to work in the smallest, low-wage firms lacking union protections. Three out of every five were in firms with fewer than 50 employees and the

same fraction were nonunion, in contrast to a 69 percent unionization rate among documented Dominicans. The undocumented were clearly in great demand as a casual labor supply by employers trying to avoid payment of employment-related taxes and benefits. This is strongly suggested by the fact that 43 percent of undocumented workers were paid in cash, over twice the percentage among the documented.

South Americans

Colombia is by far the single largest source of immigration from South America to the United States. The 143,508 Colombians counted by the 1980 census represented nearly one-fifth of the foreign-born Latin American population (excluding Mexico and Cuba). Theirs is also a recent migration, beginning in the early 1960s. Many of the first emigrants were fleeing the turmoil wrought by "*la Violencia.*" From 1948 to 1964 the country was caught up in the longest period of internal warfare and banditry in modern South American history. The death toll has been estimated at about 200,000. During the National Front period of 1958–1978, the two main political parties worked cooperatively and the worst of the civil strife ended.

Compared with most other countries in the region during the 1970s, Colombia experienced strong employment growth and some reduction in income inequality. The government offered various concessions to emigres in the hope of luring back skilled manpower, though with little success. The continued emigration of professionals and other skilled workers stems in part from the fact that the benefits of government policies accrued more to the top and bottom extremes of the population. Middle-income groups experienced a fall in their share of national income as well as a steep drop in the purchasing power of their earnings. For example, the monthly pay of salaried technicians and managers in manufacturing shrank 18 percent between 1970 and 1976.[63] The decade ended with a revival of guerrilla actions by underground political groups and the escalation of violence by powerful drug traffickers on a national scale. Coupled with evidence of rising government corruption, the violence no doubt intensified the pressure on many to leave the country.

Most Colombian migration has been to its wealthier neighbor Venezuela and, in smaller numbers, to Ecuador and Panama. Only about one-sixth of all those leaving the country have moved to the United States. Their settlement at destination has been much more geographically dispersed than Dominicans. Of all Colombians resident in the United States in 1980, 12.3 percent lived in Florida and 10.5 percent in California. But the largest single concentration (41.2 percent) is in New York State, and 9 out of 10 of these (i.e., about 36 percent of all Colombians) live in New York City.

While many migrants to nearby Latin American nations come from rural Colombia, those arriving in the United States appear to be heavily urban, with educational and occupational levels well above the Colombian average. This has been confirmed from research on migrants just before leaving Bogota and from data on those already settled in New York.[64] The most recent large-scale survey was undertaken by the Hispanic Research Center at Fordham University between June and October of 1981.[65] The main survey site was Queens, where most of the city's Colombians are concentrated in the Jackson Heights, Jamaica, and Elmhurst sections. Nine out of 10 had only been in the United States 15 years or less and almost 45 percent had been here five years or less. Over three-fifths of those surveyed had been born in an urban area with a population of 100,000 or more. Cali alone accounted for 30 percent of all migrants. By the time of emigration, 90.5 percent were urban residents. Migrants were not only more urban but also younger than the national norm. Half were between the ages of 20 and 40, compared with only 29.7 percent of the Colombian population. While the 1970s cohort had fewer college graduates than those arriving in the sixties, both waves had above average educational backgrounds. Only 26.9 percent of the urban labor force in Colombia had secondary schooling and only 4.8 percent had attended universities, but the proportions among the migrant sample were 67 percent and 9 percent, respectively. Their elite educational background was reflected in the fact that over three-fifths had white-collar occupations at home. Among males employed at home, the proportion who had held managerial and administrative positions (15.6) was nearly twice the national average. And, at a time when the official Colombian unemployment rate averaged 10 percent, none of the migrants who had been labor force participants were unemployed just before emigrating.

By contrast, at the time of the survey, 8.5 percent of the migrants were unemployed in New York. This was almost identical to the citywide rate and well below that of all Hispanics in the city (10.9 percent). But the average masks an unusually large sex differential among Colombian migrants: 13.7 percent of women were unemployed, but only 5.2 percent of men. Compared with all Hispanics in New York, Colombian women's unemployment was slightly above the female average (11.3 percent) while the Colombian male rate was less than half the rate (10.7 percent) of all Hispanic men. The high female rate reflected, in part, the increased job search by persons without employment experience before migration; 39 percent of the women had been housewives or students in Colombia but over three-fifths of them entered the labor force in New York. But a more important reason may be the high concentration of women in cyclically vulnerable industries. Manufacturing accounts for 55 percent of employed Colombian women, but only one-fourth of males.

Only 22.6 percent were in the manufacturing sector at home compared with 36.2 percent in New York. The other principal shift was into service jobs like repair, cleaning, and hotel work: 27.3 percent of men and 16.8 percent of women held U.S. jobs in this sector, a three- to fourfold increase over their premigration levels. In Colombia before emigrating, most of those with service jobs had been in higher status professional and specialized services: nearly two-fifths of men and one-third of women in the Queens sample reported previous jobs in that sector. Those who found employment in New York often experienced downward occupational mobility, at least initially. Just 3.7 percent of males' first American jobs were in managerial or administrative occupations and the fraction of initial jobs in blue-collar occupations was, for both sexes, twice as large as in their premigration distributions.

Like Dominicans and other immigrant groups, Colombians in New York are concentrated in smaller firms in manufacturing and services. Nearly 56 percent worked in small firms with total employment of 50 or less. And there is clear evidence of an ethnic job network in operation. One of every two workers was employed in a firm where the majority of coworkers were Colombians or other Hispanics. A quarter of these firms were owned or managed by Hispanics as well.

Central Americans

Over 211,000 Central Americans immigrated to the United States in the first eight years of the 1980s. The average number arriving legally each year has leapt by 86 percent since the 1970s, the greatest increase recorded from any major region of the world. This is all the more remarkable in light of the U.S. government's refusal throughout the 1980s to grant refugee status to those fleeing the political violence in El Salvador, Guatemala, and Nicaragua.[66] The number who have resorted to illegal entry is widely thought to be several times larger than the legal influx. But the Census Bureau now estimates that in the years 1980 to 1983, only about 66,000 non-Mexican undocumented aliens entered the United States from all of Latin America.[67]

The six Spanish-speaking countries stretching from the Mexican border south to Colombia are among the smallest and poorest in all Latin America. Most experienced rapid, export-driven growth in GNP during the 1960s.[68] But by 1970, only Costa Rica and Panama had per capita incomes over $1,000 per year. The seventies brought a series of economic and political crises. The oil price shock forced sharp hikes in the critical prices of insecticides, fertilizers, and industrial chemicals, which led to enormous current accounts deficits. Heavy foreign borrowing proved to be a short-lived means to sustain growth, for the oil crisis was followed by declining world prices for the region's primary products as well as the collapse of the Central American Common Market. Since 1978, both El Salvador and Nicaragua have been torn by war. Guatemala has also had considerable civil strife, though with less damage to the economy in recent years. Besides the direct human and material costs of these armed conflicts, they have discouraged foreign investment and tourism and have encouraged capital flight and emigration.

The growth of Central American immigration to the United States is too recent for much detailed economic or sociological research on it to have been completed to date.

Empirical analysis is hampered by the fact that, though increasing at a very high rate, the number of migrants from the region is still of such relatively small size that standard government population surveys have not produced enough sample observations for extensive statistical tests. But some local research projects have begun to help remedy this.

In 1979 a survey was conducted of 573 migrants to the United States from urban areas of Costa Rica and El Salvador. GDP per capita in the former averages about twice that of the latter, but by 1980 the rate of urbanization of the population in El Salvador (40 percent) was only 5 percentage points lower than in Costa Rica and both were sending growing numbers of urban migrants to the United States. In his analysis of the survey, Poitras (1983) reports that two-thirds of the migrants were male and most were young: two out of three of the Costa Ricans and three out of four Salvadorans were age 35 or under. Sixty percent of the Costa Ricans and half the Salvadorans were married, but most emigrated without their dependents.

Though relatively young, most were old enough to have accumulated some work experience. Far from being part of the marginal surplus labor pool often thought to dominate migration streams, they were invariably employed at the time of leaving the country, except for those still in school. Educational and occupational backgrounds were quite diverse, though certainly not concentrated at the low end of their national distributions. Total years of schooling completed averaged 10.8 for Costa Rican migrants and just over 10 for Salvadorans. Forty percent of the former and over one-fourth of the latter had some higher, post-secondary education. Occupationally, one in three Costa Ricans and one in four Salvadorans had been professionals, technicians, or other white-collar workers at home.

Four out of five were admitted to the United States with proper entry documents. Only 24.5 percent of the Costa Ricans and 8.1 percent of Salvadorans held the status of permanent resident aliens or temporary workers (H-2), which permitted employment. Over half of those from Costa Rica and two-fifths of Salvadorans came on tourist visas, then took advantage of lax INS enforcement to find jobs. A mere 1 percent of Costa Ricans took the riskier route of entering without documents, but 41.7 percent of Salvadorans in the sample did so, mainly by traveling the length of Mexico to slip across the northern border.

However, those surveyed overwhelmingly viewed their visit as temporary. On average, Costa Ricans stayed in the United States only two years and Salvadorans one and one-half years. Though not making a long-term commitment to their new labor market, most took full-time jobs throughout their residence. Downward mobility relative to their job status at home was the norm. Three out of four took blue-collar work like restaurant helpers, clerks, domestics, construction crewmen, and manual laborers. Though low wage by American standards, compared with their average premigration hourly earnings in Costa Rica ($1 per hour) and El Salvador ($0.80 per hour), their wages in the United States averaged a four-fold increase for both nationalities. Higher pay was typically achieved by migrants fluent in English, with more premigration work experience at above average wages, and with previous U.S. employment. Nearly three-fifths of Costa Ricans and over 56 percent of Salvadorans indicated that they would try to return later to work again in an American city.

Rodriguez (1987) has reported some suggestive early findings from a study of undocumented Central American migrants in Houston. Interviews were conducted by a team of Spanish-speaking interviewers in

1985 with 150 such migrants, located through community activities and chain sampling procedures. Just over half of the sample were Salvadorans, 21 percent were from Honduras, 19 percent from Guatemala, and 5 percent from Nicaragua. Nine out of 10 were less than 40 years old, with nearly 55 percent between the ages of 18 and 29. About 65 percent had no more than primary schooling, 28.7 percent had completed secondary school, and 6.7 percent had attended a postsecondary institution.

When questioned about their reasons for emigrating, 61 percent of those from Guatemala and 81 percent of those from Honduras said that "economic factors" were most important to them. But 36.7 percent of the Salvadorans cited "political conflict" as their main motivation for leaving, and the large number indicating "economic" motives were found to be largely referring to war-related factors: for example, former vendors cited the destruction of the town marketplace and factory workers complained of being dismissed because of damages sustained by their factory or problems in transporting raw materials or finished products over dangerous or obstructed roads.

Four out of five were employed at the time of the interview, invariably in low-wage, low-status jobs. The average hourly wage was only $3.35, the legal minimum, and 10.6 percent received less than that. These low earnings are in part attributable to the depressed state of the Houston labor market in 1985, when the unemployment rate was 12.6 percent. They also reflect the weak educational background (relative to Americans) and command of English of most migrants. But among those making just $4 an hour were a number from skilled backgrounds at home (mechanics, welders, and school teachers).

The structure of their work groups bears a striking resemblance to that observed for other recent Hispanic immigrants. Nine out of 10 Salvadorans and 84.6 percent of Honduran workers were employed in crews composed either entirely of undocumented aliens or of a mixture of the undocumented and Mexican Americans.[69] Employer interviews revealed that firms valued undocumented work crews not only for their docility but for their ability to quickly recruit other workers to meet sudden increases in business. For newly arrived migrants speaking little English, such ethnic clustering can dramatically expedite job search and on-the-job socialization and skill training.

These findings are generally consistent with those of North and Houston (1976) based on interviews with 237 apprehended undocumented migrants from Western Hemisphere nations other than Mexico. The largest component of this subsample (41.8 percent) originated in Central America and another 40 percent came from South America. Over half had lived in cities of 1 million or more inhabitants at home and a mere 10 percent had been farm workers. Nearly 17 percent had held professional or managerial occupations at origin. Compared with the Rodriguez study group, these migrants were somewhat better educated: 47.8 percent had completed more than eight years of schooling and 14 percent had some postsecondary education. Nearly half spoke some English, though only 18.8 percent felt they spoke "very well."

With an average age of 30 these migrants were younger than the American average by nine years. But they came to the United States with a mean of 12.8 years of work experience. A substantial fraction had relatives or other migrants they could ask for assistance in finding housing and employment. More than one-fourth reported a parent or sibling already in the country. The work they found involved considerable downward occupational mobility for many as well as a sectoral shift into manufacturing. The proportion with professional or managerial jobs dropped sharply to only 3.4 percent, while the proportion in service work jumped from only 6.9 percent at origin to 24.9 percent and the share of operatives and non-farm laborers from 31.2 to 48.6 percent. A threefold increase (to 52 percent) occurred in the proportion employed in manufacturing. This no doubt accounts for the tripling of the percentage in labor unions, from 9 percent at home to 29 percent after migration. Despite the cyclicity of much of manufacturing, most appear to have secured relatively continuous employment. On average they worked 2.2 years out of the 2.5 of residence in the country. More than one in three worked on the same job for two or more years. The mean wage on their most recent job was, at $3.05, higher than that of undocumented Mexicans but one-third lower than the U.S. average in 1975.

NOTES

1. According to the Census Bureau, "Other Hispanic" origin refers to persons whose origins are from Spain or to persons who identify themselves only as Hispanic, Spanish, Spanish American, Hispano, or Latino.
2. See, for example, Acuna (1981).
3. See the estimates in the valuable history by Corwin (1978).
4. See Corwin and Cardoso (1978).
5. Corwin and Cardoso (1978).
6. Clark (1908), p. 467. Quoted in Corwin (1978).
7. In fact, in 1864 Abraham Lincoln signed into law an Act to Encourage Immigration, to help ease the Civil War labor shortage in the North. It allowed private firms to recruit and pay the transportation expenses of immigrants in return for a contractual agreement that the newcomers work for the sponsoring firm exclusively for a specified period. The postwar recession of 1866 set in motion the repeal of the law two years later. On the history of immigration policies, see Briggs (1984).
8. Corwin (1978).
9. U.S. Bureau of the Census (1975a). The definition of "immigrant" on which government statistics are based has varied over time, so caution is required in comparing year-to-year counts. But the general practice has been to count as immigrants only those intending to reside in the U.S. for a substantial period. Intended stays of a minimum of six months or a year were common criteria in the earliest enumeration procedures, while the possession of permanent residence status has been the key distinction between immigrants and "nonimmigrants" (tourists, border commuters, etc.) in recent years. See the discussion in Ibid., p. 97.
10. The labor needs of the northern industrialized states during the 1920s were met by the large-scale migration of blacks from the rural South as well as by many of the 4.1 million legal immigrants who entered the country during the decade. Though less than half the record volumes of 1901–1910, this still-large number of admissions was made possible by the long delays in assigning all national quotas and fully implementing the new system.
11. U.S. Bureau of the Census (1975).
12. See, for example, Barrera (1980).
13. Corwin and Cardoso (1978).
14. See Bach (1978).
15. See the contrasting estimates and analyses in Hoffman (1978) and McWilliams (1968).
16. For useful examinations of the *bracero* program see Bustamente (1978) and Galarza (1964).
17. U.S. Bureau of the Census (1975).
18. Aspe and Beristain (1984).
19. Cockcroft (1983), p. 158.
20. For example, in 1970 the net foreign income earned on new investments in Mexico was $473.6 million (U.S.), but only $154.2 million was reinvested. See Cockcroft (1983), p. 158.
21. Barkin (1987).
22. See Appendix Table 2A.1.
23. Aspe and Beristain (1984).
24. Cockcroft (1983), p. 260.
25. Estimate for 1978 from a study conducted under the auspices of the Ministry of Labor, cited in Evans and James (1979).
26. U.S. Immigration and Naturalization Service (1989b).
27. Warren and Passel (1987).
28. The 481 Mexicans were the largest single national subsample of the total of 793 aliens, ages 16 and over, apprehended for illegal entry in May and June of 1975 at 19 sites across the country. This does not necessarily reflect their true share of the undocumented popu-

lation because the INS concentrates its enforcement effort in the Southwest and because those arriving illegally from other countries are thought to more often seek entry along the East Coast by means of improper documents. To minimize untruthful answers, the project used bilingual interviewers unaffiliated with the INS, assured the aliens that compliance was voluntary and all answers confidential, made no attempt to identify the respondents, and conducted the interviews after all INS processing was completed. Perhaps due to these assurances and the diversion the interviews offered from their boring wait for transportation back home, the nonresponse rate was only 5 percent. Confidence in the honesty of most responses is heightened by the willingness the aliens showed in giving potentially damaging information on such things as whether they intended to return to the United States (over half admitted they did).

29. Due to geographical dispersal over time, particularly among the Mexicans, 46.6 percent of the original sample was not located for the 1976 reinterviews. But 67 percent of the initial Mexican sample and 82 percent of the Cubans were reinterviewed during either the second or the third waves of the project. Portes and Bach's (1985: p. 102) tests of sample mortality bias found no significant effects on any important socioeconomic variables. But the later waves did include relatively larger proportions of those with more children, relatives, or friends in the U.S., since these members of the original sample were easier to locate.

30. CENEP (1979), Table 4.1.

31. CENEP (1979), pp. 52, 108.

32. Dietz (1986), p. 84.

33. Dietz (1986), pp. 126–29.

34. Quoted in Dietz (1986), p. 132.

35. Weisskoff and Wolff (1975).

36. Dietz (1986), Table 5.10.

37. Dietz (1986), Tables 5.5, 5.7.

38. Dietz (1986), Table 4.3.

39. CENEP (1979), Table 4.5.

40. U.S. Department of Commerce, Vol. II (1979), p. 46.

41. Safa (1985), p. 11.

42. Dietz (1986), p. 254.

43. U.S. Department of Commerce, Vol. I (1979), p. 5.

44. Weisskoff (1986), chap. 8.

45. The source of these and subsequent migration figures for Puerto Rico is the Puerto Rico Planning Board.

46. Fitzpatrick (1971), p. 15.

47. U.S. Bureau of the Census (1953), Table 4.

48. See Gray (1975).

49. See Ortiz (1986).

50. This and the following estimates of the inflows in each period are drawn from Azicri (1981); Fagen, Brody, and O'Leary (1968); and Portes and Bach (1985).

51. Fagen, Brody, and O'Leary (1968), p. 23.

52. Portes and Bach (1985), Table 62 and pp. 148–49.

53. Bach, Bach, and Triplett (1981).

54. Portes and Bach (1985), Table 39.

55. Rogg (1974), p. 28.

56. Portes and Bach (1985), Table 62 and p. 193.

57. Portes and Bach (1985), Table 64.

58. Portes and Bach (1985), Table 63.

59. For this and other selected economic and demographic data on the principal source countries, see Appendix Table 2A.2.

60. Their study traces the 300,000 figure back to an early inaccurate tabulation and interpretation of the 1981 Dominican census.

61. There is still relatively little research and many unresolved questions about the role of intermediate sectors in developing economies. See D. L. Johnson (1983).

62. Bray (1985, 1987) reports that a survey of one Dominican town indicated that 84 percent of those in the highest socioeconomic group were return migrants, compared with only 22 percent of the rural sector. Return visits of one to four months each year appeared quite common.

63. World Bank (1984).

64. See Chaney (1976).

65. For survey details and the results cited, see Urrea (1982). See also Gurak and Kritz (1983 and 1988) for comparisons of Colombian and Dominican migrants.

66. See U.S. General Accounting Office (1984).

67. Passell and Woodrow (1987).

68. On the recent economic history of the region see, for example, Weeks (1985).

69. Given the selection method employed and the small sample size, one suspects that such estimates could be biased upward. But the general finding is consistent with the results discussed earlier for other Hispanic immigrant groups in studies using quite different sampling methods.

REFERENCES

ACUNA, RODOLFO. 1981. *Occupied America: A History of Chicanos.* New York: Harper & Row.

ASPE, PEDRO, and JAVIER BERISTAIN. 1984. "The Distribution of Education and Health Opportunities and Services." In *The Political Economy of Income Distribution in Mexico,* edited by Pedro Aspe and Paul Sigmund. New York: Holmes & Meier.

BACH, ROBERT L. 1978. "Mexican Immigration and the American State." *International Migration Review* 12(4) (Winter):536–58.

BACH, ROBERT L., JENNIFER BACH, and TIMOTHY TRIPLETT. 1981–82. "The 'Flotilla Entrants.'" *Cuban Studies* 11:29–48.

BARKIN, DAVID. 1975. "Mexico's Albatross: The U.S. Economy." *Latin American Perspectives* 2 (Summer):64–80.

BARRERA, MARIO. *Race and Class in the Southwest.* South Bend, IN: Notre Dame University Press.

BRAY, D. B. 1985. "La Agricultura de Exportación, la Formación de Clases y Migración en la Republica Dominicana." *Ciencia y Sociedad* (Santo Domingo) 10 (April/June):217–36.

———. 1987. "The Dominican Exodus: Origins, Problems, Solutions." In *The Caribbean Exodus,* edited by B. B. Levine. New York: Praeger.

BRIGGS, VERNON. 1984. *Immigration Policy and the American Labor Force.* Baltimore: Johns Hopkins University Press.

BUSTAMENTE, JORGE A. 1978. *A Mexican Migration to the United States.* Cambridge, MA: MIT Press.

CENTRO DE ESTUDIOS PUERTORRIQUENOS (CENEP), City University of New York. 1979. *Labor Migration Under Capitalism: The Puerto Rican Experience.* New York: Monthly Review Press.

CHANEY, E. M. 1976. "Colombian Migration to the United States (Part 2)." In *The Dynamics of International Migration.* Washington, DC: Smithsonian Institution.

CLARK, VICTOR S. 1908. "Mexican Labor in the United States." *Bulletin of the U.S. Department of Labor* 78. Washington, DC: U.S. Department of Labor.

COCKROFT, JAMES. 1983. *Mexico.* New York: Monthly Review Press.

———. 1986. *Outlaws in the Promised Land: Mexican Immigrant Workers and America's Future.* New York: Grove Press.

CORNELIUS, WAYNE A. 1978. "Mexican Migration to the United States: Causes, Consequences, and U.S. Responses." Working paper, Center for International Studies, MIT.

CORWIN, ARTHUR. 1978. "Early Mexican American Migration." *Immigrants—and Immigrants: Perspectives on Mexican Migration to the United States,* edited by Arthur Corwin. Westport, CT: Greenwood Press.

CORWIN, ARTHUR, and LAWRENCE A. CARDOSO. 1978. "Vamos Al Norte: Causes of Mass Mexican Migration to the United States." In *Immigrants—and Immigrants: Perspectives on Mexican Migration to the United States.* Westport, CT: Greenwood Press.

DIETZ, JAMES L. 1986. *Economic History of Puerto Rico.* Princeton, NJ: Princeton University Press.

EVANS, JOHN S., and DILMUS D. JAMES. 1979. "Conditions of Employment and Income Distribution in Mexico as Incentives for Mexican Migration to the U.S." *International Migration Review* 13 (Spring):4–24.

FAGEN, RICHARD R., RICHARD A. Brody, and THOMAS J. O'LEARY. 1968. *Cubans in Exile: Disaffection and the Revolution.* Palo Alto, CA: Stanford University Press.

FITZPATRICK, JOSEPH. 1971. *Puerto Rican Americans: The Meaning of Migration to the Mainland.* Englewood Cliffs, NJ: Prentice-Hall.

GALARZA, ERNESTO. 1964. *Merchants of Labor.* Santa Barbara, CA: McNally & Loftin.

GRASMUCK, SHERRI. 1984. "Consequences of Dominican Out-Migration for National Development: The Case of Santiago." In *Americans in the New International Division of Labor,* edited by Steven Sanderson. New York: Holmes & Meier.

GRAY, LOIS S. 1975. "The Jobs Puerto Ricans Hold in New York." *Monthly Labor Review* 98 (October):12–16.

GURAK, DOUGLAS, and MARY KRITZ. 1983. "Kinship Networks and the Settlement Process: Dominican and Colombian Immigrants in New York City." Unpublished paper, Hispanic Research Center, Fordham University.

———. 1988. "New York Hispanics: A Demographic Overview." In *The Hispanic Experience in the United States,* edited by Edna Acosta-Belen and Barbara J. Sjostrom. New York: Praeger.

HOFFMAN, ABRAHAM. 1978. "Repatriation During the Great Depression: A Reappraisal." In *Immigrants—and Immigrants: Perspectives on Mexican Labor in the United States,* edited by Arthur Corwin. Westport, CT: Greenwood Press.

JOHNSON, D. L., ed. 1983. *Intermediate Classes: Historical Studies of Class Formation on the Periphery.* London: Sage.

McWilliams, Carey. 1968. *North from Mexico.* New York: Greenwood Press.

Mills, C. Wright, Clarence Senior, and Rose Goldsen. 1950. *Puerto Rican Journey.* New York: Harper & Row.

North, David, and Marian Houston. 1976. *The Characteristics and Role of Illegal Immigrants in the U.S. Labor Market.* Washington, DC: Linton.

Ortiz, Vilma. 1986. "Changes in the Characteristics of Puerto Rican Migrants from 1955 to 1980." *International Migration Review* 20 (Fall):612–28.

Passel, Jeffrey S., and Karen Woodrow. 1987. "Change in the Undocumented Alien Population in the United States: 1979–83." *International Migration Review* 21 (Winter):1304–34.

Poitras, Guy. 1983. "Through the Revolving Door: Central American Manpower in the United States." *Inter-American Economic Affairs* 36 (Spring):63–78.

Portes, Alejandro, and Robert Bach. 1985. *Latin Journey: Cuban and Mexican Immigrants to the United States.* Berkeley: University of California Press.

Rogg, Eleanor. 1974. *The Assimilation of Cuban Exiles.* New York: Aberdeen Press.

Safa, Helen. 1985. "Female Employment in the Puerto Rican Working Class." In *Women and Change in Latin America,* edited by June Nash and Helen Safa. South Hadley, MA: Bergin & Garvey.

Samora, Julian. 1971. *Los Mojados: The Wetback Story.* South Bend, IN: University of Notre Dame Press.

Ugalde, Antonio, Frank D. Bean, and Gilbert Cardenas. 1979. "International Migration from the Dominican Republic: Findings from a National Survey." *International Migration Review* 13 (Summer):235–54.

U.S. Bureau of the Census. 1953. *U.S. Census of Population 1950.* Vol. II: *Characteristics of the Population,* Part 1 (U.S. Summary) and Part 53 (Puerto Rico). Washington, DC: Government Printing Office.

———. 1964. *U.S. Census of the Population 1960.* Vol. I: *Characteristics of the Population,* Parts 1 and 53. Washington, DC: Government Printing Office.

———. 1973. *U.S. Census of the Population 1970.* Vol. 1: *Characteristics of the Population,* Parts 1 and 53. Washington, DC: Government Printing Office.

———. 1975. *Historical Statistics of the United States: Colonial Times to 1970,* Part 1. Washington, DC: Government Printing Office.

———. 1984a. *1980 Census of Population, General Social and Economic Characteristics.* Washington, DC: Government Printing Office.

———. 1984b. *1980 Census, Detailed Population Characteristics.* Washington, DC: Government Printing Office.

———. 1989a. *Current Population Reports: The Hispanic Population in the United States, March 1988.* Series P-20. Washington, DC: Government Printing Office.

———. 1989b. *Current Population Reports: The Black Population in the United States, March 1988.* Series P-20. Washington, DC: Government Printing Office.

U.S. Department of Commerce. 1979. *Economic Study of Puerto Rico,* 2 vols. Washington, DC: Government Printing Office.

U.S. General Accounting Office. 1984. *Central American Refugees: Regional Conditions and Prospects and Potential Impact on the United States.* Report to the Congress of the U.S. by the Controller General of the U.S. Washington, DC: Government Printing Office.

U.S. Immigration and Naturalization Service. 1988. *Statistical Yearbook of the Immigration and Naturalization Service, 1987.* Washington, DC: Government Printing Office.

———. 1989a. *Immigration Statistics: Fiscal Year 1988* (Advance Report). Washington, DC: Government Printing Office.

———. 1989b. *Provisional Legalization Application Statistics.* Washington, DC: INS Office of Plans and Analysis.

Urrea Giraldo, Fernando. 1982. "Life Strategies and the Labor Market: Colombians in New York City in the 1970s." *Occasional Paper* 34, Center for Latin American and Caribbean Studies, New York University.

Warren, Robert, and Jeffrey Passel. 1987. "A Count of the Uncountable: Estimates of Undocumented Aliens Counted in the 1980 Census." *Demography* 24 (August):375–93.

Weeks, John. 1985. *The Economies of Central America.* New York: Holmes & Meier.

Weisskoff, Richard. 1986. *Factories and Food Stamps: The Puerto Rican Model of Development.* Baltimore: Johns Hopkins University Press.

Weisskoff, Richard, and Edward Wolff. 1975. "Development and Trade Dependence: The Case of Puerto Rico." *Review of Economics and Statistics* 57 (November):470–77.

World Bank. 1984. *Colombia: Economic Development and Policy Under Changing Conditions.* Washington, DC: World Bank.

22

"WE'D LOVE TO HIRE THEM BUT . . ."
The Meaning of Race for Employers

Kathryn M. Neckerman • *Joleen Kirschenman*

Employers and black job applicants encounter one another in a specific context of race and class relations. Widespread publicity, emphasizing poor schools, drug use, crime, and welfare dependency, shapes the way city residents view the inner city and whom they associate with it. These perceptions shade the relations between black and white, middle class and poor, sometimes engendering suspicion, resentment, and misunderstanding (Anderson 1990).

Given the uncertainty that characterizes most hiring decisions, it is likely that these perceptions and strained relations influence employers' hiring practices. For instance, employers might recruit selectively in order to avoid inner-city residents because of expectations that they would be poor employees. Race and class misunderstanding or tension might be manifest in the job interview itself. If hiring practices are largely subjective, the influence of these perceptions about the inner city may be even more influential than would otherwise be the case.

Using data from interviews with Chicago employers, we examine employers' hiring strategies and consider their potential

for racial bias. We focus on three hiring practices: selective recruitment, job interviews, and employment tests. We examine employers' views of different categories of workers and the way these preconceptions guide their recruitment strategies, and then discuss employers' accounts of job interviews with inner-city blacks. Finally, we examine the relationship between employment testing and black representation in entry-level jobs. The research is exploratory. We cannot provide rigorous evidence about the extent of racial bias. However, our interview data lend themselves to a fine-grained description of patterns of racial bias in hiring strategies. The description can serve as the basis for future empirical work on the employment problems of disadvantaged minorities.

While there has been sustained interest in the high joblessness of blacks in the United States, most research considers skill deficiencies or spatial mismatches in labor supply and demand rather than barriers to employment that exist in the hiring process. To the extent that research examines access to jobs, most studies focus on the use of networks in filling lower-skilled positions and on inner-city blacks' lack of access to job networks (Braddock and McPartland 1987, Wilson 1987). The following survey of the literature examines the hiring process in more detail and explores how racial bias might occur at different points, from recruitment of the applicant pool to screening and interviewing.

Selective Recruitment and Racial Bias

Employers' recruitment practices are influenced by many considerations, including cost and time. For instance, employers use personal networks to recruit because they are inexpensive and fast. Small firms, lacking elaborate personnel offices, are especially likely to use informal networks, while larger firms are more likely to supplement networks with recruitment through classified ads and other formal sources.

Because screening applicants is costly, employers have an incentive to recruit selectively, excluding potential applicants they view as unpromising. Selective recruitment might be based on "statistical discrimination" or the use of nonproductive characteristics such as race to predict productive characteristics that are more difficult to observe (Aigner and Cain 1977, Bielby and Baron 1986, Phelps 1972, Thurow 1975). Employers' expectations about the productivity of different groups may be influenced by past experience, prejudice, or the mass media. Selective recruitment might also, of course, be motivated by a "taste" for discrimination or a reluctance to hire, work with, or be served by members of a particular group (Becker 1957).

Previous research suggests that employers recruit selectively based on race, ethnicity, class, and neighborhood. Of these categories, race and ethnicity have received the most attention, and empirical research has documented less favorable treatment of black and Hispanic job applicants (e.g., Braddock and McPartland 1987, Cross et al. 1990, Culp and Dunson 1986). But employers also share the larger society's perceptions of the "underclass," associating crime, illiteracy, drug use, and poor work ethic with the inner-city black population. Thus, they may look for indicators of class and "space," or neighborhood of reference,

among black workers (Kirschenman and Neckerman 1991). Studies find that employers evaluate the educational credentials and references of blacks differently depending on whether applicants are from the central city or the suburbs (Crain n.d.; see also Braddock et al. 1986). Other employers confound race, class, and "space," generalizing their negative perceptions of lower-class or inner-city workers to all black applicants (Kirschenman and Neckerman 1991).

Race Bias in the Job Interview

Almost all employers select new employees by using job interviews, usually in combination with other bases for screening such as test scores, work experience, references, and credentials. Job interviews are widely used despite psychological research showing little correlation between interviewer ratings of job applicants and measured skills or job performance.

Research on white-black interaction suggests that prejudice or cultural misunderstanding create difficulties for blacks, especially lower-class blacks who interview with white employers. While classic racism—the view of people of color as undifferentiated—has declined, race relations between strangers are often tense and shaded with fear, suspicion, and moral contempt (Blauner 1989; see also Anderson 1990). Those from different racial or ethnic groups lack the common experiences and conversation patterns that ease interaction in impersonal settings (Erickson 1975). Blacks and whites often misread each others' verbal and nonverbal cues (Kochman 1983). These misunderstandings are exacerbated when class as well as race separates people (Berg forthcoming, Glasgow 1981).

In research on employment interviews, race itself typically has little or no effect on interviewers' ratings, but race is significantly associated with interviewer ratings of nonverbal cues such as facial expression, posture, and certain aspects of voice that are known to influence employers (Arvey 1979, Parsons and Liden 1984). In one field study, for instance, black job applicants were rated significantly less favorably than whites on posture, voice articulation, voice intensity, and eye contact (Parsons and Liden 1984). Behavior or language seen as inappropriate also lowered interviewer ratings of objective characteristics such as education and experience (Hollenbeck 1984).

Race Bias in Employment Testing

Employment tests have been used for decades to measure general aptitude and specific job skills. Testing is used in hiring for perhaps one out of four high-school-level positions, with tests more common in the public sector and less common in unionized firms (Braddock and McPartland 1987, Cohen and Pfeffer 1986, Hamilton and Roessner 1972). Estimates of test validity vary. A recent meta-analysis of studies of the General Aptitude Test Battery (GATB), a widely used test of cognitive and psychomotor skills, estimated a .19 correlation between test scores and job performance (Hartigan and Wigdor 1989).

Racial bias in hiring stemming from the use of employment tests has been a long-standing concern. In 1971, the *Griggs v. Duke Power* decision required that if employment tests or other apparently neutral means of screening were shown to have an adverse impact on the hiring of protected groups, the firm must demonstrate that the test is job-related. Employers have found it difficult to validate general aptitude tests to the courts' satisfaction and have lost most testing cases since 1971 (Burstein and Pitchford 1990). However, this litigation stimulated the research on test validation. The meta-analysis cited above found that the correlation between test scores and job performance ratings was lower for minority

employees than for nonminority employees but that on average test scores did not underpredict minority job performance (Hartigan and Wigdor 1989). Tests of skills such as typing are more easily validated and have not been open to the same legal challenges.

Most research on employment testing simply compares test scores to job performance rather than comparing testing to other means of employee selection. Yet if employers do not test applicants, they may rely more heavily on selective recruitment or on subjective impressions in the job interview. Thus, even if tests introduced some racial bias, subjective means of screening might disadvantage minority applicants more. For instance, if employers base hiring decisions on their preconceptions about inner-city schools rather than on tests of individual job applicants, then *all* graduates of those schools might be screened out. This hypothesis is consistent with other research suggesting that formal job search methods work better for blacks than informal methods because the formal methods provide more objective criteria by which employers can evaluate job applicants (Holzer 1987).

The Chicago Employer Survey

Our research is based on face-to-face interviews with 185 employers in Chicago and the surrounding Cook County. The sample was stratified by location, industry, and size, and firms were sampled in proportion to the distribution of employment in Cook County.[1] Inner-city firms were oversampled.

---

[1]Given our focus on employment opportunities, the purpose of the design was to yield a sample that approximately matched the distribution of employment in Cook County. For instance, if 5 percent of Cook County jobs were in large, inner-city manufacturing firms, then 5 percent of the interviews should be in large, inner-city manufacturing firms. The sample necessarily underrepresents small *firms,* but does so in order to gain a more representative picture of employment opportunities.

Unless otherwise specified, all descriptive statistics presented here are weighted to adjust for oversampling in the inner city. As no comprehensive list exists of Chicago-area employers, the sampling frame was assembled from two directories of Illinois businesses, supplemented with the telephone book for categories of firms underrepresented in the business directories. The field period lasted from July 1988 to March 1989, and yielded a completion rate of 46 percent. In terms of industry and size, the completed sample's weighted distribution roughly matches the distribution of employment in Cook County.[2]

Our initial contacts and the majority of interviews themselves were conducted with the highest ranking official at the sampled establishment. The interviewers and respondents were not matched by race with the respondents. All of the interviewers were non-Hispanic white; 8.5 percent of the respondents were black, 1.5 percent were Hispanic, and the remainder were non-Hispanic white.

The interview schedule included both closed- and open-ended questions about employers' hiring and recruitment practices and about their perceptions of Chicago's labor force and business climate. Because of the many open-ended questions, we taped the interviews. Item nonresponse varied depending on the sensitivity and factual difficulty of the question, with most nonresponse due to lack of knowledge rather than refusal to answer. In addition, the length and detail of responses to open-ended questions varied widely. Some employers volunteered additional information in response to closed-ended questions, which provided useful context for interpretation of the survey results.

Most closed-ended questions focused on the "sample job," defined as the most typical entry-level position in the firm's modal category—sales, clerical, skilled, semi-skilled, unskilled, or service. Entry-level jobs were selected for study in order to focus on the employment of disadvantaged workers, many of whom are first-time job seekers with limited skills. Because we sampled firms by industry and size, we do not have a random sample of entry-level jobs. However, when we compared the occupational distribution of our sample jobs to that of Cook County (excluding professional, managerial, and technical categories), we found that the two distributions were quite similar. The sample job serves as the unit of analysis for the quantitative part of this research. In the text, employers are categorized based on these sample jobs.

The interview schedule included several questions that bear on issues of hiring strategies and racial bias. We asked closed-ended questions about the race and ethnicity of employees in the sample job, as well as about use of various recruitment sources, the importance of specific hiring criteria, and any credentials or skills required for the sample job. Additionally, in the context of a general discussion of the quality of the work force and of inner-city problems, we asked employers to comment on the high unemployment rates of inner-city black men and women and on any differences they saw between immigrant and native-born workers and among black, white, and Hispanic workers. . . .

Hiring Strategies and Racial Bias

During the time of the survey, the main problem most employers faced was not quantity of job applicants, but "quality."

---

[2]About 22 percent of employers we contacted refused to take part. We did not have the resources to pursue all potential respondents who were willing to be interviewed. Halfway through the field period, we set a minimum 40 percent completion rate in all industry-by-location categories and stopped pursuing unresolved cases in categories with completion rates higher than 40 percent. Response rates by industry, firm size, and location were monitored, and special efforts were made to pursue cases in categories with low completion rates.

Employers complained that Chicago's work force lacked both basic skills and job skills. They were also dissatisfied with work attitudes, with many saying that employees were not as loyal and hard-working as they once were. Also, employers' traditional ways of getting information about job applicants had become less useful. For example, respondents told us that a high school diploma was no longer a reliable indicator of good basic skills. In addition, the threat of lawsuits has made it increasingly difficult to get information from an applicant's previous employers.

In this context, careful screening has become both more important to employers and more difficult to do. To identify good workers, some employers screened applicants using skills tests, "integrity interviews," psychological profiles, and drug tests. Others tried to recruit selectively or used informal networks. Almost half of our respondents said that employee referrals were their best source of qualified applicants, and it has become more common for employers to pay recruitment bonuses to employees whose referrals are hired. One respondent estimated that he hired 80 percent of all employee referrals, compared to only 5 percent of all applicants attracted by a newspaper ad.

In the following sections, we examine the implications of these hiring strategies for black employment. We consider three ways of screening potential workers: selective recruitment, job interviews, and employment testing.

Selective Recruitment

More often than not, employers recruited selectively, limiting their search for job candidates rather than casting a wide net. Employers sometimes explained their recruitment strategies in terms of practicality, for instance the ease or low cost of using personal networks or the difficulty of screening the large numbers of applications yielded by newspaper ads. But far more often they said their recruitment strategies were intended to bring them better applicants. The criteria of applicant quality they expressed were formally race- and class-neutral, but the recruitment strategies designed to attract high-quality applicants were not. When employers targeted their recruitment efforts at neighborhoods or institutions, they avoided inner-city populations. In addition, selective recruiting was more widespread among employers in poor, black neighborhoods than among those located elsewhere. The perceptions that employers expressed of inner-city black workers are consistent with the interpretation that they avoid these applicants because on average they expect them to be lower-quality workers.

One way of screening the applicant pool is by not advertising job openings in the newspapers. More than 40 percent of our respondents did not use newspaper advertising for their entry-level jobs, and those who did place ads often did so as a last resort after employee networks had been unsuccessful. Moreover, about two-thirds of all city employers who advertised used neighborhood, suburban, or ethnic papers in addition to or instead of the metropolitan papers. Using neighborhood or ethnic papers (here, "local" papers) allowed employers to target particular populations, usually white, ethnic, or Hispanic. For instance, one downtown law firm advertised in white ethnic neighborhoods because its residents were believed to have a better work ethic. On the other hand, a few white-collar employers told us they advertised jobs in the *Defender*, a black newspaper, because of a commitment to minority hiring or simply to "keep the numbers in balance." In most cases we cannot identify the specific neighborhoods which employers targeted because respondents were not asked for this detailed information. But the effect of recruiting from local papers is evident from the survey. City employers who advertised only in local papers averaged 16 percent black in the sample job, compared to 32 percent black for those who advertised in the metropolitan papers.

Recruiting based on the quality or location of schools also provided employers with a way of screening. A downtown employer, for instance, believed that youth from suburban schools had better writing skills. Although the firm advertised over the entire metropolitan area, suburban resumes received more attention. When employers volunteered which schools they recruited from, it was usually Catholic schools and those from the city's white northwest side neighborhoods. One manufacturer posted ads at a Catholic school as well as at two of the city's magnet technical schools. A downtown bank recruited from three northwest side Catholic schools. Recruitment from Catholic schools selects white students disproportionately, but this form of recruitment was not necessarily seen in racial terms. Black Catholic school students were also viewed as more desirable employees than black public school students.

On the other hand, the state employment service and welfare programs which disproportionately refer inner-city blacks were associated with low-quality applicants, or in one respondent's words, "the dregs of the year." Neither agency screened adequately, most employers felt, and as a result tended to send inappropriate or unqualified applicants. A manufacturer who had hired white workers through Job Corps criticized the program, saying that none of them had worked out: "As a group I would be prejudiced against them." Another said:

Any time I've taken any recommendations from state agencies, city agencies, or welfare agencies I get really people who are not prepared to come to work on time, not prepared to see that a new job is carried through, that it's completed. I mean there just doesn't seem to be a work ethic involved in these people.

Most employers did not recruit through these agencies; only a third of all employers used the state employment agency, and 16 percent used welfare programs.

Employers in inner-city areas of the city were more likely than other employers to recruit selectively. For instance, they were less likely to recruit from schools or local newspapers. They tried to recruit the best of the local labor force by using labor market intermediaries such as informal networks or formal agencies to screen workers. As other research has shown, because blacks were seen as higher-risk employees, the recommendations and information provided by these intermediaries could be especially important for them (Coverdill 1990). One respondent attributed her firm's success with black workers to their heavy use of employee referrals. Another said employers were likely to be wary of a black man "unless he's got an 'in.'" A large southside employer recruited local high school or college students and added, "It gets them in the door if they're children of university people we know."

Large inner-city employers were especially likely to use formal labor market intermediaries. An inner-city day labor agency was able to place many black workers although many clients preferred "carloads of Mexicans"; its manager attributed this success partly to a computerized record-keeping system:

Having so much detail on each individual employee allows us to record in their files good performance and bad performance, and we're therefore much more able to discriminate between good workers and bad, much more so than our competitors, who would just take anybody off the street, and because they can't really monitor somebody's performance, why take a risk? Whereas we're in a position to take a risk, because if the person doesn't pan out, either he goes to a different job, or we tell him goodbye. . . . It's after they're on the payroll that you really do your screening.

An inner-city hospital developed a "feeder network" into nearby elementary and high schools, funding tutors, child care for teen mothers, and other educational assistance, and providing information about health care careers for those who went on to college. The hospital used its feeder system to "draw the best talent on the top to us. . . . They've already got the work ethic down, they've been dealing with both school and work, we also know what's going on with the schooling, the grades and all." The hospital also recruited staff through community jobs programs and employee networks, but not newspapers. "If you are just a cold applicant," the hospital's representative said, "chances of you getting in are almost nil."

Inner-city employers not large enough to develop these extensive screening mechanisms were at a disadvantage. One inner-city retailer said that young workers were disrespectful and prone to steal; she added, "I think I'm getting the best of what I've got to select from, and they're still no good. And other people in the same line of business say the same thing. I know the guy at the gas station, the guy who runs the Burger King, and all of us say the same thing." Even these smaller employers tried less elaborate means of screening. The retailer just cited recruited some employees through a youth mentoring program. A fast food manager

sent prospective workers to a distant suburb for training as a way of selecting the most motivated.

The interviews suggest that selective recruitment designed to attract higher-quality applicants disproportionately screens out inner-city blacks. Employers' perceptions of inner-city black workers are consistent with the interpretation that at least some do this deliberately. "The blacks that are employed are just not as good, not that there aren't good blacks, but it's a smaller percent than it would be of whites, for whatever reasons, cultural things, or family background, whatever," said one respondent. . . . Employers were especially likely to say that inner-city blacks lacked the work ethic, had a bad attitude toward work, and were unreliable; they also expected them to lack skills, especially basic skills. About half said that these workers had a poor work ethic. In the words of employers: "they don't want to work," "they don't know how to work," "they cannot handle the simplest of tasks," and "they come late and leave early." About 40 percent said inner-city black workers had attitude problems, including a bad attitude toward work as well as apathy and arrogance: "They've got an attitude problem. They want to be catered to . . . they want it handed to them, they don't want to do anything." Another respondent said that black men have a "chip on their shoulder; [they] resent being told what to do." One third of all employers said black workers tended to be undependable, "here today, gone tomorrow."

These perceptions of inner-city black workers are likely to underlie much of the selective recruitment discussed earlier. It is impossible for us to say whether employers avoid these applicants because of their race or their class, or for some other reason; race and class are so confounded in a setting like Chicago. But the effect of selective recruitment is to screen out disadvantaged black workers.

Social Interaction in the Job Interview

Virtually all employers interviewed job applicants, using these interviews to assess a wide range of qualities including literacy, values, common sense, integrity, dependability, intelligence, and character. Although they acknowledged the subjectivity of selection through interviews, they were confident their real world experience gave them the ability to spot good workers. The interview may take on particular importance for inner-city black applicants. Potentially, it is an arena in which they might overcome the negative images associated with their race or other markers such as neighborhood or school. One respondent described his bad experiences with black employees, but added that not all blacks were bad workers: "Well, you know when you talk to somebody you can tell a certain amount of something." Another noted that if she interviewed someone from the projects, "I would really spend a lot of time on prior work history and the types of things, the tasks that their job [requires]." These employers, and perhaps others, gave greater weight to the interview when applicants were poor or black.

Discussion of past work experience is generally an important aspect of the job interview. Searching for indications of dependability and willingness to work, employers said they probed reasons for gaps in applicants' work records. Unemployment itself did not disqualify an applicant with an acceptable excuse, such as illness or family responsibilities, and the interview provided a chance for an applicant to justify his or her work history.

In addition to relatively straightforward questions about work experience, employers often developed their own subjective "tests" of productivity and character. For instance, a manufacturer of transportation equipment

asked if applicants had a "personal philosophy about work, a personal work ethic." Another manufacturer used the interview to judge "how the person looks at life, you know, is it what's in it for me or . . . is it a positive attitude." Much depended on the "gut reaction" of the employer. When one respondent was hired, she described how she and the recruiter "just clicked. I had the stuff, but also we just, just clicked. It's real important." Many paid attention to how expressive or open an applicant was. A law firm supervisor scorned the textbook job interview methods, saying what mattered to her was how "casual, frank, and honest" people were. A real estate developer looked for "someone that appears to sit up straight, talk expressively . . . [who] appears to be intelligent, articulate, forthcoming with their answers—you don't have to drag every word out of them." A hotelier, looking for desk clerks who could handle stress, said "I think you can determine that from how forthright they are in the interview."

Complicating interaction during the job interview is many employers' distrust of job applicants in general, and perhaps minority applicants in particular. Employers complained that some applicants lied about their work record and skills. Lying on applications was one common reason for rejecting applicants at a security firm: "Well, you know, you lied about your driver's license. They have previously been suspended or a couple of your references said they don't even know you or you said you went to a certain school, you didn't go to this particular school." A clerical employer complained, "They'll come in, say they type 50, 60 words a minute, and you put them on a typewriter and they type 20. Or they'll say they have computer experience, and then it turns out they don't know what a cursor is." Another said, "They've gotten to be so good at conning people that it's just frightening." Such falsification was mentioned more often by employers who saw many minority applicants, and one respondent said that black men were more likely to falsify their applications.

Other research suggests that inner-city black applicants experience difficulty in job interview interactions, and indeed, we heard some explicit criticisms of how inner-city blacks interview. Most common were complaints about applicants dressed in shabby or inappropriate clothing or coming late to interviews. But some respondents said more generally that inner-city blacks, especially men, did not know how to interview: they "aren't prepared; they don't have the enthusiasm"; they were belligerent or had "a chip on their shoulder"; they didn't know dates of employment or provided inconsistent information. One respondent commented that black men were not willing to "play the game" and to "follow the rules."

Our question about whether employers might be wary of poor people or those from the projects drew similar responses: applicants from a poor neighborhood did not know how to present themselves. A manufacturer said that project residents would be favorably evaluated if they had a positive attitude, but that they were not well equipped to "come in and really sell themselves." A clerical employer commented. "You don't need to look at the address to know where they're from; it's how people come across; they don't know how to behave in an office." A number of respondents remarked on cultural differences between inner-city blacks and the middle-class whites who dominate in business settings. Inner-city residents come from "a different world," said one manufacturer; "we don't realize that their rules are very different than ours."

It is obvious that job interviews are biased in favor of people who are friendly and articulate. But we find evidence that interviewing well goes beyond interpersonal skills to common understandings of appropriate interaction and conversational style—in short, shared culture. Job applicants must be sensitive to verbal and nonverbal cues and to the hidden agenda underlying interviewers' questions. They may be called upon to talk about abstract matters such as philosophy of work. And in discussing their past work experience, potentially an awkward subject for inner-city applicants with few previous jobs, they must be forthcoming and honest. Because inner-city blacks have trouble with this interaction, heavy reliance on the interview to assess qualities such as honesty, intelligence, reliability, and so on is likely to disadvantage them.

Skills Tests and Black Representation

About 40 percent of the Chicago employers used formal skills tests to screen for the sample job. It is likely that this high incidence of testing is associated with city employers' distrust of the Chicago public school system and the quality of the city labor force. Only 30 percent of suburban firms in our survey used skills tests. Use of formal skills tests was much more common among clerical employers than among anyone else. More than half of all white-collar employers used conventional tests, measuring skills such as language, spelling, composition, math, typing, and filing speed. The clerical tests ranged from standard typing tests to "matching words in columns and seeing whether they know their ABCs" for filing.

Blue-collar employers also gave tests, most often informally. Skilled and craft employers often asked prospective employees to name tools or perform a given task. A precision tool manufacturer thought certification was helpful, "But most everything's going to come out on the test anyway; no matter what kind of paper people bring in, when he sets them up out there and they make the piece, it'll show." Employers of semi-skilled or unskilled blue-collar workers often screened for basic skills informally, observing how well employees filled out job applications; a few required a high school diploma as a proxy for literacy. Some had simple tests embedded in job application forms. A transportation employer described his firm's hiring process: "They fill out an application, which includes a little test—see whether they can read, write, and add." Another employer "sit[s] them down at a machine, [to] see how well they can do."

When employers have relatively objective means of getting information about job candidates, we would expect them to place less weight on more subjective and presumably more racially-biased hiring strategies. . . .

Chicago employers who test for skills, either formally or informally, tend to have higher proportions of blacks in the sample job than employers who do not test. These findings must be interpreted cautiously because there are alternative explanations for which we could not adequately test. For instance, it is possible that these employers test for skills because they attract more black applicants. It might also be that their hiring criteria differ from those of employers who do not test. However, our results suggest the need for future research to address these issues.

. . .

Our evidence suggests that negative preconceptions and strained race relations both hamper inner-city black workers in the labor market. Many respondents perceived inner-city black workers to be deficient in work ethic and work attitudes, as well as in skills. Employers commonly directed their recruitment to white neighborhoods and Catholic or magnet schools and avoided recruiting from city-wide newspapers and public agencies because they believed these recruiting strategies brought them better workers. By design or not, these practices

excluded blacks disproportionately from their applicant pool.

The job interview could be an opportunity for inner-city black job applicants to counter these negative stereotypes. But inner-city black job seekers with limited work experience and little familiarity with the white, middle-class world are also likely to have difficulty in the typical job interview. A spotty work record will have to be justified; misunderstanding and suspicion may undermine rapport and hamper communication. However qualified they are for the job, inner-city black applicants are more likely to fail subjective "tests" of productivity given during the interview.

Finally, employers who use skills tests have on average a higher proportion of black workers in the sample job than employers who do not test. Again, our results do not indicate that skills tests involve no racial bias but simply that skills tests are less biased than more subjective means of assessing job applicants. It should be emphasized that the survey on which these results were based took place in the context of legal restrictions on the use of employment tests and in a particular social context. The findings may not be generalizable to the time before these legal restrictions were enacted, nor do they indicate the likely effects of lifting these restrictions.

Our study was restricted to entry-level jobs and excluded professional, managerial, and technical positions; therefore, our results cannot be generalized to higher-level positions or to promotion rather than hiring. It is possible that promotion decisions are less prone to racial bias because employers have more information about individual job performance and need not guess about productivity based on markers such as race or class. Consistent with this, one study shows that educational credentials are more influential in hiring than in promotion (Bills 1988). On the other hand, to the extent that higher-level positions require contact with clients, supervision of staff, or interaction with executive or professional personnel, then the hiring criteria are likely to emphasize social skills and cultural compatibility, and promotion decisions may be more subjective. More research will be needed to distinguish these two effects.

The ways some employers have adapted to increasing skill demands and declining labor force quality are not race- or class-neutral. By directing recruitment away from inner-city neighborhoods, employers may provide themselves with a higher-skilled applicant pool but at the expense of qualified inner-city applicants. Attention should be given to ways that inner-city residents can demonstrate their competence, whether through certification by schools, screening by labor market intermediaries, or more extensive testing by employers. If rewards are not forthcoming for those who do improve their educational and work skills, inner-city residents' motivation to get education and training is likely to diminish.

Although we have emphasized the role of racial bias in the hiring process, the findings of this study are consistent with other interpretations of inner-city residents' employment problems. Problems of skills mismatch are evident in employers' concern with "quality" not "quantity" of applicants. Researchers' criticisms of the quality of ghetto schools are certainly echoed by employers. Finally, this work supports the emphasis others have given to job networks, suggesting that personal and institutional "connections" may be even more important in the inner city than they are elsewhere.

REFERENCES

AIGNER, DENNIS J., and GLEN C. CAIN. 1977. "Statistical Theories of Discrimination in the Labor Market." *Industrial and Labor Relations Review* 30:175–87.

ANDERSON, ELIJAH. 1990. *Streetwise: Race, Class, and Change in an Urban Community.* Chicago: University of Chicago Press.

ARVEY, RICHARD D. 1979. "Unfair Discrimination in the Employment Interview: Legal and Psychological Aspects." *Psychological Bulletin* 86:736–65.

BECKER, GARY S. 1957. *The Economics of Discrimination.* Chicago: University of Chicago Press.

BERG, LINNEA. Forthcoming. Ph.D. dissertation. Evanston, IL: Northwestern University.

BIELBY, WILLIAM T., and JAMES N. BARON. 1986. "Men and Women at Work: Sex Segregation and Statistical Discrimination." *American Journal of Sociology* 91:759–99.

BILLS, DAVID B. 1988. "Educational Credentials and Promotions: Does Schooling Do More Than Get You in the Door?" *Sociology of Education* 61:52–60.

BLAUNER, BOB. 1989. *Black Lives, White Lives: Three Decades of Race Relations in America.* Berkeley: University of California Press.

BRADDOCK, JOMILLS HENRY, II, and JAMES M. MCPARTLAND. 1987. "How Minorities Continue to Be Excluded from Equal Employment Opportunities: Research on Labor Market and Institutional Barriers." *Journal of Social Issues* 43:5–39.

BRADDOCK, JOMILLS HENRY, II, ROBERT L. CRAIN, JAMES M. MCPARTLAND, and R. L. DAWKINS. 1986. "Applicant Race and Job Placement Decisions: A National Survey Experiment." *International Journal of Sociology and Social Policy* 6:3–24.

BURSTEIN, PAUL, and SUSAN PITCHFORD. 1990. "Social-Scientific and Legal Challenges to Education and Test Requirements in Employment." *Social Problems* 37:243–57.

COHEN, YINON, and JEFFREY PFEFFER. 1986. "Organizational Hiring Standards." *Administrative Science Quarterly* 31:1–24.

COVERDILL, JAMES E. 1990. "Personal Contacts and Youth Employment." Unpublished manuscript. Evanston, IL: Northwestern University.

CROSS, HARRY, G. KEWNNEY, J. MELL, and W. ZIMMERMANN. 1990. *Employer Hiring Practices: The Differential Treatment of Hispanic and Anglo Job Seekers.* Washington, DC: Urban Institute Press, Report 90-4.

CRAIN, ROBERT L. n.d. "The Quality of American High School Graduates: What Personnel Officers Say and Do About It." Baltimore: Johns Hopkins University, Center for the Social Organization of Schools.

Culp, Jerome and Bruce H. Dunson. 1986. "Brothers of a Different Color: A Preliminary Look at Employer Treatment of White and Black Youth." Pp. 233–59 in *The Black Youth Employment Crisis,* edited by Richard B. Freeman and Harry J. Holzer. Chicago: University of Chicago Press.

Erickson, Frederick. 1975. "Gatekeeping and the Melting Pot: Interaction in Counseling Encounters." *Harvard Educational Review* 45:44–70.

Glasgow, Douglas G. 1981. *The Black Underclass: Poverty, Unemployment and Entrapment of Ghetto Youth.* New York: Vintage Press.

Hamilton, Gloria Shaw, and J. David Roessner. 1972. "How Employers Screen Disadvantaged Job Applicants." *Monthly Labor Review* 95:14–21.

Hartigan, John A., and Alexandra K. Wigdor, eds. 1989. *Fairness in Employment Testing: Validity Generalization, Minority Issues and the General Aptitude Test Battery.* Washington, DC: National Academy Press.

Hollenbeck, Kevin. 1984. *Hiring Decisions: An Analysis of Columbus Employer Assessments of Youthful Job Applicants.* Columbus: Ohio State University, National Center for Research on Vocational Education.

Holzer, Harry. 1987. "Informal Job Search and Black Youth Unemployment." *American Economic Review* 77:446–52.

Kirschenman, Joleen, and Kathryn M. Neckerman. 1991. "We'd Love to Hire Them but . . .": The Meaning of Race to Employers." Pp. 203–32 in *The Urban Underclass,* edited by Christopher Jencks and Paul Peterson. Washington, DC: Brookings Institution.

Kochman, Thomas. 1983. *Black and White Styles of Conflict.* Chicago: University of Chicago Press.

Parsons, Charles, and Robert C. Liden. 1984. "Interviewer Perceptions of Applicant Qualifications: A Multivariate Field Study of Demographic Characteristics and Nonverbal Cues." *Journal of Applied Psychology* 69:557–68.

Phelps, Edmund. 1972. "The Statistical Theory of Racism and Sexism." *American Economic Review* 62:659–61.

Thurow, Lester. 1975. *Generating Inequality.* New York: Basic Books.

Turner, Margery Austin, Michael Fix, and Raymond J. Struyk. 1991. "Opportunities Denied, Opportunities Diminished: Discrimination in Hiring." Project report. Washington, DC: Urban Institute.

Wilson, William Julius. 1987. *The Truly Disadvantaged: The Inner City, the Underclass, and Public Policy.* Chicago: University of Chicago Press.

23

WHEN THE MELTING POT BOILS OVER
The Irish, Jews, Blacks, and Koreans of New York

Roger Waldinger

Assimilation is the grand theme of American immigration research. The classic sociological position provided an optimistic counter to the dim assessments of the new immigrants prevalent at the early part of the century. Notwithstanding the marked differences that impressed contemporaries, Robert Park, Ernest Burgess, W. I. Thomas, and others contended that the new immigrant groups would lose their cultural distinctiveness and move up the occupational hierarchy. Milton

Roger Waldinger, "When the Melting Pot Boils Over: The Irish, Jews, Blacks, and Koreans of New York," from *The Bubbling Cauldron,* Michael Peter Smith and Joseph R. Feagin, eds. Copyright © 1995 by the University of Minnesota Press. Reprinted with permission from the publisher.

Gordon's now classic volume distilled the essence of the sociological view: immigrant-ethnic groups start at the bottom and gradually move up; their mobility takes place through individual advancement, not group collective action; in the process of moving up, ethnic groups lose their distinctive social structure; and as ethnics become like members of the core group, they become part of the core group, joining it in neighborhoods, in friendship, and eventually in marriage.

But the image of immigrants moving onward and upward is hard to reconcile with the darker, conflictual side of American ethnic life. Conflict, often of the fiercest kind, runs like a red thread through the history of American ethnic groups. Certainly New Yorkers evince an extraordinary propensity to come to blows over racial and ethnic differences. The latest conflicts pitting blacks against Hasidim and Koreans in Brooklyn or Chinese against Puerto Ricans in Manhattan are but the latest episodes in a longer saga, extending from the anti-Catholic crusades of the 1850s to the school conflicts of the 1890s, to the controversies engendered by the Coughlinites and the German Bund of the 1930s, to the school integration struggles of the 1960s, right up to this day.

The contradiction between ethnic assimilation and ethnic conflict is more apparent than real. Where the classic sociological model goes wrong is not in its depiction of an upward trajectory, but rather in its individualistic assumptions about the process of ethnic change. The story of ethnic progress in America can be better thought of as a collective search for mobility, in which the succession of one migrant wave after another ensures a continuous competitive conflict over resources. Groups move up from the bottom by specializing in and dominating a particular branch of economic life; that specialization goes unchallenged as long as the newest arrivals are content to work in the bottom-level jobs for which they were ini-

tially recruited. This [reading] develops the story in the form of brief episodes from the New York experience of four ethnic groups—Irish, Jews, African Americans, and Koreans. Each group is associated with the four successive waves of migration that have swept over New York in the past two hundred years.

The Irish

Nearly one and a half million Irish flocked to the United States between 1846 and 1855 in flight from famine; they converged on the eastern port cities of Boston, Philadelphia, and New York, where, lacking resources, about a quarter stayed. Low levels of education, lack of exposure to industrial or craft work, and lack of capital led the Irish into the lower ranges of manual work, with women taking domestic work and men engaging in insecure, low-paid itinerant employment, especially in construction. Irish progress from the bottom proceeded at a slow pace.

By 1900, however, the Irish had already established themselves in public employment. At the time, the public sector provided relatively few jobs, but this was soon to change. Irish employment in New York City government almost quadrupled between 1900 and 1930, increasing from just under 20,000 to 77,000, while the total number of city workers climbed from 54,000 to 148,000, less than a factor of three.[1]

Irish penetration into the public sector reflected the growing political power of the Democratic machine, which remained Irish dominated. But the machine's hold on local government was met by opposition from WASP reformers. Seeking to break the machine's power by severing the link between political activity and government employment, the reformers installed a civil service system—to little avail. The Irish encountered few effective competitors for city jobs.

There was never any serious threat that WASPs would dislodge the Irish. Moreover, the increasingly numerous Poles, Jews, Italians, and others who were just off the boat had little chance of doing well in essay-type exams against the Irish, who were, after all, native English speakers.

The liabilities of the new immigrants lasted hardly a generation; with the Jews' rapid educational and occupational advancement, another competitor entered the scene. But as long as the Irish, through Tammany Hall's grip over city government, could control municipal hiring, interethnic competition posed little threat. Competition was structured in such a way as to minimize the value of Jews' educational advantages. The patronage system functioned unencumbered throughout Tammany's dominance between 1917 and 1933.

The depression severely challenged Irish control over public jobs; LaGuardia's election in 1933 delivered the coup de grace. Keeping control of City Hall required LaGuardia to undermine the material base of Tammany's power and consolidate his support among groups not firmly under Tammany's tow—the most important of which were the Jews, who had split between LaGuardia and his Tammany opponent in 1933. Both goals could be accomplished in the same way, namely pursuing the administrative changes long championed by the reformers.[2]

The depression and LaGuardia's reforms made city jobs more attractive to highly educated workers, which, under the circumstances, mainly meant Jews. One door at which Jewish competitors knocked was teaching, previously an Irish reserve (as the 1900 statistics show). If Jewish entrance into teaching produced antagonism, far more explosive was the situation in the police force. Twenty-nine thousand men sat for the exam held in April 1939, from whom three hundred were selected to enter the department in 1940. Of these, over one-third were Jews. Not surprisingly, this class of 1940 constituted the first significant proportion of Jews to enter the police.[3]

Jewish-Irish competition produced some other episodes, but conflict between them abated, thanks to the prosperity of the postwar era and the new opportunities it provided. Outmigration to the suburbs and the Sun Belt and mobility into the middle class depleted the ranks of the city's Irish population. By the late 1950s, as Nathan Glazer and Daniel Moynihan noted, so profound was the sense of displacement that the remaining Irish New Yorkers reminded themselves, "There are still some of us left."[4]

Those who are left have kept up the long-established Irish occupational ways. Although the commissioners of the police and fire departments are black and Puerto Rican, respectively, the top brass retains a strongly Irish cast, as does the rank and file. Indeed, the fire department presents a glimpse of New York gone by, with a workforce that is 93 percent white and 80 percent Catholic. Some unions still have a distinctly Irish makeup.[5]

In the 1980s, some of the old niches at last gained new blood, as an influx of new, illegal Irish immigrants fled unemployment in the Republic of Ireland for better times in New York. Whereas black Americans still found the doors of construction unions closed, the new arrivals, dubbed "JFK carpenters," were warmly welcomed by their aging compatriots. Women also retraced the steps of the past, as could be seen from the classified pages of the *Irish Echo,* with its columns of ads for nannies, babysitters, and housekeepers.

The Jews

Although the Jewish presence in New York extends far back, almost to the city's founding, Jews did not become an important, visible element in the city's economic life until the 1880s. Rising anti-Semitism, combined with the pressures of modernization, led to a huge outflow of Jews from Eastern Europe. By 1920, New York, with two million Jews, had become the world's largest Jewish city.

The new arrivals came just when the demand for factory-made clothing began to surge. Many had been tailors in the old country, and although most had worked with needle and thread, they quickly adapted themselves to machine production. As the various components of the clothing industry grew in synergistic fashion, the opportunities for mobility through the ethnic economy multiplied. Through rags, some immigrants found riches; the sweatshop workers who moved to contracting and then to manufacturing, or possibly careers in retailing, filled the newly formed ranks of New York's *alrightniks*.[6]

The Jewish concentration in commerce and clothing manufacture defined their initial place in the ethnic division of labor. Jewish specializations seldom overlapped with the Irish: domestic service and general labor were rarities among the Russians but were common Irish pursuits; by the same token, tailoring and retailing, whether by merchant or peddler, were far more likely to engage Russians than Irish.

As Jews sought to move beyond the ethnic economy, interethnic competition and antagonism grew more intense. The relatively rapid educational progress of younger immigrants and of the second generation prepared them to work outside the ethnic economy, but gentile employers were rarely eager to hire Jews. One study, completed just before the Great Depression, found that the doors of New York's large, corporate organizations—"railroads, banks, insurance companies, lawyers' offices, brokerage houses, the New York Stock Exchange, hotels . . . and the home offices of large corporations of the first rank"—were infrequently opened to Jews.[7] The surge into the schools, and through the schools into the professions, met with resistance from the older, largely Protestant population that dominated these institutions.

In the 1930s, depression and discrimination outside the ethnic economy led many second-generation Jews to seek an alternative in public employment. Although the quest for government jobs, and in particular teaching positions, had started earlier, the straitened circumstances of the 1930s accelerated this search. The quality and quantity of Jews vying for government employment increased, heightening the competitive pressure on the Irish and yielding the antagonism we've already observed.

Jewish-Irish conflict reached its height in the late 1930s; it gradually subsided, replaced by a more explosive, deeply antagonistic relationship with blacks. Although black occupations were more similar to those of the Irish than they were to the Jews', the economic pursuits of Jews put them at odds with blacks on various counts. The Jews dominated small retail activity throughout the city and were particularly prominent in Harlem. The Jewish storeowners in Harlem sold to blacks but preferred not to employ them until protests in the mid-1930s finally forced them to relent. Antagonism toward Jewish shopkeepers in Harlem rose during the 1930s, fueled by the depression and by Jews' broader role as middlemen in the Harlem economy. Frustration boiled over in the riot of 1943, when black Harlemites burned down the stores of Jews in a fury that presaged events to come.[8] Hostility simmered thereafter, reaching the boiling point during the 1960s.

The transformation of the ethnic economy also engendered black-Jewish conflict, Rapid Jewish social mobility meant a dwindling Jewish working class; the diminishing supply of Jewish workers had a particularly notable effect on the garment industry, where Jewish factory owners were forced to hire outsiders in growing numbers—first

Italians, then blacks. In World War II, desperate for workers, Jewish employers hired blacks in great numbers. By 1950, there were 25,000 African American garment workers, 20,000 more than were working in clothing factories ten years before.[9]

But relations between blacks and Jews proved uneasy. Blacks moved into less-skilled, poorer-paying positions, from which mobility into better-remunerated positions proved difficult. Although the garment unions made explicit efforts to organize black workers and integrate them into union structures, few blacks moved up to elected offices, and none high up in the union hierarchy. To protect jobs from southern competitors, the unions adopted a policy of wage restraint, which inevitably meant a softened stance on union employers at home—much to the dismay of black New York garment workers.[10]

The garment business was the Jewish enclave of the past; Jewish mobility into the middle class had made teaching the Jewish niche of the mid-1960s. As the schools came to serve a growing black population, their role was increasingly contested by black students, parents, and protest organizations. The complaints were various, and not all directly linked to the Jews' prominent role in the school system; but the situation in which so many Jews were teachers and so many schools in black neighborhoods were staffed by Jews inevitably led to conflict. In 1968, a black-dominated school board in Brooklyn dismissed a group of white, largely Jewish teachers and replaced them with a mainly black staff; these actions set off a three-month-long strike by the Jewish-led teachers' union. Although the union eventually won, its victory was pyrrhic, at least concerning black-Jewish relations. Memory of the strike and the resentments it fueled have not significantly changed, even a generation later.[11]

What has altered, however, is the economic position of the Jews. The ethnic econ-

omy of the immigrant days remains, but in vestigial form. Although Jews are still active in the garment industry, they mainly concentrate in the designing and merchandising ends. "Goldberg" no longer runs clothing factories; his place has been taken by "Kim" and "Wong," who only employ compatriots, not blacks. The same transformations have changed the face of petty retailing and small landlording—the older flash points of black-Jewish conflict. The Jewish presence in the public sector is also fading fast: working as a city engineer or accountant used to be a Jewish occupation; now these careers engage far many more Patels than Cohens.[12] Only in teaching and in higher education do the Jewish concentrations of the past remain in full force.[13]

A distinctive Jewish role in New York's economy still lives on. It is to be found in the professions, in the persistently high rate of Jewish self-employment, in the prominence of Jews in law, real estate, finance, and the media. But the current Jewish pursuits differ crucially from the older ethnic economy in that they are detached from the dynamics of interethnic competition that characterized earlier periods. In a sense, the material basis that underlay anti-Semitic currents in New York for most of the twentieth century is gone. But its legacy and the many other resources around which groups can compete—status, politics, and territory—ensure continued conflict between Jews and their ethnic neighbors.

The Blacks

In 1890, the black share of the New York population was 1.6 percent—just about what it had been on the eve of the Civil War. But in the 1890s the South started losing blacks due to outmigration, and that loss quickly translated into New York's gain. By 1920, New York housed 150,000 black residents—who, although only 3 percent of the city's population, made New York the country's largest black urban concentration. In the next twenty years, as European immigration faltered and then stopped, and bad conditions in the rural South provided additional reasons to leave, the number of black New Yorkers tripled. Postwar prosperity and a new wave of mechanization down South launched a final, massive flow northward: by 1960, the African American population of New York numbered 1,088,000, of whom approximately 320,000 had moved to the city from other areas (mainly the South) in the previous ten years.[14]

It was not until 1940 that black New Yorkers moved out of the peripheries of the New York economy. At the turn of the century, blacks mainly found work in domestic labor, with 90 percent of black women and 55 percent of black men working in some type of domestic service occupation. Blacks' confinement to domestic service reflected, in part, the unfavorable terms of competition with immigrants, who had evicted them from trades where they had previously been accepted. The continued expansion of New York's economy slowly opened doors in a few manufacturing industries; the shutoff of immigration during World War I and its permanent demise after 1924 further accelerated dispersion into other fields.[15]

But the depression largely put an end to these gains. By 1940, 40 percent of blacks still worked in personal service—a far greater proportion than among the workforce overall.[16] With the advent of World War II doors to other jobs were finally unlocked; manufacturing, in particular, saw very large black employment gains. Yet unlike the case in Chicago or Detroit, the black sojourn in New York's manufacturing sector proved short-lived. Lacking auto factories or steel mills, New York's goods-producing sector was a concentration of low-wage jobs; white workers remained ensconced in the better-paying,

more skilled positions. Opportunities for blacks were more easily found in the burgeoning service sector—for example, health care—and in government; hence, blacks quickly dispersed into other fields.

Government, where 35 percent of native-born black New Yorkers worked in 1990,[17] has become the black niche par excellence. The history of black employment in the public sector provides yet another example of the continuing, interethnic competitive conflicts over jobs and economic resources in which New York's ethnic groups have been engaged.

In the early years of the twentieth century, local government, like most other New York employers, closed its doors to blacks: in 1911, the city only employed 511 blacks, almost all of whom were laborers. In the early 1920s, Tammany installed the leader of its black client organization, the United Colored Democracy, as a member of the three-person Civil Service Commission, but black access to public jobs changed marginally. By the late 1920s, the city counted 2,275 black workers on its payroll, of whom 900 were in laboring jobs and an additional 700 were in other noncompetitive or per diem positions.[18] The reform regime did more for blacks, pushing black employment above parity by 1940.[19] But these effects occurred as a result of the government's burgeoning payrolls, and they were mainly felt in the black concentrations of hospitals, sanitation, and public works, where more than 80 percent of the city's black job holders worked in 1935.[20] Moreover, blacks remained vulnerable to discriminatory practices, as in the city-owned subway system, where blacks only worked as porters, with the exception of a few stations in Harlem. Most important, the employment system that emerged during the depression put blacks at a structural disadvantage in competition with whites. Lacking the educational skills and credentials needed to qualify for most city jobs, blacks and

Puerto Ricans found themselves channeled into noncompetitive positions, of which the single largest concentration was found in the municipal hospital system. From here there were few routes of movement upward, as these bottom-level positions were disconnected from the competitive system, which promoted from within.

Race didn't reach the top of the government's agenda until 1965, when John Lindsay arrived in office, the first reformer elected mayor since LaGuardia.[21] Elected with the votes of liberals and minorities, Lindsay lacked his predecessors' commitments to the interests of the largely white, civil service workforce and pledged to increase black and Puerto Rican employment in city agencies. But the new mayor quickly discovered that the civil service structure was not easily amenable to change. Lindsay gradually made progress in reducing the inflated eligibility requirements inherited from the depression, but resistance proved severe when his reforms threatened established white ethnic workers in the better-paid ranks.

Lindsay's main focus, in contrast to earlier reform administrations, was to evade the civil service system and its unionized defenders. The Lindsay administration created new, less-skilled positions for which minority residents could be more easily hired. But this approach never involved large numbers and, more important, left existing eligibility requirements unchallenged, shunting minority recruits into dead-end jobs, where they were marooned.

Lindsay backed off from his confrontations with the civil service system and its defenders in the aftermath of the disastrous 1968 teachers' strike. Where the mayor could both accommodate the unions and pursue his earlier goals of increasing minority employment, he did—mainly by tripling the number of exempt workers and shifting them from agency to agency to avoid the re-

quirement of taking an examination. But in other instances, pressure from civil service interests proved overwhelming. With Abraham Beame's accession to City Hall in 1973, followed in 1977 by Edward Koch, mayoral support for black employment gains vanished for the next sixteen years.

The 1970s and 1980s nevertheless saw dramatic gains in black government employment. Like earlier white ethnic groups that had developed a concentration in public jobs, blacks benefited from simultaneous shifts in the structure of employment and in the relative availability of competing groups.

Changes in the structure of employment came from a variety of sources. The Equal Employment Opportunity (EEO) Act of 1972 prohibited discrimination in local government. By requiring local governments to maintain records on all employees by race and gender and to submit them to the Equal Employment Opportunity Commission, with the clear expectation that governments would show improvement over time, the act also led to institutional changes. As EEO functions were established in each city agency, recruitment and personnel practices changed in ways that benefited previously excluded groups, as recruitment became focused on minority and immigrant communities.

Moreover, the 1972 act provided minority employees with levers to act on more recalcitrant agencies, which they used with greatest effectiveness in the uniformed services. For example, in 1973 the Vulcan Society (the organization of black firefighters) successfully challenged the results of a 1971 exam, leading to an imposition of a 1:3 quota for the duration of that list (1973–79). In 1979, the Guardians and the Hispanic Society challenged the 1979 police officer's exam; court findings of disparate impact led to the imposition of a 33.3 percent minority quota for the duration of the list.

While the advent of affirmative action helped increase access for blacks and other minorities, other changes on the supply side hastened the growth of black employment. Although the city's attraction to its traditional white ethnic labor force had begun to diminish by the 1960s, the fiscal crisis of the mid-1970s decisively exacerbated and extended the city's recruitment difficulties among its traditional workforce. By the time large-scale hiring resumed in the early 1980s, public employment had become a less attractive option than before. Moreover, municipal salaries and benefits took a severe beating during the fiscal crisis; although compensation edged back upward during the 1980s, real gains never recaptured the losses endured during the 1970s. The strength enjoyed by New York's private sector during the 1980s pulled native white workers up the hiring queue and out of the effective labor supply for many city agencies.[22]

In a situation where "the City was hiring a great deal and not turning away anyone who was qualified," as one deputy commissioner told me in an interview, the disparity in the availability of minority and white workers led to rapid recruitment of minority workers. Minorities had constituted only 40 percent of the new workers hired in 1977, making up the majority in only two low-paid occupational categories. By 1987, minorities made up 56 percent of all hires, dominating the ranks of new recruits in five out of eight occupational categories.[23]

Thus, the Koch years of 1977 to 1989 saw the ethnic composition of the municipal workforce completely transformed, notwithstanding the mayor's opposition to affirmative action and the disfavor with which minority leaders greeted his hiring policies. By 1990, whites constituted 48 percent of the 375,000 people working for the city and just slightly more—50 percent—of the 150,000 people working in the agencies that the mayor directly controlled.[24] The declining white presence in municipal employment chiefly benefited blacks. Blacks

constituted 25 percent of the city's population and a still smaller proportion of residents who were older than eighteen and thus potentially employable, but made up 36 percent of the city's total workforce and 38 percent of those who worked in the mayoral agencies. Although blacks were still underrepresented in some of the city's most desirable jobs, the earlier pattern of concentration at the bottom was overcome. The municipal hospital system, which employed two-thirds of the city's black employees in the early 1960s, in 1990 employed less than one-fifth, reflecting the dispersion of blacks throughout the municipal sector. And higher-level jobs showed clusters of considerable black overrepresentation as well, with blacks accounting for 40 percent of the administrators and 36 percent of the professionals employed in the direct mayoral agencies.

By 1990, when David Dinkins became New York's first black mayor, the phase of black-for-white succession in municipal employment was nearly complete. Blacks held just over 35 percent of all city jobs; although unevenly represented among the city's many agencies, they were often a dominant presence, accounting for more than 40 percent of employment in six of the ten largest agencies, and more than 50 percent of employment in three of the largest ten.

The comparison with Latinos underlines blacks' advantage in the new ethnic division that has emerged in city government. Whereas the city's Latinos and black populations are equal in number, Latinos hold one-third as many municipal jobs as do blacks. The discrepancies are even greater as one moves up the occupational hierarchy into the ranks of managers and professionals. And blacks have been far more successful than Latinos in gaining new permanent civil service jobs, rather than the provisional appointments on which Latinos have mainly relied. The disparity has not gone unnoticed, as the Commission on Hispanic

Concerns pointed out in a 1986 report.[25] Of course, other answers might be invoked to explain Latinos' municipal jobs deficit relative to blacks'. But whatever the precise explanation, Mayor Dinkins's continuing conflicts with the Hispanic community suggest that earlier patterns of interethnic competition over municipal jobs remain alive and well.

The Koreans

In the mid-1960s, just when New York could no longer retain its native population, it reverted back to its role as an immigrant mecca. Immigrants began flocking to New York immediately after the liberalization of U.S. immigration laws in 1965. Their arrival has been the principal driving force of demographic and ethnic change in New York ever since—and will continue to be for the foreseeable future.

In 1965, what no one expected was the burgeoning of Asian immigration. The reforms tilted the new system toward immigrants with kinship ties to permanent residents or citizens. Since there had been so little Asian immigration in the previous fifty years, how could Asian newcomers find settlers with whom to seek reunification? The answer is that kinship connections were helpful, but not essential. The 1965 reforms also created opportunities for immigrants whose skills—as engineers, doctors, nurses, pharmacists—were in short supply. Along with students already living in the United States and enjoying easy access to American employers, these professionals made up the first wave of new Asian immigrants, creating the basis for the kinship migration of less well educated relatives.

Thus, well-educated, highly skilled immigrants have dominated the Korean influx to the United States and to New York in particular. Although Koreans constitute a small portion of New York's new immigrants—rarely more than 3 percent of the eighty thousand to ninety thousand legal immigrants who come to New York each year—they play an important and very visible role. As middle-aged newcomers with poor English-language skills and often lacking professional licenses, relatively few Koreans have managed to steer a route back into the fields for which they trained. Instead they have turned to small business, setting up new businesses at a rate that few other groups can rival.

Koreans started in fruit and vegetable stores, taking over shops in all areas of the city, regardless of neighborhood composition or customer clientele. From there, Koreans moved on to other retail specialties—dry cleaning, fish stores, novelty shops, and nail salons. By 1980, a third of New York Korean males were already self-employed. The *1991 Korean Business Directory* provides a ready indicator of commercial growth over the 1980s, listing over 120 commercial specialties in which Korean firms are to be found.[26]

The roots of the Korean ethnic economy are found in several sources. The competitive field was open. By the middle to late 1960s, the sons and daughters of Jewish and Italian storekeepers had better things to do than mind a store, and their parents, old, tired, and scared of crime, were ready to sell out to the newcomers from Korea. By the 1980s, the supply of new, native-born white entrepreneurs had virtually dried up. One survey of neighborhood businesses in Queens and Brooklyn found that almost half of the white-owned shops were run by immigrants and that most white businesses were long-established entities, in contrast to the newly founded Korean shops with which they competed.[27]

Another spur to growth came from within the ethnic community. Koreans, like every other immigrant group, have special tastes and needs that are best served by an insider: the growth of the Korean population has created business for Korean accountants, doctors, brokers, hair stylists, and restaurant owners. Although the Korean community is too small to support a huge commercial infrastructure oriented to ethnic needs, the community has utilized its ethnic connections to Korea to develop commercial activities oriented toward non-Korean markets. Active trade relations between South Korea and the United States have provided a springboard for many Korean-owned import-export businesses, of which 119 are listed in the *1991 Korean Business Directory.*

Finally, the social structure of the Korean community itself generates advantages for business success that few other immigrant groups share. Many Koreans emigrate with capital, and those who are cash poor can raise money through rotating credit associations known as *gae*. Because Koreans migrate in complete family units, family members provide a supply of cheap and trusted labor. The prevalence of self-employment means that many Koreans have close ties to other business owners, who in turn are a source of information and support, and the high organizational density of the Korean community—which is characterized by an incredible proliferation of alumni clubs, churches, businessman's associations—provides additional conduits for the flow of business information and the making of needed contacts. These community resources distinguish the Koreans from their competitors, who are less likely to be embedded in ethnic or family ties that can be drawn upon for help with business information, capital assistance, or staffing problems.

The Koreans have discovered that conflict *need not* be interethnic; there are other sources of threat, and in the 1980s they mobilized Korean merchants on a considerable scale. Like other small business owners, Koreans were unhappy with local government, usually with something that government was doing or was threatening to do. Fruit and vegetable store owners felt that sanitation officials were too conscientious about sidewalk cleanliness, especially since the result of the officials' demands was often a fine that the Korean store owner had to pay. Pressuring the city to relax inspections became a high priority for Korean organizations. In the late 1980s, as the city's fiscal crisis led it to search for new sources of revenue, fiscal planners thought of placing a special tax on dry cleaners. So Korean dry cleaners entered an unusual coalition with the white owners of commercial laundries, and the union that represented the laundryworkers, to roll back the planned tax. Like other small business owners, Korean merchants could also become dissatisfied with government's *failure* to act. The prosperity of the 1980s gave commercial landlords license to raise rents to the maximum, much to the distress of small business owners throughout the city. Koreans joined with their non-Korean counterparts to push for commercial rent control—to no avail.

Although Italians and Jews have largely deserted petty retail trade, they have remained in wholesaling, where the businesses are larger and profits more sizable. Thus Jewish and Italian fruit and vegetable or fish wholesalers have acquired a substantial Korean trade. The encounter has not always been a happy one, as Illsoo Kim recounted in his pathbreaking book: "Especially in their first years of emergence into the fruit and vegetable business, Koreans reported many incidents at the Hunts Point [wholesale] Market. The incidents ranged from unfair pricing and sale of poor-quality produce by the Italian and Jewish wholesalers, to physical threats and beatings administered by competing white retailers."[28]

Such conflicts sparked the first mass demonstration by Koreans ever in New York. Although Kim reports that Koreans were subsequently accepted by the wholesaling community, there have been continued incidents and protests, including a recent boycott by Koreans of one of the city's largest fish wholesalers.[29]

In New York, as in almost every other major American city, black neighborhoods have provided new immigrants from Asia and the Middle East with an important economic outlet. To some extent, Koreans and other immigrants have simply replaced older white groups that had long sold to blacks and were now eager to bail out of an increasingly difficult and tense situation. By opening stores in black neighborhoods Koreans were also filling the gap left by the departure of large, nonethnic chain stores, which were steadily eliminating the low-margin, high-cost operations involved in serving a ghetto clientele. Selling to black customers proved fraught with conflict. Small protests erupted in the late 1970s. In 1981 a boycott erupted along 125th Street, Harlem's main commercial thoroughfare, with black leaders calling Korean shop owners "vampires" who came to Harlem to "suck black consumers dry."[30]

Repeated security problems as well as more organized clashes led Korean store owners to establish neighborhood prosperity associations, in addition to those organizations that grouped merchants in a particular retail branch. Thus, alongside groups like the Korean Produce Association or the Korean Apparel Contractors Associations, one finds neighborhood groups like the Korean Merchant Association of the Bronx or the Uptown Korean Merchants Association, which seek "to improve Korean merchants' relations with local residents or communities" while lobbying local police for more effective support.[31]

In 1990 antagonism between black shoppers and Korean merchants erupted in picket lines set up in front of two Korean stores in the Flatbush section of Brooklyn. The clash started with a dispute between a Korean store owner and a black Haitian customer who charged assault; that claim then provoked black activist groups—of fairly dubious repute[32]—to establish a boycott that targeted not only the offending owner, but a neighboring Korean merchant against whom no injury was ever charged.

The boycott lasted for months, choking off business at both stores. Although customers disappeared, the two stores were kept alive by contributions from the organized Korean community, which perceived a broader danger to its economic viability should the boycott succeed. As time went on, government officials were inevitably involved. The boycott became a crisis for Mayor Dinkins, who was widely criticized for not actively seeking an end to the dispute.

The boycott ground to a halt, and a court threw out the legal suit brought by the aggrieved Haitian shopper. Other, fortunately short-lived boycotts were started in New York even while the Flatbush dispute lingered on. A clash in a nearby Brooklyn area between blacks and a small group of Vietnamese refugees—possibly mistaken for Koreans—showed how quickly tensions generated in one arena could move to another.

Conclusion

The story of New York's Irish, Jews, blacks, and Koreans is richer and more complicated than the occupational histories I've recounted in the preceding pages. But if the [reading's] deliberately one-sided focus provides only a partial account, it reminds us of ethnicity's continuing importance, and not simply because of feelings for one's own kind or animosities toward outsiders. Rather, ethnicity's centrality stems from its role as the mechanism whereby groups of categorically different workers have been sorted into an identifiably distinct set of jobs. In this sense, the ethnic division of labor has been the central division of labor in modern New York. Now, as in the past, distinctive roles in the ethnic division of labor impart a sense of "we-ness" and group interest—ensuring the persistence of ethnic fragmentation and conflict.

NOTES

1. Stephen Erie, *Rainbow's End* (Berkeley: University of California Press, 1988), 88–89.
2. Thomas Kessner, *Fiorella H. LaGuardia* (New York: McGraw-Hill, 1989); Charles Garrett, *The LaGuardia Years* (New Brunswick, NJ: Rutgers University Press, 1961).
3. A survey of the surviving members of the class indicates that 38 percent were Catholic and 36 percent Jewish, with Russia and Ireland the leading countries of origin of the respondents' grandparents (Richard Herrnstein et al., "New York City Police Department Class of 1940: A Preliminary Report" [unpublished manuscript, Department of Psychology, Harvard University, n.d.]).
4. Nathan Glazer and Daniel P. Moynihan, *Beyond the Melting Pot* (Cambridge, MA: MIT Press, 1969).
5. Data on the ethnic composition of the fire department are from *Equal Employment Opportunity Statistics: Agency Full Report* (New York: New York City Department of Personnel, 1990); data on the religious composition are from Center for Social Policy and Practice in the Workplace, *Gender Integration in the Fire Department of the City of New York* (New York: Columbia University School of Social Work, 1988), p. 41.
6. Roger Waldinger, *Through the Eye of the Needle* (New York: New York University Press, 1986).
7. Heywood Broun and George Britt, *Christians Only* (New York: Vantage Press, 1931), 244.
8. Dominic Capeci, *The Harlem Riot of 1943* (Philadelphia: Temple University Press, 1977), 172.
9. Waldinger, *Through the Eye of the Needle,* 109–10. Employment data calculated from the census apply to employed persons twenty-five to sixty-four years old only. "Blacks" refers to native-born African Americans only. Data calculated from the Public Use Microdata Samples (U.S. Bureau of the Census, *Census of Population, 1940,* Public Use Microdata Samples [Computer file] [Washington, DC: U.S. Dept. of Commerce, Bureau of the Census, producer, 1983; Ann Arbor, MI: Inter-university Consortium for Political and Social Research, distributor, 1984]; U.S. Bureau of the Census, Census of Population, 1950, Public Use Microdata Samples [computer file] [Washington, DC: U.S. Dept. of Commerce, Bureau of the Census, and Madison: University of Wisconsin, Center for Demography and Ecology, producers, 1984; Ann Arbor, MI: Inter-university Consortium for Political and Social Research, distributor, 1984]).
10. Hasia Diner, *In the Almost Promised Land* (Westport, CT: Greenwood Press, 1977), presents a favorable account of the response among the Jewish trade union elite to the black influx into the garment industry; see chap. 6. Herbert Hill has offered a far more critical account in numerous writings, most important, "The Racial Practices of Organized Labor: The Contemporary Record," in *Organized Labor and the Negro,* edited by Julius Jacobson (New York: Doubleday, 1968), 286–337. For a judicious balancing of the issues, see Nancy Green, "Juifs et noirs aux etats-unis: La rupture d'une 'alliance naturelle,'" *Annales, E.S.C.,* 2 (March–April 1987):445–64.
11. Diane Ravitch, *The Great School Wars* (New York: Basic Books, 1974).
12. Roger Waldinger, "The Making of an Immigrant Niche," *International Migration Review* 28(1)(1994).
13. "The Debate Goes On," *Alumnus: The City College of New York* 87(1)(Winter 1992):8–11.
14. Emmanuel Tobier, "Population," in *Setting Municipal Priorities,* edited by Charles Brecher and Raymond Horton (New York: New York University Press, 1981), 24.
15. Data are from U.S. Bureau of the Census, *Occupations at the 1900 Census* (Washington, DC: GPO, 1904). See also Herman Bloch, *The Circle of Discrimination* (New York: New York University Press, 1969).

16. Data are from the U.S. Bureau of the Census, *Census of Population, 1940.*

17. Calculated from the U.S. Bureau of the Census, *Census of Population and Housing, 1990,* Public Use Microdata Sample (a Sample): 5-Percent Sample (computer file) (Washington, DC: U.S. Dept. of Commerce, producer, 1993; Ann Arbor, MI: Inter-university Consortium for Political and Social Research, distributor, 1993).

18. Colored Citizens' Non-Partisan Committee for the Re-election of Mayor Walker, *New York City and the Colored Citizen* (n.d. [1930?]), LaGuardia Papers, Box 3530, New York Municipal Archives.

19. Calculated from U.S. Bureau of the Census, *Census of Population, 1940,* Public Use Microdata Samples. Also see Edwin Levinson, *Black Politics in New York City* (New York: Twayne, 1974).

20. Ira Katznelson, *Black Men, White Cities* (New York: Oxford University Press, 1973), 82.

21. For a more detailed discussion of the Lindsay period, see Roger Waldinger, "The Ethnic Politics of Municipal Jobs," working paper no. 248, UCLA Institute of Industrial Relations, Los Angeles, 1993.

22. Raymond Horton, "Human Resources," in *Setting Municipal Priorities,* edited by Charles Brecher and Raymond Horton (New York: New York University Press, 1986). See also Roger Waldinger, "Changing Ladders and Musical Chairs," *Politics and Society* 15(4) (1986–87): 369–402, and "Making of an Immigrant Niche."

23. City of New York, Citywide Equal Employment Opportunity Committee, *Equal Employment Opportunity in New York City Government, 1977–1987* (New York: Citywide Equal Employment Opportunity Committee, 1988), 6.

24. Data are from unpublished EEOC reports from the New York City Department of Personnel, New York Board of Education, New York City Transit Authority, and New York City Health and Hospitals Corporation.

25. City of New York, Mayor's Commission on Hispanic Concerns, *Report* (New York: Mayor's Commission on Hispanic Concerns, 1986), 109.

26. *1991 Korean Business Directory* (Long Island City, NY: Korean News, 1991).

27. Roger Waldinger, "Structural Opportunity or Ethnic Advantage: Immigrant Business Development in New York," *International Migration Review* 23(1)(1989):61.

28. Illsoo Kim, *The New Urban Immigrants* (Princeton, NJ: Princeton University Press, 1981), 51.

29. Pyong Gap Min, "Cultural and Economic Boundaries of Korean Ethnicity: A Comparative Analysis," *Ethnic and Racial Studies* 14(2)(1991):235.

30. Lucie Cheng and Yen Espiritu, "Korean Businesses in Black and Hispanic Neighborhoods," *Sociological Perspectives* 32(4)(1989): 521.

31. Illsoo Kim, "The Koreans: Small Business in an Urban Frontier," in *New Immigrants in New York,* edited by Nancy Foner (New York: Columbia University Press, 1987), 238.

32. Tamar Jacoby, "Sonny Carson and the Politics of Protest," *NY: The City Journal* 1(4)(1991): 29–40.

24

WHEN WORK DISAPPEARS

William Julius Wilson

For the first time in the twentieth century most adults in many inner-city ghetto neighborhoods are not working in a typical week. The disappearance of work has adversely affected not only individuals, families, and neighborhoods, but the social life of the city at large as well. Inner-city joblessness is a severe problem that is often overlooked or obscured when the focus is placed mainly on poverty and its consequences. Despite increases in the concentration of poverty since 1970, inner cities have always featured high levels of poverty, but the current levels of joblessness in some neighborhoods are unprecedented.

The consequences of high neighborhood joblessness are more devastating than those of high neighborhood poverty. A neighborhood in which people are poor but employed is different from a neighborhood in which people are poor and jobless. Many of today's problems in the inner-city ghetto neighborhoods—crime, family dissolution, welfare, low levels of social organization, and so on—are fundamentally a consequence of the disappearance of work.

The disappearance of work and the growth of related problems in the ghetto have aggravated an already tense racial situation in urban areas. Our nation's response to racial discord in the central city and to the growing racial divide between the city and the suburbs has been disappointing. In discussing these problems we have a tendency to engage in the kind of rhetoric that exacerbates, rather than alleviates, urban and metropolitan racial tensions. Ever since the 1992 Los Angeles riot, the media have focused heavily on the factors that divide rather than those that unite racial groups. Emphasis on racial division peaked in 1995 following the jury's verdict in the O. J. Simpson murder trial. Before the verdict was announced, opinion polls revealed that whites overwhelmingly thought Mr. Simpson was guilty, while a substantial majority of blacks felt he was innocent. The media clips showing public reaction to the verdict dramatized the racial division—blacks appeared elated and jubilant; whites appeared stunned, angry, and somber. Blacks believed that O. J. Simpson had been framed by a racist police conspiracy; whites were convinced that he was guilty of the murder of two people and was being allowed to walk free. The racial divide, as depicted in the media, seemed as wide as ever.

The implications of these developments for the future of race relations and for programs perceived to benefit blacks remain to be seen. As one observer, on the eve of the Simpson verdict, put it: "When O. J. gets off, the whites will riot the way we whites do: leave the cities, go to Idaho or Oregon or Arizona, vote for Gingrich . . . and punish the blacks by closing the day-care programs and cutting off their Medicaid."[1]

William Julius Wilson, *When Work Disappears*, pp. 567–595. Copyright © 1996 by William Julius Wilson. Reprinted by permission of Alfred A. Knopf, Inc.

[1]Frank Rich, "The L.A. Shock Treatment," *New York Times*, 4 October 1995.

The extent of the racial divisions in this country should not be minimized. The different reactions to the Simpson trial and the verdict reflect in part the fundamentally dissimilar racial experiences of blacks and whites in America—the former burdened by racial injustice, the latter largely free of the effects of bigotry and hatred. Nonetheless, the emphasis on racial differences has obscured the fact that African-Americans, whites, and other ethnic groups share many common concerns, are beset by many common problems, and have many common values, aspirations, and hopes.

Job Shrinkage in the Global Economy

Changes in the global economy are placing strains on the welfare state in both the United States and Europe and are contributing to growing social dislocations, including racial conflicts. The question that Secretary of Labor Robert Reich raised at a 1994 conference of finance and labor ministers from seven industrial democracies is central and timely: "Are we condemned to choose between more jobs but greater inequality and insecurity, as we have in this country, or better jobs but higher unemployment and a thicker social safety net, as in Europe?"[2] This question implicitly asks whether Europeans and Americans can learn from one another in the creation of programs that simultaneously address the problems of economic growth, joblessness, and wage inequality.

There is a growing recognition that proposed solutions to the problems of jobs and wages in any of the major industrial democracies cannot ignore developments in the highly integrated global market place. In-deed, because of concerns about the problem of creating good jobs in the global economy, the finance and labor ministers from the major industrial democracies (Britain, Canada, France, Germany, Italy, Japan, and the United States, or the Group of Seven, commonly called G7) held a jobs conference in Detroit in March 1994. In previous years, only heads of state and finance ministers met "to discuss high diplomacy and the high finance exchange rates and interest rate management."[3] However, that exalted approach was considered insufficient to address the concrete issue of jobs that now confronts all of these nations.

In addition to the more familiar themes, such as the importance of stimulating economic growth and of avoiding protectionist policies to safeguard shrinking job markets, the officials at the conference also agreed "that the only way to create more jobs in the face of rapid technological change was to upgrade education, particularly for those who are least skilled."[4] It was the first time the G7 policy makers had addressed, as a global problem, the widening gap in wages between skilled and unskilled workers and the strong association between low levels of education, joblessness, and poorly paid work.[5]

Although the conference did more to highlight than to solve these problems, the main hope of the ministers was that the discussions could "teach them something about what each of them has done right, and wrong, in confronting the jobs question."[6] As I examine possible policy prescriptions in cross-national perspective, a framework for discussing the appropriateness of long-term solutions to the jobs problem in the United States (solutions that take several

---

[2]Thomas L. Friedman, "World's Big Economies Turn to the Jobs Issue," *New York Times,* 14 March 1994.

[3]Ibid.
[4]Thomas L. Friedman, "Accent on Education as Talks on Jobs End," *New York Times,* 16 March 1994.
[5]Ibid.
[6]Ibid.

years before the desired ends are achieved or realized) and one for discussing more immediate solutions come to mind.

My framework for long-term solutions outlines two types of relationships in an effort to address the issues of generating good jobs and combating the growing wage inequality among workers—namely, the relationship between employment and education and family support systems and, in the metropolitan context, the relationship between the cities and the suburbs. My framework for immediate solutions delineates ways in which to either revise current programs or create new programs to decrease joblessness among disadvantaged adults. Each framework involves the integration of programs that involve both the public sector and the private sector.

I hasten to point out that the following presentation and discussion of policy frameworks is not constrained by an awareness of the current political climate in the United States. The dramatic retreat from using public policy as a means to fight social inequality has effectively discouraged calls for bold new social programs. Indeed, at the time of this writing, the trend is toward slicing or reducing social programs and the spending for such programs. The emphasis is on personal responsibility, not inequities in the larger society, and therefore the assumption is that people should help themselves and not turn to the government for handouts. It is said that the growth of joblessness and welfare receipt mainly reflects a declining commitment to the core values of society and therefore that the incentives for idleness or the factors that lead to a lack of personal and family responsibilities ought to be removed.

These arguments have been advanced with such force and consistency in public discussions since the 1994 congressional elections that even some of the most dedicated liberals feel intimidated and powerless. Accordingly, traditional programs benefiting the poor, such as Aid to Families with Dependent Children (AFDC), Medicaid, and the earned income tax credit, have either been eliminated or are being threatened with severe reductions.

This retreat from public policy as a way to alleviate problems of social inequality will have profound negative consequences for the future of disadvantaged groups such as the ghetto poor. High levels of joblessness, growing wage inequality, and the related social problems are complex and have their source in fundamental economic, social, and cultural changes. They therefore require bold, comprehensive, and thoughtful solutions, not simplistic and pious statements about the need for greater personal responsibility. Progressives who are concerned about the current social conditions of the have-nots and the future generation of have-nots not only have to fight against the current public policy strategies; they are morally obligated to offer alternative strategies designed to alleviate, not exacerbate, the plight of the poor, the jobless, and other disadvantaged citizens of America.

My aim, therefore, is to galvanize and rally concerned Americans to fight back with the same degree of force and dedication displayed by those who have moved us backward, rather than forward, in combating social inequality. I therefore do not advance proposals that seem acceptable or "realistic" given the current political climate. Rather, I have chosen to talk about what *ought to be done to address the problems of social inequality,* including record levels of joblessness in the inner-city ghetto that threaten the very fabric of our society.

Some who acknowledge the need to confront the growing social inequality also feel that new social programs should be put on hold until the huge budget deficit has been significantly reduced. In the final analysis, however, we must recognize that spending is directly related to political priorities. Decisions about budget cuts for federal programs now indisputably favor the advantaged segments of the population at the expense of the disadvantaged.

I believe that steps must be taken to galvanize Americans from all walks of life who are concerned about human suffering and the public policy direction in which we are now moving. I therefore present policy frameworks that call for the integration and mobilization of resources from both the public and the private sectors. We need to generate a public/private partnership to fight social inequality. In the final analysis, I hope to stimulate thought about what ought to be done and how we should do it among those who support positive social reforms and see the need for action now. The following policy frameworks, therefore, are suggestive and provide a basis for further discussion and debate. Let me begin by first focusing on the part of my framework for long-term solutions that involves relationships between employment and education, and family support systems.

Creating National Performance Standards for Schools

The United States can learn from industrial democracies like Japan and Germany. These countries have developed policies designed to increase the number of workers with "higher-order thinking skills," including policies that require young people to meet high performance standards before they can graduate from secondary schools and that hold each school responsible for meeting these national standards. As Ray Marshall points out, "Standards are important because they provide incentives for students, teachers and other school personnel; information to employers and postsecondary institutions; and a means for policy makers and the public to evaluate schools. Indeed, by strengthening linkages, standards have

helped fashion systems out of disjointed activities."[7]

Students who meet high standards are not only prepared for work, they are ready for technical training and other kinds of postsecondary education.[8] Currently, there are no national standards for secondary students or schools in the United States. Accordingly, students who are not in college preparatory courses have severely limited options with respect to pursuing work or secondary technical training after high school. A commitment to a system of national performance standards for every public school in the United States would be an important first step in addressing the huge gap in educational performance between the schools in advantaged and disadvantaged neighborhoods.

But because the quality of local public schools in the United States is in large measure related to the resources of local governments, national standards may not be attractive to taxpayers and local officials in some areas. Also, some schools will encounter greater difficulties in meeting a national performance standard because of fewer resources and a greater concentration of students from disadvantaged backgrounds and neighborhoods. . . .

Recent research on the nationwide distribution of science and mathematics opportunities indicates that low-income, minority, and inner-city students are in school environments that are not as conducive to learning because of less qualified teachers, fewer material resources, less engaging activities for learning in the classroom, and considerably less exposure to good training and

---

[7] Ray Marshall, "School-to-Work Processes in the United States" (paper presented at the Carnegie Corporation/ Johann Jacobs Foundation, Marbach Castle, Germany, 3–5 November 1994).
[8] Ibid.

knowledge in mathematics and science.[9] The problem of finding qualified teachers is particularly acute. Teacher shortages in many central-city and poor rural schools have resulted in a disproportionate number of underprepared and inexperienced teachers, many of whom provide instruction in fields outside their areas of preparation, and a continuous flow of short-term and long-term substitutes.[10]

A system of national performance standards should include the kind of support that would enable schools in disadvantaged neighborhoods to meet the standards that are set. State government, with federal support, not only would have to create equity in local school funding and give birth to programs that would foster teacher development (through scholarships and forgivable loans for teacher education to attract more high-quality teachers, through increased supports for teacher training in schools of education, and through reforms in teacher certification and licensing) but would also have to ensure that highly qualified teachers are distributed in local school districts in ways that provide all students with access to excellent instruction. In some cases this would require greater flexibility in the public school system, not only to attract and hire qualified teachers, but also to displace those who perform poorly in the classroom and lack a dedication to teaching. Local education agencies and state education departments should be helped to identify schools that need support in curriculum development and assessment, teacher development, educational and material resources, and so on.". . .[11]

Targeting education would be part of a national effort to raise the performance standards of all public schools in the United States to a desirable level, including schools in the inner city. Every effort should be made to enlist the support and involvement of the private sector in this national effort. Corporations, local businesses, civic clubs, community centers, churches, and community-based organizations should be encouraged to work with the schools to enhance computer-competency training. Some examples of private-sector involvement in such endeavors should be touted to spur others on. For example, Frank C. Weaver, director of the Office of Commercial Space Transportation at the U.S. Department of Transportation, reported:

> Bell Atlantic and Tele-Communications, Inc. announced in 1994 that they would provide free linkage to the information superhighways for 26,000 elementary and secondary schools in areas served by the two companies. Under the plan, known as the Basic Education Connection (BEC), the school would receive free educational cable television programming and free access to certain data and online services, such as access to the Internet.
>
> Another project, the Hughes Galaxy Classroom, is enabling 51,000 elementary school children around the country to access more of the educational resources on television available via satellite. Under the auspices of the

[9]Jeannie Oakes, *Multiplying Inequalities: The Effects of Race, Social Class and Ability Grouping on Access to Science and Mathematics Education* (Santa Monica, CA: Rand Corporation, 1990).

[10]Linda Darling-Hammond, "Teacher Quality and Equality," in *Access to Knowledge: An Agenda for Our Nation's Schools,* edited by John Goodlad and Pamela Keating (New York: College Entrance Examination Board, 1990); Darling-Hammond, "National Standards and Assessments."

[11]Darling-Hammond, "National Standards and Assessments."

Galaxy Classroom Foundation, which provides antenna dishes and related equipment to schools, the project offers a science and English curriculum beamed into classrooms through satellite transmissions. Student feedback and questions are faxed to the producers of the program for inclusion in subsequent shows. Particular attention is paid to inner-city and minority schools. There are 480 schools participating this year, and the goal for next year is 1,500 schools with 150,000 to 200,000 students.[12]

Since the creation of national performance standards would provide a clear means for the public to evaluate the different schools, data on school performances could be widely disseminated. This would enable parents of all backgrounds, including those in disadvantaged neighborhoods, to compare nearby schools and make appropriate decisions about which ones their children should attend. . . .

Improving Family Support Programs

The learning system in other industrial democracies has also been strengthened by family policies to support children. Among industrialized countries, the United States is alone in having no universal preschool, child-support, or parental leave programs. "The absence of such policies makes many of our families, particularly low-income families, very poor learning systems," states Ray Marshall. "Many of our children there-fore start school far behind their more advantaged counterparts, and subsequently receive inadequate learning opportunities at home as well as in school."[13] The family structure has undergone fundamental changes in the last several decades. There has been a sharp increase in single-parent families, and many of them are trapped in persistent poverty. Also, in many "intact" families both the husband and wife must work outside the home to make ends meet. The absence of widely available high-quality preschool and child-support assurance programs places additional stress on these families and hampers their ability to provide a learning environment that prepares children for school and reinforces the learning process.

The French system of child welfare stands in sharp contrast to the American system. In France, children are supported by three interrelated government programs—child care, income support, and medical care.[14] The child care program includes establishments for infant care, high-quality nursery schools (*écoles maternelles*), and paid leave for parents of newborns. The income support program includes child-support enforcement (so that the absent parent continues to contribute financially to his or her child's welfare), children allowances, and welfare payments for low-income single mothers. Finally, medical care is provided through a universal system of national health care financed by social security, a preventive care system for children, and a group of public health nurses who specialize in child welfare.

---

[12]Frank C. Weaver, "Preparing Our Youth for the Information Age," *Focus*, Joint Center for Political and Economic Studies, May 1995, 7. See also Richard M. Krieg, "Information Technology and Low Income Inner-City Communities," *Journal of Urban Technology* (forthcoming).

[13]Marshall, "School-to-Work Processes in the United States," 21.
[14]Barbara Bergmann, "The French Child Welfare System: An Excellent System We Could Adapt and Afford" in *Sociology and the Public Agenda,* edited by William Julius Wilson (Newbury Park, CA: Sage, 1993), 341–50.

The *école maternelle* is perhaps the most distinctive institution in the French system. Children who are no longer in diapers may enter the nursery school and attend until they are enrolled in the first grade. Because parents view participation in the *école maternelle* as highly beneficial to their children, even those mothers who are not working send their children.

As the economist Barbara Bergmann points out:

> The *école maternelle* serves the integration of all children, minority children included, to full participation in regular school and as future citizens. One of its most important functions, especially for the 4- and 5-year-olds, is getting the children ready for the regular school. Each year a child spends at an *école maternelle* reduces considerably the likelihood that the child will fail the rigorous first grade and have to repeat it. Of children from poorer backgrounds who have not attended an *école maternelle,* more than half fail the first grade. Four years of preschool attendance for such poorer children cuts their first grade failure rate in half. Children from more affluent backgrounds are also materially helped to pass.[15]

. . .

City-Suburban Economic Integration?

If the other industrial democracies offer lessons for a long-term solution to the jobs problem involving relationships between employment, education, and family support systems, they also offer lessons on the importance of another solution from a metropolitan perspective—namely, city-suburban integration and cooperation. None of the other industrialized democracies has allowed its city centers to deteriorate as has the United States. In European countries, suburbanization has not been associated with the abandonment of cities as residential areas. "The central governments continued to treat cities as a national resource to be protected and nurtured."[16] Indeed, the city centers in Europe remain very desirable places to reside because of better public transportation, more effective urban renewal programs, and good public education that is more widely available to disadvantaged students. Moreover, unlike in the United States, cheap public transportation makes suburbanized employment sites more accessible.

It will be difficult to address growing racial tensions in U.S. cities unless we tackle the problems of shrinking revenue and inadequate social services and the gradual disappearance of work in certain neighborhoods. The city has become a less desirable place in which to live, and the economic and social gap between the cities and suburbs is growing. The groups left behind compete, often along racial lines, for declining resources, including the remaining decent schools, housing, and neighborhoods. The rise of the new urban poverty neighborhoods has exacerbated these problems. Their high rates of joblessness and social disorganization have created problems that often spill over into other parts of the city at large. All of these factors aggravate race relations and elevate racial tensions.

Ideally, we need to restore the federal contribution to the city budget that existed in 1980 and to increase sharply the employment base. Regardless of changes in federal urban policy, however, the fiscal crisis in the

---

[15]Ibid., 343–44.

[16]Margaret Weir, "Race and Urban Poverty: Comparing Europe and America" (occasional paper no. 93–9, Center for American Political Studies, Harvard University, March 1993), 26.

cities would be significantly eased if the employment base could be substantially increased. Indeed, the social dislocations caused by the steady disappearance of work have led to a wide range of urban social problems, including racial tensions. Increased employment would help stabilize the new poverty neighborhoods, halt the precipitous decline in density, and ultimately enhance the quality of race relations in urban areas.

Perhaps at no other time in the nation's history has it been more important to talk about the need to promote city and suburban cooperation, not separation. The political fragmentation of many metropolitan areas in the United States has contributed to the problems of joblessness and related social dislocations of the inner-city poor. As David Rusk, the former mayor of Albuquerque, New Mexico, has pointed out, because the older cities of the East and the Midwest were unable to expand territorially through city-county consolidation or annexation, they failed to reap such benefits of suburban growth as the rise of shopping malls, offices, and industrial parks in new residential subdivisions. As areas in which poor minorities live in higher and higher concentration, these cities face an inevitable downward spiral because they are not benefitting from suburban growth. Rusk argues, therefore, that neighborhood revitalization programs, such as community development banks, nonprofit inner-city housing developments, and enterprise zones, will not be able "to reverse the downward slide of inner cities" if they are not carried out within "a framework of actions to bring down the walls between city and suburb."[17]

Efforts to promote city and suburban cooperation will not benefit cities alone. There is mounting evidence that cities and suburbs are economically interdependent. The more central cities are plagued by joblessness, dysfunctional schools, and crime, the more the surrounding suburbs undergo a decline in their own social and economic fortunes. Suburbs that experienced increases in income during the 1980s tended to be linked to a thriving urban center.[18] In the global economy, metropolitan regions continue to compete for jobs. Suburbs that will remain or become competitive are those with a well-trained workforce, good schools, a concentration of professional services, first-class hospitals, a major university and research center, and an efficient transportation network to link executives with other parts of the United States and with countries around the world. However, many of these elements cannot come solely from suburbs. They require a viable central city. It is important for Americans to realize that city-suburban *integration* is the key to the health of metropolitan regions and to the nation as a whole.

Reforms put forward to achieve the objective of city-suburban cooperation range from proposals to create metropolitan governments to proposals for metropolitan tax base sharing (currently in effect in Minneapolis/St. Paul), collaborative metropolitan planning, and the creation of regional authorities to develop solutions to common problems if communities fail to reach agreement.[19] Among the problems shared by many metropolises is a weak public transit system. A commitment to address this problem through a form of city-suburban collaboration would benefit residents of both the city and the suburbs. Theoretically, everyone

---

[17]David Rusk, *Cities Without Suburbs* (Washington, DC: Woodrow Wilson Center Press, 1993), 121.

[18]Derek Bok, "Cities and Suburbs" (paper presented for the Aspen Institute Domestic Strategy Group, Aspen Institute, Washington, DC, 1994).

[19]Ibid., 13. See also Margaret Weir, "Urban Policy and Persistent Urban Poverty" (background memorandum prepared for the Social Science Research Council Policy Conference on Persistent Urban Poverty, Washington, DC, 9–10 November 1993).

would benefit from mobility within the metropolitan areas, and inner-city residents would have greater means to prevent high joblessness.

Solutions to the Jobs Problem

The problems of joblessness and social dislocation in the inner city are, in part, related to the processes in the global economy that have contributed to greater inequality and insecurity among American workers in general, and to the failure of U.S. social policies to adjust to these processes. It is therefore myopic to view the problems of jobless ghettos as if they were separate from those that plague the larger society.

In using this cross-cultural perspective I am not suggesting that we can or even should simply import the social policies of the Japanese, Germans, or other West Europeans. As Ray Marshall has appropriately pointed out, the approaches in these other countries are embedded in their own cultures and have their "own flaws and deficiencies, as well as strengths." We should instead "learn from the approaches used in other countries and adapt the best aspects into our own homegrown solutions."[20]

The strengths of some of the approaches in other countries are apparent. For example, in Japan and Germany most high school and college graduates leave school with skills in keeping with the demands of the highly technological marketplace in the global economy.[21] In the United States, by contrast, only college graduates and those few with extra-specialized post–high school training acquire such skills. Those with only high school diplomas or less do not.

The flaws and deficiencies of some of the approaches in the other countries are also apparent. Except for Germany, European countries have the same gap in worker skills.[22] Because of the generous unemployment benefits, however, the low-skilled European workers tend to be less willing to accept the lower-paying jobs that their counterparts in the United States are often forced to take. Therefore, the problems of unskilled European workers are not only restricted to low wages, they also include high levels of unemployment. The growing problem of unemployment among low-skilled European workers is placing a strain on the welfare state. Immigrant minorities are disproportionately represented among the jobless population, and therefore tend to be publicly identified with the problem of maintaining welfare costs. These perceptions contribute to growing intergroup tensions. Accordingly, the problems of race, unemployment, and concentration of urban poverty that have traditionally plagued the United States are now surfacing in various countries in Europe.

Just as the United States can learn from some of the approaches in the other countries, the Europeans could learn from the United States how to make their workforces more flexible instead of paying them to stay unemployed indefinitely. In particular, they could learn how to get unskilled workers into low-wage jobs that would be buttressed by maintaining certain desirable aspects of the safety net, such as universal health insurance, that prevent workers from slipping into the depths of poverty, as so often happens to their American counterparts.

Expand the Earned Income Tax Credit

It is important to discuss immediate solutions to the jobs problem in the United

---

[20]Marshall, "School-to-Work Processes in the United States," 26.
[21]Ibid.

[22]Friedman, "Accent on Education as Talks on Jobs End."

States. Because of their level of training and education, the inner-city poor and other disadvantaged workers mainly have access only to jobs that pay the minimum wage or less and are not covered by health insurance. However, recent policies of the federal government could make such jobs more attractive. The United States Congress enacted an expansion of the earned income tax credit (EITC) in 1993. By 1996, the expanded EITC will increase the earnings from a minimum-wage job to $7 an hour. Families with incomes from $8,400 to $11,000 will receive cash payments of up to $3,370.[23] This expansion, and the previous expansions of the EITC in 1986 and 1990 under the Reagan and Bush administrations, reflected a recognition that wages for low-paying work have eroded and that other policies to aid the working poor—for example, the minimum wage—have become weaker.[24]

However, even when the most recent expansion of the EITC is fully in effect in 1996, it will still fall notably short of compensating for the sharp drop in the value of the minimum wage and the marked reductions in AFDC benefits to low-income working families since the early 1970s. Nonetheless, "the 1993 law set the EITC for a family with two or more children at the level that would bring a family of four with a full-time minimum wage worker to the poverty line if the family also received food stamps and the minimum wage was modestly raised."[25]

If this benefit is paid on a monthly basis and is combined with universal health care,

the condition of workers in the low-wage sector would improve significantly and would approach that of comparable workers in Europe. The passage of universal health care is crucial in removing from the welfare rolls single mothers who are trapped in a public-assistance nightmare by the health care needs of their children. It would also make low-paying jobs more attractive for all low-skilled workers and therefore improve the rate of employment.

However, at the time of this writing, not only has legislation for universal health care been shelved, but the traditional bipartisan support for the EITC is beginning to erode in the Republican-controlled Congress. In May 1995, the Senate passed a budget resolution that includes an assumption that the EITC would be cut by roughly $13 billion over five years and $21 billion over seven years. . . .

Improving Accessibility to Suburban Jobs

The mismatch between residence and the location of jobs is a special problem for some workers in America because, unlike in Europe, the public transportation system is weak and expensive. This presents a special problem for inner-city blacks because they have less access to private automobiles and, unlike Mexicans, do not have a network system that supports organized car pools. Accordingly, they depend heavily on public transportation and therefore have difficulty getting to the suburbs, where jobs are more plentiful and employment growth is greater.[26] Until public transit systems are improved in metropolitan areas, the creation of privately subsidized car-pool and van-pool networks to carry inner-city residents to the

---

[23]"Clinton Wages a Quiet but Energetic War Against Poverty," *New York Times,* 30 March 1994.

[24]Center on Budget and Policy Priorities, "Is the EITC Growing at a Rate That Is 'Out of Control'?" Washington, DC, 9 May 1995; and "The Earned Income Tax Credit Reductions in the Senate Budget Resolution," 5 June 1995.

[25]Center on Budget and Policy Priorities, "The Earned Income Tax Credit Reductions in the Senate Budget Resolution," 2.

[26]Mark Alan Hughes, "Over the Horizon: Jobs in the Suburbs of Major Metropolitan Areas" (report to Public/Private Ventures, December 1993).

areas of employment, particularly suburban areas, would be a relatively inexpensive way to increase work opportunities.[27]

In the inner-city ghettos, the problems of spatial mismatch have been aggravated by the breakdown in the informal job information network. In neighborhoods in which a substantial number of adults are working, people are more likely to learn about job openings or be recommended for jobs by working kin, relatives, friends, and acquaintances. Job referrals from current employees are important in the American labor market. Individuals in jobless ghettos are less likely to gain employment through this process. But the creation of for-profit or not-for-profit job information and placement centers in various parts of the inner city not only could significantly improve awareness of the availability of employment in the metropolitan area but could also serve to refer workers to employers.[28] . . .

Increasing Public Sector Employment

If firms in the private sector cannot use or refuse to hire low-skilled adults who are willing to take minimum-wage or subminimum-wage jobs, then the jobs problem for inner-city workers cannot be adequately addressed without considering a

policy of public-sector employment of last resort. Indeed, until current changes in the labor market are reversed or until the skills of the next generation can be upgraded before it enters the labor market, many workers, especially those who are not in the official labor force, will not be able to find jobs unless the government becomes an employer of last resort.[29] This argument applies especially to low-skilled inner-city black workers. It is bad enough that they face the problem of shifts in labor market demand shared by all low-skilled workers; it is even worse that they confront negative employer perceptions about their work-related skills and attitudes.

If jobs are plentiful even for less skilled workers during periods of economic expansion, then labor shortages reduce the likelihood that hiring decisions will be determined by subjective negative judgments concerning a group's job-related traits. Prior to the late 1970s, there was less need for the creation of public-sector jobs.[30] Not only was economic growth fairly rapid during periods of expansion, but "the gains from growth were widely shared." Before the late 1970s, public jobs of last resort were thought of in terms of "a counter-cyclical policy to be put in place during recessions and retired during recoveries. It is only since the late 1970s that the disadvantaged have been left behind during recoveries. The labor market changes . . . seem to have been permanently reduced private sector demand for less-skilled workers.[31]

Given the current need for public jobs to enhance the employment opportunities of low-skilled workers, what should be the nature of these jobs and how should they be

---

[27]Based on several local transportation programs in Chicago (especially the "JobExpress"program created by the Suburban Job Link Corporation), Public/Private Ventures, a nonprofit research organization, "has designed a research demonstration to test a transportation strategy that links inner-city residents to job opportunities outside city centers. The elements of Bridges to Work are transportation (public or private), a mechanism for connecting trained workers with available suburban jobs (a regional alliance of providers of employment services), and special support services (provided by a community agency). A four-year demonstration of the model is planned to begin in up to nine sites in Fall 1995." Annual Report, Public/Private Ventures (Philadelphia, 1994).
[28]For this short-term policy recommendation I am indebted to James S. Tobin.

[29]Sheldon Danziger and Peter Gottschalk, *America Unequal* (Cambridge, MA: Harvard University Press, 1995), 156.
[30]Ibid.
[31]Ibid., 174.

implemented? Three thoughtful recent proposals for the creation of public jobs deserve serious consideration. One calls for the creation of public-sector infrastructure maintenance jobs, the second for public service jobs for less-skilled workers, and the third, which combines aspects of the first two, for WPA-style jobs of the kind created during the Franklin D. Roosevelt administration.

Edward V. Regan has advanced a proposal for a public-investment infrastructure maintenance program. He points out that "infrastructure maintenance and upgrading can . . . benefit the economy by creating jobs, particularly for the relatively unskilled, and by raising productivity, thereby contributing to long-term economic growth."[32] According to one estimate, $1 billion spent on road maintenance will directly generate 25,000 jobs and indirectly put 15,000 people to work.[33] On the other hand, new construction creates fewer jobs at higher wages. Another study reports that new building projects or major construction employs 40 percent fewer workers than do maintenance projects.[34] Just as other low-skill jobs are made more attractive by programs of health care, child care, and earned income tax credits, so would low-skill jobs in infrastructure maintenance.

Aside from creating jobs, infrastructure maintenance could lead to higher productivity. On this point, Regan states:

> Intuitively, fixing roads and bridges means less axle damage to trucks, fewer road mishaps and congestion, lowered costs of goods, and increased

transportation productivity. Congested and deteriorated highways, broken water mains, inadequate sewage treatment, reduced transit services—all of these infrastructure deficiencies reduce productivity, drive up costs of goods and services, and inhibit people's access to employment. Any state or local government official who has tried to attract business facilities to a particular area and has watched business decision makers turn up their noses at cracked concrete and rusting bridges knows the practical meaning of those statements.[35]

Regan also points out that there are many other benefits stemming from an improved infrastructure that are not accounted for in standard economic measures, including shortened commuting times and reduced traffic congestion. If well selected, public investment in infrastructure maintenance could contribute to economic growth. According to the Congressional Budget Office, the national real rate of return for investments to maintain the current quality of the highway system would be 30 to 40 percent; those involving selected expansion in congested urban areas would be 10 to 20 percent.[36]

Although the creation of infrastructure maintenance jobs will provide some employment opportunities for low-skilled workers, the condition of today's labor market makes it unlikely that many of these jobs will actually go to high school dropouts or even to high school graduates with little or no work experience. To address this problem, the economists Sheldon Danziger and Peter Gottschalk, in a recently published book, have advocated the creation of a labor-intensive, minimum-wage public service jobs program of last resort for today's low-skilled

---

[32]Edward V. Regan, "Infrastructure Investment for Tomorrow" (Public Policy Brief no. 141, Jerome Levy Economics Institute, Bard College), 43.

[33]Michael Montgomery and David Wyes, "The Impact of Infrastructure," *DRI/McGraw-Hill U.S. Review* (October 1992).

[34]Clark Wieman, "Road Work Ahead," *Technology Review* 96 (January 1993):42–48.

---

[35]Regan, "Infrastructure Investment," 44.

[36]Ibid.

and jobless workers.[37] They have in mind jobs such as daycare aides and playground assistants who can supervise in school gyms and public parks during after-school hours. These would be jobs for poor workers who cannot find a place in the private sector, jobs providing services that the fiscally strapped cities can no longer afford to supply through local resources.

Their plan for public service jobs differs in two important respects from recent proposals aimed at increasing work requirements and work incentives for recipients of welfare. First, their proposal is directed not just at welfare recipients but at *all poor workers* adversely affected by current economic shifts, including those who have been ineligible for, or who have chosen not to participate in, welfare. Only a small proportion of those whose labor-market prospects have diminished since the early 1970s have been welfare recipients. Second, their proposal addresses changes in the demand side of the labor market by emphasizing work opportunities and earnings supplements rather than work requirements or incentives. . . .

The final proposal under consideration here was advanced by the perceptive journalist Mickey Kaus of *The New Republic*. Kaus's proposal is modeled on the Works Progress Administration (WPA), a large public works program announced in 1935 by Franklin D. Roosevelt in his State of the Union address. The public works jobs that Roosevelt had in mind included highway construction, slum clearance, housing construction, rural electrification, and so on. As Kaus points out:

> In its eight-year existence, according to official records, the WPA built or improved 651,000 miles of roads, 953 airports, 124,000 bridges and viaducts, 1,178,000 culverts, 8,000 parks, 18,000

playgrounds and athletic fields, and 2,000 swimming pools. It constructed 40,000 buildings (including 8,000 schools) and repaired 85,000 more. Much of New York City—including LaGuardia Airport, FDR Drive, plus hundreds of parks and libraries—was built by the WPA. . . . Lester Thurow has suggested that New York's infrastructure is now decaying because no WPA has existed to replace these public works in the half-century since.[38]

Kaus advances what he calls a neo-WPA program of employment for every American citizen over 18 who wants it. The program would provide useful public jobs at wages slightly below the minimum wage. Kaus's proposed program would not only eliminate the need to provide public assistance or "workfare" for able-bodied workers but, unlike welfare, the WPA-style jobs would be

> available to everybody, men as well as women, single or married, mothers and fathers alike. No perverse "anti-family" incentives. It wouldn't even be necessary to limit the public jobs to the poor. If Donald Trump showed up, he could work too. But he wouldn't. Most Americans wouldn't. There'd be no need to "target" the program to the needy. The low wage itself would guarantee that those who took the jobs would be those who needed them, while preserving the incentive to look for better work in the private sector.[39]

Kaus maintains that the work relief under his proposal, like the work relief under Roosevelt's WPA, would not carry the stigma of a cash dole. People would be earning their money. Although some workers in

---

[37]Danziger and Gottschalk, America Unequal.

[38]Mickey Kaus, *The End of Equality* (New York: Basic Books), 259.
[39]Ibid., 125.

the WPA-style jobs "could be promoted to higher-paying public service positions," most of them would advance occupationally by moving to the private sector. "If you have to work anyway," asks Kaus, "why do it for $4 an hour?"

Kaus's proposal would also place a time limit on welfare for able-bodied recipients. After a certain date they would no longer be eligible for cash payments. However, unlike the welfare program proposed in 1995 by the Republican-controlled Congress, public jobs would be available to those who move off welfare. Kaus argues that to allow poor mothers to work, government-funded day care most be provided for their children if needed. But this service has to be integrated into the larger system of child care for other families in the United States to avoid creating a "day-care ghetto" for low-income children.

In Kaus's proposal the WPA-style jobs would be supplemented with the earned income tax credit, which could be expanded at reasonable cost to lift all poor working families who work full-time throughout the year out of poverty. Because this subsidy would augment the income of all low-wage workers, those in low-level private-sector jobs would not be treated unfairly and their wages on average would be slightly higher than those in the guaranteed subminimum-wage public jobs.

Kaus maintains that there will be enough worthwhile WPA-style jobs for anyone who wants one. The crumbling infrastructure in American cities has to be repaired. Services cut back by the government for financial reasons, such as picking up trash two times a week and opening libraries every evening and on Saturdays, could be reinstated. Jobs for men and women could range from filling potholes and painting bridges to serving as nurse's aides, clerks, and cooks. "With a neo-WPA maintaining highways, schools, playgrounds, and subways, with libraries open every evening and city streets cleaned twice

a day, we would have a common life more people would find worth reclaiming.[40]. . .

Prospects

Programs proposed to increase employment opportunities, such as the creation of WPA-style jobs, should be aimed at broad segments of the U.S. population, not just inner-city workers, in order to provide the needed solid political base of support. In the new, highly integrated global economy, an increasing number of Americans across racial, ethnic, and income groups are experiencing declining real incomes, increasing job displacement, and growing economic insecurity. The unprecedented level of inner-city joblessness represents one important aspect of the broader economic dislocations that cut across racial and ethnic groups in the United States. Accordingly, when promoting economic and social reforms, it hardly seems politically wise to focus mainly on the most disadvantaged groups while ignoring other segments of the population that have also been adversely affected by global economic changes.

Yet, just when bold new comprehensive initiatives are urgently needed to address these problems, the U.S. Congress has retreated from using public policy as an instrument with which to fight social inequality. Failure to deal with this growing social inequality, including the rise of joblessness in U.S. inner cities, could seriously worsen the economic life of urban families and neighborhoods.

Groups ranging from the inner-city poor to those working- and middle-class Americans who are struggling to make ends meet will have to be effectively mobilized in order to change the current course and direction taken by policy makers. Perhaps the best way to accomplish this is through coalition

---

[40]Ibid., 137.

politics that promote race-neutral programs such as jobs creation, further expansion of the earned income tax credit, public school reform, child care programs, and universal health insurance. A broad-based political coalition is needed to successfully push such programs through the political process.

Because an effective political coalition in part depends upon how the issues to be addressed are defined, it is imperative that the political message underscore the need for economic and social reform that benefits all groups, not just America's minority poor.[41] The framers of this message should be cognizant of the fact that changes in the global economy are creating growing social inequality and situations which intensify antagonisms between different racial and ethnic groups, and that these groups, although often seen as adversaries, are potential allies in a reform coalition because they suffer from a common problem—economic distress caused by forces outside their own control.

In the absence of an effective political coalition, priorities will be established that do not represent the interests of disadvantaged groups. For example, in the House of Representatives, 67 percent of proposed spending cuts from the federal budget for the year 2000 would come from low-income programs, even though these programs represent only 21 percent of the current federal budget. Without an effective political coalition it is unlikely that Congress would be willing to finance the kinds of reforms that are needed to combat the new social inequality. At the time of this writing, the momentum is away from, not toward, social programs. Instead of recognizing and dealing with the complex and changing realities that have led to economic distress for many

Americans, policy makers seek to assign blame and associate the economic problems of families and individuals with personal shortcomings such as lack of initiative, work ethic, or motivation. Consequently, there is very little support in favor of financing any social programs—even the creation of public service jobs for the limited number of welfare recipients who reach a time limit for receipt of welfare checks. Considering the deleterious consequences this shortsighted retreat from public policy will have for so many Americans, it is distressing that progressive groups, far from being energized to reverse the public policy direction in which the country is now moving, seem to be almost intimidated and paralyzed by the rhetoric of the Republican "Contract with America."

Accordingly, the kinds of long-term and immediate-term solutions that I have proposed stand little chance of being adopted, not to mention seriously considered, in the absence of a new political coalition of groups pressing for economic and social reform. Political leaders concerned about the current shift in public policy will have to develop a unifying rhetoric, a progressive message that resonates with broad segments of the American population, a message that enables groups to recognize that it is in their interest to join a reform coalition dedicated to moving America forward.

The solutions I have outlined were developed with the idea of providing a policy framework that would be suitable for and could be easily adopted by a reform coalition. The long-term solutions, which include the development of a system of national performance standards in public schools, family policies to reinforce the learning system in the schools, a national system of school-to-work transition, and ways to promote city-suburban integration and cooperation, would be beneficial to and could draw the support of a broad range of groups in America. The

---

[41]William Julius Wilson, *The Truly Disadvantaged: The Inner City, The Underclass, and Public Policy,* 2nd ed. (Chicago: University of Chicago Press, 1980).

short-term solutions, which range from the development of job information and placement centers and subsidized car pools in the ghetto to the creation of WPA-style jobs, are more relevant to low-income Americans, but they are the kinds of opportunity-enhancing programs that Americans of all racial and class backgrounds tend to support.

Although my policy framework is designed to appeal to broad segments of the population, I firmly believe that if adopted, it would alleviate a good deal of the economic and social distress currently plaguing the inner cities. The immediate problem of the disappearance of work in many inner-city neighborhoods would be confronted. The employment base in these neighborhoods would be increased immediately by the creation of WPA-style jobs, and income levels would rise because of the expansion of the earned income tax credit. Programs such as universal health care and day care would increase the attractiveness of low-wage jobs and "make work pay."

Increasing the employment base would have an enormous positive impact on the social organization of ghetto neighborhoods. As more people become employed, crime, including violent crime, and drug use will subside; families will be strengthened and welfare receipt will decline significantly; ghetto-related culture and behavior, no longer sustained and nourished by persistent joblessness, will gradually fade. As more people become employed and gain work experience, they will have a better chance of finding jobs in the private sector when they become available. The attitudes of employers toward inner-city workers will undergo change, in part because they would be dealing with job applicants who have steady work experience and would furnish references from their previous supervisors.

This is not to suggest that all the jobless individuals from the inner-city ghetto would take advantage of these employment opportunities. Some have responded to persistent joblessness by abusing alcohol and drugs, and these handicaps will affect their overall job performance, including showing up for work on time or on a consistent basis. But they represent only a small segment of the worker population in the inner city. Most workers in the inner city are ready, willing, able, and anxious to hold a steady job.

The long-term solutions that I have advanced would reduce the likelihood that a new generation of jobless workers would be produced from the youngsters now in school and preschool. We must break the cycle of joblessness and improve the youngsters' preparation for the new labor market in the global economy.

My framework for long-term and immediate solutions is based on the notion that the problems of jobless ghettos cannot be separated from those of the rest of the nation. Although these solutions have wide-ranging application and would alleviate the economic distress of many Americans, their impact on jobless ghettos would be profound. Their most important contribution would be their effect on the children of the ghetto, who would be able to anticipate a future of economic mobility and share the hopes and aspirations that so many of their fellow citizens experience as part of the American way of life.

Race and Residence

25

AMERICAN APARTHEID
The Perpetuation of the Underclass

Douglas S. Massey • *Nancy A. Denton*

One notable difference appears between the immigrant and Negro populations. In the case of the former, there is the possibility of escape, with improvement in economic status in the second generation.
—1931 Report to President Herbert Hoover by the Committee on Negro Housing

If the black ghetto was deliberately constructed by whites through a series of private decisions and institutional practices, if racial discrimination persists at remarkably high levels in U.S. housing markets, if intensive residential segregation continues to be imposed on blacks by virtue of their skin color, and if segregation concentrates poverty to build a self-perpetuating spiral of decay into black neighborhoods, then a variety of deleterious consequences automatically follow for individual African Americans. A racially segregated society cannot be a race-blind society; as long as U.S. cities remain segregated—indeed, hypersegregated—the United States cannot claim to have equalized opportunities for

blacks and whites. In a segregated world, the deck is stacked against black socioeconomic progress, political empowerment, and full participation in the mainstream of American life.

In considering how individuals fare in the world, social scientists make a fundamental distinction between individual, family, and structural characteristics. To a great extent, of course, a person's success depends on individual traits such as motivation, intelligence, and especially, education. Other things equal, those who are more highly motivated, smarter, and better educated will be rewarded more highly in the labor market and will achieve greater socioeconomic success.

Other things generally are not equal, however, because individual traits such as motivation and education are strongly affected by family background. Parents who are themselves educated, motivated, and economically successful tend to pass these traits on to their children. Children who enter the middle and upper classes through the accident of birth are more likely than other, equally intelligent children from other classes to acquire the schooling, motivation, and cultural knowledge required for socioeconomic success in contemporary society. Other aspects of family background, moreover, such as wealth and social connections, open the doors of opportunity irrespective of education or motivation.

Yet even when one adjusts for family background, other things are still not equal, because the structural organization of society also plays a profound role in shaping the life chances of individuals. Structural variables are elements of social and economic organization that lie beyond individual control, that are built into the way society is organized. Structural characteristics affect the fate of large numbers of people and families who share common locations in the social order.

Among the most important structural variables are those that are geographically defined. Where one lives—especially, where one grows up—exerts a profound effect on one's life chances. Identical individuals with similar family backgrounds and personal characteristics will lead very different lives and achieve different rates of socioeconomic success depending on where they reside. Because racial segregation confines blacks to a circumscribed and disadvantaged niche in the urban spatial order, it has profound consequences for individual and family well-being.

Social and Spatial Mobility

In a market society such as the United States, opportunities, resources, and benefits are not distributed evenly across the urban landscape. Rather, certain residential areas have more prestige, greater affluence, higher home values, better services, and safer streets than others. Marketing consultants have grown rich by taking advantage of this "clustering of America" to target specific groups of consumers for wealthy corporate clients. The geographic differentiation of American cities by socioeconomic status does more than conveniently rank neighborhoods for the benefit of demogra-

phers, however; it also creates a crucial connection between social and spatial mobility.

As people get ahead, they not only move up the economic ladder, they move up the residential ladder as well. As early as the 1920s, sociologists at the University of Chicago noted this close connection between social and spatial mobility, a link that has been verified many times since. As socioeconomic status improves, families relocate to take advantage of opportunities and resources that are available in greater abundance elsewhere. By drawing on benefits acquired through residential mobility, aspiring parents not only consolidate their own class position but enhance their and their children's prospects for additional social mobility.

In a very real way, therefore, barriers to spatial mobility are barriers to social mobility, and where one lives determines a variety of salient factors that affect individual well-being: the quality of schooling, the value of housing, exposure to crime, the quality of public services, and the character of children's peers. As a result, residential integration has been a crucial component in the broader process of socioeconomic advancement among immigrants and their children. By moving to successively better neighborhoods, other racial and ethnic groups have gradually become integrated into American society. Although rates of spatial assimilation have varied, levels of segregation have fallen for each immigrant group as socioeconomic status and generations in the United States have increased.

The residential integration of most ethnic groups has been achieved as a by-product of broader processes of socioeconomic attainment, not because group members sought to live among native whites per se. The desire for integration is only one of a larger set of motivations, and not necessarily the most important. Some minorities may even be antagonistic to the idea of integration, but for spatial assimilation to occur, they need only be willing to put up with integration in order to gain access to socioeconomic resources that are more abundant in areas in which white families predominate.

To the extent that white prejudice and discrimination restrict the residential mobility of blacks and confine them to areas with poor schools, low home values, inferior services, high crime, and low educational aspirations, segregation undermines their social and economic well-being. The persistence of racial segregation makes it difficult for aspiring black families to escape the concentrated poverty of the ghetto and puts them at a distinct disadvantage in the larger competition for education, jobs, wealth, and power. The central issue is not whether African Americans "prefer" to live near white people or whether integration is a desirable social goal, but how the restrictions on individual liberty implied by severe segregation undermine the social and economic well-being of individuals.

Extensive research demonstrates that blacks face strong barriers to spatial assimilation within American society. Compared with other minority groups, they are markedly less able to convert their socioeconomic attainments into residential contact with whites, and because of this fact they are unable to gain access to crucial resources and benefits that are distributed through housing markets. Dollar for dollar, blacks are able to buy fewer neighborhood amenities with their income than other groups.

Among all groups in the United States, only Puerto Ricans share blacks' relative inability to assimilate spatially; but this disadvantage stems from the fact that many are of African origin. Although white Puerto Ricans achieve rates of spatial assimilation that are comparable with those found among other ethnic groups, those of African or racially mixed origins experience markedly lower abilities to convert socioeconomic attainments into contact with whites. Once race is controlled, the "paradox of Puerto Rican segregation" disappears.

Given the close connection between social and spatial mobility, the persistence of racial barriers implies the systematic exclusion of blacks from benefits and resources that are distributed through housing markets. We illustrate the severity of this black disadvantage with data specially compiled for the city of Philadelphia in 1980. The data allow us to consider the socioeconomic character of neighborhoods that poor, middle-income, and affluent blacks and whites can be expected to inhabit, holding education and occupational status constant.

In Philadelphia, poor blacks and poor whites both experience very bleak neighborhood environments; both groups live in areas where about 40% of the births are to unwed mothers, where median home values are under $30,000, and where nearly 40% of high school students score under the 15th percentile on a standardized achievement test. Families in such an environment would be unlikely to build wealth through home equity, and children growing up in such an environment would be exposed to a peer environment where unwed parenthood was common and where educational performance and aspirations were low.

As income rises, however, whites are able to escape this disadvantaged setting by relocating to a more advantaged setting. With a middle-class income ($20,000 1979 dollars), whites no longer reside in a neighborhood where unwed parenthood predominates (only 10% of births are to single mothers) and housing values are well above $30,000. At the same time, school performance is markedly better; only 17% of students in the local high school score below the 15th percentile.

Once whites achieve affluence, moreover, negative residential conditions are left far behind. Affluent whites in Philadelphia (those with a 1979 income of $32,000) live in neighborhoods where only 2% of the births are to unwed mothers, where the median home value is $57,000, and where a mere 6% of high school students score below the 15th percentile on achievement tests. Upwardly mobile whites, in essence, capitalize on their higher incomes to buy their way into improved residential circumstances.

Blacks, in contrast, remain mired in disadvantage no matter what income they achieve. Middle-income blacks live in an area where more than a quarter of the births are to unwed mothers, where housing values languish below $30,000, and where 27% of all students in the local high school score below the 15th percentile. Even with affluence, blacks achieve neighborhood environments that compare unfavorably with those attained by whites. With an income of $32,000, a black family can expect to live in a neighborhood where 17% of all births are to unwed mothers, home values are barely over $30,000, and where a fifth of high school students score below the 15th percentile.

For blacks, in other words, high incomes do not buy entrée to residential circumstances that can serve as springboards for future socioeconomic mobility; in particular, blacks are unable to achieve a school environment conducive to later academic success. In Philadelphia, children from an affluent black family are likely to attend a public school where the percentage of low-achieving students is three times greater than the percentage in schools attended by affluent white children. Small wonder, then, that controlling for income in no way erases the large racial gap in SAT scores. Because of segregation, the same income buys black and white families educational environments that are of vastly different quality.

Given these limitations on the ability of black families to gain access to neighborhood resources, it is hardly surprising that

government surveys reveal blacks to be less satisfied with their residential circumstances than socioeconomically equivalent whites. This negative evaluation reflects an accurate appraisal of their circumstances rather than different values or ideals on the part of blacks. Both races want the same things in homes and neighborhoods; blacks are just less able to achieve them. Compared with whites, blacks are less likely to be homeowners, and the homes they do own are of poorer quality, in poorer neighborhoods, and of lower value. Moreover, given the close connection between home equity and family wealth, the net worth of blacks is a small fraction of that of whites, even though their incomes have converged over the years. Finally, blacks tend to occupy older, more crowded dwellings that are structurally inadequate compared to those inhabited by whites; and because these racial differentials stem from segregation rather than income, adjusting for socioeconomic status does not erase them.

The Politics of Segregation

Socioeconomic achievement is not only a matter of individual aspirations and effort, however; it is also a matter of collective action in the political arena. Generations of immigrants have entered American cities and struggled to acquire political power as a means to enhance individual mobility. Ultimately most were incorporated into the pluralist political structure of American cities. In return for support at the polls, ethnic groups were awarded a share of public services, city contracts, and municipal jobs in rough proportion to their share of the electorate. The receipt of these public resources, in turn, helped groups consolidate their class position and gave their members a secure economic base from which to advance further.

The process of political incorporation that followed each immigrant wave grew out of shared political interests that were, to a large extent, geographically determined. Although neighborhoods may have been labeled "Polish," "Italian," or "Jewish," neighborhoods in which one ethnic group constituted a majority were rare, and most immigrants of European origin never lived in them. As a result, levels of ethnic segregation never reached the heights typical of black-white segregation today.

This geographic diversification of ethnicity created a situation in which ethnic groups necessarily shared common political interests. In distributing public works, municipal services, and patronage jobs to ethnic groups in return for their political support, resources were also allocated to specific neighborhoods, which typically contained a diverse array of ethnicities. Given the degree of ethnic mixing within neighborhoods, political patronage provided to one group yielded substantial benefits for others as well. Building a new subway stop in an "Italian" neighborhood, for example, also provided benefits to Jews, Poles, and Lithuanians who shared the area; and allocating municipal jobs to Poles not only benefited merchants in "Polish" communities but generated extra business for nearby shopkeepers who were Hungarian, Italian, or Czech.

At the same time, threats to curtail municipal services encouraged the formation of broad, interethnic coalitions built around common neighborhood interests. A plan to close a firehouse in a "Jewish" neighborhood, for example, brought protests not only from Jews but from Scandinavians, Italians, and Slovaks who shared the neighborhood and relied on its facilities. These other ethnics, moreover, were invariably connected to friends and relatives in other neighborhoods or to co-ethnic politicians from other districts who could assist them in applying political pressure to forestall the closure. In this way, residential integration structurally supported the formation of interethnic coalitions, providing a firm base for the emergence of pluralist political machines.

Residential integration also made it possible for ethnic groups to compete for political leadership throughout the city, no matter what their size. Because no single group dominated numerically in most neighborhoods, politicians from a variety of backgrounds found the door open to make a bid for elective office. Moreover, representatives elected from ethnically diverse neighborhoods had to pay attention to all voters irrespective of ethnic affiliation. The geographic distribution of political power across ethnically heterogeneous districts spread political influence widely among groups and ensured that all were given a political voice.

The residential segregation of blacks, in contrast, provided no basis for pluralist politics because it precluded the emergence of common neighborhood interests; the geographic isolation of blacks instead forced nearly all issues to cleave along racial lines. When a library, firehouse, police station, or school was built in a black neighborhood, other ethnic groups derived few, if any, benefits; and when important services were threatened with reduction or removal, blacks could find few coalition partners with whom to protest the cuts. Since no one except blacks lived in the ghetto, no other ethnic group had a self-interest in seeing them provided with public services or political patronage.

On the contrary, resources allocated to black neighborhoods detracted from the benefits going to white ethnic groups; and because patronage was the glue that held white political coalitions together, resources allocated to the ghetto automatically undermined the stability of the pluralist machine. As long as whites controlled city politics, their political interests lay in providing as few resources as possible to African Americans and as many as possible to white ethnic groups. Although blacks occasionally formed alliances with white reformers, the latter acted more from moral conviction than from self-interest. Because altruism is notoriously unreliable as a basis for political cooperation, interracial coalitions were unstable and of limited effectiveness in representing black interests.

The historical confinement of blacks to the ghetto thus meant that blacks shared few political interests with whites. As a result, their incorporation into local political structures differed fundamentally from the pluralist model followed by other groups. The geographic and political isolation of blacks meant that they had virtually no power when their numbers were small; only when their numbers increased enough to dominate one or more wards did they acquire any influence at all. But rather than entering the pluralist coalition as an equal partner, the black community was incorporated in a very different way: as a machine within a machine.

The existence of solid black electoral districts, while undermining interracial coalition-building, did create the potential for bloc voting along racial lines. In a close citywide election, the delivery of a large number of black votes could be extremely useful to white politicians, and inevitably black political bosses arose to control and deliver this vote in return for political favors. Unlike whites, who exercised power through politicians of diverse ethnicities, blacks were typically represented by one boss, always black, who developed a symbiotic and dependent relationship with the larger white power structure.

In return for black political support, white politicians granted black bosses such as Oscar DePriest or William Dawson of Chicago and Charles Anderson of Harlem a share of jobs and patronage that they could, in turn, distribute within the ghetto. Although these bosses wielded considerable power and status within the black community, they occupied a very tenuous position in the larger white polity. On issues that threatened the white machine or its constituents, the black bosses could easily be outvoted. Thus patronage, services, and jobs were allocated to the ghetto only as long as black bosses controlled racial agitation and didn't threaten the color line, and the resources they received typically compared unfavorably to those provided to white politicians and their neighborhoods.

As with black business owners and professionals, the pragmatic adaptation of black politicians to the realities of segregation gave them a vested interest in the ghetto and its perpetuation. During the 1950s, for example, William Dawson joined with white ethnic politicians to oppose the construction of public housing projects in white neighborhoods, not because of an ideological objection to public housing per se, but because integration would antagonize his white political sponsors and take voters outside of wards that he controlled.

The status quo of a powerful white machine and a separate but dependent black machine was built on shifting sand, however. It remained viable only as long as cities dominated state politics, patronage was plentiful, and blacks comprised a minority of the population. During the 1950s and 1960s, white suburbanization and black in-migration systematically undermined these foundations, and white machine politicians became progressively less able to accommodate black demands while simultaneously maintaining the color line. Given the declining political clout of cities, the erosion of their tax base, and the rising proportion of blacks in cities, municipal politics became a racially charged zero-sum game that pitted politically disenfranchised blacks against a faltering coalition of ethnic whites. . . .

Even in cities where blacks have assumed political leadership by virtue of becoming a majority, the structural constraints of segregation still remain decisive. Indeed, the political isolation experienced by blacks in places such as Newark and Detroit is probably more severe than that experienced earlier in the century, when ghetto votes were at least useful to white politicians in citywide elections. Once blacks gained control of the central city and whites completed their withdrawal to the surrounding suburbs, virtually all structural supports for interracial cooperation ended.

In the suburbs surrounding places such as Newark and Detroit, white politicians are administratively and politically insulated from black voters in central cities, and they have no direct political interest in their welfare. Indeed, money that flows into black central cities generally means increased taxes and lower net incomes for suburban whites. Because suburbanites now form a majority of most state populations—and a majority of the national electorate—the "chocolate city–vanilla suburb" pattern of contemporary racial segregation gives white politicians a strong interest in limiting the flow of public resources to black-controlled cities.

In an era of fiscal austerity and declining urban resources, therefore, the political isolation of blacks makes them extremely vulnerable to cutbacks in governmental services and public investments. If cuts must be made to balance strained city budgets, it makes political sense for white politicians to concentrate the cuts in black neighborhoods, where the political damage will be minimal; and if state budgets must be trimmed, it is in white legislators' interests to cut subventions to black-controlled central cities, which now represent a minority of most states' voters. The spatial and political isolation of blacks interacts with declining public resources to create a powerful dynamic for disinvestment in the black community.

The destructiveness of this dynamic has been forcefully illustrated by Rodrick and Deborah Wallace, who trace the direct and indirect results of a political decision in New York City to reduce the number of fire companies in black and Puerto Rican neighborhoods during the early 1970s.[1] Faced with a shortage of funds during the city's financial crisis, the Fire Department eliminated thirty-five fire companies between 1969 and 1976, twenty-seven of which were in poor minority areas located in the Bronx, Manhattan, and Brooklyn, areas where the risk of fire, was, in fact, quite high. Confronted with the unpleasant task of cutting services, white politicians confined the reductions to segregated ghetto and barrio wards where the political damage could be contained. The geographic and political isolation of blacks and Puerto Ricans meant that their representatives were unable to prevent the cuts.

As soon as the closings were implemented, the number of residential fires increased dramatically. An epidemic of building fires occurred within black and Puerto Rican neighborhoods. As housing was systematically destroyed, social networks were fractured and institutions collapsed; churches, block associations, youth programs, and political clubs vanished. The destruction of housing, networks, and social institutions, in turn, caused a massive flight of destitute families out of core minority areas. Some affected areas lost 80% of their residents between 1970 and 1980, putting a severe strain on housing in adjacent neighborhoods, which had been stable until then. As families doubled up in response to the influx of fire refugees, overcrowding increased, which led to additional fires and the diffusion of the chaos into adjacent areas. Black ghettos and Puerto Rican barrios were hollowed out from their cores.

The overcrowded housing, collapsed institutions, and ruptured support networks overwhelmed municipal disease prevention efforts and swamped medical care facilities. Within affected neighborhoods, infant mortality rates rose, as did the incidence of cirrhosis, gonorrhea, tuberculosis, and drug use. The destruction of the social fabric of black and Puerto Rican neighborhoods led to an increase in the number of unsupervised young males, which contributed to a sharp increase in crime, followed by an increase in the rate of violent deaths among young men. By 1990, this chain reaction of social and economic collapse had turned vast areas of the Bronx, Harlem, and Brooklyn into "urban deserts" bereft of normal community life.

Despite the havoc that followed in the wake of New York's fire service reductions, the cuts were never rescinded. The only people affected were minority members who were politically marginalized by segregation and thereby prevented, structurally, from finding allies to oppose the service reductions. Although residential segregation paradoxically made it easier for blacks and Puerto Ricans to elect city councillors by creating homogeneous districts, it left those that were elected relatively weak, dependent, and unable to protect the interests of their constituents.

As a result of their residential segregation and resultant political isolation, therefore, black politicians in New York and elsewhere have been forced into a strategy of angrily demanding that whites give them more public resources. Given their geographic isolation, however, these appeals cannot be made on the basis of whites' self-interest, but must rely on appeals to altruism, guilt, or fear. Because altruism, guilt, and fear do not provide a good foundation for concerted political action, the downward spiral of black neighborhoods continues and black hostility and bitterness grow while white fears are progressively reinforced. Segregation creates a political impasse that deepens the chasm of race in American society.

Under the best of circumstances, segregation undermines the ability of blacks to advance their interests because it provides ethnic whites with no immediate self-interest in their welfare. The circumstances of U.S. race relations, however, can hardly be described as "best," for not only do whites have little self-interest in promoting black welfare, but a significant share must be assumed to be racially prejudiced and supportive of policies injurious to blacks. To the extent that racism exists, of course, the geographic and political isolation of the ghetto makes it easier for racists to act on their prejudices. In a segregated society, blacks become easy targets for racist actions and policies.

The Isolation of the Ghetto

The high degree of residential segregation imposed on blacks ensures their social and economic isolation from the rest of American society. In 1980 ten large U.S. cities had black isolation indices in excess of 80 (Atlanta, Baltimore, Chicago, Cleveland, Detroit, Gary, Newark, Philadelphia, St. Louis, and Washington, D.C.), meaning that the average black person in these cities lived in a neighborhood that was at least 80% black. Averages in excess of 80% occur when a few blacks live in integrated areas, and the vast majority reside in areas that are 100% black.

Such high levels of racial isolation cannot be sustained without creating a profound alienation from American society and its institutions. Unless ghetto residents work outside of their neighborhoods, they are unlikely to come into contact with anyone else who is not also black, and if they live in an area of concentrated poverty, they are unlikely to interact with anyone who is not also *poor* and black. The structural constraints on social interaction imposed by segregation loom large when one considers that 36% of black men in central cities are either out of the labor force, unemployed, or underemployed, a figure that rises to 54% among black men aged 18 to 29.

The role that segregation plays in undermining blacks' connection to the rest of society has been demonstrated by William Yancey and his colleagues at Temple University.[2] They undertook a representative survey of people in the Philadelphia urban area and asked them to describe the race and ethnicity of their friends and neighbors. Not surprisingly, blacks were far more concentrated residentially than any other group, even controlling for social and economic background. They were also very unlikely to report friendships with anyone else but blacks, and this remarkable racial homogeneity in their friendship networks was explained entirely by their residential concentration; it had nothing to do with group size, birthplace, socioeconomic status, or organizational membership. Unlike other groups, blacks were prevented from forming friendships outside their group because they were so residentially segregated: spatial isolation leads to social isolation.

The intense isolation imposed by segregation has been confirmed by an ethnographic study of blacks living in Chicago's poorest neighborhoods.[3] Drawing on detailed, in-depth interviews gathered in William Julius Wilson's Urban Family Life Survey, Sophie Pedder found that one theme consistently emerged in the narratives: poor blacks had extremely narrow geographic horizons. Many of her informants, who lived on Chicago's South Side, had never been into the Loop (the city's center), and a large number had never left the immediate confines of their neighborhood. A significant percentage only left the neighborhood after reaching adulthood. According to Pedder, this racial isolation "is at once both real, in that movement outside the neighborhood is limited, and psychological, in that residents feel cut off from the rest of the city."[4]

Thus residents of hypersegregated neighborhoods necessarily live within a very circumscribed and limited social world. They rarely travel outside of the black enclave, and most have few friends outside of the ghetto. This lack of connection to the rest of society carries profound costs, because personal contacts and friendship networks are among the most important means by which people get jobs. Relatively few job seekers attain employment by responding to ads or canvassing employers; most people find jobs through friends, relatives, or neighbors, and frequently they learn of jobs through acquaintances they know only casually.

The social isolation imposed on blacks by virtue of their systematic residential segregation thus guarantees their economic isolation as well. Because blacks have weak links to white society, they are not connected to the jobs that white society provides. They are put at a clear disadvantage in the competition for employment, and especially for increasingly scarce jobs that pay well but require little formal skill or education. This economic isolation, moreover, is cumulative and self-perpetuating: because blacks have few connections outside the ghetto, they are less likely to be employed in the mainstream economy, and this fact, in turn, reduces the number and range of their connections to other people and institutions, which further undermines their employment chances. Given the levels of residential segregation typically found in large American cities, therefore, the inevitable result is a dependent black community within which work experience is lacking and linkages to legitimate employment are weak.

The Language of Segregation

The depth of isolation in the ghetto is also evident in black speech patterns, which have evolved steadily away from Standard American English. Because of their intense social isolation, many ghetto residents have come to speak a language that is increasingly remote from that spoken by American whites. Black street speech, or more formally, Black English Vernacular, has its roots in the West Indian creole and Scots-Irish dialects of the eighteenth century. As linguists have shown, it is by no means a "degenerate," or "illogical" version of Standard American English; rather, it constitutes a complex, rich, and expressive language in its own right, with a consistent grammar, pronunciation, and lexicon all its own. It evolved independently from Standard American English because blacks were historically separated from whites by caste, class, and region; but among the most powerful influences on black speech has been the residential segregation that blacks have experienced since early in the century.

For several decades, the linguist William Labov and his colleagues have systematically taped, transcribed, and analyzed black and white speech patterns in American cities.[5] In city after city they have found that whites "constitute a single speech community, defined by a single set of norms and a single, extraordinarily uniform structural base. Linguistic features pass freely across ethnic lines within the white community. But not across racial lines: black(s) . . . have nothing to do with these sound changes in process."[6] Divergent black and white speech patterns provide stark evidence of the structural limits to interracial communication that come with high levels of residential segregation.

Whereas white speech has become more regionally specialized over time, with lin-

guistic patterns varying increasingly between metropolitan areas, Labov and his colleagues found precisely the opposite pattern for Black English: it has become progressively more uniform across urban areas. Over the past two decades, the Black English Vernaculars of Boston, Chicago, Detroit, New York, and Philadelphia have become increasingly similar in their grammatical structure and lexicon, reflecting urban blacks' common social and economic isolation within urban America. Although black speech has become more uniform internally, however, as a dialect it has drifted farther and farther away from the form and structure of Standard American English. According to Labov's measurements, blacks and whites in the United States increasingly speak different tongues, with different grammatical rules, divergent pronunciations, and separate vocabularies. . . .

The ability to speak, write, and communicate effectively in Standard English is essential for employment in most white-collar jobs. The ability to speak Standard English, at least, is also widely demanded by employers for clerical or service positions that bring jobholders into frequent contact with the general public, most of whom are white. Employers make frequent use of language as a screening device for blue-collar jobs, even those that involve little or no interaction with the public. They assume that people who speak Black English carry a street culture that devalues behaviors and attitudes consistent with being a "good worker," such as regularity, punctuality, dependability, and respect for authority.[7]

The inability to communicate in Standard American English, therefore, presents serious obstacles to socioeconomic advancement. Black Americans who aspire to socioeconomic success generally must acquire a facility in Standard English as a precondition of advancement, even if they retain a fluency in black speech. Successful blacks who have grown up in the ghetto literally become bilingual, learning to switch back and forth between black and white dialects depending on the social context.

This "code switching" involves not only a change of words but a shift between contrasting cultures and identities. Although some people acquire the ability to make this shift without difficulty, it causes real social and psychological problems for others. For someone raised in the segregated environment of the ghetto, adopting white linguistic conventions can seem like a betrayal of black culture, a phony attempt to deny the reality of one's "blackness." As a result, black people who regularly speak Standard American English often encounter strong disapproval from other blacks. Many well-educated blacks recall with some bitterness the ridicule and ostracism they suffered as children for the sin of "talking white."

The Culture of Segregation

This struggle between "black" and "white" speech patterns is symptomatic of a larger conflict between "black" and "white" cultural identities that arises from residential segregation. In response to the harsh and isolated conditions of ghetto life, a segment of the urban black population has evolved a set of behaviors, attitudes, and values that are increasingly at variance with those held in the wider society. Although these adaptations represent rational accommodations to social and economic conditions within the ghetto, they are not widely accepted or understood outside of it, and in fact are negatively evaluated by most of American society.

Middle-class American culture generally idealizes the values of self-reliance, hard work, sobriety, and sacrifice, and adherence to these principles is widely believed to bring monetary reward and economic advancement in society. Among men, adherence to these values means that employment and financial security should precede marriage, and among women they imply that childbearing should occur only after adequate means to support the raising of children have been secured, either through marriage or through employment. In the ideal world, everyone is hardworking, self-sufficient, and not a burden to fellow citizens.

In most white neighborhoods the vast majority of working age men are employed. Because jobs are available and poverty is relatively uncommon, most residents can reasonably expect to conform to ideal values most of the time. Men generally do find jobs before marrying and women have reason to believe that men will help support the children they father. Although these ideals may be violated with some frequency, there is enough conformity in most white neighborhoods for them to retain their force as guides for behavior; there are still enough people who exemplify the values to serve as role models for others. Those failures that do occur are taken to reflect individual flaws, and most whites derive a sense of self-esteem and prestige by conforming to the broader ideals of American society.

Ghetto blacks, however, face very different neighborhood conditions created by residential segregation. A large share live in a geographically isolated and racially homogeneous neighborhood where poverty is endemic, joblessness is rife, schools are poor, and even high school graduates are unlikely to speak Standard English with any facility. Employment opportunities are limited, and given the social isolation enforced by segregation, black men are not well connected to employers in the larger economy. As a result, young men coming of age in ghetto areas are relatively unlikely to find jobs capable of supporting a wife and children, and black women, facing a dearth of potential husbands and an absence of educational institutions capable of preparing them for gainful employment, cannot realistically hope to conform to societal ideals of marriage and childbearing.

The conditions of the ghetto, in short, make it exceedingly difficult to live up to broader societal values with respect to work, marriage, and family formation, and poor blacks are thus denied the opportunity to build self-esteem and to acquire prestige through channels valued in the wider society. As a result, an alternative status system has evolved within America's ghettos that is defined *in opposition to* the basic ideals and values of American society. It is a culture that explains and legitimizes the social and economic shortcomings of ghetto blacks, which are built into their lives by segregation rather than by personal failings. This culture of segregation attaches value and meaning to a way of life that the broader society would label as deviant and unworthy. . . .

As a protection against the persistent assaults to self-esteem that are inherent in ghetto life, black street culture has evolved to legitimate certain behaviors prevalent within the black community that would otherwise be held in contempt by white society. Black identity is thus constructed as a series of oppositions to conventional middle-class "white" attitudes and behavior. If whites speak Standard American English, succeed in school, work hard at routine jobs, marry, and support their children, then to be "black" requires one to speak Black English, do poorly in school, denigrate conventional employment, shun marriage, and raise children outside of marriage. To do otherwise would be to "act white."

By concentrating poor people prone to such oppositional identities in racially homogeneous settings, segregation creates the structural context for the maintenance and perpetuation of an ongoing oppositional culture, "which includes devices for protecting [black] identity and for maintaining boundaries between [blacks] and white Americans. [Blacks] regard certain forms of behavior and certain activities or events, symbols, and meanings as *not appropriate* for them because . . . [they] are characteristic of white Americans. At the same time, they emphasize other forms of behavior and other events, symbols, and meanings as more appropriate for them because they are *not* a part of white Americans' way of life."

Ogbu and Fordham are educational specialists who have specifically documented the effect of oppositional black culture on educational achievement among black children. Their investigations show how bright, motivated, and intellectually curious ghetto children face tremendous pressure from their peers to avoid "acting white" in succeeding in school and achieving academic distinction.[8] The pressure for educational failure is most intense during the teenage years, when peer acceptance is so important and black young people live in fear of being labeled "Oreos," "Uncle Toms," or "Aunt Jemimahs" for speaking Standard English or doing well in school. If they actually achieve academic distinction, they risk being called a "brainiac," or worse, a "pervert brainiac" (someone who is not only smart but of questionable sexuality as well).

Black children who do overcome the odds and achieve academic success in inner-city schools typically go to great lengths, and adopt ingenious strategies, to lessen the burden of "acting white." Some deliberately fail selected courses, others scale back their efforts and get B's or C's rather than the A's they are capable of, and still others become class clowns, seeking to deflect attention away from their scholarly achievements by acting so ridiculous that their peers no longer take them seriously. Better to be called "crazy" or a "clown" than a "pervert brainiac."

The powerful effect of oppositional ghetto culture on black educational performance is suggested by the recent work of James Rosenbaum and his colleagues at Northwestern University.[9] Working in the Chicago area, they compared low-income black students from families assigned to scattered site housing in a white suburb (under the *Gautreaux* court decision) with comparable students from families assigned to public housing in Chicago's ghetto. Although the two groups were initially identical, once removed from ghetto high schools black students achieved higher grades, lower dropout rates, better academic preparation, and higher rates of college attendance compared with those who remained behind in ghetto institutions.

Another study by Robert Crain and Rita Mahard, who used a nationwide sample, found that northern blacks who attended racially mixed schools were more likely to enter and stay in college than those who went to all-black high schools.[10] Susan Mayer followed students who attended the tenth grade in poor and affluent high schools in 1980 and determined the likelihood of their dropping out before 1982. Controlling for family background, she discovered that students who went to affluent schools were considerably less likely to drop out than those who attended poor schools, and that girls in affluent schools were much less likely to have a child. Moreover, white students who attended predominantly black high schools were considerably more likely to drop out and have a child than those who attended predominantly white schools.

All too often, whites observe the workings of black oppositional culture and conclude that African Americans suffer from some kind of "cultural defect," or that they are somehow "culturally disadvantaged." In doing so, they blame the victims of segregation rather than the social arrangements that created the oppositional culture in the first place. It is not a self-perpetuating "culture of poverty"[11] that retards black educational progress but a structurally created and sustained "culture of segregation" that, however useful in adapting to the harsh realities of ghetto life, undermines socioeconomic progress in the wider society.

As Kenneth Clark pointed out in 1965, "the invisible walls of a segregated society are not only damaging but protective in a debilitating way. There is considerable psychological safety in the ghetto; there one lives among one's own and does not risk rejection among strangers. One first becomes aware of the psychological damage of such 'safety' when the walls of the ghetto are breached and the Negro ventures out into the repressive, frightening white world. . . . Most Negroes take the first steps into an integrated society tentatively and torn with conflict. To be the first Negro who is offered a job in a company brings a sense of triumph but also the dread of failure."[12] More recently, Shelby Steele has written of the "integration shock" that envelops blacks who enter white society directly from the isolated world of the ghetto.[13]

The origins of black oppositional culture can be traced to the period before 1920, when black migration fomented a hardening of white racial attitudes and a systematic limiting of opportunities for African Americans on a variety of fronts. Whereas urban blacks had zealously pursued education after the Civil War and were making great strides, the rise of Jim Crow in the south and de facto segregation in the north severed the links between hard work, education, sobriety, and their presumed rewards in society. Although black elites continued to promote these values, the rise of the ghetto made them look increasingly pathetic and ridiculous to the mass of recent in-migrants: in the face of pervasive barriers to social and residential mobility, the moral admonitions of the elites seemed hollow and pointless. If whites would not accept blacks on the basis of their individual accomplishments and if hard work and education went unrewarded, then why expend the effort? If one could never be accepted as white, it was just demeaning and humiliating to go through the motions of "acting white." Malcolm X summed up this attitude with his sardonic quip, "What do you call a Negro with a Ph.D.? A nigger."[14]

Unlike other groups, the force of oppositional culture is particularly powerful among African Americans because it is so strongly reinforced by residential segregation. By isolating blacks within racially homogeneous neighborhoods and concentrating poverty within them, segregation creates an environment where failure to meet the ideal standards of American society loses its stigma; indeed, individual shortcomings become normative and supported by the values of oppositional culture. As transgressions lose their stigma through repetition and institutionalization, individual behavior at variance with broader societal ideals becomes progressively more likely.

The culture of segregation arises from the coincidence of racial isolation and high poverty, which inevitably occurs when a poor minority group is residentially segregated. By concentrating poverty, segregation simultaneously concentrates male joblessness, teenage motherhood, single parenthood, alcoholism, and drug abuse, thus creating an entirely black social world in which these oppositional states are normative. Given the racial isolation and concentrated poverty of the ghetto, it is hardly surprising that black street culture has drifted steadily away from middle-class American values.

The steady divergence of black street culture from the white mainstream is clearly visible in a series of participant observer studies of ghetto life conducted over the past thirty years. Studies carried out during

the 1960s and 1970s—such as Elliot Liebow's *Tally's Corner,* Lee Rainwater's *Behind Ghetto Walls,* Ulf Hannerz's *Soulside,* and Elijah Anderson's *A Place on the Corner*—where remarkably consistent in reporting that ghetto dwellers, despite their poverty and oppression, essentially subscribed to the basic values of American society. What set ghetto blacks apart from other Americans was not their lack of fealty to American ideals but their inability to accomplish them. Specifically, the pervasiveness of poverty, unemployment, and dependency in the ghetto made it nearly impossible for them to live up to ideals they in fact held, which in turn undermined their self-esteem and thus created a psychological need for gratification through other means.

The participant observer studies indicated that feelings of personal inadequacy led black men to reject the unskilled and poorly paid jobs open to them, to denigrate the kind of work these jobs represented, and to seek gratification through more accessible channels, such as sexual liaisons or intoxication. Women and men tended to begin sexual relations at a young age, and women generally found themselves pregnant as teenagers. Childbirth was typically followed by marriage or some informal living arrangement, at least for a time; but eventually the woman's demands for financial support undermined her partner's self-esteem, and family responsibilities blocked his access to the alternate status system of the streets. Given the crosscutting pressures of poverty, joblessness, low self-esteem, family demands, and the allure of the streets, most male-female relationships were short-lived and devolved sooner or later into female-headed families.

Once they had been through this cycle of romance, pregnancy, family formation, and dissolution, black men and women came to see romantic relationships as a mutually exploitative contest whose pleasures were temporary and whose stability could not be relied upon. At the same time, the pervasive poverty of the ghetto meant that families were constantly bombarded with energy-sapping demands for assistance and debilitating requests for financial aid from extended family, friends, and neighbors. Given the association of poverty with crime and violence, moreover, they were constantly at risk of criminal victimization, injury, or even death.

In this social world, ghetto dwellers acquired a tough, cynical attitude toward life, a deep suspicion of the motives of others, and a marked lack of trust in the goodwill or benevolent intentions of people and institutions. Growing up in the ghetto, blacks came to expect the worst of others and to experience little sense of control over their lives. They adapted to these feelings by confining relationships of trust to close kin, especially maternal relatives.

Underlying this bleak portrait of ghetto life painted by studies carried out during the 1960s and 1970s was a common thread. Early participant observers saw ghetto culture as rooted in the structural conditions of poverty, dependency, and joblessness, over which ghetto residents had little control, and all characterized ghetto culture as essentially oppositional. That is, the attitudes and behaviors of ghetto blacks were fundamentally defined in opposition to the ideals of white society. Underneath the jaded rejection of conventional mores, ghetto dwellers, at least in the first or second generations, still clung to the basic values of American society. Indeed, it was because they judged themselves so harshly by broader standards that the psychological need for an oppositional identity arose in the first place.

Over time, however, as intense racial isolation and acutely concentrated poverty have continued, ghetto attitudes, values, and ideals have become progressively less connected to those prevailing elsewhere in the United States. More and more, the culture of the ghetto has become an entity unto itself, remote from the rest of American society and its institutions, and drifting even further afield. As conditions within the ghetto worsen, as the social environment grows more hostile, and as racial isolation deepens, the original connection of ghetto culture to the broader values of American society—even if only in opposition—has faded.

The new culture of the ghetto increasingly rejects the values of American society as a farce and a sham, and traits that were once clearly oppositional and therefore somehow *linked* to the rest of American society have become ends in themselves, esteemed in their own right and disconnected from their relationship to the surrounding "white" society. Under the combined pressure of isolation and poverty, black street culture has increasingly become an autonomous cultural system. Participant observer studies of ghetto life done in the 1980s have an even darker and more pessimistic tone than those carried out in earlier decades. The contrast is clearly illustrated by two studies conducted by the sociologist Elijah Anderson: one carried out in the ghetto of Chicago during the early 1970s and the other conducted in a poor black neighborhood of Philadelphia during the late 1980s.

In Anderson's first study, *A Place on the Corner*, basic American values such as hard work, honesty, diligence, respect for authority, and staying out of trouble were still very much in evidence in the thoughts and words of the poor black men gathered around the corner bar he studied. Indeed, these values provided the basis for an alternative status system that arose to confer esteem when broader standards were not met, and to encourage young men to live up to ideals despite the long odds. As a result, Anderson's subjects—who would be considered of "no account" by conventional standards—

acquire a certain nobility for their pursuit of dignity and honor in the face of adversity.

In contrast, the subjects of Anderson's latest study, *Streetwise,* scorn and ridicule conventional American ideals.[15] Symbolic of the disappearance of traditional values from the ghetto is the breakdown of the long-standing relationship between "old heads" and young boys. According to Anderson, "an old head was a man of stable means who was strongly committed to family life, to church, and, most important, to passing on his philosophy, developed through his own rewarding experience with work, to young boys he found worthy. He personified the work ethnic and equated it with value and high standards of morality; in his eyes a workingman was a good, decent individual."[16]

In the ghetto environment of earlier decades, the old head "acted as a kind of guidance counselor and moral cheerleader who preached anticrime and antitrouble messages to his charges," and "the young boy readily deferred to the old head's chronological age and worldly experience."[17] In contrast, today, "as the economic and social circumstances of the urban ghetto have changed, the traditional old head has been losing prestige and credibility as a role model. . . . When gainful employment and its rewards are not forthcoming, boys easily conclude that the moral lessons of the old head concerning the work ethic, punctuality, and honesty do not fit their own circumstances."[18]

In the past, black ghettos also used to contain numerous "female old heads," who served as "neighborhood mothers," correcting and admonishing children in the streets and instructing them in proper behavior. They "were seen as mature and wise figures in the community, not only by women and girls, but also by many young men" because of their motherly love and concern for children.[19] According to Anderson, however, these role models also have increasingly disappeared, indicating "a breakdown in feel-

ings of community. Residents . . . keep more to themselves now, [and] no longer involve themselves in their neighbors' lives as they did as recently as ten years ago."[20]

In place of traditional mores that assign value to steady work, family life, the church, and respect for others, a drug culture and its economy have arisen, with profound effects on community well-being. Anderson and others have studied and written on the appeal of the underground drug economy to young men and women from the ghetto. According to Anderson, "the roles of drug pusher, pimp, and (illegal) hustler have become more and more attractive. Street-smart young people who operate this underground economy are apparently able to obtain big money more easily and glamorously than their elders, including traditional male and female old heads. Because they appear successful, they become role models for still younger people."[21]

The proliferation of the drug culture within the ghetto has exacerbated the problems caused by segregation and its concentration of poverty, adding a powerful impetus to the cycle of neighborhood decline. Given the financial gain to be had from drugs, ghetto dealers establish aggressive marketing strategies to capture business from disillusioned young people who see little hope for improvement through work, education, or staying out of trouble. Because limited economic opportunities in the ghetto as well as drug use itself make it difficult for drug users to support themselves, the spread of drug use leads inevitably to the escalation of crime and violence. As a by-product of the new drug culture, the violent death rate has skyrocketed among black men, prostitution has spread among black women, and the number of drug-addicted babies has mushroomed. The old social order of the ghetto has increasingly broken down and veered off on an independent path dramatically different from that prevailing in the rest of American society.

At the same time, relations between the sexes, which were already antagonistic and mutually exploitative in the ghetto world of the 1960s, had by the 1980s lost all connection to conventional family values. According to Anderson, by the late 1980s sexual relations in the ghetto had degenerated into a vicious, competitive contest in which young men and women exploited each other with diametrically opposed goals. For young ghetto men, sex had become strictly a means of enhancing status among male peers and of experiencing pleasure at the expense of women. "To the young man the woman becomes, in the most profound sense, a sexual object. Her body and mind are the object of a sexual game, to be won for personal aggrandizement. Status goes to the winner, and sex is prized not as a testament of love but as testimony to control of another human being. Sex is the prize, and sexual conquests are a game whose goal is to make a fool of the young woman."[22]

In the ghetto of the 1960s, a pregnancy growing out of such casual sexual encounters was relatively likely to be followed by a marriage or some other housekeeping arrangement, however unstable or short-lived it might have been. By the late 1980s, however, this bow to conventional culture had been eliminated in black street culture. "In the social context of persistent poverty, [black men] have come to devalue the conventional marital relationship, viewing women as a burden and children as even more of one."[23] Even if a young man "admits paternity and 'does right' by the girl, his peer group likely will label him a chump, a square, or a fool."[24]

Ghetto women, for their part, seek gratification less through sex than through pregnancy and childbirth. They understand that their suitors' sweet words and well-honed "rap" are fabrications being told in order to extract sex from them, and despite a few romantic self-deceptions along the way, they realize that if they become pregnant the father is unlikely to support their child. Nonetheless, they look forward to getting pregnant, for in the contemporary ghetto "it is becoming socially acceptable for a young woman to have children out of wedlock—supported by a regular welfare check."[25]

These findings are corroborated by other ethnographic interviews gathered as part of William Julius Wilson's larger study of urban poverty in Chicago. When the sociologist Richard Taub examined the interview transcripts, he found that marriage had virtually disappeared as a meaningful category of thought and discourse among poor blacks.[26] Informants consistently stated that husband-wife relationships were neither important nor reliable as a basis for family life and child-rearing, and they were deeply suspicious of the intentions of the opposite sex.

The disappearance of marriage as a social institution was underscored by field observations that Taub and his associates undertook in black and Mexican neighborhoods. Whereas a four-block shopping strip in one of Chicago's poor Mexican neighborhoods yielded fifteen shops that provided goods or services explicitly connected to marriage, a trip to a comparable black shopping area uncovered only two shops that even mentioned marriage, and not very prominently at that.

Elijah Anderson argues that childbearing has become increasingly disconnected from marriage in the ghetto; black women now seek childbirth to signal their status as adults and to validate their worth and standing before their own peer group—namely, other young black women. A baby is a young girl's entry ticket into what Anderson calls "the baby club." This "club" consists of young black mothers who gather in public places with their children to "lobby for compliments, smiles, and nods of approval and feel very good when they are forthcoming, since they signal affirmation and pride. On Sundays, the new little dresses and suits come out and the cutest babies are passed around, and this attention serves as a social measure of the person. The young mothers who form such baby clubs develop an ideology counter to that of more conventional society, one that not only approves of but enhances their position. In effect, they work to create value and status by inverting that of the girls who do not become pregnant. The teenage mother derives status from her baby; hence, her preoccupation with the impression that the baby makes and her willingness to spend inordinately large sums toward that end."[27]

According to Anderson, sex is thus a key component in the informal status system that has evolved in the street culture of America's urban ghettos. In the absence of gratification through the conventional avenues of work and family, young men and women have increasingly turned to one commodity that lies within their reach. Through sex, young men get pleasure and a feeling of self-esteem before their peers, whereas young women get a baby and a sense of belonging within the baby club. This relationship of mutual exploitation, however, has come at a price. It has further marginalized black men from black women and has escalated the war of the sexes to new heights, a fact that is clearly revealed in the music of black street culture—rap.

An unabashedly misogynist viewpoint is extolled by rap groups such as N.W.A. ("Niggers with Attitude"), whose song "A Bitch Iz a Bitch" depicts black women as scheming, vain, whining mercenaries whose goal is to deprive black men of their self-esteem, money, and possessions. In the view of N.W.A., women are good for little more than sex, and their incessant demands for attention, constant requests for money and support, and their ever-present threats to male pride can only be checked through violence, ". . . 'cause a bitch is a bitch."[28]

The female side of the issue is aired by the female rap group H.W.A. ("Hoes [Whores] with Attitude") in songs such as "A Trick Is a Trick," "Little Dick," and "1-900-BITCHES," which attack men as vain, superficial creatures who are incompetent in their love-making, ill equipped to satisfy, and prone to meaningless violence when their inflated pride is punctured. Their metaphor for the state of male-female relations in the ghetto is that of a whorehouse, where all women are whores and men are either tricks or pimps. The liner notes leave little doubt as to the group's message: "Everybody is a pimp of some kind and pimpin' is easy when you got a Hoe Wit Attitude."[29]

The war of words between black men and women has also been fought in the black press, exemplified in 1990 by the appearance of *The Blackman's Guide to Understanding the Blackwoman*, by Shaharazad Ali, which presents a vituperative attack on black women for their supposedly historical emasculation of black men. The book advocates the violent subjugation of women by black men, advising male readers that "there is never an excuse for ever hitting a Blackwoman anywhere but in the mouth. Because it is from that hole, in the lower part of her face, that all her rebellion culminates into words. Her unbridled tongue is a main reason she cannot get along with the Blackman. . . . If she ignores the authority and superiority of the Blackman, there is a penalty. When she crosses this line and becomes viciously insulting it is time for the Blackman to soundly slap her in the mouth."[30] Ten black scholars answered to the attack in a pamphlet entitled *Confusion by Any Other Name*, hoping "to respond to the range of insulting myths, half-truths and generalized personal experiences by the author."[31]

From a sociological point of view, the specific content of these works is less important than what they illustrate about the state of relations between the sexes within the black community. After evolving for decades under conditions of intense social and economic isolation, black street culture has become increasingly divorced from basic American ideals of family, work, and respect for others. By confining large numbers of black people to an environment within which failure is endemic, negative role models abound, and adherence to conventional values is nearly impossible, segregation has helped to create a nihilistic and violent counterculture sharply at odds with the basic values and goals of a democratic society. As Kenneth Clark presciently noted in 1965, "the pathologies of the ghetto community perpetuate themselves through cumulative ugliness, deterioration, and isolation."[32]

The social environment created by segregation places a heavy burden on black parents aspiring to promote conventional attitudes and behavior in their children and increase the odds for their socioeconomic success. Although the problem is most acute for the poor, segregation confines all blacks to segregated neighborhoods regardless of social class, so working- and middle-class blacks also have a very difficult time insulating their children from the competing values and attitudes of the street. Compared with children of middle-class whites, children of middle-class blacks are much more likely to be exposed to poverty, drugs, teenage pregnancy, family disruption, and violence in the neighborhoods where they live.

As a result, it requires a great deal of concerted effort by committed parents, and no small amount of luck, to raise children successfully within the ghetto. Given the burden of "acting white," the pressures to speak Black English, the social stigma attached to "brainiacs," the allure of drug taking, the quick money to be had from drug dealing, and the romantic sexuality of the streets, it is not surprising that black educational achievement has stagnated. . . .

The Case for National Action

. . . Although race has become embroiled in partisan politics during the 1980s and 1990s, residential desegregation is not intrinsically a cause of either the right or the left; it is neither liberal nor conservative, democrat nor republican. Rather it is a bipartisan agenda in the national interest. The ghetto must be dismantled because only by ending segregation will we eliminate the manifold social and economic problems that follow from its persistence.

For conservatives, the cause of desegregation turns on the issue of market access. We have marshaled extensive evidence to show that one particular group—black Americans—is systematically denied full access to a crucial market. Housing markets are central to individual social and economic well-being because they distribute much more than shelter; they also distribute a variety of resources that shape and largely determine one's life chances. Along with housing, residential markets also allocate schooling, peer groups, safety, jobs, insurance costs, public services, home equity, and, ultimately, wealth. By tolerating the persistent and systematic disenfranchisement of blacks from housing markets, we send a clear signal to one group that hard work, individual enterprise, sacrifice, and aspirations don't matter; what determines one's life chances is the color of one's skin.

For liberals, the issue is one of unfinished business, for residential segregation is the most important item remaining on the nation's civil rights agenda. In many areas of civil life, desegregation has occurred; in the south, Jim Crow is dead, and throughout the country blacks are accepted in unions, sports, entertainment, journalism, politics, government, administration, and academia. Many barriers have fallen, but still the residential color line remains—and from residential segregation follows a host of deadly social ills that continue to undercut and overwhelm the progress achieved in other areas.

Residential desegregation should be considered an effort of national unity; any other course of action is politically indefensible. For conservatives, turning away from the task means denying the importance of markets and individual enterprise; for liberals it means sweeping the last piece of unfinished civil rights business under the rug. Ultimately, however, residential desegregation requires a moral commitment and a bipartisan leadership that have been lacking among politicians for the past two decades. Without a willingness to lead and take risks on the part of elected officials, and without a will to change on the part of the American people, none of the legal changes and policy solutions we propose will succeed.

For America, the failure to end segregation will perpetuate a bitter dilemma that has long divided the nation. If segregation is permitted to continue, poverty will inevitably deepen and become more persistent within a large share of the black community, crime and drugs will become more firmly rooted, and social institutions will fragment further under the weight of deteriorating conditions. As racial inequality sharpens, white fears will grow, racial prejudices will be reinforced, and hostility toward blacks will increase, making the problems of racial justice and equal opportunity even more insoluble. Until we face up to the difficult task of dismantling the ghetto, the disastrous consequences of residential segregation will radiate outward to poison American society. Until we decide to end the long reign of American apartheid, we cannot hope to move forward as a people and a nation.

NOTES

1. Deborah Wallace, "Roots of Increased Health Care Inequality in New York," *Social Science and Medicine* 31 (1990):1219–27; Rodrick Wallace, "Urban Desertification, Public Health and Public Order: 'Planned Shrinkage,' Violent Death, Substance Abuse, and AIDS in the Bronx," *Social Science and Medicine* 32 (1991):801–813; Rodrick Wallace, "'Planned Shrinkage,' Contagious Urban Decay, and Violent Death in the Bronx: The Implications of Synergism," Epidemiology of Mental Disorders Research Department, New York State Psychiatric Institute, 1990.
2. William L. Yancey, Eugene P. Ericksen, and George H. Leon, "The Structure of Pluralism: 'We're All Italian Around Here, Aren't We Mrs. O'Brien?'" *Ethnic and Racial Studies* 8 (1985):94–116.
3. Sophie Pedder, "Social Isolation and the Labor Market: Black Americans in Chicago" (paper presented at the Chicago Urban Poverty and Family Life Conference, 10–12 October 1991).
4. Ibid.
5. See Labov, *Language in the Inner City*; Labov, "The Logic of Nonstandard English"; William Labov, ed., *Locating Language in Space and Time* (New York: Academic Press, 1980).
6. Labov and Harris, "De Facto Segregation," 2.
7. Joleen Kirschenman and Kathryn M. Neckerman, "'We'd Love to Hire Them, but . . .': The Meaning of Race for Employers," in *The Urban Underclass*, edited by Christopher Jencks and Paul E. Peterson (Washington, DC: Brookings Institution, 1991), 203–232.
8. Signithia Fordham and John U. Ogbu, "Black Students' School Success: Coping with the 'Burden of Acting White,'" *Urban Review* 18 (1986):176–206.
9. James E. Rosenbaum and Susan J. Popkin, "Economic and Social Impacts of Housing Integration," Center for Urban Affairs and Policy Research, Northwestern University, 1990; James E. Rosenbaum, Marilynn J. Kulieke, and Leonard S. Rubinowitz, "White Suburban Schools' Responses to Low-Income Black Children: Sources of Success and Problems," *Urban Review* 20 (1988): 28–41; James E. Rosenbaum and Susan J. Popkin, "Black Pioneers: Do Their Moves to Suburbs Increase Economic Opportunity for Mothers and Children?" *Housing Policy Debate* 2 (1991):1179–1214.

10. Robert Crain and Rita Mahard, "School Racial Composition and Black College Attendance and Achievement Test Performance," *Sociology of Education* 51 (1978):81–101.

11. Susan E. Mayer, "How Much Does a High School's Racial and Socioeconomic Mix Affect Graduation and Teenage Fertility Rates?" in *The Urban Underclass*, edited by Jencks and Peterson (Washington, DC: Brookings Institution, 1991), 321–41.

12. Clark, *Dark Ghetto*, 19.

13. Shelby Steele, *The Content of Our Character* (New York: St. Martin's Press, 1990), 60.

14. Cited in Dinesh D'Souza, *Illiberal Education: The Politics of Race and Sex on Campus* (New York: Free Press, 1991), 239.

15. Elijah Anderson, *Streetwise: Race, Class, and Change in an Urban Community* (Chicago: University of Chicago Press, 1990).

16. Ibid., 69.

17. Ibid.

18. Ibid., 72.

19. Ibid., 74–75.

20. Ibid., 76.

21. Anderson, *Streetwise*, 77.

22. Ibid., 114.

23. Ibid., 120.

24. Ibid.

25. Ibid., 126.

26. Richard P. Taub, "Differing Conceptions of Honor and Orientations Toward Work and Marriage Among Low-Income African-Americans and Mexican-Americans" (paper presented at the Chicago Urban Poverty and Family Life Conference, 10–12 October 1991).

27. Anderson, *Streetwise*, 126.

28. N.W.A. and the Posse, "A Bitch Iz A Bitch" (Hollywood, CA: Priority Records, published by Ruthless Attack Muzick, 1989, ASCAP).

29. H.W.A., "Livin' in a Hoe House" (Hollywood, CA: Drive By Records, published by Thunder Publishing Company, 1990, BMI).

30. Shaharazad Ali, *The Blackman's Guide to Understanding the Blackwoman* (Philadelphia: Civilized Publications, 1990), 169.

31. Haki R. Madhubuti, ed., *Confusion by Any Other Name: Essays Exploring the Negative Impact of the Blackman's Guide to Understanding the Blackwoman* (Chicago: Third World Press, 1990).

32. Clark, *Dark Ghetto*, 12.

26

LOCAL GATEKEEPING PRACTICES AND RESIDENTIAL SEGREGATION

Judith N. DeSena

Research on the causes of residential segregation has focused on the "institutional web" created by redlining, racial steering, and market forces to explain the dual housing market in the United States

Judith N. DeSena, "Local Gatekeeping Practices and Residential Segregation" from *Sociological Inquiry*, Vol. 64, No. 3, August 1994, pp. 307–321. Reprinted by permission of the author and the University of Texas Press. All rights retained by the University of Texas Press.

(Farley 1987; Foley 1973; Kain 1968; Kain and Quigley 1975; Pearce 1979). This article examines the informal practices of local residents in perpetuating residential segregation. It is a study of the strategies used by white non-Hispanic residents in Greenpoint, Brooklyn, to maintain the segregation of Hispanics and to discourage people of color from moving into the neighborhood. An informal housing network in which available rental apartments and houses for sale are advertised by word of mouth is reinforced by the functioning of local institutions, namely, the Roman Catholic church and electoral politics. I propose that such actions reflect an invisible link between the micro-level analyses of discrimination documented by studies of real estate steering (Pearce 1979; Wienk et al. 1979) and macro-level analyses of patterns of residential segregation (Farley and Allen 1987; Lieberson 1980).

Studies on segregation in the United States have focused primarily on black-white separation. Taeuber and Taeuber (1965) analyzed census data for over two hundred cities in the United States between 1940 and 1960 and used an index of dissimilarity to measure segregation. They found segregation to be quite high, with an average index of 86.2. This analysis was followed up for 1970 (Sorenson, Taeuber, and Hollingsworth 1975) and showed a decline in segregation throughout the United States. Although there has been a slight decline in racial segregation over time, the level remained high in 1980 (Farley 1987; Farley and Allen 1987). In addition, suburbanization by blacks has continued to increase. Some blacks have settled in predominantly white communities (Spain and Long 1981). However, it is believed that "suburban ghettos" will form (Farley 1987, p. 108) as blacks who move to the suburbs locate themselves in established black areas.

Residential segregation of Hispanics has not received the same level of investigation as that of blacks. In general, Hispanics are less separated than blacks from non-Hispanic whites (Farley 1987; Massey and Denton 1987). Among Hispanic groups, Puerto Ricans experience the most segregation from non-Hispanic whites (Farley 1987; Massey and Bitterman 1985; Woolbright and Hartmann 1987), possibly because Puerto Ricans are disproportionately poor and tend to be darker in complexion than other Hispanics (Massey and Bitterman 1985, p. 326;

Woolbright and Hartmann 1987). Some studies find that Puerto Ricans are segregated at rates similar to and greater than that of blacks (Guest and Weed 1976; Hershberg et al. 1978; Kantrowitz 1978). More recently, research conducted by the federal government, which examined the contribution of housing discrimination to residential segregation, concluded that "the problem is more prevalent in New York City and its suburbs than in any of 24 other major metropolitan areas across the United States, particularly for the Spanish-speaking minority" (Lueck 1991, p. R1). This finding is especially relevant to the case of Greenpoint. White non-Hispanic residents of Greenpoint attempt to relegate Hispanic residents to the northern section of the neighborhood and seclude them there. Non-Hispanic whites accomplish residential segregation by a series of informal strategies.

On a neighborhood level, segregation has been conceptualized as ordered segmentation (Suttles 1968) and the defended neighborhood (Suttles 1972). In actual practice, attempts to maintain separation among people of different ethnic and racial groups have taken the form of restrictive covenants or zones (Krase 1982), acts of violence (Rieder 1985), and the use of local networks (DeSena 1990). This study connects the national and statistical data on segregation with the informal practices of ordinary people. It offers an additional dimension to research on segregation. The analysis presents how white non-Hispanic residents of Greenpoint, in their everyday life, contribute to the maintenance of residential segregation. This research indicates that to a large extent the "work" of segregation on a neighborhood level is done by women who serve as "gatekeepers and homeseekers" (Pearce 1979). The article begins with a description of Greenpoint followed by a discussion of the study's research design. The strategies used to accomplish residential segregation in Greenpoint will be presented, with a focus on an informal housing network and local institutional arrangements.

Description of Greenpoint

Geography

Greenpoint is a peninsula at the northernmost tip of Brooklyn bounded on the north and east by Newtown Creek and on the west by the East River. The Brooklyn-Queens Expressway (Meeker Avenue) and North 7th Street serve as Greenpoint's southern boundary (New York City Planning Commission 1969). The Brooklyn-Queens Expressway is an elevated structure as it extends through Greenpoint and breaks up the continuity of residential areas.

Population

Greenpoint is a working-class neighborhood. Since the early 1900s Greenpoint's population has been largely white ethnic, composed mostly of Irish, Italian, and Polish families. The Irish were the largest group through the 1920s. A significant influx of Polish immigration occurred in Greenpoint after World War II (Susser 1982). More recently there has been an additional wave of Polish refugees who fled martial law in Poland. The relocation efforts of these immigrants are aided by local Polish organizations and churches. Greenpoint is currently viewed as the largest Polish community in New York City.

In 1990, the population of Greenpoint was approximately 39,365.[1] Of these, 73 percent were members of white non-Hispanic ethnic groups. Since 1950 northern Greenpoint has seen an influx of Hispanic residents. In 1990 Hispanics constituted 22 percent of the neighborhood's population;[2] and Asian and Pacific Islanders totaled 4 percent and blacks 1 percent of the population. The average across ethnic groupings for median household income in 1989 was $29,121, approximately the median household income of New York City in 1989, which amounted to $29,823. In 1990, a majority of Greenpoint's residents 25 years and older had between an elementary and a high school education. Moreover, in 1990 Greenpoint's employed persons 16 years and older worked mostly in technical, sales, and administrative support occupations, as professionals and managers, and in service jobs.

Housing

A majority of Greenpoint's housing was built before 1939 and many structures were built before 1900. More than 60 percent of the residential buildings are frame dwellings (New York City Planning Commission 1974). There are a few blocks in Greenpoint that consist of brownstones and brick townhouses—remnants of Dutch settlement from the nineteenth century. These particular streets are presently part of a seven-block historic district bordered by Franklin Street, Manhattan Avenue, Calyer, and Kent Streets.

Residential structures in Greenpoint are six stories or less, and 71 percent contain four or fewer dwelling units (New York City Planning Commission 1974). In addition, "the percentage of owner-occupied buildings with rental units is usually high" (Wellisz 1982, p. R9). Most homeowners share their building with renters. In 1990 the average median rent in Greenpoint was $450, compared with $496 for New York City. Long-term residents may pay less than the median rent because of tenure and rent control laws. However, rents in Greenpoint have been escalating. Some residents report monthly rents as high as $750 to $1,000.

Religion

There are approximately twelve churches in Greenpoint. Those with the largest congregations are Roman Catholic; Catholic churches in Greenpoint are recognized by residents as the center of ethnic life. There are two types of Roman Catholic churches in Greenpoint: Diocesan churches lie within small territorial boundaries, or parishes, which in turn form, with other parishes, a larger territory, or diocese (the parishes of diocesan churches do not overlap). National churches are those that serve a particular ethnic group; they are usually located within the boundaries of a diocesan church. There are three national churches in Greenpoint: two Polish and one Italian. There is also one diocesan church that is reportedly dominated by Irish residents.

Research Methods

The findings reported here are part of a larger qualitative study in which I conducted fifty-five open-ended interviews with residents of Greenpoint for the purpose of ascertaining the strategies employed to maintain residential segregation. A technique in interviewing was used by which I asked residents to tell me about the practices of their neighbors. The respondents seemed comfortable with this approach, since the focus of discussion was not on their behavior, but on the habits of locals and the customs of the neighborhood. The respondents talked freely. Interviews lasted anywhere from 1 hour to 2.5 hours. They were recorded on tape.

The interviews were obtained by a snowball sampling technique. The sample was stratified for sex, ethnicity, and age. Since ethnicity was an important variable in this study, I began by identifying ethnic clusters through block, and block group, data from the 1980 Census. Clusters were identified for four major ethnic groups in Greenpoint: Hispanics, Irish, Italians, and Polish. Once the boundaries of these ethnic enclaves were apparent, I contacted individuals residing in each of these clusters. These

individuals became key informants, directing me to others of the same ethnic background. At the end of each interview I asked respondents to refer me to others.

I also used content analysis and reviewed written accounts of the events described in the interviews. In particular, I examined local newspapers, church bulletins, and various flyers advertising meetings in the community. This approach enabled me to use the information in subsequent interviews, to probe these matters more effectively, and to keep abreast of current issues and concerns. Data were collected between 1983 and 1990. The data collection focusing on the neighborhood dynamics presented here is ongoing.

Greenpoint: A Segregated Neighborhood

According to its residents, Greenpoint is divided into two areas: the north and the south. Northern Greenpoint is composed mainly of Poles and Hispanics. Southern Greenpoint is made up of Polish, Irish, Italian, and Hispanic groups. Because of the existence of an Hispanic community in northern Greenpoint, residents point to Greenpoint Avenue as the symbolic boundary that separates the north from the south. One northern Greenpoint resident commented: "Like I said, I've been here twenty-nine years and after Greenpoint Avenue, to me, that's the white neighborhood, and this side is more Puerto Rican."

"The boundary," Greenpoint Avenue, is a major thoroughfare and includes a bus route, truck route, and subway station. However, in many ways and for many residents, particularly those who live in southern Greenpoint, it marks the end of the area's commercial strip and the end of the neighborhood. A couple of residents from southern Greenpoint reported the following:

We never really went down that end, we had St. Anthony [Church] and we never really associated with St. Alphonsus [Church], that was like the other territory or something.

I always remember, once you cross Greenpoint Avenue, except for a few white blocks, that wasn't the good section of Greenpoint.

The urban landscape reinforces residents' differential perceptions of north and south. No banks are located north of Greenpoint Avenue and the annual street fair, and outdoor Christmas lights provided by local merchants to the south stop there. As one crosses Greenpoint Avenue going north, the ground slopes downhill. Bodegas are numerous on street corners. During the summer salsa music plays in the streets. Buildings are larger and show signs of deterioration to a greater extent than those in the south; some have been condemned and only their shells remain. Houses in the north have a lower market value than those in the south, and it is more difficult to obtain mortgages and home improvement loans for housing in the north. As one resident noted "as long as I remember, that was the poorer end of the neighborhood."

Southern Greenpoint is different. It tends to be better-maintained. Homes are renovated and building deterioration is less visible than in northern Greenpoint. Ethnic specialty stores are typically Polish, and butcher shops, bakeries, and grocery stores dot each corner. All kinds of retail stores can be found in the southern area.

White non-Hispanic respondents see a causal relationship between people of color and deteriorated living conditions. One resident reported:

Most of the Spanish people that I've seen move into homes and let them deteriorate. Maybe because most of them rent, I really don't know. . . .

But to me, it's just the way that everything is let to fall apart. They really don't care if the windows are hanging open. It's not a good feeling when you go through the blocks where the Spanish people live, and then the streets where white people live. There's no pride whatsoever.

Northern Greenpoint came to be viewed by long-term white non-Hispanic residents as the undesirable part of the community because of the clustering of Hispanic residents, and their perception that people of color create urban decay. Because of this view, non-Hispanic whites resist residence by people of color.

How Greenpoint's symbolic boundary and its attendant segregation are maintained is the focus of this study. I propose that it is through the process of an informal housing network.

Greenpoint's Informal Housing Network

It is difficult for an outsider to rent an apartment or purchase a house in southern Greenpoint. Local realtors have said that "there isn't one-, two- or three-family houses available." The local newspaper lists only a few apartments and houses for sale, while the lengths of its "Apts. Wanted" and "Houses Wanted" columns increase. Residents of southern Greenpoint are particularly cautious about renting their vacant apartments. Not only do they want to control rigidly the type of tenants they may get, but they also want to determine who will be informed about the availability of an apartment. All respondents in southern Greenpoint, regardless of ethnicity, claimed that available apartments are rented "by word of mouth."

There are some ads in the local paper, but I think most of the time it's by word of mouth. I think they mostly don't put ads in the paper, because when you put an ad in the paper, you don't know who is gonna come.

Yeh, definitely . . . when there's an apartment vacant, no one knows about it. They're very hush, or word of mouth. Even if they're not Hispanic, they still watch who they rent to.

Resident homeowners go about finding a tenant by an informal network through which they tell family, friends, and neighbors that an apartment is available. Consequently, a person who knows someone is "in the market" for an apartment will recommend the individual to the owner. In other words, individuals seeking apartments are "sponsored" by local informants to homeowners. According to residents:

Recommendations, absolutely. You want rooms, I know that Mary has rooms. I'll say "Mary, I know so and so, she seems to be a nice person, why don't you give her the rooms?"

You keep it to yourself and rent it word of mouth. If you're a friend of mine [and] you hear of an apartment, you say, "Here I got a good friend," you guarantee him.

Those who are selected as informants are assumed to have similar social characteristics as the homeowner and to possess the same values. They are the gatekeepers of the community. Most informants are local women. It is therefore presumed by both parties that an informant would sponsor only a potential tenant who is the "type" of person the homeowner is seeking. Thus, it is expected that an informant would sponsor only an individual whom the homeowner would find acceptable. As one resident stated:

What they do is, they don't want strangers that they don't know in their house. They want people to come who are recommended, or people who may be friends of people that they know. They're cautious because they're not necessarily anxious for the dollars that would be coming in. They want to have a family type of residence, people that they can get along with. They do that for their own security and for their own happiness, because sometimes you can rent to somebody and not know who they are. And, you know, they may be flamingo [sic] dancers and you're subject to this sort of stuff all the time.

The practice of sponsoring an individual as a potential tenant to a homeowner places the reputation of the sponsor "on the line." Their standing in the community could be spoiled if a tenant they sponsored turned out not to be the kind of person initially expected. One presumption is that people who are selected as informants will sponsor only white non-Hispanic ethnics, not people of color. When a neighbor is chosen as an informant by a homeowner, the homeowner does not need to list specific requirements. Informants know what homeowners expect. Likewise, homeowners select informants who they presume will know the characteristics expected in a tenant. Given this relationship between homeowners and their selected informants, most people of color are unable to gain access to apartments or houses in southern Greenpoint. One resident summed up this practice of sponsorship by saying, "They tell you because they know you're not gonna tell Spanish or black."

Intimidation is used within the informal housing network. According to respondents, neighbors sometimes pressure one another about potential tenants and homeowners. The major focus is for people of color to be unable to gain access to available apartments or houses.

This house was almost bought by a Cuban gentleman, and the lady on this side of us told our landlord that they are not welcome here, in very choice words she used; and they almost threatened him, Don't sell, and the sale did not go through.

When the guy across the street was selling his house, somebody came out and said, "I hope you're not selling to blacks."

Other respondents indicated that applying pressure is unnecessary because there is an "unwritten agreement," analogous to a "pact" among neighbors. They agree that they will not rent or sell to minority individuals.

It's a, how can I put it, it's an unwritten law. In other words, you know your family's gonna hear it if you rent to a black. . . . I know what they would go through; that's why I wouldn't really do it.

This response suggests that the "pact" operates without any overt coercion. It further suggests that residents who violate the pact will be confronted by their neighbors.

One respondent spoke about a friend who rehabilitates abandoned housing in southern Greenpoint. This developer was thinking about renting to blacks, but was advised by his friend and Greenpoint resident:

I think it will hurt you tremendously and I don't see that you should do that . . . because of their color. . . . It seems that the power brokers don't want any more minorities than they have already.

The developer was advised not to violate the pact in order to avoid unfavorable repercussions which might have caused his business to suffer.

Neighborhood Women

To a large extent, local women control who obtains housing in Greenpoint by serving as the primary gatekeepers of the community. They "pass along the word" regarding the availability of housing to family, friends, and neighbors. In this way, they have replaced local realtors. Their "work" is carried out through the maintenance of a local network in which they serve as informal brokers in the local housing market, and are involved in renting available apartments and recruiting potential tenants. Information about available housing and "homeseekers" is conveyed orally through a network of women who interact in the street, at social and religious functions, and at civic meetings. Women's activities, to a large extent, are informal. As part of their daily routine, women will meet as they shop, walk children to and from school, go to and from work, and attend community meetings at night, or play bingo. It is during these informal occasions that matters concerning housing are discussed. A local woman's anecdote illustrates this point:

I was in a butcher shop one day, and we were talking. I just happen to mention that my niece was looking for rooms. And this woman says, "Hello"; she told me who she was, and that she had rooms. So there right in the butcher shop, not that I ever got the rooms. But [if I wanted] rooms for a friend of mine or for anybody, I would spread the word around in the Society [a women's religious organization]. That would be the first place. I'd say, "Girls, anybody hears of rooms let me know." They would tell someone.

Although this research documents a housing network, the local women's network involves other aspects of neighborhood life as well. Women exchange local news. They discuss who is moving, what the implications are for friends and family seeking housing, where the best sales are, what the new priest is like, who has recently been robbed. Women's networks in communities have been trivialized as gossip and mistakenly viewed as having no purpose. Greenpoint's informal housing network is an example of the importance of women's networks in shaping communities.

In summary, by controlling accessibility to housing, residents of southern Greenpoint resist minority growth and maintain segregation. To a large extent, local women control who obtains housing. Most apartments are rented through an informal housing network by which residents sponsor individuals as tenants. Some houses are also sold this way, while others are sold through realtors who are trusted not to "blockbust" because many of the realtors are also residents. In most cases available housing never reaches the open market, but remains part of the neighborhood's "underlife" (Suttles 1972). Moreover, by keeping news of the availability of housing out of the open market, southern Greenpoint residents are not discriminating in the traditional sense (they are not turning people away). Instead, residents take an offensive position and prevent people of color from applying for housing.

Local Institutions

Local institutions also participate in making Greenpoint a segregated neighborhood. This section will focus particularly on the contributions of the Roman Catholic church and local politics.

The Church

As stated earlier, there are a number of Roman Catholic churches in Greenpoint, which are of two types: Some are national churches, while others are diocesan churches. In northern Greenpoint there is a national, Polish church called Sts. Cyril and Methodius, which is located in the heart of the Hispanic community. This church holds masses and

other services in Polish and English. It does not accommodate the Spanish-speaking community. St. Anthony–St. Alphonsus, a diocesan church located near the boundary that divides Greenpoint's northern and southern areas, offers masses in English and Spanish, thereby ministering to the Spanish-speaking community. Hispanics are not assisted by any other church. However, the Spanish-speaking and English-speaking congregations are segregated.[3] Hispanics and other ethnic groups are physically separated, not only by a different mass, but also because Spanish masses take place in the lower church (basement) of St. Anthony's church building.

In addition, parish activities are also segregated.

> Whenever it is social, for example, they don't allow it. [The parish] is going to have a dance for St. Valentine's Day but we are all going to be Spanish there, not one English speaker is going to go. They don't cross lines. I am trying to do something in that respect. Not only to bring the Hispanics into the English community, but I want to do the opposite too, take the English speakers and invite them over to our activities. Otherwise you're going to continue on and on with this problem of segregation because it's real. You have two parishes in one and I don't like that. I would like for all the people to be one.

Moreover, it was reported that parish committees are dominated by white non-Hispanics, mostly Irish parishioners.

Hence, local churches reinforce neighborhood segregation in two ways. They either block the participation of some ethnic groups, as in the case of national churches, or attend to ethnic groups separately. In northern Greenpoint, Sts. Cyril and Methodius is a Polish island in the midst of a Hispanic population. Even when all ethnic groups are aided by the local diocesan church, the Hispanic and non-Hispanic white congregations are spatially segregated in church services and activities.

Local Politics

Greenpoint has long been a stronghold for the regular Democratic party. Control of the countywide party through the years reflects the successive waves of immigrants and their assimilation. During the 1920s and 1930s, the Irish controlled the countywide party. This was also reflected in Greenpoint, where a man named Peter J. McGuinness was district leader (McGuinness had replaced Patrick McCarren). At that time in the history of New York politics, the district leader's position was a powerful one. It was a party position that carried a number of patronage "goodies" (such as jobs and dismissed traffic violations). On Thursday nights residents would line up at the clubhouse to ask for favors. The district leader, through his network of influence, would deliver these favors. McGuinness contributed to defending Greenpoint by speaking against the development of public housing in Greenpoint. McGuinness stated to the City Planning Commission, "It's nothing personal. We just don't want any of them things in Greenpoint. We're a community by ourselves."[4] Public housing was not built in Greenpoint, but it was constructed in adjacent neighborhoods such as Williamsburg, in Brooklyn, and Long Island City, in Queens.

The use of scare tactics in local political campaigns is another way that the local party resists population growth and representation of people of color. In 1980 there was a primary election held for state senator. The candidates were Thomas Bartosiewicz, the incumbent and a Greenpoint resident (who indicates ethnic succession in politics), and Lucille Rose, a black woman from Bedford-Stuyvesant. At this time, the boundaries of the district for state senator included Greenpoint, Bedford-Stuyvesant, and other areas. In an attempt to increase voter turnout in Greenpoint (the idea being that these were Bartosiewicz supporters), the local newspaper ran a front page story, "Remember: Vote on Tuesday, Sept. 9th." This article began:

> The future of Greenpoint–Williamsburg is at stake on Tuesday, September 9 as Democrats must turn out to vote in all time record numbers to support our Senator in the Primary Election. Senator Bartosiewicz is fighting against all odds in a fierce election campaign battle against boss-backed Bedford-Stuyvesant candidate Lucille Rose. (*Greenpoint Gazette,* 2 September 1980, 1)

Also on the front page were pictures of Bartosiewicz and Rose, with a caption that stated, "The Choice Is Clear." The use of pictures along with the article attempted to encourage residents to "get out and vote" for Bartosiewicz out of fear that someone black would be elected to represent Greenpoint. Moreover, on the day of the election, flyers were left on the windshields of cars in Greenpoint that had a picture of Lucille Rose with the caption, "Our New State Senator?" This was a last attempt to encourage people to vote through the use of racial overtones. Bartosiewicz won this primary and also won the general election.

These two examples demonstrate how the local political system is involved in promoting segregation. Political tactics play on residents' fears that the neighborhood will be overtaken by people of color. In this way, the red flags of public housing or public officials who are people of color enable local party leaders to easily organize residents against change.

Since 1990, Greenpoint has also been subjected to legislative reapportionment plans (mandated after every census) that have aligned Greenpoint with other, white non-Hispanic areas of Brooklyn. Rather than draw district lines that might place the community with areas like Bushwick and Bedford–Stuyvesant, which are composed largely of people of color, recent reapportionment plans have placed the neighborhood in districts with white non-Hispanic communities such as Brooklyn Heights, Park Slope, and Bay Ridge (reflecting a desire on the part of the state legislature that "safe" seats for people of color are created and to insure that Greenpoint and other white non-Hispanic communities in Brooklyn continue to be represented by European American officials).

A complication that Greenpoint faces in political defense is that as a political entity it is absorbed into larger geographic districts. In recent years, Greenpoint has remained a Democratic bastion, and has done so by joining forces with other residents in adjoining communities. For example, the dominant political club, the Seneca Club, is headed by a Jewish district leader who has managed to bridge the diverse communities of Greenpoint and Williamsburg in an electoral coalition (Orthodox Jews in Williamsburg being the other key constituency) to defeat efforts by Hispanics and blacks seeking to gain political dominance.

Local institutions of religion and politics have contributed to Greenpoint's success in remaining a defended neighborhood. Families and individual persons of color face difficulties in finding housing and running for public office, as well as in being accepted as residents in the community and as participants of local institutions. In both informal and formal areas of neighborhood life, people of color have been blocked from full integration.

Conclusions

This article illustrates how residential segregation is perpetuated in the United States through the everyday activities of individuals. In conjunction with the formal practices of institutions, the informal actions of people attempting to preserve the local culture of their neighborhoods play a major part. Casual conversations among neighbors on the streets, in church, and around political events are the medium by which the preferences of individuals are translated into macro-level patterns of residential segregation.

The basic question raised by this study is the extent to which the actions of individuals perpetuate residential segregation. Some neighborhoods, like Greenpoint, wish to maintain their local culture and therefore attempt to exclude people of color. Although the working class is sometimes accused of being racist, they in fact share this characteristic with other social classes. Affluent groups do not need to resist population growth of people of color and defend their neighborhoods in the same way as the working class. Affluent groups use their economic position to exclude others from their neighborhoods. Zoning laws and local covenants also work to the advantage of the affluent. If neighborhood change should occur, affluent groups have the economic wherewithal to move. Working-class people cannot use economics as a resource. They actively resist minority growth through the strategies described here and therefore may be more quickly accused of racism than other social classes. However, their activism is felt to be their only means of expressing control and power. They are reactive because of their limited economic position; to defend what they have, they answer most community events by actively organizing against population influx of people of color, city policy decisions, or public housing locations. When social scientists try to explain the persistence of residential segregation, the importance of everyday social exchange as a mechanism of information control should not be underestimated. Combined with the actions of institutional players such as the Roman Catholic church and political parties, what people say and don't say has the power to shape metropolitan-wide patterns of residential segregation.

NOTES

1. This information was obtained from tract data from the *1990 Census of Population and Housing*, Summary Tape File 3A.
2. Hispanics can be of any race.
3. See Molotch (1972) for a discussion of the exclusionary practices of churches.
4. "McGuinness Puts the Crimp in Any Greenpoint Rehousing," *Brooklyn Eagle*, 13 December 1939.

REFERENCES

DESENA, JUDITH N. 1990. *Protecting One's Turf: Social Strategies for Maintaining Urban Neighborhoods*. Lanham, MD: University Press of America.

FARLEY, JOHN E. 1987. "Segregation in 1980: How Segregated Are America's Metropolitan Areas?" Pp. 95–114 in *Divided Neighborhoods*, edited by Gary A. Tobin. Newbury Park, CA: Sage.

FARLEY, REYNOLDS, and WALTER R. ALLEN. 1987. *The Color Line and the Quality of Life in America*. New York: Russell Sage Foundation.

FOLEY, DONALD L. 1973. "Institutional and Contextual Factors Affecting the Housing Choices of Minority Residents." Pp. 85–147 in *Segregation in Residential Areas*, edited by Amos H. Hawley and Vincent P. Rock. Washington, DC: National Academy of Sciences.

GUEST, AVERY M., and JAMES A. WEED. 1976. "Ethnic Residential Segregation: Patterns of Change." *American Journal of Sociology* 81:1088–1111.

HERSHBERG, THEODORE, HANS BURSTEIN, EUGENE P. ERICKSEN, STEPHANIE GREENBERG, and WILLIAM L. YANCEY. 1978. "A Tale of Three Cities: Blacks and Immigrants in Philadelphia, 1850–1880, 1930, and 1970." *Annals of the American Academy of Political and Social Science* 441:55–81.

KAIN, JOHN F. 1968. "Housing Segregation, Negro Employment and Metropolitan Decentralization." *Quarterly Journal of Economics* 82:175–97.

KAIN, JOHN F., and J. M. QUIGLEY. 1975. *Housing Markets and Racial Discrimination: A Micro-Economic Analysis*. New York: National Bureau of Economic Research.

KANTROWITZ, NATHAN. 1978. "Racial and Ethnic Segregation in Boston 1930–1970." *Annals of the American Academy of Political and Social Science* 441:41–54.

KRASE, JEROME. 1982. *Self and Community in the City*. Washington, DC: University Press of America.

LIEBERSON, STANLEY. 1980. *A Piece of the Pie: Black and White Immigrants Since 1880*. Berkeley: University of California Press.

LUECK, THOMAS J. 1991. "New York Ranks High in Housing Bias." *New York Times*, November 3, real estate section.

MASSEY, DOUGLAS S., and BROOKS BITTERMAN. 1985. "Explaining the Paradox of Puerto Rican Segregation." *Social Forces* 64(2):306–331.

MASSEY, DOUGLAS S., and NANCY A. DENTON. 1987. "Trends in the Residential Segregation of Blacks, Hispanics, and Asians: 1970–1980." *American Sociological Review* 52:802–825.

MOLOTCH, HARVEY L. 1972. *Managed Integration*. Berkeley: University of California Press.

NEW YORK CITY PLANNING COMMISSION. 1969. *Plan for New York City: A Proposal*. Part 3, *Brooklyn*. New York: Author.

———. 1974. *Greenpoint: Striking a Balance Between Industry and Housing*. New York: Author.

PEARCE, DIANA M. 1979. "Gatekeepers and Homeseekers." *Social Problems* 26:325–42.

RIEDER, JONATHAN. 1985. *Canarsie: The Jews and Italians of Brooklyn Against Liberalism*. Cambridge, MA: Harvard University Press.

SORENSON, ANNEMETTE, KARL E. TAEUBER, and LESLIE J. HOLLINGSWORTH. 1975. "Indexes of Racial Residential Segregation for 109 Cities in the United States, 1940 to 1970." *Sociological Focus* 8 (April):125–42.

SPAIN, DAPHNE, and LARRY LONG. 1981. "Black Movers to the Suburbs: Are They Moving to Predominantly White Neighborhoods?" *Special Demographic Analysis*. Washington, DC: U.S. Bureau of the Census.

SUSSER, IDA. 1982. *Norman Street*. New York: Oxford University Press.

SUTTLES, GERALD D. 1968. *The Social Order of the Slum*. Chicago: University of Chicago Press.

———. 1972. *The Social Construction of Communities*. Chicago: University of Chicago Press.

TAEUBER, KARL E., and ALMA F. TAEUBER. 1965. *Negroes in Cities: Residential Segregation and Neighborhood Change.* Chicago: Aldine.

WELLISZ, CHRISTOPHER. 1982. "If You're Thinking of Living in Greenpoint." *New York Times,* December 12, R9.

WIENK, RONALD E., CLIFFORD E. REID, JOHN C. SIMONSON, and FREDERICK J. EGGERS. 1979. *Measuring Racial Discrimination in American Housing Markets: The Housing Market Practices Survey.* Washington, DC: Department of Housing and Urban Development, Office of Policy Development and Research.

WOOLBRIGHT, LOUIE ALBERT, and DAVID J. HARTMANN. 1987. "The New Segregation: Asians and Hispanics." Pp. 138–157 in *Divided Neighborhoods: Changing Patterns of Racial Segregation,* edited by Gary A. Tobin. Newbury Park, CA: Sage.

27

THE CODE OF THE STREETS

Elijah Anderson

Of all the problems besetting the poor inner-city black community, none is more pressing than that of interpersonal violence and aggression. It wreaks havoc daily with the lives of community residents and increasingly spills over into downtown and residential middle-class areas. Muggings, burglaries, carjackings, and drug-related shootings, all of which may leave their victims or innocent bystanders dead, are now common enough to concern all urban and many suburban residents. The inclination to violence springs from the circumstances of life among the ghetto poor—the lack of jobs that pay a living wage, the stigma of race, the fallout from rampant drug use and drug trafficking, and the resulting alienation and lack of hope for the future.

Simply living in such an environment places young people at special risk of falling victim to aggressive behavior. Although there are often forces in the community which can counteract the negative influences, by far the most powerful being a strong, loving, "decent" (as inner-city residents put it) family committed to middle-class values, the despair is pervasive enough to have spawned an oppositional culture, that of "the streets," whose norms are often consciously opposed to those of mainstream society. These two orientations—decent and street—socially organize the community, and their coexistence has important consequences for residents, particularly children growing up in the inner city. Above all, this environment means that even youngsters whose home lives reflect mainstream values—and the majority of homes in the community do—must be able to handle themselves in a street-oriented environment.

This is because the street culture has evolved what may be called a code of the streets, which amounts to a set of informal rules governing interpersonal public behavior, including violence. The rules prescribe both a proper comportment and a proper way to respond if challenged. They regulate the use of violence and so allow those who are inclined to aggression to precipitate violent encounters in an approved way. The rules have been established and are enforced mainly by the street-oriented, but on the streets the distinction between street and decent is often irrelevant; everybody knows that if the rules are violated, there are penalties. Knowledge of the code is thus largely defensive; it is literally necessary for operating in public. Therefore, even though families with a decency orientation are usually opposed to the values of the code, they often reluctantly encourage their children's familiarity with it to enable them to negotiate the inner-city environment.

At the heart of the code is the issue of respect—loosely defined as being treated "right," or granted the deference one deserves. However, in the troublesome public environment of the inner city, as people increasingly feel buffeted by forces beyond their control, what one deserves in the way of respect becomes more and more problematic and uncertain. This in turn further opens the issue of respect to sometimes intense interpersonal negotiation. In the street culture, especially among young people, respect is viewed as almost an external entity that is hard-won but easily lost, and so must constantly be guarded. The rules of the code in fact provide a framework for negotiating respect. The person whose very appearance—including his clothing, demeanor, and way of moving—deters transgressions feels that he possesses, and may be considered by others to possess, a measure of respect. With the right amount of respect, for instance, he can avoid "being bothered" in public. If he is bothered, not only may he be in physical danger but he has been disgraced or "dissed" (disrespected). Many of the

forms that dissing can take might seem petty to middle-class people (maintaining eye contact for too long, for example), but to those invested in the street code, these actions become serious indications of the other person's intentions. Consequently, such people become very sensitive to advances and slights, which could well serve as warnings of imminent physical confrontation.

This hard reality can be traced to the profound sense of alienation from mainstream society and its institutions felt by many poor inner-city black people, particularly the young. The code of the streets is actually a cultural adaptation to a profound lack of faith in the police and the judicial system. The police are most often seen as representing the dominant white society and not caring to protect inner-city residents. When called, they may not respond, which is one reason many residents feel they must be prepared to take extraordinary measures to defend themselves and their loved ones against those who are inclined to aggression. Lack of police accountability has in fact been incorporated into the status system: the person who is believed capable of "taking care of himself" is accorded a certain deference, which translates into a sense of physical and psychological control. Thus the street code emerges where the influence of the police ends and personal responsibility for one's safety is felt to begin. Exacerbated by the proliferation of drugs and easy access to guns, this volatile situation results in the ability of the street-oriented minority (or those who effectively "go for bad") to dominate the public spaces.

Decent and Street Families

Although almost everyone in poor inner-city neighborhoods is struggling financially and therefore feels a certain distance from the rest of America, the decent and the street family in a real sense represent two poles of value orientation, two contrasting conceptual categories. The labels "decent" and "street," which the residents themselves use, amount to evaluative judgments that confer status on local residents. The labeling is often the result of a social contest among individuals and families of the neighborhood. Individuals of the two orientations often coexist in the same extended family. Decent residents judge themselves to be so while judging others to be of the street, and street individuals often present themselves as decent, drawing distinctions between themselves and other people. In addition, there is quite a bit of circumstantial behavior—that is, one person may at different times exhibit both decent and street orientations, depending on the circumstances. Although these designations result from so much social jockeying, there do exist concrete features that define each conceptual category.

Generally, so-called decent families tend to accept mainstream values more fully and attempt to instill them in their children. Whether married couples with children or single-parent (usually female) households, they are generally "working poor" and so tend to be better off financially than their street-oriented neighbors. They value hard work and self-reliance and are willing to sacrifice for their children. Because they have a certain amount of faith in mainstream society, they harbor hopes for a better future for their children, if not for themselves. Many of them go to church and take a strong interest in their children's schooling. Rather than dwelling on the real hardships and inequities facing them, many such decent people, particularly the increasing number of grandmothers raising grandchildren, see their difficult situation as a test from God and derive great support from their faith and from the church community.

Extremely aware of the problematic and often dangerous environment in which they reside, decent parents tend to be strict in their child-rearing practices, encouraging children to respect authority and walk a straight moral line. They have an almost obsessive concern about trouble of any kind and remind their children to be on the lookout for people and situations that might lead to it. At the same time, they are themselves polite and considerate of others, and teach their children to be the same way. At home, at work, and in church, they strive hard to maintain a positive mental attitude and a spirit of cooperation.

So-called street parents, in contrast, often show a lack of consideration for other people and have a rather superficial sense of family and community. Though they may love their children, many of them are unable to cope with the physical and emotional demands of parenthood, and find it difficult to reconcile their needs with those of their children. These families, who are more fully invested in the code of the streets than the decent people are, may aggressively socialize their children into it in a normative way. They believe in the code and judge themselves and others according to its values.

In fact the overwhelming majority of families in the inner-city community try to approximate the decent-family model, but there are many others who clearly represent the worst fears of the decent family. Not only are their financial resources extremely limited, but what little they have may easily be misused. The lives of the street-oriented are often marked by disorganization. In the most desperate circumstances people frequently have a limited understanding of priorities and consequences, and so frustrations mount over bills, food, and, at times, drink, cigarettes, and drugs. Some tend toward self-destructive behavior; many street-oriented women are crack-addicted ("on the pipe"), alcoholic, or involved in complicated relationships with men who abuse them. In addition, the seeming intractability of their situation, caused in large part by the lack of well-paying jobs and the persistence of racial discrimination, has engendered deep-seated bitterness and anger in many of the most desperate and poorest blacks, especially young people. The need both to exercise a measure of control and to lash out at somebody is often reflected in the adults' relations with their children. At the least, the frustrations of persistent poverty shorten the fuse in such people—contributing to a lack of patience with anyone, child or adult, who irritates them.

In these circumstances a woman—or a man, although men are less consistently present in children's lives—can be quite aggressive with children, yelling at and striking them for the least little infraction of the rules she has set down. Often little if any serious explanation follows the verbal and physical punishment. This response teaches children a particular lesson. They learn that to solve any kind of interpersonal problem one must quickly resort to hitting or other violent behavior. Actual peace and quiet, and also the appearance of calm, respectful children conveyed to her neighbors and friends, are often what the young mother most desires, but at times she will be very aggressive in trying to get them. Thus she may be quick to beat her children, especially if they defy her law, not because she hates them but because this is the way she knows to control them. In fact, many street-oriented women love their children dearly. Many mothers in the community subscribe to the notion that there is a "devil in the boy" that must be beaten out of him or that socially "fast girls need to be whupped." Thus much of what borders on child abuse in the view of social authorities is acceptable parental punishment in the view of these mothers.

Many street-oriented women are sporadic mothers whose children learn to fend for themselves when necessary, foraging for food and money any way they can get it. The children are sometimes employed by drug dealers or become addicted themselves. These children of the street, growing up with little supervision, are said to "come up hard." They often learn to fight at an early age, sometimes using short-tempered adults around them as role models. The street-oriented home may be fraught with anger, verbal disputes, physical aggression, and even mayhem. The children observe these goings-on, learning the lesson that might makes right. They quickly learn to hit those who cross them, and the dog-eat-dog mentality prevails. In order to survive, to protect oneself, it is necessary to marshal inner resources and be ready to deal with adversity in a hands-on way. In these circumstances physical prowess takes on great significance.

In some of the most desperate cases, a street-oriented mother may simply leave her young children alone and unattended while she goes out. The most irresponsible women can be found at local bars and crack houses, getting high and socializing with other adults. Sometimes a troubled woman will leave very young children alone for days at a time. Reports of crack addicts abandoning their children have become common in drug-infested inner-city communities. Neighbors or relatives discover the abandoned children, often hungry and distraught over the absence of their mother. After repeated absences, a friend or relative, particularly a grandmother, will often step in to care for the young children, sometimes petitioning the authorities to send her, as guardian of the children, the mother's welfare check, if the mother gets one. By this time, however, the children may well have learned the first lesson of the streets: survival itself, let alone respect, cannot be taken for granted; you have to fight for your place in the world.

Campaigning for Respect

These realities of inner-city life are largely absorbed on the streets. At an early age, often even before they start school, children from street-oriented homes gravitate to the streets, where they "hang"—socialize with their peers. Children from these generally permissive homes have a great deal of latitude and are allowed to "rip and run" up and down the street. They often come home from school, put their books down, and go right back out the door. On school nights eight- and nine-year-olds remain out until nine or ten o'clock (and teenagers typically come in whenever they want to). On the streets they play in groups that often become the source of their primary social bonds. Children from decent homes tend to be more carefully supervised and are thus likely to have curfews and to be taught how to stay out of trouble.

When decent and street kids come together, a kind of social shuffle occurs in which children have a chance to go either way. Tension builds as a child comes to realize that he must choose an orientation. The kind of home he comes from influences but does not determine the way he will ultimately turn out—although it is unlikely that a child from a thoroughly street-oriented family will easily absorb decent values on the streets. Youths who emerge from street-oriented families but develop a decency orientation almost always learn those values in another setting—in school, in a youth group, in church. Often it is the result of their involvement with a caring "old head" (adult role model).

In the street, through their play, children pour their individual life experiences into a common knowledge pool, affirming, confirming, and elaborating on what they have observed in the home and matching their skills against those of others. And they learn to fight. Even small children test one another, pushing and shoving, and are ready to hit other children over circumstances not to their liking. In turn, they are readily hit by other children, and the child who is toughest prevails. Thus the violent resolution of disputes, the hitting and cursing, gains social reinforcement. The child in effect is initiated into a system that is really a way of campaigning for respect.

In addition, younger children witness the disputes of older children, which are often resolved through cursing and abusive talk, if not aggression or outright violence. They see that one child succumbs to the greater physical and mental abilities of the other. They are also alert and attentive witnesses to the verbal and physical fights of adults, after which they compare notes and share their interpretations of the event. In almost every case the victor is the person who physically won the altercation, and this person often enjoys the esteem and respect of onlookers. These experiences reinforce the lessons the children have learned at home: might makes right, and toughness is a virtue, while humility is not. In effect they learn the social meaning of fighting. When it is left virtually unchallenged, this understanding becomes an ever more important part of the child's working conception of the world. Over time the code of the streets becomes refined.

Those street-oriented adults with whom children come in contact—including mothers, fathers, brothers, sisters, boyfriends, cousins, neighbors, and friends—help them along in forming this understanding by verbalizing the messages they are getting through experience: "Watch your back." "Protect yourself." "Don't punk out." "If somebody messes with you, you got to pay them back." "If someone disses you, you got to straighten them out." Many parents actually impose sanctions if a child is not sufficiently aggressive. For example, if a child loses a fight and comes home upset, the parent might respond, "Don't you come in here crying that somebody beat you up; you better get back out there and whup his ass. I didn't raise no punks! Get back out there and whup his ass. If you don't whup his ass, I'll whup your ass when you come home." Thus the child obtains reinforcement for being tough and showing nerve.

While fighting, some children cry as though they are doing something they are ambivalent about. The fight may be against their wishes, yet they may feel constrained to fight or face the consequences—not just from peers but also from caretakers or parents, who may administer another beating if they back down. Some adults recall receiving such lessons from their own parents and justify repeating them to their children as a way to toughen them up. Looking capable of taking care of oneself as a form of self-defense is a dominant theme among both street-oriented and decent adults who worry about the safety of their children. There is thus at times a convergence in their child-rearing practices, although the rationales behind them may differ.

Self-Image Based on "Juice"

By the time they are teenagers, most youths have either internalized the code of the streets or at least learned the need to comport themselves in accordance with its rules, which chiefly have to do with interpersonal communication. The code revolves around the presentation of self. Its basic requirement is the display of a certain predisposition to violence. Accordingly, one's bearing must send the unmistakable if sometimes subtle message to "the next person" in public that one is capable of violence and mayhem when the situation requires it, that one can take care of oneself. The nature of this communication is largely determined by the demands of the circumstances but can include facial expressions, gait, and verbal expressions—all of which are geared mainly to deterring aggression. Physical appearance, including clothes, jewelry, and grooming, also plays an important part in how a person is viewed; to be respected, it is important to have the right look.

Even so, there are no guarantees against challenges, because there are always people around looking for a fight to increase their share of respect—or "juice," as it is sometimes called on the street. Moreover, if a person is assaulted, it is important, not only in the eyes of his opponent but also in the eyes of his "running buddies," for him to avenge himself. Otherwise he risks being "tried" (challenged) or "moved on" by any number of others. To maintain his honor he must show he is not someone to be "messed with" or "dissed." In general, the person must "keep himself straight" by managing his position of respect among others; this involves in part his self-image, which is shaped by what he thinks others are thinking of him in relation to his peers.

Objects play an important and complicated role in establishing self-image. Jackets, sneakers, gold jewelry, reflect not just a person's taste, which tends to be tightly regulated among adolescents of all social classes, but also a willingness to possess things that may require defending. A boy wearing a fashionable, expensive jacket, for example, is vulnerable to attack by another who covets the jacket and either cannot afford to buy one or wants the added satisfaction of depriving someone else of his. However, if the boy forgoes the desirable jacket and wears one that isn't "hip," he runs the risk of being teased and possibly even assaulted as an unworthy person. To be allowed to hang with certain prestigious crowds, a boy must wear a different set of expensive clothes—sneakers and athletic suit—every day. Not to be able to do so might make him appear socially deficient. The youth comes to covet such items—especially when he sees easy prey wearing them.

In acquiring valued things, therefore, a person shores up his identity—but since it is an identity based on having things, it is highly precarious. This very precariousness gives a heightened sense of urgency to staying even with peers, with whom the person is actually competing. Young men and women who are able to command respect through their presentation of self—by allowing their possessions and their body language to speak for them—may not have to campaign for regard but may, rather, gain it by the force of their manner. Those who are unable to command respect in this way must actively campaign for it—and are thus particularly alive to slights.

One way of campaigning for status is by taking the possessions of others. In this context, seemingly ordinary objects can become trophies imbued with symbolic value that far exceeds their monetary worth. Possession of the trophy can symbolize the ability to violate somebody—to "get in his face," to take something of value from him, to "dis" him, and thus to enhance one's own worth by stealing someone else's. The trophy does not have to be something material. It can be another person's sense of honor, snatched away with a derogatory remark. It can be the outcome of a fight. It can be the imposition of a certain standard, such as a girl's getting herself recognized as the most beautiful. Material things, however, fit easily into the pattern. Sneakers, a pistol, even somebody else's girlfriend, can become a trophy. When a person can take something from another and then flaunt it, he gains a certain regard by being the owner, or the controller, of that thing. But this display of ownership can then provoke other people to challenge him. This game of who controls what is thus constantly being played out on inner-city

streets, and the trophy—extrinsic or intrinsic, tangible or intangible—identifies the current winner.

An important aspect of this often violent give-and-take is its zero-sum quality. That is, the extent to which one person can raise himself up depends on his ability to put another person down. This underscores the alienation that permeates the inner-city ghetto community. There is a generalized sense that very little respect is to be had, and therefore everyone competes to get what affirmation he can of the little that is available. The craving for respect that results gives people thin skins. Shows of deference by others can be highly soothing, contributing to a sense of security, comfort, self-confidence, and self-respect. Transgressions by others which go unanswered diminish these feelings and are believed to encourage further transgressions. Hence one must be ever vigilant against the transgressions of others or even *appearing* as if transgressions will be tolerated. Among young people, whose sense of self-esteem is particularly vulnerable, there is an especially heightened concern with being disrespected. Many inner-city young men in particular crave respect to such a degree that they will risk their lives to attain and maintain it.

The issue of respect is thus closely tied to whether a person has an inclination to be violent, even as a victim. In the wider society people may not feel required to retaliate physically after an attack, even though they are aware that they have been degraded or taken advantage of. They may feel a great need to defend themselves *during* an attack, or to behave in such a way as to deter aggression (middle-class people certainly can and do become victims of street-oriented youths), but they are much more likely than street-oriented people to feel that they can walk away from a possible altercation with their self-esteem intact. Some people may even have the strength of character to flee, without any thought that their self-respect or esteem will be diminished.

In impoverished inner-city black communities, however, particularly among young males and perhaps increasingly among females, such flight would be extremely difficult. To run away would likely leave one's self-esteem in tatters. Hence people often feel constrained not only to stand up and at least attempt to resist during an assault but also to "pay back"—to seek revenge—after a successful assault on their person. This may include going to get a weapon or even getting relatives involved. Their very identity and self-respect, their honor, is often intricately tied up with the way they perform on the streets during and after such encounters. This outlook reflects the circumscribed opportunities of the inner-city poor. Generally people outside the ghetto have other ways of gaining status and regard, and thus do not feel so dependent on such physical displays.

By Trial of Manhood

On the street, among males these concerns about things and identity have come to be expressed in the concept of "manhood." Manhood in the inner city means taking the prerogatives of men with respect to strangers, other men, and women—being distinguished as a man. It implies physicality and a certain ruthlessness. Regard and respect are associated with this concept in large part because of its practical application: if others have little or no regard for a person's manhood, his very life and those of his loved ones could be in jeopardy. But there is a chicken-and-egg aspect to this situation: one's physical safety is more likely to be jeopardized in public *because* manhood is associated with respect. In other words, an existential link has been created between the idea of man-

hood and one's self-esteem, so that it has become hard to say which is primary. For many inner-city youths, manhood and respect are flip sides of the same coin; physical and psychological well-being are inseparable, and both require a sense of control, of being in charge.

The operating assumption is that a man, especially a real man, knows what other men know—the code of the streets. And if one is not a real man, one is somehow diminished as a person, and there are certain valued things one simply does not deserve. There is thus believed to be a certain justice to the code, since it is considered that everyone has the opportunity to know it. Implicit in this is that everybody is held responsible for being familiar with the code. If the victim of a mugging, for example, does not know the code and so responds "wrong," the perpetrator may feel justified even in killing him and may feel no remorse. He may think, "Too bad, but it's his fault. He should have known better."

So when a person ventures outside, he must adopt the code—a kind of shield, really—to prevent others from "messing with" him. In these circumstances it is easy for people to think they are being tried or tested by others even when this is not the case. For it is sensed that something extremely valuable is at stake in every interaction, and people are encouraged to rise to the occasion, particularly with strangers. For people who are unfamiliar with the code—generally people who live outside the inner city—the concern with respect in the most ordinary interactions can be frightening and incomprehensible. But for those who are invested in the code, the clear object of their demeanor is to discourage strangers from even thinking about testing their manhood. And the sense of power that attends the ability to deter others can be alluring even to those who know the code without being heavily invested in it—the decent inner-city youths. Thus a boy who has been leading a basically decent life can, in trying circumstances, suddenly resort to deadly force.

Central to the issue of manhood is the widespread belief that one of the most effective ways of gaining respect is to manifest "nerve." Nerve is shown when one takes another person's possessions (the more valuable the better), "messes with" someone's woman, throws the first punch, "gets in someone's face," or pulls a trigger. Its proper display helps on the spot to check others who would violate one's person and also helps to build a reputation that works to prevent future challenges. But since such a show of nerve is a forceful expression of disrespect toward the person on the receiving end, the victim may be greatly offended and seek to retaliate with equal or greater force. A display of nerve, therefore, can easily provoke a life-threatening response, and the background knowledge of that possibility has often been incorporated into the concept of nerve.

True nerve exposes a lack of fear of dying. Many feel that it is acceptable to risk dying over the principle of respect. In fact, among the hard-core street-oriented, the clear risk of violent death may be preferable to being "dissed" by another. The youths who have internalized this attitude and convincingly display it in their public bearing are among the most threatening people of all, for it is commonly assumed that they fear no man. As the people of the community say, "They are the baddest dudes on the street." They often lead an existential life that may acquire meaning only when they are faced with the possibility of imminent death. Not to be afraid to die is by implication to have few compunctions about taking another's life. Not to be afraid to die is the quid pro quo of being able to take somebody else's life—for the right reasons, if the situation demands it. When others believe this is one's position, it gives one a real sense of power on the streets. Such credibility is what many inner-city youths strive to achieve, whether they are decent or street-oriented, both because of its practical defensive value and because of the positive way it makes them feel about themselves. The difference between the decent and the street-oriented youth is often that the decent youth makes a conscious decision to appear tough and manly; in another setting—with teachers, say, or at his part-time job—he can be polite and deferential. The street-oriented youth, on the other hand, has made the concept of manhood a part of his very identity; he has difficulty manipulating it—it often controls him.

Girls and Boys

Increasingly, teenage girls are mimicking the boys and trying to have their own version of "manhood." Their goal is the same—to get respect, to be recognized as capable of setting or maintaining a certain standard. They try to achieve this end in the ways that have been established by the boys, including posturing, abusive language, and the use of violence to resolve disputes, but the issues for the girls are different. Although conflicts over turf and status exist among the girls, the majority of disputes seem rooted in assessments of beauty (which girl in a group is "the cutest"), competition over boyfriends, and attempts to regulate other people's knowledge of and opinions about a girl's behavior or that of someone close to her, especially her mother.

A major cause of conflicts among girls is "he say, she say." This practice begins in the early school years and continues through high school. It occurs when "people," particularly girls, talk about others, thus putting their "business in the streets." Usually one girl will say something negative about another in the group, most often behind the person's back. The remark will then get back to the person talked about. She may retaliate or her friends may feel required to "take up for" her. In essence this is a form of group gossiping in which individuals are negatively assessed and evaluated. As with much gossip, the things said may or may not be true, but the point is that such imputations can cast aspersions on a person's good name. The accused is required to defend herself against the slander, which can result in arguments and fights, often over little of real substance. Here again is the problem of low self-esteem, which encourages youngsters to be highly sensitive to slights and to be vulnerable to feeling easily "dissed." To avenge the dissing, a fight is usually necessary.

Because boys are believed to control violence, girls tend to defer to them in situations of conflict. Often if a girl is attacked or feels slighted, she will get a brother, uncle, or cousin to do her fighting for her. Increasingly, however, girls are doing their own fighting and are even asking their male relatives to teach them how to fight. Some girls form groups that attack other girls or take things from them. A hard-core segment of inner-city girls inclined toward violence seems to be developing. As one thirteen-year-old girl in a detention center for youths who have committed violent acts told me, "To get people to leave you alone, you gotta fight. Talking don't always get you out of stuff." One major difference between girls and boys: girls rarely use guns. Their fights are therefore not life-or-death struggles. Girls are not often willing to put their lives on the line for "manhood." The ultimate form of respect on the male-dominated inner-city street is thus reserved for men.

"Going for Bad"

In the most fearsome youths such a cavalier attitude toward death grows out of a very limited view of life. Many are uncertain about how long they are going to live and believe they could die violently at any time. They ac-cept this fate; they live on the edge. Their manner conveys the message that nothing intimidates them; whatever turn the encounter takes, they maintain their attack—rather like a pit bull, whose spirit many such boys admire. The demonstration of such tenacity "shows heart" and earns their respect.

This fearlessness has implications for law enforcement. Many street-oriented boys are much more concerned about the threat of "justice" at the hands of a peer than at the hands of the police. Moreover, many feel not only that they have little to lose by going to prison but that they have something to gain. The toughening-up one experiences in prison can actually enhance one's reputation on the streets. Hence the system loses influence over the hard core who are without jobs, with little perceptible stake in the system. If mainstream society has done nothing *for* them, they counter by making sure it can do nothing *to* them.

At the same time, however, a competing view maintains that true nerve consists in backing down, walking away from a fight, and going on with one's business. One fights only in self-defense. This view emerges from the decent philosophy that life is precious, and it is an important part of the socialization process common in decent homes. It discourages violence as the primary means of resolving disputes and encourages youngsters to accept nonviolence and talk as confrontational strategies. But "if the deal goes down," self-defense is greatly encouraged. When there is enough positive support for this orientation, either in the home or among one's peers, then nonviolence has a chance to prevail. But it prevails at the cost of relinquishing a claim to being bad and tough, and therefore sets a young person up as at the very least alienated from street-oriented peers and quite possibly a target of derision or even violence.

Although the nonviolent orientation rarely overcomes the impulse to strike back in an encounter, it does introduce a certain confusion and so can prompt a measure of soul-searching, or even profound ambivalence. Did the person back down with his respect intact or did he back down only to be judged a "punk"—a person lacking manhood? Should he or she have acted? Should he or she have hit the other person in the mouth? These questions beset many young men and women during public confrontations. What is the "right" thing to do? In the quest for honor, respect, and local status—which few young people are uninterested in—common sense most often prevails, which leads many to opt for the tough approach, enacting their own particular versions of the display of nerve. The presentation of oneself as rough and tough is very often quite acceptable until one is tested. And then that presentation may help the person pass the test, because it will cause fewer questions to be asked about what he did and why. It is hard for a person to explain why he lost the fight or why he backed down. Hence many will strive to appear to "go for bad," while hoping they will never be tested. But when they are tested, the outcome of the situation may quickly be out of their hands, as they become wrapped up in the circumstances of the moment.

An Oppositional Culture

The attitudes of the wider society are deeply implicated in the code of the streets. Most people in inner-city communities are not totally invested in the code, but the significant minority of hard-core street youths who are have to maintain the code in order to establish reputations, because they have—or feel they have—few other ways to assert themselves. For these young people the standards of the street code are the only game in town. The extent to which some children—particularly those who through upbringing have become most alienated and those

lacking in strong and conventional social support—experience, feel, and internalize racist rejection and contempt from mainstream society may strongly encourage them to express contempt for the more conventional society in turn. In dealing with this contempt and rejection, some youngsters will consciously invest themselves and their considerable mental resources in what amounts to an oppositional culture to preserve themselves and their self-respect. Once they do, any respect they might be able to garner in the wider system pales in comparison with the respect available in the local system; thus they often lose interest in even attempting to negotiate the mainstream system.

At the same time, many less alienated young blacks have assumed a street-oriented demeanor as a way of expressing their blackness while really embracing a much more moderate way of life; they, too, want a nonviolent setting in which to live and raise a family. These decent people are trying hard to be part of the mainstream culture, but the racism, real and perceived, that they encounter helps to legitimate the oppositional culture. And so on occasion they adopt street behavior. In fact, depending on the demands of the situation, many people in the community slip back and forth between decent and street behavior.

A vicious cycle has thus been formed. The hopelessness and alienation many young inner-city black men and women feel, largely as a result of endemic joblessness and persistent racism, fuels the violence they engage in. This violence serves to confirm the negative feelings many whites and some middle-class blacks harbor toward the ghetto poor, further legitimating the oppositional culture and the code of the streets in the eyes of many poor young blacks. Unless this cycle is broken, attitudes on both sides will become increasingly entrenched, and the violence, which claims victims black and white, poor and affluent, will only escalate.

Race and the Media

28

PUT ON A HAPPY FACE
Masking the Differences Between Blacks and Whites

Benjamin DeMott

At the movies these days, questions about racial injustice have been amicably resolved. Watch *Pulp Fiction* or *Congo* or *A Little Princess* or any other recent film in which both blacks and whites are primary characters and you can, if you want, forget about race. Whites and blacks greet one another on the screen with loving candor, revealing their common humanity. In *Pulp Fiction,* an armed black mobster (played by Samuel L. Jackson) looks deep into the eyes of an armed white thief in the middle of a holdup (played by Tim Roth) and shares his version of God's word in Ezekiel, whereupon the two men lay aside their weapons, both more or less redeemed. The moment inverts an earlier scene in which a white boxer (played by Bruce Willis) risks his life to save another black mobster (played by Ving Rhames), who is being sexually tortured as a prelude to his execution.

Pulp Fiction (gross through July: $107 million) is one of a series of films suggesting that the beast of American racism is tamed and harmless. Close to the start of *Die Hard with a Vengeance* (gross through July: $95 million) the camera finds a white man wearing sandwich boards on the corner of Amsterdam Avenue and 138th Street in Harlem. The boards carry a horrific legend: I HATE NIGGERS. A group of young blacks approach the man with murderous intent, bearing guns and knives. They are figures straight out of a national nightmare—ugly, enraged, terrifying. No problem. A black man, again played by Jackson, appears and rescues the white man, played by Willis. The black man and white man come to know each other well. In time the white man declares flatly to the black, "I need you more than you need me." A moment later he charges the black with being a racist—with not liking whites as much as the white man likes blacks—and the two talk frankly about their racial prejudices. Near the end of the film, the men have grown so close that each volunteers to die for the other.

Pulp Fiction and *Die Hard with a Vengeance* follow the pattern of *Lethal Weapon 1, 2,* and *3,* the Danny Glover/Mel Gibson buddy vehicles that collectively grossed $357 million, and *White Men Can't Jump,* which, in the year of the L. A. riots, grossed $76 million. In *White Men Can't Jump,* a white dropout, played by Woody

Harrelson, ekes out a living on black-dominated basketball courts in Los Angeles. He's arrogant and aggressive but never in danger because he has a black protector and friend, played by Wesley Snipes. At the movie's end, the white, flying above the hoop like a stereotypical black player, scores the winning basket in a two-on-two pickup game on an alley-oop pass from his black chum, whereupon the two men fall into each other's arms in joy. Later, the black friend agrees to find work for the white at the store he manages.

WHITE (helpless): I gotta get a job. Can you get me a job?

BLACK (affectionately teasing): Got any references?

WHITE (shy grin): You.

Such dialogue is the stuff of romance. What's dreamed of and gained is a place where whites are unafraid of blacks, where blacks ask for and need nothing from whites, and where the sameness of the races creates a common fund of sweet content.[1] The details of the dream matter less than the force that makes it come true for both races, eliminating the constraints of objective reality and redistributing resources, status, and capabilities. That cleansing social force supersedes political and economic fact or policy; that force, improbably enough, is friendship.

Watching the beaming white men who know how to jump, we do well to remind

---

[1] I could go on with examples of movies that deliver the good news of friendship: *Regarding Henry, Driving Miss Daisy, Forrest Gump, The Shawshank Redemption, Philadelphia, The Last Boy Scout, 48 Hours I–II, Rising Sun, Iron Eagle I–II, Rudy, Sister Act, Hearts of Dixie, Betrayed, The Power of One, White Nights, Clara's Heart, Doc Hollywood, Cool Runnings, Places in the Heart, Trading Places, Fried Green Tomatoes, Q & A, Platoon, A Mother's Courage: The Mary Thomas Story, The Unforgiven, The Air Up There, The Pelican Brief, Losing Isaiah, Smoke, Searching for Bobby Fischer, An Officer and a Gentleman, Speed,* etc.

ourselves of what the camera shot leaves out. Black infants die in America at twice the rate of white infants. (Despite the increased numbers of middle-class blacks, the rates are diverging, with black rates actually rising.) One out of every two black children lives below the poverty line (as compared with one out of seven white children). Nearly four times as many black families exist below the poverty line as white families. More than 50 percent of African American families have incomes below $25,000. Among black youths under age twenty, death by murder occurs nearly ten times as often as among whites. Over 60 percent of births to black mothers occur out of wedlock, more than four times the rate for white mothers. The net worth of the typical white household is ten times that of the typical black household. In many states, five to ten times as many blacks as whites age eighteen to thirty are in prison.

The good news at the movies obscures the bad news in the streets and confirms the Supreme Court's recent decisions on busing, affirmative action, and redistricting. Like the plot of *White Men Can't Jump,* the Court postulates the existence of a society no longer troubled by racism. Because black-white friendship is now understood to be the rule, there is no need for integrated schools or a congressional Black Caucus or affirmative action. The Congress and state governors can guiltlessly cut welfare, food assistance, fuel assistance, Head Start, housing money, fellowship money, vaccine money. Justice Anthony Kennedy can declare, speaking for the Supreme Court majority last June, that creating a world of genuine equality and sameness requires only that "our political system and our society cleanse themselves . . . of discrimination."

The deep logic runs as follows: *Yesterday white people didn't like black people, and accordingly suffered guilt, knowing that the dislike was racist and knowing also that as moral persons they would have to atone for the guilt. They would have to ante up for welfare and Head Start and halfway houses and free vaccine and midnight basketball and summer jobs for schoolkids and graduate fellowships for promising scholars and craft-union apprenticeships and so on, endlessly. A considerable and wasteful expense. But at length came the realization that by ending dislike or hatred it would be possible to end guilt, which in turn would mean an end to redress: no more wasteful ransom money. There would be but one requirement: the regular production and continuous showing forth of evidence indisputably proving that hatred has totally vanished from the land.*

I cannot tell the reader how much I would like to believe in this sunshine world. After the theater lights brighten and I've found coins for a black beggar on the way to my car and am driving home through downtown Springfield, Massachusetts, the world invented by *Die Hard with a Vengeance* and America's highest court gives way only slowly to the familiar urban vision in my windshield—homeless blacks on trash-strewn streets, black prostitutes staked out on a corner, and signs of a not very furtive drug trade. I know perfectly well that most African Americans don't commit crimes or live in alleys. I also know that for somebody like myself, downtown Springfield in the late evening is not a good place to be.

The movies reflect the larger dynamic of wish and dream. Day after day the nation's corporate ministries of culture churn out images of racial harmony. Millions awaken each morning to the friendly sight of Katie Couric nudging a perky elbow into good buddy Bryant Gumbel's side. My mailbox and millions of demographically similar others are choked with flyers from companies (Wal-Mart, Victoria's Secret) bent on publicizing both their wares and their social bona fides by displaying black and white models at cordial ease with one another. A torrent of goodwill messages about race arrives daily—revelations of corporate largesse, commercials, news features, TV specials, all proclaiming that whites like me feel strongly positive impulses of friendship for blacks and that those same admirable impulses are effectively eradicating racial differences, rendering blacks and whites the same. BellSouth TV commercials present children singing "I am the keeper of the world"—first a white child, then a black child, then a white child, then a black child. Because Dow Chemical likes black America, it recruits young black college grads for its research division and dramatizes, in TV commercials, their tearful-joyful partings from home. ("Son, show 'em what you got," says a black lad's father.) American Express shows an elegant black couple and an elegant white couple sitting together in a theater, happy in one another's company. (The couples share the box with an oversized Gold Card.) During the evening news I watch a black mom offer Robitussin to a miserably coughing white mom. Here's *People* magazine promoting itself under a photo of John Lee Hooker, the black bluesman. "We're these kinds of people, too," *People* claims in the caption. In the current production of *Hamlet* on Broadway, Horatio is played by a black actor. On *The 700 Club,* Pat Robertson joshes Ben Kinchlow, his black sidekick, about Ben's far-out ties.

What counts here is not the saccharine clumsiness of the interchanges but the bulk of them—the ceaseless, self-validating gestures of friendship, the humming, buzzing background theme: *All decent Americans extend the hand of friendship to African Americans; nothing but nothing is more auspicious for the African American future than this extended hand.* Faith in the miracle cure of racism by change-of-heart turns out to be so familiar as to have become unnoticeable. And yes, the faith has its benign aspect. Even as they nudge me and others toward belief in magic (instant pals and no-money-down equality), the images and messages of devoted relationships between blacks and whites do exert a humanizing influence.

Nonetheless, through these same images and messages the comfortable majority tells itself a fatuous untruth. Promoting the fantasy of painless answers, inspiring groundless self-approval among whites, joining the Supreme Court in treating "cleansing" as *inevitable,* the new orthodoxy of friendship incites culture-wide evasion, justifies one political step backward after another, and greases the skids along which, tomorrow, welfare block grants will slide into state highway-resurfacing budgets. Whites are part of the solution, says this orthodoxy, if we break out of the prison of our skin color, say hello, as equals, one-on-one, to a black stranger, and make a black friend. We're part of the problem if we have an aversion to black people or are frightened of them, or if we feel that the more distance we put between them and us the better, or if we're in the habit of asserting our superiority rather than acknowledging our common humanity. Thus we shift the problem away from politics— from black experience and the history of slavery—and perceive it as a matter of the suspicion and fear found within the white heart; solving the problem asks no more of us than that we work on ourselves, scrubbing off the dirt of ill will.

The approach miniaturizes, personalizes, and moralizes; it removes the large and complex dilemmas of race from the public sphere. It tempts audiences to see history as irrelevant and to regard feelings as decisive—to believe that the fate of black Americans is shaped mainly by events occurring in the hearts and minds of the privileged. And let's be frank: the orthodoxy of friendship feels *nice.* It practically *consecrates* self-flattery. The "good" Bill Clinton who attends black churches and talks with likable ease to fel-

low worshipers was campaigning when Los Angeles rioted in '92. "White Americans," he said, "are gripped by the isolation of their own experience. Too many still simply have no friends of other races and do not know any differently." Few black youths of working age in South-Central L.A. had been near enough to the idea of a job even to think of looking for work before the Rodney King verdict, but the problem, according to Clinton, was that whites need black friends.

Most of the country's leading voices of journalistic conscience (editorial writers, television anchorpersons, syndicated columnists) roundly endorse the doctrine of black-white friendship as a means of redressing the inequalities between the races. Roger Rosenblatt, editor of the *Columbia Journalism Review* and an especially deft supplier of warm and fuzzy sentiment, published an essay in *Family Circle* arguing that white friendship and sympathy for blacks simultaneously make power differentials vanish and create interracial identity between us, one by one. The author finds his *exemplum* in an episode revealing the personal sensitivity, to injured blacks, of one of his children.

"When our oldest child, Carl, was in high school," he writes, "he and two black friends were standing on a street corner in New York City one spring evening, trying to hail a taxi. The three boys were dressed decently and were doing nothing wild or threatening. Still, no taxi would pick them up. If a driver spotted Carl first, he might slow down, but he would take off again when he saw the others. Carl's two companions were familiar with this sort of abuse. Carl, who had never observed it firsthand before, burned with anger and embarrassment that he was the color of a world that would so mistreat his friends."

Rosenblatt notes that when his son "was applying to colleges, he wrote his essay on that taxi incident with his two black friends. . . . He was able to articulate what he could not say at the time—how ashamed and impotent he felt. He also wrote of the power of their friendship, which has lasted to this day and has carried all three young men into the country that belongs to them. To all of us."

In this homily white sympathy begets interracial sameness in several ways. The three classmates are said to react identically to the cabdrivers' snub; i.e., they feel humiliated. "[Carl] could not find the words to express his humiliation and his friends *would* not express theirs."

The anger that inspires the younger Rosenblatt's college-admission essay on racism is seen as identical with black anger. Friendship brings the classmates together as joint, equal owners of the land of their birth ("the country that belongs to [all of] them"). And Rosenblatt supplies a still larger vision of essential black-white sameness near the end of his essay: "Our proper hearts tell the truth," he declares, "which is that we are all in the same boat, rich and poor, black and white. We are helpless, wicked, heroic, terrified, and we need one another. We need to give rides to one another."

Thus do acts of private piety substitute for public policy while the possibility of urgent political action disappears into a sentimental haze. "If we're looking for a formula to ease the tensions between the races," Rosenblatt observes, then we should "attack the disintegration of the black community" and "the desperation of the poor." Without overtly mocking civil rights activists who look toward the political arena "to erase the tensions," Rosenblatt alludes to them in a throwaway manner, implying that properly adjusted whites look elsewhere, that there was a time for politicking for "equal rights" but we've passed through it. Now is a time in which we should listen to our hearts at moments of epiphany and allow sympathy to work its wizardry, cleansing and floating

us, blacks and whites "all in the same boat," on a mystical undercurrent of the New Age.

Blacks themselves aren't necessarily proof against this theme, as witness a recent essay by James Alan McPherson in the Harvard journal *Reconstruction*. McPherson, who received the 1977 Pulitzer Prize for fiction for his collection of stories *Elbow Room*, says that "the only possible steps, the safest steps . . . small ones" in the movement "toward a universal culture" will be those built not on "ideologies and formulas and programs" but on experiences of personal connectedness.

"Just this past spring," he writes, "when I was leaving a restaurant after taking a [white] former student to dinner, a black [woman on the sidewalk] said to my friend, in a rasping voice, 'Hello, girlfriend. Have you got anything to spare?'" The person speaking was a female crack addict with a child who was also addicted. "But," writes McPherson, when the addict made her pitch to his dinner companion, "I saw in my friend's face an understanding and sympathy and a shining which transcended race and class. Her face reflected one human soul's connection with another. The magnetic field between the two women was charged with spiritual energy."

The writer points the path to progress through interpersonal gestures by people who "insist on remaining human, and having human responses. . . . Perhaps the best that can be done, now, is the offering of understanding and support to the few out of many who are capable of such gestures, rather than devising another plan to engineer the many into one."

The elevated vocabulary ("soul," "spiritual") beatifies the impulse to turn away from the real-life agenda of actions capable of reducing racial injustice. Wherever that impulse dominates, the rhetoric of racial sameness thrives, diminishing historical catastrophes affecting millions over centuries and inflating the significance of tremors of tenderness briefly troubling the heart or conscience of a single individual—the boy waiting for a cab, the woman leaving the restaurant. People forget the theoretically unforgettable—the caste history of American blacks, the connection between no schools for longer than a century and bad school performance now, between hateful social attitudes and zero employment opportunities, between minority anguish and majority fear.

How could this way of seeing have become conventional so swiftly? How did the dogmas of instant equality insinuate themselves so effortlessly into courts and mass audiences alike? How can a white man like myself, who taught Southern blacks in the 1960s, find himself seduced—as I have been more than once—by the orthodoxy of friendship? In the civil rights era, the experience for many millions of Americans was one of discovery. A hitherto unimagined continent of human reality and history came into view, inducing genuine concern and at least a temporary setting aside of self-importance. I remember with utter clarity what I felt at Mary Holmes College in West Point, Mississippi, when a black student of mine was killed by tailgating rednecks; my fellow tutors and I were overwhelmed with how shamefully wrong a wrong could be. For a time, we were released from the prisons of moral weakness and ambiguity. In the year or two that followed—the mid-Sixties—the notion that some humans are more human than others, whites more human than blacks, appeared to have been overturned. The next step seemed obvious: society would have to admit that when one race deprives another of its humanity for centuries, those who have done the depriving are obligated to do what they can to restore the humanity of the deprived. The

obligation clearly entailed the mounting of comprehensive *long-term* programs of developmental assistance—not guilt-money handouts— for nearly the entire black population. The path forward was unavoidable.

It was avoided. Shortly after the award of civil rights and the institution, in 1966, of limited preferential treatment to remedy employment and educational discrimination against African Americans, a measure of economic progress for blacks did appear in census reports. Not much, but enough to stimulate glowing tales of universal black advance and to launch the good-news barrage that continues to this day (headline in the *New York Times,* June 18, 1995: "Moving On Up: The Greening of America's Black Middle Class").

After Ronald Reagan was elected to his first term, the new dogma of black-white sameness found ideological support in the form of criticism of so-called coddling. Liberal activists of both races were berated by critics of both races for fostering an allegedly enfeebling psychology of dependency that discouraged African Americans from committing themselves to individual self-development. In 1988, the charge was passionately voiced in an essay in these pages, "I'm Black, You're White, Who's Innocent?" by Shelby Steele, who attributed the difference between black rates of advance and those of other minority groups to white folks pampering. Most blacks, Steele claimed, could make it on their own—as voluntary immigrants have done—were they not held back by devitalizing programs that presented them, to themselves and others, as somehow dissimilar to and weaker than other Americans. This argument was all-in-the-same-boatism in a different key; the claim remained that progress depends upon recognition of black-white sameness. Let us see through superficial differences to the underlying, equally distributed gift for success. Let us teach ourselves—in the words of the

Garth Brooks tune—to ignore "the color of skin" and "look for . . . the beauty within."

Still further support for the policy once known as "do-nothingism" came from points-of-light barkers, who held that a little something might perhaps be done *if* accompanied by enough publicity. Nearly every broadcaster and publisher in America moves a bale of reportage on pro bono efforts by white Americans to speed the advance of black Americans. Example: McDonald's and the National Basketball Association distribute balloons when they announce they are addressing the dropout problem with an annual "Stay in School" scheme that gives schoolkids who don't miss a January school day a ticket to an all-star exhibition. The publicity strengthens the idea that these initiatives will nullify the social context—the city I see through my windshield. Reports of white philanthropy suggest that the troubles of this block and the next should be understood as phenomena in transition. The condition of American blacks need not be read as the fixed, unchanging consequence of generations of bottom-caste existence. Edging discreetly past a beggar posted near the entrance to Zabar's or H&H Bagels, or, while walking the dog, stepping politely around black men asleep on the sidewalk, we need not see ourselves and our fellows as uncaring accomplices in the acts of social injustice.

Yet more powerful has been the ceaseless assault, over the past generation, on our knowledge of the historical situation of black Americans. On the face of things it seems improbable that the cumulative weight of documented historical injury to African Americans could ever be lightly assessed. Gifted black writers continue to show, in scene after scene—in their studies of middle-class blacks interacting with whites—how historical realities shape the lives of their black characters. In *Killer of Sheep,* the brilliant black filmmaker Charles Burnett dramatizes the daily encounters that suck poor blacks into will-lessness and contempt for white fairy tales of interracial harmony; he quickens his historical themes with images of faceless black meat processors gutting undifferentiated, unchoosing animal life. Here, say these images, as though talking back to Clarence Thomas, here is a basic level of black life unchanged over generations. Where there's work, it's miserably paid and ugly. Space allotments at home and at work cramp body and mind. Positive expectation withers in infancy. People fall into the habit of jeering at aspiration as though at the bidding of physical law. Obstacles at every hand prevent people from loving and being loved in decent ways, prevent children from believing their parents, prevent parents from believing they themselves know anything worth knowing. The only true self, now as in the long past, is the one mocked by one's own race. "Shit on you, nigger," says a voice in *Killer of Sheep.* "Nothing you say matters a good goddamn."

For whites, these works produce guilt, and for blacks, I can only assume, pain and despair. The audience for tragedy remains small, while at the multiplex the popular enthusiasm for historical romance remains constant and vast. During the last two decades, the entertainment industry has conducted a siege on the pertinent past, systematically excising knowledge of the consequences of the historical exploitation of African Americans. Factitious renderings of the American past blur the outlines of black-white conflict, redefine the ground of black grievances for the purpose of diminishing the grievances, restage black life in accordance with the illusory conventions of American success mythology, and present the operative influences on race history as the same as those implied to be pivotal in *White Men Can't Jump* or a BellSouth advertisement.

Although there was scant popular awareness of it at the time (1977), the television miniseries *Roots* introduced the figure of the Unscathed Slave. To an enthralled audience of more than 80 million the series intimated that the damage resulting from generations of birth-ascribed, semi-animal status was largely temporary, that slavery was a product of motiveless malignity on the social margins rather than of respectable rationality, and that the ultimate significance of the institution lay in the demonstration, by freed slaves, that no force on earth can best the energies of American Individualism. ("Much like the Waltons confronting the depression," writes historian Eric Foner, a widely respected authority on American slavery, "the family in 'Roots' neither seeks nor requires outside help; individual or family effort is always sufficient.") Ken Burns's much applauded PBS documentary *The Civil War* (1990) went even further than *Roots* in downscaling black injury; the series treated slavery, birth-ascribed inferiority, and the centuries-old denial of dignity as matters of slight consequence. (By "implicitly denying the brutal reality of slavery," writes historian Jeanie Attie, Burns's programs crossed "a dangerous moral threshold." To a group of historians who asked him why slavery had been so slighted, Burns said that any discussion of slavery "would have been lengthy and boring.")

Mass media treatments of the civil rights protest years carried forward the process, contributing to the "positive" erasure of difference. Big-budget films like *Mississippi Burning,* together with an array of TV biographical specials on Dr. Martin Luther King and others, presented the long-running struggle between disenfranchised blacks and the majority white culture as a heartwarming episode of interracial unity; the speed and caringness of white response to the oppression of blacks demonstrated that broadscale race conflict or race difference was inconceivable.

A consciousness that ingests either a part or the whole of this revisionism loses touch with the two fundamental truths of race in America; namely, that because of what happened in the past, blacks and whites cannot yet be the same; and that because what happened in the past was no mere matter of ill will or insult but the outcome of an established caste structure that has only very recently begun to be dismantled, it is not reparable by one-on-one goodwill. The word "slavery" comes to induce stock responses with no vital sense of a grinding devastation of mind visited upon generation after generation. Hoodwinked by the orthodoxy of friendship, the nation either ignores the past, summons for it a detached, correct "compassion," or gazes at it as though it were a set of aesthetic conventions, like twisted trees and fragmented rocks in nineteenth-century picturesque painting—lifeless phenomena without bearing on the present. The chance of striking through the mask of corporate-underwritten, feelgood, ahistorical racism grows daily more remote. The trade-off—whites promise friendship, blacks accept the status quo—begins to seem like a good deal.

Cosseted by Hollywood's magic lantern and soothed by press releases from Washington and the American Enterprise Institute, we should never forget what we see and hear for ourselves. Broken out by race, the results of every social tabulation from unemployment to life expectancy add up to a chronicle of atrocity. The history of black America fully explains—to anyone who approaches it honestly—how the disaster happened and why neither guilt money nor lectures on personal responsibility can, in and of themselves, repair the damage. The vision of friendship and sympathy placing blacks and whites "all in the same boat," rendering them equally able to do each other favors, "to give rides to one another," is a smiling but monstrous lie.

29

MADONNA
Plantation Mistress or Soul Sister?

bell hooks

*Subversion is contextual, historical, and
above all social. No matter how exciting
the "destabilizing" potential of texts,
bodily or otherwise, whether those texts
are subversive or recuperative or both
or neither cannot be determined
by abstraction from actual social practice.*
—SUSAN BORDO

White women "stars" like Madonna, Sandra Bernhard, and many others publicly name their interest in, and appropriation of, black culture as yet another sign of their radical chic. Intimacy with that "nasty" blackness good white girls stay away from is what they seek. To white and other non-black consumers, this gives them a special flavor, an added spice. After all it is a very recent historical phenomenon for any white girl to be able to get some mileage out of flaunting her fascination and envy of blackness. The thing about envy is that it is always ready to destroy, erase, take-over, and consume the desired object. That's exactly what Madonna attempts to do when she appropriates and commodifies aspects of black culture. Needless to say this kind of fascination is a threat. It endangers. Perhaps that is why so many of the grown black women I spoke with about Madonna had no interest in her as a cultural icon and said things like, "The bitch can't even sing." It

bell hooks, *Black Looks: Race and Representation,* South End Press, 1992, pp. 157–164. Reprinted by permission from the publisher, South End Press, 116 Saint Botolph Street, Boston, MA 02115.

was only among young black females that I could find die-hard Madonna fans. Though I often admire and, yes at times, even envy Madonna because she has created a cultural space where she can invent and reinvent herself and receive public affirmation and material reward, I do not consider myself a Madonna fan.

Once I read an interview with Madonna where she talked about her envy of black culture, where she stated that she wanted to be black as a child. It is a sign of white privilege to be able to "see" blackness and black culture from a standpoint where only the rich culture of opposition black people have created in resistance marks and defines us. Such a perspective enables one to ignore white supremacist domination and the hurt it inflicts *via* oppression, exploitation, and everyday wounds and pains. White folks who do not see black pain never really understand the complexity of black pleasure. And it is no wonder then that when they attempt to imitate the joy in living which they see as the "essence" of soul and blackness, their cultural productions may have an air of sham and falseness that may titillate and even move white audiences yet leave many black folks cold.

Needless to say, if Madonna had to depend on masses of black women to maintain her status as cultural icon she would have been dethroned some time ago. Many of the black women I spoke with expressed intense disgust and hatred of Madonna. Most did not respond to my cautious attempts to suggest that underlying those negative feelings might lurk feelings of envy, and dare I say it, desire. No black woman I talked to declared that she wanted to "be Madonna." Yet we have only to look at the number of black women entertainers/stars (Tina Turner, Aretha Franklin, Donna Summer, Vanessa Williams, Yo-Yo, etc.) who gain greater cross-over recognition when they demonstrate that, like Madonna, they too, have a healthy dose of "blonde ambition." Clearly their careers have been influenced by Madonna's choices and strategies.

For masses of black women, the political reality that underlies Madonna's and our recognition that this is a society where "blondes" not only "have more fun" but where they are more likely to succeed in any endeavor is white supremacy and racism. We cannot see Madonna's change in hair color as being merely a question of aesthetic choice. I agree with Julie Burchill in her critical work *Girls on Film,* when she reminds us: "What does it say about racial purity that the best blondes have all been brunettes (Harlow, Monroe, Bardot)? I think it says that we are not as white as we think. I think it says that Pure is a Bore." I also know that it is the expressed desire of the non-blonde Other for those characteristics that are seen as the quintessential markers of racial aesthetic superiority that perpetuate and uphold white supremacy. In this sense Madonna has much in common with the masses of black women who suffer from internalized racism and are forever terrorized by a standard of beauty they feel they can never truly embody.

Like many black women who have stood outside the culture's fascination with the blonde beauty and who have only been able to reach it through imitation and artifice, Madonna often recalls that she was a working-class white girl who saw herself as ugly, as outside the mainstream beauty standard. And indeed what some of us like about her is the way she deconstructs the myth of "natural" white girl beauty by exposing the extent to which it can be and is usually artificially constructed and maintained. She mocks the conventional racist defined beauty ideal even as she rigorously strives to embody it. Given her obsession with exposing the reality that the ideal female beauty in this society can be attained by artifice and social construction it should come as no surprise that many of her fans are gay men, and that the majority of nonwhite men, particularly black men, are among that group. Jennie Livingston's film *Paris Is Burning* suggests that many black gay men, especially queens/divas, are as equally driven as Madonna by "blonde ambition." Madonna never lets her audience forget that whatever "look" she acquires is attained by hard work—"it ain't natural." And as Burchill comments in her chapter "Homosexual Girls":

> I have a friend who drives a cab and looks like a Marlboro Man but at night is the second best Jean Harlow I have ever seen. He summed up the kind of film star he adores, brutally and brilliantly, when he said, "I like actresses who look as if they've spent hours putting themselves together—and even then they don't look right."

Certainly no one, not even die-hard Madonna fans, ever insists that her beauty is not attained by skillful artifice. And indeed, a major point of the documentary film *Truth or Dare: In Bed with Madonna* was to demonstrate the amount of work that goes into the construction of her image. Yet when the chips are down, the image Madonna most exploits is that of the quintessential "white girl." To maintain that image she must always position herself as an outsider in relation to black culture. It is that position of outsider that enables her to colonize and appropriate black experience for her own opportunistic ends even as she attempts to mask her acts of racist aggression as affirmation. And no other group sees that as clearly as black females in this society. For we have always known that the socially constructed image of innocent white womanhood relies on the continued production of the racist/sexist sexual myth that black women are not innocent and never can be. Since we are coded always as "fallen" women in the racist cultural iconography we can never, as can Madonna, publicly "work" the image of ourselves as innocent female daring to be bad. Mainstream culture always reads the black female body as sign of sexual experience. In part, many black women who are disgusted by Madonna's flaunting of sexual experience are enraged because the very image of sexual agency that she is able to project and affirm with material gain has been the stick this society has used to justify its continued beating and assault on the black female body. The vast majority of black women in the United States, more concerned with projecting images of respectability than with the idea of female sexual agency and transgression, do not often feel we have the "freedom" to act in rebellious ways in regards to sexuality without being punished. We have only to contrast the life story of Tina Turner with that of Madonna to see the different connotations "wild" sexual agency has when it is asserted by a black female. Being represented publicly as an active sexual being has only recently enabled Turner to gain control over her life and career. For years the public image of aggressive sexual agency Turner projected belied the degree to which she was sexually abused and exploited privately. She was also materially exploited. Madonna's career could not be all that it is if there were no Tina Turner and yet, unlike her cohort Sandra Bernhard, Madonna never articulates the cultural debt she owes black females.

In her most recent appropriations of blackness, Madonna almost always imitates phallic black masculinity. Although I read many articles which talked about her appropriating male codes, no critic seems to have noticed her emphasis on black male experience. In his *Playboy* profile, "Playgirl of the Western World," Michael Kelly describes Madonna's crotch grabbing as "an eloquent visual put-down of male phallic pride." He points out that she worked with choreographer Vince Paterson to perfect the gesture. Even though Kelly tells readers that Madonna was consciously imitating Michael Jackson, he does not contextualize his interpretation of the gesture to include this act of appropriation from black male culture. And in that specific context the groin grabbing gesture is an assertion of pride and phallic domination that usually takes place in an all male context. Madonna's imitation of this gesture could just as easily be read as an expression of envy.

Throughout much of her autobiographical interviews runs a thread of expressed desire to possess the power she perceives men have. Madonna may hate the phallus, but she longs to possess its power. She is always first and foremost in competition with men to see who has the biggest penis. She longs to assert phallic power, and like every other group in this white supremacist society, she clearly sees black men as embodying a quality of maleness that eludes white men. Hence, they are often the group of men she most seeks to imitate, taunting white males with her own version of "black masculinity." When it comes to entertainment rivals, Madonna clearly perceives black male stars like Prince and Michael Jackson to be the standard against which she must measure herself and that she ultimately hopes to transcend.

Fascinated yet envious of black style, Madonna appropriates black culture in ways that mock and undermine, making her presentation one that upstages. This is most evident in the video "Like a Prayer." Though I read numerous articles that discussed public outrage at this video, none focused on the issue of race. No article called attention to the fact that Madonna flaunts her sexual agency by suggesting that she is breaking the ties that bind her as a white girl to white patriarchy, and establishing ties with black men. She, however, and not black men, does the choosing. The message is directed at white men. It suggests that they only labeled black men rapists for fear that white girls would choose black partners over them. Cultural critics commenting on the video did not seem at all interested in exploring the reasons Madonna chooses a black cultural backdrop for this video, i.e., black church and religious experience. Clearly, it was this backdrop that added to the video's controversy.

In her commentary in the *Washington Post,* "Madonna: Yuppie Goddess," Brooke Masters writes: "Most descriptions of the controversial video focus on its Catholic imagery: Madonna kisses a black saint, and develops Christ-like markings on her hands. However, the video is also a feminist fairy tale. Sleeping Beauty and Snow White waited for their princes to come along, Madonna finds her own man and wakes him up." Notice that this writer completely overlooks the issue of race and gender. That Madonna's chosen prince was a black man is in part what made the representation potentially shocking and provocative to a white supremacist audience. Yet her attempt to exploit and transgress traditional racial taboos was rarely commented on. Instead critics concentrated on whether or not she was violating taboos regarding religion and representation.

In the United States, Catholicism is most often seen as a religion that has little or no black followers and Madonna's video certainly perpetuates this stereotype with its juxtaposition of images of black non-Catholic representations with the image of the black saint. Given the importance of re-

ligious experience and liberation theology in black life, Madonna's use of this imagery seemed particularly offensive. For she made black characters act in complicity with her as she aggressively flaunted her critique of Catholic manners, her attack on organized religion. Yet, no black voices that I know of came forward in print calling attention to the fact that the realm of the sacred that is mocked in this film is black religious experience, or that this appropriative "use" of that experience was offensive to many black folk. Looking at the video with a group of students in my class on the politics of sexuality where we critically analyze the way race and representations of blackness are used to sell products, we discussed the way in which black people in the video are caricatures reflecting stereotypes. They appear grotesque. The only role black females have in this video is to catch (i.e., rescue) the "angelic" Madonna when she is "falling." This is just a contemporary casting of the black female as Mammy. Made to serve as supportive backdrop for Madonna's drama, black characters in *Like a Prayer* remind one of those early Hollywood depictions of singing black slaves in the great plantation movies or those Shirley Temple films where Bojangles was trotted out to dance with Miss Shirley and spice up her act. Audiences were not supposed to be enamored of Bojangles, they were supposed to see just what a special little old white girl Shirley really was. In her own way Madonna is a modern day Shirley Temple. Certainly her expressed affinity with black culture enhances her value.

Eager to see the documentary *Truth or Dare* because it promised to focus on Madonna's transgressive sexual persona, which I find interesting, I was angered by her visual representation of her domination over not white men (certainly not over Warren Beatty or Alek Keshishian), but people of color and white working-class women. I was too angered by this to appreciate other aspects of the film I might have enjoyed. In *Truth or Dare* Madonna clearly revealed that she can only think of exerting power along very traditional, white supremacist, capitalistic, patriarchal lines. That she made people who were dependent on her for their immediate livelihood submit to her will was neither charming nor seductive to me or the other black folks that I spoke with who saw the film. We thought it tragically ironic that Madonna would choose as her dance partner a black male with dyed blonde hair. Perhaps had he appeared less like a white-identified black male consumed by "blonde ambition" he might have upstaged her. Instead he was positioned as a mirror, into which Madonna and her audience could look and see only a reflection of herself and the worship of "whiteness" she embodies—that white supremacist culture wants everyone to embody. Madonna used her power to ensure that he and the other non-white women and men who worked for her, as well as some of the white subordinates, would all serve as the backdrop to her white-girl-makes-good drama. Joking about the film with other black folks, we commented that Madonna must have searched long and hard to find a black female that was not a good dancer, one who would not deflect attention away from her. And it is telling that when the film directly reflects something other than a positive image of Madonna, the camera highlights the rage this black female dancer was suppressing. It surfaces when the "subordinates" have time off and are "relaxing."

As with most Madonna videos, when critics talk about this film they tend to ignore race. Yet no viewer can look at this film and not think about race and representation without engaging in forms of denial. After choosing a cast of characters from marginalized groups—non-white folks, heterosexual and gay, and gay white folks—Madonna publicly describes them as "emotional crip-

ples." And of course in the context of the film this description seems borne out by the way they allow her to dominate, exploit, and humiliate them. Those Madonna fans who are determined to see her as politically progressive might ask themselves why it is she completely endorses those racist/sexist/classist stereotypes that almost always attempt to portray marginalized groups as "defective." Let's face it, by doing this, Madonna is not breaking with any white supremacist, patriarchal *status quo;* she is endorsing and perpetuating it.

Some of us do not find it hip or cute for Madonna to brag that she has a "fascistic side," a side well documented in the film. Well, we did not see any of her cute little fascism in action when it was Warren Beatty calling her out in the film. No, there the image of Madonna was the little woman who grins and bears it. No, her "somebody's got to be in charge side," as she names it, was most expressed in her interaction with those representatives from marginalized groups who are most often victimized by the powerful. Why is it there is little or no discussion of Madonna as racist or sexist in her relation to other women? Would audiences be charmed by some rich white male entertainer telling us he must "play father" and oversee the actions of the less powerful, especially women and men of color? So why did so many people find it cute when Madonna asserted that she dominates the inter-racial casts of gay and heterosexual folks in her film because they are crippled and she "like[s] to play mother." No, this was not a display of feminist power, this was the same old phallic nonsense with white pussy at the center. And many of us watching were not simply unmoved—we were outraged.

Perhaps it is a sign of a collective feeling of powerlessness that many black, non-white, and white viewers of this film who were disturbed by the display of racism, sexism, and heterosexism (yes, it's possible to hire gay people, support AIDS projects, and still be biased in the direction of phallic patriarchal heterosexuality) in *Truth or Dare* have said so little. Sometimes it is difficult to find words to make a critique when we find ourselves attracted by some aspect of a performer's act and disturbed by others, or when a performer shows more interest in promoting progressive social causes than is customary. We may see that performer as above critique. Or we may feel our critique will in no way intervene on the worship of them as a cultural icon.

To say nothing, however, is to be complicit with the very forces of domination that make "blonde ambition" necessary to Madonna's success. Tragically, all that is transgressive and potentially empowering to feminist women and men about Madonna's work may be undermined by all that it contains that is reactionary and in no way unconventional or new. It is often the conservative elements in her work converging with the *status quo* that has the most powerful impact. For example: Given the rampant homophobia in this society and the concomitant heterosexist voyeuristic obsession with gay lifestyles, to what extent does Madonna progressively seek to challenge this if she insists on primarily representing gays as in some way emotionally handicapped or defective? Or when Madonna responds to the critique that she exploits gay men by cavalierly stating: "What does exploitation mean? . . . In a revolution, some people have to get hurt. To get people to change, you have to turn the table over. Some dishes get broken."

I can only say this doesn't sound like liberation to me. Perhaps when Madonna explores those memories of her white working-class childhood in a troubled family in a way that enables her to understand intimately the politics of exploitation, domination, and submission, she will have a deeper connection with oppositional black culture. If and when this radical critical self-interrogation takes place, she will have the power to create new and different cultural productions, work that will be truly transgressive—acts of resistance that transform rather than simply seduce.

30

AFRICAN AMERICANS ACCORDING TO TV NEWS

Robert M. Entman

While journalists strive to portray the news objectively (or at least fairly), it is no secret that constructing the news requires subjective judgments. Limited in resources and time, under great competitive pressure, TV news organizations in particular must select, simplify and organize the day's events into a meaningful and visually compelling narrative.

My research suggests a disturbing by-product of television's news-making processes. The choices TV journalists make appear to feed racial stereotypes, encouraging white hostility and fear of African Americans. TV news, especially local news, paints a picture of blacks as violent and threatening toward whites, self-interested and demanding toward the body politic—continually causing problems for the law-abiding, tax-paying majority.

We have all heard that sensationalism and entertainment values are on the rise in TV news. My studies indicate these trends aren't simply professional embarrassments and frustrations for journalists. They may also be making urban America less governable, deepening the chasm of misunderstanding and distrust between blacks and whites.

Scholars believe that people process information by using stored categories called schemas. Schemas are like mental filing cabinets that allow the individual to group like objects together in the mind. By assimilating new data with what's already stored in a schema, individuals interpret and make sense of the bits and pieces of new information they encounter.

But this mental organizational system can create the inaccurate beliefs and negative emotions that underpin prejudiced thinking: stereotypes. If the new information an individual keeps encountering fits the negative categories, prejudiced thinking can develop and grow.

Despite considerable progress, white Americans still exhibit a high degree of racial prejudice. For example, in the 1992 National Election Study (the authoritative academic public opinion survey from the University of Michigan), 57.4 percent of white respondents rated blacks as lazier than whites; 66 percent of whites rated blacks as more violence-prone; 49.4 percent of whites said blacks were less intelligent. Since there is a demonstrated tendency for whites to misrepresent their true racial feelings (it is socially undesirable to express overt anti-black bigotry to strangers such as survey interviewers), these data probably understate the degree of racial stereotyping. It seems reasonable to assume at least half the white audience is bigoted and susceptible to having their negative stereotypes confirmed, deepened and activated by TV news.

A series of scholarly studies on images of blacks in TV news that I have conducted suggests that newsroom procedures and definitions of news combine with selected aspects of the real world to encourage negative stereotypes about blacks. My research focuses mainly on local Chicago news, but other work indicates similar patterns elsewhere, including that of Erna Smith at San Francisco State University on coverage of the Los Angeles riots, and Kathleen Hall Jamieson at the University of Pennsylvania on local news in several urban markets. Network news differs as a genre from typical local newscasts, but some images of African Americans presented by the networks appear equally problematic. The damage comes especially from reporting on crime and violence, politics and poverty.

Research reveals that for the three dominant network affiliates in Chicago, eight or nine minutes out of about 14 given to news on an average half-hour broadcast in late 1993 and early 1994 concerned the threat of violence to humans. A steady drumbeat of frightening information dominates local news. And there's a racial skew to this scary stuff. For example, black defendants were more likely to be shown in still photos or mug shots, with no name appearing on the screen. White defendants, on the other hand, were more frequently named, and were represented through a variety of visual images, particularly, still photos and motion video. Such subtle visual differences may contribute to white perceptions of blacks as an undifferentiated group, while whites, named and portrayed in more detail, retain individual identities.

At the same time, blacks are significantly more likely to appear in the physical custody of police officials than are whites. The symbolic message is that, even when accused of similar crimes, blacks are more dangerous than whites. A negative and emotional stereotype may be unconsciously reinforced by whites' year-in, year-out exposure to this pattern of images.

The basic scholarly understanding of prejudiced thinking is that people from the dominant "in group" (whites) perceive members of the disliked "outgroup" (blacks) as homogeneous, and blanket them with negative associations. The key element of anti-black racism is whites' tendency to lump all or most blacks together as possessing undesirable traits.

Finally, the research showed that local TV news was far more likely to depict whites than minorities in an official law enforcement capacity, or in unofficial "helper" or "good Samaritan" roles. In my latest research, about 12 white law enforcers were shown for every black one, a ratio that underrepresents the true proportion of blacks in metropolitan Chicago police departments. As for helpers, the local news sample included 450 minutes devoted to showing white samaritans, 33 minutes to stories depicting black samaritans. The overall image of crime and violence from local news is one in which minorities, especially blacks, play a heavy role in causing violence but contribute disproportionately little toward helping society cope with it.

Additional analysis probed the image of blacks in political news, and findings were no more positive. Direct quotes (sound bites) from black activists, politicians or officials made them appear much more selfish and demanding than their white counterparts. In one study, some 33 percent of all assertions made by blacks endorsing or criticizing a government policy demanded attention to the black community. Whites explicitly promoted their ethnic group interests only 5 percent of the time. Indeed, white leaders were shown more often explicitly defending black political interests than openly advancing their own group's self-interests.

This image of black politics is not wholly a creation of journalists. It reflects real characteristics of the political system. Having been shut out of the power structure for so long, African-American leaders may indeed speak up largely for black interests. But it is highly unlikely that white political actors are as purely civic-minded as they appear. Since white politicians already dominate, they do not have to use an overt rhetoric of white power. To protect the status quo and their group's position in it, they need only speak of the public interest or nonracial values such as meritocracy or low taxes.

In theory, the depictions of black demands could be offering a powerful platform for African Americans. But academic theories of modern American racism suggest a boomerang effect: White audiences may infer that blacks seek a lot from government, receive quite a bit of support from whites, but fail to return the favor by supporting policy beneficial to whites. Moreover, the presentation of black spokespersons often includes snippets of loud, angry or emotional rhetoric: The televisual sound bite predominates over the calm analysis and justification of the black community's legitimate grievances.

Negative images of blacks in politics are not restricted to local TV news. In one year of network news coverage, more than one-third of the stories mentioning black leaders included an accusation that the leader committed a crime. Here again, the news reflects some aspects of reality—there are few blacks in top federal leadership positions that are automatically newsworthy. Thus, black leaders receive prolonged media attention only when they are involved in some kind of crime or controversy. The result is a comparatively more positive picture of white leadership in network news.

Consider reporting on Washington Mayor Marion Barry. In the year sampled, Barry was the second most commonly mentioned black figure (Clarence Thomas was number one). The coverage of Barry's drug arrest accurately reflected the experience of a scurrilous politician who happened to be black. But there are hundreds of effective, conscientious black mayors toiling around the United States who together attained only a fraction of the network visibility accorded Barry. That the Barry stories comprised a high proportion of network images of black politicians is due to news standards that emphasize unusual controversy and drama—to the extraordinary videotape showing Barry committing apparent crimes—not to a reality that the typical black mayor uses drugs and consorts with shady characters. Nonetheless, given how prejudiced people process information, we can predict that the accurate but frequent and sensational reports of Barry's crimes, arrest and conviction promoted inaccurate stereotypes among many whites.

Beyond its active contribution to stereotyping, TV news may be having deleterious effects on black-white relations through omission and indirection in covering poverty. Television news seldom addresses poverty and its causes explicitly. Rather, TV makes implicit arguments about poverty by showing images of its symptoms. For example, stories on violent crime, drug abuse and gangs contain visual images of urban blight and stereotyped references to geographic locations that provide implicit links to poverty. One story included in the research portrayed the murder of a little girl, allegedly by her mother. Viewers learned the crime was committed in an "abandoned building" in a "drug-infested neighborhood" by somebody with a history of mental illness. The report associated one poverty symptom—violent crime—with others—drug abuse, mental illness—and visually linked them to poverty by showing pictures of blighted buildings and identifying the neighborhood as Chicago's South Side, widely known for its high concentration of poor residents.

The visual and verbal images of poverty symptoms suggest poverty is overwhelmingly concentrated among blacks, so much so that merely showing black persons appears to be a TV code for the involvement of poor people in the news event. The connection between "black" and "poor" exists even though poverty is not the lot of most black persons, and more whites are poor than black. The concepts of "black person" and "poverty" are so thoroughly intertwined in television news that the white public's perceptions of poverty appear difficult to disentangle from their thinking about African Americans. (A national survey by Mark Peffley of the University of Kentucky and his colleagues supports this notion.) That connection promotes a stereotyped and inaccurate understanding of the economic and social diversity of the African-American community, a misapprehension that itself could feed bigotry and lower support among whites for public policy that tackles poverty.

Because television news offers only implicit information about the relationship between poverty, race and crime, viewers are left with no coherent explanation of poverty issues. Only indirectly does TV news suggest, for example, that racial discrimination might have something to do with poverty, which in turn may help explain all that crime. Beyond the common visual links, there is little in the news to draw poverty symptoms together as interrelated causes and consequences that are not merely the individual doing of the poor. Even the non-racist white audience receives few messages that might allow them to reconcile their legitimate self-interest in low taxes and personal safety with what might be called their moral self-interest, their desire to alleviate the human suffering of the poor.

But the inattention to poverty as a policy problem is hardly TV's fault alone. Television news is locked in a self-reinforcing political climate with politicians who see few votes to be gained in speaking sympathetically about the poor. The lack of serious political rhetoric about poverty causes a dearth in TV coverage of poverty

as a policy issue—the public fails to see poverty as a pressing matter—and that discourages politicians still more from targeting poverty.

Determining whether this pattern of images and gaps actually affects audiences is a difficult proposition, but scientific surveys designed to measure racist attitudes suggest a connection between exposure to television news and the extent of anti-black racism in the public. While these findings are far from definitive, they do indicate that the images of blacks in the news contribute to the perpetuation of anti-black stereotypes. A survey of Chicago-area residents found that whites who rely on television for their news were more likely than those who rely on print or radio to deny that blacks are discriminated against. Similarly, heavy television viewers were more likely than light viewers to stereotype blacks as being unskilled and lazy. (This analysis controlled for education and other demographic traits.)

The absence of a visual dimension to radio news and the infrequent use of photographs in print stories involving blacks means that for these media, the race of individuals in stories is seldom known. But television's visuals tend to make race an explicit part of the news text. A lack of much exposure to print news may prevent opportunities to have stereotypes challenged. At the same time, those with less racial sympathy may be more willing to put up with the unflattering images of blacks that permeate TV news.

Racial stereotypes in the news pose a difficult problem for television journalists. Reporters do not construct messages from scratch. The images that dominate local and network TV news are grounded in elements of reality. Young black males are statistically more likely to commit violent crime than young white males; black leaders may more often express demands for government services than white leaders whose constituents are on average better off; most American cities do have poverty-ridden black neighborhoods. Therefore, one could argue, the news merely reflects unfortunate reality. But for the media to achieve a comprehensive accuracy in portraying any reality is impossible. The news can offer only partial, selective representations. While individual stories about blacks may accurately reflect a particular slice of reality, they may over time construct a distorted impression in the minds of white (and black) audience members.

And this is the crux of the problem TV journalists face: Is their responsibility limited to creating an accurate verbal and visual record in each individual news text, or does it include stimulating an accurate mental representation in the audience's mind? Presumably helping the audience understand truth is what justifies professional news standards and practices. Textual accuracy for its own sake seems an unlikely candidate for journalism's ultimate goal.

Television news is uniquely poised to reduce racial stereotyping. But to do so, TV journalists must realize that their words and images, however accurate on a story-by-story basis, accumulate over time to exacerbate racial tensions. A deliberate choice to introduce more complexity and variety in images of African Americans could, on balance, make TV news less likely to arouse white antagonism rooted in misunderstanding and stereotype—while offering a more comprehensively accurate depiction of African-American life.

Innovations in news could include an increase in serious reporting on policy issues which, unlike single violent episodes that directly affect only a few people, speak to almost everyone in the audience. This is not to gainsay the importance of reporting on violence, or to minimize the suffering it

causes. But mere cataloging of the day's unfortunate victims, uncontrollable disasters, and scary criminals appears to inflame more than inform the public. Other changes might include less frequently revealing the ethnicity of accused perpetrators through pictures; minimizing the use of frightening images (wounded people on stretchers, flashing lights of police cars, flames); and reordering priorities so that news of individual violent incidents receive less news time and prominence.

We must acknowledge, however, that actions taken to ameliorate one false impression could heighten another. For example, reducing images of black crime and victimization could instill among whites an unwarranted sense of progress in the inner city. Similarly, deliberate use of successful black experts as sources, while perhaps counterbalancing all the criminals and victims, could simultaneously feed the complacency of whites who insist racial discrimination has ceased. And correcting the implication that blacks are more demanding of government responsiveness than whites could lead to airtime for safe, white-anointed black leaders who enjoy slim legitimacy in the African-American community.

While there is no easy way out of such dilemmas, they point to the familiar need for context. By routinely contextualizing, TV news could reveal the continued prevalence of discrimination, illuminate structural forces that make crime attractive in the ghetto, and explain why so many black political leaders adopt a confrontational style. But complex, nuanced context is difficult for daily TV news to convey. Perhaps the first step toward improving accuracy and social responsibility in the portrayal of blacks on television news is acknowledging these difficulties.

31

DISTORTED REALITY
Hispanic Characters in TV Entertainment

S. Robert Lichter • *Daniel R. Amundson*

The Past as Prologue

It takes diff'rent strokes to move the world.
—"Diff'rent Strokes" Theme Song

When Kingfish uttered his last "Holy Mackerel, Andy!" in 1953, it marked the end of television's most controversial depiction of blacks. Ironically, the departure of "Amos 'n' Andy" also signaled the end of a brief period of ethnic diversity that would not reappear in prime time for two decades. Several of the earliest family sitcoms were transplanted radio shows set in America's black or white ethnic subcultures. "The Goldbergs" followed the lives of a Jewish immigrant family in New York for twenty years on radio before switching to the new medium in 1949. It featured Gertrude Berg as Molly Goldberg, everyone's favorite Jewish mother. An even more successful series that premiered the same year was "Mama," which chronicled a Norwegian immigrant family in turn-of-the-century San Francisco. Theme music by Grieg added to the "ethnic" atmosphere, as did accents that made Aunt "Yenny" into a popular character. These white ethnic shows were soon joined by the all-black "Amos 'n' Andy" as well as

"Beulah," which starred the black maid of a white middle-class family.

All these shows relied on stereotypical dialogue and behavior for much of their humor. But social standards were changing, and the new medium created its own demands and perceptions. For example, not only Amos and Andy but even Beulah had been portrayed on radio by white males. When the popular radio show "Life with Luigi" made the switch to TV in 1952, Italian American groups protested its stereotyped portrayal of Italian immigrants. Black groups were equally outraged over "Amos 'n' Andy," which had been an institution on radio since 1929. As the program evolved, it centered on the schemes of George "Kingfish" Stevens, who combined the soul of Sgt. Bilko with the fate of Ralph Kramden. A small-time con man with big plans that never panned out, he became an immensely popular, lovable loser. His schemes usually pulled in the ingenuous cabbie Andy and the slow-moving janitor Lightnin'.

From Kingfish's fractured syntax ("I'se regusted") to Lightnin's shuffle and falsetto "yazzuh," the series drew on overtly racial stereotypes. The NAACP blasted the portrayal of blacks as "inferior, lazy, dumb, and dishonest," and urged a boycott of Blatz beer, the sponsor. The pressure from civil rights groups probably helped bring the series to a premature end, since it attracted sizeable audiences throughout its two year run.

• • •

S. Robert Lichter and Daniel R. Amundson, "Distorted Reality" from *Latin Looks*, edited by Clara Rodriguez, pp. 57–72. Copyright 1997 by WestviewPress. Reprinted by permission of WestviewPress.

While controversy surrounded "Amos and Andy," little debate attended television's earliest and most high profile Latino portrayal. From 1950 through 1956, Ziv productions sold 156 episodes of "The Cisco Kid" in syndication to individual stations across the country. Resplendent in his heavily embroidered black costume, Cisco rode across the southwest righting wrongs and rescuing damsels in distress. He was accompanied by his portly sidekick, Pancho, who served as a comic foil. Pancho was loyal and brave, but his English was every bit as fractured as the Kingfish's. Further, although Cisco and Pancho were positive and even heroic characters, they were often outnumbered by evil and frequently criminal Latino adversaries. In its simplistic presentation that combined positive and negative ethnic stereotypes, "Cisco" set the tone for the "Zorro" series that would follow it on ABC from 1957 through 1959. Thus, these early high-profile representations of Latinos proved a mixed bag, as television's conventions of the day were applied to both network and syndicated fare.

The All-White World

"Cisco" and "Zorro," which were aimed at children, outlasted the first generation of ethnic sitcoms for general audiences. By the 1954 season "Mama" was the only survivor of this once-thriving genre. Thus, by the time our study period began, TV's first era of ethnic humor had already come and gone. The urban ethnic sitcoms were replaced by homogeneous suburban settings. There was nothing Irish about the life of Chester Riley, nothing Scandinavian about Jim and Margaret Anderson. The new family shows were all-American, which meant vaguely northern European and carefully noncontroversial. The few remaining eth-

nics were mostly relegated to minor roles or single episodes.

Just how homogeneous was this electronic neighborhood? From 1955 through 1964, our coders could identify only one character in ten as anything other than northern European on the basis of name, language, or appearance. Such a small slice of the pie got cut up very quickly, and many groups got only crumbs. Just one character in fifty was Hispanic, fewer than one in a hundred was Asian, and only one in two hundred was black.

. . .

Hispanics had virtually no starring roles. For most Hispanic characters, life consisted of lounging in the dusty square of a sleepy Latin town, waiting for the stars to come on stage. Occasionally Hispanics would show up as outlaws in the Old West, but even then mostly as members of someone else's gang. Their comic roles were epitomized by Pepino Garcia, a farmhand for "The Real McCoys," who functioned mainly as a target of Grandpa Amos McCoy's tirades. Pepino and "The Real McCoys" were replaced in 1963 by Jose Jimenez in the "Bill Dana Show."

Like their black colleagues, a few stars stood out in a sea of marginal and insignificant roles. A notable exception was Cuban band leader Ricky Ricardo in "I Love Lucy," played by Desi Arnaz. As the co-star of one of the most popular shows on TV (and co-owner of Desilu Productions, along with wife Lucille Ball), Arnaz was a prominent figure in Hollywood. When exasperated by Lucy's schemes and misadventures, Ricky added a comic touch with displays of "Latin" temper and lapses into Spanish. "I Love Lucy" made its mark on television comedy and TV production in general, but it did little for Hispanic characters. The same could be said of another early show with a Hispanic setting, which nonetheless cast

Anglos in the major roles. Guy Williams played Don Diego, alias Zorro, the masked champion of the poor and oppressed in old Los Angeles. Their oppressors were evil, greedy Spanish governors and landowners. In one episode Annette Funicello, fresh from the Mickey Mouse Club, showed up as the singing senorita Anita Cabrillo. Despite its "Hispanic" characters, the show was not a generous portrayal of either the people or the culture.

The departure of "Amos and Andy" and "Beulah" all but eliminated black stars. Jack Benny's valet Rochester was one of the few major roles still held by a black in the late 1950s. Black characters didn't even show up in the backgrounds of early shows. Urban settings might feature a black delivery man, porter, or waiter, but black professionals and businessmen were virtually nonexistent. Some westerns like "Rawhide" and "Have Gun, Will Travel" presented a few black cowboys riding the range with their white counterparts. Aside from such occasional and insignificant roles, black characters were simply not a part of the early prime time world.

The Return of Race

In the mid-1960s, the portrayal of ethnic and racial minorities underwent major changes. The proportion of non–northern European roles doubled over the next decade. Before 1965, all racial and ethnic groups to the south or east of England, France, and Germany had scrambled for the one role in ten available to them. Now nonwhite characters alone could count on better than one role in ten. From the first to the second decade in our study [1955–1975], the proportion of English characters was cut in half, while Hispanics became half again as numerous and the proportion of Asians doubled.

Blacks were the biggest winners, gaining a dramatic fourteen-fold increase in what had been virtually an all-white landscape.

The invisibility of Hispanics during this period remained more than metaphorical. They were simply not part of television's new ethnic "relevance." Latinos had few continuing prime time roles of any sort during the late 1960s, and certainly no major star parts like Bill Cosby's Alexander Scott. In fact, most Latinos who were cast during this period showed up in episodes of international espionage series that used Central and South American locales. "I Spy" had many episodes set in Mexico, bringing the agents into contact with some positive and many more negative Hispanic characters. In other espionage shows, such as "Mission Impossible," the action often centered on a fictitious Central American country, which was inevitably run by a jack-booted junta that could only be stopped by the enlightened Anglo-led team from north of the border.

One of the few exceptions to this pattern was the western "High Chaparral." Rancher John Cannon had settled in the Arizona territory to found a cattle empire. When his first wife was killed by Apaches, John married Victoria Montoya, the daughter of a wealthy Mexican rancher. The marriage was as much a business move as a romance, since it united the two families. Once tied by marriage, Don Montoya helped John build his herds and produce good breeding stock. Together the two families fought off Apaches and other marauders. Culture clashes between the two families occurred, but usually as a minor part of the plot. Unlike most Mexicans shown in previous westerns, the Montoyas were rich, powerful, sophisticated, and benevolent. In most episodes, Victoria attempted to civilize her more rustic husband and establish a proper home on the range. To be sure, this series still presented semiliterate Hispanic ranch-hands, but these portrayals were overshadowed by the Montoyas.

The other exception was the short-lived social relevancy series "Man and the City." This series presented more contemporary problems of Latinos in an unnamed southwestern city. The show was notable for frequently asserting the dignity and rights of Latinos. For example, in a 1971 segment, a cop is killed in the city's barrio. The police department pulls out all the stops to catch the killers, imposing a curfew and holding suspects incommunicado without legal counsel. All the suspects are Hispanics from the barrio who have little connection to the case. The mayor is forced to intervene and remind the police chief that the city has laws. He demands that all suspects, including minority groups, be given their full rights. The police are reluctant, believing this will impede their investigation. The mayor insists and the police obey his order. They eventually capture a key suspect who helps them catch the killers. There is no indication that racial tensions in the city have ended, merely that one violent episode is over. The groups involved have not learned to like each other; nor are they presented as peacefully coexisting. The point here is that all people have rights and deserve to be treated with dignity and equality. This seems to be the only series that attempted to derive socially relevant plotlines from the barrio.

Not only did the proportion of black characters jump to 7 percent between 1965 and 1975, but the range and quality of roles expanded even more dramatically. In adventure series like "I Spy" and "Mission: Impossible," blacks moved into their first starring roles in over a decade. Not only were these roles more prominent, they offered a new style of character. Alexander Scott of "I Spy" and Barney Collier of "Mission: Impossible" were competent, educated professionals. These men were highly successful agents whose racial backgrounds were clearly secondary to their bravery and skill. They opened the way for blacks to appear in roles that did not require the actor to be black. There was no more use of poor English, servile shuffling, or popeyed double takes for comic effect. Instead, Collier was presented as an electronics expert and Scott as a multilingual Rhodes Scholar.

The new visibility of blacks quickly moved beyond the secret agent genre. In 1968 the first of television's relevance series managed to convert a negative stereotype into a positive one by casting a young black rebel as a member of "The Mod Squad." Linc Hayes' militant credentials included an afro haircut, aviator sunglasses, and an arrest during the Watts riots. Not to worry, though. This brooding black rebel was working with the good guys on the L.A.P.D.'s undercover "youth squad," where the dirty dozen met the counterculture every Tuesday at 7:30.

While ABC was coopting the Black Panthers into the establishment, NBC looked to the black middle class for "Julia," the first black-oriented sitcom in fifteen years. As a dedicated nurse and loving mother in an integrated world, the Julia Baker character looked ahead to "The Cosby Show" rather than backward to "Amos 'n' Andy." She certainly had more in common with Claire Huxtable than with Kingfish's nagging wife, Sapphire. Unfortunately, she also lacked the vitality and wit of either Sapphire or future mother figures who would be more firmly rooted in black culture, like "Good Times" Florida Evans.

"Julia" suffered from the dullness of being a prestige series, just as "The Mod Squad" labored under the hype that attended the relevance series. What they had in common with better-written shows like "I Spy" and "Mission Impossible" was a tendency to replace the old negative black stereotypes with new positive ones. The authors of

Watching TV wrote with a touch of hyperbole, "They were no longer bumbling, easygoing, po' folk like Beulah, but rather articulate neo-philosophers just descended from Olympus, though still spouting streetwise jargon."[1] Having discovered that blacks didn't have to be cast as valets and janitors, white writers turned them into James Bonds and Mary Tyler Moores. Thus, as blacks suddenly began to appear on the tube after a decade's absence, they remained invisible in Ralph Ellison's sense. The frantic search for positive characters smothered individuality with good intentions.

Let a Hundred Flowers Bloom

In the early 1970s TV began to broadcast a different message about minorities. The unlikely agent of change was an equal opportunity bigot named Archie Bunker, who excoriated "spics," "jungle bunnies," "chinks," "yids," and every other minority that ever commanded an epithet. When "All in the Family" became the top-rated show within five months of its 1971 premiere, it attracted a barrage of criticism for making the tube safe for ethnic slurs. The producer of public television's "Black Journal" found it "shocking and racist."[2] Laura Hobson, who wrote "Gentlemen's Agreement," an attack on anti-Semitism, decried its attempt to sanitize bigotry, "to clean it up, deodorize it, make millions of people more comfy about indulging in it."[3] Of course, the point of the show was to poke fun at Archie and all he stood for, as the script and laugh track tried to make clear.

Norman Lear's strategy was to educate audiences by entertaining them instead of preaching at them. So he created a kind of politicized Ralph Kramden, whom audiences could like in spite of his reactionary views, not because of them. He intended that the contrast between Archie's basic de-

cency and his unattractive rantings would prod viewers to reexamine the retrograde ideas they permitted themselves. As Lear put it, the show "holds up a mirror to our prejudices. . . . We laugh now, swallowing just the littlest bit of truth about ourselves, and it sits there for the unconscious to toss about later."[4] As a tool for improving race relations, this approach may have been too subtle for its own good. Several studies suggest that liberals watched the show to confirm their disdain for Archie's views, while conservatives identified with him despite his creator's best intentions.[5] But another legacy of the program was to pioneer a more topical and (by television's standards) realistic portrayal of ethnic relations.

An immediate consequence of "All in the Family" was to introduce the first sitcoms populated by black families since "Amos 'n' Andy." A year after demonstrating the audience appeal of a white working class milieu not portrayed successfully since "The Honeymooners," Lear and his partner Bud Yorkin transferred the setting to a black ghetto in "Sanford and Son." Unlike the integrated middle class world of TV blacks in the late 1960s, "Sanford and Son" revolved around the foibles of a junk dealer in a poor black section of Los Angeles. "Sanford" proved so popular that it soon trailed only "All in the Family" in the Nielsen ratings.

Meanwhile, in an irony Archie would not have appreciated, "All in the Family" spawned not one but two additional black family sitcoms. "The Jeffersons" featured Archie's one-time neighbor George Jefferson as an upwardly mobile businessman whose snobbishness and inverted racism made him almost a black Archie Bunker. "Good Times" was actually a second-generation spinoff. When Archie's liberal nemesis Maude got her own show in 1972, the scriptwriters gave her a quick-witted and tart-tongued black maid named Florida Evans. Two years later the popular Florida got her own show as the matriarch of a family living in a Chicago housing project. This series developed the "Sanford" technique of finding sometimes bitter humor among lower status characters trying to cope with life in the ghetto while looking for a way out of it. Scripts featured ward heelers, loan sharks, abused children, and other facets of life on the edge, in sharp contrast to the comfortable middle class world of "Julia" or the glamorous and exotic locales of "I Spy."

By this time, other producers, stimulated by Norman Lear's enormous success, were providing sitcoms that drew their characters from minority settings. "What's Happening!!" followed the adventures of three big city high school kids. "Diff'rent Strokes" created an unlikely "accidental family" in which a wealthy white man raised two black kids from Harlem in his Park Avenue apartment, without any serious clash of cultures. This trend almost never extended from the ghetto to the barrio. The one great exception was "Chico and the Man," a generation-gap sitcom that paired an ebullient young Mexican American with an aging Bunkerish Anglo garage owner. This odd couple clicked with audiences, but the show's success was cut short by the suicide of comedian Freddy Prinze (Chico) in 1977.

Like the black sitcoms, "Chico" used minority culture as a spark to enliven a middle class white world that seemed bland or enervated by comparison. Minority characters of the early 1970s prided themselves not on their similarity to mainstream culture, but on their differences from it. Assimilated characters like Alexander Scott, Barney Collier, and Julia Baker gave way to the racial pride of George Jefferson, Fred of "Sanford and Son," and Rooster on "Starsky and Hutch." Where would Fred Sanford or George Jefferson be without their jive talk and street slang? Language was just one way of stressing the differences between racial and ethnic groups.

Minority characters also picked up flaws as they took on more complete roles. Fred Sanford was domineering and could appear foolish. George Jefferson could be as stubborn and narrow-minded as his one-time next-door neighbor. By badgering the interracial couple living upstairs and labelling their daughter a "zebra," he left no doubt about his views. But the thrust of the ethnic sitcom was not to ridicule minority cultures. Instead, racial and ethnic backgrounds were used as an educational tool. The religious, cultural, and other traditions that differentiate minorities from the mainstream were now treated as beneficial rather than problematic. Removed from the confines of the melting pot, these groups offered new approaches to old problems. Television charged them with the task of teaching new ways to the often obstinate world around them. Blacks and Hispanics participated in this era of racial and cultural re-education. It was Chico Rodriguez who taught Ed Brown to relax and be more tolerant on "Chico and the Man." Benson, the sharp-tongued butler, tried to maintain order amidst the chaos of "Soap," while steering his employers onto the right track. In one episode he even saved young Billy from the clutches of a religious cult.

The most spectacularly successful effort to combine education with entertainment was a hybrid of the miniseries and "big event" genres. Indeed, "Roots" became the biggest event in television history. This adaptation of Alex Haley's best-selling novel traced the history of four generations of a black family in America, beginning with Kunta Kinte, an African tribesman sold into slavery. It ran for eight consecutive nights in January 1977. When it was over, 130 million Americans had tuned in, including 80 million who viewed the final episode. Seven of the eight episodes ranked among the all-time top ten at that point in television's history. "Roots" created a kind of national town meeting comparable to the televised moon landing or the aftermath of President Kennedy's assassination. It was blamed for several racial disturbances but credited for stimulating a productive national debate on the history of American race relations.

While blacks could look to the high-profile presentation of African American history presented by "Roots," there was no similar presentation of Hispanic history. If Anglos relied exclusively on Hollywood for information on Latino contributions to American history, their knowledge would extend little further than John Wayne's defense of "The Alamo" against the Mexican "invaders." Illustrations of Latino culture were equally rare. In fact, the only high-profile Hispanic character during this period was Chico Rodriguez. Despite its popularity, "Chico and the Man" was not known as a series that explored Latino culture or Hispanic contributions to American history and culture.

Despite occasional failures, ethnic comedies became the hottest new programming trend of the 1970s. "All in the Family" was the top-rated show for an unprecedented five straight seasons, surpassing previous megahits "I Love Lucy" and "Gunsmoke." Other top twenty regulars included "Sanford and Son," "The Jeffersons," black comic Flip Wilson's variety show, and "Chico and the Man." The ethnic wave crested during the 1974–75 season, when a remarkable six of the seven top-rated shows were ethnic sitcoms—"All in the Family," "Sanford," "Chico," "Jeffersons," "Rhoda," and "Good Times."

If the new decade offered an unaccustomed array of new roles for minorities, it contained some traps as well. Ethnic characters gained more prominent and desirable roles, but also more unflattering ones. Bumblers, buffoons, and bimbos took their place alongside heroes and sages. For example, Vinnie Barbarino and Juan Epstein were two of the uneducated underachievers on "Welcome Back Kotter." Barbarino's Italian heritage added ethnic color to his machismo

image, while Epstein's ethnic background was contrived for comic effect. He was presented as Buchanan High School's only Puerto Rican Jew. "Good Times" created some negative black characters, such as insensitive building supervisors and abusive politicians. In "What's Happening," the Thomas family made do without their con man father after he walked out on them. His occasional visits home were usually in search of money for some new scheme. A steady stream of minority characters began to show up as criminals in cop shows like "Kojak," "Baretta," and "Barney Miller."

"Barney Miller" also deserves note as one of the most multicultural shows of the time. In the 1975–76 season the squad room contained Polish detective Wojohowicz, Asian American Nick Yemana, African American Harris, and Puerto Rican Chano Amenguale. While Chano was far from perfect he appeared to be a capable officer and no more eccentric than his colleagues on the squad. In the next season Chano was replaced by Detective Baptista, who was a fiery Latina, but not as significant in the squad as Chano. These characters at least served to offset the Hispanic criminals they often arrested.

The late 1970s retained a mix of ethnic heroes and fools in some of the most popular shows of the day. But ethnic characters were beginning to lose their novelty. For instance, "CHiPs" ran from 1977 through 1983 and one of the starring characters was Officer Frank Poncherello. Even though Poncherello was played by the well-known Eric Estrada, Poncherello's Hispanic heritage was all but invisible. It no longer mattered in this series that one of the leads was a Latino. During the 1979 season, three dramatic series were launched with black leads, but none came close to the ratings necessary for renewal. "Paris" starred James Earl Jones as a supercop who ran the station house during the day and taught criminology at night. "The Lazarus Syndrome" featured Louis Gossett as the chief of cardiology in a large hospital. "Harris and Company" focused on the problems of a single parent raising a family. The twist was that this black family was held together not by a matriarch but a middle-aged widower. Thus, Hollywood was at least trying to create some positive role models for black males. But no such efforts extended to Latinos. There were no network series built around a Latino family, Hispanic high school kids, or any of the other patterns found in sitcoms featuring blacks. It would be several years before the short-lived ABC series "Condo" would prominently cast Latinos as middle class characters.

Overall, the 1980s offered little that was new to racial or ethnic minority portrayals in the wake of TV's ethnic revival. These groups continued to be presented more or less as they were in the late 1970s. Despite the continuing presence of racial and ethnic diversity, however, racial themes were no longer in vogue. Integration was assumed as a backdrop, as the prime time world became less polarized. The age of pluralism had arrived, but the thrill was gone. The riots were over, the battles won, and characters got back to their other plot functions. Among these were crime and other wrongdoing. Comedies like "Taxi," "White Shadow," and "WKRP in Cincinnati" continued to present integrated casts, but ethnic characters in dramatic series were often on the dark side of the law.

Ironically, television's multicultural world of the 1980s provided an updated version of the stereotypical Hispanic banditos who populated the westerns thirty years earlier. In the fall of 1980, ABC's controversial sitcom "Soap" introduced a remake of Frito Bandito. Carlos "El Puerco" Valdez was a South American revolutionary playing a love interest of Jessica Tate. They had met when his band kidnapped her for ransom. This plan failed, but after things took a passionate turn, she became a benefactor of his revolution. "El Puerco" led a bumbling, low-budget revolution and he was not above taking time out to romance his new gringo benefactor. "El Puerco" was both Latin lover and bandito with a measure of Jerry Lewis buffoonishness thrown in. Thus, it was down this line that the Frito Bandito's sombrero had been passed—to a fatigue-wearing ne'er-do-well.

There were also more sinister turns in Latino portrayals. Crime shows like "Miami Vice," "Hill Street Blues," and "Hunter" presented Hispanic drug lords as a major nemesis. Trafficking in human misery made these characters rich enough to own cities and sometimes even small countries. They were among the nastiest criminals on TV in the 1980s. There were also petty Hispanic criminals in the slums of "Hill Street Blues" and "Cagney & Lacey." These small-time hoods, drug addicts, and pimps were less flamboyant than their big-league counterparts, but no less unsavory. Altogether, TV's latest crop of Hispanics included a cruel and vicious group of criminals.

"Miami Vice" was not only a source of criminal Hispanics—after all the squad was led by the enigmatic Lieutenant Martin Castillo and on the distaff side of the unit was detective Gina Navarro. However inconsistently, the show did attempt to show successful law-abiding Latinos mixed in with the criminal crop. For all of its flaws "Miami Vice" at least attempted to reflect the presence of Latinos in Miami. Contrast this attempt with more contemporary shows like "Baywatch," "Acapulco H.E.A.T.," and others that rarely if ever reference the Hispanic populations in their host cities.

There were occasional attempts to base shows on Hispanic casts, but all proved unsuccessful. In 1983 the Lear-wannabee sitcom "Condo" briefly pitted a bigoted WASP against his Latino next-door neighbors. The following season, the equally short-lived

"A.K.A. Pablo" dealt somewhat more seriously with ethnic questions. Focusing on struggling young comic Pablo Rivera and his extended family, the series wrestled with questions about ethnic humor and the preservation of Hispanic culture. Pablo made many jokes about his family and his Mexican American heritage in his nightclub act. This frequently offended his traditionalist parents, who expected him to treat his heritage more respectfully. Despite its brief run, this series was one of the few to deal explicitly with aspects of Latino culture.

A more mixed portrayal appeared in the 1987 series "I Married Dora." In this fractured fairy tale, Dora Calderon was the housekeeper for widower Peter Farrell and his family. When faced with deportation, Dora and Peter joined in a marriage of convenience. Like many television housekeepers before her, Dora was the voice of wisdom and compassion in the household, but her own illegal status gave her role an ambiguous twist. In 1988, a series called "Trial and Error" was based on Latino characters from the barrio in East Los Angeles. The show revolved around a free-wheeling entrepreneur who ran a souvenir T-shirt company and his upwardly mobile roommate, who was a newly minted lawyer. This series had a lighter touch with less attention to Hispanic culture, but it met with the same quick demise as its predecessors.

Both "A.K.A. Pablo" and "Trial and Error" sprang from the efforts of comedian Paul Rodriguez. It is not uncommon for bankable stars to get their own television series. This is particularly true for stand-up comics, who have taken their nightclub acts into successful series like "Roseanne," "Home Improvement," "Grace Under Fire," and "Seinfeld." This approach has proven to be a very important avenue onto the screen for blacks. Several exclusively black shows currently on the air are the result of the work of a bankable star. Among those who have followed in the footsteps of Bill Cosby are Keenan Ivory Wayans of "In Living Color," Martin Lawrence of "Martin," Mark Curry of "Hangin' with Mr. Cooper," and Charles Dutton of "Roc." Unfortunately, this approach has so far been a dead end for Latinos.

Blacks fared better in the 1980s, largely escaping the criminal portrayals of other minorities. When black characters did turn to crime, they were usually small-time criminals driven by desperation. There were even times when their criminal acts were presented as social commentary. For instance, in an episode of "Hill Street Blues," a black militant occupies a housing project and takes hostages. He threatens to kill them unless the city agrees to keep the project open and fix it up. The man is frustrated and angry that weeks of negotiating led to nothing. The city simply set a new closing date and moved on. Rage and desperation drive him to act and a tense standoff ensues. In the end, he is mistakenly shot by a police sniper. Everyone is shocked by his desperate act and his tragic death.

Meanwhile, TV turned out numerous positive black role models as diverse as "The Cosby Show's" Heathcliff Huxtable, Mary Jenkins of "227," Rico Tubbs on "Miami Vice," and Bobby Hill of "Hill Street Blues." These shows suggest the diversity of major roles that were at last becoming available to blacks. "227" and "Amen" continued the sharp-tongued tradition of 1970s sitcoms, without the abrasive or objectionable images that had brought criticism. Tubbs and Hill both carried on the tradition of "salt and pepper" law enforcement teams. Hill also represented the educative function of minorities by helping to wean his partner Renko, a southerner, away from residual racist tendencies.

Of course, "Cosby" was the biggest hit of all. This series further developed the low-key humanistic colorblind approach that Bill Cosby has popularized over two decades as

"I Spy's" Alexander Scott, high school teacher Chet Kincaid on "The Bill Cosby Show," and finally in a black version of "Father Knows Best." The enormous success of this venture led some critics to snipe at Cosby for playing black characters in white-face to maximize audience appeal. Black psychiatrist Alvin Pouissant, retained by the show to review scripts for racial authenticity, notes that the criticisms come from white reporters more often than black viewers: "Sometimes it seems they want the show to be 'culturally black' . . . and sometimes it seems they would be happier to see them cussing out white people, a sort of protest sitcom. Some seem to feel that because the family is middle class with no obvious racial problems, that constitutes a denial or dismissal of the black person."[6]

Compared to the plight of TV's Hispanics, debates over whether the Huxtables are divorced from the black experience may seem a luxury, a sign that a one-time outgroup has reached a mature phase in its relationship with the Hollywood community. In 1979 organized opposition even persuaded Norman Lear to withdraw a new comedy series at the last minute. "Mister Dugan," a sitcom about a black congressman, was scheduled to premier on CBS a week after Lear arranged a special screening for the Congressional Black Caucus. The screening was a disaster, with Congressman Mickey Leland calling the lead character "a reversion to the Steppin' Fetchit syndrome."

Lear promptly pulled the show from the schedule. He remarked at the time, "We have a high social conscience, and we want to get the story right. We do not favor the short-term gain over the long-term public interest. Dropping the show was an exercise in that commitment."[7] This was an extraordinary episode in a business often excoriated for caring only about the bottom line. When the medium's most successful producer is willing to withdraw a series on the eve of its broadcast, writing off a $700,000 investment, it shows the power of social commitment in television. The only question is the strength and direction of that commitment.

Moreover, such criticism is belied by the top ten ratings obtained by such diverse families as the Sanfords, Jeffersons, and Evans, not to mention Kunta Kinte and his kin. The success of upper and lower class, matriarchal and patriarchal black family series suggests that television has gone beyond using black characters as a sign of racial diversity. It has begun to show diversity within the black community as well, at last recognizing both the cultural distinctiveness and the universal humanity of this group of Americans. Unfortunately, Hispanics have never played a significant role in television's debate over race relations. When television has explored discrimination, prejudice, or the appropriateness of inter-racial relationships, it has almost always staged them as a black versus white issue. Whatever racial tensions exist between Latinos and other groups in American society, they have very rarely made it to the small screen.

A Tale of Two Minorities

Black representation continued to increase during the 1990s, as the number of shows with all-black or mostly black casts jumped. Driven largely by the Fox network's quest for new audiences and trademark shows, these new series drew heavily on the struttin' and jivin' characters of the 1970s. Both the 1992 and 1993 seasons featured ten such series, including hits like "Hangin' with Mr. Cooper," "Family Matters," "Martin," and "Fresh Prince of Bel Air." Intense debate has ensued over the quality of these roles and portrayals, which critics disparage as latter-day minstrel show stereotypes. However, such complaints have not diminished the popularity of these shows, particularly among black audiences.

Despite continuing controversy, television's portrayal of blacks is in many ways more diverse and substantive than ever before. For instance, on Monday nights viewers could contrast the wealthy Banks family on "Fresh Prince of Bel Air" with the working class Cumberbatches in "704 Hauser Street." On Tuesday, they could see the struggles of a single mother in "South Central," followed by the stable two-parent extended family in "Roc." Then there were the Winslows, a comfortably middle class black family that was a cornerstone of Friday night viewing for years. In addition there were numerous black characters in integrated series such as "L.A. Law," "Law & Order," "Evening Shade," "Love & War," "NYPD Blue," "In the Heat of the Night," and "seaQuest DSV." African Americans were seen as lawyers, judges, police captains, and a host of other roles in these shows.

While shows that were exclusively or mainly about blacks comprised about one eighth of the prime time schedule in 1992–93, only one series in the previous three seasons was based on a Latino family or character. Moreover, that series—the short-lived "Frannie's Turn"—mainly used Hispanic traditions as a comic foil for feminist putdowns. This series revolved around the marriage of a Cuban emigré named Joseph Escobar and his wife, Frannie, an Anglo of unclear ethnic origins. Whatever ethnic and cultural differences may have existed between them were rarely played upon, since most of the plots dealt with Frannie's quest for equality. However, when aspects of heritage did come up, they frequently reflected poorly on Latinos. For instance, the first episode dealt with Frannie's discovery that Joseph has been sending money to a Cuban liberation movement while telling her to cut the household budget. At one point in the ensuing argument,

she suggests sarcastically, "Who knows, maybe they'll send you the Bay of Pigs decoder ring." In the few episodes that aired, the couple's children seemed oblivious to their heritage, and no effort was made to teach them about their father's culture. Overall, this series made no greater use of ethnicity than "I Love Lucy" did almost forty years earlier.

Otherwise, Latino characters remained largely supporting players or background figures in the prime time schedule. The highest profile in 1992–93 was enjoyed by Daniel Morales, who replaced Victor Sifuentes on "L.A. Law." Most other recent Latino roles involved lower status jobs or far less airtime in low-rated series. Examples include Chuy Castillo, the cook at the "Golden Palace"; Jennifer Clemente, a very junior attorney in the U.S. Justice Department on "The Round Table"; and detective Rafael Martinez on the "Hat Squad." There was also Mahalia Sanchez, a bus station cashier in the "John Larroquette Show," rookie detective James Martinez in "NYPD Blue," and Paco Ortiz in "Nurses," none of them starring roles.

The cultural diversity within the Latino community was almost completely absent from prime time. Most Hispanic characters on television came from a "generic" background without reference to national origin or past. Television has rarely pointed out the cultural, historical, or economic differences among different groups within the Latino community. The few shows to make such distinctions, from "Miami Vice" to "Frannie's Turn," usually did so to place a particular nationality in a negative light. In "Miami Vice," differing national origins were connected with different types of illegal activities, while in "Frannie's Turn" a Cuban heritage was not a badge of honor. Sadly, the highest-profile Latino characters of the season were Eric and Lyle Menendez, whose murder trial was featured in two made-for-television movies.

TABLE 1   Traits of TV Characters, 1955–1986

	White	Black	Latino
All characters	89%	6%	2%
Social background*			
Attended college	72	44	**
Lacked high school diploma	25	49	**
Low economic status	22	47	40
Professional or executive	22	17	10
Unskilled laborer	13	16	22
Plot functions			
Starring role	17	15	8
Character succeeded	65	72	54
Character failed	23	16	34
Positive portrayal	40	44	32
Negative portrayal	31	24	41
Committed crime	11	7	22

*Characters were coded only if their backgrounds were clearly indicated by the script.

**Two few characters were coded for meaningful comparisons.

Source: Based on a content analysis of 7,639 prime time characters that appeared in 620 entertainment programs between 1955 and 1986.

An Update

As we have seen, before 1965, prime time was a nearly all-white world populated mainly by generic northern Europeans, save for the occasional black servant or Mexican bandito. Soon thereafter, the spectrum widened to embrace an array of ethnic and cultural traditions. But various minority groups shared unequally in television's new search for ethnic roots.

Some of these disparities are summarized in Table 1. As the table makes clear, between 1955 and 1986, proportionately fewer Hispanic characters were professionals or executives and more were unskilled laborers. Fewer Hispanics had starring roles, were positively portrayed, or succeeded in attaining their goals. Indeed, according to our 1994 study,[8] the more villainous the character, the sharper the group differences that emerged. Hispanic characters were twice as likely as whites and three times as likely as blacks to commit a crime. Once TV's roster of Hispanic stereotypes solely included the grin-ning bandito criss-crossed with ammunition belts. More recently, as scriptwriter Ben Stein has observed, "Any time a Cuban or Colombian crosses the tube, he leaves a good thick trail of cocaine behind."[9]

In addition, because of their negative and criminal roles, Latinos stood apart from other characters in the methods they adopted to attain their goals. They were more likely than either whites or blacks to use violence and deceit. If Latinos were distinctive in the means they used to pursue their goals, they also differed in their motivations. Hispanic characters were much more likely to be driven by greed than other characters. More broadly, black characters managed to attain whatever they strove for more often than either whites or Hispanics. In fact, the failure rate among Hispanics was more than double that of blacks. Perusing these figures, it is difficult to resist the conclusion that Hollywood has cracked open the door to black concerns while letting Hispanics serve as window dressing.

Examining character portrayals in 1992, we found that compared to both Anglos and African Americans, television's Hispanics were low in number, low in social status, and lowdown in personal character, frequently portraying violent criminals. The worst offenders were "reality" shows, whose version of reality often consisted of white cops chasing black and Hispanic robbers. Utilizing the same scientific content analysis approach, we examined the more recent 1994–95 season. We focused on a composite month of prime time entertainment programs broadcast on the four major broadcast networks and in first-run syndication. We found some welcome progress in television's portrayal of Hispanics, combined with some lingering sins of both omission and commission. (These results reflect our analysis of 5,767 characters who appeared on 528 different episodes of 139 prime time series.)

The proportion of Hispanic characters was up but still far below the proportion of Hispanic Americans in the real world. Latinos were "ghettoized" in a handful of series, few of which are still on the air, and few portrayed prosperous, well-educated, authoritative characters. The most striking and hopeful result, however, was a dramatic decline in the portrayal of Hispanics as criminals. Among the major findings:

- *Visibility.* TV's Hispanic presence doubled from 1992 levels. And these characters were more likely to play major roles when they appeared. But the rise was from only 1 to 2 percent of all characters, far below the 10 percent of Americans with Hispanic ancestry in real life. And a majority appeared in only two series, one of which has been canceled.

- *Criminality.* Hispanic characters were less likely to play villains than they were in the 1992 network prime time schedules. The drop in criminal portrayals was down 63 percent (from 16 percent of all Hispanic characters in 1992 and 6 percent in 1994). But even this level of criminality was higher than the 4 percent we found among whites and 2 percent among blacks.

- *New "Realities."* The most striking changes appeared in the cops-and-robbers "reality" shows, such as "COPS" and "America's Most Wanted." In 1992, a staggering 45 percent of all Hispanics and 50 percent of African Americans who appeared in these shows committed crimes. In 1994–95, the "crime rate" for both minorities plummeted to less than half the previous levels—down from 45 to 16 percent of Latinos and from 50 to 20 percent of blacks portrayed.

NOTES

1. Harry Castleman and Walter Podrazik, *Watching TV: Four Decades of American Television* (New York: McGraw-Hill, 1982), 208.
2. Ibid., 226.
3. Laura Z. Hobson, quoted in Christopher Lasch, "Archie Bunker and the Liberal Mind," *Channels,* October/November 1981, 34.
4. Quoted in Castleman and Podrazik, *Watching TV,* 227.
5. See Richard Adler, ed., *All in the Family: A Critical Appraisal* (New York: Praeger, 1979).
6. Quoted in William Raspberry, "Cosby Show: Black or White?" *Washington Post,* 5 November 1984.
7. Quoted in *Time,* 19 March 1979, 85.
8. S. Robert Lichter and Daniel R. Amundson, *Distorted Reality: Hispanic Characters in TV Entertainment* (Washington, DC: Center for Media and Public Affairs, 1994).
9. Quoted in *Time,* 19 March 1979, 85.

32

THE 1997 RACIAL REPORT CARD

Richard E. Lapchick with Kevin J. Matthews

Introduction

Northeastern University's Center for the Study of Sport in Society has completed its ninth annual Racial Report Card regarding the racial composition of players, coaches, and front office employees in the National Basketball Association, National Football League, and Major League Baseball. Gender comparisons are also provided where they are relevant. *The 1997 Racial Report Card (RRC)* represents the first time that the Center has included comparative data for college sport.

It was a year of expanded coverage of the issue of race due to 1997 being the 50th anniversary of Jackie Robinson breaking Major League Baseball's color barrier. Special attention was paid to the issue of race in professional sport in public forums, in the media and on college campuses. The report is being issued just after the 25th anniversary of the death of Roberto Clemente on December 31, 1997. The explosion of Latino talent in baseball in 1997, especially in the post-season and the World Series, also lent a special interest to Latinos in sports.

The results showed no significant overall breakthroughs in any of the categories covered in professional sport. Both the NFL and the NBA showed some improvement in selected categories but there were no gen-

eral trends observable. The NBA made the most dramatic move with Commissioner David Stern's announcement at the NBA League meetings in September that the NBA would provide workshops on diversity for all league employees and all 29 teams in 1998, thus becoming the first professional sports organization to initiate this.

By including college sport, the most notable conclusion for 1997 was that college sport, often assumed to be a more equitable arena in terms of race and gender, was actually behind pro sport in most categories in which comparisons could be made.

The percentage of Black players went down slightly in the NBA and the NFL while it remained the same in Major League Baseball. The percentage of Latino players broke new ground in baseball. The proportion of Black student-athletes in colleges was at its lowest point since 1991 while that of Latino student-athletes went up slightly.

The 1997 Racial Report Card is especially timely not only in light of the Robinson and Clemente anniversaries but also because President Clinton has inaugurated a national discussion of race in America. The Presidential Commission, headed by historian John Hope Franklin, may turn to the issue of race and sport early in 1998.

Whatever points are up for criticism in this report, whatever the shortcomings of sport may be when it comes to ideals and reality, sport remains the one national plane where people of color and whites seem to have the greatest opportunity to set a national example for the rest of the country.

Richard E. Lapchick with Kevin J. Matthews, from *The 1997 Racial Report Card*, 1997. Reprinted by permission of the author and Northeastern University's Center for the Study of Sport in Society.

RACIAL REPORT CARD

Highlights

- Regarding hiring of women and people of color in management, the NBA has the best record while Major League Baseball the worst in pro sport
- College sport has worst record of all for hiring practices for women and people of color
- Gains for women outstrip those for minorities
- The "glass ceiling" severely limits opportunities for women and people of color in top management positions on teams
- League offices do far better than teams regarding hiring practices
- The number of Black players decreased in pro and college sports
- Majority ownership for people of color does not exist
- The NFLPA and NBPA score highly while the MLBPA is far behind regarding opportunities for women and people of color
- Positional segregation or stacking is once again an issue in the NFL and Major League Baseball

---

Overview

As has been the case since the publication of the first *RRC*, no league received A's at the critical level of team front office hiring practices. The categories in this classification are team top management, team senior administration and team administration in general. The same would have been true for colleges with positions of athletics director, assistant and associate AD.

The NBA has had the highest grade in virtually every major category for all nine years of the publication of *The Racial Report Card*. Thus, it was not surprising that when all categories were combined, the National Basketball Association came out on top for the ninth straight year with an **A–** overall.

The National Football League received a **B–**, slightly down from its **B** of the previous three years. Major League Baseball received a *conditional* **C** because so much data usually supplied by the League was not available in 1996 and 1997.

In the 1996–97 season, the NBA improved to an **A** in the areas of coaching (head and assistant) and had an **A+** for player opportunities and an **A–** for people of color in the Commissioner's office. However, when we viewed opportunities on the individual teams, the NBA's grades were lower for top management (**C**), and in the categories of team senior administration (**B**) and for administration in general (**B+**). Women did better at the team level in senior administration and administration categories as well as in professional positions in the League office, far surpassing the status of women in the other sports.

The NFL had a **B+** for professional positions in the Commissioner's office. It held its **A+** for player opportunities. Like the NBA, the NFL received its lowest marks in the categories of team top management (**C–**), senior management (**C**) and for team administration in general (**C**). . . . The status of women improved in the NFL League office and at the team level in senior administration and administrative categories.

Once again, Major League Baseball did not issue its own report. Baseball continues to present a difficult problem for analysis because officials have not compiled the necessary data. Thus, we are able to issue grades only in the verifiable categories. Baseball had a **B** for Latino and Black managers combined; an **A** for player opportunities. Baseball had an **F** in top management with only a 5 percent total, which represented nearly half of the percentage in the NFL and the NBA. The status of women as professionals in Major League Baseball was not determinable from the data obtained by the Center.

The issue of stacking or positional segregation was, once again, one that the NFL and Major League Baseball would have to pay attention to after seeming to fade from the ranks of pro sports in the 1995 season and creeping back in 1996.

The Center will not issue grades for college sport in 1997. Nonetheless, it needs to be noted that college sport had the lowest rate of player opportunities for student-athletes of color. It also had the smallest percentage of people of color among head coaches, athletic directors (the college equivalent of general managers), senior administrators and administrators in general. The NCAA headquarters had a good record at the top but a weaker record for mid-level managers and other professionals than the respective pro league offices. It should be noted that the basis for most of the college

data was a 1995–96 NCAA Minority Opportunities and Interest Committee survey which had not been reviewed by the Committee and had not been publicly released at the time of the publication of *The 1997 Racial Report Card.*

There is clearly room for progress, especially in professional baseball and football and in college sport.

The Center publishes *The Racial Report Card* to indicate areas of improvement, stagnation and regression in the racial and gender composition of professional and college sports personnel and to contribute to the improvement of integration in front office and college athletics department positions.

As in previous reports, the 1997 data shows that professional sport's front office hiring practices do not nearly reflect the number of minority players competing in the game. However, to give it perspective for sports fans, the Center issues the grades in relation to overall patterns in society. Federal affirmative action policies state that the workplace should reflect the percentage of the people in the racial group in the population. Thus, with approximately 12 percent of the population being Black, if 12 percent of the positions were held by Blacks the sport received a **B.** It got a **C** if it had only 9 percent and an **A** if it doubled it to 24 percent.

While Commissioners David Stern (NBA) and Paul Tagliabue (NFL) continued to actively lobby for improved hiring practices for minorities in the front office and in the coaching and managerial ranks in the NBA and NFL respectively, the results at the team levels clearly showed the limits of what they were able to accomplish. Baseball's Equal Opportunity Committee performed the same role. The commissioners can set an important tone, but they cannot mandate change at the club level. The same is true with individual colleges and the NCAA where Executive Director Cedric Dempsey has taken a very strong position on racial hiring practices.

This report covers the seasons of 1996–97 in the NBA, 1997 in Major League Baseball and 1997 in the NFL, and the 1995–96 academic year for colleges. All coaching and general manager changes were updated as of December 12, 1997.

Minorities Playing Professional and College Sports

Because of its milestones in 1997, it is fitting to start with Major League Baseball.

Baseball has always been filled with ironies on the issue of race. As the first sport in the modern era to integrate, it has for decades had the fewest minority players among the three major sports. At one point during this historic year, the Dodgers, the team that broke the barriers in 1947, did not have a single African-American player on the team.

League-wide, the percentage of African-American players in 1997 hovered near a two decade low at 17 percent.

On the other hand, the percentage of Latinos in Major League Baseball has continued its upward climb, rising from 20 percent in 1996 to 23.7 percent in 1997. This dramatic rise represents the biggest increase of Latino players in the 1990s. Other than the 6 percent rise in the percentage of African-American players in the NFL between 1991 and 1992, this year's increase in Latino players in baseball is sport's biggest single-season swing for minorities playing sport. In 1997, the combined total of African-American and Latino players on Major League rosters increased from 37 to 41 percent, an all-time combined high.

In total percentage of players, the NBA continues to lead the way in pro sport for player opportunities for Blacks. At the outset of the 1996–97 season, 79 percent of NBA players were Black, down slightly from last year's 80 percent. However, it should be noted that the 1996–97 figures marked the

TABLE 1 Racial Composition of Players

	NBA	NFL	MLB
1991–92			
White	25%	36%	68%
Black	75%	62%	17%
Latino	0%	2%	14%
1992–93			
White	23%	30%	67%
Black	77%	68%	16%
Latino	0%	<1%	16%
Other	0%	1%	<1%
1993–94			
White	21%	35%	64%
Black	79%	65%	18%
Latino	0%	0%	18%
1994–95			
White	18%	31%	62%
Black	82%	68%	19%
Latino	0%	0%	19%
Other	0%	1%	0%
1995–96			
White	20%	31%	62%
Black	80%	67%	17%
Latino	0%	0%	20%
Other	<1%	<2%	1%
1996–97			
White	20%	31%	58%
Black	79%	66%	17%
Latino	<1%	<1%	24%
Other	<1%	2%	1%

second consecutive decrease of Blacks playing in the NBA in the 1990s. It is a trend worth watching.

As the 1997 season opened, 66 percent of the NFL players were Black. This is the second straight year that the percentage of Blacks has decreased in the game. While the proportion of whites remained constant in the NFL, it increased by 1 percent in the NBA. The difference in the NFL was made up with the increase of Pacific Islanders and Latinos, thus leaving the percentage of minority players in the NFL the same.

At the NCAA Division I level in 1996, Black males made up 61 percent of the basketball student-athletes, 52 percent of football student-athletes and only 6.5 percent of baseball student-athletes. Those percentages represent a decline in basketball and baseball and a 5 percent increase in football since 1991. It should be noted that while the percentages of Black college student-athletes have declined (as have the percentages of whites) their numbers, like those of whites and Latinos, have increased.

Latinos made up 1.6 percent of the basketball student-athletes, 1.8 percent of football student-athletes and 4.1 percent of baseball student-athletes in 1996. That represented between a half and one percent increase in the three sports.

In Division I in 1996, Black females made up 15.5 percent of all female student-athletes. Latino females accounted for 2.2 percent; and Native American/Alaskan-American made up 0.5 percent of all female student-athletes, an increase from 0.3 percent in 1991.

The Commissioners League Offices and the NCAA Headquarters

The league offices in the three sports have always had better records for hiring practices than their individual teams.

The 1997 RRC reveals that minority representation in both the NBA and NFL league offices increased. The percentages of Blacks, Latinos, and Asians all rose in the NBA league office in 1997 to a combined 23 percent. There were 101 new professional staff positions filled in the NBA league office, NBA Properties, and NBA Entertainment. The total number of minorities increased from 81 in 1996 to 109 in 1997. This was important since *The 1997 Racial Report Card* showed that the proportion of minorities in

the NBA league office, especially Blacks, had decreased for the first time in the 1990's.

Black vice presidents in the league office include: Steve Mills (Senior Vice President/Basketball Development), John Rose (Senior Vice President/Players Relations and Administration), Marcia Sells (Vice President/Organization Development), Tom Sanders (Vice President/Player Programs), Horace Balmer (Vice President/Security), and Leah Wilcox (Vice President/Player and Talent Relations). The NBA continues to lead in both race and gender hiring in the league offices.

Forty-four percent of all league professionals were women in 1997. A total of 26 more women were in such positions in 1997 but since 101 new positions were added, this represented a decline from 49 percent in 1996.

The percentage of Blacks, Latinos, Asians and women who held support staff positions in the league offices all increased in 1997.

The total percentage of all minorities combined in support positions increased 9 percent to nearly 50 percent and the percentage of women increased by 5 percent to 65 percent.

Commissioner David Stern also chose to address the issue of race in the NBA league meetings in September 1997. The Commissioner announced that diversity workshops would be held for all NBA league employees and for the staff of all 29 NBA teams in 1997–98. It was the first time the issue was ever raised in an open league-wide meeting of any professional sport in America and the workshops are the first of their kind.

The percentage of Black, Latino, Asian and women professionals all rose in the NFL for the 1997 season. Nearly 20 percent of all professional positions were held by minorities in the NFL's league office at the start of the 1997 season. This was up almost 3 percent from the previous year. The proportion of management positions held by women rose by 4 percent to 26 percent. There were

25 additional management positions in the NFL in 1997; the number of minorities increased by 10 and number of women increased by 14. Dr. Lem Burnham, who is Black, was promoted from Director of Player Programs to Vice President for Player and Employee Relations. Harold Henderson remains as the head of the powerful NFL Management Council.

The percentage of minorities in support staff positions increased from 19 to 32 percent overall while the percentage of women increased from 64 to 84 percent.

Major League Baseball has, as of the issue date of *The 1997 RRC*, not published or supplied its data for its central offices for more than two years. For informational purposes, we have supplied the most recent data available.

Len Coleman, who is Black, is the President of the National League in Major League Baseball. Coleman is arguably the highest ranking person of color in professional sport.

Dan Boggan was appointed as the chief operating officer (COO) for the National Collegiate Athletic Association in 1996. He is the highest ranking Black person in the organization. At the time he first joined the NCAA in 1994, Boggan became the first Black member of the eight-person Executive Directors Advisory Team of the NCAA in its history. In 1997, there were two Black group executive directors out of seven people holding this vice-presidential equivalent level post: Celeste Rose, Group Executive Director for Public Affairs, and Ron Stratten, Group Executive Director for Educational Services. Prior to the leadership of Cedric Dempsey as NCAA Executive Director, the NCAA was far behind pro sport. It is now doing well at the top levels.

At the next level, there are 38 chief aides. Three of the 38 are minorities. They are Stan Johnson, Alfred White, and Lydia Sanchez. There are 53 managers. Five man-

agers are Black (one woman and four men); one is a Latino female. Thirty percent of managers are women. Of the 106 professional staff, 53 percent are women; 27 percent are minorities (including 21% Black, 1% Asian and 3% Latino). There are eight professional technical staff members and 14 members of the sales staff. Women hold 50% and 71% of those posts, respectively. There are two Black women on the technical staff and one Latino female in sales. There are no minority men in either category.

At the clerical level, women hold 94 percent of the positions; white women hold 90.4%; Blacks occupy 6.7% of the posts; Asians and American-Indians hold 1.5% each. There are no Latinos in clerical positions.

In total, 14.9% of all 323 NCAA employees are minorities; 66.3% are women. Nearly half (148) are clerical workers.

Ownership

Few teams in Major League Baseball, the National Basketball Association or the National Football League are owned entirely by one individual. Most organizations have a group of investors that has part ownership in a franchise. Generally, a single individual is typically designated as the chief executive officer of the organization. While a chief executive officer is often classified as "owner," they are not necessarily the majority owner or senior partner.

There are no majority owners in Major League Baseball, the National Basketball Association or the National Football League who are Black or Latino.

Our current data identifies several limited partners in Major League Baseball, the NBA and the NFL who are Black or Latino. Black part-owners are Isiah Thomas (Toronto Raptors), Henry Aaron and Rubye M. Lucas (Atlanta Braves), Louis W. Smith (Kansas City Royals), William Simms

(Carolina Panthers), Deron L. Cherry (Jacksonville Jaguars), Earvin Johnson (L.A. Lakers), and Edward and Bettiann Gardner (Chicago Bulls).

Latino part-owners include Julio Iglesias and Amancio Suarez of the Miami Heat. Minoru Arakawa, who is Asian-American, is a limited partner in the Seattle Mariners franchise. Hiroshi Yamauchi, a resident of Japan, is the Mariners majority owner.

Marge Schott, the owner of the Cincinnati Reds, is the sole woman majority owner in Major League Baseball. Georgia Frontiere, the owner of the St. Louis Rams, is the sole woman majority owner in the National Football League. Women part-owners in the NBA include Bettiann Gardner, Ann Lurie and Carol P. Norton of the Chicago Bulls, Betsy DeVos, Helen DeVos, Maria DeVos, Pam DeVos, and Cheri Vander Weide of the Orlando Magic, Cassandra Carr of the San Antonio Spurs, and Teri E. Popp, Joyce Sexton, and Glenda Taylor of the Minnesota Timberwolves.

In the NFL, women part-owners are Denise DeBartolo-York (San Francisco 49ers), Rosalind S. Richardson and Ashley Allen of the Carolina Panthers, Carroll Smith Walraven, Dorothy Smith Knox and Karen Smith Owen of the Atlanta Falcons, and Donna Dewitt Lambert (St. Louis Rams).

In Major League Baseball, women part-owners include Jessica Mallory, Jennifer S. Swindal, Charlotte Whitkind, and Joan Steinbrenner (N.Y. Yankees), Marian Ilitch (Detroit Tigers), Pam Shriver (Baltimore Orioles), Claire S. Betz (Philadelphia Phillies), [and] Eloise Pohlad (Minnesota Twins).

Head Coaching and Baseball Managing Positions

Other than players, head coaches and big league managers hold the most visible positions in pro sports. This has always seemed to be the most logical place for Blacks and Latinos to get jobs. After all, who knows sport better than the athletes who played it? It is natural—although not always true—to believe that a former player could transmit the knowledge and skills accumulated over the course of many years of playing to younger players. Many athletes of all colors and ethnic backgrounds have shared this dream. It is far more likely to become a reality if you are white.

Jackie Robinson had two dreams for sport: increased player opportunities and similar increases for front office and coaching positions. The first dream has been overwhelmingly fulfilled. The latter is overwhelmingly unfulfilled.

At the beginning of the 1997 season, Major League Baseball had Felipe Alou of the Montreal Expos as its only Latino manager; Dusty Baker was with the San Francisco Giants, Cito Gaston led the Toronto Blue Jays, and Don Baylor was with the Colorado Rockies as the sport's three Black managers. As the season ended, Baker was named 1997 Manager of the Year for the second time after leading the Giants from last place to first. Gaston, who had won back-to-back World Series championships for Toronto, was fired after the Blue Jays had a dismal season. In December of 1997, Jerry Manuel, a Black man, was hired as the manager of the Chicago White Sox.

The 1996–97 NBA season began with seven head coaches who were Black: Darrell Walker of the Toronto Raptors, Stu Jackson of the Vancouver Grizzlies, Bernie Bickerstaff of the Denver Nuggets, Jim Cleamons of the Dallas Mavericks, M. L. Carr of the Boston Celtics, Lenny Wilkens of the Atlanta Hawks, and Johnny Davis of the Philadelphia 76ers. That was the high point since 1992–93 when there were also seven Black head coaches. The NBA's 24 percent in the category of head coaches who are Black was more than double the percentage for Black coaches in either the NFL or Major League Baseball. By the end of the season, Bickerstaff, Davis, and Carr were no longer in these positions. Bickerstaff replaced Jim Lyman in midseason at the newly renamed Washington Wizards. Later in the season Edgar Jordan, who is Black, replaced Garry St. Jean at the Sacramento Kings. By the start of the 1997–98 season, there were five coaches who were Black. Jim Cleamons was fired early in the season, leaving only four NBA coaches who are Black as of this writing. For clarity, the NBA's grade in this category was taken—as with all leagues—from the season being reported on, that is, 1996–97.

The 1997 NFL season started with the same three Black head coaches who finished the 1996 season: Dennis Green (Minnesota Vikings), Tony Dungy (Tampa Bay Buccaneers), and Ray Rhodes (Philadelphia Eagles). The NFL was last in this visible category. Commissioner Tagliabue's office paid special attention to the issue when 10 openings occurred at the end of the 1996 season and no Blacks were hired or seriously considered. The Commissioner held two closed meetings with five owners, 10 executives and Dungy and Green in New York to address his concerns with them. The NFL has commissioned a national head-hunting team to compile a database of all potential head coaches.

The college ranks were worse.

To try to make the most valuable comparisons, *The 1997 Racial Report Card* looks at Division IA football and Division I men's basketball and baseball. *The 1997 RCC* will use this basis of comparison throughout.

Eight of the 110 Division IA schools had Black football coaches (7.2 percent) as did two of 101 Div. IAA (1.9 percent)—excluding the historically Black institutions—in 1997. At the end of the 1996 season, there were 25 openings for head coaching positions in Division IA. New Mexico State, the last of the 25 to choose, was reportedly the

only school to even interview a Black candidate. It chose Tony Samuel who joined Ron Dickerson (Temple), Jim Caldwell (Wake Forest), Ron Cooper (Louisville), Tyronne Willingham (Stanford), Robert Simmons (Oklahoma State), Mat Simon (North Texas) and John Blake (Oklahoma) as the only Black head football coaches in NCAA Division IA. At the end of the season Cooper was fired and Dickerson resigned. There were 12 openings at the end of the 1997 season. No blacks were interviewed. Floyd Keith (Rhode Island) and Alex Woods (James Madison) were the only Blacks coaching in Division IAA. In the entire history of college football, there were only six other Black head coaches in Division IA. In that history, there have been thousands of college football teams that took the field: 51 have been led by a Black head coach!

In college basketball, there were 50 head coaches at the 289 Division I schools (17.3 percent). In college baseball, there is not a single Black head coach at any of the 249 Division I schools, while there were six "other minority" head coaches. As can be seen, college sports at this top level does not match up to the pros: Division IA football at 7.2 percent vs. the NFL's 11 percent; Division I basketball at 17.3 percent vs. the NBA's 24 percent; and Division I college baseball's 0 percent Blacks and 2.4 percent "other" vs. Major League Baseball's 14 percent Black and Latino managers.

While the following data may not compare directly to professional sport, the Center believes it can stand alone as a look at all of college sport. *The 1997 RCC* will do this throughout the report.

In 1995–96 in all NCAA men's sports, there were 7,101 head coaching opportunities with the historically Black institutions excluded. Of those, there were 304 teams with a head coach who was Black or 4.2 percent of the total. (Three Black women coached men's tennis.)

There were 547 college football teams and only 15 (2.7%) with Black head coaches. There were four "other minority" football coaches for a total of 3.4 percent. The NFL, which has the lowest percentage of the three major pro sports, more than doubled that with 10 percent.

In all of college basketball, 11.3 percent of the jobs were held by Black men; another 1.5 percent were held by "other minorities." The NBA nearly doubled that with 24 percent in the 1996–97 season.

In college baseball, a mere six Black men (0.8%) and 12 other minorities (1.6%) led any of the 764 college baseball teams. In Major League Baseball, there were three Black managers (11%) and one Latino manager (3%).

Eleven of the 21 sports listed by the NCAA, which has more than 900 members, had less than five Black men as head coaches. Of the 301 Black male head coaches, 205 coached either basketball (98), track (61) or cross country (46). Another 39 coached tennis (24), soccer (20) and football (15). That means that there were 41 (1.5%) Black male head coaches among the 2,733 teams in those other sports.

Black women coached 1.5 percent (106) of the 6,881 college women's teams; 52 "other minority" women coached 0.8 percent of the women's teams. Twice as many Black or minority men coached women's teams as Black or minority women (331 vs. 158). In fact, in 1995–96, only 44 percent of women's teams were coached by women.

Many recent news stories have glamorized NCAA Division III sports as college sports' largest reservoir of "pure sport," or as "sport as it was meant to be played." While there is a great deal of truth to this romantic notion, we should not ignore how race and gender play out at Division III: only 3.1 percent of the men's teams and 3.3 percent of the women's teams were coached by Blacks and 2.9 percent of the women's teams were coached by "other mi-norities." Only 57 Blacks or "other minority" women were head coaches of the 2,921 women's teams. In total, women only coached 48.1 percent of women's teams in Division III.

Assistant Coaches

Many believe that the ranks of assistant coaches in the NBA and NFL and coaches in baseball and college sports are the pipelines to head coaching and managing jobs.

The outlook improved significantly for Latinos in Major League Baseball where the percentage of Latino coaches jumped from 7 to 11 percent between 1996 and 1997. That took on added significance since the percentage had actually dropped from 1995 to 1996.

The news was not as good for Black baseball coaches. The portion of coaching positions held by Blacks dropped from 18 to 14 percent between 1996 and 1997.

At the beginning of the 1996–97 season, 34 percent of the assistant coaches in the NBA were Black. That was a drop from an all-time high of 41 percent in 1995–96. At the beginning of the 1997–98 season there were 34 Black assistant coaches which constituted 37 percent of these positions in the NBA.

The NFL had the only reported improvement in this category with an increase from 23 to 26 percent of the jobs held by people of color.

To continue to make the most valuable comparisons for assistants, *The 1997 Racial Report Card* looks at Division I football and Division I men's basketball and baseball for such positions.

In Division I basketball, whites made up 68 percent of the assistant coaches. Blacks made up 31.2 percent and "others" made up the remaining 0.8 percent of the total. In college football we looked at assistant coaches in all of Division I. Whites were 79.8 percent of the total; Blacks were 18 percent and "other minorities" were 2.2 percent. White assistant coaches in Division I baseball were 93.2 percent of the total with Blacks consisting of 1.3 percent and "others" the remaining 5.5 percent.

In the NFL, by comparison, 26 percent of the assistant coaches were Black or "other minorities." In the NBA, Blacks held 34 percent of the assistant positions in the 1996–97 season. In Major League Baseball, 14 percent of the coaches were Black and 11 percent were Latino.

As with head coaches, the following data may not compare directly to professional sport. However, the Center believes it needs to stand alone as part of a public look at all of college sport.

In 1995–96 in all men's college sports, there were 9,720 assistant coaching opportunities with the historically Black institutions excluded. Of those, there were 1,143 Black male and 73 Black female assistant coaches or 12.6 percent of the total. That was less than half of the total percentage for Black assistants in any of the three major pro sports.

There were 3,208 college football assistant coaches. Of those, 481 or 15 percent were Black. There were another 56 minority football assistant coaches for a total of 1.7 percent. In the NFL, 26 percent of the coaches were Black or "other minorities."

In college basketball, 23.9 percent of the assistant jobs were held by Blacks. Another 1.8 percent were held by "other minorities." In the NBA, Blacks held 34 percent of the assistant positions in the 1996–97 season.

In college baseball, only 2.2 percent of the assistant jobs were held by Blacks and 3.7 percent by an "other minority." In Major League Baseball, 14 percent of the coaches were Black and 11 percent were Latino.

In 12 of the 21 sports listed by the NCAA, less than 5 percent of the assistant coaches were Black men. There were 3.2 percent of the assistant jobs held by "other minorities." The vast majority of these were in baseball, basketball, football, track and field, and soccer.

Only 333 of the women's assistant jobs were held by Black women (5%). Another 96 (1.5%) of the assistants were "other minority" women.

There were almost as many Black or minority men as assistant coaches of women's teams as Black or minority women (424 vs. 429). In fact, in 1995–96, only 50.3 percent of women's assistant coaching positions were occupied by women.

As with head coaching positions, NCAA Division III sports had the worst record for hiring women and people of color as assistant coaches.

Only 8.3 percent of the men's assistant coaching jobs were held by Blacks; 6.2 percent of the women's teams were coached by Blacks; only 2.3 percent of the assistant coaching jobs on men's teams and 3 percent of the women's teams were coached by "other minorities."

In 10 of the 16 sports listed for women, there were two or less than two Black women as assistant coaches *in all of Division III.* There were none in six of the 16 sports *in all of Division III.* Only two of the 16 sports had more than two other "minority women" *in all of Division III.*

Top Management

For the purposes of *The 1997 Racial Report Card,* top management positions on professional sports teams include chairman of the board, president, chief executive officer, vice president and general manager.

The data clearly shows that the proverbial "glass ceiling" was very prominent for women and people of color at this level in baseball and was better, but had not disappeared, in the NFL and the NBA.

There were no people of color in the NFL or Major League Baseball who were board chairs, presidents or CEOs. Marge Schott is baseball's only woman in such a post.

The NBA had the best record in these categories. When all team figures were combined, the NBA had 9 percent of its top management posts held by Blacks at the beginning of the 1996–97 season. Women made up 6 percent of the top management of the NBA.

The percentage of Blacks in the top management of the National Football League at the beginning of the 1997 season was 8 percent. Women held 3 percent of these NFL posts.

Major League Baseball was at the bottom rung in this category with only 5 percent of top management positions held by Blacks and 1 percent by Latinos. Women made up 3 percent of the top management.

At the beginning of the 1996–97 NBA season, there were three Black CEOs: Bernie Bickerstaff (Denver Nuggets), Stu Jackson (Vancouver Grizzlies), and Wayne Embry (Cleveland Cavaliers). There was one woman CEO, Susan O'Malley of the Washington Bullets. There were no minority CEOs in the NFL in 1997 or in Major League Baseball. Terdema Ussery, who is a Black man, was named as president of the Dallas Mavericks at the start of the 1997–98 season.

For the purposes of *The 1997 Racial Report Card,* the term "principal in charge of day-to-day team operations" includes the positions of general manager and director of player personnel.

At the start of the 1996–97 NBA season, there were eight Black men filling one of these positions. They were Mel Daniels (Director/Player Personnel, Indiana Pacers), M. L. Carr (Director of Player Development, Boston Celtics), Stu Jackson (General Manager, Vancouver Grizzlies), and Wes Unseld (General Manager, Washington Bullets). Isiah Thomas (Toronto Raptors), Elgin Baylor (L.A. Clippers), Bickerstaff (Denver Nuggets), and Embry (Cleveland Cavaliers)

also played these roles for their teams, making a total of eight teams with a Black man in charge of the day-to-day team dealings. For the 1997 season there were six Blacks in this position. They were Elgin Baylor, Billy King (Philadelphia 76ers), Wes Unseld, Mel Daniels, Stu Jackson and Wayne Embry.

In the 1997 NFL season there were five Blacks fitting the job description of "principal in charge of day-to-day team operations": Bobby Grier (Vice President of Player Personnel, New England Patriots), Dick Daniels (Director of Football Operations, Philadelphia Eagles), Clyde Powers (Director of Pro Player Personnel, Indianapolis Colts), Ozzie Newsome (Vice President of Player Personnel, Baltimore Ravens), and Michael Huygue (Jacksonville Jaguars).

Bob Watson was baseball's only Black or Latino General Manager in both 1996 and 1997. When the New York Mets hired Omar Minaya, in 1997, he became baseball's first *Assistant* General Manager who is Latino.

At the college level, the top management post would be the athletic director.

For direct comparison to the pros, we look at the 287 Division I ADs in 1995–96. Of those, 9.1 percent were Black men, 1.0 percent were "other minority" men, 1.0 percent were Black women, and 0.3 were "other minority" women. The combined figure was 11.4 percent of the total Division I ADs being held by people of color. Another 6.3 percent were held by white women.

When we look at all NCAA divisions, there were 939 ADs in 1995–96. Of those, 6.9 percent were Black men, 0.7 percent were "other minority" men, 0.6 were Black women and 0.4 were "other minority" women. The combined figure is 8.6 percent of the total.

The 265 Division II schools had the best record for minority opportunities for ADs: 9.8 percent were Black men, 0.8 percent were "other minority" men, 0.8 percent were Black women, and 0.4 percent were "other minority" women. The combined figure was 11.8 percent of the total in 1995–96.

The ceiling dropped in Division III where there were 385 ADs in 1995–96. Of those, only 3.4 percent were Black men, 0.5 were "other minority" men, 0.3 percent were Black women, and 0.5 were "other minority" women. The combined figure was 4.7 percent of the total.

Most of the minority ADs were appointed in the 1990s. With them in key positions, the opportunities for "other minority" candidates within college athletics would seem to be brighter.

Nonetheless, at a combined 11.4 percent of the total, Division I college ADs have smaller percentages of minorities than general managers in the NBA (28 percent) and the NFL (17 percent). The Division I colleges do better than Major League Baseball's 3 percent.

Vice Presidents

There were 15 Black vice presidents during the 1996–97 season in the NBA, an increase of two from the previous year. They were Elgin Baylor (Vice President Basketball Operations, Los Angeles Clippers), Al Attles (Vice President and Assistant General Manager, Golden State Warriors), Billy Knight (Vice President Basketball Operations, Indiana Pacers), Michael A. McCollough (Vice President Marketing and Broadcasting, Sacramento Kings), Wes Unseld (Executive Vice President and General Manager, Washington Bullets), Ronald O. Sally (Senior Vice President and General Counsel, Denver Nuggets), Isiah Thomas, Executive Vice President of Basketball, Toronto Raptors), Wally Scales (Vice President/Special Events, Portland Trail Blazers), Wali Jones (Vice President Community Relations, Miami Heat), Earvin Johnson (Vice President, Los Angeles Lakers), M. L. Carr (Vice President and Director of Basketball Operations, Boston Celtics), Robert Barr (Senior Executive Vice President of Basketball Affairs, Houston Rockets), Ed Tapscott (Vice President, Administration and Scouting, New York Knicks), Willis Reed (Senior Vice President/Basketball Operations, New Jersey Nets), and a Black woman, Judy Holland (Vice President of Community Relations, Washington Bullets).

There were 10 Black vice presidents in the NFL in the 1997 season: Bob Wallace Sr. (Vice President/Administration, General Counsel) and Kevin Warren (Vice President/Player Programs, Legal Counsel, both with the St. Louis Rams), Frank Gilliam (Vice President/Player Personnel, Minnesota Vikings), Bobby Grier (Vice President/Player Personnel) and Don Lowery (Vice President/Public and Community Relations, both with the New England Patriots), Larry Lee (Vice President/Football Administration, Detroit Lions), Richard Leigh (Vice President and Associate General Counsel, Seattle Seahawks), Ozzie Newsome (Vice President/Player Personnel, Baltimore Ravens), and Michael Huygue (Senior Vice President/Football Operations, Jacksonville Jaguars).

There were 10 women vice presidents in the NFL for the 1997 season, more than double the number of the previous year. They were Veronica Costello (Tampa Bay Buccaneers), Charlotte Anderson (Dallas Cowboys), Linda Bogdan (Buffalo Bills), Mimi Box (Philadelphia Eagles), Jill R. Strafaci (Miami Dolphins), Judy Seldin (Jacksonville Jaguars), Jody Patton (Seattle Seahawks), Lisa DeBartolo (San Francisco 49ers), and Jackie Curley (Tennessee Oilers). Adrian E. Barr was the only Black woman who was a vice president (St. Louis Rams).

Although vice president is not in their titles, Katherine Blackburn (General Counsel/Corporate Secretary for the Cincinnati Bengals) and Amy Trask (Chief Executive for the Oakland Raiders) are both at an equivalent high level in their respective organizations.

Senior Administrators

The category of senior administrators consists of personnel who hold the title of director, coordinator or manager. In the NBA, 89 percent of the senior administrators on teams were white, 11 percent were Black and 31 percent were female. In the NFL, 10 percent of senior administration were Black and 16 percent were women. There was no comparable data for baseball.

The highest ranking financial officer on a team is generally referred to as a chief financial officer, vice president of finance, or controller. During the 1996–97 NBA season, Dwayne Redmon was the only black person that held the position with an NBA franchise; Pablo Garcia held that position with the L.A. Clippers.

Women who held such a position were Julie Wagner (Detroit Pistons), Pauline Winick (Miami Heat), Jean Sullivan (Minnesota Timberwolves) and Lori Warren (San Antonio Spurs).

At the beginning of the 1997 NFL season, there was only one Black CFO, Adrian E. Barr (St. Louis Rams). There were four more women CFOs: Jackie Curley (Tennessee Oilers), Jill R. Strafaci (Miami Dolphins), Jeanne Bonk (San Diego Chargers) and Mimi Box (Philadelphia Eagles).

The position of public relations director can be crucial in the determination of which players are presented to the media and how these players are portrayed.

Arthur Triche (Atlanta Hawks) and Travis Stanley (Sacramento Kings) were the only Black male public relations directors in the NBA. In the 1996–97 season, 17 percent of NBA teams employed female public relations directors. These public relations directors were Marilynn Bowler (Charlotte Hornets), Julie Marvel (Golden State Warriors), Juli Fie (Phoenix Suns), Cheri White (Seattle Supersonics) and Jodi Silverman (Philadelphia 76ers).

There were six (20 percent) P.R. directors who were Black in the NFL. They are Rod St. Clair (Tennessee Oilers), Rob Boulware (Pittsburgh Steelers), Mike Taylor (Oakland Raiders), Rodney Knox (San Francisco 49ers), Don Lowery (New England Patriots) and Reggie Roberts (Tampa Bay Buccaneers).

The position of director of community relations is where you most frequently will find a person of color or a woman. In the NBA, 48 percent (up from 42 percent in 1995–96) were occupied by Blacks and 31 percent by women (up 10 percent from 1995–96). In the NFL, 32 percent of community relations directors were Black (up from 25 percent in 1996). It is widely believed that this is the case because most teams play in cities with large Black and Latino populations.

At the college level, the senior administrative positions would be the associate and assistant athletic director posts. In order to provide a direct comparison to pro sports, *The 1997 RCC* first presents the data for Division I: 66 percent (997) of all those college opportunities for minorities are in Division I. Of those posts, 7.5 percent were held by Black men, 1.1 percent were "other minority" men, and 1.8 percent were Black women. There was a single "other minority" woman in all of Division I in one of these posts. The combined figure was 10.5 percent of the total.

In taking a broader look at all of college sport, there were 1,523 associate and assistant director posts in 1995–96. The ceiling seemed to drop across the board for these key appointments. Of them, 6.0 percent were Black men, 1 percent were "other minority" men, 2 percent were Black women, and 0.2 were "other minority" women. The combined figure was 9.2 percent of the total. Thus, the training pipeline for the AD position was not filled with minority candidates.

In 1995–96, the 265 Division II schools had 226 such positions (less than one per school, according to NCAA data): 4.4 percent were Black men, 3.5 percent were Black women. In all of Division II, there were only two "other minority" men and two "other minority" women. The combined figure was 9.7 percent of the total assistant and associate ADs in Division II.

In Division III, there were 297 associates and assistants in 1995–96 (like Division II, less than one per school). Of those, only 3.7 percent were Black men, 1 percent were "other minority" men, and 1.7 percent were Black women. Only one "other minority" woman held such a Division III appointment. The combined figure was 6.7 percent of the total.

As stated earlier, with more Black ADs there seemed to be more opportunities for other minority candidates within college athletics. More attention needs to be paid to where they may come from since there are so few assistant and associate ADs in all NCAA schools.

One area is the post of senior woman administrator. In Division I, 8.4 percent were Black women and 1.3 percent were "other minority" women; 89.8 percent were white women.

For all divisions, 9.1 percent were Black women and 0.7 percent were "other minority" women; 87.2 percent were white women.

Another is the faculty athletics representative. While not an employee of athletics, this is an appointment with considerable policy influence. In Division I, white men had 76.2 percent of the rep assignments; white women were at 15.4 percent; Black men had 6.1 percent; Black women had 1.3 percent. "Other minority" men and women combined held slightly less than 1 percent of these positions.

For all divisions, white men had 76 percent of the rep assignments; white women were at 17 percent; Black men had 5.0 percent; Black women had 1 percent. "Other minority" men and women combined held slightly more than 1 percent of these positions.

Administration (Front Office)

In professional team sports, the categories under administration include, but are not restricted to, professionals who work in business operations, marketing, promotions, publications, and various other positions. Our administration classification excludes secretaries, administrative assistants, staff assistants, receptionists and other support level staff.

The record of NBA teams has steadily built up during the last two seasons after undergoing a reversal during the 1994–95 season when only 10 percent of these posts were occupied by Blacks. In 1996–97, Blacks reached an all-time high in NBA administration with 14% of these positions; other minorities held 3 percent for a total of 17 percent. Women were in 38% of the posts.

On the other hand, positions for people of color in the NFL dropped from 12 percent in 1996 to 10 percent in 1997. Blacks dropped from 11 percent of the total to 8 percent. Women increased from 15 to 18 percent.

At NCAA institutions, jobs that fit this category are academic advisor, counselor, compliance coordinator, managers for business, equipment, fundraiser/development, facilities, promotions/marketing, and tickets, the sports information director and assistant directors, and strength coaches.

In Division I, whites held 90 percent of the above positions. White men held 62 percent while white women held 28 percent. The remaining 10 percent was divided into: Black men (5%), Black women (2%), "other minority" men (2%) and "other minority" women (1%).

There were 5,791 of the above positions at the 939 NCAA schools in 1995–96. Whites held nearly 89 percent of these administrative positions: white women occupy 25 percent while white men retain approximately 64 percent of these positions; Black women and "other minority" men have 2 percent

TABLE 2   NBA and NFL Administration*

	NBA 1993–94	NFL 1993
White	84%	88%
Black	13%	9%
Latino	2%	1%
Asian-American	<1%	<1%
Other	<1%	<1%

	NBA 1994–95	NFL 1994
White	87%	89%
Black	10%	11%
Latino	<1%	<1%
Asian-American	<1%	0%
Other	1%	<1%
Women	32%	12%

	NBA 1995–96	NFL 1995
White	84%	88%
Black	13%	11%
Other	<3%	1%
Women	45%	15%

	NBA 1996–97	NFL 1997
White	83%	90%
Black	14%	8%
Other	3%	2%
Women	38%	18%

*Similar data was not available for Major League Baseball.

each; Black men have 7 percent of the assignments; "other minority" women hold less than 1 percent of these jobs. The colleges, thus, do slightly better than the NFL and worse than the NBA in professional administrative jobs.

Medical Staff

Each team in Major League Baseball, the National Basketball Association and the National Football League retains one doctor as a senior physician or primary doctor. A majority of teams list a number of other physicians in their media guides, but generally the teams do not employ these doctors full-time.

There are no Black doctors listed as senior club physicians in any of the three leagues. The NBA, NFL and Major League Baseball each have one consulting physician who is Black. In the NBA it is Steven Brooks with the Orlando Magic. In the NFL, it is Dr. Warren Strudwick of the Oakland Raiders. In Major League Baseball it is Dr. Norman Elliot of the Atlanta Braves.

The Dallas Mavericks retain Dr. J. R. Zamarano, a Latino, as well as Dr. T. O. Souryal, who is Indian. The Dallas Cowboys also employ Dr. Zamarano as a team physician. Other Latino physicians include Dr. Robert Flores, a consultant with the Oakland A's, and Dr. Carlos Tandron, who is retained by the Jacksonville Jaguars. Dr. Jeff Tanji (Sacramento Kings) and Dr. Craig Young (Milwaukee Brewers) are Asian-American.

The league offices of the NBA and the NFL each employ a Black physician to head up their drug testing programs. Dr. Lloyd Baccus is with the NBA and Dr. Lawrence Brown is with the NFL.

According to the Bureau of the Census, 3.2 percent of the physicians in the United States are Black, 4.4 percent are Latino, and 20.7 percent are women. In the three pro sports leagues combined, three percent of the physicians are minorities and none are women.

In the NBA, only 14 percent of the head trainers are Black. They are Kevin Carroll (Philadelphia 76ers), Kevin Johnson (Washington Bullets), Keith Jones (Houston Rockets), and Roger Hinds (Dallas Mavericks). In the NFL there are three head trainers who are Black: Rod Medlin (Atlanta Falcons), James Collins (Philadelphia Eagles), and Ronnie Barnes (N.Y. Giants). That represents a 3 percent increase over the previous season.

Radio and Television Announcers

The percentages of Black broadcasters in the NBA decreased from 18 percent in 1996 to 16 percent in 1997 while Latino broadcasters in the NBA have remained at 3 percent.

The number of Black broadcasters more than doubled in the NFL while the percentage of minority broadcasters dropped by 1 percent. Sixteen percent of MLB broadcasters were Latino, an all-time high. The number of minority broadcasters in MLB increased 1 percent.

Referees and Game Officials

The NBA continued to surpass the other sports regarding the percentage of minority referees, which reached 30 percent (16 of 60) in the 1996–97 season. At the start of 1997–98, two women refs were added to the NBA's roster. They were Dee Kantner and Violet Palmer, who is a black woman.

The NFL maintained 112 on-field officials. There were 19 Blacks and 93 whites. In the NBA, the officials are overseen by one director, who is white, and three supervisors— two of whom are Black. Of the three members of Major League Baseball's Umpire Evaluation System, two were Black. Baseball-wide totals for all umpires were not available.

Support Staff

As might be expected, women were well represented in support staff positions in the NBA and the NFL. As stated earlier, *The 1997 Racial Report Card* has distinguished administrative assistants, secretaries, receptionists, staff assistants, and aides from professional staff. Categorizing support staff and top executives under the umbrella term

of front office staff makes it impossible to differentiate between secretaries and department heads.

At the outset of the 1996–97 season in the NBA, Blacks filled 16 percent of the support staff posts on franchises, down 1 percent from last year. Women held 62 percent of these positions.

Ten percent of the support positions on NFL teams in 1997 are held by minorities (7 percent were Black, 2 percent were Latino and 1 percent were Asian-American). That represented a 1 percent rise for Blacks, and a similar decrease for Latinos. The total percentage for minorities on support staffs remained the same. Women held 48 percent of the support staff positions in the NFL.

Stacking or Positional Segregation in Professional Sports

Whenever it is brought up, the issue of stacking or positional segregation is as hotly discussed as any issue in pro sport. When it comes to hiring practices, no one seems to dispute what the numbers and percentages mean.

However, when it comes to the numbers and percentages of which positions are played by which racial groups, debate becomes intense. League officials adamantly deny that race plays any factor in positions on the field. As trends shifted, *The 1995 Racial Report Card* noted that stacking had become almost entirely eliminated and had become a "non-issue" for all positions except quarterback in football. *The 1996 Racial Report Card* added a note of caution that "key positions once again suggest possible stacking."

As *The 1997 Racial Report Card* shows, stacking is again a serious issue in the NFL and Major League Baseball. The data seems to suggest that coaches, like administrators

TABLE 3   Positions in the NFL by Race—Offense

Offense	% of White Players				% of Black Players			
	1983	1993	1995	1997	1983	1993	1995	1997
Quarterback	99	93	91	91	1	7	9	7
Running back	12	8	10	7	88	92	91	90
Wide receiver	23	10	9	8	77	90	91	89
Center	97	79	84	72	3	18	16	20
Guard	77	64	60	72	23	32	35	23
Tight end	52	39	44	52	48	60	54	48
Tackle	68	51	46	49	32	47	52	47

TABLE 4   Positions in the NFL by Race—Defense

Defense	% of White Players				% of Black Players			
	1983	1993	1995	1997	1983	1993	1995	1997
Cornerback	8	1	0	2	92	99	100	98
Safety	43	18	13	10	57	80	87	89
Linebacker	53	27	26	24	47	72	74	74
Defensive end	31	27	20	15	69	71	78	83
Defensive tackle	47	30	30	24	53	63	64	71

Note: 66% of all players in NFL are Black. 31% of all players in NFL are White. 3% of all players in NFL are either Pacific Islander, Latino or Asian-American. Any totals of less than 100% are due to the third category, "other."

TABLE 5   Major League Baseball: Positional Breakdown

Pos.	% of White Players				% of Black Players				% of Latino Players			
	'83	'93	'96	'97	'83	'93	'96	'97	'83	'93	'96	'97
P	86	82	76	73	7	5	7	6	7	12	17	20
C	93	87	73	74	0	1	1	2	7	12	25	24
1B	55	69	70	67	38	19	21	21	7	11	9	12
2B	65	58	51	55	21	13	11	16	14	26	37	29
3B	82	75	70	68	5	12	13	10	13	12	17	22
SS	73	42	39	40	11	8	17	16	9	50	43	44
OF	45	33	28	29	46	50	54	50	9	17	18	21

in front offices, make decisions, either consciously or subconsciously, as to who plays certain positions based on race. Some positions rely more on physical qualities such as speed and reactive time than thinking, decision-making and leadership ability. In the NFL, such positions include running back, wide receiver, cornerback, and safety.

Can it be a coincidence that in 1997, Blacks held 90, 89, 98 and 89 percent of those positions respectively? Or that 91 percent of the quarterbacks and 72 percent of the centers were white?

In Major League Baseball, the 6 percent of pitchers who were Black in 1997 was a smaller percentage than in 1983 when it was

7 percent. Only 2 percent of the catchers were Black in 1997. Those were baseball's two central positions, ones that managers say require intelligence, quick thinking and decision-making.

Baseball's most notable speed and reactive positions are the outfield positions. Fifty-one percent of the outfielders were Black. The only positions which Blacks occupied in proportion to their percentage in baseball are the infield positions. Latino players did not seem to fit any pattern of stacking.

The Center will continue to monitor this closely as it is clearly an area of concern that there has been so little change over so long a period of time.

The Players Associations: Hiring Practices

This is the third year that the Center is reporting on the racial compositions of the players unions. As can be readily seen, the racial composition of the players association in the NBA and NFL better represents those playing in their sport. Both have executive directors who are Black: Billy Hunter at the NBPA and Gene Upshaw at the NFLPA.

National Basketball Players Association

Billy Hunter was in his second year as the head of the NBPA, which he took over after there were two executive directors and one acting director in the previous two years.

There were 10 members of the Executive Committee and one vice president of the NBPA; 10 of the 11 were Black. They were all current players and were elected by their fellow players.

Of the five department heads, two were Black and one was a woman. Five of the six men who worked regionally around the country in the respective player programs were Black. All were former players. Support staff consisted of four whites, three Blacks and one Latino.

National Football League Players Association

Upshaw has been the NFLPA's executive director for more than a decade. The board of directors, made up of current players, consisted of 60% Blacks and 40% whites. They were elected by fellow players. Six of the 11 NFLPA vice-presidents were Black.

The NFLPA had an outstanding record in 1995 and 1996, both in terms of racial and gender diversity. Their record at the NFLPA headquarters got even better in 1997: 31 percent of department heads were Black and 63 percent were women.

Support staff was 67 percent female, 62 percent Black, 33 percent White and 5 percent Asian.

Both the NFLPA and the NBPA have maintained outstanding records for equal opportunity.

Major League Baseball Players Association

The Major League Baseball Players Association did not submit a report for *The 1996* or *1997 Racial Report Card*. The Center requested the information by mail and by phone without success. It was unfortunate that they could not verify the information we received from other sources.

This was especially true since they had the lowest grade among all the leagues and players associations in 1995, receiving a "C–" as they had employed no Blacks and one Latino in professional positions.

To our knowledge, in 1997 there is still one Latino professional and a Black person employed as an assistant bookkeeper out of 30 full-time employees at the Major League Baseball Players Association.

Conclusion

There was no notable increase in the intensity of the effort to change front office and on-field hiring practices in professional sport to include more people of color and women in this, the 50th year of the anniversary of Jackie Robinson breaking into Major League Baseball. In fact, baseball, while celebrating Robinson in stadiums across the nation, failed to issue its own report on the racial issue with the data pertaining to the last two years.

Perhaps the saddest finding of *The 1997 Racial Report Card* is for college sport. While Division I does better than all NCAA divisions combined, college sport has a worse record in nearly every comparable category with professional sport. *The 1998 Racial Report Card* will mark the first time that Northeastern University's Center will issue grades at the college level. If they were given in 1997, they would be poor indeed.

Possibly the best news was that the NBA, so long the leader on racial and gender issues, is going a step further in 1998 with the Commissioner's announcement of league-wide diversity workshops. The NBA remained far ahead of the NFL, baseball and college sport in almost all categories covered by the report. Other than in the area of player opportunities, the NBA was near its peak levels in most other areas.

The decade-long, steady increases for Blacks playing sport seem to have ended with declines in the NBA, the NFL and a hold on MLB. It was the year of the Latino in baseball as Latino players reached new peaks regarding numbers, performance and opportunities for endorsements.

Women continued to make inroads in the league offices and in administrative positions on teams, especially in the NBA. However, few have opportunities at the highest level executive positions of team front offices in the three leagues.

The media continues to focus on hiring former players, making it easy to forget that there are many positions for skilled professionals on each team. Few are filled by minorities or women. The sports industry has made little progress regarding diversity in positions such as physician, attorney or team counsel, accountant, financial officer, and vendors.

On the issue of providing significant opportunities for former players, the National Basketball Players Association and National Football League Players Associations are way ahead of the leagues and teams. This was not true of the Major League Baseball Players Association.

Finally, it seems clear that stacking or positional segregation is, once again, an issue to monitor in the NFL and Major League Baseball.

The goal in publishing *The 1997 Racial Report Card* is to help professional—and now college— sport recognize that sport, which is America's most integrated workplace for players, is not much better than society in who it hires in front office and decision-making positions. There is widely acknowledged enlightened leadership on issues of diversity in the league offices of the NBA and the NFL. It also exists within Baseball's Executive Committee and at the top of the NCAA. Nonetheless, white males control the operations on most franchises and in the colleges.

If we couldn't celebrate more victories for diversity in the year of Jackie's 50th, perhaps sport can commit to refocus so it really can lead the nation to find a better way to serve the principle of equal opportunity for all.

PART IV

Color-Blind or Color Bind: Thinking Through the American Dilemma

A nationally distributed, full-page magazine advertisement placed by IBM depicts nine of their employees at a business meeting. The employees, presumably managers, are focusing on a white-haired man who is pointing to a chart. The activity depicted is rather mundane—meetings of this type take place thousands of times every business day. What makes this ad exceptional is what it is selling. In large letters across the top of the page, the text of the ad announces that "Diversity Works." The employees shown in the hand-drawn advertisement consist, in order, of an older white woman, a black woman, an Asian woman, a white man, an older black man with white hair, two men of ambiguous racial identity, and a white woman in a wheelchair. The racial and ethnic makeup of the cartoon characters in this ad is intended to convey to readers that IBM, as the supporting text tells us, "values individual differences." What is particularly interesting is the lack of white men in this rendering of the inner workings of a large corporation.

IBM may indeed value diversity, but the reality is that the upper ranks of corporate management are still the domain of white men. The bipartisan Glass Ceiling Commission found that white men "hold about 95 of every 100 senior management positions, defined as vice president or above." How corporate America presents its work force to the public and how diverse the organization actually is, especially as one moves up the occupational ranks, is a contradiction. Perhaps there is a reason this advertisement was a drawing and not an actual photograph of a diverse work environment. What occupations or organizations can you name in which high-status positions reflect the racial, ethnic, and gender composition of the United States? Think about the racial and ethnic composition of members of Congress, or the CEOs of the Fortune 500 companies, or the fifty state governors, or tenured college professors. What is the race and gender of your university or college president? What about the racial or ethnic background of sports or entertainment celebrities? What patterns emerge, and what do they mean?

We are an incredibly diverse nation. We are reminded of this by the advertisements promoting diversity from corporations like IBM, McDonald's, Texaco, Denny's, and Du Pont. We are reminded of this when we are repeatedly told that by the year 2050, about half of U.S. residents will be white and the other half will be black, Asian, and Latino. We are reminded of this when we debate the relative merits of affirmative action, bilingual education, or immigration quotas.

In the public imagination, the idea of ethnic and racial diversity seems to be simultaneously celebrated, feared, and reviled. The United States is promoted as the land of opportunity, but some groups have had more opportunity than others. Why? The United States is defined as a country of immigrants, yet many citizens are fearful that the "new wave" of immigrants will radically change "American" culture. Why? The United States is proclaimed a color-blind nation, yet inequities based on race and ethnicity are still the norm for a sizable part of the population. Why?

The readings in Part IV examine these contradictions. The five readings in the first section of Part IV focus on the changing complexion of the United States. Stephen Steinberg examines how often social and economic mobility are reflections of the opportunity structure immigrants experienced when they arrived in the United States. Mary Waters and Nicholas Lemann tap themes of mobility and racial identity construction to explore how race, ethnicity, and opportunity shape the experiences of Puerto Ricans and Afro-Caribbeans, respectively, in New York City. Pyong Gap Min provides a concise overview of some of the obstacles Asian immigrants experience. Lillian Rubin presents a narrative of immigration that is rather unpleasant, recounting how many individuals blame immigrants for their own lack of economic mobility.

The next four readings focus on how different social conditions can exacerbate racial and ethnic relations. Michael Eric Dyson argues that it is harmful to promote the idea of a color-blind society without addressing racial disparities in education, income, and employment. Robert Staples suggests that racial equality is an illusion, that the social and economic standing of racial minorities has improved over time, but that many obstacles remain. Mary Waters and Charles Gallagher each examine how whites view their own ethnic and racial identity and what a racially diversifying population means to the dominant group.

The final four readings suggest possible ways to improve racial and ethnic relations in the United States. Randall Kennedy re-jects the idea that skin color in and of itself creates an "obligation" to members of that race, asking whether color or morality or one's behavior should be what links individuals. In a similar way, Cornel West maintains that moral reasoning, not "racial reasoning," should be what guides our political, social, and moral agendas. Speaking from a public policy perspective, Melvin Oliver and Thomas Shapiro discuss what social issues need to be addressed if economic and social justice are to be realized. Finally, Jennifer Hochschild outlines how political coalitions might be built in the next century and what that implies for the future of racial and ethnic relations.

QUESTIONS TO FRAME YOUR READINGS

- How and in what ways does the historical timing of a group's entry (for example, Irish, Jews, Italians, and Afro-Caribbeans) into the United States affect its economic and social mobility?

- Why do some whites, as the dominant racial group in the United States, feel threatened about current trends in immigration?

- How does shrinking economic opportunity create racial antagonisms?

- Are we moving toward a color-blind society? Why or why not?

- How might you link attitudes with economics and politics to improve racial and ethnic relations in the United States?

The Changing Complexion of the United States: Race, Ethnicity, and Immigration

33

WHY IRISH BECAME DOMESTICS AND ITALIANS AND JEWS DID NOT

Stephen Steinberg

"I hate the very words 'service' and 'servant.' We came to this country to better ourselves, and it's not bettering to have anybody ordering you around."

> The Daughter of an Irish Domestic, quoted in Helen Campbell, *Prisoners of Poverty*, 1889

The familiar plaint that "it's hard to find good help these days" dates back to the earliest days of this country, when American-born women refused to work as domestics. According to one writer in 1904, "the servant class was never native American; even in Colonial days domestics came as indentured servants who ultimately moved up to higher-status jobs once their service was over."[1] In the South, of course, domestic work was a "negro job," but even in the North, as one writer commented in 1860, "domestic service certainly is held to be so degrading . . . that no natives will do it."[2] Those native women who did enter the labor market could usually find more attractive employment as teachers, bookkeepers, saleswomen, clerks, secretaries, and nurses.

While native-born Americans were loath to work as domestics, immigrants sometimes viewed domestic work more favorably. As a Norwegian wrote to a newspaper back home in 1868:

> America is an excellent country for capable and moral servant girls, because usually young American women show a decided unwillingness to submit to the kind of restraint connected with the position of a servant. . . . People are constantly looking for Norwegian and Swedish servant girls; and as they are treated very well, especially in Yankee families, there is no one whom I can so safely advise to emigrate as diligent, moral, and well-mannered young girls.[3]

Stephen Steinberg, "Why Irish Became Domestics and Jews Did Not." Reprinted with the permission of Scribner, a Division of Simon & Schuster, from *The Ethnic Myth* by Stephen Steinberg. Copyright © 1981 Stephen Steinberg.

[1]Frances A. Kellor, "Immigration and Household Labor," *Charities* XII (1904). Reprinted in Lydio F. Tomasi, ed., *The Italian in America* (New York: Center for Migration Studies, 1972), 39.

[2]Thomas Kettel, *Southern Wealth and Northern Profits* (New York: G. W. & J. A. Wood, 1860), 102.
[3]Theodore C. Blegen, ed., *Land of Their Choice* (St. Paul: University of Minnesota Press, 1955), 435–36.

As can be inferred from this passage, "the service" was not regarded with the opprobrium in Europe as in America. This can be traced to a number of demographic and economic factors.

As industrialization advanced in England, France, and other European countries, the hiring of servants became an integral part of the life-style of the new middle classes. At the same time, conditions of poverty and overpopulation in the countryside induced marginal peasants to apprentice their excess children to work as domestics in adjacent cities.[4] As one British historian notes, domestic service became "the major setting for female urban labour force participation during the transitional stages of industrialization."[5] It was often viewed as a respectable path for single young women, one that would indoctrinate them into the values and manners of the middle class, provide them with domestic skills, and in both these respects, prepare them for marriage. Thus, the prevailing cultural attitude sanctioned what was at bottom a matter of economic necessity. For poor country girls, domestic service functioned as a channel of social and economic mobility, and especially before there was a demand for female labor in the nascent textile industries, it provided rural women with an important stimulus for migrating to cities. It provided others with their only opportunity to emigrate to the United States.

From the vantage point of their employers, immigrants made ideal servants. In the first place, they could be paid little, since they had few alternative sources of employment. Perhaps for the same reason, or perhaps because they came from societies where rank was taken for granted, foreigners also tended to make more pliable and less disgruntled servants. As one observer wrote in 1904: "Although the immigrant so frequently lacks training, she is strong, asks few privileges, is content with lower wages and long hours, and has no consciousness of a social stigma attaching to her work."[6] The pariah status of immigrants also meant that their employers ran little risk that compromising details of their lives might be revealed to anyone in their own milieu.

While it is easy to see why immigrant women were in demand as servants, it might seem curious that immigrants in pursuit of the American Dream would accept such low-status employment. Actually, at the end of the nineteenth century there was only one other major avenue of employment open to immigrant women. That was in the needle trades, an industry that includes dressmakers, milliners, seamstresses, and tailoresses, and could be stretched to include workers in textile mills. Both domestic labor and the needle trades were extensions of traditional female roles, in that they involved work that was similar to household tasks. Domestics, of course, were employed to do the household work of other women. In the case of the needle trades, women were engaged in clothing production that once had been carried out in the home, but by the end of the nineteenth century had been mechanized and transferred to small shops and factories. Among immigrant women in the labor force in 1900, a solid majority worked in these two occupations.[7]

However, women of different ethnic backgrounds differed greatly in their propensity to work as domestics or as workers in the needle trades. Though some Irish women were employed in mills scattered across small industrial towns in the North-

---

[4]Theresa M. McBride, *The Domestic Revolution* (New York: Holmes & Meier, 1976), 38.
[5]Ibid., 14.

[6]Kellor, "Immigration and Household Labor," 39.
[7]*Report of the United States Immigration Commission,* Vol. I (Washington, DC: Government Printing Office, 1911), 830–38.

east, the vast majority worked as domestics. The proportion varied, depending on time and place, but its high point occurred during the famine migration of the 1850s. Of the 29,470 domestics that show up in the 1855 census of New York City, 23,386 were Irish.[8] Though Irish were about one-quarter of New York's population, they were over three-quarters of the domestic labor force. Germans were the other major immigrant group during this period, but the German proportion in the domestic labor force was exactly the same as in the city's population—15 percent. Not only were most domestics Irish, but it was also the case that virtually all Irish women who worked did so as domestics.

Of course, the peak of Irish immigration preceded by several decades the burgeoning of the garment industry. However, even after the waves of Jewish and Italian immigration at the end of the century, it was still the Irish who dominated the ranks of domestic workers. According to figures collected by the United States Immigration Commission in 1900, 71 percent of immigrant Irish women in the labor force were classified as "domestic and personal" workers; 54 percent were specifically classified as "servants and waitresses." In contrast, only 9 percent of Italian female workers and 14 percent of Jewish female workers were classified as "servants and waitresses." And whereas 38 percent of Italian women and 41 percent of Jewish women were in the needle trades, the figure for Irish was only 8 percent.[9]

How is this ethnic division to be explained? Why were Italian and Jewish women generally able to avoid working at one of the most menial and low-status jobs in the labor force, and why should so many Irish flock to it? As with occupations connoting success, social scientists have stressed the operation of cultural factors in explaining why some groups were more likely than others to become domestics.

For example, in *Blood of My Blood*, Richard Gambino implies that Italian women never deigned to work as domestics. As he writes:

> No matter how poor, the Italian-American woman to this day does not work as a domestic. For to work in the house of another family (sometimes an absolute economic necessity in the old land) is seen as a usurpation of family loyalty by her family *and by her.* And if one loses one's place in *la via vecchia*, there is no self-respect. In American history, there is no Italian counterpart of Irish, German, black, Spanish-speaking, English, Scandinavian, and French maids.[10]

How is it that Italians were able to escape a fate that befell all these other groups? Gambino implies that a stubborn ethnic pride, buttressed by a strong family system, protected Italian women from the indignities of domestic labor. Would he then suggest that other groups were lacking in these traits? And if domestic labor was "an absolute economic necessity" in Italy, as Gambino says, why was this not so in America?

In her recent history of Italians in Buffalo, New York, Virginia Yans-McLaughlin also suggests that family pride, reinforced by a strong patriarchal tradition, protected Italian women from having to work as domestics:

> Truly enterprising women seeking year-round wages could become domestics; but the Italian women were

---

[8]Robert Ernst, *Immigrant Life in New York City, 1825–1863* (Port Washington, NY: Ira J. Friedman, 1949), 219.

[9]*Report of the United States Immigration Commission,* 834–36.

[10]Richard Gambino, *Blood of My Blood* (Garden City, NY: Anchor, 1975), 14.

more likely to take in boarders because the men rarely permitted their wives to work as maids, cleaning women, or factory hands. The Italian ideal was to keep women at home.[11]

For Yans-McLaughlin, the "decision" not to work as domestics constituted an "occupational choice," one that was governed by "cultural tradition." As she put it: "Culture, then, acted as an interface between family and economy, dictating which options were acceptable and which were not."[12]

Acting on the same assumptions, other writers have suggested that the Irish lacked the cultural repugnance that supposedly deterred Italians and Jews from working as domestics. As one historian comments: "The Irish community viewed domestic service favorably and no ethnic taboos or language barriers prevented Irish women from working in other people's homes."[13]

Are these writers correct in positing ethnic and cultural factors as the explanation of why some ethnic women became domestics and others did not? On reflection, it makes little sense to take the Irish "tolerance" of domestic work at face value. This is hardly a calling that any group would define as an ideal worth striving for, and, for better or worse, the idea that woman's place is in the home is no less characteristic of Irish than of Italians and Jews. As will be seen, it was not a different cultural norm but a different set of historical circumstances that explains why Irish became domestics and Italians and Jews did not.

Though both domestics and needle-trade workers were engaged in traditionally female occupations, there was one fundamental difference between them: needle-trade workers returned to their homes when the workday was finished, whereas domestics typically lived in with a family, usually occupying a single small room in the rear of the residence specifically designed for this purpose. Although some domestics worked in households where there were other servants and a clear-cut division of labor, most households employed a single domestic. Her daily regimen consisted of preparing and serving three meals, doing household cleaning according to a prescribed weekly schedule, and being "on call" for whatever demands might be made outside of her routine duties. The average day began at six in the morning and lasted until late into the evening. Most domestics worked seven days a week, though a generous employer might give servants Sunday and perhaps one evening off.[14]

By comparison, needle-trade workers clearly labored under more adverse physical conditions. Indeed, Marx and Engels singled out textile factories as typifying the most inhumane and brutalizing aspects of capitalism. Sweatshops and factories were notoriously dirty, crowded, and often dangerous, and the work itself had a relentless tedium. For meager wages, workers were reduced to repeating a single minute task under the watchful eye of a boss or foreman, and the average workweek lasted between fifty and sixty hours. In her 1919 study of *Italian Women in Industry*, Louise Odencrantz reported that a typical workday began at eight and went until six; Saturday was sometimes, though not always, a short day.[15]

Yet factory workers had decided advantages over domestics. The fact that they returned to their own homes necessarily limited the authority of their bosses to the

[11]Virginia Yans-McLaughlin, *Family and Community* (Ithaca, NY: Cornell University Press, 1977), 53.
[12]Ibid.
[13]Barbara Klaczynska, "Why Women Work: A Comparison of Various Groups—Philadelphia, 1910–1930," *Labor History* 17 (Winter 1976):81.

[14]Daniel Katzman, *Seven Days a Week* (New York: Oxford University Press, 1978), 110–12.
[15]Louise C. Odencrantz, *Italian Women in Industry* (New York: Russell Sage Foundation, 1919), 317.

workplace, and even there, once unions were organized, workers could place restraints on their employers and strike for better wages. Degraded as they were by the conditions that prevailed in textile factories, they still belonged to a class of free labor, and as the early garment-trade unions demonstrated, could realistically hope to achieve a measure of dignity.

Domestic work, in contrast, had the earmarks of feudalism. Lacking a separation between work and home, the domestic was, in effect, bonded to her employer, and scarcely an aspect of her life escaped scrutiny and regulation. The domestic had virtually no time, and except for the limited privacy of her maid's room, no space that she could claim as her own. Isolated from other workers, she was powerless to change the conditions of her employment. To be sure, she was nominally free to quit, but lacking a home of her own, she could hardly risk the perils of being unemployed.

Furthermore, the nature of her work involved an exploitation of the whole person. Motivated solely by profit, the factory owner took little interest in the personal lives of his workers so long as they executed their assigned tasks. Though the textile worker might be reduced to a commodity, paradoxically, her inner self was left intact. But the employers of a domestic need to be sure that the person with whom they share the intimacies of their lives, and to whom they entrust their children, are decent, kind, affable, well mannered, and so on. In this sense, it is not just labor that is purchased, but the laborer as well.[16]

Domestic servants implicitly understood the feudalistic aspects of their employment, as was revealed by a survey of over 5,000 domestics conducted in 1889 by an enterprising professor from Vassar College, Lucy Maynard Salmon.[17] Though only 1,000 responded to Salmon's survey, they provide valuable insight into the private sentiments of domestic laborers during this period.

A common complaint among Salmon's respondents was that they felt lonely. This may seem curious since domestics lived in such close quarters to others and often developed personal ties with the families they served. However, one of Salmon's respondents eloquently describes the loneliness of the household domestic:

> Ladies wonder how their girls can complain of loneliness in a house full of people, but oh! it is the worst kind of loneliness—their share is but the work of the house, they do not share in the pleasures and delights of a home. One must remember that there is a difference between a *house,* a place of shelter, and a *home,* a place where all your affections are centered. Real love exists between my employer and myself, yet at times I grow almost desperate from the sense of being cut off from those pleasures to which I had always been accustomed.[18]

Another complaint among Salmon's respondents was that they had little time of their own; several said bluntly that they felt like prisoners. This feeling was articulated by an Irish woman in another 1889 survey who

---

[16]Lewis Coser has suggested that the servant is engulfed by a "greedy institution" that demands total allegiance. As he writes: "The master's family operates as a 'greedy organization' in relation to the servant. It does not rest content with claiming a segment of the time, commitment, and energy of the servant, as is the case with other occupational arrangements in the modern world, but demands—though it does not always receive—full-time allegiance. Moreover, while in other occupational roles the incumbent's duties are largely independent of personal relationships with this or that client or employer, particularistic elements loom very large in the master-servant relationship." *Greedy Institutions* (New York: Free Press, 1974), 69.

[17]Lucy Maynard Salmon, *Domestic Service* (New York: Macmillan, 1901).

[18]Ibid., 151.

explained why she chose to work in a paper box factory instead of "the service":

> It's freedom that we want when the day's work is done. I know some nice girls . . . that make more money and dress better and everything for being in service. They're waitresses, and have Thursday afternoon out and part of every other Sunday. But they're never sure of one minute that's their own when they're in the house. Our day is ten hours long, but when it's done it's done, and we can do what we like with the evenings. That's what I've heard from every nice girl that ever tried service. You're never sure that your soul's your own except when you are out of the house, and I couldn't stand that a day. Women care just as much for freedom as men do. Of course they don't get so much, but I know I'd fight for mine.[19]

When Salmon asked her respondents why more women do not choose housework as regular employment, the most common answer alluded to a loss of pride. Above all else, they bristled at being called "servants," a term that has a spasmodic history.

During Colonial times "servant" referred to indentured servants, but fell into disuse after the Revolution, apparently reflecting the democratic spirit of that period. Instead the term "help" was used, though "servant" was still applied to blacks in the South. With the influx of Irish and other foreigners in the second half of the nineteenth century, however, "servant" again came into vogue. Salmon herself acknowledged that it was "a mark of social degradation" that discouraged women from entering this occupation. There were efforts to substitute the term "maid" or "working housekeeper," but

according to Salmon, this "excited little more than ridicule."[20]

A less offensive nomenclature, however, could hardly disguise the stigma of servitude that was inescapably associated with domestic work. It is endemic to a master-servant relationship that even friendly gestures on the part of employers inevitably assume a patronizing cast, and unwittingly frustrate the servant's need to maintain a modicum of social distance. For example, Salmon's respondents complained that their employers took the liberty of addressing them by their Christian names. "It may seem a trifling matter," Salmon commented, "yet the fact remains that domestic employees are the only class of workers, except day laborers, who are thus addressed."[21] Domestics also objected to the cap and apron as still another badge of social inferiority.

What kinds of women, then, were willing to submit to the indignities of a cap and apron, and what kinds opted instead for the drudgery of the sweatshop? And why should Irish go one way, and Italians and Jews another?

The answer, in a nutshell, has to do with the fact that comparatively large numbers of Irish female immigrants were unmarried and unattached to families. Italian and Jewish women rarely immigrated unless they were accompanied or preceded by husbands or fathers, but it was common for Irish women to migrate on their own. For an unattached woman in an alien country—impoverished, uprooted, and often isolated from friends and family—domestic work had practical appeal. At least, it provided them with a roof over their head and a degree of personal security until they were able to forge a more desirable set of circumstances.

The reasons why Irish women were far more likely than either Italians or Jews to be

---

[19]Helen Campbell, *Prisoners of Poverty* (Boston: Roberts Brothers, 1889), 224.

[20]Salmon, *Domestic Service*, 156.
[21]Ibid.

single has to do with conditions in their respective countries of origin. In the case of Italians, an economic crisis in agriculture induced men to emigrate in pursuit of industrial labor and higher wages, and there was an overwhelming preponderance of males in the immigration pool. Between 1899 and 1910, nearly two million Italian men, but fewer than half a million Italian women entered the United States.[22] In some cases the men planned to send for their families once they had accumulated some savings; more often, they planned to return to Italy. An excerpt from a 1903 study on the Italian colonies in New York City describes this immigration pattern:

> The Italian population in this country is predominantly male. The reason for this is plainly seen. In nine cases out of ten, the father of a family decides to emigrate to America; he would like to take with him his wife and children, but since the least cost of a steerage ticket is something over $30, it becomes an impossibility for the entire family to come at once. The result is the wife and children are left behind and the father comes. On the other hand, few women indeed come here of their own accord—they are brought or sent for by husband or prospective husband.[23]

Thus, few Italian women immigrated as independent breadwinners. Invariably, a husband or family member preceded them, sometimes by many years, and by the time the women arrived, they were already part of families that had established at least a tenuous economic foothold. Married women generally stayed out of the job market altogether, though some took in lodgers or homework. Those women who did enter the job market generally found employment in the manufacturing sectors, especially in the expanding needle trades. In other words, neither economic necessity nor circumstances forced Italian women into domestic labor.

In Italy the situation was different. According to a study of women's employment in Milan in 1881, 23,000 women, or 20 percent of all female workers, were employed as domestics.[24] If few Italian women worked as domestics in America, this can hardly be attributed to a distinctively Italian attitude toward women and the home.

Immigrant Jewish women, like their Italian counterparts, rarely immigrated alone, though for very different reasons. Eastern European Jews were refugees from religious persecution and political violence, and unlike Italians, those who left harbored no thoughts of returning. As a consequence, Jews typically immigrated as families. Whereas there were nearly four Italian men for every woman among those who immigrated between 1899 and 1910, Jews had a much more even sexual balance—608,000 men and 467,000 women.[25] That Jews tended to immigrate as families is also indicated by the fact that a quarter of all Jewish immigrants during this period were children under fourteen years of age. Thus, most Jewish women came to America with husbands or fathers. Few were independent breadwinners, and when they did work, they usually found employment in the burgeoning garment industry. Often they worked in small shops with other family members.

The demographic character of Irish immigration was different from that of either Italians or Jews in that it included large

---

[22]*Report of the United States Immigration Commission*, 97.
[23]Antonio Mangano, "The Italian Colonies of New York City," in *Italians in the City* (New York: Arno Press, 1975), 13.

[24]Louise A. Tilly, "Urban Growth, Industrialization, and Women's Employment in Milan, Italy, 1881–1911," *Journal of Urban History* 3 (August 1977):476–78.
[25]*Report of the United States Immigration Commission*, 97.

numbers of single women. Unfortunately, no data exist on the marital status of immigrants, and consequently there is no exact measure of how many were unmarried. However, a rough estimate can be gleaned from examining the sex ratios of the various immigrant pools. In contrast to the situation among Italians and Jews, there were actually more women than men among Irish immigrants around the turn of the century. Specifically, among Irish arriving between 1899 and 1910, there were 109 women for every 100 men. Among Jews, there were 77 women for every 100 men; among Italians, only 27 women for every 100 men.[26] Not only were Irish women far less likely to be married when they immigrated, but the sex ratio did not favor their finding Irish husbands after they arrived.

A similar situation existed earlier in the century as well. For example, according to the 1860 census, New York's Irish-born population consisted of 87,000 males, but 117,000 females. Not surprisingly, the marriage rates of Irish in American cities were generally lower than those for other groups throughout the nineteenth century. Hence, from a demographic standpoint, Irish women were an ideal source of live-in domestics. That they also spoke English made them all the more desirable.

Further impetus was given to the immigration of Irish domestics by agencies that sprang up on both sides of the Atlantic. Beginning in the 1850s, a number of British emigration societies were organized to encourage and assist the emigration of surplus population, especially single women of childbearing age who were unlikely to emigrate on their own. They bore imposing names like the London Female Emigration Society, the British Ladies Emigration Society, the Girls' Friendly Society, and the Travelers' Aid Society for Girls and Women.

With philanthropic pretense, these societies recruited indigent women, paid for their steerage, escorted them to the port of embarkation, and dispatched them to the New World where they were commonly placed in private households as domestic servants.[27] Not all the recipients of this dubious largess were Irish, and many were sent to Canada and other British colonies. Nevertheless, the very existence of these societies testifies to the popular currency given to the idea of sending poor young girls across the Atlantic to work as domestic servants.

There were also employment agencies in the United States that recruited and transported young foreign girls to work as domestics in New York. According to one account, in 1904 there were as many as 300 "intelligence offices" in New York City alone.[28] To some extent, then, "Bridget" was the creation of employment agencies that engaged in this human commerce and collected fees for supplying households with Irish domestics.

There is still other evidence that many Irish women emigrated with the express purpose of finding work as domestics. Among immigrants arriving between 1899 and 1910, 40 percent of the Irish were classified as servants; in contrast, the figure for both Italians and Jews was only 6 percent.[29] Only 14 percent of Irish immigrants were classified as having "no occupation," a category that consisted mostly of children and women who considered themselves homemakers. The comparable figure for Southern Italians was 23 percent; for Jews it was 45 percent. From this it is reasonable to assume that most Irish women who immigrated around the turn of the century planned to enter the labor force,

---

[26]Ibid.

[27]Stanley C. Johnson, *A History of Emigration from the United Kingdom to North America, 1763–1812* (London: Frank Case, 1966 [1913]), chap. 11, 264.

[28]Kellor, "Immigration and Household Labor," 39.

[29]*Report of the United States Immigration Commission*, 173.

presumably in the servant occupation that they named when asked their occupation at the port of entry.

The reasons why so many young women left Ireland just to become servants in America must be traced to a series of economic crises in the nineteenth century, and the social and cultural changes that ensued. The infamous potato famine of the late 1840s was only one such crisis. Almost as important was a process of land consolidation that, between 1849 and 1851 alone, involved the dispossession of some million people from the land and the physical destruction of their homes.[30] To make matters worse, English colonial policy had reduced Ireland to a producer of wool and food, and the island had no industrial base that might have absorbed its surplus rural population. Irish emigration reached its peak during the potato famine, but it was already gaining momentum before the famine and it continued at substantial levels long after. Incredibly, Ireland's population in 1900 was almost half of what it had been in 1850.[31]

Ireland's prolonged economic depression played havoc with the family system. Traditionally, marriage was bound up with the inheritance of land, and as land became more scarce, there was a tendency to postpone marriage. For nearly a century after the famine, as one recent study has shown, "the average age at marriage increased, the marriage rate decreased, and the percentage who remained permanently celibate increased."[32] In 1891, for example, two-thirds of men and half the women between the ages of 25 and 34 were single. Even among those between 35 and 44, a third of the men

and a quarter of the women were single. One out of six of each sex never married.

The impact of these trends was especially harsh on women, since they were forced onto a labor market that was hardly favorable to them. Against this background it is easy to understand why young women, even more often than men, decided to emigrate. And given their vulnerability as single women in an alien country, as well as the limited alternatives that existed, it is also easy to understand why "the service" provided at least a temporary solution to their dilemma. It made emigration possible, provided them with food and lodging, and carried them over until such time as they could find either husbands or more desirable employment.

If historical circumstances and economic necessity forced immigrant Irish women to accept work as domestics, this was not a trend that continued into the second generation. Table 1 reports the occupations in 1900 of first- and second-generation Irish, Italian, and Jewish women. The most striking observation is that whereas 71 percent of immigrant Irish women were classified as working in "domestic and personal service," only 25 percent of their children were so classified. Thus, by the second generation, Irish were not much more likely than other groups to work as domestics.

What the female children of Irish immigrants did was to follow in the footsteps of Italian and Jewish immigrants. As can also be seen in Table 1, by 1900 they were entering the needle trades and other branches of manufacturing, precisely at the point when second-generation Italian and Jewish women were abandoning these occupations in favor of work as saleswomen, bookkeepers, clerks, and the like. In a sense, Irish women started out on a lower occupational threshold than either Italians or Jews, and remained one generational step behind. But as far as domestic service is concerned, by

---

[30]Oscar Handlin, *Boston's Immigrants* (New York: Atheneum, 1968), 46.

[31]Walter F. Willcox, ed., *International Migrations*, Vol. II (New York: National Bureau of Economic Research, 1931), 274.

[32]Richard Stivers, *A Hair of the Dog* (University Park: Pennsylvania State University Press, 1976), 56.

TABLE 1   Occupations of First- and Second-Generation Irish, Italian, and Jewish Female Breadwinners, 1900

Ethnic Group	Irish		Italian		Jews	
Generation	*First*	*Second*	*First*	*Second*	*First*	*Second*
Occupation*						
Domestic & personal service (includes waitresses)	71%	25%	21%	15%	18%	21%
Needle trades & textiles	16	29	48	33	44	26
Other manufacturing	6	17	20	28	23	17
Saleswomen, bookkeepers, clerks, etc.	5	19	10	20	14	31
Professional	2	10	1	4	1	5
	100%	100%	100%	100%	100%	100%
Number of cases	(245,792)	(388,108)	(20,307)	(5,751)	(35,030)	(5,781)

*The small number of cases whose occupations could not be classified are excluded from the percentages.

Source: Adapted from the *Reports of the United States Immigration Commission,* Vol. 1 (Washington, DC: Government Printing Office, 1911), 834–36.

the second generation few women in any of these groups were so employed.

Culture and family morality have little or nothing to do with explaining why Irish became domestics and Italians and Jews did not. It was not that Irish husbands were less protective of their wives, but rather that immigrant Irish women were less likely to have husbands in the first place. It was not that as a group Irish had less aversion to working in other people's homes, but that their choices were far more limited. For these courageous women who migrated alone to the New World, domestic work was merely a temporary expedient to allow them to forge new lives. That the Irish had no cultural tolerance for domestic work is pointed up by the fact that they fled "the service" just as quickly as they could establish families of their own or gain access to more desirable employment. If other groups were spared the indignities of domestic labor, it is not that they had better cultural defenses or a superior moral code, but because their circumstances did not compel them to place economic survival ahead of their pride.

34

ETHNIC AND RACIAL IDENTITIES OF SECOND-GENERATION BLACK IMMIGRANTS IN NEW YORK CITY

Mary C. Waters

The growth of nonwhite voluntary immigrants to the United States since 1965 challenges the dichotomy that once explained different patterns of American inclusion and assimilation—the ethnic pattern of assimilation of European immigrants and the racial pattern of exclusion of America's nonwhite peoples. The new wave of immigrants includes people who are still defined racially in the United States but who migrate voluntarily and often under an immigrant preference system that selects for people with jobs and education that puts them well above their coethnics in the economy. Do the processes of immigration and assimilation for nonwhite immigrants resemble the processes for earlier white immigrants? Or do these immigrants and their children face very different choices and constraints because they are defined racially by other Americans?

This [reading] examines a small piece of this puzzle—the question of the development of an ethnic identity among the second generation of black immigrants from the Caribbean. While there has been a substantial amount of interest in the identities and affiliations of these immigrants, very little research has been conducted on the identi-

ties of their children. The children of black immigrants in the United States face a choice about whether to identify as black American or whether to maintain an ethnic identity reflecting their parents' national origins. First-generation black immigrants to the United States have tended to distance themselves from American blacks, stressing their national origins and ethnic identities as Jamaican or Haitian or Trinidadian, but they also face overwhelming pressures in the United States to identify only as blacks (Foner 1987; Kasinitz 1992; Stafford 1987; Sutton and Makiesky 1975; Woldemikael 1989). In fact, they have been described as "invisible immigrants" (Bryce-Laporte 1972), because rather than being contrasted with other immigrants (for example, contrasting how Jamaicans are doing relative to Chinese), they are compared with black Americans. The children of black immigrants, because they lack their parents' distinctive accents, can choose to be even more invisible as ethnics than their parents. Second-generation West Indians in the United States most often will be seen by others as merely "American"—and must actively work to assert their ethnic identities.

The types of racial and ethnic identities adopted by a sample of second-generation West Indians[1] and Haitian Americans in New York City are explored here, along with subjective understandings these youngsters have of being American, being black American, and being their ethnic identity. After a short discussion of current theoretical approaches to understanding assimilation among the second generation, three types of identities adopted by the second generation are described and the different experiences of race relations associated with these identities are traced. Finally this [reading] suggests some implications for future patterns of identity development. . . .

Interviews with first-generation immigrants and their American coworkers reveal a great deal of tension between foreign-born and American-born blacks in both the working-class and the middle-class work sites. Long-standing tensions between newly arrived West Indians and American blacks have left a legacy of mutual stereotyping. (See Kasinitz 1992.) The immigrants see themselves as hardworking, ambitious, militant about their racial identities but not oversensitive or obsessed with race, and committed to education and family. They see black Americans as lazy, disorganized, obsessed with racial slights and barriers, with a disorganized and laissez-faire attitude toward family life and child raising. American blacks describe the immigrants as arrogant, selfish, exploited in the workplace, oblivious to racial tensions and politics in the United States, and unfriendly and unwilling to have relations with black Americans. The first generation believes that their status as foreign-born blacks is higher than American blacks, and they tend to accentuate their identities as immigrants. Their accent is usually a clear and unambiguous signal to other Americans that they are foreign born.

The dilemma facing the second generation is that they grow up exposed to the negative opinions voiced by their parents about American blacks and to the belief that whites respond more favorably to foreign-born blacks. But they also realize that because they lack their parents' accents and other identifying characteristics, other people, including their peers, are likely to identify them as American blacks. How does the second generation handle this dilemma? Do they follow their parents' lead and identify with their ethnic identities such as Jamaican or Haitian or West Indian? Or do they try to become "American" and reject their parents' ethnic immigrant identities? . . .

Theoretical Approaches to Assimilation

Theories derived from the experiences of European immigrants and their children in the early twentieth century predicted that the more time spent in the United States, the more likely second-generation youths were to adopt an "American identity" and to reduce ties to the ethnic identities and culture of their parents. This "straight-line" assimilation model assumes that with each succeeding generation, the groups become more similar to mainstream Americans and more economically successful. For instance, Warner and Srole's (1945) study of ethnic groups in Yankee City (Newburyport, Massachusetts) in the early 1930s describes the generational march from initial residential and occupational segregation and poverty to residential, occupational, and identificational integration and Americanization.

However, the situation faced by immigrant blacks in the 1990s differs in many of the background assumptions of the straight-line model. The immigrants do not enter a society that assumes an undifferentiated monolithic American culture but rather a consciously pluralistic society in which a variety of subcultures and racial and ethnic identities coexist. In fact, if these immigrants assimilate, they become not just Americans but black Americans. The immigrants generally believe that it is higher social status to be an immigrant black than to be an American black. Second, the economic opportunity structure is very different now from what it was at the beginning of the twentieth century. The unskilled jobs in manufacturing that enhanced job mobility for immigrants' children at the turn of the century have been lost as economic restructuring in the United States has shifted to a service economy (Gans 1992). The immigrants also are quite varied in the skills they bring with them. Some arrive with advanced educations and professional qualifications to take relatively well-paying jobs, which put them ahead of native American blacks (for example, Jamaican nurses). Others are less skilled and face difficulties finding work in the United States. Finally, the degree of residential segregation faced by blacks in the United States, whether foreign born or American born, has always been, and continues to be, of a much higher order than the segregation faced by foreign-born white immigrants (Lieberson 1980; Massey 1990). Thus, even with occupational mobility, it is not clear that blacks would be able to move into higher-status neighborhoods in the orderly progression that Warner and Srole (1945) describe in their Yankee City study of European ethnic succession. A further complication for the black second generation is that part of being a black American involves dealing with American racism. Because immigrants and black Americans report a large difference in the perception and expectation of racism in American society, part of becoming American for the second generation involves developing a knowledge and perception of racism and its subtle nuances. . . .

Patterns in the Second Generation

The interviews suggest that while the individuals in this study vary a great deal in their identities, perceptions, and opinions, they can be sorted into three general types: identifying as Americans, identifying as ethnic Americans with some distancing from black Americans, or identifying as an immigrant in a way that does not reckon with American racial and ethnic categories.

A black American identity characterized the responses of approximately 42 percent of the eighty-three second-generation respondents interviewed. These youngsters identified with other black Americans. They did not see their "ethnic" identities as important to their self-image. When their parents or friends criticized American blacks or described what they perceived as fundamental differences between Caribbean-origin people and American blacks, these youngsters disagreed. They tended to downplay a national-origin identity and described themselves as American.

Another 30 percent of the respondents adopted a very strong ethnic identity that involved a considerable amount of distancing from American blacks. It was important for these respondents to stress their ethnic identities and for other people to recognize that they were not American blacks. These respondents tended to agree with parental judgments that there were strong differences between Americans and West Indians. This often involved a stance that West Indians were superior to American blacks in their behaviors and attitudes.

A final 28 percent of respondents had an immigrant attitude toward their identities, as opposed to American-identified youth or ethnic-identified youth. Most, but not all, of these respondents were more recent immigrants themselves. A crucial factor for these youngsters is that their accents and styles of clothing and behavior clearly signaled to others that they were foreign born. In a sense, their identity as an immigrant people precluded having to make a "choice" about what kind of American they were. These respondents had a strong identity, such as Jamaican or Trinidadian, but did not evidence much distancing from American blacks. Rather their identities were strongly linked to their experiences on the islands, and they did not worry much about how they were seen by other Americans, white or black.

A number of factors influence the type of identity the youngsters develop. They include the class background of the parents, the social networks in which the parents are involved, the type of school the child attends, and the family structure. All of these factors affect the ability of parents and other family members to shield children from neighborhood peer groups that espouse antischool values.

The type of identity and outlook on American race and ethnic relations that the youngsters developed was strongly related to their social class and its trajectory. The ethnic-identified youngsters were most likely to come from a middle-class background. Of the eighty-three second-generation teens and young adults interviewed, 57 percent of the middle-class teens identified ethnically, whereas only 17 percent of the working-class and poor teens identified ethnically.[2] The poorest students were the most likely to be immigrant or American identified. Only one out of the twelve teens whose parents were on public assistance identified ethnically. The American identified, perhaps not surprisingly, were also more likely to be born in the United States—67 percent of the American identified were born in the United States, as opposed to only 13 percent of the immigrant identified and 42 percent of the ethnically identified.

Parents with more education and income were able to provide better schools for their offspring. Among the respondents, some of the middle class had moved from the inner-city neighborhoods they had originally settled in to middle-class neighborhoods in the borough of Queens or to suburban areas where the schools were of higher academic quality and more likely to be racially integrated. Other middle-class parents sent their children to Catholic parochial schools or to citywide magnet schools such as Brooklyn Tech or Stuyvesant. Thus, the children were far more likely to attend schools with other immigrant children and with other middle-class whites and blacks, although some of the Catholic high schools were all black in enrollment.

The children of middle-class parents who did attend the local high schools were likely to be recent immigrants who had an immigrant identity. Because of their superior education in the West Indies, these students were the best in the local high schools, attended honors classes, and were bound for college. The children of middle-class parents who identified as American and were pessimistic about their own future opportunities and adopted antischool ideologies were likely to have arrived early in their lives and to have attended New York City public schools in inner-city areas from an early age.

The social networks of parents also influenced the type of identity the children developed. Regardless of social class, parents who were involved in ethnic voluntary organizations or heavily involved in their churches seemed to instill a strong sense of ethnic identity in their children. Parents whose social networks transcended neighborhood boundaries seemed to have more ability to provide guidance and social contacts for their children.

The two neighborhood schools where we interviewed the teenagers were among the five most dangerous schools in New York City—they were inadequate facilities with crumbling physical buildings, high dropout rates, and serious problems with violence. Both schools were all minority, with over 90 percent of the student body composed of black students, both American and foreign born. The students who attended these schools and were not in the separate honors tract (which was overwhelmingly filled with newly arrived immigrants) faced very limited future options, even if they managed to graduate.

Finally, the family structure and the experience of migration itself have a profound effect on the degree of control parents have over teenage children. Many families are composed of single working mothers and children. These mothers have not been able to supervise their children as much as they would like, and many do not have any extended family or close friends available to help with discipline and control. Even families with two spouses present often have been apart for long periods because one spouse preceded the family in migration. Often children have been left in the islands or sent ahead with relatives to New York, with the parents often struggling to reassert authority after the family reunites. The generational conflict that ensues tends to create greater pressure for students to want to be "American" to differentiate themselves from parents.

Ethnic Response

All of the teenage respondents reported comments by their parents about American blacks that were very similar to those recorded in our interviews with the first generation. The differences were in how the teens interpreted what their parents were saying. In general, the ethnic-identified teens agreed with their parents and reported seeing a strong difference between themselves and black Americans, stressing that being black is not synonymous with being black American. They accept their parents' and the wider society's negative portrayals of poor blacks and wanted to avoid any chance that they will be identified with them. They described the culture and values of lower-class black Americans as lacking discipline, a work ethic, good child-rearing

practices, and respect for education. They contrast these failures with the values of their parents' ethnic groups, which include an emphasis on education, strict discipline for children, a strong work ethic, and social mobility. They try to impress that they are Jamaican or Haitian and most definitely not black American. This allows them less dissonance with their parents' negative views of American blacks. They do not reject their parents' culture and identities but rather reject the American social system that would identify them as black American and strongly reject the African American peer group culture to which they would be assigned by whites and others if they did not consciously transmit their ethnic identities.

Although society may define the second generation on the basis of skin color, the second-generation ethnic teens believed that being black American involves more than merely having black skin. One young woman criticized American blacks in this way:

> Some of them [black Americans] think that their heritage includes not being able to speak correctly or walk correctly, or act loud and obnoxious to make a point. I don't think they have to do that. Just when I see black Americans, it depends on how I see you on the street. Walking down the street with that walk that moves a little bit too much. I would say, I'd think you dropped out of high school.

These teens also differentiated themselves from black Americans in terms of their sensitivity to racism, real or imagined. Some of the ethnic-identified second generation echo the feelings we heard from the first generation that American blacks are too quick to use race as an explanation or excuse for not doing well:

> There was a time back in the '40s and '50s and '60s or whenever when people

was actually trying to keep down black people and stuff like that. But, you know, some black people now, it's like they not actually trying to make it better, you know? Some are just like, people are like, oh, this place is trying to keep me down, and they sulk and they cry about it, and they're not really doing that much to help themselves. . . . It's just like hyping the problem if they keep [saying] everything is racial, everything is racial.

The second-generation teens who are doing well try to understand how it is that they are so successful when black Americans are not—and often they chalk it up to family values. They say that their immigrant families have close-knit family values that stress education. Aware of, and sometimes sharing, the negative images of black Americans that the whites they encounter believe, the second generation also perceives that whites treat them better when they realize they are not "just" black Americans. When asked if they benefited ever from their ethnicity, they responded "yes": "It seems white Americans don't tend to put you in the same category as black Americans." Another respondent said:

The West Indians tend to go that extra step because they, whites, don't usually consider them really black Americans, which would be working class. They don't consider them, I guess, as black. They see them as a person.

The dilemma for the second generation is that while they have a strong sense of their own identities as very different from black Americans, this was not clear to other people. Often both whites and blacks saw them as just black Americans and did not notice that they were ethnically different. When people did comment on their ethnic difference it was often because of the way they

talked and the way they walked. These two characteristics were cited as reasons that whites and other blacks gave for thinking those of the second generation were not "really black." Whites tend to let these children know that they think of them as exceptions to the rule, with the rule being that most blacks are not good people. However, these young people also know that unless they tell people of their ethnicity, most whites have no idea they are not black Americans.

Many of these teens coped with this dilemma by devising ways to telegraph their identities as second-generation West Indians or Haitians. One girl carried a Guyanese map as part of her key chain so that when people looked at her keys they would ask her about it and she could tell them that her parents were from Guyana. One young woman described having her mother teach her an accent so that she could use it when she applied for a job or a place to live. Others just try to work it into conversation when they meet someone. This means that their self-identification is almost always at odds with the identifications others make of them in impersonal encounters in American society and that, as a result, they must consciously try to accentuate their ethnic identity:

Q: When a form or survey asks for your race what do you put down?
A: Oh boy, that is a tough one. It's funny because, you know, when we fill applications I never know what to check off, you know. I'm serious. 'Cause they have Afro-American, but they never have like Caribbean. They do have white, Chinese. To tell the truth, I would like to be called Caribbean, West Indian. Black West Indian.

The teens who were around many black Americans felt pressure from their peers to be part of the group and identify as black American. These teens would consciously talk about passing for American at some points and passing for Haitian or Jamaican at others by changing the way they talked or acted:

> When I'm at school and I sit with my black friends and, sometimes I'm ashamed to say this, but my accent changes. I learn all the words. I switch. Well, when I'm with my friends, my black friends, I say I'm black, black American. When I'm with my Haitian-American friends, I say I'm Haitian. Well, my being black, I guess that puts me when I'm with black Americans, it makes people think that I'm lower class. . . . Then, if I'm talking like this [regular voice] with my friends at school, they call me white.

American-Identified Second Generation

The American-identified second-generation teenagers differed in how little they stressed their immigrant or ethnic identities to the interviewers. They follow a path that is more similar to the model posed in the straight-line theory. They stress that they are American because they were born here, and they are disdainful of their parents' lack of understanding of the American social system. Instead of rejecting black American culture, it becomes their peer culture, and they embrace many aspects of it. This brings them in conflict with their parents' generation, most especially with their parents' understandings of American blacks. They most definitely assimilate to black America; they speak black English with their peers, they listen to rap music, and they accept the peer culture of their black American friends. They are aware of the fact that they are considered black American by others and that they can be accused of "acting white" if they don't speak black English and behave in particular ways. Most included their ethnic identities as background, but none of them adopted the stance that they were not, in a major sense, black American. When asked about ethnic background and how other people think of it, one respondent replied:

Q: What is your ethnic background?
A: I put down American because I was born up here. I feel that is what I should put down. . . .
Q: What do other people think you are?
A: Black American because if I don't say. . . . Like if they hear my parents talk or something they always think they are from Jamaica. . . . But they just think I am black American because I was born up here.

Many of these teens discuss how they do not control how others see them:

> Some people just think I am American because I have no accent. So I talk like American people. I don't talk Brooklynese. They think I am from down south or something. . . . A lot of people say you don't look Haitian. I think I look Haitian enough. I don't know, maybe they are expecting us to look fresh off the boat. I was born here and I grew up here, so I guess I look American and I have an American accent.

Q: If people think you are black American do you ever do anything about it?
A: No, I don't. If they ask me if I am American, I say yes. If they ask me where my parents are from, I tell them Haiti.

In fact, they imply that being a black American is more stylish and "with it" than being from the islands:

> I consider myself a black American. When I think of a black American I don't think of them as coming from the West Indies.

Q: Any characteristics that come to mind?

A: I would not think of someone in a suit. I would think of a regular teenager. I would think of a regular person. I think of someone that is in style.

Q: What about someone from the islands?

A: Jamaicans. They dress with neon colors. Most of the girls wear gold and stuff like that.

Some of the young people told us that they saw little if any difference between the ethnic blacks and the American blacks. Many stressed the Caribbeanization of black New York and described how all the Americans were interested in being Caribbean now:

> It use to be Jamaicans and American blacks did not get along because everyone was afraid of Jamaicans. But now I guess we are closer now. You tell an American that you are Jamaican and it is no big deal. Americans are acting more like Jamaicans. Jamaicans are acting like Americans.

Q: What do you mean by acting like each other?

A: Sure there are a lot of Americans out there speaking patois. And then all the Jamaicans are coming over here and they are like "Yo, what's up" and they are like that. Pretty soon you can't really tell who is Jamaican and who is American.

However, the parents of the American-identified teens have expressed to their children the same negative impressions of American blacks that the ethnic-identified teens reported. These teenagers report many negative appraisals of American blacks by their parents:

> They always say Haiti is better in this way or in that way. They say the kids here have no respect. The kids here are brought up without any supervision. My father is always talking about they

[American blacks] be hanging out on the corner. And he says you won't find Haitians doing that. My mom always says you will marry a Haitian. Why are you talking to those American boys?

This young Haitian American teen tries to disagree with her mother and to temper her mother's interpretations of American blacks:

Q: Are there any characteristics or traits that come to mind about Haitian Americans?

A: Not really. I don't really—cause most people are Haitian American if they are born here. . . . Like me, I don't know if I act like a Haitian or do I have Haitian characteristics, but I'm mostly—like everything I do or like is American. My parents, they do not like American blacks, but they feel that they are lazy. They don't want to work and stuff like that from what they see. And I feel that, um, I feel that way too, but sometimes it won't be that person's fault, so I try to stick up for them. And my mother is like, yeah, you're just too American.

In marked contrast to the ethnic-identified teens, though, the American-identified teens disagreed with their parents' statements about American blacks, reluctantly agreed with some of it but provided qualifications, or perhaps, most disturbingly, accepted the appraisals as true of American blacks in general and themselves as American blacks. This young Trinidadian American swallows her parents' stereotypes and applies them directly to herself:

Q: How close do you feel in your ideas about things to West Indians?

A: Not very close. My feelings are more like blacks than theirs. I am lazy. I am really lazy and my parents are always making comments and things about how I am lazy. They are always like, in

Trinidad you could not be this lazy. In Trinidad you would have to keep on working.

The fact that the teens are identifying as American and that their parents have such negative opinions of Americans causes some conflict. The teens either adopt a negative opinion of themselves or disagree with their parents' assessments of American blacks. But it is not just their parents who criticize black Americans. These youngsters are very aware of the generalized negative view of blacks in the wider culture. In answer to the question, "Do whites have an image of blacks?" all of them responded that whites have a negative view of blacks, seeing them as criminal, lazy, violent, and uncaring about family. Many of the teenagers prefaced their remarks by saying that they did not know any whites but that they knew this is what whites thought through the mass media and through the behaviors of whites they encountered in buses, trains, and stores. This mostly involved incidents such as whites protecting their handbags when the teenagers arrived or store clerks following them and expecting them to shoplift. This knowledge that the society in which they live devalues them because of their skin color and their identity affected these teens deeply.

Immigrant-Identified Teens

The more recently arrived young people who still identify as immigrant differed from both the ethnic- and the American-identified youth. They did not feel as much pressure to "choose" between identifying with or distancing from black Americans as did either the American or the ethnic teens. Strong in their national-origin identities, they were neutral toward American distinctions between ethnics and black Americans. They tended to stress their nationality or

their birthplace as defining their identity. They also pointed to their experiences growing up and attending school in a different country. This young man had dreadlocks and a strong Jamaican accent. He stresses his African roots and lets his Jamaican origin speak for itself:

Q: What is your ethnicity? For example, when forms or surveys ask what your ethnic group or ancestry is what do you put?

A: African.

Q: Do you ever put Jamaican or anything?

A: No, not really. Only where Jamaican comes up is if someone asks where you're from. I'll say I am from Jamaica.

Q: What do people usually think you are?

A: They say I am Jamaican.

Q: They know that immediately?

A: Yeah.

Q: How do they know?

A: I change my voice. I don't have to tell them. I think it's also because of my locks sometimes and the way I carry myself, the way I dress.

While an ethnic-identified Jamaican American is aware that she might be seen by others as American and thus actively chooses to present herself as Jamaican, an immigrant-identified Jamaican could not conceive of herself as having a choice, nor could she conceive of being perceived by others as American. While an ethnic-identified teen might describe herself as Jamaican American, for the immigrant teen Jamaican would be all the label needed. Most teens in this category were recent immigrants. The few U.S.-born teens classified as immigrant identified had strong family roots on the islands, were frequent visitors to the islands, and had plans to return to live there as adults. A crucial factor that allows these youngsters to maintain this identity is that their accents and styles of clothing and behavior clearly signaled to others that they were foreign born.

Q: How important is it to you that your friends think of you in terms of your ethnicity?

A: Oh, very important. You know, I try hard not to lose my roots, you know, when I come to the United States. A lot of people who come here try to lose their accent, you know. Even in the workplace, you know, because they fear what other people might think of them. Even in the workplace. Me, I never try to change, you know, the way I am. I always try to, you know, stay with them, the way of my culture.

Q: So it's something you want people to recognize?

A: Yeah, definitely, definitely, absolutely.

Q: Why?

A: Why? I'm proud of who I am, you know. I'm proud of where I'm from and I'm not going to change because somebody might not like the way I walk, talk or dress, you know.

The importance of birthplace was stressed repeatedly by the immigrant identified as they stressed their difference from American-born coethnics:

Q: What would you put on a form or survey that asked about your ethnicity?

A: I'll say I'm Jamaican. You gotta say where you come from.

Q: And do you think of yourself more as a Jamaican or more as an American?

A: I think of more of a Jamaican 'cause it's, I wasn't born here. I was born in Jamaica and was there for fourteen years.

Q: And what about kids who are born in America, but their parents were born in Jamaica?

A: Well, you see that is the problem. You see, kids whose parents are Jamaican, they think that, well, they are Jamaican. They need to recheck that they're Americans 'cause they was born in the country and they wasn't born outside the coun-

try. So I think they should, you know, know more about American than Jamaican.

Some who adopt this strong identity with the immigrant country were born in the United States, but the combination of strong family roots on the island, frequent visits, and plans to go live there when they are older allows them to think of themselves as not really American at all. This is especially easy to do in the public high schools where there are large numbers of freshly arrived youngsters from the islands.

Q: What do you think your race is?

A: Well, I'm black. I consider myself black. I don't consider myself black American, Afro-American and stuff like that because it's hard to determine, you know, for a person as an individual to determine himself to be Afro-American. . . . I'll be more a Guyanese person because certain things and traditions that I am accustomed to back home, it's still within the roots of me. And those things have not changed for a long period of time, even though you have to adapt to the system over here in order to get ahead and cope with what is going on around you.

While the ethnics tended to describe people as treating them better when they described their ethnic origins, and the Americans tended to stress the antiblack experiences they have had and the lack of difference between the foreign born and the American, the immigrant teens spoke about anti-immigrant feelings and discrimination and responded with pride in their national origins.

Contrasting Identities

In some sense one can see each of these identities as an embrace of one identity and an opposition to another. The American-identified youth are assimilating, in fact, to the American black subculture in the neighborhood. They are adapting to American black cultural forms, and they do so in distinction to their parents' ethnic identities and the wider mainstream white identities. These students adopt some of the "oppositional" poses that American black teenagers show toward academic achievement: the idea of America, the idea of opportunity, and the wider society (Fordham 1988; Ogbu 1990; Portes and Zhou 1993). They also are opposed to their parents' outlooks and ideas, stressing that what worked as a life strategy and a child-raising technique in the islands does not work in the United States. These teens tend to adopt a peer culture of racial solidarity and opposition to school authorities. What is clear from the interviews is that this stance is in part a socialized response to a peer culture, but the vast majority of it comes about as a reaction to their life experiences. Most specifically, the teens respond to their experiences with racial discrimination and their perceptions of blocked social mobility. The lives of these youngsters basically lead them to reject their parents' immigrant dream of individual social mobility and to accept their peers' analysis of the United States as a place with blocked social mobility where they will not move far.

The American-identified teens do not seem aware of the scholarly literature and the perceptions among ethnic- and immigrant-identified youngsters that the foreign born are of higher social status than the American born. In the peer culture of the neighborhood and the school, these teenagers describe a situation in which being American offers higher social status than being ethnic. For instance, several youngsters described "passing" as black American in order not to be ridiculed or picked on in school:

> I used to be scared to tell people that I was Haitian. Like when I was in eighth grade there were lots of Haitians in the ESL classes, and people used to beat them up. They used to pick on them. I said to myself I am going to quiet down, say I am American.

When asked about the images others held of being from the islands, most of the teens described neutral attributes, such as styles of dress. However, many who identified as Americans also described negative associations with the immigrants' identities. The Jamaicans said most people thought of drug dealers when they thought of Jamaicans. A few of the teens also intimated that people from the islands were backward in not knowing how to live in a big city, both in appreciating the wonders of the city and being street smart to avoid crime and hassles with other people. In terms of the former attribute, the teens described people from the islands who were not accustomed to shopping in big malls or having access to a wide variety of consumer goods.

Not one of the American-identified teens voiced the opinion of the overwhelming majority of the ethnic teens that whites were more likely to like the foreign born. In part, this reflected the differences the groups had in their contact with whites. Most of the inner-city ethnic-identified teens had almost no contact with whites, except for teachers. They also are in schools where the vast majority of the students are foreign born or second generation. The larger number of middle-class teens who were ethnic-identified were more likely to have white classmates in citywide magnet high schools, in parochial schools, or in suburban schools or workplaces.

The inner-city American-identified teens also voiced more positive appraisals of black Americans than did the immigrant- or the ethnic-identified teens. Their descriptions reflect the reality of living in neighborhoods where there is crime and violence. A majority of the American-identified teens said that a good trait of black Americans is that they work hard and they struggle. These are the very same children whose parents describe black Americans primarily as lazy and unwilling to take advantage of the opportunities available to them. The children seem to be perceiving a reality that the parents cannot or will not.

Many of these teens live in neighborhoods that are all black and also attend schools that are all black. So, aside from teachers, these young people have almost no contact with white Americans. This does not stop them from absorbing the fact that whites have negative stereotypic views of blacks. But unlike the middle-class blacks who come in contact with whites who tell them that they are "good blacks," these youths live in the urban areas associated with crime, they dress like the typical black urban youth, and they talk with Brooklyn accents and black American slang. When they do encounter whites in public places, the whites do not ask about their parents' backgrounds.

Q: Have you ever experienced any discrimination or hostility in New York?
A: From being Trinidadian no. But because of being black, you know, everybody stereotypes. And they say "blacks, they tend to steal, and stuff like that." So, like, if I am walking down the street and a white lady go by and they smile and I smile. They put their bag on the other side.

The parents of these teens grew up in situations where blacks were the majority. The parents do not want their children to be "racial" in the United States. They define "being racial" as being overly concerned with race and with using race as an excuse or explanation for lack of success at school or on the job. The first generation tends to believe that, while racism exists in the United States, it can be overcome or circumvented through hard work, perseverance, and the right values and attitudes. The second generation experiences racism and discrimination constantly and develops perceptions of the overwhelming influence of race on their lives. These teens experience being hassled by police and store owners, not being given jobs, even being attacked on the streets if they venture into white neighborhoods. The boys adopt black American culture in their schools, wearing flattops, baggy pants, and certain types of jewelry. This contributes to the projection of the "cool pose," which in turn causes whites to be afraid of them. This makes them angry and resentful. The media also tells these youngsters that blacks are disvalued by American society. While parents tell their children to strive for upward mobility and to work harder in the face of discrimination, the American-identified teens think the rewards for doing so will be very slim.

This causes a wide gulf between the parents and their children. These parents are absolutely terrified of their children becoming Americans. For the children, to be American is to have freedom from the strict parental controls of the immigrant parents. This is an old story in the immigrant saga, one visible in novels and movies about conflicts between Jewish and Italian immigrants and their children. But the added dimension here is that these parents are afraid of the downward social mobility that becoming an American black represents to them. And this idea is reinforced constantly to these parents by whites who tell them that they are better than American blacks.

One question about how things had changed since the civil rights movement shows the different perceptions of the teens about race in American society. The ethnically identified gave answers I suspect most white Americans would give. They said that things are much better for blacks now. They state that blacks now can ride at the front of the bus and go to school with whites. The irony, of course, is that I was sitting in an all-black school when they told this story. The vast majority of the American-identified teens state that things are not better since the civil rights movement; the change is that discrimination now is "on the down low," covered up, more crafty. Some pointed out that we were in an all-black school. The result of these different world views is that the parents' view of an opportunity structure that is open to hard work is systematically undermined by their children's peer culture and, more important, by the actual experience of these teens.

On the other hand, the ethnic-identified teens, whose parents are more likely to be middle class and doing well or who attend parochial or magnet schools, see clearer opportunities and rewards ahead, despite the existence of racism and discrimination. Their parents' message that hard work and perseverance can circumvent racial barriers does not fall on unreceptive ears. The ethnic-identified youngsters embrace an identity derived directly from their parents' immigrant identity. Such an identity is in opposition to their peers' identities and in solidarity with their parents' identities. These youngsters stress that they are Jamaican Americans and that, while they may be proud of their racial identity as black, they see strong differences between themselves and black Americans. They specifically see their ethnic identities as keys to upward social mobility, stressing, for instance, that their parents' values of hard work and strict discipline help them to succeed in the United States when black Americans fail. This ethnic identity is very much an American-based identity—it is in the context of American social life that these youngsters base their assumptions of what

it means to be Jamaican or Trinidadian. In fact, the pan-ethnic identities of Caribbean or West Indian often are the most salient label for these youngsters, as they see little differences among the groups and it is more important to differentiate themselves as second-generation Americans. The distancing that these teens show from black Americans often leads them to accept many negative stereotypes of black Americans. These youngsters tend to have ethnic friends from a West Indian background, white American friends, and very few, if any, black American friends.

The immigrant-identified teens are different from either of the other two, because of how they think about who they are not as well as how they think about who they are. These teens have a strong identity as Jamaican or Trinidadian, but this identity tends to be related to their interactions with other Jamaicans or Trinidadians rather than their interactions with black or white Americans. These youngsters identify with their homelands or their parents' homelands, but not in opposition to black Americans or in opposition to white Americans. They tend to be immersed in the immigrant community, to have friends who are all the same ethnicity or from other islands. They tend to be more recent arrivals. Unlike the ethnically identified, however, they do not distance themselves from American blacks, and they have neutral or positive attitudes and relations with them. At the same time, they see themselves as different from, but not opposed to, black Americans.

These identities are fluid and change over time and in different social contexts. We found cases of people who describe identifying very strongly as black American when they were younger and who became more immigrant identified when they reached high school and found a large immigrant community. Most new arrivals to the United

States start out as immigrant identified, and the longer they stay in the United States, the more they begin to think of themselves in terms of American categories. The kind of social milieu the child faces, especially the school environment, has a strong influence on the outcome. A school with many black Americans creates pressure to identify racially; likewise a neighborhood and school with many immigrants makes it possible to avoid thinking much about American categories. In the face of much pressure not to follow the rules and not to succeed academically, youngsters who are doing well in school and do value education increasingly come to stress their ethnic backgrounds as an explanation for their ambition and success.

The American racial classification system that pushes toward an either/or—"black or white"—designation of people makes the immigrant option harder to hold onto. When others constantly identify the individual as black and refuse to make distinctions based on black ethnicity, pressure builds for the individual to adapt his or her identity to that outside identification—either to say "Yes, I am black," and to accept categorization with black Americans or to resent the characterization and strongly make an ethnic identification as Trinidadian American. The American myopia about ethnic differences within the black community makes the middle-ground immigrant identity unstable. Because every young person is aware of the negative images held by whites and the wider society of black Americans, the acceptance of an American black identity also means the acceptance of the oppositional character of that identity. Oppositional identities, as Ogbu (1990) clearly argues, are self- and group-affirming identities for stigmatized groups—defining as good and worthy those traits and characteristics that are the opposite of those valued by the majority group. This tends to draw the aspirations of the teens downward.

Implications of the Patterns

Some of the distancing shown by the ethnic-identified teens vis-à-vis underclass black identity is the same as that exhibited by middle-class black Americans. Elijah Anderson (1990) has noted that middle-class blacks in a gentrifying neighborhood in Philadelphia use various verbal and nonverbal strategies to convey to others that they are not from the ghetto and that they disapprove of the ghetto-specific behaviors of the blacks who live there. Being an ethnic black in interactions with whites seems to be a shorthand way of conveying distance from the ghetto blacks. Thus, the second generation reserves their ethnic status for use as an identity device to stress their distance from poor blacks and to stress their cultural values, which are consistent with American middle-class values. This same use of an ethnic identity is present among first-generation immigrants of all social classes, even those in racially segregated poor neighborhoods in New York.

The second generation in the segregated neighborhoods, with little chance for social mobility, seems to be unaware that status as a black ethnic conveys higher social status among whites, in part because they have not had much contact with whites. The mass media conveys to them the negative image of American blacks held by whites but does not convey to them the image among intellectuals, middle-class whites, and conservative scholars, such as Thomas Sowell, that they have cultural capital by virtue of their immigrant status. They do get the message that blacks are stereotyped by whites in negative ways, that the all-black neighborhoods they live in are violent and dangerous, and that the neighborhoods of whites are relatively safe. They also encounter a peer culture that values black American cultural forms. The immigrant culture of struggle, hard work, and educational success that their parents try to enforce is experienced in negative ways by these youngsters. They see their parents denying them privileges that their American peers enjoy and, unlike the middle-class youth, they do not automatically associate hard work, lack of dating and partying, and stress on scholastic achievement with social mobility. In the peer culture of the school, immigrant- and ethnic-identified teens tend to be the best students. In the neighborhood inner-city schools, newly arrived immigrants who have attended better schools in the islands tend to outperform the students who have spent their lives in substandard New York City public schools. This tends to reinforce the association between ethnicity and school success—and the more American-identified teens adopt an adversarial stance toward school.

Warner and Srole (1945), in their study of Yankee City in the 1930s, report that it is the socially mobile white ethnics whose ties to the ethnic group and the ethnic identity decline. In their work, those individuals stuck in the lower classes turned to their ethnic identities and groups as a sort of consolation prize:

> Our class system functions for a large proportion of ethnics to destroy the ethnic subsystems and to increase assimilation. The mobile ethnic is much more likely to be assimilated than the non-mobile one. The latter retains many of the social characteristics of his homeland. . . . Some of the unsuccessfully mobile turn hostile to the host culture, develop increasing feelings of loyalty to their ethnic traditions, become active in maintaining their ethnic

subsystems, and prevent others from becoming assimilated. But, generally speaking, our class order disunites ethnic groups and accelerates their assimilation. (p. 284)

It could be that the process will be exactly the opposite for black immigrants and black ethnics. In this case, the more socially mobile cling to ethnic identity as a hedge against their racial identity. The less mobile blacks see little advantage to stressing an ethnic identity in the social worlds in which they travel, which are shared mostly with black Americans. Stressing an ethnic identity in that context risks being described as "acting white," being seen as rejecting the race and accepting the white stereotypes, which they know through their everyday lives are not true.

The changes in race relations in the United States since the 1960s are very complicated and most surely involve a mixing of class and race. Some white Americans are trying to see the difference between ghetto inner-city blacks, whom they fear and do not like, and middle-class blacks, whom they do not fear and with whom they would like to have contact, if only to prove to themselves that they are not racist or, in a more formal sense, to meet their affirmative goals.

Middle-class blacks realize this and try to convey their class status in subtle and not so subtle ways (Feagin 1991). The immigrants also utilize the fact that New Yorkers tend to use foreign-born status as a proxy for the class information they are seeking. The white New Yorkers we interviewed do notice differences among blacks, and they use ethnic differences as clues for class differences. If the association found here between social class and ethnic identity is widespread, this perception could become a self-fulfilling prophesy. It could be that the children of poor parents will not keep an ethnic identity and the children whose parents achieve social mobility will keep the ethnic identity. This will reinforce the image in the minds of whites that the "island people" are "good blacks," thus giving the edge in employment decisions and the like to ethnic blacks over American blacks.

On the other hand, it remains to be seen how long the ethnic-identified second generation will continue to identify with their ethnic backgrounds. This also is related to the fact that whites tend to make racial judgments about identity when it comes to blacks. The second generation does not have an accent or other clues that immediately telegraph their ethnic status to others. They are aware that, unless they are active in conveying their identities, they are seen as black Americans, and that often in encounters with whites, the status of their black race is all that matters. It could be that by the time they have children, they will have decided that the quest not to be seen as a black American will be a futile one.

NOTES

1. The families of the teens were from twelve different countries including Jamaica (31 percent); Trinidad (21 percent); Guyana (16 percent); Barbados (10 percent); Haiti (10 percent); Grenada (5 percent); and a few each from the smaller islands of Montserrat, Saint Thomas, Anguilla, Saint Lucia, Dominica, and Nevis.
2. Middle class was defined as having at least one parent with a college degree or a professional or business position. Working class was defined as a parent with a low-skill job; poor were students whose parents were not currently employed.

REFERENCES

ANDERSON, E. 1990. *Streetwise: Race, Class, and Change in an Urban Community.* Chicago: University of Chicago Press.

FEAGIN, J. R. 1991. "The Continuing Significance of Race—Antiblack Discrimination in Public Places." *American Sociological Review* 56(1): 101–116.

FONER, N. 1987. "The Jamaicans: Race and Ethnicity Among Migrants in New York City." In *New Immigrants in New York,* edited by N. Foner. New York: Columbia University Press.

FORDHAM, S. 1988. "Racelessness as a Factor in Black Students' School Success: Pragmatic Strategy or Pyrrhic Victory?" *Harvard Education Review* 58(1) (February).

GANS, H. J. 1992. "Second-Generation Decline: Scenarios for the Economic and Ethnic Futures of Post-1965 American Immigrants." *Ethnic and Racial Studies* 15 (April):173–92.

KASINITZ, P. 1992. *Caribbean New York: Black Immigrants and the Politics of Race.* Ithaca, NY: Cornell University Press.

LIEBERSON, A. 1980. *A Piece of the Pie: Blacks and White Immigrants Since 1980.* Berkeley: University of California Press.

MASSEY, D. 1990. "American Apartheid: Segregation and the Making of the Underclass." *American Journal of Sociology* 96(2) (September): 329–57.

OGBU, J. U. 1990. "Minority Status and Literacy in Comparative Perspective." *Daedalus* 119(2) (Spring):141–68.

PORTES, A., and M. ZHOU. 1993. "The New Second Generation: Segmented Assimilation and Its Variants." *Annals of the American Academy of Political and Social Sciences* 530 (November):74–96.

STAFFORD, S. B. 1987. "Language and Identity: Haitians in New York City." In *Caribbean Life in New York City: Sociocultural Dimensions,* edited by C. R. Sutton and E. M. Chaney. New York: Center for Migration Studies.

SUTTON, C. R., and S. P. MAKIESKY. 1975. "Migration and West Indian Racial and Ethnic Consciousness." In *Migration and Development: Implications for Ethnic Identity and Political Conflict,* edited by H. I. Safa and B. M. Du Toit. Paris: Mouton.

WARNER, W. L., and L. SROLE. 1945. *The Social Systems of American Ethnic Groups.* New Haven, CT: Yale University Press.

WOLDEMIKAEL, T. M. 1989. *Becoming Black American: Haitian and American Institutions in Evanston, Illinois.* New York: AMS Press.

35

THE OTHER UNDERCLASS

Nicholas Lemann

The term "Hispanic," which is used to describe Spanish-speaking American ethnic groups—mainly Mexican-Americans, but also Cubans, Puerto Ricans, Dominicans, Colombians, Salvadorans, Nicaraguans, and immigrants from other Latin American countries—may wind up having only a brief run in common parlance. It has been in official governmental use for only a few years; the Census Bureau did not extensively use the term "Hispanic" until the 1980 census. Now it faces two threats: First, although most Hispanic groups are comfortable with the term, another name, "Latino," is gaining favor, especially on campuses, because it implies that Latin America has a distinctive indigenous culture, rather than being just a stepchild of Spain. Second, the very idea that it is useful to try to understand all Americans with Spanish-speaking backgrounds as members of a single group tends to crumble on examination.

Cubans, who are much more prosperous than the other Hispanic subgroups, have now risen above the national mean in family income. They are concentrated in Florida. Mexican-Americans, who make up about two thirds of the country's 22.4 million Hispanics, live mainly in the Southwest, especially California and Texas. Puerto Ricans are the second-largest Hispanic group—2.75 million people in the mainland

United States. A third of them live in one city—New York.

As soon as the Hispanic category is broken down by group, what leaps out at anyone who takes even a casual look at the census data is that Puerto Ricans are the worst-off ethnic group in the United States. For a period in the mid-1980s nearly half of all Puerto Rican families were living in poverty. It seems commonsensical that for Hispanics poverty would be a function of their unfamiliarity with the mainland United States, inability to speak English, and lack of education. But Mexican-Americans, who are no more proficient in English than Puerto Ricans, less likely to have finished high school, and more likely to have arrived here very recently, have a much lower poverty rate. The *Journal of the American Medical Association* reported earlier this year that, as the newsletter of a leading Puerto Rican organization put it, "On almost every health indicator . . . Puerto Ricans fared worse" than Mexican-Americans or Cubans. Infant mortality was 50 percent higher than among Mexican-Americans, and nearly three times as high as among Cubans.

The statistics also show Puerto Ricans to be much more severely afflicted than Mexican-Americans by what might be called the secondary effects of poverty, such as family breakups, and not trying to find employment—which work to ensure that poverty will continue beyond one generation. In 1988 females headed 44 percent of Puerto Rican families, as opposed to 18 percent of Mexican-American families. Mexican-Americans had a slightly higher unemployment rate, but Puerto Ricans had a substantially higher rate in the sociologically ominous category "labor force nonparticipation," meaning the percentage of people who haven't looked for a job in the previous month.

Practically everybody in America feels some kind of emotion about blacks, but Puerto Rican leaders are the only people I've ever run across for whom the emotion is pure envy. In New York City, black median family income is substantially higher than Puerto Rican, and is rising more rapidly. The black home-ownership rate is more than double the Puerto Rican rate. Puerto Rican families are more than twice as likely as black families to be on welfare, and are about 50 percent more likely to be poor. In the mainland United States, Puerto Ricans have nothing like the black institutional network of colleges, churches, and civil-rights organizations; there isn't a large cadre of visible Puerto Rican successes in nearly every field; black politicians are more powerful than Puerto Rican politicians in all the cities with big Puerto Rican populations; and there is a feeling that blacks have America's attention, whereas Puerto Ricans, after a brief flurry of publicity back in *West Side Story* days, have become invisible.

The question of why poverty is so widespread, and so persistent, among Puerto Ricans is an urgent one, not only for its own sake but also because the answer to it might prove to be a key to understanding the broader problem of the urban underclass. "Underclass" is a supposedly nonracial term, but by most definitions the underclass is mostly black, and discussions of it are full of racial undercurrents. Given the history of American race relations, it is nearly impossible for people to consider issues like street crime, unemployment, the high school dropout rate, and out-of-wedlock pregnancy without reopening a lot of ancient wounds. To seek an explanation for poverty

among Puerto Ricans rather than blacks may make possible a truly deracialized grasp of what most experts agree is a nonrace-specific problem. Although there is no clear or agreed-upon answer, the case of Puerto Ricans supports the view that being part of the underclass in the United States is the result of a one-two punch of economic factors, such as unemployment and welfare, and cultural ones, such as neighborhood ambience and ethnic history.

The First Emigration

Puerto Rico was inhabited solely by Arawak Indians until 1493, when Christopher Columbus visited it on his second voyage to the New World. The island became a Spanish colony, and it remained one until 1898. In that year an autonomous Puerto Rican government was set up, with Spain's blessing, but it functioned for only a few days; American troops invaded during the Spanish-American War and the island became a possession of the United States shortly thereafter. The U.S. conquest of Puerto Rico was not the bloody kind that resonates psychologically through the generations; there was little resistance, and the arrival of the troops was cheered in many places. In 1917 all Puerto Ricans were granted U.S. citizenship and allowed to elect a senate, but until after the Second World War the island was run by a series of colonial governors sent from Washington.

During this period Puerto Rico underwent an economic transformation, as big U.S. sugar companies came in and established plantations. Previously the island's main crops had been grown on small subsistence farms up in the hills. The sugar plantations induced thousands of people to move down to the coastal lowlands, where they became what the anthropologist Sidney Mintz calls a "rural proletariat," living in hastily constructed shantytowns and often paid in company scrip. The most salient feature of Puerto Rico throughout the first half of the twentieth century, at least in the minds of non–Puerto Ricans, was its extreme poverty and overpopulation. "What I found appalled me," John Gunther wrote, in *Inside Latin America* (1941), about his visit to Puerto Rico. "I saw native villages steaming with filth— villages dirtier than any I ever saw in the most squalid parts of China. . . . I saw children bitten by disease and on the verge of starvation, in slum dwellings—if you can call them dwellings—that make the hovels of Calcutta look healthy by comparison." Gunther reported that more than half of Puerto Rican children of school age didn't go to school, that the island had the highest infant-mortality rate in the world, and that it was the second most densely populated place on earth, after Java.

From such beginnings Puerto Rico became, after the Second World War, one of the great economic and political successes of the Latin American Third World. The hero of the story is Luis Muñoz Marin (the son of the most important Puerto Rican political leader of the early twentieth century), who founded the biggest Puerto Rican political party and, after the United States decided to allow the island to elect its own governor, was the first Puerto Rican to rule Puerto Rico, which he did from 1949 to 1964. Muñoz was the leading proponent of the idea of commonwealth status, as opposed to statehood or independence, for Puerto Rico. Under the system he helped to institute, Puerto Ricans forfeited some rights of U.S. citizenship, such as eligibility for certain federal social-welfare programs and the right to participate in national politics, and in return remained free of certain responsibilities, mainly that of paying federal income taxes. (Local taxes have always been high.)

Muñoz's main goal was the economic development of the island. He accomplished it by building up the educational system tremendously at all levels, by using the tax breaks to induce U.S. companies to locate manufacturing plants in Puerto Rico, and perhaps (here we enter a realm where the absolute truth is hard to know) by encouraging mass emigration. Michael Lapp, a professor at the College of New Rochelle, unearthed memoranda from several members of Muñoz's circle of advisers during the 1940s in which they discuss schemes to foster large-scale emigration from Puerto Rico as a way of alleviating the overpopulation problem. "They speculated about the possibility of resettling a breathtakingly large number of people," Lapp wrote in his doctoral dissertation, and described several never-realized plans to create agricultural colonies for hundreds of thousands of Puerto Ricans elsewhere in Latin America.

It's doubtful that the Muñoz government would ever have been able to export Puerto Ricans en masse to Brazil or the Dominican Republic, but in any case the issue became moot, because heavy voluntary emigration to an extremely nonagricultural venue—New York City—was soon under way. In 1940 New York had 70,000 Puerto Rican residents, in 1950 it had 250,000, and in 1960 it had 613,000. In general, what brought people there was economic prospects vastly less dismal than those in Puerto Rico. Back home, at the outset of the migration, industrialization was still in its very early stages, sugar prices were depressed, and thousands of people who had moved from the hills to the lowlands a generation earlier now had to move again, to notorious slums on the outskirts of urban areas, such as La Perla ("the pearl") and El Fanguito ("the little mudhole"). "The whole peasantry of Puerto Rico was displaced," says Ramón Daubón, a former vice-president of the National Puerto Rican Coalition. Among Muñoz's many works was the construction of high-rise housing projects to replace the slums, but during the peak years of Puerto Rican emigration little decent housing for the poor was available locally.

In particular what set off the migration was the institution of cheap air travel between San Juan and New York. During the 1940s and 1950s a one-way ticket from San Juan to New York could be bought for less than $50, and installment plans were available for those without enough cash on hand. Muñoz's government may not have invented the emigration, but it did do what it could to help it along—first by allowing small local airlines to drive down air fares, and second by opening, in 1948, a Migration Division in New York, which was supposed to help Puerto Ricans find jobs and calm any mainland fears about the migration which might lead to its being restricted, as had been every previous large-scale migration of an ethnic group in the twentieth century.

The South Bronx Becomes the South Bronx

At first the center of Puerto Rican New York was 116th Street and Third Avenue, in East Harlem. This was part of the congressional district of Vito Marcantonio, the furthest-to-the-left member of the House of Representatives and a staunch friend of the Puerto Ricans. A rumor of the time was that he was "bringing them up" because Italian-Americans were moving out of Harlem and he needed a new group of loyal constituents. But the migration increased after Marcantonio lost his seat in the 1950 election. By the end of the 1950s the Puerto Rican center had begun to shift two miles to the north, to 149th Street and Third Avenue, in the Bronx, which is where it is today.

At the time, the South Bronx was not a recognized district. A series of neighborhoods at the southern tip of the Bronx—Mott Haven, Hunts Point, Melrose—were

home to white ethnics who had moved there from the slums of Manhattan, as a step up the ladder. These neighborhoods were mostly Jewish, Italian, and Irish. Most of the housing stock consisted of tenement houses, but they were nicer tenements than the ones on the Lower East Side and in Hell's Kitchen. From there the next move was usually to the lower-middle-class northern and eastern Bronx, or to Queens. During the boom years after the Second World War whites were leaving the South Bronx in substantial numbers. Meanwhile, urban renewal was displacing many blacks and Puerto Ricans from Manhattan, and the city was building new high-rise public housing—much of it in the South Bronx. During the mid-1960s another persistent rumor was that Herman Badillo, who had been appointed the city's relocation commissioner in 1961, tried to engineer the placement of as many Puerto Ricans as possible in the South Bronx, so that he would have a base from which to run for office. (Badillo was elected borough president of the Bronx in 1965, and in 1970 he became the first Puerto Rican elected to the U.S. Congress.)

For most of the Puerto Ricans moving to the South Bronx, though, the neighborhood was just what it had been for the area's earlier occupants—a step up (usually from East Harlem). All through the 1950s and 1960s it was possible to see Puerto Ricans as a typical rising American immigrant group (rising more slowly than most, perhaps), and their relocation to the South Bronx was part of the evidence. The idea that New York was going to be continually inundated by starving Puerto Rican peasants for whom there was no livelihood at home had faded, because spectacular progress was being made back on the island: per capita income increased sixfold from 1940 to 1963; the percentage of children attending school rose to 90.

In a new preface for the 1970 edition of *Beyond the Melting Pot,* Nathan Glazer and

Daniel Patrick Moynihan wrote, "Puerto Ricans are economically and occupationally worse off than Negroes, but one does find a substantial move in the second generation that seems to correspond to what we expected for new groups in the city." In keeping with the standard pattern for immigrants, Puerto Ricans were beginning to achieve political power commensurate with their numbers in the city. And the War on Poverty and the Model Cities program created a small but important new cache of jobs for Puerto Ricans which were more dignified and better-paying than jobs in the garment district and hotel dining rooms and on loading docks and vegetable farms.

But the 1970s were a nightmare decade in the South Bronx. The statistical evidence of Puerto Rican progress out of poverty evaporated. After rising in the 1960s, Puerto Rican median family income dropped during the 1970s. Family structure changed dramatically: the percentage of Puerto Ricans living in families headed by a single, unemployed parent went from 9.9 in 1960 and 10.1 in 1970 to 26.9 in 1980. The visible accompaniment to these numbers was the extraordinary physical deterioration of the South Bronx, mainly through arson. Jill Jonnes, in *We're Still Here: The Rise, Fall, and Resurrection of the South Bronx,* wrote:

> There was arson commissioned by landlords out for their insurance. . . . Arson was set by welfare recipients who wanted out of their apartments. . . . Many fires were deliberately set by junkies—and by that new breed of professional, the strippers of buildings, who wanted to clear a building so they could ransack the valuable copper and brass pipes, fixtures, and hardware. . . . Fires were set by firebugs who enjoyed a good blaze and by kids out for kicks. And some were set by those who got their revenge with fire, jilted

lovers returning with a can of gasoline and a match. . . .

Exact numbers are difficult to come by, but it seems safe to say that the South Bronx lost somewhere between 50,000 and 100,000 housing units during the 1970s, and this produced the vistas of vacant, rubble-strewn city blocks by which the outside world knows the South Bronx. Two Presidents, Jimmy Carter and Ronald Reagan, paid well-publicized visits to burned-out Charlotte Street. Theories abound about why, exactly, the South Bronx burned: the excessive strictness of rent control in New York, the dispiriting effects of welfare and unemployment, the depredations of drugs. It is not necessary to choose among them to be able to say that the burning took place because most parties had abandoned any commitment to maintaining a functional society there. It is rare for the veneer of civilization to be eroded so rapidly anywhere during peacetime. Fernando Ferrer, the Bronx's borough president, says, "I remember in 1974 walking around Jennings Street. One weekend everything's going, stores, et cetera. The next week, boom, it's gone. It hit with the power of a locomotive. In '79, '80, it seemed like *every* goddamn thing was burning."

By virtue of the presidential visits and its location in New York City (and its prominence in *Bonfire of the Vanities*), the South Bronx has become the most famous slum in America. To visit it today is to be amazed by how much less completely devastated it is than we've been led to expect. The area around 149th Street and Third Avenue, which is known as the Hub, is a thriving retail district, complete with department stores and the usual *bodegas* (corner stores) and *botanicas* (shops selling religious items and magic potions). A neighborhood like Lawndale in Chicago, in contrast, hasn't had any substantial commercial establishments for more than twenty years. During the daytime the Hub area feels lively and safe. Also, there is new and rehabilitated housing all over the South Bronx, including incongruous ranch-style suburban houses lining Charlotte Street, row houses on Fox Street, and fixed-up apartment houses all over the old tenement districts from Hunts Point to Mott Haven.

What accounts for the signs of progress is, first, a decision during the prosperous 1980s by the administration of Mayor Ed Koch ("kicking and screaming," Ferrer says) to commit a sum in the low billions to the construction and rehabilitation of housing in the South Bronx. This has led to the opening of many thousands of new housing units. Some of them are very unpopular in the neighborhood, because they are earmarked to house homeless people who are being moved out of welfare hotels in Manhattan. Community leaders in the Bronx grumble that there's a master plan to export Manhattan's problems to their neighborhood.

Several impressive community-development groups, including the Mid-Bronx Desperadoes, Bronx Venture Corporation, and Banana Kelly, have played a part in the rehabilitation of the neighborhood, by using funds from the city and foundations to fix up and then manage apartment buildings. Nationally, a generation's worth of efforts to redevelop urban slums haven't worked well on the whole. The lesson of the community groups' success in the Bronx seems to be that if the focus of redevelopment is on housing rather than job creation, and if there is money available to renovate the housing, and if the groups are permitted to function as tough-minded landlords, then living conditions in poor neighborhoods can be made much more decent.

The biggest community-development organization in the South Bronx is the South East Bronx Community Organization, which is run by Father Louis Gigante. Gigante, a Catholic priest, is a legendary figure in the Bronx. He is the brother of Vincent "The Chin" Gigante, the reputed head of the Genovese organized-crime family. He has been associated with St. Athanasius Church in Hunts Point since 1962, but he is an atypical priest: he is tough, combative, politically active (he served on the New York city council, and once ran for Congress), and immodest. The area surrounding St. Athanasius is an oasis of clean streets and well-kept housing, which Gigante runs in the manner of a benevolent dictator. He is known for his tough tenant-screening policy. "You've got to house a base of people with economic strength," he told me recently. "We look at family structure—how do they live? We visit everyone. We look in their background and see if there are extensive social problems, like drugs or a criminal record. Back in the late seventies, I'd only take ten or twelve percent of people on some government subsidy—including pensions. I was looking for working-class people. You cannot put a whole massive group of social problems all together in one place. They're going to kill you. They're going to destroy you. They're going to eat you up with their problems."

For many years the politics of Hunts Point was dominated by a rivalry between Gigante and Ramon Velez, another legendary figure who was also a New York city councilman. Velez ran the Hunts Point Multi-Service Center, a large, government-funded social-services dispensary that provided him with a base of political-patronage jobs. Born in Puerto Rico, Velez came to the South Bronx as a welfare caseworker in 1961, the year before Gigante arrived. A fiery street-corner speaker, he quickly became the kind of up-from-the-streets community leader that the War on Poverty liked to fund. He made the multi-service center into a big organization, ran for Congress once, registered hundreds of thousands of Puerto Rican voters, became a power in the Puerto Rican Day parade, and led demonstrations that helped induce the city to rebuild a large South Bronx hospital, which has been by far the most significant new source of jobs in the area. He was investigated and audited many times because of government money unaccounted for at his organizations. His aides were rumored to carry weapons and to threaten political rivals with violence. (Velez says this isn't true.) Once Velez and Gigante got into a fistfight after Velez called Gigante a *maricón* ("queer"). (Velez insists that this never happened.)

Today Gigante and Velez are both in their late fifties, gray-haired (at least they were until recently, when Velez dyed his hair black), and mellowed. Each professes to have developed a grudging respect for the other. No doubt they will soon be representatives of a certain period of the past—the rough-and-tumble period when the Bronx was just becoming Puerto Rican. Fernando Ferrer, on the other hand, is part of the first generation of Puerto Ricans born and raised in the Bronx to come to power. He has been groomed for leadership ever since; as a teenager, he joined a program for promising Puerto Rican kids called ASPIRA.

A different group—Dominicans—is now streaming into New York (mainly Washington Heights, in Manhattan, but also the South Bronx) but is too recently arrived to have produced the kind of leaders whose names are widely recognized. A common Dominican route to the United States is to pay a smuggler $800 or $1,000 for boat passage from the Dominican Republic to Puerto Rico, and then to buy a plane ticket from San Juan to New York. Estimates of the number of Dominicans who have moved to New York City in the past decade run between a half million and a million. Dominicans are known for their industriousness, and many of them are illegal aliens ineligible for any kind of social-welfare program; they have gone into the undesirable, illegal, or disorganized end of the labor market, working in

sweatshops, driving gypsy cabs, dealing drugs, and operating nightclubs and other perilous small businesses. In New York City, according to Ramon Velez, 6,500 "Puerto Rican-Judases" have sold their *bodegas* to Dominicans. Gigante says that many of his tenants are now Dominican. Partly because the Dominican migration is predominantly male and the Puerto Rican family in the South Bronx is predominantly female-headed, Dominican–Puerto Rican marriages and liaisons are becoming common. Surely the Dominican migration is partly responsible for the increased vitality that the South Bronx has begun to display.

I don't mean to make the South Bronx sound happier than it is. Only a block and a half from the Hub, at the corner of 148th Street and Bergen Avenue, is an outdoor drug market, one of many in the area. There is still a great deal of deteriorated housing and vacant land where housing used to be. I spent a couple of mornings recently at Bronx Venture Corporation, a job-placement and community-development organization in the Hub, talking to Puerto Ricans who had come in to get help finding work. Without exception they wanted to leave the South Bronx. They complained about absent fathers, angry mothers, brothers in jail, sisters on welfare; about ruthless competition with the Dominicans for jobs, shoot-outs between drug dealers, high schools where nobody learns, domestic violence, alcoholism, a constant sense of danger. Something is badly wrong there.

Why Is There a Puerto Rican Underclass?

There is no one-factor explanation of exactly what it is that's wrong. In fact, most of the leading theorists of the underclass could find support for their divergent positions in the Puerto Rican experience.

One theory, which fits well with William Julius Wilson's argument that the underclass was created by the severe contraction of the unskilled-labor market in the big northeastern and midwestern cities, is that Puerto Ricans who moved to the mainland during the peak years of the migration were unlucky in where they went. New York City lost hundreds of thousands of jobs during the 1970s. Particularly unfortunate for Puerto Ricans was the exodus of much of the garment industry to the South. "What I see is a community that came here and put all its eggs in one basket, namely the garment industry and manufacturing," says Angelo Falcón, the president of the Institute for Puerto Rican Policy. When the unskilled jobs in New York began to disappear, Puerto Ricans, who had little education and so were not well prepared to find other kinds of work, began to fall into drugs, street crime, and family dissolution.

The ill effects of unemployment have been exacerbated by the nature of Puerto Rican sex roles and family life. The tradition on the island is one of strong extended-family networks. These deteriorated in New York. "You find the extended family in Puerto Rico and the nuclear family here," says Olga Mendez, a Puerto Rican state senator in New York. The presence of relatives in the home would make it easier for Puerto Rican mothers to work; their absence tends to keep mothers at home, and so does the island ethic that women shouldn't work. In 1980 in New York City, 49 percent of black women and 53 percent of white women were out of the labor force—and 66 percent of Puerto Rican women. Even this low rate of labor-force participation is much higher than the rate for Puerto Rican women on the island. In the United States today the two-income family is a great generator of economic upward mobility, but it is a rare institution among poor Puerto Ricans, whose men are often casualties of the

streets, addicted or imprisoned or drifting or dead. Also rare is the female-headed family in which the woman works. "That poverty rates soared for Puerto Rican families while they have declined for black families largely can be traced to the greater success of black women in the labor market," says a 1987 paper by Marta Tienda and Leif Jensen, two of the leading experts on Puerto Ricans.

Conservatives who emphasize the role of the welfare system in creating the underclass would say that since other Hispanic groups have labor-force participation rates and family structures markedly different from those of Puerto Ricans, the real issue must be the availability of government checks, not jobs. Other than Cubans, Puerto Ricans are the only Spanish-speaking ethnic group for whom full U.S. citizenship (and therefore welfare eligibility) in the immigrant generation is the rule rather than the exception. "What should be an advantage for Puerto Ricans—namely, citizenship—has turned into a liability in the welfare state," Linda Chavez writes in *Out of the Barrio: Toward a New Politics of Hispanic Assimilation.* "They have been smothered by entitlements."

In the community of underclass experts the role of pure skin-color prejudice is not much stressed these days, but the case can be made that it has contributed to the woes of poor Puerto Ricans. A staple of Puerto Rican reminiscence, written and oral, is the shock and hurt that dark-skinned Puerto Ricans feel when they come here and experience color prejudice for the first time. Blacks were enslaved on Puerto Rico for centuries—emancipation took place later there than here—but the structure of race relations was different from what it was in the American South. Plantations were relatively unimportant in pre-emancipation Puerto Rico, blacks were always a minority of the island's population, and there was a much higher proportion of free blacks than in the United States. Puerto Rico never developed the kind of rigid racial caste system that characterized places with plantation economies and black majorities. Intermarriage was common, and there was no bright legal and social line between those having African blood and whites. (The U.S. Census Bureau no longer asks Puerto Ricans to identify themselves by race.) In Puerto Rico, the prosperous classes tend to be lighter-skinned, but dark-skinned people who acquire money don't find the same difficulty in being accepted in neighborhoods and social clubs that they do here.

On the mainland racial prejudice may play a role in shutting Puerto Ricans out of jobs, in ensuring that they live in ghettos, and in instilling an internalized, defeatist version of the wider society's racial judgments. But what's striking about the racial consciousness of Puerto Ricans as against that of African-Americans is the much lower quotient of anger at society. The whole question of who is at fault for the widespread poverty—the poor people or the United States—seems to preoccupy people much less when the subject is Puerto Ricans. For example, conservatives now commonly attribute the persistent poverty of the black underclass to the "victim mentality" expressed by black professors and leadership organizations. I think that the victim mentality among blacks is much more a part of the life of the upper-middle class than of the poor. But even if we grant the premise that ethnic groups are ideologically monolithic, the Puerto Rican case would indicate that the victim mentality doesn't have anything to do with persistent poverty: the Puerto Rican leadership does not have a victim mentality, but persistent poverty is much more severe among Puerto Ricans than among blacks. The National Puerto Rican Coalition publishes first-rate studies about Puerto Rican poverty that take different sides on

the question of whether or not it's completely society's fault—something it's difficult to imagine of the NAACP.

Va y Ven

A final theory about why Puerto Ricans are so poor as a group has to do with migration patterns. During the peak years of migration from Puerto Rico to the mainland, the people who migrated were apparently worse off than the people who didn't. A paper by Vilma Ortiz, of the Educational Testing Service, cites figures showing that in 1960 a group of recent Puerto Rican immigrants had a lower percentage of high school and college graduates than a control group on the island. Ortiz's view that it was not a migration of the most ambitious and capable—that people with less education and lower-status occupations were likelier to move—fits with the idea that for Muñoz emigration was a way to reduce the crush of destitute former peasants on the island. Since about 1970, most experts believe, the pattern has been changing and better-educated Puerto Ricans have become more likely to leave the island, because of a shortage of middle-class jobs there. Oscar Lewis wrote in *La Vida*, his 1965 book about Puerto Rican poverty, "The majority of migrants in the New York sample had made a three-step migration—from a rural birthplace in Puerto Rico to a San Juan slum to New York." (Lewis did a lifetime of work on Latin American poverty which contains a great deal of interesting material, but he is rarely quoted anymore; his reputation is in total eclipse in academic circles because he invented the phrase "culture of poverty," which is now seen as a form of blaming the victim.)

Social critics commonly complain that Puerto Ricans lack a true immigrant mentality—that they aren't fully committed to making it on the mainland, so they don't put down deep neighborhood and associational roots, as other immigrants do, and they are constantly moving back and forth from Puerto Rico. Glazer and Moynihan wrote,

> In 1958–1959, 10,600 children were transferred from Puerto Rican schools, and 6,500 were released to go to school in Puerto Rico. . . . Something new perhaps has been added to the New York scene—an ethnic group that will not assimilate to the same degree as others do. . . .

This is known as the *va y ven* syndrome; those who dispute its existence say that the heavy air traffic back and forth between New York and San Juan is evidence that Puerto Ricans visit their relatives a lot, not that they relocate constantly. "Where's your data [about constant relocation]?" Clara Rodriguez, a sociologist at Fordham University, asks. "There's nothing but travel data."

The migration patterns of middle-class, as well as poor, Puerto Ricans have become an issue in recent years. As has been the case with other ethnic groups, the well-educated and employed Puerto Ricans leave the slums. For Puerto Ricans who came to New York during the 1940s and 1950s—in slang, "Nuyoricans"—the most common sequence of moves was from the island to East Harlem to the South Bronx to Soundview, a blue-collar neighborhood just across the Bronx River from Hunt's Point, and then to the middle-class North Bronx, Queens, New Jersey, or Connecticut.

The consequent isolation of the Puerto Rican poor seems to be even more pronounced than the isolation of the black poor. Churches in black ghettos are all-black institutions often dominated by middle-class blacks; the major churches in the South Bronx are Catholic and aren't run by Puerto Ricans. The work force of the New York City government is a third black and only a tenth

Puerto Rican, meaning that middle-class blacks are much more likely than middle-class Puerto Ricans to return to the slums during the workday to perform professional social-service functions. The most common form of upward mobility in the South Bronx is supposed to be military service (South Bronx soldiers were often in the news during the Gulf War), but that makes people more successful by taking them thousands of miles away from the neighborhood.

The leaders of the South Bronx often don't live there. Ramon Velez has a residence in the Bronx but also ones in Manhattan and Puerto Rico; Ferrer and Badillo live in more prosperous sections of the Bronx; Robert Garcia, Badillo's much-loved successor in Congress, who resigned in a scandal, owned a house north of the New York City suburbs during the time he was in Congress; Yolanda Rivera, who as the head of Banana Kelly is one of the most promising young community leaders in the South Bronx, keeps a house in Old Saybrook, Connecticut. The Reverend Earl Kooperkamp, an Episcopal minister who was recently transferred to a South Bronx church after tours of duty in several poor black neighborhoods in New York City, says, "Anybody who was living here before and making anything got the hell out. In Harlem, East New York, Bushwick, Bedford Stuyvesant, you had the occasional professional. There are no lawyers and doctors in this community."

When middle-class blacks move out of black ghettos, they usually relocate to more prosperous black neighborhoods, which form a nonblighted locus of the ethnic culture. Puerto Ricans who leave the South Bronx for other parts of the New York area tend to melt into more integrated neighborhoods, where it's much harder to maintain the fierce concern with "the race" that has historically existed in the black middle class. Ramon Daubón, of the National Puerto

Rican Coalition, goes so far as to say, "There is no distinctive middle-class Puerto Rican neighborhood in the United States."

There *is* a Levittown for Puerto Ricans who are pursuing the standard dream of escape to suburban comfort—just outside San Juan. "If a Puerto Rican makes fifty or sixty thousand a year here, he wants to move back," says Ramon Velez. "He wants to buy land, build a house." Black middle-class emigrants from ghettos tend to remain in the same metropolitan area. Middle-class Puerto Ricans who move back to Puerto Rico can hardly function as role models, political leaders, counselors, or enlargers of the economic pie for the people in the South Bronx. "Look around in Puerto Rico," Velez says. "The legislature, all the influential people—they're all from New York. Two of my former employees are in the state senate. Those who are able to achieve something here and make money, they go back."

When young middle-class Puerto Ricans leave the island for the mainland because they can't find work as doctors or engineers at home, they often gravitate not to New York but to Sun Belt destinations like Orlando and Houston. The Puerto Rican population of Florida rose by 160 percent in the 1980s. New York now has a reputation on the island as the place that poor people move to, and later leave if they make any money. The percentage of mainland Puerto Ricans who live in New York has dropped steadily over the years, and if you exclude Nuyoricans from the social and economic statistics, Puerto Ricans look much less like an underclass.

Douglas Gurak and Luis Falcón, in a 1990 paper on Puerto Rican migration patterns, argue that poverty, nonparticipation in the labor force, and unstable marriages were often characteristic of the Puerto Ricans who are now poor here, rather than resulting from the economic and social conditions of New York. They write,

It is clear that the selectivity of the migration process . . . results in an over-representation of women in the New York region who are characterized by traits associated with poverty. Those with less labor force experience, less education, more children, and more marital instability are the ones most likely to migrate to the mainland. Those with more stable unions, fewer children and more education are more likely to return to the island.

In Puerto Rico, especially rural Puerto Rico, common-law marriage and out-of-wedlock childbearing are long-established customs. Before Muñoz's modernization efforts brought the rates down, a quarter of all marriages on the island were consensual, and one-third of all births were out of wedlock. (Muñoz himself had two daughters out of wedlock, and married their mother only when he was about to assume the governorship of Puerto Rico.) Female immigrants to New York, Gurak and Falcón say, tend to come out of this tradition, and they are more likely than those who don't emigrate to have recently gone through the breakup of a marriage or a serious relationship. Other Hispanic emigrants, such as Dominicans and Colombians, tend to rank higher than non-emigrants on "human capital" measures like education, family structure, and work history; and Puerto Rican immigrants who settle outside New York aren't generally more disadvantaged than people who remain in Puerto Rico. The overall picture is one of entrenched Puerto Rican poverty becoming increasingly a problem in New York City rather than nationwide.

Although their explanations vary, experts on Puerto Rican poverty tend to agree on how to ameliorate it: both Marta Tienda and Douglas Gurak, for example, call for special educational and job-training efforts.

There is something about black-white race relations in America that leads people in all camps to dismiss those kinds of anti-poverty efforts in behalf of blacks as unimaginative, old-fashioned, vague, unworkable, or doomed to failure. The self-defeating view that the problem is so severe that it could be solved only through some step too radical for the political system ever to take seems to evaporate when the subject is Puerto Ricans rather than blacks.

The Status Question

Or it may be that the reason for the relatively calm and undramatic quality of discussions of Puerto Rican poverty is that the whole issue is really only a sideshow. The consuming policy matter for Puerto Ricans, including mainland Puerto Ricans, is what's known as the status question: the issue of whether Puerto Rico should become a state, become independent, or remain a commonwealth. "It affects our psyche, our opportunity, our identity, our families," says Jorge Batista, a Puerto Rican lawyer who is a former deputy borough president of the Bronx. "The only analogy for you is the Civil War. It permeates all our lives."

Puerto Rico occupies an unusual economic middle ground—worse off than the United States, better off than most of the rest of Latin America. Progress is now coming much more slowly than it did in the Muñoz years. Muñoz retired in 1964, after handpicking his successor. During the next four years, however, Muñoz's commonwealth party split into factions, and in 1968 Luis Ferré, the head of the archrival statehood party, won the governorship. Muñoz, then in retirement in Spain but still a god in Puerto Rico, handpicked another successor, Rafael Hernández Colón. Hernández unseated Ferré in the 1972 election, and the statehood party passed into the hands of

Carlos Romero Barceló. The next few gubernatorial elections pitted Hernández against Romero: Romero won in 1976 and 1980, and Hernández won in 1984, and was re-elected against a different opponent in 1988.

The essential features of commonwealth are federal-income-tax exemption, only partial participation in the U.S. welfare system, and a lack of voting representation in Congress. Psychically, commonwealth status implies a certain distance from the United States—a commitment to the preservation of the Spanish language and of Puerto Rican culture. Like other liberal parties of long standing around the world, the commonwealth party is perceived as both the party of the establishment—of the way things are done in Puerto Rico—and the party of the common man. The party's symbol is the *jíbaro,* the agrarian peasant from the mountains, the closest thing there is to an emblematic national figure. The typical Puerto Rican is no longer a *jíbaro,* but that doesn't matter—the typical Texan is no longer a pickup-driving country boy named Bubba, either. Puerto Rico's idea of itself is as an island of earthy, unpretentious, good-hearted people who treat each other with *dulce cariño,* "sweet caring." It's easy to see how American culture could be perceived as a threat to this ethos, and thus something that should be kept at arm's length.

The statehood party is prepared to take the plunge into American life, although it promises, by way of soothing people's fears, to establish an *estatidad jíbara.* Politically, the statehood party is to the right of the commonwealth party (and far to the right of the small, left-wing independence party) on the classic Latin American issue of whether or not to view the United States as a benign force in the hemisphere.

In terms of what would actually happen under statehood, though, the party, conservative though it may be, would bring into being a conservative counter-utopia. As a state, Puerto Rico would have two U.S. senators and five or six congressmen, all of whom might well be Democrats. And if Puerto Rico became a state, Republicans could find it more difficult to maintain their opposition to making the District of Columbia, even more solidly Democratic, a state too. Taxes on the island might rise significantly, because Section 936 of the Internal Revenue Code, the big Puerto Rican tax break, would be abolished; businesses would presumably relocate elsewhere. Puerto Rico is now given parts of the U.S. social-welfare benefits package, and 1.4 million people, nearly half the island's population, receive food assistance. Statehood would bring full benefits and the welfare rolls of the new state might swell tremendously, not just with islanders but possibly also with mainland Puerto Ricans who would move back. A bitter controversy could be expected to emerge over whether to make English the island's official language.

Robert L. Bartley, the editorial-page editor of *The Wall Street Journal,* who in conservative battles can usually be relied on to side with the ideologues against the pragmatists, recently concluded after a visit to Puerto Rico that "what the statehood issue really needs is a good vacation." Advocates of statehood—a mixture of business interests and the rising lower and middle classes, like Margaret Thatcher's coalition in Britain—acknowledge that it would be worse in the short term, and stress the over-riding historical importance of the island's becoming fully American.

The last time the status question was put to a vote in Puerto Rico was in 1967; commonwealth won. There the matter rested until 1989, when Governor Hernández, at his inauguration, issued a surprise call for resolution of the status question—and then, even more surprising, President Bush announced that he favors Puerto Rican statehood in his first address to Congress.

Bush's Puerto Rico policy is usually explained as an example of his tendency to make decisions more on the basis of personal loyalty than of political analysis. Luis Ferré, the first statehood-party governor, now an eighty-seven-year-old patriarch, is an old friend of Bush's, and endorsed him for President in 1980. Soon after the 1988 election Don Luis came to Washington and stayed as a guest in the Bush home. There, the rumor goes, Bush asked him what he wanted as his reward now that the long crusade for the White House was over, and Ferré said, "Before I die, I would like to hear a President of the United States say before a joint session of Congress that he wants statehood for Puerto Rico."

Bush's remarks in favor of statehood set off a two-year process in Congress to arrange another plebiscite in Puerto Rico. It was supposed to take place this year, but negotiations fell apart over such issues as whether the results would be binding on Congress and whether mainland Puerto Ricans would be allowed to vote. Now the plebiscite is sure to be put off until a year or two after the 1992 election. In the meantime, the commonwealth party's dream is that the U.S. Congress will allow it to be represented on the ballot by an option called "enhanced commonwealth," which would give Puerto Rico greater political autonomy, including the right to negotiate with foreign governments; even if this happens, it is not a foregone conclusion that the commonwealth option will win the plebiscite.

Every possible outcome of the status question would have some effect on Puerto Rican poverty on the mainland. In the almost completely unlikely event of independence, the new Puerto Rican nation would be unable to offer anything like the current level of food-stamp benefits, and presumably there would be another mass emigration of the poor to the United States, motivated by fear of privation; when independence took effect, islanders would lose the right of free immigration to the mainland that they now have as U.S. citizens. Statehood would raise food assistance and other benefits on the island to their mainland levels, and so would engender some migration of the poor from the mainland to the island, thus making the problem of Puerto Rican poverty less severe in New York and other big eastern cities.

Enhanced commonwealth is the only one of the three status options that holds any real promise of spurring economic development on the island in the near future. Even a muted reprise of Muñoz's economic miracle could surely be expected to help al-

leviate Puerto Rican poverty in New York, by drawing people back to the island to find the unskilled jobs that they can no longer find on the mainland.

Obviously, a great deal could be done on the mainland to reduce Puerto Rican poverty. That it can even be discussed as an island problem, susceptible to island solutions, may be the most important of all the differences between the situations of Puerto Ricans and blacks. For many blacks there is, psychologically, a homeland offstage, in the South or in Africa, but nobody can really think of it as a place where the wrenching difficulties of the present might be worked out.

36

MAJOR ISSUES RELATING TO ASIAN AMERICAN EXPERIENCES

Pyong Gap Min

This [reading] introduces major issues relating to Asian American experiences. Some are practical issues with policy implications, such as anti-Asian violence. Other issues concern Asian American experiences that have both theoretical and practical implications. For example, Asian Americans' degree of socioeconomic success is a question of interpretation, using a particular theoretical perspective, as much as a practical question concerning the economic well-being of Asian Americans. Therefore,

whenever necessary, I will introduce a theoretical orientation useful for understanding the issue under consideration.

Depending on our ideological and/or theoretical position, we have different views about which issues are important to the experiences of Asian Americans. As stated in the introductory chapter, this book emphasizes structural factors such as institutional barriers, discrimination, and disadvantages facing Asian Americans, rather than the cultural mechanisms employed for their successful adjustment. This structural approach and the related theoretical perspectives have largely determined which issues concerning Asian Americans are presented [here].

In the 1970s, the U.S. media and many scholars portrayed Asian Americans as successful minority groups that overcame disadvantages through hard work, family ties, and emphasis on children's education (Bell 1985; Kitano 1974; Kitano and Sue 1973; Oxnam 1986; Peterson 1966; Ramirez 1986). Largely in reaction to this "model minority" thesis, Asian American scholars began to emphasize the structural barriers facing Asian Americans. The revisionist critique of the model minority thesis currently has a powerful influence in Asian American scholarship (Chan 1991, pp. 167–71; Chun 1980; Crystal 1989; Divoky 1988; Endo 1980; Furuto et al. 1990; Gould 1988; Hurh and Kim 1982, 1989; Kwong 1987; Okihiro 1988; Osajima 1988; Suzuki 1977; Takaki 1989, pp. 474–84; Wong 1985). The attack on the model minority thesis is not limited to academic research. Activists, social workers in Asian American communities, Asian American faculty members, and the U.S. Commission on Civil Rights have also expressed concerns about the negative consequences of the success image (Asian Pacific American Education Advisory Committee, California State University, 1990; U.S. Commission on Civil Rights 1992; Yun 1989). This [reading] will introduce many issues that revisionist critics of the model minority thesis consider important.

Asian Americans' Underreward and Underemployment

Several topics discussed as major issues [here] concern socioeconomic adjustment. A question underlying all these issues is whether Asian Americans are socioeconomically successful. Traditionally, the U.S. media and many researchers have emphasized Asian American success stories. Those who considered Asian Americans successful focused on their high family incomes (relative to white family incomes) and their high educational levels.

However, revisionist critics claim that this traditional interpretation has little validity. They concede that Asian Americans excel in education and earn relatively high incomes. But they point out that to assess Asian Americans' success in socioeconomic adjustment, we must compare their incomes to their educational levels. Revisionist critics argue that Asian American workers do not receive economic rewards comparable to their education. To support this argument, many researchers have shown, using regression analysis, that Asian workers receive smaller economic rewards for their education than white workers (Cabezas and Kawaguchi 1988; Cabezas, Shinagawa, and Kawaguchi 1987; Hurh and Kim 1989; Tsukada 1988; U.S. Commission on Civil Rights 1988; Wong 1982). This means that Asian Americans need more education to maintain economic parity with white Americans.

Asian American workers' unequal rewards for their human capital investments suggest that they, like other racial minority members and women, encounter structural barriers in the labor market. Dual labor market theory is useful for understanding this social phenomenon. Dual labor market theory was created as an alternative to the human capital investment model to explain earnings. Dual labor market theorists distinguish between primary and secondary labor markets. The primary labor market is characterized by high wages, fringe benefits, job security, unionization, and opportunity for promotion; the secondary labor market has the opposite characteristics. The theory's central argument is that the kind of market a worker is located in is a more accurate predictor of his/her earnings than the worker's human capital investments (Edwards, Reigh, and Gordon 1975; Gordon 1972).

Using dual labor market theory, several sociologists (Bluestone, Murphy, and Stevenson 1973; Doeringer and Piore 1971; Piore 1979) argue that a large proportion of minority members and new immigrants, regardless of their education, are trapped in the secondary labor market. Some revisionist scholars (Cabezas et al. 1987; Cabezas and Kawaguchi 1988; Hurh and Kim 1982; Lee 1989; Toji and Johnson 1992) use dual labor market theory as a frame of reference to discuss Asian Americans' unequal rewards for their education. Partly because of racial discrimination, a higher proportion of Asian Americans work in the secondary labor market than their education levels might indicate. Some scholars (Shin and Chang 1988; Taylor and Kim 1980) show that even Asian workers in the primary labor market, such as Korean immigrant physicians and Asian American government employees, are concentrated in periphery specialty areas or less influential positions.

Moreover, revisionist critics also point out that Asian Americans' high median family income compared to whites' is not a good indicator of their socioeconomic position. Critics provide three reasons for not using family income to measure Asian American economic success. First, the relatively high median family income among Asian Americans is misleading because all Asian ethnic groups have more workers per family than whites. Asian Americans generally need more workers per family to maintain parity with white Americans. Second, Asian ethnic groups' median family incomes do not accurately reflect their standards of living, because Asian Americans are concentrated in San Francisco, Los Angeles, New York City, and Honolulu, where living expenses are much higher than in the United States as a whole. Finally, revisionist scholars argue that average family income is misleading because Asian ethnic groups are socioeco-

nomically polarized. We will come back to this point in the next section.

Negative Effects of the Success Image on Welfare Benefits

Revisionist critics argue that the success image is not only invalid but also detrimental to the welfare of Asian Americans. They point out that because Asian Americans are assumed to be economically well-off, they are eliminated from affirmative action and other programs designed to help disadvantaged minorities. As Hurh and Kim (1989) forcefully argue, "Asian Americans are considered by the dominant group as 'successful' and 'problem free' and not in need of social programs designed to benefit disadvantaged minorities such as blacks and Mexican Americans" (p. 528). Nakanishi (1985–1986) points out that the alleged success of Asian Americans "disguises their lack of representation in the most significant national arenas and institutions" (p. 2). Several revisionist scholars also point out that the success stories of Asian Americans have stimulated anti-Asian sentiment and violence on college campuses and communities during recent years (Osajima 1988; Takaki 1989, p. 479; U.S. Commission on Civil Rights 1986, 1992; Wong 1991). In addition, Hurh and Kim claim that by defining Asian Americans as a model minority, the dominant group has led Asian Americans to develop "false consciousness." Many Asian Americans believe that they have attained middle-class status without realizing they are underemployed and overworked.

Revisionist scholars also point out that the positive stereotype of Asian Americans negatively affects other minority groups as well. By emphasizing the importance of cultural traits and values in Asians' successful adjustment, the success image in effect blames other less successful minority groups for their own failure. It thus legitimates the openness of American society. As one writer (Crystal 1989) comments:

> The existence of a "model minority" supports the belief that democracy "works" and that the racism about which some ethnic groups complain is the product of their own shortcomings and is not inherent in society. To be able to make an assertion is, as one might imagine, extremely important to many persons in power. (p. 407)

The above criticism becomes significant because when politicians and journalists talk about the success stories of Asian Americans, they may intend to suggest that blacks and other minority groups have not succeeded because of their cultural deficiencies.[1]

Revisionist critics have made us aware that the positive stereotypes of Asian Americans can have negative consequences. However, one could argue that the revisionist critics fail to recognize the positive effects the model minority thesis has had on Asian Americans while overemphasizing its negative effects. Positive stereotypes are likely to lead policy makers to be less sensitive to the needs of Asian Americans and to stimulate anti-Asian sentiments among less successful whites and minorities. However, positive stereotypes are also likely to lead many Americans—managers, teachers, community leaders, and home owners—to hold more favorable views of Asian Americans and treat them more favorably. The connection between the positive stereotypes of Asian Americans and their favorable treatment in the classroom, job hiring, and housing is so obvious that we need not provide evidence to support this argument. Nevertheless, there is one empirical study that focused on the positive effects of these stereotypes. In her Westinghouse project, Choi (1988) showed that high school teachers expect Asian students to perform better in science and math

and to be more motivated than white students. Based on the findings, she concluded that "the high expectation feedback the Asian students receive from their teachers might push them a little further than if teachers had a lower expectation of them" (Choi 1988, pp. 17–18).

Underrepresentation in Executive and Managerial Positions

Another important issue regarding Asian Americans' socioeconomic adjustment is their underrepresentation in important administrative, executive, and managerial positions in corporate and public sectors. Asian Americans are well-represented in professional occupations mainly because they are highly educated and obtain professional certificates. However, they are severely underrepresented in high-ranking executive and administrative positions (Chan 1989; Tang 1993; Tom 1988). For example, only two Asian Americans currently serve as presidents of major universities, although Asian American professors constitute a large proportion of the total faculty in American colleges and universities. Few Asian Americans hold important positions in local and federal governments.

Asian Americans may be at a disadvantage for these administrative positions because they lack communication and leadership skills, a result of the authoritarian child socialization techniques practiced in many Asian American families. However, it is also true that many well-qualified Asian Americans are not given these desirable positions because Asians are stereotyped as docile and lacking leadership skills. Compared to blacks, Asian Americans are severely underrepresented in leadership positions, particularly in higher education institutions and government, partly because affirmative action does not apply to them.

Closely related to the underrepresentation of Asian Americans in high-ranking executive and administrative positions is the so-called "glass ceiling." Glass ceiling refers to a situation in which people cannot advance beyond a certain level in their careers. The term can be applied to the mobility barrier facing women and minority members. However, the term is largely used to indicate the difficulty that highly educated Asian Americans encounter in reaching the top of the occupational ladder (Der 1993; Duleep and Sanders 1992; Rajagopal 1990; Tang 1993; U.S. Commission on Civil Rights 1992, pp. 131–35). For example, analyzing the career histories of 12,200 Caucasian and Asian engineers, Tang (1993) showed that there was more racial disparity in managerial representation and upward mobility than in earnings. The glass cciling has been the topic of many seminars and conferences on Asian Americans' occupational adjustment.

Class Homogeneity Versus Class Division

When people claim that Asian Americans are socioeconomically successful, they assume that Asian Americans are more or less homogeneous in socioeconomic status. However, as noted in the previous chapter, Asian Americans are not a socioeconomically homogeneous group. Indochinese refugees and immigrants from mainland China are far behind other Asian groups in socioeconomic status. There are also significant intraethnic differentials in socioeconomic status. Those who emphasize Asian American success in socioeconomic adjustment use statistical averages as the indicators. However, revisionist critics argue that averages are misleading because some Asian ethnic groups are socioeconomically polarized. Statistically speaking, Asian Americans have a bipolar distribution, with proportionally far more people both above and below the average. Occupationally, larger proportions of Asian Americans than white Americans occupy both the highest and the lowest tiers of the occupational hierarchy. Economically, a much larger proportion of Asian Americans than white Americans is at the poverty level, although proportionally more of them belong to the high-income brackets. The Chinese American community is extremely polarized along class lines.

Asian American children's educational performance is also polarized. Using standardized test results as indicators, Asian American students as a group do much better than other minority students, even better than white students. Asian Americans stand well above white Americans in college enrollment.[2] However, as Hu (1989) indicates, Asian American students have the largest proportions of both the highest and the lowest Scholastic Achievement Test scores. Compared to whites, Asian American students include proportionally larger numbers of both super students and poor students. Revisionist scholars criticize the American media for focusing on Asian American students' success stories, giving the impression that most Asian American students are super students.

Ethnic Solidarity Versus Class Conflict

The issue of class homogeneity versus class division is closely related to another issue: the issue of ethnic solidarity versus class conflict. Researchers traditionally emphasized each Asian community's strong ethnic ties based on common culture and national origin (Light 1972; Miyamoto 1939; Montero 1975). For example, in his study of the Japanese community in Seattle, Miyamoto (1939) described ethnic solidarity as its most conspicuous characteristic. However, since the late 1970s, an increasing number of Asian American scholars have shown class conflicts in Asian ethnic communities. The Chinatown study by Light and Wong (1975) highlighted the class division between business owners and ethnic employees and their conflicts over economic interests. Based on his analysis of the Chinese community in Toronto, Thompson (1979) also indicated that class conflict affected the structure of a North American Chinese community. In another article (Thompson 1980), he discussed major classes in Chinatowns in North America and suggested that a modified Marxian class model best describes the current structure of Chinese ethnic communities.

In the 1980s, several researchers showed the economic disadvantages of Chinese workers employed in ethnic businesses in Chinatowns in New York and San Francisco, jobs characterized by low wages and poor working conditions (Mar 1984; Ong 1984; Sanders and Nee, 1987). They suggested that Chinatown business owners achieve economic mobility largely by exploiting co-ethnic employees. The emphasis on economic exploitation is in sharp contrast with the enclave economy thesis, which emphasizes the economic benefits to both business owners and employees in an ethnic enclave (Portes and Bach 1985; Wilson and Portes 1980; Zhou 1992). In his New York Chinatown study, Kwong (1987) stressed the Chinese community's polarization into the working and professional classes. Other scholars consider class division in the Chinese community important in understanding the differences, not only in their life chances, but also in lifestyles, including their family system (Glenn 1983; Huang 1981; Tasi 1980; Wong 1988).

Japanese Americans are culturally and socioeconomically more homogeneous than Chinese Americans and may therefore be less suitable for class analysis. Nevertheless, researchers have recently criticized the research tradition for overemphasizing the homogeneity and solidarity of Japanese Americans (Okihiro 1988). Researchers have increasingly emphasized the class conflict of the early Japanese community rather than its ethnic solidarity (Chan 1991, p. 70; Ichioka 1976, 1988). For example, in his study of first-generation Japanese, Ichioka (1988) highlighted the exploitative relationship between Japanese labor contractors and Japanese labor immigrants. Glenn (1980, 1986) analyzed the difficulty of Japanese American women engaged in domestic service, who were doubly exploited both as Asian Americans and as women.

Family Ties Versus Family Conflicts

Traditionally, the U.S. media and researchers depict Asian Americans as maintaining strong family ties, which facilitate their adjustment in American society. They emphasize that the harmony between husband and wife and parents and children in Asian American families, particularly Asian immigrant families, is based on traditional family values brought from Asian countries.

To what extent Asian Americans maintain family ties is an empirical question that can be determined by comparing Asian American families with white American families. However, our perception may be shaped by our particular approach or theoretical orientation. The traditional interpretation—that family ties facilitate Asian immigrants' adjustment—is the cultural approach, in that it tries to explain Asian Americans' adjustment in terms of their cultural mechanism, family ties. In reaction, more and more researchers now apply the structural approach, paying great attention to the effects of structural conditions on Asian American families. As Kibria

(1993) states in her introduction to Vietnamese immigrant families:

> In contrast to such cultural explanations, I suggest that immigrant families must be analyzed in relation to the external structural conditions encountered by immigrants in the "host" society. These structural conditions provide the fundamental parameters—opportunities and conditions—within which immigrants must construct their family life. (p. 22)

Kibria (1993) indicates that the increase in Vietnamese women's control over economic and social resources and the concomitant decline in Vietnamese men's earning power and social status, contributed, along with other factors, to a shift in relative power from men to women. This shift in power, although desirable from the egalitarian point of view, brings about conflicts and tensions in marital relations as Vietnamese women challenge men's traditional patriarchal authority. The loss of parental social and economic resources and exposure to the American socioeconomic environment have also liberated Vietnamese children from parental control, increasing generational conflicts in Vietnamese immigrant families (see also Tran 1988; see also Min 1993 for marital conflicts in Korean immigrant families).

Glenn's (1983) study of Chinese families was probably the first significant work to examine Asian American families using a structural approach. She emphasized the "changing structure of Chinese-American families resulting from the interplay between shifting institutional constraints and the efforts of the Chinese Americans to maintain family life in the face of these restrictions" (p. 35). Based on a historical analysis, she described three types of Chinese American families that emerged in three different periods: split household,

small producer, and dual-wage worker. Similarly, Wong analyzes four types of Chinese families existing in four different periods. This structural approach to Chinese families is a good contrast to the cultural approach, which emphasized the effects of the Confucian ideology on Chinese American families (Hsu 1971).

Asian Americans' Underutilization and the Myth of Their Mental Health

Another important issue with policy implications is the underuse of mental health services by Asian Americans and the myth of their mental well-being. Data show that, compared to white Americans, Asian Americans are underrepresented as mental health patients (Kitano 1969; Snowden and Cheung 1990; Sue and McKinney 1980). Based on the data, policy makers and non-Asian social scientists assume that Asian Americans have lower rates of mental disturbance than the U.S. general population. They also assume that through strong family ties and informal ethnic networks, Asian Americans can adequately care for mental health patients informally without depending on formal service agencies.

Asian American social workers argue that both of the above assumptions are wrong. Asian American underrepresentation among mental health patients does not imply that they have lower rates of mental disturbance than the general population; it reflects their help-seeking behavior rather than their mental health status (Crystal 1989). That is, moderately disturbed Asian Americans are reluctant to seek help from mental health services (Sue and Morishima 1980). And their reluctance has much to do with cultural values emphasizing avoidance of shame and family integrity (Tsai, Teng, and Sue 1975). Several studies reveal that

Asian Americans, particularly Asian immigrants, have a high level of stress and other mental health problems, higher than white Americans (Hurh and Kim 1990; Kuo 1984; Loo, Tong, and True 1989; Ying 1988). Overall, recent Asian immigrants have more mental problems than native-born Asian Americans. Elderly Asian American immigrants, middle-aged immigrant women, and Southeast Asian refugees in particular have been identified as high risk (Crystal 1989; Kim 1988; Sue 1993).

Asian Americans' mental disturbance is a serious issue. But Asian American social workers and community leaders consider their underuse of mental health services a more serious issue. Funding agencies and policy makers tend to allot funds for mental health services based on use and therefore underestimate Asian Americans' needs for mental health services. Asian American social workers argue that need, rather than demand, should determine funding targets and program policy. As Crystal (1989) states:

> Underutilization is an important issue for the Asian American community because it is still used by governmental agencies to buttress the belief that Asian Americans have low rates of mental disturbance. The criterion of use rather than need determines funding targets and program policy. What must be recognized is the distinction between needs and demands: Low demand as reflected in low utilization should not be misconstrued as an absence of need. (p. 408)

Asian American social workers recommend that mental health service agencies hire more bilingual and bicultural staff members to serve Asian American mental health patients with language difficulties and cultural differences. They also recommend that community education be given to Asian Americans

so that they do not consider mental health problems shameful and private (Sue 1993).

Lack of Political Representation

As previously discussed, Asian Americans have problems in their socioeconomic adjustment. Nevertheless, Asian Americans generally do well due to their success in education and their readiness to work long hours for economic mobility. Although Asian Americans are underrepresented in corporate businesses, they are well-represented in the small-business sector. Compared to blacks and Hispanics, Asian Americans are well-represented in professional occupations and small businesses. However, Asian Americans are greatly underrepresented in politics, far below blacks and Hispanics. As of 1992, there were only four U.S. Congress members of Asian ancestry: two in Hawaii and two in California. In contrast, there were 38 black and 20 Hispanic members of Congress. Outside of Hawaii, where Asians are numerically dominant, only five Asian Americans were elected to the state legislatures, all in Western states. There is only one Asian American on the city council in Los Angeles, the largest Asian American city on the U.S. mainland. Although New York City had nearly 550,000 Asian Americans in 1992, it has never had an Asian American on its city council.

Several factors contribute to Asian American underrepresentation in politics (see Espiritu 1992, pp. 157–63; U.S. Commission on Civil Rights 1992, pp. 157–63). First, because most Asian Americans are recent immigrants, most are not eligible to vote. Moreover, Asian Americans who can vote have lower voter participation rates than other populations (Nakanishi 1985–1986). For example, a survey of California voters found that only 69% of Asian American citizens voted in 1984, compared to 80% of non-Hispanic white and black citizens (U.S. Commission on Civil Rights 1992, p. 158). Their lack of interest in American politics and lack of knowledge about the American political system contribute to their relatively low voter participation rate.[3]

Even if eligible Asian Americans voted in a higher proportion than other populations, they would have difficulty getting Asian American candidates elected to Congress or state legislatures due to their small population size and low level of segregation. Although the Asian American population has radically increased over the last 20 years, it remains small compared to black and Hispanic populations. Outside of Hawaii, there is no congressional district where Asian Americans make up the majority of the population. Even in areas of California where Asian Americans compose a large proportion of residents, Asian American candidates have two additional disadvantages. As already discussed, the Asian American population is characterized by diverse ethnic groups, social classes, generations, and political ideologies. This diversity hinders Pan-Asian solidarity in electoral politics (Espiritu 1992, p. 59). Furthermore, discriminatory apportionment schemes split Asian American voters in one area into several districts. For example, Koreatown, Chinatown, and Filipinotown in Los Angeles are each divided among several city council districts (U.S. Commission on Civil Rights 1992, p. 159).

Discrimination in College Admission

Their cultural tradition stressing education and their higher professional socioeconomic status enable Asian immigrants to successfully educate their children, although there are big intergroup differences in terms of socioeconomic status and national origin (Wang 1993). Although the United States is an achievement-oriented society, Asian societies put more emphasis on children's education. Many Asian immigrants made the trans-Pacific migration mainly in search of a better education for their children. A disproportionately large number of recent Asian immigrants were able to send their children to elite universities. Also, a large number of Asian students annually come to major universities for undergraduate and graduate study. As a result, Asian American enrollment at many prestigious American colleges and universities has increased dramatically. Several campuses of the University of California system have witnessed a phenomenal increase in the number of Asian American students since the mid-1970s. Over the last 20 years, the proportion of Asian American students has also significantly increased in several private universities with national reputations.

Administrators in prestigious universities, perhaps concerned about the radical increase in Asian American students, have taken measures to lessen the increase. Asian American students, faculty members, and community leaders charge that these elite universities used quotas to limit the enrollment of Asian American applicants (Takagi 1990). Recent internal and external investigations suggest that these universities discriminated against Asian American students in granting admission. This is a controversial issue (Biemiller 1986; Lindsey 1987; Reynolds 1988; Takagi 1990, 1992; Takaki 1982; Wang 1988).[4]

The following are some of the major findings from several investigations (see Takagi 1992):

1. A smaller proportion of Asian American applicants received admission than white applicants in several elite universities.

2. Both Asian applicants and Asian students admitted to Brown University had higher SAT averages than white counterparts.

3. A minimum score of 400 on the SAT verbal test was imposed at UC Berkeley to deny admissions to eligible Asian American immigrant applicants.

4. Asian American applicants to UC Berkeley who were eligible for the Educational Opportunity Program were automatically redirected to other University of California campuses.

5. The preferences given to children of alumni and to recruited athletic applicants largely explained the admission rate disparity between white and Asian applicants at Harvard.

Whether or not elite universities discriminated against Asian American students is a complicated issue that cannot be deciphered by statistical facts alone. As Takagi (1990) nicely analyzed, participants in the admissions controversy interpreted the same facts in different ways to justify their claims and counterclaims. In admissions policy, UC Berkeley and other universities combine strict academic criteria with supplemental criteria such as personal essays, extracurricular activities, and extra European foreign language courses. Asian American organizations argue that using supplemental criteria discriminates against Asian American students, who are generally disadvantaged in these areas. However, university officials justify the supplementary criteria in the name of student body *diversity*. That is, they claim that the supplemental criteria add diversity to the class by admitting students with more attributes than good grades and high test scores.

Conservative white politicians have used the Asian American student admissions controversy to attack affirmative action. They argue that elite universities use discriminatory quotas against Asian American students to create a floor for underrepresented black and Hispanic students. They suggest that abolishing affirmative action policies in admissions would eliminate discrimination against Asian American students. However, Asian American leaders object to the pairing of Asian American admissions with an attack on affirmative action. They argue that because Asian American students do not compete with black or Hispanic students, their admission is a separate issue from affirmative action.

When Jewish students in Ivy League schools increased in the first half of the 20th century, Jewish applicants encountered restrictive admission measures. Asian American students will continue to increase in major universities in the future. To lessen the increasing proportion of Asian American students, more restrictive measures may be taken in colleges and universities. However, any such restrictive measure is likely to meet a strong Pan-Asian opposition. If university officials attempt to use measures to curb the increase in Asian American students, it will be interesting to see what arguments they will use and how Asian American organizations will challenge their arguments.

Anti-Asian Violence

Minority members in the United States are often subject to "hate crimes" or "bias crimes"—crimes motivated by animosity toward victims because of their race, religion, sexual orientation, or national origin. In the 1980s, civil rights laws and ordinances were passed to protect minority citizens. Nevertheless, there is evidence that hate crimes against Asian Americans have increased since the early 1980s. The U.S. Commission on Civil Rights monitors and collects data on the violations of minority rights. It regularly releases reports on cases of discrimination and violence against minority members. The reports on anti-Asian discrimination and violence released by the agency in 1986 and 1992 both concluded that anti-Asian violence is on the rise (U.S. Commission on Civil Rights 1986, 1992). Reports released by Los Angeles County in 1990 and 1991 also indicate that hate crimes against people of Asian ancestry have recently increased. Because the Hate Crimes Statistics Act enacted in 1990 requires the U.S. Attorney General to collect and report data on hate crimes, more accurate information on hate crimes against Asian Americans will be available in the future.

Several factors have contributed to the rise in hate crimes against Asian Americans. First of all, the great increase in the Asian American population has contributed to the rise in anti-Asian crimes. As previously noted, Asian Americans currently constitute a large proportion of the population in many cities. The increase in the Asian American population simply increases the likelihood that more Asian Americans will interact with members of non-Asian groups, and thus more of them will be targets of hate crimes. Moreover, the increase in Asian immigrants with language barriers and different customs is likely to increase the prejudice against Asian Americans.

Second, economic factors play an important role in the increase of anti-Asian violence. The economic recession that began in the mid-1970s coincided with the influx of Asian immigrants. Many Americans, both black and white, feel that new Asian immigrants took over their jobs and businesses, although research shows that this was not the case (Borjas 1989; Simon 1989). Many Korean immigrants established businesses in black inner-city neighborhoods as living conditions of the black underclass became increasingly worse. Korean merchants all over the country have been targets of black hostility in the form of physical assault, boycott, arson, murder, and press attack. Black hostility toward Korean merchants culminated during the Los Angeles race riots in the spring of 1992, when more than 2,000 Korean-owned stores were burned and/or looted. Undoubtedly, black people's perception that Korean immigrants economically exploit them is mainly responsible for black hostility toward Koreans.

Another economic factor influencing the recent rise in anti-Asian violence cases is the trade deficit between the United States and Japan and the general perception that Japanese imports cause economic problems in the United States. Vincent Chin, a Chinese American, was murdered in 1982 by two white auto workers who, mistaking him for a Japanese, sought a scapegoat for their economic problems (Wong 1991). As the U.S. economic situation further deteriorated in 1991, U.S. media and high-ranking politicians blamed the Japanese for the trade imbalance. The high unemployment rate and the political controversy over trade deficits heightened anti-Japanese sentiments all over the country. Recent Japan bashing culminated in the murder of a Japanese businessman in his home in Ventura County, California, in February 1992. Two weeks before he was stabbed to death, he was threatened by two white young men, who blamed Japan for causing economic problems in the United States ("A Japanese," 1992).

Closely related to the economic factors in anti-Asian violence is the success image of Asian Americans. As previously discussed, both the U.S. media and scholars depict Asian Americans as "successful model minorities," which has negative effects on the interests of Asian Americans. The success image can heighten the resentment toward Asian American academic and economic success and in turn increase hate crimes against them. Many white Americans, particularly those in the lower tiers of the socioeconomic hierarchy, are jealous and resentful of Asian Americans' success. Out of their status anxiety, they believe that Asian Americans belong to an "inferior race." Asian Americans' success image only strengthens their status anxiety.

NOTES

1. Since the late 1960s, various cultural explanations have been severely criticized in the field of race and ethnic relations in the United States mainly because of this conservative implication, the implication that they "blame the victims."
2. For example, the 1990 census indicates that 54.1% of Asian Americans 20 to 21 years old were enrolled in school in comparison to only 33.3% of their white counterparts (U.S. Bureau of the Census 1993, pp. 1, 97, 98).
3. Survey studies have shown that Asian American immigrants are more interested in home country politics than politics in the United States.
4. Takagi's book (1992) most systematically analyzed the controversy.

REFERENCES

Asian Pacific American Education Advisory Committee, California State University. 1990. *Enriching California's Future: Asian Pacific Americans in the CSU.* Long Beach: Office of the Chancellor, California State University.

BELL, D. A. 1985. "The Triumph of Asian-Americans: America's Greatest Success Story." *New Republic,* July 15, pp. 22, 24–31.

BIEMILLER, L. 1986. "Asian Students Fear Top Colleges Use Quota Systems." *The Chronicle of Higher Education,* November 19, p. 3.

BLUESTONE, B., W. MURPHY, and M. STEVENSON. 1973. *Low Wages and the Working Poor.* Ann Arbor: Institute of Labor and Industrial Relations, University of Michigan.

BORJAS, G. 1989. *Friends or Strangers: Impacts of Immigrants on U.S. Economy.* New York: Basic Books.

CABEZAS, A., and G. KAWAGUCHI. 1988. "Empirical Evidence for Continuing Asian American Income Inequality: The Human Capital Model and Labor Market Segmentation." Pp. 144–64 in *Reflections on Shattered Windows: Promises and Prospects for Asian American Studies,* edited by G. Y. Okihiro, S. Hune, A. A. Hansen, and J. M. Liu. Pullman: Washington State University Press.

CABEZAS, A., L. SHINAGAWA, and G. KAWAGUCHI. 1987. "New Inquiries into the Socioeconomic Status of Pilipino Americans in California." *Amerasia Journal* 13:1–22.

CHAN, S. 1989. "Beyond the Affirmative Action: Empowering Asian American Faculty." *Change* (November/December):48–51.

CHAN, S. 1991. *Asian Americans: An Interpretive History.* Boston: Twayne.

CHOI, M. 1988. *Race, Gender and Eyeglasses: Teachers' Perceptions of Asian, Black and White Students.* Paper submitted to Westinghouse Science Talent Search, Stuyvesant High School, New York City.

CHUN, K. T. 1980. "The Myth of Asian American Success and Its Educational Ramifications." *IRCD Bulletin* 15:1–12.

CRYSTAL, D. 1989. "Asian Americans and the Myth of the Model Minority." *Social Casework* 70:405–413.

DER, H. 1993. "Asian Pacific Islanders and the 'Glass Ceiling'—New Era of Civil Rights Activism." Pp. 215–32 in *The State of Asian Pacific America: Policy Issues to the Year 2000,* edited by LEAP Asian Pacific Islander Public Policy Institute and UCLA Asian American Studies Center. Los Angeles: LEAP Asian Pacific Islander Public Policy Institute and UCLA Asian American Studies Center.

DIVOKY, D. 1988. "The Model Minority Goes to School." *Phi Delta Kappan* 70:219–22.

DOERINGER, P. B., and M. PIORE. 1971. *Internal Labor Market and Manpower Analysis.* Lexington, MA: Heath.

DULEEP, H. O., and S. SANDERS. 1992. "Discrimination at the Top: American-Born Asian and White Men." *Industrial Relations* 31: 416–32.

EDWARDS, R., M. REIGH, and D. GORDON, eds. 1975. *Labor Market Segmentation.* Lexington, MA: Heath.

ENDO, R. 1980. "Asian Americans and Higher Education." *Phylon* 41:367–78.

ESPIRITU, Y. L. 1992. *Asian American Panethnicity: Bridging Institutions and Identities.* Philadelphia: Temple University Press.

FURUTO, S. M., R. BISWAS, D. K. CHUNG, K. MURASE, and F. ROSS-SHERIFF, eds. 1990. *Social Work Practice with Asian Americans.* Newbury Park, CA: Sage.

GLENN, E. N. 1980. "The Dialectics of Wage Work: Japanese-American Women and Domestic Service, 1905–1940." *Feminist Studies* 6:432–71.

———. 1983. "Split Household, Small Producer and Dual Wage Earner: An Analysis of

Chinese American Family Strategies." *Journal of Marriage and the Family* 45:35–46.

———. 1986. *Issei, Nisei, War Bride: Three Generations of Japanese American Women in Domestic Service.* Philadelphia: Temple University Press.

GORDON, D. M. 1972. *Theories of Poverty and Underemployment.* Lexington, MA: Lexington Books.

GOULD, K. H. 1988. "Asian and Pacific Islanders: Myth and Reality." *National Association of Social Workers* 37:142–47.

HSU, F. L. K. 1971. *The Challenge of the American Dream: The Chinese in the United States.* Belmont, CA: Wadsworth.

HU, A. 1989. "Asian Americans: Model or Double Minority?" *Amerasia Journal* 15(1):243–57.

HUANG, L. J. 1981. "The Chinese American Family." Pp. 115–41 in *Ethnic Families in America: Patterns and Variations,* 2nd ed., edited by C. H. Mindel and R. W. Habenstein. New York: Elsevier.

HURH, W. M., and K. C. KIM. 1982. "Race Relations Paradigm and Korean-American Research: A Sociology of Knowledge Perspective." Pp. 219–46 in *Koreans in Los Angeles: Prospects and Promises,* edited by Eui-Young Yu, E. Phillips, and Eun Sik Yang. Los Angeles: Center for Korean and Korean-American Studies, California State University.

———. 1989. "The 'Success' Image of Asian Americans: Its Validity and Its Practical Implications." *Ethnic and Racial Studies* 12:512–38.

———. 1990. "Correlates of Korean Immigrants' Mental Health." *Journal of Nervous and Mental Disease* 178:703–711.

ICHIOKA, Y. 1976. "Early Issei Socialists and the Japanese Community." Pp. 47–62 in *Counterpoint: Perspectives on Asian America,* edited by E. Gee. Los Angeles: Asian American Studies Center, University of California at Los Angeles.

———. 1988. *The Issei: The World of the First Generation Japanese Immigrants, 1885–1924.* New York: Free Press.

"A Japanese Businessman Was Stabbed to Death." 1992. *Korea Times Los Angeles,* February 26, p. 2.

KIBRIA, N. 1993. *Family Tightrope: The Changing Lives of Vietnamese Americans.* Princeton, NJ: Princeton University Press.

KIM, U. C. 1988. *Acculturation of Korean Immigrants to Canada: Psychological, Demographic and Behavioral Profiles of Emigrating Koreans, Non-Emigrating Koreans, and Korean-Canadians.* Unpublished doctoral dissertation, Queens University at Kingston, Canada.

KITANO, H. 1969. "Japanese-American Mental Illness." Pp. 256–84 in *Changing Perspectives in*
Mental Illness, edited by S. C. Plog and R. B. Edgerton. New York: Holt, Rinehart & Winston.

———. 1974. "Japanese Americans: The Development of a Middleman Minority." *Pacific Historical Review* 43:500–519.

KITANO, H., and S. SUE. 1973. "The Model Minorities." *Journal of Social Issues* 29:1–9.

KUO, W. H. 1984. "Prevalence of Depression Among Asian Americans." *Journal of Nervous and Mental Disease* 172:449–57.

KWONG, P. 1987. *The New Chinatown.* New York: Noonsday.

LEE, S. 1989. "Asian Immigration and American Race-Relations: From Exclusion to Acceptance." *Ethnic and Racial Studies* 12:368–90.

LIGHT, I. 1972. *Ethnic Enterprise in North America: Business and Welfare Among Chinese, Japanese, and Blacks.* Berkeley: University of California Press.

LIGHT, I., and C. C. WONG. 1975. "Protest or Work: Dilemmas of the Tourist Industry in American Chinatown." *American Journal of Sociology* 80:1342–68.

LINDSEY, R. 1987. "Colleges Accused of Biases to Stem Asians' Gains." *The New York Times,* January 19, p. 6.

LOO, C., B. TONG, and R. TRUE. 1989. "A Bitter Bean: Mental Health Status and Attitudes in Chinatown." *Journal of Community Psychology* 17:183–296.

MAR, D. 1984. "Chinese Immigrant Women and the Ethnic Labor Market." *Critical Perspectives of Third World America* 2:62–74.

MIN, P. G. 1993. "Korean Immigrant Wives' Overwork." *Korea Journal of Population and Development* 21:23–36.

MIYAMOTO, S. F. 1939. *Social Solidarity Among the Japanese in Seattle* (publications in the Social Sciences, Vol. 11, No. 2). Seattle: University of Washington.

MONTERO, D. M. 1975. *The Japanese American Community: A Study of Generational Changes in Ethnic Affiliation.* Doctoral dissertation, University of California, Los Angeles.

NAKANISHI, D. T. 1985–1986. "Asian American Politics: An Agenda for Research." *Amerasia Journal* 12(2):1–27.

OKIHIRO, G. Y. 1988. "The Idea of Community and a 'Particular Type of History.'" Pp. 175–83 in *Reflections on Shattered Windows,* edited by G. Y. Okihiro, S. Hune, A. A. Hansen, and J. M. Liu. Pullman: Washington State University Press.

ONG, P. 1984. "Chinatown Unemployment and the Ethnic Labor Market." *Amerasia Journal* 11:35–54.

OSAJIMA, K. 1988. "Asian Americans as a Model Minority: An Analysis of the Popular Press Image in the 1960s and the 1980s." Pp. 165–74 in *Reflections on Shattered Windows*, edited by G. Y. Okihiro, S. Hune, A. Hansen, and J. Liu. Pullman: Washington University Press.

OXNAM, R. 1986. "Why Asians Succeed Here." *New York Times Magazine*, November 30, pp. 89–90, 92.

PETERSON, W. 1966. "Success Story, Japanese-American Style." *New York Times Magazine*, January 9, pp. 20–21, 33, 36, 38, 40–41, 43.

PIORE, M. 1979. *Birds of Passage: Migrant Labor and Industrial Societies*. London: Cambridge University Press.

PORTES, A., and R. BACH. 1985. *Latin Journey: Cuban and Mexican Immigrants in the United States*. Berkeley: University of California Press.

RAJAGOPAL, I. 1990. "The Glass Ceiling in the Vertical Mosaic: Indian Immigrants in Canada." *Canadian Ethnic Studies* 22:96–105.

RAMIREZ, A. 1986. "America's Super Minority." *Fortune Magazine*, November 24, pp. 148–49, 152, 156, 160.

REYNOLDS, W. B. 1988. *Discrimination Against Asian Americans in Higher Education: Evidence, Causes, and Cures*. Washington, DC: Civil Rights Division, Department of Justice.

SANDERS, J., and V. NEE. 1987. "The Limits of Ethnic Solidarity in the Enclave Economy." *American Sociological Review* 52:745–67.

SHIN, E. H., and K. S. CHANG. 1988. "Peripherization of Immigrant Professionals: Korean Physicians in the United States." *International Migration Review* 22:609–626.

SIMON, J. 1989. *The Economic Consequences of Immigration*. Cambridge, MA: Basil Blackwell.

SNOWDEN, L. R., and F. K. CHEUNG. 1990. "Use of Inpatient Mental Health Services by Members of Ethnic Minority Groups." *American Psychologists* 45:347–55.

SUE, S. 1993. "The Changing Asian American Population: Mental Health Policy." Pp. 79–93 in *The State of Asian Pacific America: Policy Issues to the Year 2020*, edited by LEAP Asian Pacific American Public Policy Institute and UCLA Asian American Studies Center. Los Angeles: LEAP Asian Pacific American Public Policy Institute and UCLA Asian American Studies Center.

SUE, S., and H. MCKINNEY. 1980. "Asian Americans in the Community Mental Health Care System." Pp. 291–310 in *Asian Americans: Social and Psychological Perspectives*, Vol. 2, edited by R. Endo, S. Sue, and N. Wagner. Palo Alto, CA: Science and Behavior Books.

SUE, S., and J. MORISHIMA. 1980. *The Mental Health of Asian Americans*. San Francisco: Jossey-Bass.

SUZUKI, B. H. 1977. "Education and the Socialization of Asian Americans: A Revisionist Analysis of the 'Model Minority' Thesis." *Amerasia Journal* 4:23–51.

TAKAGI, D. Y. 1990. "From Discrimination to Affirmative Action: Facts in the Asian American Admissions Controversy." *Social Problems* 37:578–92.

———. 1992. *The Retreat from Race: Asian-American Admissions and Racial Politics*. New Brunswick, NJ: Rutgers University Press.

TAKAKI, R. 1982. "The Myth of Ethnicity: Scholarship of the Anti-Affirmative Action Backlash." *Journal of Ethnic Studies* 10:17–42.

———. 1989. *Strangers from a Different Shore: A History of Asian Americans*. Boston: Little, Brown.

TANG, J. 1993. "The Career Attainment of Caucasian and Asian Engineers." *The Sociological Quarterly* 34:467–96.

TASI, F. W. 1980. "Diversity and Conflict Between Old and New Chinese Immigrants in the United States." Pp. 324–37 in *Source Book on New Immigration*, edited by R. S. Bryce-Laporte. New Brunswick: Transaction.

TAYLOR, P. A., and S. S. KIM. 1980. "Asian Americans in the Federal Civil Service, 1977." *California Sociologist* 3:1–16.

THOMPSON, R. H. 1979. "Ethnicity vs. Class: An Analysis of Conflict in a North American Chinese Community." *Ethnicity* 6:306–326.

———. 1980. "From Kinship to Class: A New Model of Urban Overseas Chinese Social Organization." *Urban Anthropology* 9:265–93.

TOJI, D. S., and J. H. JOHNSON. 1992. "Asian and Pacific Islander American Poverty: The Working Poor and the Jobless Poor." *Amerasia Journal* 18(1):83–91.

TOM, G. 1988. "The Bifurcated World of the Chinese American." *Asian Profile* 16:1–10.

TRAN, T. V. 1988. "The Vietnamese American Family." Pp. 276–302 in *Ethnic Families in America: Patterns and Variations*, 3rd ed., edited by C. Mindel, R. Habenstein, and R. Wright, Jr. New York: Elsevier.

TSAI, M., L. N. TENG, and S. SUE. 1975. "Mental Status of Chinese in the United States." *American Journal of Orthopsychiatry* 45:111–18.

TSUKADA, M. 1988. "Income Parity Through Different Paths: Chinese Americans, Japanese Americans, and Caucasians in Hawaii." *Amerasia Journal* 14(2):47–60.

U.S. Bureau of the Census. 1993. *1990 Census of Population, General Population Characteristics, the United States* (CP-1-1). Washington, DC: U.S. Government Printing Office.

U.S. Commission on Civil Rights. 1986. *Recent Activities Against Citizens and Residents of Asian Descent*. Washington, DC: U.S. Government Printing Office.

————. 1988. *The Economic Status of Americans of Asian Descent: An Exploratory Investigation*. Washington, DC: U.S. Government Printing Office.

————. 1992. *Civil Rights Issues Facing Asian-Americans, 1990*. Washington, DC: U.S. Government Printing Office.

WANG, L. C. 1988. "Meritocracy and Diversity in Higher Education: Discrimination Against Asian Americans in the Post-Bakke Era." *Urban Review* 20:189–209.

————. 1993. "Trends in Admissions for Asian Americans in Colleges and Universities." Pp. 49–59 in *The State of Asian Pacific America,* edited by LEAP Asian Pacific American Policy Institute and UCLA Asian American Studies Center. Los Angeles: LEAP Asian Pacific American Public Policy Institute and UCLA Asian American Studies Center.

WILSON, K., and A. PORTES. 1980. "Immigrant Enclaves: An Analysis of the Labor Market Experiences of Cubans in Miami." *American Journal of Sociology* 86:305–319.

WONG, E. F. 1985. "Asian American Middleman Minority Theory: The Framework of an American Myth." *Journal of Ethnic Studies* 13:51–88.

WONG, M. 1982. "The Cost of Being Chinese, Japanese and Filipino in the United States, 1960, 1970, 1976." *Pacific Sociological Review* 5:59–78.

————. 1988. "The Chinese American Family." Pp. 230–57 in *Ethnic Families in America: Patterns and Variations,* edited by C. H. Mindel, R. W. Habenstein, and R. Wright, Jr. New York: Elsevier.

————. 1991. *Rise in Hate Crimes Against Asians in the United States*. Paper presented at the Annual Meeting of the American Sociological Association, Cincinnati.

YING, Y. 1988. "Depressive Symptomatology Among Chinese Americans as Measured by the CES-D." *Journal of Clinical Psychology* 44:739–46.

YUN, G., ed. 1989. *A Look Beyond the Model Minority Image*. New York: Minority Rights Groups, Asian and Pacific American Project.

ZHOU, M. 1992. *Chinatown: The Socioeconomic Potential of an Urban Enclave*. Philadelphia: Temple University Press.

37

"IS THIS A WHITE COUNTRY, OR WHAT?"

Lillian B. Rubin

They're letting all these coloreds come in and soon there won't be any place left for white people," broods Tim Walsh, a 33-year-old white construction

worker. "It makes you wonder: Is this a white country, or what?"

It's a question that nags at white America, one perhaps that's articulated most often and most clearly by the men and women of the working class. For it's they who feel most vulnerable, who have suffered the economic contractions of recent decades most keenly, who see the new immigrants most clearly as direct competitors for their jobs.

It's not whites alone who stew about immigrants. Native-born blacks, too, fear the newcomers nearly as much as whites—and for the same economic reasons. But for whites the issue is compounded by race, by the fact that the newcomers are primarily people of color. For them, therefore, their economic anxieties have combined with the changing face of America to create a profound uneasiness about immigration—a theme that was sounded by nearly 90 percent of the whites I met, even by those who are themselves first-generation, albeit well-assimilated, immigrants.

Sometimes they spoke about this in response to my questions; equally often the subject of immigration arose spontaneously as people gave voice to their concerns. But because the new immigrants are predominantly people of color, the discourse was almost always cast in terms of race as well as immigration, with the talk slipping from immigration to race and back again as if these are not two separate phenomena. "If we keep letting all them foreigners in, pretty soon there'll be more of them than us and then what will this country be like?" Tim's wife, Mary Anne, frets. "I mean, this is *our* country, but the way things are going, white people will be the minority in our own country. Now does that make any sense?"

Such fears are not new. Americans have always worried about the strangers who came to our shores, fearing that they would corrupt our society, dilute our culture, debase our values. So I remind Mary Anne, "When your ancestors came here, people also thought we were allowing too many foreigners into the country. Yet those earlier immigrants were successfully integrated into the American society. What's different now?"

"Oh, it's different, all right," she replies without hesitation. "When my people came, the immigrants were all white. That makes a big difference."

"Why do you think that's so?"

"I don't know; it just is, that's all. Look at the black people; they've been here a long time, and they still don't live like us—stealing and drugs and having all those babies."

"But you were talking about immigrants. Now you're talking about blacks, and they're not immigrants."

"Yeah, I know," she replies with a shrug. "But they're different, and there's enough problems with them, so we don't need any more. With all these other people coming here now, we just have more trouble. They don't talk English; and they think different from us, things like that."

Listening to Mary Anne's words I was reminded again how little we Americans look to history for its lessons, how impoverished is our historical memory. For, in fact, being white didn't make "a big difference" for many of those earlier immigrants. The dark-skinned Italians and the eastern European Jews who came in the late nineteenth and early twentieth centuries didn't look very white to the fair-skinned Americans who were here then. Indeed, the same people we now call white—Italians, Jews, Irish—were seen as another race at that time. Not black or Asian, it's true, but an alien other, a race apart, although one that didn't have a clearly defined name. Moreover, the racist fears and fantasies of native-born Americans were far less contained then than they are now, largely because there were few social constraints on their expression.

When, during the nineteenth century, for example, some Italians were taken for blacks and lynched in the South, the incidents passed virtually unnoticed. And if Mary Anne and Tim Walsh, both of Irish ancestry, had come to this country during the great Irish immigration of that period, they would have found themselves defined as an inferior race and described with the same language that was used to characterize blacks: "low-browed and savage, grovelling and bestial, lazy and wild, simian and sensual."[1] Not only during that period but for a long time afterward as well, the U.S. Census Bureau counted Irish as a distinct and separate group, much as it does today with the category it labels "Hispanic."

But there are two important differences between then and now, differences that can be summed up in a few words: the economy and race. Then, a growing industrial economy meant that there were plenty of jobs for both immigrant and native workers, something that can't be said for the contracting economy in which we live today. True, the arrival of the immigrants, who were more readily exploitable than native workers, put Americans at a disadvantage and created discord between the two groups. Nevertheless, work was available for both.

Then, too, the immigrants—no matter how they were labeled, no matter how reviled they may have been—were ultimately assimilable, if for no other reason than that they were white. As they began to lose their alien ways, it became possible for native Americans to see in the white ethnics of yesteryear a reflection of themselves. Once this shift in perception occurred, it was possible for the nation to incorporate them, to take them in, chew them up, digest them, and spit them out as Americans—with subcultural variations not always to the liking of those who hoped to control the manners and mores of the day, to be sure, but still recognizably white Americans.

Today's immigrants, however, are the racial other in a deep and profound way. It's true that race is not a fixed category, that it's no less an *idea* today than it was yesterday. And it's also possible, as I have already suggested, that we may be witness to social transformation from race to ethnicity among some of the most assimilated—read: middle-class—Asians and Latinos. But even if so, there's a long way to go before that metamorphosis is realized. Meanwhile, the immigrants of this era not only bring their own language and culture, they are also people of color—men, women, and children whose skin tones are different and whose characteristic features set them apart and justify the racial categories we lock them into.[2] And integrating masses of people of color into a society where race consciousness lies at the very heart of our central nervous system raises a whole new set of anxieties and tensions.

It's not surprising, therefore, that racial dissension has increased so sharply in recent years. What is surprising, however, is the passion for ethnicity and the preoccupation with ethnic identification among whites that seems suddenly to have burst upon the public scene. . . .

. . .

What does being German, Irish, French, Russian, Polish mean to someone who is an American? It's undoubtedly different for recent immigrants than for those who have been here for generations. But even for a relative newcomer, the inexorable process of becoming an American changes the meaning of ethnic identification and its hold on the internal life of the individual. Nowhere have I seen this shift more eloquently described than in a recent op-ed piece published in the *New York Times*. The author, a Vietnamese refugee writing on the day when Vietnamese either celebrate or mourn the fall of Saigon, depending on which side of the conflict they were on, writes:

> Although I sometimes mourn the loss of home and land, it's the American landscape and what it offers that solidify my hyphenated identity. . . . Assimilation, education, the English language, the American 'I'—these have carried me and many others further from that beloved tropical country than the C-130 ever could. . . . When did this happen? Who knows? One night,

America quietly seeps in and takes hold of one's mind and body, and the Vietnamese soul of sorrows slowly fades away. In the morning, the Vietnamese American speaks a new language of materialism: his vocabulary includes terms like career choices, down payment, escrow, overtime.[3]

A new language emerges, but it lives, at least for another generation, alongside the old one; Vietnamese, yes, but also American, with a newly developed sense of self and possibility—an identity that continues to grow stronger with each succeeding generation. It's a process we have seen repeated throughout the history of American immigration. The American world reaches into the immigrant communities and shapes and changes the people who live in them.[4] By the second generation, ethnic identity already is attenuated; by the third, it usually has receded as a deeply meaningful part of life.

Residential segregation, occupational concentration, and a common language and culture—these historically have been the basis for ethnic solidarity and identification. As strangers in a new land, immigrants banded together, bound by their native tongue and shared culture. The sense of affinity they felt in these urban communities was natural; they were a touch of home, of the old country, of ways they understood: Once within their boundaries, they could feel whole again, sheltered from the ridicule and revulsion with which they were greeted by those who came before them. For whatever the myth about America's welcoming arms, nativist sentiment has nearly always been high and the anti-immigrant segment of the population large and noisy.

Ethnic solidarity and identity in America, then, was the consequence of the shared history each group brought with it, combined with the social and psychological experience of establishing themselves in the new land. But powerful as these were, the connections among the members of the group were heightened and sustained by the occupational concentration that followed—the Irish in the police departments of cities like Boston and San Francisco, for example, the Jews in New York City's garment industry, the east central Europeans in the mills and mines of western Pennsylvania.[5]

As each ethnic group moved into the labor force, its members often became concentrated in a particular occupation, largely because they were helped to find jobs there by those who went before them. For employers, this ethnic homogeneity made sense. They didn't have to cope with a babel of different languages, and they could count on the older workers to train the newcomers and keep them in line. For workers, there were advantages as well. It meant that they not only had compatible workmates, but that they weren't alone as they faced the jeers and contempt of their American-born counterparts. And perhaps most important, as more and more ethnic peers filled the available jobs, they began to develop some small measure of control in the workplace.

The same pattern of occupational concentration that was characteristic of yesterday's immigrant groups exists among the new immigrants today, and for the same reasons. The Cubans in Florida and the Dominicans in New York,[6] the various Asian groups in San Francisco, the Koreans in Los Angeles and New York—all continue to live in ethnic neighborhoods; all use the networks established there to find their way into the American labor force.[7]

For the white working-class ethnics whose immigrant past is little more than part of family lore, the occupational, residential, and linguistic chain has been broken. This is not to say that white ethnicity has ceased to be an observable phenomenon in American life. Cities like New York, Chicago, and San Francisco still have white ethnic districts that influence their culture, especially around food preferences and eating habits. But as in San Francisco's North Beach or New York's Little Italy, the people who once created vibrant neighborhoods, where a distinct subculture and language remained vividly alive, long ago moved out and left behind only the remnants of the commercial life of the old community. As such transformations took place, ethnicity became largely a private matter, a distant part of the family heritage that had little to do with the ongoing life of the family or community.

What, then, are we to make of the claims to ethnic identity that have become so prominent in recent years? Herbert Gans has called this identification "symbolic ethnicity"—that is, ethnicity that's invoked or not as the individual chooses.[8] Symbolic ethnicity, according to Gans, has little impact on a person's daily life and, because it is not connected to ethnic structures or activities—except for something like the wearing of the green on St. Patrick's Day—it makes no real contribution to ethnic solidarity or community.

The description is accurate. But it's a mistake to dismiss ethnic identification, even if only symbolic, as relatively meaningless. Symbols, after all, become symbolic precisely because they have meaning. In this case, the symbol has meaning at two levels: One is the personal and psychological, the other is the social and political.

At the personal level, in a nation as large and diverse as ours—a nation that defines itself by its immigrant past, where the metaphor for our national identity has been the melting pot—defining oneself in the context of an ethnic group is comforting. It provides a sense of belonging to some recognizable and manageable collectivity—an affiliation that has meaning because it's connected to the family where, when we were small children, we first learned about our relationship to the group. As Vilma

Janowski, a 24-year-old first-generation Polish-American who came here as a child put it: "Knowing there's other people like you is really nice. It's like having a big family, even if you don't ever really see them. It's just nice to know they're there. Besides, if I said I was American, what would it mean? Nobody's just American."

Which is true. Being an American is different from being French or Dutch or any number of other nationalities because, except for Native Americans, there's no such thing as an American without a hyphen somewhere in the past. To identify with the front end of that hyphen is to maintain a connection—however tenuous, illusory, or sentimentalized—with our roots. It sets us apart from others, allows us the fantasy of uniqueness—a quest given particular urgency by a psychological culture that increasingly emphasizes the development of the self and personal history. Paradoxically, however, it also gives us a sense of belonging—of being one with others like ourselves—that helps to overcome some of the isolation of modern life.

But these psychological meanings have developed renewed force in recent years because of two significant sociopolitical events. The first was the civil rights movement with its call for racial equality. The second was the change in the immigration laws, which, for the first time in nearly half a century, allowed masses of immigrants to enter the country.

It was easy for northern whites to support the early demands of the civil rights movement when blacks were asking for the desegregation of buses and drinking fountains in the South. But supporting the black drive to end discrimination in jobs, housing, and education in the urban North was quite another matter—especially among those white ethnics whose hold on the ladder of mobility was tenuous at best and with whom blacks would be most likely to compete, whether in the job market, the neighborhood, or the classroom. As the courts and legislatures around the country began to honor some black claims for redress of past injustices, white hackles began to rise.

It wasn't black demands alone that fed the apprehensions of whites, however. In the background of the black civil rights drive, there stood a growing chorus of voices, as other racial groups—Asian Americans, Latinos, and Native Americans—joined the public fray to seek remedy for their own grievances. At the same time that these home-grown groups were making their voices heard and, not incidentally, affirming their distinctive cultural heritages and calling for public acknowledgment of them, the second great wave of immigration in this century washed across our shores.

After having closed the gates to mass immigration with the National Origins Act of 1924, Congress opened them again when it passed the Immigration Act of 1965.[9] This act, which was a series of amendments to the McCarran-Walter Act of 1952, essentially jettisoned the national origins provisions of earlier law and substituted overall hemisphere caps. The bill, according to immigration historian Roger Daniels, "changed the whole course of American immigration history" and left the door open for a vast increase in the numbers of immigrants.[10]

More striking than the increase in numbers has been the character of the new immigrants. Instead of the large numbers of western Europeans whom the sponsors had expected to take advantage of the new policy, it has been the people of Asia, Latin America, and the Caribbean who rushed to the boats. "It is doubtful if any drafter or supporter of the 1965 act envisaged this result," writes Daniels.[11] In fact, when members of Lyndon Johnson's administration, under whose tenure the bill became law, testified before Congress, they assured the legislators and the nation that few Asians would come in under the new law.[12]

This is a fascinating example of the unintended consequences of a political act. The change in the law was sponsored by northern Democrats who sought to appeal to their white ethnic constituencies by opening the gates to their countrymen once again—that is, to the people of eastern and southern Europe whom the 1924 law had kept out for nearly half a century. But those same white ethnics punished the Democratic Party by defecting to the Republicans during the Reagan-Bush years, a defection that was at least partly related to their anger about the new immigrants and the changing social balance of urban America.

During the decade of the 1980s, 2.5 million immigrants from Asian countries were admitted to the United States, an increase of more than 450 percent over the years between 1961 and 1970, when the number was slightly less than half a million. In 1990 alone, nearly as many Asian immigrants—one-third of a million—entered the country as came during the entire decade of the 1960s. Other groups show similarly noteworthy increases. Close to three-quarters of a million documented Mexicans crossed the border in the single year of 1990, compared to less than half a million during all of the 1960s. Central American immigration, too, climbed from just under one hundred thousand between 1961 and 1970 to more than triple that number during the 1980s. And immigrants from the Caribbean, who numbered a little more than half a million during the 1960s, increased to over three-quarters of a million in the years between 1981 and 1989.[13]

Despite these large increases and the perception that we are awash with new immigrants, it's worth noting that they are a much smaller proportion of the total population today, 6.2 percent, than they were in 1920, when they were a hefty 13.2 percent of all U.S. residents.[14] But the fact that most immigrants today are people of color gives them greater visibility than ever before.

Suddenly, the nation's urban landscape has been colored in ways unknown before. In 1970, the California cities that were the site of the original research for *Worlds of Pain* were almost exclusively white. Twenty years later, the 1990 census reports that their minority populations range from 54 to 69 percent. In the nation at large, the same census shows nearly one in four Americans with African, Asian, Latino, or Native American ancestry, up from one in five in 1980.[15] So dramatic is this shift that whites of European descent now make up just over two-thirds of the population in New York State, while in California they number only 57 percent. In cities like New York, San Francisco, and Los Angeles whites are a minority—accounting for 38, 47, and 37 percent of residents, respectively. Twenty years ago the white population in all these cities was over 75 percent.[16]

The increased visibility of other racial groups has focused whites more self-consciously than ever on their own racial identification. Until the new immigration shifted the complexion of the land so perceptibly, whites didn't think of themselves as white in the same way that Chinese know they're Chinese and African Americans know they're black. Being white was simply a fact of life, one that didn't require any public statement, since it was the definitive social value against which all others were measured. "It's like everything's changed and I don't know what happened," complains Marianne Bardolino. "All of a sudden you have to be thinking all the time about these race things. I don't remember growing up thinking about being white like I think about it now. I'm not saying I didn't know there was coloreds and whites; it's just that I didn't go along thinking, *Gee, I'm a white person.* I never thought about it at all. But now with all the different colored people around,

you have to think about it because they're thinking about it all the time."

"You say you feel pushed now to think about being white, but I'm not sure I understand why. What's changed?" I ask.

"I told you," she replies quickly, a small smile covering her impatience with my question. "It's because they think about what they are, and they want things their way, so now I have to think about what I am and what's good for me and my kids." She pauses briefly to let her thoughts catch up with her tongue, then continues. "I mean, if somebody's always yelling at you about being black or Asian or something, then it makes you think about being white. Like, they want the kids in school to learn about their culture, so then I think about being white and being Italian and say: What about my culture? If they're going to teach about theirs, what about mine?"

To which America's racial minorities respond with bewilderment. "I don't understand what white people want," says Gwen Tomalson. "They say if black kids are going to learn about black culture in school, then white people want their kids to learn about white culture. I don't get it. What do they think kids have been learning about all these years? It's all about white people and how they live and what they accomplished. When I was in school you wouldn't have thought black people existed for all our books ever said about us."

As for the charge that they're "thinking about race all the time," as Marianne Bardolino complains, people of color insist that they're forced into it by a white world that never lets them forget. "If you're Chinese, you can't forget it, even if you want to, because there's always something that reminds you," Carol Kwan's husband, Andrew, remarks tartly. "I mean, if Chinese kids get good grades and get into the university, everybody's worried and you read about it in the papers."

While there's little doubt that racial anxieties are at the center of white concerns, our historic nativism also plays a part in escalating white alarm. The new immigrants bring with them a language and an ethnic culture that's vividly expressed wherever they congregate. And it's this also, the constant reminder of an alien presence from which whites are excluded, that's so troublesome to them.

The nativist impulse isn't, of course, given to the white working class alone. But for those in the upper reaches of the class and status hierarchy—those whose children go to private schools, whose closest contact with public transportation is the taxicab—the immigrant population supplies a source of cheap labor, whether as nannies for their children, maids in their households, or workers in their businesses. They may grouse and complain that "nobody speaks English anymore," just as working-class people do. But for the people who use immigrant labor, legal or illegal, there's a payoff for the inconvenience—a payoff that doesn't exist for the families in this study but that sometimes costs them dearly.[17] For while it may be true that American workers aren't eager for many of the jobs immigrants are willing to take, it's also true that the presence of a large immigrant population—especially those who come from developing countries where living standards are far below our own—helps to make these jobs undesirable by keeping wages depressed well below what most American workers are willing to accept.[18]

Indeed, the economic basis of our immigration policies too often gets lost in the lore that we are a land that says to the world, "Give me your tired, your poor, your huddled masses, yearning to breathe free."[19] I don't mean to suggest that our humane impulses are a fiction, only that the reality is far more complex than Emma Lazarus' poem suggests. The massive immigration of the nineteenth and early twentieth centuries didn't just happen spontaneously. America may have been known as the land of opportunity to the Europeans who dreamed of coming here—a country where, as my parents once believed, the streets were lined with gold. But they believed these things because that's how America was sold by the agents who spread out across the face of Europe to recruit workers—men and women who were needed to keep the machines of our developing industrial society running and who, at the same time, gave the new industries a steady supply of hungry workers willing to work for wages far below those of native-born Americans.

The enormous number of immigrants who arrived during that period accomplished both those ends. In doing so, they set the stage for a long history of antipathy to foreign workers. For today, also, one function of the new immigrants is to keep our industries competitive in a global economy. Which simply is another way of saying that they serve to depress the wages of native American workers.

It's not surprising, therefore, that working-class women and men speak so angrily about the recent influx of immigrants. They not only see their jobs and their way of life threatened, they feel bruised and assaulted by an environment that seems suddenly to have turned color and in which they feel like strangers in their own land. So they chafe and complain: "They come here to take advantage of us, but they don't really want to learn our ways," Beverly Sowell, a 33-year-old white electronics assembler, grumbles irritably. "They live different than us; it's like another world how they live. And they're so clannish. They keep to themselves, and they don't even *try* to learn English. You go on the bus these days and you might as well be in a foreign country; everybody's talking some other language, you know, Chinese or Spanish or something.

Lots of them have been here a long time, too, but they don't care; they just want to take what they can get."

But their complaints reveal an interesting paradox, an illuminating glimpse into the contradictions that beset native-born Americans in their relations with those who seek refuge here. On the one hand, they scorn the immigrants; on the other, they protest because they "keep to themselves." It's the same contradiction that dominates black–white relations. Whites refuse to integrate with blacks but are outraged when they stop knocking at the door, when they move to sustain the separation on their own terms—in black theme houses on campuses, for example, or in the newly developed black middle-class suburbs.

I wondered, as I listened to Beverly Sowell and others like her, why the same people who find the lifeways and languages of our foreign-born population offensive also care whether they "keep to themselves."

"Because like I said, they just shouldn't, that's all," Beverly says stubbornly. "If they're going to come here, they should be willing to learn our ways—you know what I mean, be real Americans. That's what my grandparents did, and that's what they should do."

"But your grandparents probably lived in an immigrant neighborhood when they first came here, too," I remind her.

"It was different," she insists. "I don't know why; it was. They wanted to be Americans; these here people now, I don't think they do. They just want to take advantage of this country."

She stops, thinks for a moment, then continues, "Right now it's awful in this country. Their kids come into the schools, and it's a big mess. There's not enough money for our kids to get a decent education, and we have to spend money to teach their kids English. It makes me mad. I went to public school, but I have to send my kids to Catholic school because now on top of the black kids, there's all these foreign kids who don't speak English. What kind of an education can kids get in a school like that? Something's wrong when plain old American kids can't go to their own schools.

"Everything's changed, and it doesn't make sense. Maybe you get it, but I don't. We can't take care of our own people and we keep bringing more and more foreigners in. Look at all the homeless. Why do we need more people here when our own people haven't got a place to sleep?"

"Why do we need more people here?"— a question Americans have asked for two centuries now. Historically, efforts to curb immigration have come during economic downturns, which suggests that when times are good, when American workers feel confident about their future, they're likely to be more generous in sharing their good fortune with foreigners. But when the economy falters, as it did in the 1990s, and workers worry about having to compete for jobs with people whose standard of living is well below their own, resistance to immigration rises. "Don't get me wrong; I've got nothing against these people," Tim Walsh demurs. "But they don't talk English, and they're used to a lot less, so they can work for less money than guys like me can. I see it all the time; they get hired and some white guy gets left out."

It's this confluence of forces—the racial and cultural diversity of our new immigrant population; the claims on the resources of the nation now being made by those minorities who, for generations, have called America their home; the failure of some of our basic institutions to serve the needs of our people; the contracting economy, which threatens the mobility aspirations of working-class families—all these have come together to leave white workers feeling as if everyone else is getting a piece of the action while they get nothing. "I feel like white people are left out in the cold," protests Diane Johnson, a 28-year-old white single mother who believes she lost a job as a bus driver to a black woman. "First it's the blacks; now it's all those other colored people, and it's like everything always goes their way. It seems like a white person doesn't have a chance anymore. It's like the squeaky wheel gets the grease, and they've been squeaking and we haven't," she concludes angrily.

Until recently, whites didn't need to think about having to "squeak"—at least not specifically as whites. They have, of course, organized and squeaked at various times in the past—sometimes as ethnic groups, sometimes as workers. But not as whites. As whites they have been the dominant group, the favored ones, the ones who could count on getting the job when people of color could not. Now suddenly there are others—not just individual others but identifiable groups, people who share a history, a language, a culture, even a color—who lay claim to some of the rights and privileges that formerly had been labeled "for whites only." And whites react as if they've been betrayed, as if a sacred promise has been broken. They're white, aren't they? They're *real* Americans, aren't they? This is their country, isn't it?

NOTES

1. David R. Roediger, *The Wages of Whiteness* (New York: Verso, 1991), 133.
2. I'm aware that many Americans who have none of the characteristic features associated with their African heritage are still defined as black. This is one reason why I characterize race as an idea, not a fact. Nevertheless, the main point I am making here still holds—that is, the visible racial character of a people makes a difference in whether white Americans see them as assimilable or not.
3. *New York Times,* 30 April 1993.
4. For an excellent historical portrayal of the formation of ethnic communities among the east central European immigrants in Pennsylvania, the development of ethnic identity, and the process of Americanization, see Ewa Morawska, *For Bread with Butter* (New York: Cambridge University Press, 1985).
5. Ibid.
6. Alejandro Portes and Ruben G. Rumbaut, *Immigrant America* (Berkeley: University of California Press, 1990).
7. One need only walk the streets of New York to see the concentration of Koreans in the corner markets and the nail care salons that dot the city's landscape.
   In San Francisco the Cambodians now own most of the donut shops in the city. It all started when, after working in such a shop, an enterprising young Cambodian combined the family resources and opened his own store and bakery. He now has 20 shops and has been instrumental in helping his countrymen open more, all of them buying their donuts from his bakery.
8. Herbert Gans, "Symbolic Ethnicity: The Future of Ethnic Groups and Cultures in America," *Ethnic and Racial Studies* 2 (1979):1–18.
9. Despite nativist protests, immigration had proceeded unchecked by government regulation until the end of the nineteenth century. The first serious attempt to restrict immigration came in 1882 when, responding to the clamor about the growing immigration of Chinese laborers to California and other western states, Congress passed the Chinese Exclusion Act. But European immigration remained unimpeded. In the years between 1880 and 1924, twenty-four million newcomers arrived on these shores, most of them eastern and southern Europeans, all bringing their own language and culture, and all the target of pervasive bigotry and exploitation by native-born Americans. By the early part of the twentieth century, anti-immigration sentiments grew strong enough to gain congressional attention once again. The result was the National Origins Act of 1924, which established the quota system that sharply limited immigration, especially from the countries of southern and eastern Europe.
10. Roger Daniels, *Coming to America: A History of Immigration and Ethnicity in American Life* (New York: HarperCollins, 1990), 338–44.

11. Daniels, *Coming to America*, 341, writes further, "In his Liberty Island speech Lyndon Johnson stressed the fact that he was redressing the wrong done [by the McCarran-Walter Act] to those 'from southern or eastern Europe,' and although he did mention 'developing continents,' there was no other reference to Asian or Third World immigration."

12. For a further review of the Immigration Act of 1965, see chapter 13 (pp. 328–49) of *Coming to America*.

13. *Statistical Abstract*, U.S. Bureau of the Census (1992), Table 8, p. 11.

14. Ibid, Table 45, p. 42.

15. Ibid., Table 18, p. 18, and Table 26, p. 24.

16. U.S. Bureau of the Census, *Population Reports*, 1970 and 1990. Cited in Mike Davis, "The Body Count," *Crossroads* (June 1993). The difference in the racial composition of New York and San Francisco explains, at least in part, why black–white tensions are so much higher in New York City than they are in San Francisco. In New York, 38 percent of the population is now white, 30 percent black, 25 percent Hispanic, and 7 percent Asian. In San Francisco, whites make up 47 percent of the residents, blacks 11 percent, Hispanics 14 percent, and Asians 29 percent. Thus, blacks in New York reflect the kind of critical mass that generally sparks racial prejudices, fears, and conflicts. True, San Francisco's Asian population—three in ten of the city's residents—also form that kind of critical and noticeable mass. But whatever the American prejudice against Asians, and however much it has been acted out in the past, Asians do not stir the same kind of fear and hatred in white hearts as do blacks.

17. Zoë Baird, the first woman ever to be nominated to be attorney general of the United States, was forced to withdraw when it became known that she and her husband had hired an illegal immigrant as a nanny for their three-year-old child. The public indignation that followed the revelation came largely from people who were furious that, in a time of high unemployment, American workers were bypassed in favor of cheaper foreign labor.

18. This is now beginning to happen in more skilled jobs as well. In California's Silicon Valley, for example, software programmers and others are being displaced by Indian workers, people who are trained in India and recruited to work here because they are willing to do so for lower wages than similarly skilled Americans (*San Francisco Examiner*, 14 February 1993).

19. From Emma Lazarus' "The New Colossus," inscribed at the base of the Statue of Liberty in New York's harbor, the gateway through which most of the immigrants from Europe passed as they came in search of a new life.

Trapped in Race? The Black–White Dichotomy

38

IN A COLOR-BLIND SOCIETY, WE CAN ONLY SEE BLACK AND WHITE
Why Race Will Continue to Rule

Michael Eric Dyson

The rules may be color-blind, but people are not. The question remains, therefore, whether the law can truly exist apart from the color-conscious society in which it exists, as a skeleton devoid of flesh; or whether law is the embodiment of society, the reflection of a particular citizenry's arranged complexity of relations.

PATRICIA J. WILLIAMS,
The Alchemy of Race and Rights, 1991

"Michael Eric Dyson . . . any sense of why these things are going on?" Charlie Gibson, the literate host of *Good Morning America*, asked me.

He was referring to the recent rash of burnings that have gutted nearly seventy black churches since January 1, 1995. In the brief time I had—shared with eloquent guests Deval Patrick, U.S. Assistant Attorney General for Civil Rights, and Morris Dees, Director of the Southern Poverty Law Center—I suggested two factors. First, black churches are vulnerable targets for white

Michael Eric Dyson, *Race Rules: Navigating the Color Line,* pp. 213–224. Copyright © 1996 by Michael Eric Dyson. Reprinted by permission of Addison Wesley Longman.

rage, especially since even rural churches symbolize black presence and progress. Second, the burnings are an outgrowth of our nation's lethal racial climate.

To be honest, no one can say for certain why black churches are being targeted for fiery destruction, mostly in the South. In the '60s black churches were the headquarters for those enlisted in the army of nonviolent resistance to state-sponsored apartheid. The church kitchen provided nourishment to famished troops, offices became war rooms to develop strategies, and sanctuaries became rallying posts where the charge to battle was sounded. In the perverse reasoning of white supremacists, it made sense to bomb and burn churches as a way to terrorize blacks, to discourage them from fighting for racial justice.

While the church remains at the center of black life in the '90s, it is now more venerable than threatening. In part, that's a reflection of how our times have evoked less dramatic demonstrations of the church's role in social transformation. In that light, it is curious that black churches—not the large, urban, affluent ones, but mostly modest, rural houses of worship—are once again being consumed by more than the Holy Spirit.

The fact that we can't get a good grip on what's going on, that we can't draw from these church burnings the clear conclusions that old-style racism made possible, is an ironic sign of progress. In the '60s and before, acts of hatred had symbolic clarity because blacks and whites shared an ecology of race. I'm not suggesting that blacks and whites agreed about what each group saw as the source of racial conflict. In fact, like today, they often didn't even agree about what they saw: many whites saw roses where many blacks saw thorns. Blacks and whites also bitterly disagreed about what they should do about the problems that existed. Still, the racial environment they inherited and shaped made the discerning of racist symbols easier. A church burning was undisguised racial hatred. A cross burning was meant to intimidate "uppity" blacks. And a lynching was the ultimate expression of a white supremacist desire to control the black body.

But in our more racially murky era—an era in which the ecology of race is much more complex and choked with half-discarded symbols and muddied signs—our skills of interpretation have to be more keen, our readings more nuanced. There's little doubt that most of the vitriolic expressions of racism have been forced underground by the success of '60s black freedom struggles. But symptoms of racial antipathy persist, even if they're harder to prove and far more difficult to analyze.

Our current racial climate, which encourages the belief that we do, or should, live in a color-blind society, has made many commentators wary of claiming a connection between the church burnings. Some commentators claim that these burnings are more religious than racial, since so many white churches have also been burned. Some commentators believe that claiming a connection between the burnings might give heart to isolated racists by exaggerating

the degree to which a concerted effort to rattle black folk even exists among the perpetrators. In other words, these commentators seek to avoid claiming that a conspiracy to destroy black churches exists. Well, if not all racial meanings have been driven underground, some of them are hidden in plain sight. We miss them because they're right in front of our faces.

There are various reasons for some of the black church burnings: teenage vandalism, mental derangement, and, in a couple of cases, insurance fraud. (Though we should ask why a black church is viewed as a viable target for a disgruntled teen or a confused young adult.) Among those twelve arsonists already convicted of burning black churches in the '90s, however, there is a definite pattern of racial hostility. A couple of them felt they were being cheated at a black-owned juke joint in Tennessee, while another was angered that his daughter had run off with a black man. Torching a black church was a way to get revenge.

All twelve of the arsonists are white, and all of them were convicted under a 1965 federal civil rights law. Two other arsonists, both white, are in jail awaiting trial, as federal prosecutors prepare to charge them under civil rights law.

The twelve share other similarities. Ten didn't finish high school. Half were unemployed, while others were stuck in low-paying jobs. Ten are young, ranging in age from seventeen to twenty-three. Half lived at home with their parents, most in rural areas near the churches they burned. And three had explicit ties to racist groups.

The perpetrators' profiles made it clear that black churches symbolize to them—and perhaps to other arsonists as well—not the civil rights threat of old, but a local sign of black survival, of black success. The rural black church in particular captures the utility—it is a major outlet for social recreation—and the invincibility of black

Christian faith. Ironically, those very qualities have made it newly vulnerable to another generation of confused, disgruntled, racist whites. We need not hunt for a Grand Conspiracy to explain what's going on. It would then be easy to scapegoat poor whites. Rather, our very racial ecology—littered with code words, hidden racial meanings, thinly veiled racial assumptions, and confused racial rules, while witnessing the emergence of racist militias and the resurgence of white hate groups—conspires against racial justice. Church burnings are merely the most obvious sign of a more dangerous racial fire raging in our nation.

To make matters worse, many of the guardians of our legal and political culture are busy retarding real racial progress by invoking the same principles of justice and equality for which blacks heroically fought and often died. One of the bitter ironies of this situation is that many of the former opponents of racial equality are now charged with dispensing racial justice in local, state, and federal governments. The fox who once terrorized the chicken coop is now expected to be fair to the chickens—to know best what they need, and to determine what measures are just in their pursuit of equality with the foxes.

That bitter irony is compounded by the fact that laws aimed at equality and justice are often interpreted by those who have done little of the suffering that brought the laws into existence. As a result, the spirit of struggle that helped make the laws a vibrant fulfillment of democracy is nullified. And the history of racial conflict that shaped how those laws should be understood and applied is obscured, distorted, or simply erased.

I'm certainly not arguing that one has to have been victimized by slavery, a denial of rights after Reconstruction, or the rule of Jim Crow to interpret or apply laws meant to realize racial justice. That kind of petty identity politics is harmful to historically wronged blacks who are much larger and more complex than the labels of suffering they wear. Neither am I arguing that blacks should demonize those who disagree with us about how to bring about justice and equality. It's one thing to say let freedom ring. It's another matter to determine who gets to strike the liberty bell, when it should be rung, and what our responses should be to what we hear. Still, there's no denying that, in terms of racial politics, where you stand—and the history that makes that stance both possible and plausible—determines what you see and hear. If the Rodney King beating, and the riots that followed his molesters' acquittal, didn't make that clear, then the O. J. Simpson trial and its aftermath should leave little doubt that it's true.

The most recent example of our tragic confusion about how racial justice should be conceived and applied is the 1996 Supreme Court decisions that ruled four congressional districts—one in North Carolina and three in Texas—unconstitutional. The Court invalidated the districts because race played a predominant role in their creation. The four districts had been created after the 1990 census to give minorities more just electoral representation. The Supreme Court's 5–4 rulings buttress three previous decisions in which the Court said race should not be the main reason for drawing odd-shaped districts that pull together minority voters to maximize their electoral strength. So while districts may be legally redrawn to protect political incumbents, they cannot be drawn to support previously and presently excluded minority voters.

What's tragic about the Court's decision is that it is based in large part on an ahistorical interpretation of the Fourteenth Amendment. We should recall that the Fourteenth Amendment was passed after the Civil War to extend to former slaves equal protection under the law. In his majority decision against the district (in the North Carolina case, *Shaw v. Hunt*), Chief Justice William Rehnquist argued that racial "classifications are antithetical to the Fourteenth Amendment, whose central purpose was to eliminate racial discrimination emanating from official sources in the States."

But what Rehnquist fails to address is how congressional districts drawn with race in mind are a response to the 1965 Voting Rights Act, passed to guarantee the right to vote for blacks who should already have been protected by the Fourteenth Amendment. If that amendment was insufficient to help enforce legal enfranchisement for blacks, it is ironic that the supposed failure to abide by it is now evoked by the Supreme Court to further erode electoral representation for those same blacks.

Before the 1990 census led to the creation of majority-minority districts, there were 26 black members in Congress. In 1992 that number rose to 39, and in 1994 there were 41 black members in Congress. In North Carolina, two majority-minority districts helped send the first two black North Carolina legislators to Congress since George White was forced out of Congress in 1901 by the state's ratification of a disfranchisement amendment. In the words of white turn-of-the-century North Carolina Democratic leader Charles Aycock, the ratification of the disfranchisement amendment was "the final settlement of the negro problem." Unsurprisingly, Aycock was elected governor of North Carolina in the same election in 1901. When Congresswoman Eva Clayton, of North Carolina's first district, and Congressman Melvin Watt, of the twelfth district, took their seats in the House in 1993, the promise of the Fourteenth Amendment, reinforced by the Voting Rights Act of 1965, was at long last realized.

An even greater irony is that the Court ruled against the majority-minority districts because they failed to satisfy the Court's criteria, established in a 1993 ruling, that a "compelling state interest" be reflected in the drawing of the districts, and that the districts should be drawn in a way that was "narrowly tailored" to serve that interest. Certainly the proportional representation of black voters is a "compelling state interest." But Rehnquist wrote: "an effort to alleviate the effects of societal discrimination is not a compelling interest."

And according to Justice Sandra Day O'Connor's opinion for the majority in the Texas case, *Bush v. Vera*, more judicial weight is given to the geographical shape of a district than to its political utility in realizing the aims of the Fourteenth Amendment and the Voting Rights Act. "The bizarre shape and noncompactness demonstrated by the districts . . . cause constitutional harm insofar as they convey the message that political identity is, or should be, predominantly racial," O'Connor writes. With one stroke of her pen, O'Connor denies the role that race has historically played in shaping political identity. She also completely ignores how racial identity is politicized, since it doesn't exist in a protected zone outside our nation's profound political conflicts. One can only conclude that, at least when it comes to racial politics and majority-minority districts, Freud was right. Anatomy *is* destiny.

Of course, alternatives to district-based representation, and hence, to racial redistricting, have been put forth. Alas, they have gone the way of all political flesh, or at least such ideas have been castigated as "profoundly antidemocratic." Lani Guinier, for instance, suggested that geographically based constituencies deny individual representation of the voter. She has written that "the use of geographic districts as the basis for establishing representational constituencies is at its very heart a system of group-based representation."

What to do? Guinier suggested an alternative to the winner-take-all manner of our current single-member congressional districts. Instead, we might have multiseat congressional districts where each voter has several votes that can be distributed among many candidates. Or we might have preference voting, where voters rank their votes in order of preference. But Guinier's notions of cumulative and preference voting got her dubbed a "quota queen" in the *Wall Street Journal*. She was widely dismissed as a fringe radical whose ideas made her unfit for the Assistant Attorney General for Civil Rights post, for which her nomination was withdrawn by President Clinton in 1993. A year later, without any controversy, Supreme Court Justice Clarence Thomas, in an opinion for a voting rights case, wrote that in "principle, cumulative voting and other non-district-based methods of effecting proportional representation are simply more efficient and straightforward mechanisms for achieving what has already become our tacit objective: roughly proportional allocation of political power according to race."

It is clear from the Supreme Court's decisions about majority-minority districts and other recent decisions severely undermining the scope of affirmative action, and from the effect its decisions have had on black communities, that the Court is failing miserably as the guardian of racial justice. Justice O'Connor is worried that by creating majority-minority districts, we will forget that "voters are more than racial statistics." What she fails to understand is that without legal guarantees of equal protection and just representation, the interests of black voters will remain largely unrepresented. The Supreme Court's judgments underscore a

dilemma the Court has failed to successfully address: how our nation can overcome racism without taking race into account.

The Supreme Court has consistently, at least recently, argued for the ideal of a color-blind society. Ironically, that ideal has led the Court, and other would-be advocates of black interests, to overlook the history of sacrifice, suffering, and struggle that made the Fourteenth Amendment and the Voting Rights Act necessary. (In fact, Robinson Everett, the Duke law professor who instigated the North Carolina suit, and who argued it before the Supreme Court, is a self-described "yellow dog Democrat" who believes in a color-blind politics inspired by 1960s social activism. Everett and other southern white Democrats are heartened by the Supreme Court ruling because it will spread blacks throughout districts where white politicians have a better chance of being elected, since blacks vote overwhelmingly Democratic. This is another instance where alleged black allies inflict the deepest wounds to black interests with the double-edged sword of political opportunism sharpened on either side by race.)

Over the last decade, the Supreme Court has consistently failed to appreciate the complexities of the history of race in America. As Justice John Paul Stevens writes in his dissenting opinion, it is unfortunate that the Court should intervene "into a process by which federal and state actors, both black and white, are jointly attempting to resolve difficult questions of politics and race that have long plagued North Carolina." Stevens recognizes that the Court's ruling means, in effect, that all sorts of political interests can be legally protected save those that are based on race. Stevens doesn't "see how our constitutional tradition can countenance the suggestion that a State may draw unsightly lines to favor farmers or city dwellers, but not to create districts that benefit the very group whose history inspired the Amendment that the Voting Rights Act was designed to implement."

The disagreement about race in America's highest court reflects the fatal disagreements that continue to bewitch our nation. Those courageous black souls who fought to make America all that it should be were not interested in what is presently meant by a color-blind society. True enough, they were interested in shaping an American society that wasn't obsessed with race, that didn't use race to unfairly dispense goods or allocate resources. But most were not naive enough to believe that we could ever, in the foreseeable future, arrive at a place where race didn't make a huge difference in how we live our lives, how we view one another, how we are granted or denied social privilege.

The tragedy of our condition is that we have a Supreme Court, and many other Americans, who have ignored the rules of race, how race continues to shape American life. Worse yet, they blame those who resist the color-blind myth for extending, rather than exposing, the hold race still has on American character. But we cannot overcome the history of racial oppression in our nation without understanding and addressing the subtle, subversive ways race continues to poison our lives. The ostrich approach of burying our collective head in the sands of historical amnesia or political denial will not work. We must face race head on.

The ideal of a color-blind society is a pale imitation of a greater, grander ideal: of living in a society where our color won't be denigrated, where our skin will be neither a badge for undue privilege nor a sign of social stigma. Because skin, race, and color have in the past been the basis for social inequality, they must play a role in righting the social wrongs on which our society has been built. We can't afford to be blind to color when extreme color consciousness continues to mold the fabric and form of our nation's history. Color consciousness is why black churches continue to burn. Color consciousness is why Supreme Court justices bend over backwards to repress the memory and present manifestation of racial inequality.

But we can strive for a society where each receives his or her just due, where the past in all its glory and grief is part of the equation of racial justice and social equality. Then we won't need to be blind to color, which in any case is a most morbid state of existence. Then we can embrace our history and our ideals with the sort of humane balance that makes democracy more than a distant dream.

39

THE ILLUSION OF RACIAL EQUALITY
The Black American Dilemma

Robert Staples

Never in the history of *Homo sapiens* has a society brought together so many cultural, religious, and racial groups in one country as the twentieth-century United States. Protestants, Catholics, Jews, Buddhists, Muslims, Italians, Africans, Chinese, Mexicans, Indians, all live together under the same government and operate in the same economy. This diversity is all the more striking when it is noted that none of these groups are at war with each other, that they coexist peaceably. This situation runs counter to the experiences of other countries in the world, where conflicts between ethnic and religious groups are epidemic. In 1986, more than five million people worldwide died as a result of ethnic and religious conflicts.[1]

As a society dominated by people of European ancestry, the U.S.A. appears to have accommodated people of different national origins while European governments are besieged and in danger of being toppled by the small number of non-European immigrants allowed into their countries. Whereas most countries, in the latter part of the twentieth century, have permitted immigration on the basis of labor demand and personal wealth, American immigration policies have favored the family ties and refugee status of American citizens. Consequently, 85 percent

of the legal immigration to the United States for the last twenty years has involved citizens of Latin America, Asia, the Caribbean, and Africa. The white, non-Hispanic population in 1990 was recorded as 75 percent of the American population and, if current immigration and birthrate trends prevail, fewer than half of this country's citizens will be non-Hispanic whites in the year 2080.[2] Further testament to the efficacy of the melting-pot theory is the high rate of intermarriage between these different groups. Most telling is the statistic that shows that Jews, a group that has faced persecution for most of its existence on this planet, have a minority of their members married within the same faith.[3]

It is within the Afro-American community that America's blend of free-wheeling capitalism and political democracy has produced the most startling success stories—or so it seems. Having come to the American continent, first as indentured servants, later as slaves, suffering from the most vicious form of segregation and discrimination in the postslavery era, they have risen to heights never envisioned for any group that occupied such low status. Jesse Jackson's slogan "From the outhouse to the White House" belies the struggle of this nation to keep its black population in a perpetually subjugated condition since their arrival. Having used their labor, destroyed their culture and family life, the American version of apartheid and the caste system was erected after the official end of slavery. The white South created dual public institutions to degrade them, and states outside Dixie used informal rules to establish a ceiling on their aspirations and status. The black condition was best summed up in the saying: "No black shall ever rise above the lowest status of a white man."

Perforce, 1990s America has witnessed a dramatic turnaround of this country's determination to see and treat all black Americans as subhumans. This reversal did not come without a great deal of turmoil for a country whose self-definition is "the world's greatest democracy." It fought a bloody civil war over the issue of black slavery, perverted many of its institutions to protect racial inequality, endured mass demonstrations and protest against Jim Crow over a twenty-year period before officially eliminating the practice, and witnessed its major cities in flames during the 1960s as rebellions by blacks occurred throughout the nation. Because the civil rights movement and urban rebellions transpired during the expansionist and neo-colonial phase of capitalism, the pragmatic captains of industry and government decided that the caste line had to be abolished. Civil rights laws, recruitment of blacks into heretofore excluded positions, affirmative action regulations, loans, scholarships, social programs, set asides, and so on were gradually used to reduce the absolute caste line extant in 1940.

Those measures bore fruit in the 1990s when the world's largest black middle class was created. Overall, black Americans had a total income of $300 billion a year, a figure that equals the income of the twelfth-largest nation in the world. The median household income of black married couples, in 1990, was $33,893, giving them almost the highest standard of living in the world. Blacks also have a median educational level of 12.2 years, higher than most Europeans. More than a million blacks were enrolled in institutions of higher learning in 1991.[4] More than other

people of color, blacks appear to be integrated into the institutional life of American society. On the political level, they serve in the president's cabinet as his advisers, on the Supreme Court, as governors of states, as presidential candidates, as the head of the military, and as mayors of the nation's largest cities. In the major sports, amateur and professional, blacks dominate and earn millions of dollars in salaries and commercial endorsements. Three of the five wealthiest entertainers in America are black, the biggest box-office stars and highest-rated TV shows have, in the past, been black, and the largest sales of a record album are by a black performer. Not all blacks in the entertainment industry are performers. In 1991, two dozen theatrical films were directed by blacks, starring black actors and actresses.

One might think that 1990s America is a racial utopia—or close to it. Certainly a black sociologist from Harvard, Orlando Patterson, believed it to be true when he wrote in *The New York Times* that "the sociological truths are that America, while still flawed in its race relations and its stubborn refusal to institute a national, universal welfare system, is now the least racist white majority society in the world; has a better record of legal protection of minorities than any other society, white or black; offers more opportunities to a greater number of black persons than any other society, including those of Africa; and has gone through a dramatic change in its attitude toward miscegenation over the past 25 years."[5] Professor Patterson is regarded as a color-blind neo-conservative, which helps to explain his pollyannaish view of race relations. Another view is held by an Afro-American filmmaker, who has earned millions in the movie industry. Douglas McHenry is quoted as saying: "Today there is probably more segregation and less tolerance than there was. More than ever, there are two Americas."[6]

Ironically, both men are essentially correct. The U.S., with a white majority, has made more accommodations to its racial diversity than any other country largely composed of Europeans. Even South American countries, with their pervasive pattern of miscegenation, have reserved the most powerful and prestigious positions for those most clearly identified as of European ancestry. The Patterson argument is most flawed when it depicts the U.S. as "the least racist white majority society in the world." However one defines racism in the 1990s, this country is more racially segregated and its institutions more race driven than any country outside South Africa. This fact, at least for the Euro-American population, has been disguised by the emerging racial ideology of the "color-blind theory." This theory has as its main premise that after 365 years of slavery and legal segregation, only 25 years of governmental laws and actions were necessary to reverse the historical systematic and legalized segregation and inequality in this country, and no further remedial effort is needed. The net effect of the color-blind theory is to institutionalize and stabilize the status quo of race relations for the twenty-first century: white privilege and black deprivation. Most notable among the proponents of the color-blind theory are the ideological descendants of the theories that slavery was necessary to make Christians out of African savages, that the South could operate separate but equal facilities and Jim Crow could not be abolished because it interfered with states' rights.

The color-blind theory ignores the reality of 1990s America: that race determines everyone's life chances in this country. In any area where there is significant racial diversity, race impacts on where people live and go to school, whom they vote for, date, and marry, with whom they do business, who they buy from or sell to, how much they pay, and so on. This does not sound like the racial utopia Martin Luther King dreamed of. Indeed, it may have been his

worst nightmare. Yet there could be a worse nightmare for the prophet of racial equality. How would he have felt if he had watched his former lieutenants endorse the right-wing Ronald Reagan for president in 1980, or the organization he founded, the Southern Christian Leadership Conference, remain neutral on the appointment of Clarence Thomas to the U.S. Supreme Court—a neutrality tantamount to the support provided by Strom Thurmond, Jesse Helms, and David Duke (former Grand Dragon of the Ku Klux Klan). The complexities of race in 1990s America are enough to confuse any outsider who has read the history of race relations in the U.S.

In part, to sort out the contradictions in American race relations, it is necessary to look at the other side of the black success story. Despite the largest black middle class in the world, the average black household income is only 56 percent of white household income. More than 32 percent of black households have incomes below the poverty line. The high income of black married-couple households is a function of multiple workers in those households. Moreover, poverty in the U.S. is increasingly synonymous with people of color. Only 8 percent of whites are considered poor, and they are disproportionately found among the elderly, women with children, and rural and farm families. Of all Western nations, the United States has the greatest inequality of wealth. According to an international study, poverty in the U.S. is more widespread and more severe: poor families here stay poor longer; and government programs of assistance are the least able to lift families with children out of poverty.[7]

Poverty also is more likely to be spread among the nonelderly households and to be widely distributed across all age and family groups. It is this class of poor people of color that make up a majority. In the more racially homogeneous countries of Europe, Australia, and New Zealand, government welfare programs and subsidies have eliminated the kind of massive poverty found among young households in this country. The tolerance of pervasive poverty, malnutrition, and homelessness can only be related to the perception that it is people of color who bear the brunt of American poverty and the reasons attributed to are their failure to get an education and work hard. When asked if the Federal Government should see to it that every person has a job and a good standard of living, 65 percent of blacks said it should, but only 24 percent of whites thought so. Euro-Americans were more inclined to give support to the idea of "individuals getting ahead on their own," versus government intervention.[8] Surely the racial differences in attitude toward government assistance are linked to the fact that unemployment, for white male heads of households, is less than 6 percent, and as many as 46 percent of Black males sixteen to sixty-two years of age are not in the labor force. Moreover, money is not the only measure of wealth in 1990s America. Noncash assets are easily convertible to cash. They include stocks, bonds, businesses, property, and so on, a total of $10 trillion. Given the concentration of wealth in the U.S., Euro-Americans will control 97 percent of those assets. Most blacks have only their homes and automobiles as assets. Because black homes tend to be located in black neighborhoods, their value is inherently less than those of similar homes in white neighborhoods.[9]

Based on any variable that can be statistically measured, blacks have not achieved racial equality in any area of American life. And they are overrepresented on every negative variable except suicide, itself a mixed blessing since black suicide rates are highest among its young people in contrast to white suicide rates weighted toward its oldest members. And the direction of change in the U.S. has made come conditions worse than in the era before the civil rights movement. In 1950 the black unemployment rate was double that of whites: in 1990 it was triple. Housing and school segregation are worse outside the South in 1990 than in 1950. The inequality of wealth is greater in 1990 than in 1950, when most people earned money from wages. In the 1990s, people earn money, in larger numbers, from stocks, bonds, property, leveraged buyouts, etc. The percent of intact black families vis-à-vis white families was much higher in 1950 than in 1990, as was the lower number of black children born in wedlock. The times they are changing but things remain the same.[10]

For some reason this society documents but does not change many of its discriminatory practices. There are numerous studies, most of them conducted by Euro-Americans, showing the retention of racial discrimination in employment, housing, education, health care, and so on. One study found that 75 percent of black men seeking employment were discriminated against.[11] In another investigation of housing discrimination, it was discovered that blacks face discrimination 56 percent of the time they seek to rent a house and 59 percent of the time they try to buy a home.[12] Other studies reveal that black patients in a hospital were more likely to be sent to inexperienced medical doctors and that car dealers were likely to charge Afro-Americans and women higher prices than white males. The number of studies showing racial discrimination in every facet of American life makes a mockery of the color-blind theory and Patterson's claim that this is the least-racist white majority society in the world.

Adding to the scholarly studies of racial discrimination are the TV shows, like *60 Minutes,* which showed an employment agency using special codes to avoid sending black applicants to employers for jobs. On September 26, 1991, the show *Prime Time Live* showed a nationwide audience what it's like to be black in 1990s America. They sent two twenty-eight-year-old men, Glen Brewer, black, and John Kuhnen, white, to shop in the same stores, attempt to rent the same apartment, and apply for the same job. Here are the results of their experiment in the city of St. Louis:

> At several stores, Mr. Kuhnen gets instant service; Mr. Brewer is ignored except at a record store, where a salesman keeps a close eye on him, without offering any assistance. When they go for a walk, separately on the same street, a police car passes Mr. Kuhnen but slows down to give Mr. Brewer a once-over. At a car dealership, Mr. Kuhnen is offered a lower price and better financing terms than Mr. Brewer. Inquiring about a job at a dry cleaner that has advertised for help, Mr. Kuhnen is told jobs are still available; Mr. Brewer is told, "The positions are taken." Following up a for-rent sign, Mr. Kuhnen is promptly offered an apartment, which he does not take; ten minutes later, Mr. Brewer is told it has been rented for hours.[13]

That program gave Euro-Americans a visual lesson in the mundane indignities that many Afro-Americans experience day after day. Of course, only the most naive white viewer should have been surprised at the results. Despite the color-blind theory, white claims of reverse racism and preferential treatment for blacks, there is no queue of whites claiming black heritage to qualify for the "benefits" of black membership. The color-blind theory is a smokescreen to mask the persistence of a racial hierarchy in American life. Blacks who buy into the theory are easily manipulated, compare themselves to their poorer brothers on the African continent, and measure their progress by those standards, and a small but increasing number of black opportunists

who seek to reap the rewards of catering to Euro-American prejudices. The illusion of racial equality seems real because tokenism begins at the top and slowly trickles down to the bottom. Only a small number of elite positions are available in 1990s America and they are often visible to everyone. Few Euro-Americans make claims on the elite positions albeit they are very desired. Selection or appointment is very subjective and the qualifications ambiguous. Thus, it is easier to integrate the elite positions, such as Miss America or head of the military, involving a few thousand people than provide equal employment opportunities for millions of black and white workers. The blacks see their members in elite positions and take pride in their achievements, although their own situations have not improved—reflected glory. Euro-Americans see those same blacks and can rationalize a dramatic change in the racial character of American society while thinking that the poor, homeless, and criminals could have made similar achievements if they had gotten an education and worked hard.

The illusions of racial equality are best exemplified in the two areas in which blacks appear to dominate: entertainment and sports. While three of the five wealthiest entertainers are black (Oprah Winfrey, Bill Cosby, and Michael Jackson), they are not the wealthiest people in the entertainment industry.[14] Those people are white and own and/or manage record companies, talent-management agencies, movie studios, and so on. Because black entertainers often have unique skills and American society highlights all black entry into elite positions, they have a visibility difficult for Euro-American entertainers to attain. However, there are thousands of Euro-Americans we do not know about earning millions yearly from the entertainment industry. There are comparatively few black millionaires in show business and we tend to know them all. Moreover, even among the wealthy black entertainers, their income is divided up among agents, attorneys, accountants, producers, and so on. In most cases those people are white. There is virtually no white entertainer who shares any significant portion of his/her income with a black person.

It is possible that Euro-Americans take 97 percent of the dollars spent on entertainment produced in this country and distributed to the rest of the world. Thus, black success in the entertainment world is racial tokenism at its worst. And the constraints of race dictate the kind of entertainment product that blacks are allowed to exhibit. Although people of color buy 38 percent of the movie tickets, almost all the blacks starring in movies are men and comedians. Former basketball star Wilt Chamberlain has written, "The movie industry is still back in the 1930's and 1940's. The Eddie ("Rochester") Andersons and Stepin Fetchits of today are the Eddie Murphys and Richard Pryors. Producers give starring roles to comedians and let them make a lot of money, but they never cast people of color in the roles of real heroes."[15] The same is true of prime-time television, where blacks are frequently relegated to scattered token roles or the clownish context of a situation comedy. With the exception of the now defunct Cosby show, most of the prime-time sitcoms featuring blacks portray them in particularly stereotyped roles. One NAACP study found that "no Black executive makes final decisions in the motion picture or television industry, that only a handful of Afro-Americans hold executive positions with film studios or television networks."[16]

Anyone watching the popular American sports on television would have to be impressed with the number of black athletes. In the case of basketball, the starting players are often all Afro-Americans. The sports pages are replete with the million-dollar salaries of professional athletes and

their commercial endorsement deals. While the most popular sports, football, baseball, and basketball, are the ones dominated by blacks, those athletes do not necessarily earn the highest incomes. Because of sponsor tie-ins, endorsement deals, and appearance fees, the top ten of the highest-paid athletes are mostly whites in the less popular sports of tennis, golf, and racing.[17] Since those sports appeal to a better demographic group (i.e., higher-status whites), corporations pay more per audience than in the more popular sports. It might be noted that the white-dominated sports have fewer injuries and greater longevity for their participants. As true of show business, black athletes share their incomes with agents, accountants, investors, and so on, almost all of them Euro-Americans. And it is essential that a black player be superior to any white rivals for his position. He will rarely be allowed to be a part-time or reserve player in any sport. Those positions are reserved for Euro-Americans. Few blacks can remain in their sports, after finishing their careers, as managers, coaches, or front-office employees. In sports where the top ten players are all Afro-Americans it was rare to find an Afro-American clerk-typist in the front office of most professional teams.

On the amateur level, the exploitation of black athletes is most blatant. Afro-Americans constitute almost 75 percent of the players in the major revenue sports at the collegiate level. While they ostensibly do not get paid except for tuition and expenses, the alleged advantage of college athletes is a college education for four years' sports performance and a chance to enter the lucrative professional sports arena. Yet only a fraction will join a professional sports team, and 70 percent of black college athletes do not attain a college degree within four years.[18] Adding insult to injury, the revenues received from the black-dominated sports programs are generally used to subsidize the less-popular, Euro-American-dominated sports such as lacrosse, volleyball, baseball, wrestling, and tennis.

Throughout American society the illusion of racial equality is promoted as a reality. Although black political participation increased dramatically, once blacks were permitted access to the voting booths as a result of the Voting Rights Act of 1965, Afro-Americans hold less than 2 percent of all political offices in the United States while comprising 13 percent of its population.[19] As a result of at-large elections and political gerrymandering, black candidates cannot win elective office in political districts where blacks are not a majority. With few exceptions, Euro-Americans vote for Euro-Americans, regardless of the political party, gender, or other variable. Race transcends everything in politics. Until recently, no Afro-American had been elected mayor of a major city with a majority of the Euro-American vote. That explains why blacks rarely win state-wide offices, because no American state has a majority black population. Afro-American politicians are generally dependent on getting 90 percent of the black vote and 20–40 percent of the white vote in order to win elective office. Once they are in office, their appointments are often of Euro-Americans to the most important positions—a tactic designed to reassure the business community of their "color-blindness" and to pacify Euro-American voters worried about black "domination." With a black mayor in charge, blacks lose the right to charge racism in their governance. Seemingly they also lose the desire to change black mayors, as relatively few black incumbents are ever voted out of office by their black constituents.

The structural inequality, based on race, poses a vicious circle for Afro-Americans. A high rate of unemployment creates a class of impoverished blacks, particularly males, who resort to illegal activity in order to survive. While representing less than 6 percent of the American population, Afro-American men comprise 47 percent of the prison population. Almost one of four black men aged twenty to thirty are in jail or on probation or parole. The United States has the highest percentage of its population behind bars of any country in the world, and a majority of them are poor and people of color. Blacks make up 40 percent of prisoners awaiting death penalties. The majority of those death-row black prisoners have been convicted of murdering Euro-Americans. In the last forty-seven years, no white person has been executed for murdering an Afro-American.[20] The inescapable conclusion is that the American legal system, and its participants, place a greater value on white life than on black life.

Other examples abound on racial difference and the question of value. In a bizarre case of a sperm-bank mixup resulting in a white woman's giving birth to a black child, the white "victim" was awarded $400,000 because of the mistake.[21] Imagine the anguish of millions of black mothers who have no choice but to give birth to black children. Had the situation been reversed, a black woman inseminated with a white man's sperm, the baby would still be considered black, and it is doubtful that a jury would award a black woman $400,000 for giving birth to a biracial child. It is these countless racial insults that make most Afro-Americans feel they live in the United States at the discretion of Euro-Americans, even those most recently arrived. The case of Rodney King, the black male beaten by Los Angeles police officers, certainly did little to reassure Afro-Americans that they have the same citizenship rights as Euro-Americans. His case was not an isolated incident. A commission assigned to investigate the Los Angeles Police Department found over seven hundred racist, homophobic, and sexist remarks typed by officers into the department's car-communication systems over the previous eighteen months.[22] One of the most eloquent testimonies to the legacy of racism is the number of prominent blacks stopped and abused by police officers in this country, ranging from famous athletes to singers and movie stars. Comparable situations with Euro-American celebrities are almost unheard of.

Racial indignities affect the black middle class the most. They have played by the rules, achieved some degree of success, and find they are still below the lowest-ranking Euro-American. As one Afro-American woman was quoted, "Life in general requires a lot of psychic energy for Black people on racial things."[23] A professor of philosophy wrote an article entitled "In My Next Life, I'll Be White." He speaks of the fact that black men rarely enjoy the public trust of Euro-Americans, that they are always regarded as possible thieves, criminals, violent and dangerous until proven innocent. The essence of his argument is that while white males have committed more evil cumulatively than any other class of people in the world, a suit and tie suffice to make one of them respectable.[24] Black women, while regarded as less dangerous, encounter the same suspicion that they are shoplifters or morally loose. The important point is that being denied the public trust leaves a deep psychic scar of discrimination, which festers and becomes the fountainhead of low self-esteem and self-hate for those who have no emotional salve.

Those Afro-Americans who do not have their self-esteem destroyed often suffer from a quiet anger at their treatment. This anger is currently being manifested in a racial chauvinism almost as virulent as its white counterpart. It is expressed in a kind of dysfunctional racial solidarity that has left the race victim to a series of charlatans and racial demagogues. Any black who yells racism when accused of misconduct is as-sumed to be innocent without being required to prove that innocence. This anger and this racial solidarity reached their most extreme form in the nomination of black jurist Clarence Thomas to replace Thurgood Marshall on the U.S. Supreme Court. Nominated by the titular head of the Republican party, the party which had captured the presidency of the nation largely through its use of racial appeals to white voters, Thomas had a record considered so anti-black that one black political scientist called him a "racist by proxy."[25] Another columnist wrote, "Stripped of his color, Clarence Thomas is just another Republican conservative apparatchik come to Washington to seek his fortune by protecting the already powerful from the weak and disenfranchised."[26]

That Thomas had the support of former and current arch segregationists, such as Strom Thurmond, Jesse Helms, and David Duke, seems not to have mattered or was not known to his black supporters. When Professor Anita Hill, an Afro-American woman, accused him of sexually harassing her, the low-esteem, angry black population rallied to his defense, representing 60 percent of the blacks polled on the matter.[27] White Southern Democrats claimed their vote to appoint him was from the fear of black anger if they did not. Observers of the situation speculate that Thomas's anti–civil rights record will be reinforced by his anger at black groups for attempting to derail his appointment. Meanwhile, the party of Strom Thurmond, Jesse Helms, and David Duke is talking about a massive defection of blacks from the Democratic party because of their support of Clarence Thomas. One black leader's explanation for this weird marriage between blacks and the leaders of American racialism, Roger Wilkins, says, "Blacks have been terribly deprived throughout our history and we've been deprived among other things of symbols of pride occupying high places. So that when a Black is presented for such a position, there is an instinctive reaction to support that person."[28]

The controversy over Clarence Thomas revealed some widening splits in the Afro-American community and the Euro-American political strategies for the twenty-first century. Those splits are along gender and class lines. Gender lines are dividing because some black men feel that black women are given preference over them, that white men like to put black women in between themselves and black men. Many blacks accused Anita Hill of acting as a tool for white men to ruin the life of a black man at the peak of his career. That many black leaders did not share that view is reflected in the statement of Jesse Jackson that Anita Hill will rank in history along with civil rights pioneer Rosa Parks.[29] Representative Craig Washington put it best when he said, "It is not Black women who have lynched Black men. It is white racism that has been tolerated for so long by many of Judge Thomas's supporters. It is a problem that will not be addressed by attacking and demeaning Black women."[30] Thomas's claim that he was the victim of racism was the real irony. Most of the racists in America were his supporters, and the white supporters of civil rights were his opponents.

Class divisions are a more serious matter. Since the desegregation of public facilities and the rise of racial tokenism, blacks have been less united as a race on many matters that affect one class more than the other. Younger blacks have become ahistorical and simply want to enter mainstream America. The Republican party has been in power for eighteen of the last twenty-two years, by controlling the White House. They attained power by developing a political strategy to appeal to southern whites resentful of the civil rights gains in the 1960s. In the 1980s the Republican presidents Reagan and Bush both had past histories of publicly

supporting racial segregation. As the party of white America, there was little room for blacks, except those who supported the racist and classist views of the Republican party. Clarence Thomas was an opportunist who decided to jump on the Republican bandwagon at exactly the time this bandwagon was crushing millions of Afro-Americans into deeper economic misery. One columnist noted: "Thomas has spent a lot of his life seeking to please people who hate him, currying favor with the man, being available as a token and symbol."[31] Thousands of other blacks, hungry for some political power, will join the Republican party because the line for political participation is shorter. Race traitors are in short supply, even in 1990s America. If the Republicans believe that replacing white overseers with black ones will make blacks accept slavery, that may be the greatest illusion of them all.

The double-consciousness that Du Bois wrote about still exists, except that the racial identity of blackness threatens to overtake the national identity of Americans. White America is imposing this choice upon many of its black inhabitants. Being human—also American—seems beyond the pale of consideration for people of African descent. For all the progress that has been made on so many fronts, it is still true that Afro-Americans have their worth measured by the darkness of their skin, not the content of their characters. In a society where there is no scarcity of decent jobs, housing, and education, nonracial factors may become the criteria for the perception and treatment of black Americans. Du Bois also recognized that the class factor was intertwined with the racial factor. It is unlikely that the problems of race and class will be resolved in this generation's lifetime. Until the problem of class division is resolved, the problem of the twenty-first century will continue to be the problem of the color line.

NOTES

1. "Report Says Five Million Died in Wars During Year of Peace." *San Francisco Chronicle,* 18 June 1987, p. A1.
2. A. Carlson, "Collapse of Birthrates in Industrial Democracies," *San Francisco Chronicle,* 14 May 1986, p. A4.
3. Paul Spickard, *Mixed Blood: Intermarriage and Ethnic Identity in Twentieth Century America* (Madison: University of Wisconsin Press, 1989).
4. U.S. Bureau of the Census, *The Black Population in the United States: March 1990 and 1989* (Washington, DC: U.S. Government Printing Office, 1991).
5. Orlando Patterson, "Race, Gender and Liberal Fallacies," *The New York Times,* 20 October 1991, p. A15.
6. Quoted in Greg B. Smith, "Director's No. 1 Hope for House Party 2," *San Francisco Examiner,* 23 October 1991, p. D1.
7. Arch Parsons, "Poverty in U.S. Worse Than in 7 Western Nations," *Oakland Tribune,* 19 September 1991, p. A8.
8. F. Harris and L. Williams, "JCPS/Gallup Poll Reflects Changing Views on Political Issues," *Focus* 14 (October 1986), p. 4.
9. "Wealth, in Black and White," *The New York Times,* 24 July 1986, p. A1.
10. U.S. Bureau of the Census, *The Black Population in the United States: March 1990 and 1989.*
11. Manning Marable, "The New Racism: The Etiquette of Racial Prejudice," *The Oklahoma Eagle,* 10 October 1991, p. 26.
12. "Housing Survey Shows Bias Against Blacks, Hispanics," *San Francisco Chronicle,* 31 August 1991, p. A2.
13. Walter Goodman, "Looking Racism in the Face," *The New York Times,* 26 September 1991, p. B5.
14. "The World's 40 Highest Paid Performers," *Parade Magazine,* 10 November 1991, p. 28.
15. Quoted in Liz Smith, "Wilt's Claim Sounds like a Tall Tale," *San Francisco Chronicle,* 17 October 1991, p. E1.
16. "Study Says Hollywood Still Shuts Blacks Out," *San Francisco Chronicle,* 24 September 1991, p. A2.
17. Michael Hiestand, "Blacks Popular but Scarce as Product Endorsers," *USA Today,* 19 December 1991, p. C9.
18. Jim Myers, "Whites Still Get Most Athletic Scholarships," *USA Today,* 18 December 1991, p. C4.
19. U.S. Bureau of the Census, *Voting and Registration in the Election of November 1988* (Washington, DC: U.S. Government Printing Office, 1989).
20. Alan M. Dershowitz, "Justice Isn't Color Blind," *San Francisco Examiner,* 8 October 1991, p. A15.
21. "White Woman Who Had Black Baby in Sperm Bank Mixup Awarded $400,000." *Jet Magazine,* 19 August 1991, p. 6.
22. Marable, "The New Racism," 26.
23. Delores Watson quoted in Ronald Smothers, "South's New Blacks Find Comfort Laced with Strain," *The New York Times,* 23 September 1991, p. A1.
24. Laurence Thomas, "In My Next Life, I'll Be White," *Ebony,* December 1990, p. 84.
25. J. Owens Smith, "Clarence Thomas's Nomination Unveils Crisis Among Black Intellectuals," *California Black Faculty and Staff Newsletter* 16 (September-October 1991), p. 2.
26. Bill Mandel, "Truth, Justice and the American Way," *San Francisco Chronicle,* 18 October 1991, p. A4.
27. "New Polls Show Most Americans Favoring Thomas," *San Francisco Examiner,* 14 October 1991, p. A9.
28. Roger Wilkins quoted in Peter Applebome, "Despite Talk of Sexual Harassment, Thomas Hearings Turned on Race Issue," *The New York Times,* 19 October 1991, p. Y7.
29. Teresa Moore, "Jesse Jackson Gives Hill a Spot in History," *San Francisco Chronicle,* 14 October 1991, p. A2.
30. Representative Craig Washington quoted in "Black Caucus Decries Thomas Racism Defense," *San Francisco Chronicle,* 16 October 1991, p. A9.
31. Alexander Cockburn, "Democrats Let Thomas Off the Hook," *San Francisco Examiner,* 21 October 1991, p. A21.

40

OPTIONAL ETHNICITIES
For Whites Only?

Mary C. Waters

This paper reviews the current meaning of ethnicity for the descendants of nineteenth- and early twentieth-century European immigrants to the United States and contrasts that experience with the identities of people with non-European origins—the descendants of earlier forced immigrants and conquered peoples and the growing number of voluntary immigrants from non-European countries. The paper proceeds as follows. First the proposition that ethnic identity is optional for most Americans of European background is put forth. Empirical evidence that this is the case is reviewed. The social and historical forces that allow ethnicity to be an option are described.

The experience of non-Whites in the United States is then contrasted. Non-Whites have much more limited options with regard to their ethnicity because of particular historical and social circumstances in the United States. Using the example of current relations on college campuses between Blacks and Whites, I trace the influence that different degrees of options have on everyday encounters between people and the everyday social psychological consequences of failing to recognize this key difference between race and ethnicity.

Ethnic Identity for Whites in the 1990s

What does it mean to talk about ethnicity as an option for an individual? To argue that an individual has some degree of choice in their ethnic identity flies in the face of the common sense notion of ethnicity many of us believe in—that one's ethnic identity is a fixed characteristic, reflective of blood ties and given at birth. However, social scientists who study ethnicity have long concluded that while ethnicity is based in a *belief* in a common ancestry, ethnicity is primarily a *social* phenomenon, not a biological one (Alba 1985, 1990; Barth 1969; Weber [1921] 1968, p. 389). The belief that members of an ethnic group have that they share a common ancestry may not be a fact. There is a great deal of change in ethnic identities across generations through intermarriage, changing allegiances, and changing social categories. There is also a much larger amount of change in the identities of individuals over their life than is commonly believed. While most people are aware of the phenomenon known as "passing"—people raised as one race who change at some point and claim a different race as their identity—there are similar life course changes in ethnicity that happen all the time and are not given the same degree of attention as "racial passing."

White Americans of European ancestry can be described as having a great deal of choice in terms of their ethnic identities. The two major types of options White Americans can exercise are (1) the option of whether to claim any specific ancestry, or to just be "White" or American (Lieberson [1985] called these people "unhyphenated Whites"), and (2) the choice of which of their European ancestries to choose to include in their description of their own identities. In both cases, the option of choosing how to present yourself on surveys and in everyday social interactions exists for Whites because of social changes and societal conditions that have created a great deal of social mobility, immigrant assimilation, and political and economic power for Whites in the United States. Specifically, the option of being able to not claim any ethnic identity exists for Whites of European background in the United States because they are the majority group—in terms of holding political and social power, as well as being a numerical majority. The option of choosing among different ethnicities in their family backgrounds exists because the degree of discrimination and social distance attached to specific European backgrounds has diminished over time.

The Ethnic Miracle

When European immigration to the United States was sharply curtailed in the late 1920s, a process was set in motion whereby the European ethnic groups already in the United States were for all intents and purposes cut off from any new arrivals. As a result, the composition of the ethnic groups began to age generationally. The proportion of each ethnic group made up of immigrants or the first generation began to gradually decline, and the proportion made up of the children, grandchildren, and eventually great-grandchildren began to increase. Consequently, by 1990 most European-origin ethnic groups in the United States were composed of a very small number of immi-

grants, and a very large proportion of people whose link to their ethnic origins in Europe was increasingly remote.

This generational change was accompanied by unprecedented social and economic changes. The very success of the assimilation process these groups experienced makes it difficult to imagine how much the question of the immigrants' eventual assimilation was an open one at the turn of the century. At the peak of immigration from southern and central Europe there was widespread discrimination and hostility against the newcomers by established Americans. Italians, Poles, Greeks, and Jews were called derogatory names, attacked by nativist mobs, and derided in the press. Intermarriage across ethnic lines was very uncommon—castelike in the words of some sociologists (Pagnini and Morgan 1990). The immigrants and their children were residentially segregated, occupationally specialized, and generally poor.

After several generations in the United States, the situation has changed a great deal. The success and social mobility of the grandchildren and great-grandchildren of that massive wave of immigrants from Europe has been called "The Ethnic Miracle" (Greeley 1976). These Whites have moved away from the inner-city ethnic ghettos to White middle-class suburban homes. They are doctors, lawyers, entertainers, academics, governors, and Supreme Court justices. But contrary to what some social science theorists and some politicians predicted or hoped for, these middle-class Americans have not completely given up ethnic identity. Instead, they have maintained some connection with their immigrant ancestors' identities—becoming Irish American doctors, Italian American Supreme Court justices, and Greek American presidential candidates. In the tradition of cultural pluralism, successful middle-class Americans in the late twentieth century maintain some degree of identity with their ethnic backgrounds. They have remained "hyphenated Americans." So while social mobility and declining discrimination have created the option of not identifying with any European ancestry, most White Americans continue to report some ethnic background.

With the growth in intermarriage among people of European ethnic origins, increasingly these people are of mixed ethnic ancestry. This gives them the option of which ethnicity to identify with. The U.S. census has asked a question on ethnic ancestry in the 1980 and 1990 censuses. In 1980, 52 percent of the American public responded with a single ethnic ancestry, 31 percent gave multiple ethnic origins (up to three were coded, but some individuals wrote in more than three), and only 6 percent said they were American only, while the remaining 11 percent gave no response. In 1990 about 90 percent of the population gave some response to the ancestry question, with only 5 percent giving American as a response and only 1.4 percent reporting an uncodeable response such as "don't know" (McKenney and Cresce 1992; U.S. Bureau of the Census 1992).

Several researchers have examined the pattern of responses of people to the census ancestry question. These analyses have shown a pattern of flux and inconsistency in ethnic ancestry reporting. For instance, Lieberson and Waters (1986, 1988, p. 93) have found that parents simplify children's ancestries when reporting them to the census. For instance, among the offspring in situations where one parent reports a specific single White ethnic origin and the other parent reports a different single White origin, about 40 percent of the children are not described as the logical combination of the parents ancestries. For example, only about 60 percent of the children of English-German marriages are labeled as English-German or German-English. About 15 percent of the children of

these parents are simplified to just English, and another 15 percent are reported as just German. The remainder of the children are either not given an ancestry or are described as American (Lieberson and Waters 1986, 1993).

In addition to these intergenerational changes, researchers have found changes in reporting ancestry that occur at the time of marriage or upon leaving home. At the ages of eighteen to twenty-two, when many young Americans leave home for the first time, the number of people reporting a single as opposed to a multiple ancestry goes up. Thus while parents simplify children's ancestries when they leave home, children themselves tend to report less complexity in their ancestries when they leave their parents' homes and begin reporting their ancestries themselves (Lieberson and Waters 1986, 1988; Waters 1990).

These individual changes are reflected in variability over time in the aggregate numbers of groups determined by the census and surveys. Fairly (1991) compared the consistency of the overall counts of different ancestry groups in the 1979 Current Population Survey, the 1980 census, and the 1986 National Content Test (a pretest for the 1990 census). He found much less consistency in the numbers for northern European ancestry groups whose immigration peaks were early in the nineteenth century—the English, Dutch, Germans, and other northern European groups. In other words each of these different surveys and the census yielded a different estimate of the number of people having this ancestry. The 1990 census also showed a great deal of flux and inconsistency in some ancestry groups. The number of people reporting English as an ancestry went down considerably from 1980, while the number reporting German ancestry went up. The number of Cajuns grew dramatically. This has led officials at the Census Bureau to assume that the examples used in the instructions strongly influence the responses people give. (Cajun was one of the examples of an ancestry given in 1990 but not in 1980, and German was the first example given. English was an example in the 1980 instructions, but not in 1990.)

All of these studies point to the socially variable nature of ethnic identity—and the lack of equivalence between ethnic ancestry and identity. If merely adding a category to the instructions to the question increases the number of people claiming that ancestry, what does that mean about the level of importance of that identity for people answering the census? Clearly identity and ancestry for Whites in the United States, who increasingly are from mixed backgrounds, involve some change and choice.

Symbolic Ethnicities for White Americans

What do these ethnic identities mean to people and why do they cling to them rather than just abandoning the tie and calling themselves American? My own field research with suburban Whites in California and Pennsylvania found that later-generation descendants of European origin maintain what are called "symbolic ethnicities." Symbolic ethnicity is a term coined by Herbert Gans (1979) to refer to ethnicity that is individualistic in nature and without real social cost for the individual. These symbolic identifications are essentially leisure time activities, rooted in nuclear family traditions and reinforced by the voluntary enjoyable aspects of being ethnic (Waters 1990). Richard Alba (1990) also found later-generation Whites in Albany, New York, who chose to keep a tie with an ethnic identity because of the enjoyable and voluntary aspects to those identities, along with the feelings of specialness they entailed. An example of symbolic ethnicity is individuals who identify as Irish, for example, on occasions such as Saint

Patrick's Day, on family holidays, or for vacations. They do not usually belong to Irish American organizations, live in Irish neighborhoods, work in Irish jobs, or marry other Irish people. The symbolic meaning of being Irish American can be constructed by individuals from mass media images, family traditions, or other intermittent social activities. In other words, for later-generation White ethnics, ethnicity is not something that influences their lives unless they want it to. In the world of work and school and neighborhood, individuals do not have to admit to being ethnic unless they choose to. And for an increasing number of European-origin individuals whose parents and grandparents have intermarried, the ethnicity they claim is largely a matter of personal choice as they sort through all of the possible combinations of groups in their genealogies.

Individuals can choose those aspects of being Italian, for instance, that appeal to them, and discard those that do not. Or a person whose father is Italian, and mother part Polish and part French, might choose among the three ethnicities and present herself as a Polish American. For instance, a nineteen-year-old college student, interviewed in California in 1986, told me he would have answered Irish on the 1980 census form that asked about ethnic ancestry. These are his reasons:

Q: Why would you have answered that?
A: Well my Dad's name is Kerrigan and my mom's name is O'Leary, and I do have some German in me, but if you figure it out, I am about 75% Irish, so I usually say I am Irish.
Q: You usually don't say German when people ask?
A: No, no, I never say I am German. My dad just likes being Irish. . . . I don't know I just never think of myself as being German.

Q: So your dad's father is the one who immigrated?

A: Yes. On his side is Irish for generations. And then my grandmother's name is Dubois, which is French, partly German, partly French, and then the rest of the family is all Irish. So it is only the maternal grandmother who messes up the line. (Waters 1990, p. 10)

Thus in the course of a few questions, this man labeled himself Irish, admitted to being part German but not identifying with it, and then as an afterthought added that he was also part French. This is not an unusual case. With just a little probing, many people will describe a variety of ancestries in their family background, but do not consider these ancestries to be a salient part of their own identities. Thus the 1990 census ancestry question, which estimated that 30 percent of the population is of mixed ancestry, most surely underestimates the degree of mixing among the population. My research, and the research of Richard Alba (1990), shows that many people have already sorted through what they know of their ethnic ancestries and simplified their responses before they ever answer a census or survey question (Waters 1990).

But note that this freedom to include or exclude ancestries in your identification to yourself and others would not be the same for those defined racially in our society. They are constrained to identify with the part of their ancestry that has been socially defined as the "essential" part. African Americans, for example, have been highly socially constrained to identify as Blacks, without other options available to them, even when they know that their forebears included many people of American Indian or European background. Up until the mid-twentieth century, many state governments had specific laws defining one as Black if as little as one-thirty-second of one's an-

cestors were defined as Black (Davis 1991; Dominguez 1986; Spickard 1989). Even now when the one drop rule has been dropped from our legal codes, there are still strong societal pressures on African Americans to identify in a particular way. Certain ancestries take precedence over others in the societal rules on descent and ancestry reckoning. If one believes one is part English and part German and identifies in a survey as German, one is not in danger of being accused of trying to "pass" as non-English and of being "redefined" English by the interviewer. But if one were part African and part German, one's self identification as German would be highly suspect and probably not accepted if one "looked" Black according to the prevailing social norms.

This is reflected in the ways the census collects race and ethnic identity. While the ethnic ancestry question used in 1980 and 1990 is given to all Americans in the sample regardless of race and allows multiple responses that combine races, the primary source of information on people defined racially in the United States is the census race question or the Hispanic question. Both of these questions require a person to make a choice about an identity. Individuals are not allowed to respond that they are both Black and White, or Japanese and Asian Indian on the race question even if they know that is their background. In fact, people who disobey the instructions to the census race question and check off two races are assigned to the first checked race in the list by the Census Bureau.

In responding to the ancestry question, the comparative latitude that White respondents have does not mean that Whites pick and choose ethnicities out of thin air. For the most part people choose an identity that corresponds with some element of their family tree. However, there are many anecdotal instances of people adopting ethnicities when they marry or move to a strongly identified neighborhood or community. For instance Micaela di Leonardo (1984) reported instances of non-Italian women who married into Italian American families and "became Italian." Karen Leonard (1992) describes a community of Mexican American women who married Punjabi immigrants in California. Some of the Punjabi immigrants and their descendants were said to have "become Mexican" when they joined their wives' kin group and social worlds. Alternatively she describes the community acknowledging that Mexican women made the best curry, as they adapted to life with Indian-origin men.

But what do these identities mean to individuals? Surely an identity that is optional in a number of ways—not legally defined on a passport or birth certificate, not socially consequential in terms of societal discrimination in terms of housing or job access, and not economically limiting in terms of blocking opportunities for social mobility—cannot be the same as an identity that results from and is nurtured by societal exclusion and rejection. The choice to have a symbolic ethnicity is an attractive and widespread one despite its lack of demonstrable content, because having a symbolic ethnicity combines individuality with feelings of community. People reported to me that they liked having an ethnic identity because it gave them a uniqueness and a feeling of being special. They often contrasted their own specialness by virtue of their ethnic identities with "bland" Americanness. Being ethnic makes people feel unique and special and not just "vanilla" as one of my respondents put it. For instance, one woman describes the benefits she feels from being Czech American:

> I work in an office and a lot of people in there always talk about their background. It's weird because it is a big office and people are of all different backgrounds. People are this or that. It is interesting I think to find out. Especially when it is something you do not

hear a lot about. Something that is not common like Lithuania or something. That's the good part about being Czech. People think it is something different. (Waters 1990, p. 154)

Because "American" is largely understood by Americans to be a political identity and allegiance and not an ethnic one, the idea of being "American" does not give people the same sense of belonging that their hyphenated American identity does. When I asked people about their dual identities—American and Irish or Italian or whatever—they usually responded in a way that showed how they conceived of the relationship between the two identities. Being an American was their primary identity; but it was so primary that they rarely, if ever, thought about it—most commonly only when they left the country. Being Irish American, on the other hand, was a way they had of differentiating themselves from others whom they interacted with from day to day—in many cases from spouses or in-laws. Certain of their traits—being emotional, having a sense of humor, talking with their hands—were understood as stemming from their ethnicity. Yet when asked about their identity as Americans, that identity was both removed from their day-to-day consciousness and understood in terms of loyalty and patriotism. Although they may not think they behave or think in a certain way because they are American, being American is something they are both proud of and committed to.

Symbolic ethnicity is the best of all worlds for these respondents. These White ethnics can claim to be unique and special, while simultaneously finding the community and conformity with others that they also crave. But that "community" is of a type that will not interfere with a person's individuality. It is not as if these people belong to ethnic voluntary organizations or gather as a group in churches or neighborhoods or union halls. They work and reside within the mainstream of American middle-class life, yet they retain the interesting benefits—the "specialness"—of ethnic allegiance, without any of its drawbacks.

It has been suggested by several researchers that this positive value attached to ethnic ancestry, which became popular in the ethnic revival of the 1970s, is the result of assimilation having proceeded to an advanced stage for descendants of White Europeans (Alba 1985; Crispino 1980; Steinberg 1981). Ironically, people celebrate and embrace their ethnic backgrounds precisely because assimilation has proceeded to the point where such identification does not have that much influence on their day-to-day life. Rather than choosing the "least ethnic" and most bland ethnicities, Whites desire the "most ethnic" ones, like the once-stigmatized "Italian," because it is perceived as bringing the most psychic benefits. For instance, when an Italian father is married to an English or a Scottish or a German mother, the likelihood is that the child will be reported to the census with the father's Italian ancestry, rather than the northern European ancestries, which would have been predicted to have a higher social status. Italian is a good ancestry to have, people told me, because they have good food and a warm family life. This change in the social meaning of being Italian American is quite dramatic, given that Italians were subject to discrimination, exclusion, and extreme negative stereotyping in the early part of the twentieth century.

Race Relations and Symbolic Ethnicity

However much symbolic ethnicity is without cost for the individual, there is a cost associated with symbolic ethnicity for the society. That is because symbolic ethnicities of the type described here are confined to White Americans of European origin. Black Americans, Hispanic Americans, Asian Americans, and American Indians do not have the option of a symbolic ethnicity at present in the United States. For all of the ways in which ethnicity does not matter for White Americans, it does matter for non-Whites. Who your ancestors are does affect your choice of spouse, where you live, what job you have, who your friends are, and what your chances are for success in American society, if those ancestors happen not to be from Europe. The reality is that White ethnics have a lot more choice and room to maneuver than they themselves think they do. The situation is very different for members of racial minorities, whose lives are strongly influenced by their race or national origin regardless of how much they may choose not to identify themselves in terms of their ancestries.

When White Americans learn the stories of how their grandparents and great-grandparents triumphed in the United States over adversity, they are usually told in terms of their individual efforts and triumphs. The important role of labor unions and other organized political and economic actors in their social and economic successes are left out of the story in favor of a generational story of individual Americans rising up against communitarian, Old World intolerance and New World resistance. As a result, the "individualized" voluntary, cultural view of ethnicity for Whites is what is remembered.

One important implication of these identities is that they tend to be very individualistic. There is a tendency to view valuing diversity in a pluralist environment as equating all groups. The symbolic ethnic tends to think that all groups are equal; everyone has a background that is their right to celebrate and pass on to their children. This leads to the conclusion that all identities are equal and all identities in some sense are interchangeable—"I'm Italian

American, you're Polish American. I'm Irish American, you're African American." The important thing is to treat people as individuals and all equally. However, this assumption ignores the very big difference between an individualistic symbolic ethnic identity and a socially enforced and imposed racial identity.

My favorite example of how this type of thinking can lead to some severe misunderstandings between people of different backgrounds is from the *Dear Abby* advice column. A few years back a person wrote in who had asked an acquaintance of Asian background where his family was from. His acquaintance answered that this was a rude question and he would not reply. The bewildered White asked Abby why it was rude, since he thought it was a sign of respect to wonder where people were from, and he certainly would not mind anyone asking HIM about where his family was from. Abby asked her readers to write in to say whether it was rude to ask about a person's ethnic background. She reported that she got a large response, that most non-Whites thought it was a sign of disrespect, and Whites thought it was flattering:

> Dear Abby,
> I am 100 percent American and because I am of Asian ancestry I am often asked "What are you?" It's not the personal nature of this question that bothers me, it's the question itself. This query seems to question my very humanity. "What am I? Why I am a person like everyone else!"
>
> Signed, A REAL AMERICAN

> Dear Abby,
> Why do people resent being asked what they are? The Irish are so proud of being Irish, they tell you before you even ask. Tip O'Neill has never tried to hide his Irish ancestry.
>
> Signed, JIMMY

In this exchange JIMMY cannot understand why Asians are not as happy to be asked about their ethnicity as he is, because he understands his ethnicity and theirs to be separate but equal. Everyone has to come from somewhere—his family from Ireland, another's family from Asia—each has a history and each should be proud of it. But the reason he cannot understand the perspective of the Asian American is that all ethnicities are not equal; all are not symbolic, costless, and voluntary. When White Americans equate their own symbolic ethnicities with the socially enforced identities of non-White Americans, they obscure the fact that the experiences of Whites and non-Whites have been qualitatively different in the United States and that the current identities of individuals partly reflect that unequal history.

In the next section I describe how relations between Black and White students on college campuses reflect some of these asymmetries in the understanding of what a racial or ethnic identity means. While I focus on Black and White students in the following discussion, you should be aware that the myriad other groups in the United States—Mexican Americans, American Indians, Japanese Americans—all have some degree of social and individual influences on their identities, which reflect the group's social and economic history and present circumstance.

Relations on College Campuses

Both Black and White students face the task of developing their race and ethnic identities. Sociologists and psychologists note that at the time people leave home and begin to live independently from their parents, often ages eighteen to twenty-two, they report a heightened sense of racial and ethnic identity as they sort through how much of their beliefs and behaviors are idiosyncratic to their families and how much are shared with other people. It is not until one comes in close contact with many people who are different from oneself that individuals realize the ways in which their backgrounds may influence their individual personality. This involves coming into contact with people who are different in terms of their ethnicity, class, religion, region, and race. For White students, the ethnicity they claim is more often than not a symbolic one—with all of the voluntary, enjoyable, and intermittent characteristics I have described above.

Black students at the university are also developing identities through interactions with others who are different from them. Their identity development is more complicated than that of Whites because of the added element of racial discrimination and racism, along with the "ethnic" developments of finding others who share their background. Thus Black students have the positive attraction of being around other Black students who share some cultural elements, as well as the need to band together with other students in a reactive and oppositional way in the face of racist incidents on campus.

Colleges and universities across the country have been increasing diversity among their student bodies in the last few decades. This has led in many cases to strained relations among students from different racial and ethnic backgrounds. The 1980s and 1990s produced a great number of racial incidents and high racial tensions on campuses. While there were a number of racial incidents that were due to bigotry, unlawful behavior, and violent or vicious attacks, much of what happens among students on campuses involves a low level of tension and awkwardness in social interactions.

Many Black students experience racism personally for the first time on campus. The upper-middle-class students from White suburbs were often isolated enough that

their presence was not threatening to racists in their high schools. Also, their class background was known by their residence and this may have prevented attacks being directed at them. Often Black students at the university who begin talking with other students and recognizing racial slights will remember incidents that happened to them earlier that they might not have thought were related to race.

Black college students across the country experience a sizeable number of incidents that are clearly the result of racism. Many of the most blatant ones that occur between students are the result of drinking. Sometimes late at night, drunken groups of White students coming home from parties will yell slurs at single Black students on the street. The other types of incidents that happen include being singled out for special treatment by employees, such as being followed when shopping at the campus bookstore, or going to the art museum with your class and the guard stops you and asks for your I.D. Others involve impersonal encounters on the street—being called a nigger by a truck driver while crossing the street, or seeing old ladies clutch their pocketbooks and shake in terror as you pass them on the street. For the most part these incidents are not specific to the university environment, they are the types of incidents middle-class Blacks face every day throughout American society, and they have been documented by sociologists (Feagin 1991).

In such a climate, however, with students experiencing these types of incidents and talking with each other about them, Black students do experience a tension and a feeling of being singled out. It is unfair that this is part of their college experience and not that of White students. Dealing with incidents like this, or the ever-present threat of such incidents, is an ongoing developmental task for Black students that takes energy, attention, and strength of character. It should be clearly understood that this is an asymmetry in the "college experience" for Black and White students. It is one of the unfair aspects of life that results from living in a society with ongoing racial prejudice and discrimination. It is also very understandable that it makes some students angry at the unfairness of it all, even if there is no one to blame specifically. It is also very troubling because, while most Whites do not create these incidents, some do, and it is never clear until you know someone well whether they are the type of person who could do something like this. So one of the reactions of Black students to these incidents is to band together.

In some sense then, as Blauner (1992) has argued, you can see Black students coming together on campus as both an "ethnic" pull of wanting to be together to share common experiences and community, and a "racial" push of banding together defensively because of perceived rejection and tension from Whites. In this way the ethnic identities of Black students are in some sense similar to, say, Korean students wanting to be together to share experiences. And it is an ethnicity that is generally much stronger than, say, Italian Americans. But for Koreans who come together there is generally a definition of themselves as "different from" Whites. For Blacks reacting to exclusion, there is a tendency for the coming together to involve both being "different from" but also "opposed to" Whites.

The anthropologist John Ogbu (1990) has documented the tendency of minorities in a variety of societies around the world, who have experienced severe blocked mobility for long periods of time, to develop such oppositional identities. An important component of having such an identity is to describe others of your group who do not join in the group solidarity as devaluing and denying their very core identity. This is why it is not common for successful Asians to be

accused by others of "acting White" in the United States, but it is quite common for such a term to be used by Blacks and Latinos. The oppositional component of a Black identity also explains how Black people can question whether others are acting "Black enough." On campus, it explains some of the intense pressures felt by Black students who do not make their racial identity central and who choose to hang out primarily with non-Blacks. This pressure from the group, which is partly defining itself by not being White, is exacerbated by the fact that race is a physical marker in American society. No one immediately notices the Jewish students sitting together in the dining hall, or the one Jewish student sitting surrounded by non-Jews, or the Texan sitting with the Californians, but everyone notices the Black student who is or is not at the "Black table" in the cafeteria.

An example of the kinds of misunderstandings that can arise because of different understandings of the meanings and implications of symbolic versus oppositional identities concerns questions students ask one another in the dorms about personal appearances and customs. A very common type of interaction in the dorm concerns questions Whites ask Blacks about their hair. Because Whites tend to know little about Blacks, and Blacks know a lot about Whites, there is a general asymmetry in the level of curiosity people have about one another. Whites, as the numerical majority, have had little contact with Black culture; Blacks, especially those who are in college, have had to develop bicultural skills—knowledge about the social worlds of both Whites and Blacks. Miscommunication and hurt feelings about White students' questions about Black students' hair illustrate this point. One of the things that happens freshman year is that White students are around Black students as they fix their hair. White students are generally quite curious about Black students' hair—they have basic questions such as how often Blacks wash their hair, how they get it straightened or curled, what products they use on their hair, how they comb it, etc. Whites often wonder to themselves whether they should ask these questions. One thought experiment Whites perform is to ask themselves whether a particular question would upset them. Adopting the "do unto others" rule, they ask themselves, "If a Black person was curious about my hair would I get upset?" The answer usually is "No, I would be happy to tell them." Another example is an Italian American student wondering to herself, "Would I be upset if someone asked me about calamari?" The answer is no, so she asks her Black roommate about collard greens, and the roommate explodes with an angry response such as, "Do you think all Black people eat watermelon too?" Note that if this Italian American knew her friend was Trinidadian American and asked about peas and rice the situation would be more similar and would not necessarily ignite underlying tensions.

Like the debate in *Dear Abby*, these innocent questions are likely to lead to resentment. The issue of stereotypes about Black Americans and the assumption that all Blacks are alike and have the same stereotypical cultural traits has more power to hurt or offend a Black person than vice versa. The innocent questions about Black hair also bring up a number of asymmetries between the Black and White experience. Because Blacks tend to have more knowledge about Whites than vice versa, there is not an even exchange going on; the Black freshman is likely to have fewer basic questions about his White roommate than his White roommate has about him. Because of the differences historically in the group experiences of Blacks and Whites there are some connotations to Black hair that don't exist about White hair. (For instance, is straightening your hair a form of assimila-

tion, do some people distinguish between women having "good hair" and "bad hair" in terms of beauty and how is that related to looking "White"?) Finally, even a Black freshman who cheerfully disregards or is unaware that there are these asymmetries will soon slam into another asymmetry if she willingly answers every innocent question asked of her. In a situation where Blacks make up only 10 percent of the student body, if every non-Black needs to be educated about hair, she will have to explain it to nine other students. As one Black student explained to me, after you've been asked a couple of times about something so personal you begin to feel like you are an attraction in a zoo, that you are at the university for the education of the White students.

Institutional Responses

Our society asks a lot of young people. We ask young people to do something that no one else does as successfully on such a wide scale—that is to live together with people from very different backgrounds, to respect one another, to appreciate one another, and to enjoy and learn from one another. The successes that occur every day in this endeavor are many, and they are too often overlooked. However, the problems and tensions are also real, and they will not vanish on their own. We tend to see pluralism working in the United States in much the same way some people expect capitalism to work. If you put together people with various interests and abilities and resources, the "invisible hand" of capitalism is supposed to make all the parts work together in an economy for the common good.

There is much to be said for such a model—the invisible hand of the market can solve complicated problems of production and distribution better than any "visible hand" of a state plan. However, we have learned that unequal power relations among the actors in the capitalist marketplace, as well as "externalities" that the market cannot account for, such as long-term pollution, or collusion between corporations, or the exploitation of child labor, means that state regulation is often needed. Pluralism and the relations between groups are very similar. There is a lot to be said for the idea that bringing people who belong to different ethnic or racial groups together in institutions with no interference will have good consequences. Students from different backgrounds will make friends if they share a dorm room or corridor, and there is no need for the institution to do any more than provide the locale. But like capitalism, the invisible hand of pluralism does not do well when power relations and externalities are ignored. When you bring together individuals from groups that are differentially valued in the wider society and provide no guidance, there will be problems. In these cases the "invisible hand" of pluralist relations does not work, and tensions and disagreements can arise without any particular individual or group of individuals being "to blame." On college campuses in the 1990s some of the tensions between students are of this sort. They arise from honest misunderstandings, lack of a common background, and very different experiences of what race and ethnicity mean to the individual.

The implications of symbolic ethnicities for thinking about race relations are subtle but consequential. If your understanding of your own ethnicity and its relationship to society and politics is one of individual choice, it becomes harder to understand the need for programs like affirmative action, which recognize the ongoing need for group struggle and group recognition, in order to bring about social change. It also is hard for a White college student to understand the need that minority students feel to band together against discrimination. It also is easy,

on the individual level, to expect everyone else to be able to turn their ethnicity on and off at will, the way you are able to, without understanding that ongoing discrimination and societal attention to minority status makes that impossible for individuals from minority groups to do. The paradox of symbolic ethnicity is that it depends upon the ultimate goal of a pluralist society, and at the same time makes it more difficult to achieve that ultimate goal. It is dependent upon the concept that all ethnicities mean the same thing, that enjoying the traditions of one's heritage is an option available to a group or an individual, but that such a heritage should not have any social costs associated with it.

As the Asian Americans who wrote to *Dear Abby* make clear, there are many societal issues and involuntary ascriptions associated with non-White identities. The developments necessary for this to change are not individual but societal in nature. Social mobility and declining racial and ethnic sensitivity are closely associated. The legacy and the present reality of discrimination on the basis of race or ethnicity must be overcome before the ideal of the pluralist society, where all heritages are treated equally and are equally available for individuals to choose or discard at will, is realized.

REFERENCES

ALBA, RICHARD D. 1985. *Italian Americans: Into the Twilight of Ethnicity.* Edgewood Cliffs, NJ: Prentice-Hall.

_____. 1990. *Ethnic Identity: The Transformation of White America.* New Haven, CT: Yale University Press.

BARTH, FREDERICK. 1969. *Ethnic Groups and Boundaries.* Boston: Little, Brown.

BLAUNER, ROBERT. 1992. "Talking Past Each Other: Black and White Languages of Race." *American Prospect* (Summer):55–64.

CRISPINO, JAMES. 1980. *The Assimilation of Ethnic Groups: The Italian Case.* Staten Island, NY: Center for Migration Studies.

DI LEONARDO, MICAELA. 1984. *The Varieties of Ethnic Experience: Kinship, Class and Gender Among Italian Americans.* Ithaca, NY: Cornell University Press.

DOMINGUEZ, VIRGINIA. 1986. *White by Definition: Social Classification in Creole Louisiana.* New Brunswick, NJ: Rutgers University Press.

FARLEY, REYNOLDS. 1991. "The New Census Question About Ancestry: What Did It Tell Us?" *Demography* 28:411–29.

FEAGIN, JOE R. 1991. "The Continuing Significance of Race: Antiblack Discrimination in Public Places." *American Sociological Review* 56:101–117.

GANS, HERBERT. 1979. "Symbolic Ethnicity: The Future of Ethnic Groups and Cultures in America." *Ethnic and Racial Studies* 2:1–20.

GREELEY, ANDREW M. 1976. "The Ethnic Miracle." *Public Interest* 45 (Fall):20–36.

LEONARD, KAREN. 1992. *Making Ethnic Choices: California's Punjabi Mexican Americans.* Philadelphia: Temple University Press.

LIEBERSON, STANLEY. 1985. "Unhyphenated Whites in the United States." *Ethnic and Racial Studies* 8:159–80.

LIEBERSON, STANLEY, and MARY WATERS. 1986. "Ethnic Groups in Flux: The Changing Ethnic Responses of American Whites." *Annals of the American Academy of Political and Social Science* 487:79–91.

_____. 1988. *From Many Strands: Ethnic and Racial Groups in Contemporary America.* New York: Russell Sage.

_____. 1993. "The Ethnic Responses of Whites: What Causes Their Instability, Simplification, and Inconsistency?" *Social Forces* 72(2):421–50.

McKENNEY, NAMPEO R., and ARTHUR R. CRESCE. 1992. "Measurement of Ethnicity in the United States: Experiences of the U.S. Census Bureau." Paper presented at the Joint Canada–United States Conference on the Measurement of Ethnicity, Ottawa, Canada, April 1–3.

SPICKARD, PAUL R. 1989. *Mixed Blood.* Madison: University of Wisconsin Press.

STEINBERG, STEPHEN. 1981. *The Ethnic Myth: Race, Ethnicity, and Class in America.* Boston: Beacon Press.

U.S. BUREAU OF THE CENSUS. 1992. *Census of Population and Housing, 1990: Detailed Ancestry Groups for States.* Supplementary Reports CP-S-1–2. Washington, DC: U.S. Government Printing Office.

WATERS, MARY C. 1990. *Ethnic Options: Choosing Identities in America.* Berkeley and Los Angeles: University of California Press.

WEBER, MAX. 1921. *Economy and Society: An Outline of Interpretive Sociology,* edited by Guenther Roth and Claus Wittich, translated by Ephraim Fischoff. New York: Bedminster Press.

41

WHITE RACIAL FORMATION
Into the Twenty-First Century

Charles A. Gallagher

Charles A. Gallagher, "White Racial Formation," from *Critical White Studies: Looking Behind the Mirror*, Richard Delgado and Jean Stefancic, eds., Temple University Press, 1997. Copyright © 1997 Charles A. Gallagher.

Whiteness is in a state of change. One only need browse book stands or news racks for examples of how the idea of whiteness is being interpreted, defined, reinterpreted, and contested by popular writers and journalists. Whites perceive themselves, according to one account, as being part of a distinctly different, colorblind, sympathetic generation that has learned to look beyond "the color of the skin" to "the beauty within."[1]

Whereas some whites see a common humanity with their nonwhite counterparts, others see whiteness as a liability. A white sergeant with the Los Angeles County Sheriff's Office announced creation of the Association of White Male Peace Officers, with the goal of defending the rights of white officers who are "distinctly averse to the proposal that, as a class, we be punished or penalized for any real or purported transgressions of our forbears."[2] This "class" of white men seeks the same types of legal protection afforded to other groups organized around their race or gender. Samuel Francis, an editorial writer for the *Washington Times* and advisor to Patrick Buchanan's presidential campaign, declared that "whites must reassert our identity and our solidarity . . . in explicitly racial terms through the articulation of racial consciousness as whites."[3] Francis believes whites have ignored or disregarded their racial identity and must (re)unite as whites to stop the influx of nonwhite immigrants. It is no wonder many whites feel confused and overwhelmed about who they are racially and how they fit into American race relations.

The meaning of whiteness is not to be found in any single one of the preceding descriptions of how whites imagine themselves or come to understand their racial identity. The contemporary meaning is an amalgamation of these white narratives. Whites can be defined as naive because they attach little meaning to their race, humane in their desire to reach out to nonwhites, defensive as self-defined victims, and reactionary in their calls for a return to white solidarity.

It is not surprising, then, that my respondents would generate similar disparate (and at times schizophrenic) renderings when asked what meaning they attach to their race. As in the anecdotes above, the extent to which whiteness was a salient form of identity for my respondents varied greatly, ranging from the naive, to the reactionary, to the situational. Some de-

scribed their sense of whiteness as being partially veiled, becoming visible and salient only when they felt they were a racial minority. This momentary minority status and the anxiety often associated with this experience colored how respondents saw themselves and their relationship to other racial groups. For other respondents, whiteness had been made explicitly visible at some earlier point in their lives. Their understanding of the concept was often no more than a list of what they were not, why they should not feel guilty about being white, or why their race was now being held against them. The extent to which a sense of whiteness was just emerging for some and had already evolved as an overt identity for others obscures an obvious and important finding: If whiteness was ever invisible for these respondents, it no longer is.

What, however, have we learned about the social, political, and cultural construction of whiteness? How is the construction of whiteness linked sociologically to the structural elements that shape those meanings? Respondents may "know they are white," but what does that mean and what are its political and social consequences? A number of patterns emerged in my data, each of which delineates a particular facet of how white racial identity is constructed and made salient. These patterns point to one clear and significant finding: Whiteness is in the midst of fundamental transformation. White identity is not only a reaction to the entrance of historically marginalized racial and ethnic groups into the political arena and the ensuing struggle over social resources. The construction of whiteness is based, at least among the respondents in my study, on a perception of current and future material deprivation and the need to delineate white culture in a nondemonized fashion. The majority of whites in this study have come to understand themselves and their interests as white. Many of my respondents now think about themselves as whites, not as ethnics; they see themselves as individuals who are members of a racial category with its own particular set of interests. They have attached new meanings to being white and have used those meanings as the basis for forging an identity centered around race. They have, to borrow Michael Omi and Howard Winant's term, gone through the process of racialization. The factors shaping white racialization include the decline of ethnicity, the rise of identity politics, the perception that whiteness is a social and economic liability, and the precepts of neoconservative racial politics. While I do not suggest whiteness is constructed in a uniform, linear fashion, I do believe that white racialization has emerged at this particular moment due to a confluence of these trends. I see them as being linked in the following ways.

The Ethnic Vacuum

A lack of ethnic identity among my respondents has created an emptiness that is being filled by an identity centered on race. Almost fifty years ago, W. Lloyd Warner observed: "The future of American ethnic groups seems to be limited; it is likely that they will quickly be absorbed. When this happens one of the great epochs of American history will end, and another, that of race, will begin."[4] My interviews and survey data bear out Warner's prediction. For the majority of the white respondents in my study, little is left in the way of ethnic solidarity, ethnic identity, or even symbolic nostalgia for the ethnic traditions of their older kin. When asked to define themselves in ethnic or racial terms (or both), the majority of students labeled themselves as white or Caucasian, ignoring such labels as Italian-American. Like most whites their

age, these students have undergone such extensive generational assimilation and convergence of cultural experiences that only a few chose to describe themselves as "plain old American," "mutt," or "nothing." The young whites I interviewed were so removed from the immigrant experience that even the small minority who defined themselves in ethnic terms acknowledged that their ethnicity was in name only. As one remarked, he thought of his mixed Polish heritage only when he ate kielbasa at Christmas. Ethnicity is a subjective series of choices (or, as Mary Waters writes, an "option") in constructing an identity, but the majority of white students I interviewed and surveyed came from families where very little in the way of "ethnic options" existed because the symbolic ethnic practices had all but died out.

Young whites selectively resurrect their ethnicity through "immigrant tales" mainly when they feel white privilege is being contested, even though their perceived ethnic history does not necessarily concern a specific nation but rather a generalized idea of a European origin. This common, yet fuzzy, connection to the "old country" provides the historical backdrop and cultural space for the construction of white identity, or "a yearning for a usable past."[5] As the importance of ethnicity wanes in the lives of young whites, the immigration experience of older (or dead) kin becomes a mythologized narrative providing a historical common denominator of passage, victimization, and assimilation. As white students often tell it, blacks can point to the middle passage and slavery; Japanese and Chinese can speak of internment and forced labor, respectively; and whites have the immigrant experience. In a sense, past group victimization or hardship is part of the American experience; young whites, when confronted by real or perceived charges of racism, can point to the mistreatment of their older relatives when they were newly arrived immigrants in the United States.

Although whites did experience prejudice and discrimination when they arrived in the United States, it is unlikely that their descendants encounter anything remotely similar today. Unlike the case of the white ethnic revival movement of the 1960s and 1970s, it is now impossible to mobilize young whites politically based on their ethnicity; an ethnic identity no longer exists, as it did for their parents or grandparents.

The markers of ethnic identity have all but disappeared. A "subjective belief in common descent" did not exist for the majority of my respondents. These students could not speak, nor had they been exposed to, a "mother tongue." They did not feel obligated to marry or date people from similar ethnic backgrounds. Nor did they derive a "sense of honor" from being part of an ethnic group or draw on their heritage to become a "carrier of 'interests,' economic or political, which the members of an ethnic group lay claim to or defend."[6] The generation of older whites who were part of the "ethnic revival" and who used their ethnicity as the basis for group claims has been displaced by one that feels increasingly comfortable using their racial identity as the sole carrier of their interests.

Race matters for my respondents because it is racial, not ethnic, identity that is bound up in popular culture and the political order. As David Roediger sees it, "*Among whites,* racial identity (whiteness) and ethnic identity are distinct."[7] I would argue, on the contrary, that for many respondents there is no distinction because ethnic identity has all but vanished. After generations of assimilation, only whiteness is left as an identity with any real social or political import. The decline of ethnicity among later-generation whites has created an identity vacuum, one that has been at least partially replaced by an identity grounded in race.

White Identity Politics

The second influence on white racialization is how identity politics has raised white consciousness. The generation of whites I studied, born around 1975, grew up with a brand of racial politics and media exposure that are unique. This generation is the first to witness the full social, political, and cultural effects of identity politics. As Herbert Blumer puts it, "To characterize another racial group is, by opposition, to define one's own."[8] The political and cultural mobilization of racially defined minorities has forced many of my white respondents to think about who they are racially in relation to other racial groups.

The racially charged and politically conservative environment of the late 1980s and 1990s has reinterpreted whiteness as a liability. The cultural mythology that has become today's commonsense understanding of race relations is a definition of society that is color blind. The ascendancy of color blindness as the dominant mode of race thinking and the emergence of liberal individualism as a source of white entitlement and racial backlash was a central finding in my work. It is, I believe, a view that is not specific to the student population at Urban University. Stanley Fish sums up how color blindness has been twisted politically to maintain white privilege. "When the goal was to make discrimination illegal," he argues, color blind meant lifting barriers to full citizenship, but the term now means blind to the effects of prejudice on people because of their color.[9]

The social movements that challenged the racial status quo unfolded over twenty-five years. The first "revolution" my respondents witnessed, however, was President Reagan's attack on civil rights legislation in the name of democracy and fair play. They grew up hearing that the United States was a color-blind nation, saw the rise of a black and Asian middle class, and were told stories about a federal government that "blocks opportunities for white workers."[10] Whites of this generation "have no knowledge of the disciplined, systematic, and collective *group* activity that has structured white identities in American society."[11]

Racial Politics: The Right and White Victimization

The belief that whites were subject to racial discrimination (reverse discrimination) appeared as a dominant theme throughout my research. One example of this belief was the perception that a racial double standard exists on campus. In the majority of my interviews and focus groups, white students felt that race-based organizations at Urban University were a form of reverse discrimination. Twenty-nine of 119 campus organizations used race as their primary organizing principle. Mainly cultural and political, these groups encourage an affirmation of racial identity and provide a safe, supportive space for students of color to develop social and professional networks. The latent effect of these organizations, however, is that they transform and contribute to redefining the meaning of racial identity for whites on campus. When they are excluded, white students get a taste of what it is like to be reduced to a racial category. They are generally unnerved by this experience and quickly slip into reactionary, defensive posturing. The resentment, anger, and frustration white students express because they are excluded provide the foundation for a white identity based on the belief that whites are now under siege. Student groups like the Black Pre-Law Society or the Korean Cultural Club were sanctioned by the university, but, as was said many times in my interviews, if whites tried to establish an or-

ganization and it had "white" in the title a major controversy would ensue and the group and its members would be labeled racist. Nor could white respondents retreat into an Italian-American House or a Hibernians Club, because there was no basis for solidarity around an ethnic identity.

If a loss of ethnic identity has created a void among many of my respondents, and if identity politics has made whiteness a visible racial category, then the perception that being white is now a social liability has most certainly raised white consciousness. The social cost of whiteness arose whenever issues of affirmative action on and off campus were discussed. The majority of white students felt that contemporary affirmative action measures were unfair because issues of overt racism, discrimination, and equal opportunity had been addressed by their parents' generation in the 1960s. A majority of white students argued that the United States is a meritocracy where nonwhites have every advantage whites do (and in some cases more because of affirmative action). Most of my respondents want to believe the United States is an egalitarian, "color-blind" society because to think otherwise would raise the irritating issue of white privilege. The working- and middle-class young people I interviewed do not see themselves as privileged or benefiting from their skin color. It becomes difficult for working-class college students to think about white privilege when they are accumulating college debt, forced to live with their parents, working twenty-five hours a week on top of their studies, and are concerned that Starbucks or the Gap may be their future employer.

A fundamental transformation of how young whites define and understand themselves racially is taking place. The white students I interviewed believe that the American class system is fair and equitable: Anyone who delays gratification, works hard, and follows the rules will succeed regardless of color. Black television stars, the media's treatment of the black middle class, and stereotypes of Asians as model minorities have provided young whites with countless nonwhite success stories. For many of them, the "leveled playing field" argument has rendered affirmative action policies a form of reverse discrimination and a source of resentment. White students who believe social equality has been achieved are able to assert a racial identity and not regard themselves as racist—they are merely affirming their identity in ways similar to the language and actions of other racially defined groups. On the individual level, the racism most prevalent among the respondents was not the cultural stereotypes some white students used to counter charges of white privilege but the racist projections many made about how blacks perceive whites.

In large part, white identity is a reaction to the entry of historically marginalized racial and ethnic groups into the political arena and the ensuing struggle over social resources. But it is not only that. Whiteness as an explicit cultural product may be taking on a life of its own, developing its own racial logic and essence as it is molded by the political right. The rhetoric of neoconservatives serves to legitimate the benefits that accrue to whites based on skin color. Starting with the false premise of social equality and equal opportunity, neoconservatives can speak of America's Western roots and traditions in racial terms but not appear racist. This ostensibly nonracist "white" space that is being carved out of our cultural landscape allows whites to be presented like any other racial contender in the struggle over political and cultural resources and self-definition.

NOTES

1. Benjamin Demott, *The Trouble with Friendship: Why Americans Can't Think Straight About Race* (New York: Atlantic Monthly Press, 1995), 45.
2. "Police Officer Starts Group to Defend White Men," *New York Times,* 19 November 1995, p. 36.
3. *New York Times,* 23 February 1995, p. A23.
4. Quoted in Michael Banton, *Racial and Ethnic Competition* (London: Cambridge University Press, 1983), 64.
5. Bob Blauner, "Talking Past Each Other: Black and White Languages of Race," in *Race and Ethnic Conflict,* edited by Howard J. Ehrlich and Fred L. Pincus (Boulder, CO: Westview Press, 1994), 27.
6. Richard Alba suggests that these beliefs are the fundamental benchmark of what it means to be part of an ethnic group. See *Ethnic Identity: The Transformation of White America* (New Haven, CT: Yale University Press), 313.
7. David Roediger, *Towards the Abolition of Whiteness* (New York: Verso Press, 1994), 182.
8. Herbert Blumer, "Race Prejudice as a Sense of Group Position," *Pacific Sociology Review* 1(1):4.
9. Stanley Fish, "How the Right Hijacked the Magic Words," *New York Times,* 13 August 1995, section 4, p. 15.
10. Frederick R. Lynch, "Race Unconsciousness and the White Male," *Society* 29 (2):31. Lynch is quoting the pollster Stanley Greenberg.
11. George Lipsitz, "The Possessive Investment in Whiteness: Racialized Social Democracy and the 'White' Problem in American Studies," *American Quarterly,* 47 (3) (September 1995): 369.

Constructing a Nonracist World: Obstacles and Opportunities

42

MY RACE PROBLEM—AND OURS

Randall Kennedy

What is the proper role of race in determining how I, an American black, should feel toward others? One response is that although I should not dislike people because of their race, there is nothing wrong with having a special—a *racial*—affection for other black people. Indeed, many would go further and maintain that something would be wrong with me if I did not sense and express racial pride, racial kinship, racial patriotism, racial loyalty, racial solidarity—synonyms for that amalgam of belief, intuition, and commitment that manifests itself when blacks treat blacks with more solicitude than they do those who are not black.

Some conduct animated by these sentiments has blended into the background of daily routine, as when blacks who are strangers nonetheless speak to each other— "Hello," "Hey," "Yo"—or hug or give each other a soul handshake or refer to each other as "brother" or "sister." Other manifestations are more dramatic. For example, the Million Man March, which brought at least 500,000 black men to Washington, D.C., in 1995, was a demonstration predicated on the notion that blackness gives rise to racial

obligation and that black people should have a special, closer, more affectionate relationship with their fellow blacks than with others in America's diverse society.

I reject this response to the question. Neither racial pride nor racial kinship offers guidance that is intellectually, morally, or politically satisfactory.

Racial Pride

I eschew racial pride because of my conception of what should properly be the object of pride for an individual: something that he or she has accomplished. I can feel pride in a good deed I have done or a good effort I have made. I cannot feel pride in some state of affairs that is independent of my contribution to it. The color of my skin, the width of my nose, the texture of my hair, and the various other signs that prompt people to label me black constitute such a state of affairs. I did not achieve my racial designation. It was something I inherited—like my nationality and socio-economic starting place and sex—and therefore something I should not feel proud of or be credited with. In taking this position I follow Frederick Douglass, the great nineteenth-century reformer, who declared that "the only excuse for pride in individuals . . . is in the fact of their own achievements." If the sun has created curled hair and tanned skin, Douglass observed, "let the sun be proud of its achievement."

It is understandable why people have often made inherited group status an honorific credential. Personal achievement is difficult to attain, and the lack of it often leaves a vacuum that racial pride can easily fill. Thus even if a person has little to show for himself, racial pride gives him status.

But maybe I am misconstruing what people mean by racial pride; perhaps it means simply that one is unashamed of one's race. To that I have no objection. No one should be ashamed of the labeling by which she or he is racially categorized, because no one chooses her or his parents or the signs by which society describes and sorts people. For this very same reason, however, no one should congratulate herself on her race insofar as it is merely an accident of birth.

I suspect, however, that when most black people embrace the term "racial pride," they mean more than that they are unembarrassed by their race. They mean, echoing Marcus Garvey, that "to be [black] is no disgrace, but an honor." Thus when James Brown sings "Say It Loud—I'm Black and I'm Proud," he is heard by many blacks as expressing not just the absence of shame but delight and assertiveness in valuing a racial designation that has long been stigmatized in America.

There is an important virtue in this assertion of the value of black life. It combats something still eminently in need of challenge: the assumption that because of their race black people are stupid, ugly, and low, and that because of their race white people are smart, beautiful, and righteous. But within some of the forms that this assertiveness has taken are important vices—including the belief that because of racial kinship blacks ought to value blacks more highly than others.

Racial Kinship

I reject the notion of racial kinship. I do so in order to avoid its burdens and to be free to claim what the distinguished political theorist Michael Sandel labels "the unencumbered self." The unencumbered self is free and independent, "unencumbered by aims and attachments it does not choose for itself," Sandel writes. "Freed from the sanctions of custom and tradition and inherited status, unbound by moral ties antecedent to choice, the self is installed as sovereign, cast as the author of the only obligations that constrain." Sandel believes that the unencumbered self is an illusion and that the yearning for it is a manifestation of a shallow liberalism that "cannot account for certain moral and political obligations that we commonly recognize, even prize"—"obligations of solidarity, religious duties, and other moral ties that may claim us for reasons unrelated to a choice," which are "indispensable aspects of our moral and political experience." Sandel's objection to those who, like me, seek the unencumbered self is that they fail to appreciate loyalties and responsibilities that should be accorded moral force partly because they influence our identity, such that living by these attachments "is inseparable from understanding ourselves as the particular persons we are—as members of this family or city or nation or people, as bearers of that history, as citizens of this republic."

I admire Sandel's work and have learned much from it. But a major weakness in it is a conflation of "is" and "ought." Sandel privileges what exists and has existed so much that his deference to tradition lapses into historical determinism. He faults the model of the unencumbered self because, he says, it cannot account for feelings of solidarity and loyalty that most people have not chosen to impose upon themselves but that they cherish nonetheless. This represents a fault, however, only if we believe that the unchosen attachments Sandel celebrates should be accorded moral weight. I am not prepared to do that simply on the basis that such attachments exist, have long existed, and are passionately felt. Feelings of primordial attachment often represent mere prejudice or superstition, a hangover of the childhood socialization from which many people never recover.

One defense of racial kinship takes the shape of an analogy between race and family. This position was strikingly advanced by the nineteenth-century black-nationalist intellectual Alexander Crummell, who asserted that "a race *is* a family," that "race feeling, like the family feeling, is of divine origin," and that the extinction of race feeling is thus—fortunately, in his view—just as impossible as the extinction of family feeling.

Analogizing race to family is a potent rhetorical move used to challenge those who, like me, are animated by a liberal, individualistic, and universalistic ethos that is skeptical of, if not hostile to, the particularisms—national, ethnic, religious, and racial—that seem to have grown so strong recently, even in arenas, such as major cosmopolitan universities, where one might have expected their demise. The central point of the challenge is to suggest that the norms I embrace will, or at least should, wobble and collapse in the face of claims on familial loyalty. Blood, as they say, is thicker than water.

One way to deal with the race-family analogy is to question its aptness on the grounds that a race is so much more populous than what is commonly thought of as a family that race cannot give rise to the same, or even similar, feelings of loyalty. When we think of a family, we think of a small, close-knit association of people who grow to know one another intimately over time. A race, in contrast, is a conglomeration of strangers. Black men at the Million Man

March assuredly called one another brothers. But if certain questions were posed ("Would you be willing to lend a hundred dollars to this brother, or donate a kidney to that one?"), it would have quickly become clear that many, if not most, of those "brothers" perceived one another as strangers—not so distant as whites, perhaps, but strangers nonetheless.

However, I do not want to rest my argument here. Rather, I want to accept the race-family analogy in order to strengthen my attack on assumptions that privilege status-driven loyalties (the loyalties of blood) over chosen loyalties (the loyalties of will). In my view, many people, including legislators and judges, make far too much of blood ties in derogation of ties created by loving effort.

A vivid illustration is provided by the following kind of child-custody decision. It involves a child who has been separated from her parents and placed with adults who assume the role of foster parents. These adults nurture her, come to love her, and ultimately seek legally to become her new parents. If the "blood" parents of the child do not interfere, the foster parents will have a good chance of doing this. If, however, the blood parents say they want "their" child back, authorities in many jurisdictions will privilege the blood connection and return the child—even if the initial separation is mainly attributable to the fault of the blood parents, even if the child has been with the foster parents for a long time and is prospering under their care, even if the child views the foster parents as her parents and wants to stay with them, and even if there is good reason to believe that the foster parents will provide a more secure home setting than the child's blood parents. Judges make such rulings in large part because they reflect the idolatry of "blood," which is an ideological cousin to the racial beliefs I oppose.

Am I saying that, morally, blood ties are an insufficient, indeed bad, basis for preferring one's genetic relatives to others? Yes. I will rightly give the only life jacket on the sinking ship to my mother as opposed to your mother, because I love my mother (or at least I love her more than yours). I love my mother, however, not because of a genetic tie but because over time she has done countless things that make me want to love her. She took care of me when I could not take care of myself. She encouraged me. She provided for my future by taking me to the doctor when appropriate, disciplining me, giving me advice, paying for my education. I love her, too, because of qualities I have seen her exhibit in interactions with others—my father, my brother, my sister, neighbors, colleagues, adversaries. The biological connection helped to create the framework in which I have been able to see and experience her lovable qualities. But it is deeds, not blood—doing, not being—that is the morally appropriate basis for my preference for my mother over all other mothers in the world.

Solidarity with Viola Liuzzo

Some contend, though, that "doing" is what lies at the foundation of black racial kinship—that the reason one should feel morally compelled by virtue of one's blackness to have and show racial solidarity toward other blacks is that preceding generations of black people did things animated by racial loyalty which now benefit all black people. These advocates would contend that the benefits bestowed—for instance, *Brown v. Board of Education,* the Civil Rights Act of 1964, the Voting Rights Act of 1965, and affirmative-action programs—impose upon blacks correlative racial obligations. This is what many are getting at when they say that all blacks, but particularly affluent ones, have a racial obligation to "give back" to the black community.

I agree that one should be grateful to those who have waged struggles for racial justice, sometimes at tremendous sacrifice. But why should my gratitude be racially bounded? Elijah Lovejoy, a white man murdered in Alton, Illinois, in 1837 for advocating the abolition of slavery, participated just as fervently in that great crusade as any person of my hue. The same could be said of scores of other white abolitionists. Coming closer to our time, not only courageous black people, such as Medgar Evers, Vernon Dahmer, and James Chaney, fought white supremacy in the shadow of death during the struggle for civil rights in the Deep South. White people like James Reeb and Viola Liuzzo were there too, as were Andrew Goodman and Michael Schwerner. Against this history I see no reason why paying homage to the struggle for racial justice and endeavoring to continue that struggle must entail any sort of racially stratified loyalty. Indeed, this history suggests the opposite.

"One's People"

Thus far I have mainly argued that a black person should not feel morally bound to experience and show racial kinship with other blacks. But what do I say to a person who is considering whether to *choose* to embrace racial kinship?

One person who has made this choice is Stephen L. Carter, a professor at Yale Law School and a well-known author. In a contribution to an anthology titled *Lure and Loathing: Essays on Race, Identity, and the Ambivalence of Assimilation,* Carter writes about his racial love for black people, declaring at one point that "to love one's people is to crave a kind of familyhood with them." Carter observes that this feeling of racial kinship influences his life concretely, affecting the way in which he values people's opinions of him. "The good opinions of black people . . . matter to me more," he writes, than the good opinions of white people. "That is my choice, and I cannot imagine ever making another." In *Reflections of an Affirmative Action Baby,* Carter gives another example of how racial kinship affects his life.

> Each December, my wife and I host a holiday dessert for the black students at the Yale Law School. . . . Our hope is to provide for the students an opportunity to unwind, to escape, to renew themselves, to chat, to argue, to complain—in short, to relax. For my wife and myself, the party is a chance to get to know some of the people who will lead black America (and white America, too) into the twenty-first century. But more than that, we feel a deep emotional connection to them, through our blackness: we look at their youthful, enthusiastic faces and see ourselves. There is something affirming about the occasion—for them, we hope, but certainly for us. It is a reminder of the bright and supportive side of solidarity.

I contend that in the mind, heart, and soul of a teacher there should be no stratification of students such that a teacher feels closer to certain pupils than to others on grounds of racial kinship. No teacher should view certain students as his racial "brothers and sisters" while viewing others as, well, mere students. Every student should be free of the worry that because of race, he or she will have less opportunity to benefit from what a teacher has to offer.

Friends with whom I have debated these matters object to my position, charging that I pay insufficient attention to the complexity of the identities and roles that individuals assume in society, and that I thus ignore or minimize the ability of a black professor to be both a good teacher who serves all his students well *and* a good

racial patriot who feels a special, racial affection for fellow blacks. These friends assert that I have no valid basis for complaint so long as the professor in his official duties is evenhanded in his treatment of students. By "official duties" they mean his conduct in the classroom, his accessibility during office hours, and his grading of students' academic performance. If these duties are met, they see no problem if the black professor, paying homage to his feelings of racial kinship, goes beyond what is officially required in his dealings with black students.

I see a variety of problems. For one thing, I find it inconceivable that there would be no seepage from the personal sphere into the professional sphere. The students invited to the professor's home are surely being afforded an opportunity denied to those who are not invited—an opportunity likely to be reflected in, for instance, letters of recommendation to Judge So-and-So and Law Firm Partner Such-and-Such.

Another problem is that even in the absence of any tangible, dollars-and-cents difference, the teacher's racial distinctions are likely to make a difference psychologically to the students involved. I have had the great benefit of being taught by wonderful teachers of various races, including white teachers. I never perceived a racial difference in the way that the best of these teachers treated me in comparison with my white classmates. Neither John McCune nor Sanford Levinson nor Eric Foner nor Owen Fiss ever gave me reason to believe that because of my color I took a back seat to any of my classmates when it came to having a claim on their attention. My respect for their conduct is accompanied by disappointment in others who seemed for reasons of racial kinship to invest more in white than in black students—who acted, in other words, in a way that remains unfortunately "normal" in this society.

Am I demanding that teachers make no distinctions between pupils? No. Distinctions should be made. I am simply insisting that sentiments of racial kinship should play no role in making them.

Am I demanding that teachers be blind to race? No. It seems to me bad policy to blind oneself to any potentially useful knowledge. Teachers should be aware of racial differences and differentiations in our society. They should be keenly aware, for instance, that historically and currently the dominant form of racial kinship in American life, the racial kinship that has been best organized and most destructive, is racial kinship mobilized in behalf of whites. This racial kinship has been animated by the desire to make and keep the United States "a white man's country." It is the racial kinship that politicians like Patrick Buchanan and Jesse Helms openly nurture and exploit. This is also the racial kinship that politicians take care to avoid challenging explicitly. A teacher should be aware of these and other racial facts of life in order to satisfactorily equip students with knowledge about their society.

The fact that race matters, however, does not mean that the salience and consequences of racial distinctions are good or that race must continue to matter in the future. Nor does the brute sociological fact that race matters dictate what one's response to that face should be.

Assuming that a teacher is aware of the different ways in which the race problem bears down upon his students, how should he react? That depends on the circumstances.

Consider a case, for instance, in which white students were receiving considerable attention from teachers while black students were being widely ignored. In this case it would be morally correct for a professor, with his eyes focused on race, to reach out with special vigor to the black students. In this circumstance the black students would be more in need than the white students, whose needs for mentorship were already being abundantly met. This outreach, however, would be based not on racial kinship but on distributive justice.

Our Problems

The distinction is significant. For one thing, under the rationale of giving priority of attention to those most in need, no racial boundary insulates professors from the obligation to attend to whatever maldistributions of mentorship they are in a position to correct. White professors are at least as morally obligated to address the problem as are black or other professors.

This is a point with ramifications that reach far beyond the university. For it is said with increasing urgency by increasing numbers of people that the various social difficulties confronting black Americans are, for reasons of racial kinship, the moral responsibility of blacks, particularly those who have obtained some degree of affluence. This view should be rejected. The difficulties that disproportionately afflict black Americans are not "black problems" whose solutions are the special responsibility of black people. They are *our* problems, and their solution or amelioration is the responsibility of us all, irrespective of race. That is why it is proper to object when white politicians use the term "you people" to refer to blacks. This happened when Ross Perot addressed the NAACP annual convention during the 1992 presidential election campaign. Many of those who objected to Perot's reference to "you people," however, turned right around and referred to blacks as "our people," thereby replicating the racial boundary-setting they had denounced.

A second reason why the justification for outreach matters is that unlike an appeal to racial kinship, an appeal to an ideal untrammeled by race enables any person or group to be the object of solicitude. No person or group is racially excluded from the possibility of assistance, and no person or group is expected to help only "our own." If a professor reaches out in response to student need, for instance, that means that whereas black students may deserve special solicitude today, Latino students or Asian-American students or white students may deserve it tomorrow. If Asian-American students have a greater need for faculty mentorship than black students, black professors as well as other professors should give them priority.

Some will argue that I ignore or minimize the fact that different groups are differently situated and that it is thus justifiable to impose upon blacks and whites different standards for purposes of evaluating conduct, beliefs, and sentiments. They will maintain that it is one thing for a white teacher to prefer his white students on grounds of racial kinship and a very different thing for a black teacher to prefer his black students on grounds of racial kinship. The former, they will say, is an expression of ethnocentrism that perpetuates racist inequality, whereas the latter is a laudable expression of racial solidarity that is needed to counter white domination.

Several responses are in order.

First, it is a sociological fact that blacks and whites are differently situated in the American polity. But, again, a brute fact does not dictate the proper human response to it. That is a matter of choice—constrained, to be sure, but a choice nonetheless. In choosing how to proceed in the face of all that they encounter, blacks should insist, as did Martin Luther King Jr., that acting with moral propriety is itself a glorious goal. In seeking to attain that goal, blacks should be attuned not only to the all too human cruelties and weaknesses of others but also to the all too human cruelties and weaknesses in

themselves. A good place to start is with the recognition that unless inhibited, every person and group will tend toward beliefs and practices that are self-aggrandizing. This is certainly true of those who inherit a dominant status. But it is also true of those who inherit a subordinate status. Surely one of the most striking features of human dynamics is the alacrity with which those who have been oppressed will oppress whomever they can once the opportunity presents itself. Because this is so, it is not premature to worry about the possibility that blacks or other historically subordinated groups will abuse power to the detriment of others.

Moreover, at long last blacks have sufficient power to raise urgent concerns regarding the abuse of it. Now, in enough circumstances to make the matter worth discussing, blacks are positioned to exploit their potential racial power effectively. Hence black attorneys wonder whether they should seek to elicit the racial loyalties of black jurors or judges in behalf of clients. Black jurors and judges face the question of whether they should respond to such appeals. Black professors face the question of whether racial loyalty should shape the extent to which they make themselves available to their students. Black employers or personnel directors face the question of whether racial loyalties should shape their hiring decisions. Were blacks wholly bereft of power, as some commentators erroneously assert, these and similar questions would not arise. Thus I evaluate arguments in favor of exempting blacks from the same standards imposed upon whites and conclude that typically, though perhaps not always, such arguments amount to little more than an elaborate camouflage for self-promotion or group promotion.

A second reason I resist arguments in favor of asymmetrical standards of judgment has to do with my sense of the requirements of reciprocity. I find it difficult to accept that

it is wrong for whites to mobilize themselves on a racial basis solely for purposes of
white advancement but morally permissible
for blacks to mobilize themselves on a racial
basis solely for purposes of black advancement. I would propose a shoe-on-the-
other-foot test for the propriety of racial sentiment. If a sentiment or practice would be
judged offensive when voiced or implemented by anyone, it should be viewed as
prima facie offensive generally. If we would
look askance at a white professor who wrote
that on grounds of racial kinship he values
the opinions of whites more than those of
blacks, then unless given persuasive reasons
to the contrary, we should look askance at a
black professor who writes that on grounds
of racial kinship he values the opinions of
blacks more than those of whites.

In some circumstances it is more difficult for blacks to give up the consolations of
racial kinship than for whites to do so, insofar as whites typically have more resources
to fall back on. But that should not matter, or
at least should not matter decisively, if my
underlying argument—that the sentiments
and conduct of racial kinship are morally
dubious—is correct. After all, it is surely
more difficult for a poor person than for a
rich one to give up the opportunity to steal
untended merchandise. But we nevertheless
rightly expect the poor person to give up
that opportunity.

A third consideration is prudential. It is
bad for the country if whites, blacks, or any
other group engages in the politics of racial
kinship, because racial mobilization prompts
racial countermobilization, further entrench-
ing a pattern of sterile racial competition.

Beyond Racial Loyalty

I anticipate that some will counter that this
is what is happening, has happened, and
will always happen, and that the best that

blacks can expect is what they are able to
exact from the white power structure
through hard bargaining. In this view, racial
unity, racial loyalty, racial solidarity, racial
kinship—whatever one wants to call it—is
absolutely essential for obtaining the best
deal available. Therefore, in this view, my
thesis is anathema, the most foolhardy ide-
alism, a plan for ruination, a plea for unilateral disarmament by blacks in the face of a
well-armed foe with a long history of bad
intentions.

This challenge raises large issues that
cannot be exhaustively dealt with here. But
I should like to conclude by suggesting the
beginning of a response, based on two
observations.

First, it is noteworthy that those who
have most ostentatiously asserted the im-
peratives of black racial solidarity—I think
here particularly of Marcus Garvey, Elijah
Muhammad, and Louis Farrakhan—are also
those who have engaged in the most divisive,
destructive, and merciless attacks on "brothers" and "sisters" who wished to follow a different path. My objection to the claims of
racial pride and kinship stems in part from
my fears of the effect on interracial relations.
But it stems also in large part from my fears
of the stultifying effect on intraracial relations. Racial pride and kinship seem often to
stunt intellectual independence. If racial loyalty is deemed essential and morally virtuous, then a black person's adoption of
positions that are deemed racially disloyal
will be seen by racial loyalists as a supremely
threatening sin, one warranting the harsh
punishments that have historically been visited upon alleged traitors.

Second, if one looks at the most admirable efforts by activists to overcome
racial oppression in the United States, one
finds people who yearn for justice, not
merely for the advancement of a particular
racial group. One finds people who do not
replicate the racial alienations of the larger

society but instead welcome interracial intimacy of the most profound sorts. One finds people who are not content to accept the categories of communal affiliation they have inherited but instead insist upon bringing into being new and better forms of communal affiliation, ones in which love and loyalty are unbounded by race. I think here of Wendell Phillips and certain sectors of the abolitionist movement. I also think of James Farmer and the early years of the Congress of Racial Equality, and John Lewis and the early years of the Student Nonviolent Coordinating Committee. My favorite champion of this ethos, however, is a person I quoted at the beginning of this article, a person whom the sociologist Orlando Patterson aptly describes as "undoubtedly the most articulate former slave who ever lived," a

person with whose words I would like to end. Frederick Douglass literally bore on his back the stigmata of racial oppression. Speaking in June of 1863, only five months after the Emancipation Proclamation and before the complete abolition of slavery, Douglass gave a talk titled "The Present and Future of the Colored Race in America," in which he asked whether "the white and colored people of this country [can] be blended into a common nationality, and enjoy together . . . under the same flag, the inestimable blessings of life, liberty, and the pursuit of happiness, as neighborly citizens of a common country." He answered: "I believe they can."

I, too, believe we can, if we are willing to reconsider and reconstruct the basis of our feelings of pride and kinship.

43

THE PITFALLS OF RACIAL REASONING

Cornel West

Insistence on patriarchal values, on equating black liberation with black men gaining access to male privilege that would enable them to assert power over black women, was one of the most significant forces undermining radical struggle. Thorough critiques of gender would have compelled leaders of black liberation struggles to envision new strategies and to talk about black subjectivity in a visionary manner.

BELL HOOKS, *Yearning: Race, Gender, and Cultural Politics* (1990)

The most depressing feature of the Clarence Thomas/Anita Hill hearings was neither the mean-spirited attacks of the Republicans nor the spineless silences of the Democrats—both reveal the predictable inability of most white politicians to talk candidly about race and gender. Rather what was most disturbing was the low level of political discussion in black America about these hearings—a crude discourse about race and gender that bespeaks a failure of nerve of black leadership.

This failure of nerve already was manifest in the selection and confirmation process of Clarence Thomas. Bush's choice of Thomas caught most black leaders off guard. Few had the courage to say publicly that this was an act of cynical tokenism concealed by outright lies about Thomas being the most qualified candidate regardless of race. Thomas had an undistinguished record as a student (mere graduation from Yale Law School does not qualify one for the Supreme Court); he left thirteen thousand age discrimination cases dying on the vine for lack of investigation in his turbulent eight years at the EEOC; and his performance during his short fifteen months as an appellate court judge was mediocre. The very fact that no black leader could utter publicly that a black appointee for the Supreme Court was *unqualified* shows how captive they are to white racist stereotypes about black intellectual talent. The point here is not simply that if Thomas were white they would have no trouble shouting this fact from the rooftops. The point is also that their silence reveals that black leaders may entertain the possibility that the racist stereotype may be true. Hence their attempt to cover Thomas's mediocrity with silence. Of course, some privately admit his mediocrity while pointing out the mediocrity of Justice Souter and other members of the Court—as if white mediocrity were a justification of black mediocrity. No double standards here, the argument goes; if a black man is unqualified one can defend and excuse him by appealing to other unqualified white judges. This chimes well with a cynical tokenism of the lowest common denominator—with little concern for the goal of shattering the racist stereotype or for furthering the public interest of the nation. It also renders invisible highly qualified black judges who deserve serious consideration for selection to the Court.

How did much of black leadership get in this bind? Why did so many of them capitulate to Bush's cynical strategy? First, Thomas's claim to racial authenticity—his birth in Jim Crow Georgia, his childhood as

the grandson of a black sharecropper, his undeniably black phenotype degraded by racist ideals of beauty, and his gallant black struggle for achievement in racist America. Second, the complex relation of this claim to racial authenticity to the increasing closing-ranks mentality in black America. Escalating black nationalist sentiments—the notion that America's will to racial justice is weak and therefore black people must close ranks for survival in a hostile country—rests principally upon claims to racial authenticity. Third, the way in which black nationalist sentiments promote and encourage black cultural conservatism, especially black patriarchal (and homophobic) power. The idea of black people closing ranks against hostile white Americans reinforces black male power exercised over black women (e.g., to protect, regulate, subordinate, and hence usually, though not always, to use and abuse women) in order to preserve black social order under circumstances of white literal attack and symbolic assault.

Most black leaders got lost in this thicket of reasoning and hence got caught in a vulgar form of racial reasoning: black authenticity → black closing-ranks mentality → black male subordination of black women in the interests of the black community in a hostile white racist country. Such a line of racial reasoning leads to such questions as: "Is Thomas really black?" "Is he black enough to be defended?" "Is he just black on the outside?" In fact, these kinds of questions were asked, debated, and answered throughout black America in barber shops, beauty salons, living rooms, churches, mosques, and schoolrooms.

Unfortunately, the very framework of racial reasoning was not called into question. Yet as long as racial reasoning regulates black thought and action, Clarence Thomases will continue to haunt black America—as Bush and other conservatives sit back, watch, and prosper. How does one undermine the framework of racial reasoning? By dismantling each pillar slowly and systematically. The fundamental aim of this undermining and dismantling is to replace racial reasoning with moral reasoning, to understand the black freedom struggle not as an affair of skin pigmentation and racial phenotype but rather as a matter of ethical principles and wise politics, and to combat the black nationalist attempt to subordinate the issues and interests of black women by linking mature black self-love and self-respect to egalitarian relations within and outside black communities. The failure of nerve of black leadership is its refusal to undermine and dismantle the framework of racial reasoning.

Let us begin with the claim to racial authenticity—a claim Bush made about Thomas, Thomas made about himself in the hearings, and black nationalists make about themselves. What is black authenticity? Who is really black? First, blackness has no meaning outside of a system of race-conscious people and practices. After centuries of racist degradation, exploitation, and oppression in America, being black means being minimally subject to white supremacist abuse and being part of a rich culture and community that has struggled against such abuse. All people with black skin and African phenotype are subject to potential white supremacist abuse. Hence, all black Americans have some interest in resisting racism—even if their interest is confined solely to themselves as individuals rather than to larger black communities. Yet how this "interest" is defined and how individuals and communities are understood vary. Hence any claim to black authenticity—beyond that of being a potential object of racist abuse and an heir to a grand tradition of black struggle—is contingent on one's political definition of black interest and one's ethical understanding of how this interest relates to individuals and communities in and outside black America. In short,

blackness is a political and ethical construct. Appeals to black authenticity ignore this fact; such appeals hide and conceal the political and ethical dimension of blackness. This is why claims to racial authenticity trump political and ethical argument—and why racial reasoning discourages moral reasoning. Every claim to racial authenticity presupposes elaborate conceptions of political and ethical relations of interests, individuals, and communities. Racial reasoning conceals these presuppositions behind a deceptive cloak of racial consensus—yet racial reasoning is seductive because it invokes an undeniable history of racial abuse and racial struggle. This is why Bush's claims to Thomas's black authenticity, Thomas's claims about his own black authenticity, and black nationalist claims about black authenticity all highlight histories of black abuse and black struggle.

But if claims to black authenticity are political and ethical conceptions of the relation of black interests, individuals, and communities, then any attempt to confine black authenticity to black nationalist politics or black male interests warrants suspicion. For example, black leaders failed to highlight the problematic statements Clarence Thomas made about his sister, Emma Mae, regarding her experience with the welfare system. In front of a conservative audience in San Francisco, Thomas implied she was a welfare cheat dependent on state support. Yet, like most black women in American history, Emma Mae is a hard-working person. She was sensitive enough to take care of her sick aunt even though she was unable to work for a short period of time. After she left welfare, she worked two jobs—until 3:00 in the morning! Thomas's statements reveal his own lack of integrity and character. But the failure of black leaders to highlight his statements discloses a conception of black authenticity confined to black male interests, individuals, and communities. In short, the refusal by most black leaders to give weight to the interests of black women was already apparent before Anita Hill appeared on the scene.

The claims to black authenticity that feed on the closing-ranks mentality of black people are dangerous precisely because this closing of ranks is usually done at the expense of black women. It also tends to ignore the divisions of class and sexual orientation in black America—divisions that require attention if *all* black interests, individuals, and communities are to be taken into consideration. Thomas's conservative Republican politics do not promote a closing-ranks mentality; instead Thomas claims black authenticity for self-promotion, to gain power and prestige. All his professional life he has championed individual achievement and race-free standards. Yet when it looked as though the Senate would not confirm his appointment to the Supreme Court, he played the racial card of black victimization and black solidarity at the expense of Anita Hill. Like his sister, Emma Mae, Anita Hill could be used and abused for his own self-interested conception of black authenticity and racial solidarity.

Thomas played this racial card with success—first with appeals to his victimization in Jim Crow Georgia and later to his victimization by a "hi-tech lynching"—primarily because of the deep cultural conservatism in white and black America. In white America, cultural conservatism takes the form of a chronic racism, sexism, and homophobia. Hence, only certain kinds of black people deserve high positions, that is, those who accept the rules of the game played by white America. In black America, cultural conservatism takes the form of an inchoate xenophobia (e.g., against whites, Jews, and Asians), systemic sexism, and homophobia. Like all conservatisms rooted in an quest for order, the pervasive disorder in white and, especially, black America fans and fuels the channeling of rage toward the most vulnerable and degraded members of the community. For white America, this means primarily scapegoating black people, women, gay men, and lesbians. For black America, this means principally attacking black women and black gay men and lesbians. In this way, black nationalist and black male-centered claims to black authenticity reinforce black cultural conservatism. The support of Louis Farrakhan's Nation of Islam for Clarence Thomas—despite Farrakhan's critique of Republican Party racist and conservative policies—highlights this fact. It also shows how racial reasoning leads different and disparate viewpoints in black America to the same dead end—with substantive ethical principles and savvy wise politics left out.

The undermining and dismantling of the framework of racial reasoning—especially the basic notions of black authenticity, closed-ranks mentality, and black cultural conservatism—lead toward a new framework for black thought and practice. This new framework should be a *prophetic* one of moral reasoning with its fundamental ideas of a mature black identity, coalition strategy, and black cultural democracy. Instead of cathartic appeals to black authenticity, a prophetic viewpoint bases mature black self-love and self-respect on the moral quality of black responses to undeniable racist degradation in the American past and present. These responses assume neither a black essence that all black people share nor one black perspective to which all black people should adhere. Rather, a prophetic framework encourages *moral* assessment of the variety of perspectives held by black people and selects those views based on black dignity and decency that eschew putting any group of people or culture on a pedestal or in the gutter. Instead, blackness is understood to be either the perennial possibility of white supremacist abuse or the distinct styles and dominant modes of expression found in black cultures and communities. These styles and modes are diverse—yet they do stand apart from those of other groups (even as they are shaped by and shape those of other groups). And all such styles and modes stand in need of ethical evaluation. Mature black identity results from an acknowledgment of the specific black responses to white supremacist abuses and a moral assessment of these responses such that the humanity of black people does not rest on deifying or demonizing others.

Instead of a closing-ranks mentality, a prophetic framework encourages a coalition strategy that solicits genuine solidarity with those deeply committed to antiracist struggle. This strategy is neither naive nor opportunistic; black suspicion of whites, Latinos, Jews, and Asians runs deep for historical reasons. Yet there are slight though significant antiracist traditions among whites, Asians, and especially Latinos, Jews, and indigenous people that must not be cast aside. Such coalitions are important precisely because they not only enhance the plight of black people but also because they enrich the quality of life in America.

Last, a prophetic framework replaces black cultural conservatism with black cultural democracy. Instead of authoritarian sensibilities that subordinate women or degrade gay men and lesbians, black cultural democracy promotes the equality of black women and men and the humanity of black gay men and lesbians. In short, black cultural democracy rejects the pervasive patriarchy and homophobia in black American life.

If most black leaders had adopted a prophetic framework of moral reasoning rather than a narrow framework of racial reasoning, the debate over the Clarence Thomas/Anita Hill hearings would have proceeded in a quite different manner in black America. For example, both Thomas and Hill would be viewed as two black Re-publican conservative supporters of some of the most vicious policies to besiege black working and poor communities since Jim and Jane Crow segregation. Both Thomas and Hill supported an unprecedented redistribution of wealth from working people to well-to-do people in the form of regressive taxation, deregulation policies, cutbacks and slowdowns in public service programs, take-backs at the negotiation table between workers and management, and military buildups at the Pentagon. Both Thomas and Hill supported the unleashing of unbridled capitalist market forces on a level never witnessed in the United States before that have devastated black working and poor communities. These market forces took the principal form of unregulated corporative and financial expansion and intense entrepreneurial activity. This tremendous ferment in big and small businesses—including enormous bonanzas in speculation, leverage buyouts and mergers, as well as high levels of corruption and graft—contributed to a new kind of culture of consumption in white and black America. Never before has the seductive market way of life held such sway in nearly every sphere of American life. This market way of life promotes addictions to stimulation and obsessions with comfort and convenience. Addictions and obsessions—centered primarily around bodily pleasures and status rankings—constitute market moralities of various sorts. The common denominator is a rugged and ragged individualism and rapacious hedonism in quest of a perennial "high" in body and mind.

In the hearings, the image of Clarence Thomas that emerged was one of an exemplary hedonist, a consumer of pornography, captive to a stereotypical self-image of the powerful black man who revels in sexual prowess in a racist society. Anita Hill appeared as the exemplary careerist addicted to job promotion and captive to the stereotypical self-image of the sacrificial black woman who suffers silently and alone. There was reason to suspect that Thomas was not telling the whole truth. He was silent about *Roe v. Wade,* his intentions in the antiabortion essay on Lewis Lehrmann, and the contours of his conservative political philosophy. Furthermore, his obdurate stonewalling in regard to his private life was disturbing. There also should be little doubt that Anita Hill's decision to testify was a break from her careerist ambitions. On the one hand, she strikes me as a person of integrity and honesty. On the other hand, she indeed put a premium on job advancement—even at painful personal cost. Yet her speaking out disrupted this pattern of behavior and she found herself supported only by people who opposed the very conservative Republican policies she otherwise championed, namely, progressive feminists, liberals, and some black folk. How strange she must feel being a hero to her former foes. One wonders whether Judge Bork supported her as fervently as she did him a few years ago.

A prophetic framework of moral reasoning would have liberated black leaders from the racial guilt of opposing a black man for the highest court in the land and of the feeling that one had to choose between a black woman and a black man. Like the Black Congressional Caucus (minus one?), black people could have simply opposed Thomas based on qualifications and principle. And one could have chosen between two black right-wing figures based on their sworn testimonies in light of the patterns of their behavior in the recent past. Similarly, black leaders could have avoided being duped by Thomas's desperate and vulgar appeals to racial victimization by a white male Senate committee who handled him gently (no questions about his private life). Like Senator Hollings, who knows racial intimidation when he sees it (given his past experiences with it), black leaders could have seen

through the rhetorical charade and called a moral spade a moral spade.

Unfortunately, most black leaders remained caught in a framework of racial reasoning—even when they opposed Thomas and/or supported Hill. Rarely did we have a black leader highlight the moral content of a mature black identity, accent the crucial role of coalition strategy in the struggle for justice, or promote the ideal of black cultural democracy. Instead, the debate evolved around glib formulations of a black "role model" based on mere pigmentation, an atavistic defense of blackness that mirrors the increasing xenophobia in American life, and circled around a silence about the ugly authoritarian practices in black America that range from sexual harassment to indescribable violence against women. Hence a grand opportunity for substantive discussion and struggle over race and gender was missed in black America and the larger society. And black leadership must share some of the blame. As long as black leaders remain caught in a framework of racial reasoning, they will not rise above the manipulative language of Bush and Thomas—just as the state of siege (the death, disease, and destruction) raging in much of black America creates more urban wastelands and combat zones. Where there is no vision, the people perish; where there is no framework of moral reasoning, the people close ranks in a war of all against all. The growing gangsterization of America results in part from a market-driven racial reasoning that links the White House to the ghetto projects. In this sense, George Bush, David Duke, and many gangster rap artists speak the same language from different social locations—only racial reasoning can save us. Yet I hear a cloud of witnesses from afar—Sojourner Truth, Wendell Phillips, Emma Goldman, A. Phillip Randolph, Ella Baker, Myles Horton, Fannie Lou Hamer, Michael Harrington, Abraham Joshua Heschel, Tom Hayden, Harvey Milk,

Robert Moses, Barbara Ehrenreich, Martin Luther King, Jr., and many anonymous others who championed the struggle for freedom and justice in a prophetic framework of moral reasoning. They understood that the pitfalls of racial reasoning are too costly in mind, body, and soul—especially for a downtrodden and despised people like black Americans. The best of our leadership recognized this valuable truth—and more must do so in the future if America is to survive with any moral sense.

44

GETTING ALONG
Renewing America's Commitment to Racial Justice
Melvin L. Oliver • *Thomas M. Shapiro*

In America, though, life seems to move faster than anywhere else on the globe and each generation is promised more than it will get; which creates, in each generation, a furious, bewildered rage, the rage of people who cannot find solid ground beneath their feet.

—JAMES BALDWIN,
"The Harlem Ghetto"

Can we all just get along?
—RODNEY KING, Los Angeles, 1992

Introduction: The Meaning of Money

Wealth is money that is not typically used to purchase milk, shoes, or other necessities. Sometimes it bails families out of financial and personal crises, but more often it is used to create opportunities, secure a desired stature and standard of living, or pass along a class status already obtained to a new generation. We have seen how funds transferred by parents to their children both before and after death are often treated as very special money. Such funds are used for down payments on houses, closing costs on a mortgage, start-up money for a business, maternal and early childhood expenses, private education, and college costs. Parental endowments, for those fortunate enough to receive them, are enormously consequential in shaping their recipients' opportunities, life chances, and outlooks on life.

A common literary theme shows how money debases character, love, and relationships. In *A Room of One's Own* Virginia Woolf reminds us that the absence of money also deeply corrupts. As a woman, Virginia Woolf thought that her financial inheritance would be more important in her life than even gaining the right to vote. Suppose a black person inherited a good deal of money (let's not inquire about the source) at about the time the slaves were emancipated in

1863. Of the two events—the acquisition of wealth and the attainment of freedom—which would be more important in shaping the life of this person and his or her family? John Rock, the abolitionist, pre–Civil War orator, and first African American attorney to argue before the Supreme Court, lectured that "you will find no prejudice in the Yankee whatsoever," when the avenues of wealth are opened to the formerly enslaved.[1]

Over a century and a third later Ellis Cose disagrees with this assessment in *The Rage of a Privileged Class.* His book illustrates the daily discriminations, presumptions, and reproaches to which even very successful upper-middle-class blacks are subject. Cose reminds us that the color of the hand holding the money matters. The former mayor of New York, David Dinkins, stated pointedly: "a white man with a million dollars is a millionaire, and a black man with a million dollars is a nigger with a million dollars."[2] Even highly accomplished and prosperous black professionals bitterly lament that their personal success does not translate into status, at least not outside the black community.

This notion is further elaborated in *Living with Racism* by Joe Feagin and Melvin Sikes, a book based on the life experiences of two hundred black middle-class individuals. Feagin and Sikes found that no amount of hard work and achievement, or money and resources, provides immunity for black people from the persistent, commonplace injury of white racism. Modern racism must be understood as lived experience, as middle-class blacks "tell of mistreatment encountered as they traverse traditionally white places."[3] Occasions of serious discrimination are immediately painful and stressful, and they have a cumulative impact on individuals, their psyches, families, and communities. The repeated experience of racism affects a person's understanding of and outlook on life. It is from the well of institutionalized racism that daily incidents of racial hostility are drawn.

One's sense of autonomy and security about the future is not merely or necessarily characterological; it is also a reflection of one's personal position and status. "The secret point of money and power in America is neither the things that money can buy nor power for power's sake . . . but absolute personal freedom, mobility, privacy," according to the writer Joan Didion. Money allows one "to be a free agent, live by one's own rules."[4]

Mary Ellen comes from an upper-middle-class business- and property-owning black family and is well on the road to building her own wealth portfolio. She talks about how her background helped shape her attitudes toward economic security and risk-taking.

> I think that growing up as I did, I think my mindset is a little different because I don't feel like I'm going to fall back. I don't feel that. A lot of people I talk to feel that. They don't see options that I see. They don't take as many risks. You know, I could always run home to my parents if something drastic happened. A lot of people don't have those alternatives.

As the twentieth century draws to a close the mixed legacy of racial progress and persistent racial disadvantage continues to confront America and shape our political landscape. Our focus in this book on assets has yielded a fuller comprehension of the extent and the sources of continued racial inequality. But how can we use this understanding to begin to close the racial gap?

This [reading] steps back from the detailed examination of wealth to place our major substantive findings into the larger picture. Our exploration of racial wealth differences began with theoretical speculations about how wealth differences might force us to revise previous thinking about racial inequality. The unreflective use of income as the standard way to measure inequality has contributed to a serious underestimation of the magnitude and scope of the racial disadvantage, revealing only one of its causes. If income disparities are not the crux of the problem, then policies that seek to redress inequality by creating equal opportunities and narrowing racial differences are doomed to fail, even when such programs succeed in putting blacks in good jobs. The more one learns about patterns of racial wealth differences, the more misguided current policies appear. One of our greatest hopes is [bringing] to widespread attention the urgent need for new thinking on the part of those in the world of policymaking. Given the role played by racial wealth differences in reproducing inequality anew, we are more convinced than ever that well-intended current policies fail not simply because they are inadequately funded and prematurely curtailed but, perhaps more important, because they are exclusively focused on income. In some key respects our analysis of racial wealth differences forms an agenda for the future.

Why Racial Wealth Inequality Persists

The contemporary effects of race are vividly depicted in the racial pattern of wealth accumulation that our analysis has exposed. We have compiled a careful, factual account of how contemporary discrimination along demographic, social, and economic lines results in unequal wealth reservoirs for whites and blacks. Our examination has proven insightful in two respects. It shows that unequal background and social conditions result in unequal resources. Whether it be a matter of education, occupation, family sta-

tus, or other characteristics positively correlated with income and wealth, blacks are most likely to come out on the short end of the stick. This is no surprise.

Our examination of contemporary conditions also found, more surprisingly, that equally positioned whites and blacks have highly unequal amounts of wealth. Matching whites and blacks on key individual factors correlated with asset acquisition, demonstrated the gnawing persistence of large magnitudes of wealth difference. Because it allows us to look at several factors at once, regression analysis was then called into play. Even when whites and blacks were matched on all the identifiably important factors, we could still not account for about three-quarters of the racial wealth difference. If white and black households shared all the wealth-associated characteristics we examined, blacks would still confront a $43,000 net worth handicap!

We argue, furthermore, that the racialization of the welfare state and institutional discrimination are fundamental reasons for the persistent wealth disparities we observed. Government policies that have paved the way for whites to amass wealth have simultaneously discriminated against blacks in their quest for economic security. From the era of slavery on through the failure of the freedman to gain land and the Jim Crow laws that restricted black entrepreneurs, opportunity structures for asset accumulation rewarded whites and penalized blacks. FHA policies then thwarted black attempts to get in on the ground floor of home ownership, and segregation limited their ability to take advantage of the massive equity build-up that whites have benefited from in the housing market. As we have also seen, the formal rules of government programs like social security and AFDC have had discriminatory impacts on black Americans. And finally, the U.S. tax code has systematically privileged whites and those with assets over and against asset-poor black Americans.

These policies are not the result of the workings of the free market or the demands of modern industrial society; they are, rather, a function of the political power of elites. The powerful protect and extend their interests by way of discriminatory laws and social policies, while minorities unite to contest them. Black political mobilization has removed barriers to black economic security, but the process is uneven. As blacks take one step forward, new and more intransigent legislative or judicial decisions push them back two steps. Nowhere has this trend been more evident than in the quest for housing. While the Supreme Court barred state courts from enforcing restrictive covenants, they did not prevent property owners from adhering to these covenants voluntarily, thereby denying black homeowners any legal recourse against racist whites. Similarly, while the Fair Housing Act banned discrimination by race in the housing market, it provided compensation only for "individual victims of discrimination," a fact that blunts the act's effectiveness as an antidiscrimination tool. These pyrrhic victories have in no way put an end to residential segregation, and black fortunes continue to stagnate.[5]

Our empirical investigation of housing and mortgage markets demonstrates the way in which racialized state policies interact with other forms of institutional discrimination to prevent blacks from accumulating wealth in the form of residential equity. At each stage of the process blacks are thwarted. It is harder for blacks to get approved for a mortgage—and thus to buy a home—than for whites, even when applicants are equally qualified. More insidious still, African Americans who do get mortgages pay higher interest rates than whites. Finally, given the persistence of residential segregation, houses located in black communities do not rise in value nearly as much as those in white neighborhoods. The average racial difference in home equity amounts to over $20,000 among those who currently hold mortgages.

The inheritance of accumulated disadvantages over generations has, in many ways, shortchanged African Americans of the rather dramatic mobility gains they have achieved. While blacks have made stunning educational strides, entered middle-class occupations at an impressive rate, and moved into political positions in numbers unheard of a quarter of a century ago, they have been unable to surmount the historical obstacles that inhibit their accumulation of wealth. Still today, they bear the brunt of the sedimentation of racial inequality.

The Substantive Implications of Our Findings

What are the implications of our findings? First, our research underscores the need to include in any analysis of economic well-being not only income but private wealth. In American society, a stable economic foundation must include a command over assets as well as an adequate income flow. Nowhere is this observation better illustrated than by the case of black Americans. Too much of the current celebration of black success is related to the emergence of a professional and middle-class black population that has access to a steady income. Even the most visibly successful numbers of the black community—movie and TV stars, athletes, and other performers—are on salary. But, income streams do not necessarily translate into wealth pools. Furthermore, when one is black, one's current status is not easily passed on to the next generation. The presence of assets can pave the way for an extension and consolidation of status for a family over several generations.

This is not, however, an analysis that emphasizes large levels of wealth. The wealth that can make a difference in the lives of families and children need not be in the million-dollar or six-figure range. Nonetheless, it is increasingly clear that a significant amount of assets will be needed in order to provide the requisites for success in our increasingly technologically minded society. Technological change and the new organization of jobs have challenged our traditional conception of how to prepare for a career and what to expect from it. Education in the future will be lifelong, as technological jobs change at a rapid pace. Assets will play an important role in allowing people to take advantage of training and retraining opportunities. In the economy of the twenty-first century children will require a solid educational foundation, and parents will most likely need to develop new skills on a regular basis. The presence or absence of assets will have much to say about the mobility patterns of the future.

Second, our investigation of wealth has revealed deeper, historically rooted economic cleavages between the races than were previously believed to exist. The interaction of race and class in the wealth accumulation process is clear. Historical practices racist in their essence have produced class hierarchies that, on the contemporary scene, reproduce wealth inequality. As important, contemporary racial disadvantages deprive those in the black middle class from building on their wealth assets at the same pace as similarly situated white Americans. The shadow of race falls most darkly, however, on the black underclass, whose members find themselves at the bottom of the economic hierarchy. Their inability to accumulate assets is thus grounded primarily in their low-class backgrounds. The wealth deficit of the black middle class, by contrast, is affected more by the racial character of certain policies deriving in part from the

fears and anxieties that whites harbor regarding lower-class blacks than by the actual class background of middle-class blacks. As Raymond Franklin suggests in his *Shadows of Race and Class:*

> The overcrowding of blacks in the lower class . . . casts a shadow on middle-class members of the black population that have credentials but are excluded and discriminated against on racial grounds.

Given the mutually reinforcing and historically accumulated race and class barriers that blacks encounter in attempting to achieve a measure of economic security, we argue that a focus on job opportunity is not sufficient to the task of eradicating racial disadvantage in America. Equal opportunity, even in the best of circumstances, does not lead to equality. This is a double-edged statement. First, we believe that equal opportunity policies and programs, when given a chance, do succeed in lowering some of the more blatant barriers to black advancement. But given the historically sedimented nature of racial wealth disparities, a focus on equal opportunity will only yield partial results. Blacks will make some gains, but so will whites, with initial inequalities persisting at another level. As blacks get better jobs and higher incomes, whites also advance. Thus, as Edwin Dorn points out in *Rules and Racial Equality:*

> To say that current inequality is the result of discrimination against blacks is to state only half the problem. The other half—is discrimination in favor of whites. It follows that merely eliminating discrimination is insufficient. The very direction of bias must be reversed, at least temporarily. If we wish to eliminate substantive inequality we waste effort when we debate whether some form of special treatment for the

disadvantaged group is necessary. What we must debate is how it can be accomplished.

How do we link the opportunity structure to policies that promote asset formation and begin to close the wealth gap? In our view we must take a three-pronged approach. First, we must directly address the historically generated as well as current institutional disadvantages that limit the ability of blacks, as a group, to accumulate wealth resources. Second, we must resolutely promote asset acquisition among those at the bottom of the social structure who have been locked out of the wealth accumulation process, be they black or white. Third, we must take aim at the massive concentration of wealth that is held by the richest Americans. Without redistributing America's wealth, we will not succeed at creating a more just society. Even as we advance this agenda, policies that safeguard equal opportunity must be defended. In short, we must make racial justice a national priority.

Toward a More Equal Equality

Our recommendations are designed to move the discourse on race in America beyond "equality of opportunity" and toward the more controversial notion of "equality of achievement." The traditional debate in this area is between fair shakes and fair shares. The thrust of our examination allows us to break into this debate with a different perspective. We have demonstrated that equal achievement does not return equal wealth rewards—indeed, our results have shown vast inequality. Of course, this may simply be another way of saying that wealth is not only a function of achievement; rather, it can rise or fall in accordance with racially differential state policies and in the presence or absence of an intergenerational bequest.

We are not left, however, with a pessimistic, nothing-can-be-done message. Instead, the evidence we have presented clearly suggests the need for new approaches to the goal of equality. We have many ideas related to this topic and several concrete suggestions for change that can lead to increased wealth for black and poor families. On the individual and family level, proposals are already on the table concerning the development of asset-based policies for welfare, housing, education, business, and retirement. On the institutional level we have a whole series of recommendations on how to tighten up the enforcement of existing laws that supposedly prohibit racial discrimination on the part of banks and saving and loans. After presenting those recommendations we shall broach the sensitive, yet wholly defensible strategy of racial reparations. Then we will reflect on the leadership role that the black community must play in closing the wealth gap.

Promoting Asset Foundation for Individuals and Families[6]

In the United States, as in advanced welfare states the world over, social policies for the poor primarily focus on ways to maintain an essential supply of consumptive services like housing, food, heat, clothing, health care, and education. Welfare is premised on the notion that families from time to time or on a more permanent basis lack adequate income sources to furnish these goods and services, in which case the government steps in to fill the breach. Questions about how well, adequately, or even if government should perform this function fuel public policy concerns.

In *Assets and the Poor* Michael Sherraden challenges conventional wisdom regarding the efficacy of welfare measures designed to reduce poverty and offers a fresh and imaginative approach to a persistent problem. He argues that the welfare state in its current and historical guise has not fundamentally reduced poverty or class or racial divisions and that it has not stimulated economic growth. He identifies a focus on income as the theoretically unquestioned and deficient basis of an imperfect welfare policy. Welfare as we know it provides income maintenance for the poor; welfare policies for the non-poor, by contrast, emphasize tax and fiscal measures that facilitate the acquisition of wealth. Sherraden suggests that "asset accumulation and investment, rather than income and consumption, are the keys to leaving poverty," concluding that "welfare policy should promote asset accumulation—stakeholding—by the poor."[7] Welfare for the poor should be designed to provide the same capacity for asset accumulation that tax expenditures now offer the non-poor. By giving individuals a "stake" in their society, Sherraden believes that this type of policy will channel them along more stable and productive paths. Sherraden's asset-based welfare policy combines maintenance of the consumptive goods and services with economic development. While the claim that stakeholding would provide a wide range of psychological and behavioral benefits is probably overly optimistic, and too deterministic in our view, Sherraden is clearly onto something.

Our analysis of assets and Sherraden's bold challenge to existing welfare policies spring from similar concerns, namely, that a family's life chances and opportunities emanate from the resources, or lack thereof, at its command. Sherraden's critique of the income-maintaining and consumptive welfare state leads him to advocate asset-based welfare policies. Our work points to how the welfare state has developed along racial lines, grafting new layers of accumulated disadvantage onto inequalities inherited from the past. It corroborates Sherraden's

findings on the subject of asset accumulation among members of the middle class and the exclusion of the poor from the asset game. But it also shows how a racialized welfare state, both historically and in modern times, has either systematically excluded African Americans or made it very difficult for them to accumulate assets. Furthermore, our examination of assets reveals that assets, or the lack thereof, are a paramount issue: one in three American families possesses no assets whatsoever, and only 45 percent possess enough to live above the poverty line for three months in times of no income.

A number of policy implications follow from our focus on resources, economic well-being, and the racialization of the welfare state. Existing programs such as AFDC must be reexamined. In particular, the amount of assets an AFDC recipient may hold and remain eligible for benefits must be increased. Poor people should not be forced to draw down existing assets in order to meet draconian eligibility requirements any more than seniors should have to pass an asset-means test to receive social security. Personal and business assets should be separated so that recipients can engage in self-employment activities. The work-search requirement should be redefined to make it possible for the part-time self-employed individual to qualify for benefits as well.

Mechanisms to Promote Asset Formation

Welfare does not help young people prepare for the future, nor is it designed to. At best it allows young people and their families to survive at the subsistence level. Sherraden's *Assets and the Poor* is the most fruitful work in this area, and since its analysis of asset poverty and its effects is similar to ours, we believe that some of Sherraden's key policy ideas merit serious consideration. Sherraden suggests that maintenance income and services should be supplemented by broad-based asset accounts. In many situations, where accumulation is desirable and feasible, asset-based policies are preferable to those based on income. Some of the most promising areas include education, home ownership, start-up capital for businesses, self-employment, and funds for retirement. Each year a given sum of money could be invested in an asset account restricted to a specific purpose, and the accounts would have monetary limits. These accounts could be established at different points over the life course. Standard initial deposits could be matched by federal grants on the basis of a sliding scale for poor individuals who also meet asset criteria.

Education and Youth Asset Accounts

The global economy stresses job flexibility, training in multiple areas, and technological and computer literacy. Education, training, continual skill enhancement, lifelong learning, and the ability to shift fields are the new hallmarks of modern employability. Formal schooling is a minimum requirement, with college education best preparing people for opportunities in the global marketplace. Blacks and the poor, we fear, are falling further behind in their quest to secure credentials necessary to qualify for the kinds of jobs and careers that lead to economic well-being. Since 1976 black college enrollment and completion rates have declined sharply, threatening to wipe out the gains of the civil rights era. The growing racial discrepancy in higher education is caused by blacks' increasing inability to afford the ever-soaring cost of college tuition, government's flagging fiscal commitment to higher education, and poverty rates that are more than twice as high for blacks as for whites. Without assets to fall back on, the average black family simply has no way to finance college.

Instead of asking students to assume heavy debts to foot the bill for college, Sherraden suggests establishing universal nontaxable educational asset accounts. Deposits would be linked to benchmark events: say, a one-thousand-dollar deposit at birth, a five-hundred-dollar deposit for completing each grade, and twenty-five hundred dollars for high school graduation. Student fund-raising projects and businesses could underwrite other contributions to these accounts. A year of military or civilian national service might earn a five-thousand-dollar deposit. While anyone could establish such an account, the government would subsidize these accounts for poor people on a sliding scale. For example, a poor child's family might deposit $250 with the government matching that amount. With the interest that they earn and their nontaxed status, educational asset accounts would be a wise investment in any child's future. The primary purpose of the accounts would be to provide resources upon high school graduation, after which funds would be available only for postsecondary education and training of the recipient's choosing. Such accounts would not only allow children from poor families to obtain a college education or other, equivalent training but also go a considerable distance toward closing the-quality-of-education gap. After a certain age individuals could transfer the funds in their account to their children or grandchildren. Or they could cash out their account withdrawing only their original deposits and earnings, not the government's matched share, less a 10 percent penalty. They would pay income taxes on the full amount withdrawn.

Housing Asset Accounts

We have continually stressed how essential homeownership is to the American Dream:

owning a home is not only a source of residential security, stability, and pride, but also a potential means of increasing one's wealth. We suggest here several ways to close the racial home owning and housing-appreciation gap. Homeownership rates declined significantly during the late 1980s and early 1990s. First-time buyers are edged out of the market when the rise in housing prices exceeds the rise in wages for most Americans. Down payments and closing costs are the most critical barriers to homeownership, and thus housing asset accounts should focus on accumulating funds for these purposes. We have taken Michael Sherraden's suggestions as a model of how a housing asset program might work.

Beginning at age eighteen individuals who are first-time homebuyers or who have not owned a home for longer than three years may open a housing asset account. These nontaxable interest-earning accounts would be open to everyone on the sole basis of housing status. There would be an annual deposit limit of two thousand dollars per individual account, with an overall family limit not exceeding 20 or 25 percent of the price of a region's median home. Individuals who fall below specified income and asset levels would be eligible for matching grants from the federal government, for up to 90 percent of their annual deposit. The government would thus match or supplement the deposits made by poor individuals, on a sliding scale, but would not match the deposits of those not in need. Funds accumulated in housing asset accounts would be available only for down payments and other costs associated with buying or owning a home. After ten years unused funds could be transferred to educational or housing accounts for children or grandchildren or else cashed in on the same terms we outlined in the case of educational asset accounts.

Self-Employment and Business Accounts

Self-employment is one of the most celebrated paths to economic self-sufficiency in American society. Even though self-employment is enshrouded in Horatio Alger–like cultural myths, and even though most small ventures fail within the first five years, the rewards of success, financial independence, and autonomy have been many. Severe economic restrictions have historically prevented many African Americans from establishing successful businesses. These include segregation, legal prohibition, acts of violence, discrimination, and general access only to so-called black markets. We want to emphasize the very risky nature and often low returns of self-employment. Yet, given a progressively less-favorable labor market, high unemployment rates in the black community, and the often entrepreneurial essence of the American Dream, we believe that for certain individuals self-employment represents an important path to economic well-being. Successful black businesses also contribute to community development. The absence of start-up capital is, among the asset-poor, one of the most formidable barriers to self-employment. Credit is needed to seed most businesses and the banking record on this score leaves much to be desired. Self-employment accounts would provide another option.

We have already discussed proposals to restructure AFDC criteria and payments that would remove some of the disincentives to self-employment or the establishment of small business by poor people. Michael Sherraden's work proposes a more expansive program to encourage self-employment and business ventures. Self-employment asset trusts would be open to anyone eighteen or older to be used only for start-up money for business ventures. Annual deposits of $500 would be permitted, with an overall limit of

$15,000. These accounts would be nontaxable as long as they were used for starting a new business or for family expenses associated with running the business, such as child care. Income-poor individuals who meet certain asset criteria would be eligible for 50 percent matching contributions from the federal government. These funds could be used without penalty, according to Sherraden, "only after a business plan is developed and approved by a voluntary local review board made up of businesspeople."[8] Individuals could pool their accounts with others in order to launch a joint venture. Funds not used as seed capital after ten years could be disbursed, the fundholder receiving only his or her original contributions and earnings, less a 10 percent penalty; income tax would be paid on the full amount.

Removing Institutional Barriers to Asset Formation

The Homeowner Deduction

Our explication of the racialization of the welfare state draws attention to the ways in which a host of government programs and policies have historically assisted the white middle class to acquire, secure, and expand assets. One case in point is the nation's largest annual housing subsidy, a subsidy that goes not to the poor or to stimulate low-cost housing but to often well-heeled homeowners in the form of $54 billion in tax deductions for mortgage interest and property taxes. While the homeowner deduction primarily benefits the affluent, fewer than one in five low-income Americans receive federal housing assistance. Those with the highest incomes and the most expensive homes get the lion's share of federal subsidies. The Congressional Joint Taxation Committee analysis of taxation data shows that

more than one-third (38.5 percent) of the $54 billion government subsidy goes to the 5 percent of taxpayers who have incomes above $100,000.[9]

The homeowner deduction has come under increasing scrutiny, however, and several reforms have been suggested. Recognizing that through the tax code the state has assisted home ownership and asset formation among certain groups, notably the middle class, that this aid has increasingly benefited the affluent, and that whites are far more likely than blacks to profit from current tax policy, many have suggested that a corrective is clearly in order. The goal of helping families purchase homes could be maintained and expanded in order to apply to more moderate income families, and thereby proportionately more minorities. Simultaneously, tax reform could place benefits to affluent Americans within a progressive context. Current home mortgage interest and property tax deductions should be scrapped and replaced by a simple homeowner tax credit available to all taxpayers, not just those who itemize deductions. The credit would apply to one's primary residence and could be capped at a specific amount or tied progressively to income, thus limiting subsidies for the wealthy while preserving them for the middle class and extending the goal of homeownership to moderate-income Americans. A homeowner tax credit could make the difference between renting and owning for millions of working families now shut out of the American Dream. Such a policy would enable more blacks to buy homes than can do so under the current tax law and thereby represent a step in the direction of greater racial equity.

Capital Gains Tax

All sources of earnings are not treated equally under America's tax laws. Most notably, net proceeds from financial assets are privileged over paycheck earnings. In 1993 the top tax bracket for wages, tips, and salaries was fixed at 39.6 percent on earnings over $250,000. Capital gains, by contrast—the profits from selling something for an amount more than it cost, whether it be stocks, bonds, homes, property, or works of art—are taxed at the more favorable top rate of 28 percent, a rate that can go down as low as 14 percent in some situations. Barlett and Steele in *America; Who Really Pays the Taxes?* refers to "different dollar bills; different rates.[10] They report that one twenty-fifth of one percent of Americans filing taxes collects one-third of all capital gains incomes. Conversely, 93 percent of all persons filing tax returns have no need to fill out a Schedule D form because they have no capital gains. We doubt if more than a relative handful of blacks are among the small affluent group advantaged by this favored child of free marketers and conservatives.

Reform of the capital gains tax would help simplify the tax forms and end an unfair subsidy designed for the rich. Income from playing the stock market should be treated just like income from work, and capital gains should be taxed at the same rates as earnings. Changes would affect only those in the highest income brackets, leaving people with modest investment unaffected.

Inheritance Tax

Donald Barlett and James Steele write in *America: Who Really Pays the Taxes?* that one of the most cherished tax privileges of the very rich resides in the ability of that group to pass along its accumulated wealth in stocks, bonds, and other financial instruments to heirs free of capital gains tax. Taxpayers who sell financial assets to fund a child's education, make a down payment on a house, or weather a financial crisis pay a capital gains tax on the increased value of their investment. But under current tax law, stocks, bonds, and other capital assets can be passed along at death and escape all capital gains. "Better still," according to Barlett and Steele, "when you inherit the stock it gets a new 'original' value—the price at which it was selling on the day you received it." Thus, one can sell the stock immediately and pocket the entire proceeds without paying any capital gains tax. In large part, Barlett and Steele go on to say, "this is how the rich stay rich—by passing on from generation to generation assets that have appreciated greatly in value but on which they never pay capital gains taxes."[11]

The wealth of many families has thus escaped taxes since the establishment of the income tax in 1924. The time has come to seriously challenge this capital gains tax exemption. Just how large is the inheritance tax break for the very rich? *America: Who Really Pays the Taxes?* cites a Treasury Department and Office of Management and Budget calculation that the very rich escaped paying $24 billion in 1991 alone because of this exemption. While Americans do not begrudge their fellow citizens the opportunity of becoming rich, they might not be so willing to accept the extent to which the very wealthy and powerful rig the rules to hold onto their wealth at everybody else's expense.

Antidiscrimination Laws

In the 1960s and 1970s Congress passed important legislation and strengthened the banking regulatory structure so that all groups would have access to credit and communities would not be written off by unscrupulous financial institutions. The Reagan administration weakened this regulatory system, and some banks read its change as an opportunity to revert to past practices and ignore or prey upon minority and low-income neighborhoods. We estimate that discriminatory mortgage practices, higher interest-rate charges, and biased housing inflation cost the black community approximately $83 billion. Both the private and public sectors have a lot of work ahead of them if they are to redress this history of institutional discrimination.

Bankers do not sit down with a map and census tract data and draw red lines around low-income and minority neighborhoods. As we have seen, however, some have policies and practices that effectively do the same thing. Banks that set minimum loan amounts effectively exclude whole neighborhoods from the conventional mortgage market. Lenders must discontinue this practice.[12]

We have also seen that the tiering of interest rates for mortgages has a disparate impact on minority and female applicants, and on minority, integrated, and ethnic neighborhoods. Because of tiered interest rates, minorities and low-income home buyers pay more to borrow less. This policy, too, must be changed.

Every good business designs a marketing strategy to capture the market it wants to serve. Lenders need to review the media they use to reach minority and low-income consumers as well as the messages they send. A bank becomes known, or fails to do so, not only by its advertising efforts but also by the services it offers to a community. A bank must be conveniently located and accessible to the consumers it wants to attract. The services it offers should be tailored to meet the needs and interests of its customers. To respond to their needs, some banks offer investment seminars free of charge to their high-income customers. They should also be offering free seminars on how to buy a home or start a small business to their low-income depositors. These ideas are not new, and they have had a public hearing. Their implementation is long overdue.

Closing the Gap is the name of a brochure put together in 1993 by the Federal Reserve Bank of Boston for lending institutions. It starts, "Fair lending is good business. Access to credit, free from considerations of race or national origin, is essential to the economic health of both lenders and borrowers."[13] The brochure proposes a series of practices and standards designed to constitute "good banking" and to close the mortgage loan gap. Its recommendations include reviewing minimum loan amounts because they negatively affect low-income applicants and giving special consideration to applicants who have demonstrated an ability to cover high housing expenses (relative to income) in the past. Lenders should allow down payment and closing costs to be paid by gifts, grants, and loans from relatives or agencies. Credit history criteria should be reviewed and made more sensitive to the needs of those with no credit history, problem histories, or low incomes. *Closing the Gap* also points out that subjective aspects of property and neighborhood appraisal using terms like "desirable area," "pride of ownership," "homogeneous neighborhood," and "remaining economic life" allow room for racial bias and bias against urban areas. It advocates the elimination of such concepts from the process of property appraisal. The brochure further advises lenders to distinguish between length of employment and employment stability in reviewing an applicant's work history, pointing out that many low-income people work in sectors of the economy where job changes are frequent. Lenders should focus on an applicant's ability to maintain or increase income levels, not on the number of jobs he or she has held.

"Good-Neighbor Mortgages" and Banking Restitution

"Good-Neighbor Mortgages" are new mortgage products featuring little or no down payment and minimal or no closing costs, often below-market interest rates, expanded debt-to-income ratios, no costly private mortgage insurance, and an open option to refinance at 100 percent of a home's appraised value. These mortgages can be used for purchase and rehabilitation, so homes in distressed communities can be revitalized. Credit for small business, on comparable terms, can also be obtained as part of a comprehensive community revitalization effort. The key to the success of Good-Neighbor programs is not only their generous terms but commitment on the part of the bank. Such programs should not be viewed as a penalty paid by a bank to redress past discriminatory practices; instead, they must be seen as establishing a new partnership designed to meet the needs of a once prejudicially underserved community.

In 1994 Fleet Financial Group, a corporation that has drawn a lot of fire because of its biased community-lending policies, announced a stunning settlement with one of its most severe critics. The bank had been in trouble with community activists in Boston and Atlanta and with the Federal Reserve Bank because of its practice of redlining large sections of central cities and then quietly backing small second-mortgage companies that loaned money at pawnbroker rates. It set aside an $8 billion loan pool aimed at inner-city, low-income, and small-business borrowers. One Fleet insider ominously told the *Wall Street Journal* that "Fleet did nothing that wasn't common practice in the consumer-finance business. But we took the heat."[14]

An alternative and supplement to private-sector banks could come in the form of community development banks. These federally sponsored banks would give creative people in inner-city areas the tools with which to rebuild strong supportive communities and help poor people to develop assets for the future. They would hark back to the strong financial institutions that once helped American communities save their own money, invest, borrow, and grow.

Modeled after Chicago's famous South Shorebank, enabling legislation sponsored by Senator Bill Bradley of New Jersey envisions developing a range of community-based financial institutions, all of which will respond to the capital and savings needs in their service areas.

The Racial Reparations Movement

A growing social movement within the black community for racial reparations attempts to address the historical origins of what House Resolution 40 in 1993 called the "lingering negative effects of the institution of slavery and discrimination" in the United States.[15] With a host of community-based organizations agitating and educating with respect to the issue, this movement has taken off since the passage of the legislation approving reparations for Japanese Americans interned during World War II. For the torment and humiliation suffered at that time each family was awarded $20,000. Since 1989 black Representative John Conyers of Michigan has introduced into the House Judiciary Committee each year a bill to set up a commission to study whether "any form of compensation to the descendants of African slaves is warranted." While the bill has yet to reach the floor of Congress, it has opened up this issue to public debate and discussion.

Given the historical nature of wealth, monetary reparations are, in our view, an appropriate way of addressing the issue of racial inequity. The fruits of their labor and the ability to accumulate wealth was denied African Americans by law and social custom during two hundred fifty years of slavery. This initial inequality has been aggravated during each new generation, as the artificial head start accorded to practically all whites has been reinforced by racialized state policy and economic disadvantages to which

536 *Melvin L. Oliver and Thomas M. Shapiro*

only blacks have been subject. We can trace the sedimented material inequality that now confronts us directly to this opprobrious past. Reparations would represent both a practical and a moral approach to the issue of racial injustice. As the philosopher Bernard Boxill argues:

> One of the reasons for which blacks claim the right to compensation for slavery is that since the property rights of slaves to "keep what they produce" were violated by the system of slavery to the general advantage of the white population, and, since the slaves would presumably have exercised their libertarian-right to bequeath their property to their descendants, their descendants, the present black population, have rights to that part of the wealth of the present white population derived from violating black property rights during slavery . . . [Whites] also wronged [the slaves] by depriving them of their inheritance—of what Kunta Kinte would have provided them with, and passed on to them, had *he* been compensated—a stable home, education, income, and traditions.

While reparations based on similar logic have occurred in both the United States and other societies, it may be a testament to the persistence of antiblack racial attitudes in America that the prospects for such compensation are minimal. The objections are many: Are present-day whites to blame for the past? Who among blacks should receive such reparations? Would reparations of this sort really improve the economic situation of blacks today? We are not sure that racial reparations are the choice—political or economic—that America should make at this historical juncture. They may inflame more racial antagonism than they extinguish. But the reparations debate does open up the issue of how the past affects the present; it can focus

attention on the historical structuring of racial inequality and, in particular, wealth. What we fear most is the prospect of reparations becoming a settlement, a payoff for silence, the terms of which go something like this: "Okay. You have been wronged. My family didn't do it, but some amends are in order. Let's pay it. But in return, we will hear no more about racial inequality and racism. Everything is now colorblind and fair. The social programs that were supposed to help you because you were disadvantaged are now over. No more!" Instead, racial reparations should be the first step in a collective journey to racial equality.

Any set of policy recommendations that requires new revenues and implies a redistribution of benefits toward the disadvantaged faces formidable political and ideological obstacles. In an era of stagnant incomes for the working and middle classes, race has become even more of an ideological hot button in the arena of national politics. The conservative cast of American political discourse in the 1990s is in large measure rooted in white opposition to the liberal policies of the sixties. According to Thomas and Mary Edsall's *Chain Reaction,* a pernicious ideology that joins opposition to opportunities for blacks and a distrust of government has "functioned to force the attention of the public on the costs of federal policies and programs."[16]

We believe that the program we have outlined could be put into place within the fiscal confines of present budget realities. For example, the tax structure reforms we discussed would help defray the expenses associated with asset development accounts and other increased social welfare benefits. But when it comes to race and social policy, ideology tends to reign. Despite the cost effectiveness of our program it is likely that it would be opposed mostly on ideological grounds. As Martin Carnoy in *Faded Dreams* resignedly notes:

The negative intertwining of race with "tax and spend," "welfare state" economic policy remains a potentially highly successful conservative political card . . . There is absolutely no doubt that the card will be played and played repeatedly.[17]

To move beyond the present impasse we must embark on a national conversation that realistically interprets our present dilemmas as a legacy of the past that if not addressed will forever distort the American Dream.

The African American Community's Role in Wealth Creation

Our interviews with African Americans revealed the importance of barriers to wealth creation that our policy proposals are designed to address. However, many interviewees also placed significant responsibility for the lack of assets in the black community on blacks themselves. Implicit in these criticisms was a feeling that blacks can do much to help themselves in creating greater wealth and using it more productively. The desire to increase wealth in the black community is seen in many ways as the civil rights theme of the twenty-first century. "The black community will not be free until we control the wealth in it," said one respondent. Three ideas continued to come up in our interviews regarding what the black community could do to increase wealth: entrepreneurship and business development, better education and information on the subject of financial planning, and networking to develop capital and economic opportunity.

The lack of business development was one of the key factors cited by one respondent as a barrier to black wealth accumulation: "I do believe that we really need to get into our own businesses." A lack of capital

was cited as the most important barrier to business creation. As Mary Ellen, who left the corporate world to join her father's family business, noted, problems "in the banking system" stopped many people that she knew from being able to make their dream of self-employment a reality. Many of those who did start businesses had the age-old problem of being "undercapitalized." As Mary Ellen summarized, "You know you just can't succeed in a business without having capital. And we just don't have it."

While the lack of material resources was seen as important, our respondents were just as concerned about the dearth of social capital, particularly information and ways to communicate it, in the black community. Many worry that the kind of education that prepares one to take advantage of investment and business opportunities is not as available in the black community as it is elsewhere. Some of the information blacks are less apt to have access to is formal in nature: "People are not taught about entrepreneurship . . . in the universities . . . to go into business for themselves. . . . In school we learn how to add and subtract and divide and all that, but you really aren't taught . . . about finances." Much crucial information is transmitted informally, however. Interviewees often spoke of a separate "dialogue that goes on in the white community," generating investment information that is inaccessible to those in the black community. African Americans as a group are seen as "isolated" from basic knowledge pertaining to investment instruments, business opportunities, and financial markets. On a subtler level one respondent suggested that the real rules of the game are unknown to African Americans. As a consequence

the playing field is not level—we do everything as we're supposed to do— we go through all the right channels. We don't know the back doors.

Our interviewees looked to the self-organization and self-activity of the black community for solutions to these problems. While supporting policies to force mainstream financial institutions to be more responsive to blacks, these respondents were quite pessimistic that any other aid would come from the wider society. They looked instead to actions that could be taken within, for, and by the black community. Pointing out significant increases in assets and financial knowledge in certain sectors of the black community (e.g., successful African American entrepreneurs), they argued that these resources had to be socially shared in order to help the less fortunate lay claim to a wealth stake. Over and over again respondents spoke of the way in which the well-off had to give back to the community. Our most affluent black respondent, the owner of several businesses, spoke of how she is

> attempting to help as many young people as I can now. I have a program now that is doing exactly that with a female organization. Business Opportunities Unlimited [a pseudonym] is helping young minorities open businesses. And I mentor young people that want to do that. The funding is there. The grants are there. It's knowing how to go in there and fill them out. Instead of training our children as my parents trained us, you know, work for the County, City, or State. Those are good stable jobs [laughter]. You gotta tell them, look, you're gonna take some risks. You know, you're young. What do you have to lose? You got the education. If you fall down, you pick yourself up again.

Another person in business talked about creating "rotating credit associations" that would help generate capital for new businesses and other financial opportunities.

> If banks are not going to give us money, we're going to get an investment pool together to help each other . . . Basically what they [immigrants] do is everybody puts in ten thousand dollars into a pot, and let's say there are ten people in the pool. So there's a hundred thousand dollars. We give this hundred thousand to Johnny. He starts a business and gets it growing. Then it goes to the next person and they can start a business. Or they can borrow against this pool, so they have their own internal banking system.

Blacks need to "network" with each other in order to socialize people in the culture of business and finances, as well as to circulate the crucial information one needs to be successful. As an example Camille spoke of how her success is owed in part to the advice and business counsel that she has received from a successful black real estate entrepreneur. He informs her of "easy-ins without huge sums of money. Someone's losing something. Dell will say, Camille, I have five thousand dollars. Do you have five thousand dollars? Let's pick this up. You know, that kind of thing."

Despite the concerns of our respondents, more and more blacks are taking advantage of financial self-employment opportunities—both formal and informal. Entrepreneurship programs are erupting everywhere. Schools and community-based organizations are teaching youth about the essentials of self-employment. In Los Angeles, the African American community's dominant response to the civil disorders that rocked the city in 1992 has been to "promote entrepreneurship among community residents as a primary job creation and wealth accumulation strategy."[18] Traditional black self-help organizations like the First African Methodist Episcopal Church (FAME) have launched entrepreneurial development programs that help fund and provide counseling and business services to budding businesspeople. Likewise, a recent spate of self-help books have begun to celebrate the power of networking for blacks.[19] One of the most successful black magazines is *Black Enterprise,* which, under the leadership of its editor, Earl Graves, has served as a clearinghouse for information about black business and investment opportunities. National organizations like the NAACP and the Nation of Islam have also joined this effort.

We applaud these initiatives. They will help energize African Americans to seek ownership and control of their community. They will in time increase by some as yet unknown factor the wealth of some members of that community. The limits of unilateral community-based self-help measures also need to be recognized, however. Two interrelated concerns are paramount. First, the emphasis on owning and controlling business in the black community re-creates many of the negative features of the segregated market that characterized the economic detour described earlier. The purchase of small retail and service establishments within the black community places black entrepreneurs in unnecessarily restrictive economic markets. The key to growth is to break out of segregated markets and into the wider economic mainstream. Second, a primary focus on traditional retail and service outlets may very well leave blacks out of the most dynamic parts of the economy. Each period of economic growth in America has been ushered in by new industrial and technological breakthroughs. The winners have increasingly been those who have been able to master these technologies and to market them rapidly and economically. In order to succeed African American business in the twenty-first century needs to set its sights on the next great frontier of economic growth: information processing. An empha-

sis on retail and service will divert the energies of able black businesspeople away from the most fertile area of economic growth.

Any viable strategy for enhancing black wealth must include both the development of local community-based entrepreneurs and their penetration into the newest and most profitable sectors of the wider economy. Neither goal can be accomplished without the kinds of redistributive and wealth accumulation policies that we have outlined.

Conclusion

Racial inequality is still the unsolved American dilemma. The nation's character has been forged on the contradiction of the promise of equality and its systematic denial. For most of our nation's history we have allowed racial inequality to fester. But there are other choices. These choices represent a commitment to equality and to closing the gap as much as possible, and in so doing redefine the values, preferences, interests, and ideals that define us. Fundamental change must be addressed before we can begin to affirmatively answer Rodney King's poignant plea: "Can we all just get along?"

To address these fundamental issues, to rejuvenate America's commitment to racial justice, we must first acknowledge the real nature of racial inequality in this country. We must turn away from explanations of black disadvantage that focus exclusively on the supposed moral failings of the black community and attempt to create the kinds of structural supports that will allow blacks to live full and socially productive lives. The effort will require an avowedly egalitarian antiracist stance that transcends our racist past and brings blacks from the margin to the mainstream.

In her novel *Beloved* Toni Morrison tells the tale of forty-seven men on a chain gang in Alfred, Georgia. They all want to be free, but because they are chained together, no individual escape is possible. If "one lost, all lost," Morrison says, "the chain that held them would save all or none."[20] The men learn to work together, to converse, because they have to. When the opportunity presents itself, they converse quietly with one another and slip out of prison together. Like the convicts in Morrison's story, we need to realize a future undivided by race because we have to. No individual solution is possible. The chain that holds us all will save all or none.

NOTES

1. Quote on no prejudice in the Yankee see Rock 1858.
2. The quote is from Cose 1993, 28.
3. The quote is from Feagin and Sikes 1994, 15.
4. The quote is from Didion's 1967 essay "7000 Romaine, Los Angeles" reprinted in Didion 1968, 71.
5. On restrictive covenants see Zarembka 1990, 101–102. On the Fair Housing Act see ibid., 106.
6. Our emphasis on asset acquisition is not meant to discount the need for income and employment policy. On the contrary, we believe that it is imperative to institute policies that encourage full employment at wages consistent with a decent standard of living. In fact, many of our proposals assume that people have some kind of income. However, to dwell on the intricacies of this area would divert our attention from the unique implications of our argument. There are several important proposals already under discussion that merit serious consideration (see Carnoy 1994; Ellwood 1988; Weir 1992; Wilson 1987).
7. The quote is from Sherraden 1991, 294.
8. The quote is from Sherraden 1991, 256–57.
9. See Dreier and Atlas 1994.
10. The quote is from Barlett and Steele 1994, 29.
11. The quotes are from Barlett and Steele 1994, 335.
12. Our focus is on the role of financial institutions in providing mortgages. However, an equally important aspect of the low wealth accumulation of black households has been persistent residential segregation. Massey and Denton (1993, 186–216) have provided a blueprint for policy in this area that we need not rehash here. Their proposals, if implemented, would be an important complement to the ones we suggest regarding lending discrimination.
13. The quote is from Federal Reserve Bank of Boston 1993.
14. The quote is from Ryan and Wilke 1994, A5.
15. The quote is from U.S. House of Representatives 1993.
16. The quote is from Edsall and Edsall 1991, 11.
17. The quote is from Carnoy 1994, 225–26.
18. On efforts to "promote entrepreneurship among [black] community residents" in Los Angeles see Jackson, Johnson, and Farrell 1994.
19. On self-help books see Anderson 1994 and Fraser 1994.
20. The quote is from Morrison 1987, 110.

REFERENCES

ANDERSON, CLAUD. 1994. *Black Labor, White Wealth: The Search for Power and Economic Justice.* Edgewood, MD: Duncan & Duncan.

BARLETT, DONALD L., and JAMES B. STEELE. 1994. *America: Who Really Pays the Taxes?* New York: Touchstone.

BOXILL, BERNARD. 1984. *Blacks and Social Justice.* Totawa, NJ: Rowman & Allanheld.

CARNOY, MARTIN. 1994. *Faded Dreams: The Politics and Economics of Race in America.* Cambridge: Cambridge University Press.

COSE, ELLIS. 1993. *The Rage of a Privileged Class.* New York: HarperCollins.

DORN, EDWIN. 1979. *Rules and Racial Equality.* New Haven, CT: Yale University Press.

DREIER, PETER, and JOHN ATLAS. 1994. "Tax Break for the Rich: Reforming the Mansion Subsidy." *The Nation* 258(17), pp. 592–95.

EDSALL, THOMAS BYRNE, and MARY EDSALL. 1991. *Chain Reaction.* New York: Norton.

FEAGIN, JOE R., and MELVIN P. SIKES. 1994. *Living with Racism: The Black Middle-Class Experience.* Boston: Beacon Press.

FRANKLIN, RAYMOND S. 1991. *Shadows of Race and Class.* Minneapolis: University of Minnesota Press.

FRASER, GEORGE C. 1994. *Success Runs in Our Race: The Complete Guide to Networking in the African-American Community.* New York: Morrow.

JACKSON, MARIA-ROSARIO, JAMES H. JOHNSON, JR., and WALTER C. FARRELL, JR. 1994. "After the Smoke Has Cleared: An Analysis of Selected Responses to the Los Angeles Civil Unrest of 1992." *Contention* 3(3) (Spring):3–22.

MASSEY, DOUGLAS S., and NANCY A. DENTON. 1993. *American Apartheid: Segregation and the Making of the Underclass.* Cambridge, MA: Harvard University Press.

ROCK, JOHN S. 1858. "Address to Boston Antislavery Society, March 5." *Antislavery Collection.* Rare Book Division, Boston Public Library.

RYAN, SUZANNE ALEXANDER, and JOHN R. WILKE. 1994. "Banking on Publicity, Mr. Marks Got Fleet to Lend Billions." *Wall Street Journal,* February 11, pp. A1, A5.

SHERRADEN, MICHAEL. 1991. *Assets and the Poor: A New American Welfare Policy.* New York: Sharpe.

WOOLF, VIRGINIA. 1929. *A Room of One's Own.* New York: Harcourt.

ZAREMBKA, ARLENE. 1989. *The Urban Housing Crisis.* New York: Greenwood Press.

45

AMERICAN RACIAL AND ETHNIC POLITICS IN THE 21ST CENTURY
A Cautious Look Ahead

Jennifer L. Hochschild

The course of American racial and ethnic politics over the next few decades will depend not only on dynamics within the African-American community, but also on relations between African Americans and other racial or ethnic groups. Both are hard to predict. The key question within the black community involves the unfolding relationship between material success and attachment to the American polity. The imponderable in ethnic relations is how the increasing complexity of ethnic and racial coalitions and of ethnicity-related policy issues will affect African-American political behavior. What makes prediction so difficult is not that there are no clear patterns in both

areas. There are. But the current patterns are highly politically charged and therefore highly volatile and contingent on a lot of people's choices.

Material Success and Political Attachment

Today the United States has a thriving, if somewhat tenuous, black middle class. By conventional measures of income, education, or occupation at least a third of African Americans can be described as middle class, as compared with about half of whites. That is an astonishing—probably historically unprecedented—change from the early 1960s, when blacks enjoyed the "perverse equality" of almost uniform poverty in which even the best-off blacks could seldom pass on their status to their children. Conversely, the depth of

Jennifer L. Hochschild, "American Racial and Ethnic Politics in the 21st Century: A Cautious Look Ahead," *The Brookings Review,* Spring 1988, pp. 43–46. Reprinted with permission from Brookings Institute Press.

poverty among the poorest blacks is matched only by the length of its duration. Thus, today there is greater disparity between the top fifth and the bottom fifth of African Americans, with regard to income, education, victimization by violence, occupational status, and participation in electoral politics, than between the top and bottom fifths of white Americans.

An observer from Mars might suppose that the black middle class would be highly gratified by its recent and dramatic rise in status and that persistently poor blacks would be frustrated and embittered by their unchanging or even worsening fate. But today's middle-class African Americans express a "rage," to quote one popular writer, that has, paradoxically, grown along with their material holdings. In the 1950s and 1960s, African Americans who were well-off frequently saw *less* racial discrimination, both generally and in their own lives, than did those who were poor. Poor and poorly educated blacks were *more* likely than affluent or well-educated blacks to agree that "whites want to keep blacks down" rather than to help them or simply to leave them alone. But by the 1980s blacks with low status were perceiving *less* white hostility than were their higher-status counterparts.

Recent evidence confirms affluent African Americans' greater mistrust of white society. More college-educated blacks than black high school dropouts believe that it is true or might be true that "the government deliberately investigates black elected officials in order to discredit them," that "the government deliberately makes sure that drugs are easily available in poor black neighborhoods in order to harm black people," and that "the virus which causes AIDS was deliberately created in a laboratory in order to infect black people." In a 1995 *Washington Post* survey, when asked whether "discrimination is the major reason for the economic and social ills blacks face,"

84 percent of middle-class blacks, as against 66 percent of working-class and poor blacks, agreed.

Ironically, today most poor and working-class African Americans remain committed to what Gunnar Myrdal called "the great national suggestion" of the American Creed. That is a change; in the 1960s, more well-off than poor blacks agreed that "things are getting better . . . for Negroes in this country." But, defying logic and history, since the 1980s poor African Americans have been much more optimistic about the eventual success of the next generation of their race than have wealthy African Americans. They are more likely to agree that motivation and hard work produce success, and they are often touchingly gratified by their own or their children's progress.

Assume for the moment that these two patterns, of "succeeding more and enjoying it less" for affluent African Americans, and "remaining under the spell of the great national suggestion" for poor African Americans, persist and grow even stronger. That suggests several questions for political actors.

It is virtually unprecedented for a newly successful group of Americans to grow more and more alienated from the mainstream polity as it attains more and more material success. One exception, David Mayhew notes, is South Carolina's plantation owners in the 1840s and 1850s. That frustrated group led a secessionist movement; what might embittered and resource-rich African Americans do? At this point the analogy breaks down: the secessionists' actions had no justification, whereas middle-class blacks have excellent reason to be intensely frustrated with the persistent, if subtle, racial barriers they constantly meet. If more and more successful African Americans become more and more convinced of what Orlando Patterson calls "the homeostatic . . . principle of the . . . system of racial domination"—racism is squelched in one place, only to arise with renewed force in another—racial interactions in the political arena will be fraught with tension and antagonism over the next few decades.

In that case, ironically, it may be working-class blacks' continued faith in the great national suggestion that lends stability to Americans' racial encounters. If most poor and working-class African Americans continue to care more about education, jobs, safe communities, and decent homes than about racial discrimination and antagonism per se, they may provide a counterbalance in the social arena to the political and cultural rage of the black middle class.

But if these patterns should be reversed—thus returning us to the patterns of the 1960s—quite different political implications and questions would follow. For example, it is possible that the United States is approaching a benign "tipping point," when enough blacks occupy prominent positions that whites no longer resist their success and blacks feel that American society sometimes accommodates them instead of always the reverse. That point is closer than it ever has been in our history, simply because never before have there been enough successful blacks for whites to *have* to accommodate them. In that case, the wealth disparities between the races will decline as black executives accumulate capital. The need for affirmative action will decline as black students' SAT scores come to resemble those of whites with similar incomes. The need for majority-minority electoral districts will decline as whites discover that a black representative could represent *them*.

But what of the other half of a reversion to the pattern of 1960s beliefs, when poor blacks mistrusted whites and well-off blacks, and saw little reason to believe that conventional political institutions were on their side? If that view were to return in full force, among people now characterized by widespread ownership of firearms and iso-

lation in communities with terrible schools and few job opportunities, there could indeed be a fire next time.

One can envision, of course, two other patterns—both wealthy and poor African Americans lose all faith, or both wealthy and poor African Americans regain their faith that the American creed can be put into practice. The corresponding political implications are not hard to discern. My point is that the current circumstances of African Americans are unusual and probably not stable. Political engagement and policy choices over the next few decades will determine whether affluent African Americans come to feel that their nation will allow them to enjoy the full social and psychological benefits of their material success, as well as whether poor African Americans give up on a nation that has turned its back on them. Racial politics today are too complicated to allow any trend, whether toward or away from equality and comity, to predominate. Political leaders' choices, and citizens' responses, are up for grabs.

Ethnic Coalitions and Antagonisms

America is once again a nation of immigrants, as a long series of recent newspaper stories and policy analyses remind us. Since 1990 the Los Angeles metropolitan region has gained almost a million residents, the New York region almost 400,000, and the Chicago region 360,000—almost all from immigration or births to recent immigrants. Most of the nation's fastest-growing cities are in the West and Southwest, and their growth is attributable to immigration. More than half of the residents of New York City are immigrants or children of immigrants. How will these demographic changes affect racial politics?

Projections show that the proportion of Americans who are neither white nor black will continue to increase, dramatically so in some regions. By 2030, whites will become a smaller proportion of the total population of the nation as a whole, and their absolute numbers will begin to decrease. The black population, now just over 13 percent, will grow, but slowly. The number of Latinos, however, will more than double, from 24 million in 1990 to almost 60 million in 2030 (absent a complete change in immigration laws). The proportion of Asians will also double.

A few states will be especially transformed. By 2030 Florida's population is projected to double; by then its white population, now about seven times as large as either the black or Latino population, will be only three or four times as large. And today, of 30 million Californians, 56 percent are white, 26 percent Latino, 10 percent Asian, and 7 percent black. By 2020, when California's population could grow by as much as 20 million (10 million of them new immigrants), only 35 percent of its residents are projected to be white; 40 percent will be Latino, 17 percent Asian, and 8 percent black.

These demographic changes may have less dramatic effects on U.S. racial politics than one might expect. For example, the proportion of *voters* who are white is much higher than the proportion of the *population* that is white in states such as California and Florida, and that disproportion is likely to continue for some decades. Second, some cities, states, and even whole regions will remain largely unaffected by demographic change. Thus racial and ethnic politics below the national level will be quite variable, and even in the national government racial and ethnic politics will be diluted and constrained compared with the politics in states particularly affected by immigration. Third, most Latino and Asian immigrants are eager to learn English, to become Americans, and to be less insulated in ethnic communities, so their basic political framework

may not differ much from that of native-born Americans.

Finally, there are no clear racial or ethnic differences on many political and policy issues; the fault lines lie elsewhere. For example, in the 1995 *Washington Post* survey mentioned earlier, whites, blacks, Latinos, and Asians showed similar levels of support for congressional action to limit tax breaks for business (under 40 percent), balance the budget (over 75 percent), reform Medicare (about 55 percent), and cut personal income taxes (about 50 percent). Somewhat more variation existed in support for reforming the welfare system (around 75 percent support) and limiting affirmative action (around a third). The only issue that seriously divided survey participants was increased limits on abortion: 24 percent support among Asian Americans, 50 percent support among Latinos, and 35 percent and 32 percent support among whites and blacks respectively. Other surveys show similar levels of interethnic support for proposals to reduce crime, balance the federal budget, or improve public schooling.

But when political disputes and policy choices are posed, as they frequently are, along lines that allow for competition among racial or ethnic groups, the picture looks quite different. African Americans are overwhelmingly likely (82 percent) to describe their own group as the one that "faces the most discrimination in America today." Three in five Asian Americans agree that blacks face the most discrimination, as do half of whites. But Latinos split evenly (42 percent to 40 percent) over whether to award African Americans or themselves this dubious honor. The same pattern appears in more specific questions about discrimination. Blacks are consistently more likely to see bias against their own race than against others in treatment by police, portrayals in the media, the criminal justice system, promotion to management positions, and the ability to get mortgages and credit loans. Latinos are split between blacks and their own group on all these questions, whereas whites see roughly as much discrimination against all three of the nonwhite groups and Asians vary across the issues.

Perhaps the most telling indicator of the coming complexity in racial and ethnic politics is a 1994 National Conference survey asking representatives of the four major ethnic groups which other groups share the most and the least in common with their own group. According to the survey, whites feel most in common with blacks, who feel little in common with whites. Blacks feel most in common with Latinos, who feel least in common with them. Latinos feel most in common with whites, who feel little in common with them. Asian Americans feel most in common with whites, who feel least in common with them. Each group is running after another that is fleeing from it. If these results hold up in political activity, then American racial and ethnic politics in the 21st century are going to be interesting, to say the least.

Attitudes toward particular policy issues show even more clearly the instability of racial and ethnic coalitions. Latinos support strong forms of affirmative action more than do whites and Asians, but sometimes less than do blacks. In a 1995 survey, whites were much more likely to agree strongly than were blacks, Asians, and Latinos that Congress should "limit affirmative action." But the converse belief—that Congress should *not* limit affirmative action—received considerable support only from African Americans. Across a variety of surveys, blacks are always the most likely to support affirmative action for blacks; blacks and Latinos concur frequently on weaker though still majority support for affirmative action for Latinos, and all groups concur in lack of strong support for affirmative action for Asians. Exit polls on California's Proposition 209 banning affirmative action found that 60 percent of white voters, 43 percent of Asian voters, and just over one-quarter of black and Latino voters supported the ban.

What might seem a potential coalition between blacks and Latinos is likely to break down, however—as might the antagonism between blacks and whites—if the issue shifts from affirmative action to immigration policy. The data are too sparse to be certain of any conclusion, especially for Asian Americans, but Latinos and probably Asians are more supportive of policies to encourage immigration and offer aid to immigrants than are African Americans and whites. A recent national poll by the Princeton Survey Research Associates suggests why African Americans and whites resemble each other and differ from Latinos in their preferences for immigration policy: without exception they perceive the effects of immigration—on such things as crime, employment, culture, politics, and the quality of schools—to be less favorable than do Latinos.

Taking Advantage of the Possibilities

We can only guess at this point about how the complicated politics of racial and ethnic competition and coalition-building will connect with the equally complicated politics of middle-class black alienation and poor black marginality. These are quintessentially political questions; the economic and demographic trajectories merely set the conditions for an array of political possibilities ranging from assimilation to a racial and ethnic cold war. I conclude only with the proposal that there is more room for racial and ethnic comity than we sometimes realize because most political issues cut across group lines—but achieving that comity will require the highly unlikely combination of strong leadership and sensitive negotiation.